UNITED STATES
CONSTITUTIONAL
AND
LEGAL HISTORY

A TWENTY VOLUME SERIES
REPRODUCING OVER 450 OF THE MOST
IMPORTANT ARTICLES ON THE TOPIC

Edited with Introductions by
KERMIT L. HALL

A GARLAND SERIES

CONTENTS OF THE SERIES

MAIN THEMES IN UNITED STATES CONSTITUTIONAL AND LEGAL HISTORY

MAJOR HISTORICAL ESSAYS

Edited with an Introduction by
KERMIT L. HALL

GARLAND PUBLISHING, INC.
NEW YORK • LONDON 1987

Library of Congress Cataloging-in-Publication Data

Main themes in United States constitutional and legal history.

   (United States constitutional and legal history ; v. 1)
   Bibliography: p.
   1. Law—United States—History and criticism.
2. United States—Constitutional history.
I. Hall, Kermit. II. Series.
KF352.A2M35 1987 349.73'09 86-31897
ISBN 0-8240-0129-X 347.3009

The volumes in this series have been printed on acid-free,
250-year-life paper.

Printed in the United States of America.

ACKNOWLEDGMENTS

Randall Bridwell, "Theme v. Reality in American Legal History," *Indiana Law Journal* 53 (1978): 449–496. Reprinted by permission of Fred B. Rothman and Company.

Stephen Diamond, "Legal Realism and Historical Method: J. Willard Hurst and American Legal History," *Michigan Law Review* 77 (1979): 784–794. Reprinted by permission of the Michigan Law Review Association.

David H. Flaherty, "An Approach to American History: Willard Hurst as Legal Historian." This article originally appeared in the *American Journal of Legal History*, Vol. 14, July 1970, pages 222–234.

John P. Frank, "American Legal History: The Hurst Approach," Journal of Legal Education 18 (1966): 395–410. Reprinted by permission of the *Journal of Legal Education* .

Lawrence M. Friedman, "Heart Against Head: Perry Miller and the Legal Mind." Reprinted by permission of the Yale Law Journal Company and Fred B. Rothman & Company from *The Yale Law Journal*, Vol.77, pp.1244–1259.

Lawrence M. Friedman, "Notes Toward a History of American Justice," *Buffalo Law Review* (1974). Reprinted by permission of the *Buffalo Law Review.*

Julius Goebel, Jr., "Constitutional History and Constitutional Law," *Columbia Law Review* 38 (April 1938): 555–577. Reprinted by permission of Fred B. Rothman & Company.

Robert W. Gordon, "Introduction: J. Willard Hurst and the Common Law Tradition in American Legal Historiography" *Law and Society Review* 20 (Fall 1975): 9–56. Reprinted by permission of the *Law and Society Review*, copyright (c) the Law and Society Association.

Wythe Holt, "Morton Horwitz and the Transformation of American Legal History," *William and Mary Law Review* 23 (Summer 1982): 663–723. Reprinted by permission. Copyright (c) 1982 by the College of William and Mary.

JUN 3 1987

James W. Hurst, "Legal Elements in United States History,"
    Perspectives in American History, 5 (1971): 3–94. Reprinted
    by permission of the author.
James W. Hurst, "The Law in United States History," *Proceedings
    of the American Philosophical Society* 104 (no. 5, 1960): 518–
    526. Reprinted by permission of the American Philosophical
    Society.
James W. Hurst, "Old and New Dimensions of Research in United
    States Legal History." This article originally appeared in the
    American Journal of Legal History, Vol. 23, 1979, pages
    1–20.
Stanley N. Katz, "Looking Backward: The Early History of
    American Law," *University of Chicago Law Review* 33
    (1966): 867–884. Reprinted by permission of the *University
    of Chicago Law Review*.
Paul L. Murphy, "Time to Reclaim: The Current Challenge of
    American Constitutional History," *American Historical Review*
    69 (October 1963): 64–79. Reprinted by permission of the
    American Historical Association.
A. E. Keir Nash, "*In Re* Radical Interpretations of American Law:
    The Relation of Law and History," *Michigan Law Review* 82
    (1983): 274–345. Reprinted by permission of the Michigan
    Law Review Association.
Stephen B. Presser, "'Legal History' or the History of Law: A
    Primer on Bringing the Law's Past into the Present,"
    Vanderbilt Law Review 35 (May 1982): 849–890. Reprinted
    by permission of the author.
Stephen B. Presser, "Book Review: Revising the Conservative
    Tradition: Towards a New American Legal History," 52
    N.Y.U.L. Rev. 700 (1977). Reprinted by permission of the
    New York University Law Review.
James G. Randall, "The Interrelation of Social and Constitutional
    History," *American Historical Review* 35 (October 1929):
    1–13. Reprinted by permission of the American Historical
    Association.
Harry N. Scheiber, "American Constitutional History and the New
    Legal History: Complementary Themes in Two Modes,"
    Journal of American History 68 (September 1981): 337–350.
    Reprinted by permission.
Harry N. Scheiber, "At the Borderland of Law and Economic
    History: The Contributions of Willard Hurst," *American
    Historical Review* 75 (February 1970) 744–756. Reprinted by
    permission
Calvin Woodard, "History, Legal History, and Legal Education,"
    Virginia Law Review 53 (January 1967): 89–121. Reprinted
    by permission of Fred B. Rothman & Company.

CONTENTS

INTRODUCTION

"This abstraction called the Law," Justice Oliver Wendell Holmes, Jr., once observed, is "a magic mirror, [wherein] we see reflected, not only our own lives but the lives of all men that have been!"[1] Holmes thought his "magic mirror" offered historians an extraordinary source through which to analyze the social choices and moral imperatives of previous generations. The law, constitutions (state and federal), and legal institutions, of course, have figured prominently in American history, and since the turn of this century some historians have identified themselves with one of two related subfields— constitutional or legal history. In the past three decades, scholarly productivity in both has exploded. More writing, for example, was published in legal history in the period 1979–1980 than in all the years prior to 1960.

The separation of legal and constitutional history into subfields stems from a traditional distinction between private and public law. All law is a system of social choice backed by the power of the state. But the state has varying degrees of interest in those choices. Private law, although implemented through public courts, aims to resolve disputes in which the interests of individuals, rather than the state, are directly involved. The state, for example, has a direct interest in whether you speed or murder your neighbor, but it has only an indirect interest in whether you keep a promised contractual agreement with that neighbor. Private law, therefore, encompasses the major categories of substantive legal rules, such as contracts, real property, and torts. Private law is private because of the character of the parties in dispute and the absence of a *direct* state interest.

Public law, on the other hand, involves social choices where the state has a direct interest. Public law embraces those rules that affect the organization of the state, the relations between the state and the people who compose it (including control over the means of legitimate violence and punishment of deviant social acts), the responsibilities of the officers of the state to each other and to the public, and the relations of states within the nation to one another. Public law, like private law, also has several categorical divisions. It consists of criminal, administrative, international, and constitutional law. The last of these, constitutional law, treats the establishment, construction, and interpretation of constitutions and the validity of legal enactments passed under them.

Constitutional historians have concentrated on one category of public law—constitutional law. They have probed problems of sovereignty, individual rights, separation of power, federalism, judicial review, and such in the formation and implementation of the federal Constitution and, less frequently, state constitutions. Constitutional history has been intellectual and institutional history, and constitutional historians have lavished attention on the framers of the constitution, the Philadelphia Convention of 1787, the decisions of the Supreme Court, and the lives of its justices. The emphasis on the high court has made sense, in as much as the American constitutional order grants to that body the power to determine conclusively whether laws and other acts of government and its officers are constitutional.

Legal historians carved a broader field of inquiry. They have concentrated on the changing nature of private law, some public law issues (criminal and administrative law) neglected by constitutional historians, legal institutions (courts, the police, law schools, the bench and bar) and legal ideas. Legal historians attempt to explain the development of those areas of human action that most persons would commonly identify with the word "law." Constitutional historians, by contrast, have devoted attention to matters most of the citizenry has never directly confronted and would have doubtless described as esoteric and impenetrable if they had.

"Today it would be presumptuous," William E. Nelson has written, "to attempt to define the boundaries of the discipline of legal history or to specify the sorts of scholarship upon which practioners within the field should work."[2] Yet if the exact agenda of legal historians remains murky, three themes do emerge clearly from the recent literature, and in each instance they owe something to the work of James Willard Hurst.

First, historians have increasingly viewed public and private law concerns as reciprocal and reinforcing. As Harry Scheiber has written, legal and constitutional history are emerging as "complementary themes in two modes."[3] As another scholar has observed, the merging of public and private law concerns will ultimately push scholars to develop a history of "American legal culture."[4] The quest to understand American law in its entirety is accompanied by the usual sense of loss as older and narrower boundaries, and the sense of definition that went with them, blur. But this sense of loss is more than compensated for by richer lines of inquiry that connect writing about the history of American legal culture to the historiography of American history.

Second, and related to the first, historians of American legal culture recognized that they must ground their findings in society. It is no longer enough to discover what the law was; now it is important to explain its social and economic consequences. This concern with the social bases of American law is part and parcel of the social history revolution that has swept writing about the American past. As new Ph.D.s have emerged from graduate schools, they have brought with them a concern about law as a social reality rather than as an intellectual abstraction. So, too, law school professors, once concerned exclusively with teaching legal history as a means of explaining doctrinal development, have become "legal realists"—they want to know what the distributive economic and social consequences of legal change have been.

Third, there is a sustained debate about what those effects have been. Beginning in the late 1960s and continuing today, a radical interpretation of the history of American legal culture has emerged. Morton J. Horwitz, Robert Gordon, and Mark V. Tushnet, for example, have posed serious questions about the pluralist-consensus interpretation of James Willard Hurst, the dean of American legal historians. Scholars associated with the Critical Legal Studies movement in American law schools have argued that, contrary to the findings of Hurst, the law has been neither neutral nor stable at its core. Rather, it has consistently reflected the priorities of dominant social and political elites.

The essays in this volume deal with these multiple themes in the history of American legal culture. That students of it disagree about what constitutes its proper research agenda presents a challenge quite unlike that in any other area of contemporary writing about the American past. It is, in sum, the fate of historians of American legal culture to live in interesting times.

Kermit L. Hall

Notes

1. Oliver Wendell Holmes, Jr., *The Speeches of Oliver Wendell Holmes* (1891), p.17.
2. William E. Nelson, "Legal History Before the 1960s," in Nelson and Reid, eds., *The Literature of American Legal History* (1985), p.1
3. Harry N. Scheiber, "American Constitutional History and the New Legal History: Complementary Themes in Two Modes," *The Journal of American History* 68 (September 1981): 337–350.
4. Kermit L. Hall, "The Magic Mirror: American Constitutional and Legal History," *International Journal of Social Education* 1 (1986): 29.

ADDITIONAL READING

Lawrence M. Friedman, *A History of American Law*, 2nd Edition (1985).

Lawrence M. Friedman and Harry N. Scheiber, eds., *American Law and the Constitutional Order: Historical Perspectives* (1978).

Kermit L. Hall "The Magic Mirror: American Constitutional and Legal History, " *International Journal of Social Education* 1 (1986): 22–48.

James Willard Hurst, *The Growth of American Law: The Law Makers* (1950).

William E. Nelson and John Phillip Reid, *The Literature of American Legal History* (1985).

Theme v. Reality in American Legal History: A Commentary on Horwitz, *The Transformation of American Law, 1780-1860,* and on the Common Law in America

R. RANDALL BRIDWELL*

> While the events of the past are the source of the experience of the human race, their opinions are determined not be the objective facts but by the records and interpretations to which they have access. Few men will deny that our views about the goodness or badness of different institutions are largely determined by what we believe to have been their effects in the past. There is scarcely a political ideal or concept which does not involve opinions about a whole series of past events, and there are few historical memories which do not serve as a symbol of some political aim. Yet the historical beliefs which guide us in the present are not always in accord with the facts; sometimes they are even the effects rather than the cause of political beliefs.
>
> F. A. Hayek**

INTRODUCTION

Morton Horwitz's *The Transformation of American Law, 1780-1860*[1] is a serious and thoughtful attempt to describe some of the basic, general themes in American law during one of its most energetic and creative periods. Professor Horwitz assembles a vast body of data consisting principally of judicial opinions and doctrinal writing, but which also extends to economic, social and political history. He attempts to extrapolate from this data the common

---

* Professor of Law, University of South Carolina School of Law. Portions of this article were based upon a recently published treatise, R. BRIDWELL AND R. WHITTEN, THE CONSTITUION AND THE COMMON LAW, THE DECLINE OF THE DOCTRINES OF SEPARATION OF POWERS AND FEDERALISM. Lexington Books, D.C. Heath and Co. (1977). The author wishes to express his thanks to D.C. Heath and Co. for permitting the use of some of the material herein, as well as to Professor Ralph U. Whitten, who developed many of the ideas herein with the author. Thanks are also due to Professor Maurice Holland of Indiana University School of Law, who read the manuscript of this article and offered many valuable suggestions. For a more complete treatment of the subjects discussed here, the treatise should be consulted.

**F. HAYEK, CAPITALISM AND THE HISTORIANS at 3-4 (1954).

[1]Harvard University Press (1971) [hereinafter cited as HORWITZ]. For some recent reviews of Horwitz's book, see Gilmore, Book Review, 86 YALE L.J. 788 (1977); Kettner, Book Review, 8 J. INTERDISCIPLINARY HIST. 390 (1977); Genovese, Book Review, 91 HARV. L. REV. 776 (1978); Wroth, Book Review, 28 HARV. LAW SCHOOL BULLETIN at 30 (1977); Foner, Book Review, THE NEW YORK REVIEW OF BOOKS (1977); Reid, Book Review, 55 TEX. L. REV. 1307 (1977); Hurst, Book Review, 21 AM. J. LEGAL HIST. 175 (1977); Winship, Book Review, 31 SOUTHWESTERN L.J. 751 (977). The best review to appear thus far is Presser, Book Review, 52 N.Y.U. LAW REV. 100 (1977).

threads and general patterns which can give the reader genuinely fundamental insights into our legal process, indeed into the nature of the process by which common law is generated, or as some say "created" and applied by the judiciary.[2] In his description of precise causes for the emergence of much nineteenth century doctrine, Professor Horwitz's work is much more thematic than similar recent attempts to present comprehensive insights into our legal history,[3] and much more reliant on his own interpretations of original sources of a general nature. He also extends his inquiry beyond the more regional or localized works, though many of the essentially local studies certainly have broader, national implications.[4] Thus, in the breadth of both the raw material analysed and the ambition of the monograph to expand upon the narrower doctrinal treatment of its parts, Professor Horwitz should be commended.[5] However, neither the ambitious scope of such a work, nor the laudibile intent of its author to raise the level of his inquiry above that of our previous historical pioneers who sought to reveal the substance and general character rather than the often confusing particulars of our legal past,[6] are the final measure of success. For, though Professor Horwitz has attempted to prove much, what he has *actually* proved may be summarized with rather startling brevity. Relatedly, the points upon which his proof and analysis can with all charity he said to have failed utterly are rather numerous.[7] Moreover, among his numerous errors one may readily see one central mistake more fundamental than the others, indeed one which in all probability produced the others. This recurrent problem concerns the method by which Professor Horwitz seeks to demonstrate the major themes of his book—his most essential proof is clumsily lifted completely out of its context so that its significance

---

[2]More than anything else Horwitz seeks to illuminate the common law process as an instrument for legal change "[s]ince few historians have . . . thought through the problems of using this concept in a comment law context." HORWITZ, *supra* note 1 at XV. Indeed, emphasis on the judicial role is the keynote of Horwitz's whole analysis. It is precisely this facet of his study that is the weakest. The ingenious way in which Horwitz distorts the common law process is of primary interest to anyone who wished to thoroughly understand this book and appraise its worth.

[3]*See* L. FRIEDMAN, A HISTORY OF AMERICAN LAW(1973). Professor Friedman relied mainly on secondary materials for his work, and his presentation of the major themes in American legal history is more various and diverse than Horwitz's focused economic interpretations.

[4]*See* W. NELSON, THE AMERICANIZATION OF THE COMMON LAW (1975).

[5]*See* Holt, *Now and Then: The Uncertain State of Nineteenth Century American Legal History*, 7 IND. L. REV. 615, 626 (1974), where Holt quotes Horwitz's dissatisfaction with too much "detail" in the writing of American legal history, to the neglect of "broader interpretative themes." Indeed Horwitz in his new book allows that "This study attempts to challenge certain features of 'concensus' history that has continued to dominate American historiography since the Second World War." HORWITZ, *supra* note 1, at xiii. In producing much of this history, "Even sophisticated lawyers, who regularly address themselves to the policies imbedded in contemporary legal rules, tried to treat the historical study of law with an arid formalism that is striking and surprising." *Id.* at xi - xii, A distaste for the particulars of legal rules, and their technicalities forms a large part of the new preference for thematic "intellectual" history.

[6]For example, see R. POUND, THE FORMATIVE ERA OF AMERICAN LAW (1950) for an attempt to synthesize and explain a great mass of doctrinal detail.

[7]This point is developed further in later parts of this article. See notes 21-124 *infra* & text accompanying.

is invariably distorted and its meaning thoroughly changed.[8] In this respect
alone, Professor Horwitz's book exemplifies the increasing prevalent condition
of American legal historical scholarship more vividly than any book in
decades. Even more importantly the apparent reason for this spirit of even
handed distortion is an erroneous conception of the common law process,
particularly the English common law system. Horwitz's misconstruction of the
common law system is a product of his failure to treat any of the major legal
issues analysed in their broader historical context. More than any other factor, this causes Professor Horwitz to conceive of each chosen piece of legal
datum as evidence of a novel or revolutionary change in the legal system.
Thus a great amount of evidence which appears quite conventional in context
is by extraction and narrow presentation made to fit into his "transformation"
motif.

More than anything else, Horwitz's book purports to be about the common law process. This is of course one of the most debated themes in
American legal history, and one with much relevance to current issues of
judicial authority and discretion. Much has been said and written about the
powers which judges have traditionally enjoyed in our legal system and their
capacity to discretionarily employ their authority to apply, or perhaps also
provide, binding rules aimed at serving particular social or economic purposes, as well as the appropriate sources of the legal rules so applied.[9]
Naturally what the judges did in the past is highly relevant to the analysis of
the broader issue of the current status of the common Law. Ironically, it is in
describing the concept and practice of common law adjudication in our early
national period that Horwitz's new book fails the most. It will therefore be
useful to analyze particular examples of Horwitz's method of proof, and to
discuss at some length the operation of this common law system in certain
areas critical to his proof in order to illustrate the broader context and the

3

---

[8]Though almost any attempt to isolate legal or Constitutonal phenonamena rends the
"seamless webb" of history and to some degree inevitably distorts the truth.

However, there is a vast difference in the distortion caused by the interjection of the
observer and his inevitable selectivity and focus upon particular data, and the overly narrow partial representation of a phenomena such as the common law process, resulting in a mistatement
of its content. It is the latter, more serious, flaw which charactrizes Horwitz's book.

[9]Professor Horwitz's current book is in large measure an attempt to expand upon and provide further proof for the thesis of his earlier writing in article form, as his introduction indicates. See Horwitz, *The Emergence of an instrumental Conception of American Law 1780-1820*
in V. PERSPECTIVES IN AMRICAN HISTORY 287 (1971); Horwitz, *The Transformation ifn the Conception of Property 1780-1860*, 40 U. CHI. L. REV. 248 (1973); Horwitz, *The Rise of Legal Formalism*, 19 AM. J. LEGAL HIST. 251 (1976). As Professor Nelson aptly observed

"The key point, however, is that legal rules and traditions do service beyond the period
of their immediate usefulness to dominate groups, and in doing so, take on a status
that is autonomous to the immediate political interests of those groups. This semi-
autoumonous body of law, which can and does serve as a restraint on decision makers,
surely is a legitimate object of historical study." Nelson, *Legal History—Annual Survey
of American Law*, 1973-74 N.Y.U. L. REV. 625, 640. See BURGER, GOVERNMENT BY
JUDICARY (1977).

operational rules and principles of decision-making which his artificial selectivity has managed to obscure. If as Professor Nelson claims this is "one of the five most significant books ever published in the field of American legal History,"[10] the book and the developments it analyses certainly deserve this extended treatment. The process by which this demonstrable distortion has been produced can than be placed in the context of broader tends in the writing of legal history, and some observations can be made on a much debated subject: the efficient relationship between legal and historical training and methods of investigation and analysis.[11] This may be accomplished by considering the following: (a) a description of *what* Professor Horwitz attempts to prove, that is, his central theme; (b) the methods he employs in attempting this proof and the particular errors associated with several elements of it; and (c) a description of certain of the broader subject matter areas critical to Horwitz's analysis of the common law process and to his basic theme, including a more thorough description of the common law precess itself in the context of two extremely important elements in Horwitz's thesis—the general commercial law and the conflict of laws. Also thoroughly analyzed and evaluated will be one of William Crosskey's controversial themes as it applies to the common law process in the federal courts,[12] and Horwitz's

---

[10]"The comment is attributed to William A. Nelson, Yale University." S. Bremer, Book Review, 52 N.Y.U. L. REV. 700, 716 n.52 (1977).

[11]As Frederick Maitland remarked, though lawyers seldom seem to make good historians and the lawyers method often conflicts with historical objectivity, legal training is nonetheless important in doing good legal historical work. "But we can say this, that a thorough training in modern law is almost indispensable for anyone who wishes to do good work on legal history." Maitland, *Why the History of England Law Was Not Written*, in FREDRICK WILLIAM MAITLAND, HISTORIAN 132, 140 (R. Schuyler ed. 1960). Horwitz has elsewhere observed that a reasoning process common to the lawyer's technique, has produced a "conservative tradition in the writing of our legal history." In comparing the effect of legal reasoning process upon historical objectivity, Horwitz draws a comparison to the writing of scientific history, in which " 'earlier ages are implicitly represented as having worked upon the same set of fixed problems and in accordance with the same set of fixed cannons that the most recent revolution in scientific method has made seem scientific." Horwitz, *The Conservative Tradition in the Writing of American Legal History*, 17 AM. J. LEGAL HIST. 275 (1973), quoting, T. KUHN, THE STRUCTURES OF SCIENTIFIC REVOLUTIONS at 137-38 (2d ed. 1970). In other words, the lawyer's attempt to synthesize a current postulate or principle from past data, which may represent disorder and conflict rather than a continuum, results in a distortion of the acutal past condition analyzed. Amazingly enough, some recent writers have regarded the recognition of "ideological conservatism" in the writing of legal history as a path-breaking insight. See *Auerbach*, Book Review, 85 YALE L.J. 855 (1976). This particular observation is, however, one of the older recognized historiographic themes. See W. HOLDSWORTH, THE HISTORIAN OF ANGLO AMERICAN LAW 138-41 (1928); C. FIFOOT, LAW AND HISTORY IN THE NINETEENTH CENTURY 8, 14-15 (1956). In evaluating Professor Horwitz's books, we shall isolate and discuss the relationship between legal methods of investigation and analysis of data.

[12]The reference is, of course, to W. CROSSKEY, POLITICS AND THE CONSTITUTION IN THE HISTORY OF THE UNITED STATES (1953). For a detailed discussion of parts of Professor Crosskey's work particularly his interpretation of the development of conflict of laws and commercial law rules in the federal courts. See note 56 *supra* & text accompanying. For an excellent account of the "reception" of the controversy generated by Crosskey's famous work, see Wollan, *Crosskey's Once and Future Constituion*, 6 POLITICAL SCI. REVIEWER 129 (1975). One objective here is to supply some much needed data and analysis relevant to these excerpts of Crosskey's work, as they have not been forthcoming since its publication nearly twenty-five years ago.

treatment of it. Our objective will then be to briefly illustrate and critique Horwitz's theory and methodology in a selective fashion, and to test his theories against the broader and more fully developed background of a major subject matter area. The conclusion will emphasize the thematic and subjective characteristics of much of our modern legal literature, and hopefully provide some sound insights into the relevance of the lawyer's craft to the analysis of legal historical data. Not only may the worth of Horwitz's book and its contribution to our understanding be thereby better appraised; but also what this and numerous other articles purport to describe—the role of the judge in the American system—may be better understood.

BASIC THEMES

The central themes of Horwitz's monograph may be stated briefly. During the years in question, 1780-1860, a wholly novel theory emerged in American law, and appeared in judicial decisions in the area of private law. This new "conception" of American law resulted from the collapse of the older theory of the common law as a body of just principles autonomous from human institutions, but discernable by the application of human reason.[13] In its place emerged a theory of law, including common law, which identified legal rules wholly with human will, thus coming full circle from the old view. As Horwitz puts it, "The result of this transformation in the underlying basis for legitimacy of the common law was that jurists began to conceive of the common law as an instrument of will."[14] This dramatic shift in legal theory also led to an equally dramatic shift in the judges' conception of their own role and their ultimate objectives in the common law process. "As judges began to conceive of common adjudication as a process of making and not merely discovering legal rules, they were led to frame general doctrines based on a self conscious consideration of social and economic policies."[15] The shift from the supposed "discovery" of legal rules to rational and "self conscious articulation" of them heightened the judicial awareness that what was being

5

---

[13] The characterization which Horwitz places upon the old or eighteenth century conception of the common law is entirely incomplete and misleading. Characteristically, he confines his discussion of this complex phenomenon to certain parts only, and contrasts the supposed change in legal theory to the single narrow facet of the common law process which he has chosen to represent it. A whole or more sophisticated explanation of the common law process, as it was conceived in the eighteenth century, will render all of Horwitz's evidence of novelty and change quite conventional. The recurrent practice of taking evidence out of context—such as the narrow view of the common law—which Horwitz uses to create the appearance of change whenever other data is compared to the extracted artificially limited evidence of the common law thus accelerates and distorts the observer's sense of movement away from old doctrine.

[14] HORWITZ, *supra* note 1, at 22.

[15] *Id.* at 2, appearing in a chapter entitled "The Emergence of an Instrumental Conception of American Law," which is the name Horwitz gives to this new judicial rulemaking power. Likewise Horwitz asserts, "What dramatically distinguished nineteenth century law from its eighteenth century counterpart was the extent to which common law judges came to play a central role in directing the course of social change." *Id.* at 1.

done was the making and enforcement of far ranging social policy. "For the first time, lawyers and judges can be found with some regularity to reason about the social consequences of particular legal rules."[16] Similarly, jurists began to frame legal arguments in terms of "the importance of the present decision to the commercial character of our country."[17] Thus, not only did a large number of new legal rules, new precedent, emerge during this period, but both the *way* in which the rules were created and their *purpose* were also novel. These features and their effect on the judicial role in our common law processes are central to Horwitz's work.[18]

Equally important, however, is the *result* of this jurisprudential change, for as it concentrated far ranging power in the courts, Horwitz argues, the precise conception of the social and economic policies resulting from the new power also became clear. The new direction pursued by the judiciary armed with their novel and instrumental theory of law was to support dominant, growing capital and economic forces, that is "big business" and the commercial classes, by restructuring the private law in order to create an extensive system of legal subsidies. As Horwitz contends "Having destroyed or neutralized earlier protective or regulatory doctrines at the same time as they limited power of juries to mete out the rough and discretionary standards of commercial justice, a newly established procommercial elite was able to align itself with aggressive business interests."[19] Thus, "[I]n the period between 1790 and 1820 we see the development of an important new set of relationships that make this position of dominance [of commercial interests] possible: *the forging of an alliance between legal and commercial interests.*"[20] The judiciary,

---

[16]*Id.* at 2.

[17]*Id.* (*quoting* Liebert v. The Emperor, Bee's Admir. Rep. 339, 343 (Pa. 1785)).

[18]*See* note 2 *supra.*

[19]HORWITZ. *supra* note 1, at 211.

[20]*Id.* at 140 (emphasis added). The results of the alliance and the emerging system of private law subsidy rules, Horwitz alleges, did no good for the economically weaker elements of society. "It does seem quite likely that they did contribute to an increase in inequality by throwing a disproportionate share of the burdens of economic growth on the weakest and least organized group in American society." *Id.* at 101.

For seventy or eighty years after the American Revolution of major direction of common law policy reflected the overthrow of eighteenth century precommercial and antidevelopmental values. As political and economic power shifted to merchant and entreprenurial groups in the postrevolutionary period, they began to forge an alliance with the legal profession to advance their own interests through a transformation of the legal system.

. . . .

Law, once conceived of as protective, regulative, paternalistic and, above all, a paramount expression of the moral sense of the community, had come to be thought of as facilitative of individual desires and as simply reflective of the existing organization of economic and political power.

. . . .

By the middle of the nineteenth century the legal system had been reshaped to the advantage of men of commerce and industry at the expense of farmers, workers, consumers, and other less powerful groups within the society. Not only had the law come to establish legal doctrines that maintained the new distribution of economic and

then, employed a new conception of their common law authority to shake off
the restraints of earlier common law substantive principles, and in so doing
conspired with the business world to redistribute society's resources in a manner favorable to the commercial elite.[21] The thesis is straightforward enough,
but the proof of these claims must be tested. That requires a discussion of the
data used by Horwitz to support this transformation theme and the method
of its presentation.

In discussing the law lectures of James Wilson delivered in Philadelpia in
the 1790's, Horwitz remarks: "Wilson revealed the extent to which he had
come under the spell of modern [sic] conception of law as a sovereign command."[22] In the passage Horwitz quotes from Wilson, a hypothotical dispute
is put by Wilson as an illustration of the principle legitimizing positive rules
of law. Wilson denies the asserted duty to obey a particular principle simply
because it may arguably be moral to do so, because such an "injunction",
without more "possessed no human authority."[23] Horwitz concludes,

> "Thus the bases for obedience to law was set entirely within the modern
> framework of a will theory of law . . . This definition of the basis of obliga-
> tion in terms of popular will was a far cry from the eighteenth century con-
> ception of obligation derived from the inherent rightness or justice of law.
> The result was distinctly postrevolutionary phenomenon: an attempt to
> reconstruct the legitimacy not simply of statues, but of common law rules, on
> a consensual foundation. Wilson, for example, insisted that custom was in-
> trinsic evidence of consent."[24]

Indeed, as Wilson put it, in the continuance of customary rules revealed
"the operations of consent universally predominant."[25] "Thus," says Horwitz,

---

political power, but, wherever it could, it actively promoted a legal redistribution of
wealth against the weakest groups in society.
Id. at 253-54.
    At one point Horwitz allows that this massive overhaul in the private law may have come
"only by inadvertance" thus avoiding a flat statement of a conscious "conspiracy theory" involving
lawyers, judges and businessmen. The degree of consciousness is, however, irrelevant to whether
the doctrinal changes actually took place outside conventional common law theories and according to a new conception of law.
    Even if Horwitz's theory of a rather unified class oriented activism in the early American
judiciary is accepted, the economic interpretations which he makes of the case law are very questionable. *See* R. POSNER, ECONOMIC ANALYSIS OF LAW 183-85 (2d ed. 1977), discussing Horwitz's
economic interpretations of certain features of nineteenth century contract law in Horwitz, *The
Historical Foundations of Modern Contract Law*, 87 HARV. L. REV. 917 (1974). Full consideration of Horwitz's economic analysis is beyond the scope of this paper.
    [21]*See* HORWITZ, *surpa* note 1, at xvi, citing R.H. Coase's famous theorem on the effect of
legal rules on efficiency. Though it is debatable whether efficiency is affected by altering the
legal rules without "transaction costs, distribution of resources is an entirely different matter.
    [22]HORWITZ, *supra* note 1, at 19.
    [23]*Id.*, citing 1 THE WORKS OF JAMES WILSON 180 (R. McCLoskey ed. 1967) [hereinafter
cited as WILSON]. See WILSON at 112-14.
    [24]HORWITZ, *supra* note 1, at 19. See WILSON at 122.
    [25]*Id.*

"Wilson had significantly concluded that the obligatory force of the common law rested on nothing else but free and voluntary consent."[26]

What, precisely, is the *old* view with which Wilson's remarks are contrasted? According to Horwitz, it is "the inherent rightness or justice" of a particular rule, which is very different from consent. In understanding Horwitz's method, several things must be noted. For one thing, this characterization is an artificial and misleading characterization of the old view of law, albeit a characterization absolutely indispensable to Horwitz's claim of novelty and ultimately to the transformation theme of the book. Even more importantly, however, the contention that purely consensual explanations of the common law were in Wilson's time new is simply an error.[28] In fact, "natural law" or "law of reason" justifications for common law rules *and* consensual explanations of their origins were both a part of the common law tradition long before the American Revolution.[29] Horwitz's vision of a "law of nature"

---

[26]HORWITZ, *supra* note 1, at 19. See WILSON at 184-85.

[27]HORWITZ, *supra* note 1, at 19.

[28]A thorough description of the different views of the precise relationship between natural theory and the positive law, particularly customary law, is beyond the scope of this work. It is enough for our purposes to note the conjunctive use of natural law and consensual explanations for the obligatory force of legal rules. Horwitz ignores this highly important fact by presenting the older theory of legal obligation in terms of a completely unexplained reference to the "discovery" principle of common law adjudication. As Professor Christie has observed "The ability of the natural-law tradition to attract sustained widespread intellectual interest in modern times has not been helped by the tendency of supporters and detractors of the tradition to carry on their debate by means of cliches." G. CHRISTIE, JURISPRUDENCE 78 (1973). Moreover, as he remarked, "[T]here really is no such thing as a coherent natural law tradition with a common core of specific intellectual and moral concerns but only a constant groping by many diverse thinkers for the essence of law." *Id.* The important point to remember, however, is that the structure of the analysis of natural law has not been along the mutually exclusive lines of consent and "discovery" of disembodied devine principles, but has integrated the latter theoretical explanation for the 'essence of law" with consensual forms of positive rulemaking, which characteristically include custom or common law. See C. ST. GERMAIN, DOCTOR AND STUDENT OR DIALOGUES BETWEEN A DOCTOR OF DIVINTY AND A STUDENT OF THE LAWS OF ENGLAND 14 (16th ed. 1761) [hereinafter cited as GERMAIN]; F. POLLOCK, ESSAYS IN THE LAW, 179 (1922).

Much of the influential writing on the subject also recognized the compatability of the process of exercising human will to create positive law with essentially "devine" and natural principles of a supposedly immountable and universal character. *SEe* T. AQUINAS, SUMMA THEOLOGICA SECUNDA PAR, Q 90. Arts I and II (1273-76), from Dominican Province Translation (London, 1915). As Aaninas remarked upon the related or compatible exercise of human will and the devine standards that governed and validated the exercise, "[T]his participation in the external law in the rational creature is called natural law." *Id.* at Q 91, Art. III. "Therefore all laws insofar as they partake of right reason, are derived from the external law." *Id.* Q 93, art. III. "Natural reason" was regarded as a "general condition" to which positive laws must conform, though each mainfestation of reason in the form of positive laws entails *different* positive principles among different people or different places. See *id.* Q. 91, art IV. But most importantly "the consent of the whole people expressed by a custom" was a well understood function of the natural law. *Id.*, Q. 97, Art III. We will later herein more thoroughly consider the manifestations of this particular aspect of natural law theory in the case law. At any rate, regardless of the particular espistomological problems with the theory, its compatability with positive customary rules of law of a recognized consensual nature was perfectly evident in the classical philosophy and judicial exigesis of the natural law system.

[29]J. POCOCK, THE ANCIENT CONSTITUTION AND THE FEUDAL LAW 32 (1957); F. POLLOCK, ESSAYS IN THE LAW 64 (1922).

8

rationale yielding to the consensual one is grossly overstated, for both elements had long been regarded as essential to a complete description of the common law process. Moreover, even if one accepted Horwitz' view, it is not clear why the alleged emphasis on consent would cause the *judiciary* to emerge as the most significant and powerful element in the legal system. Such a persuasive preoccupation with consent would rather seem to be an invitation to legislate, and perhaps tend to reduce rather than encourage the extensive judicial activity which Horwitz points to in support of his thesis. If such a new conception were really widely or deeply held, one would expect more than a passing remark from the judiciary in defense of the massive doctrinal overhaul which they were producing.

METHOD OF PROOF: FLAWS IN EVIDENCE

It is clear that Horwitz's proof for the existence of the new "instrumental" theory of law, and the procommercial results it was consciously used to produce, rests mainly upon the demonstration that nineteenth century judicial action was itself novel in character. In the styles of decisionmaking which typified it, and in the effects it was capable of producing, this judicial action is described by Horwitz as being thoroughly novel. This is of course indispensable to the argument that a new theory of judicial action, a new conception, was born; for unless Horwitz can successfully argue that this era represented a new jurisprudence, his primary contribution would simply be the identification of doctrinal changes which had *some* impact on the distribution of societies resources. It is thus critical for Horwitz to show that the *way* is which rules of common law were changed was novel, and not just that some novel rules emerged.

One of the first and most important indicators of the evidence of an instrumental conception concerns the manner in which the older common law authority was, according to Horwitz, harmonized by the courts with an allegedly modern theory—the "will theory" of law. Two facets of the argument which provide evidence of this new rationalization are critical to Horwitz's argument: (1) the characterization of the *old* concept of common law authority—(i.e. what legitimized common law rules), and (2) the identification of a *new* explanation in contrast with the old. In the treatment of these elements, illustrating a process of proof that is quite literally pathological to Horwitz's work, the data representing the old view is narrowed and completely removed from context—and in some cases left entirely unexplained—so that the evidence tendered as representing the new view will assume an exaggerated contrast when compared with the old, thus appearing strikingly distinct. The important point, however, is the fact that abundant evidence from the English common law system demonstrates a pre-eighteenth century awareness of both the consensual rational for common law authority and the utility of judicially fashioned rules—two elements which Horwitz defines as

9

"distinctly postrevolutionary."[30] (For example, in the *Case of Tanistry,* decided by the King's Bench in 1608 all the trappings of the instrumental conception of law are apparent.) The question there was whether a customary rule of Irish law—the tenure of tanistry—or the English common law rule of primogeniture should prevail.[31] Both the source of legal obligation in the common law system and the utility of these competing rules were discussed by the court. As the reporter described the principles relating to the common law:

> "[A] custom, in the intendment of law, is such an usage as hath obtained the force of a law, and is in truth a binding law to such particular place, persons or things as it concerns; and such custom cannot be established by the king's grant . . . nor by act of parliament, but is *lex non scripta,* and *made by the people* only of such place, where the custom runs."[32]

Is the phrase "made by the people" suggestive of some consensual explanation of the common law process, or merely the jargon of the old "discovery" theory of the common law?[33] The case places the source of common law obligation within a voluntary or consensual process. As the case continues: "For where the people find any act to be good and beneficial, and apt and agreeable to their nature and disposition, they use and practice it from time to time . . ."[34] Further underscoring the conceptual justifications thought to apply to common law rules, the court disallowed the alleged custom of tanistry, and illuminated the relationship between the determination of reasonableness and consent itself by characterizing such allegedly binding customary rules as "prejudicial to a multitude of subjects or to the common wealth in general, and commenced by wrong and oppression, and not be voluntary consent of the people. . ." and as such "they are adjudged unreasonable."[35]

---

[30] HORWITZ, *supra* note 1, at 19.

[31] See 80 Eng. Rep. 516 (1608). Under the Irish custom, property descended to "oldest and most worthy man of the blood and surname."

[32] 80 Eng. Rep. 519 (1608).

[33] HORWITZ, *supra* note 1, at 248 referring to "common law rules, which were thought to be discovered from 'immutable principles of natural law and abstract justice.' "

[34] 88 Eng. Rep. 520 (1608).

[35] 88 Eng. Rep. 520-21 (1608). The court elsewhere sets up a distinction between a custom and "positive law," stating that "chescun custome nest unreasonable give est contrarie at particular rule ou maxine del positive ley," and also between these two elements and the "law of reason." As to a custom contrary to the public good or somehow injurious to the multitude and favoring only some particular person, "tiel custome est repugnant al ley de reason, gives est desuis touts positive leyes," that is, repugnant to the law of reason which transcends even positive laws. 80 Ens. Rep. 520 (1608). Under this heirarchy of legitimizing principles a custom may prevail, if not "unreasonable," or against a "positive law" but neither avail if contrary to the law of reason. This will be discussed in § C, *infra* in the description of the common law process. The most important point is that all were viewed as compatible with consent, and consensual explanations were ordinarily given conjuctively with the others. It is necessary to delay full discussion of the common law process and its legitimizing principles until the later section, because it is too complex and important to allow piecemeal examination.

Thus, autonomous and regular party behavior could be observed by the courts under standards principally involving general acceptance, continuity and certainty, and could become a governing rule of decision. The consensual explanation as the overriding source of legitimacy of the rule was a familiar element in the language of the common law, and was employed in a manner compatible with what Horwitz describes as a separate and exclusive "natural justice" or discovery" rationale.[36] Indeed, consent was employed in a manner which demonstrated its essential relationship to the transcendent requirement of "reasonableness."[37]

---

[36]HORWITZ, *supra* notre at 19.

[37]Moreover, the classical debate about the natural law from the middle ages onward embraced consensual explanations for customary law. As St. Thomas Aquinas observed in *Summa Theologia* of 1273-76, "[T]he consent of the whole people expressed by a custom counts far more in favour of a particular observance, than does the authority of the sovereign, who has not the power to frame laws, except as representing the people." T. AQUINAS, SUMMA THEOLOGICA, SEUCNDA PARS, O. 97, Art. III (1273-76) from the Dominican Province Translation (London 1915). Indeed the language of "reason," "reasonableness" or "natural law" was merely a theoretical justification of the processes of the common law. Rather than signifying some detached process of discretionary selection among certain disembodies natural rules, such language was the companion of the "consensual" description and theory behind the process of evolving rules of decision. As Matthew Hale, writing in 1671, remarked of the common law:

> [T]here is great reason for it; for it is not only a very just and excellent law in itself, but it is singularly accommodated to the frames of English Government, and to the disposition of the English nation, and such as by long experience and use is as it were incorporated into their very temperament, and, as a manner, became the complection and constitution of the English Commonwealth.

THE HISTORY OF THE COMMON LAW OF ENGLAND 30 (C. Gray ed. 1973). Thus, the language of consent was one of *the* most familiar elements in both municipal law and private international law in the eighteenth century, and during earlier periods. As Christopher St. Germain pointed out in describing the elements of the common law within English jurisprudence of the early sixteenth century, customs were observable facts, to be "determined by the justices," which derived their authority from their acceptance "by our lord the king, and his progenitors and all his subjects." GERMAIN *supra* note 28, at 19. As Horwitz remarked in his attempts to describe the supposed novelty of Wilson's views, "however much Wilson argued over whose will ultimately legitimized legal commands," a description of the principles of legitimation in terms of consent was "entirely modern." HORWITZ, *surpa* note 1, at 19. It was not, and however much one debates such procedures for identifying consent, the theoretical and consensual justification for the rules themselves may have been modern for Christopher St. Germain, writing in 1523 but a 250 year discrepancy in Horwitz case for novelty is hardly insignificant!

Other evidence of the older consensual view abounds in the literature of the Engligh common law, and was largely adopted with the rationale for the common law system in America. For example, in the introductory remarks to his report of cases from the King's Bench from 1601-1621, Sir William Davies remarked on the principles from which the rules of the common law — indeed the common law process — derived legitimacy and obligatory force.

> Therefore as the law of nature, which the Schoolman calls *jus commun* and which is also *jus non scriptum*, being written only in the heart of man, is better than all the written hours on the world to make man honest and happy in this life, if they would observe the rules therof: so the customary law of England, which we do believe call *jus commun*, as coming nearest to the law of nature . . . and which is also *jus non Scriptum*.

Davies Report 4 (1615). In contrasting statutory laws, which are "imposed upon the subject," with common law rules, which must be "tried and approved" before they assume the status of governing rules, Davies was merely reiterating the familiar theory of common law rules as

11

In describing postrevolutionary American legal theory, Horwitz asserts that much of the historical evidence clearly reveals the growing recognition of unprecedented judicial descretion. For example, Horwitz quotes Zepheniah Swift from his *System of Laws of Connecticut* (1795) as arguing that "If a determination has been founded as mistaken principles, or the rule adopted by it be inconvenient, or repugnant to the general tenor of law, a subsequent court assumes the power to vary from it or contradict it. In such cases they do not determine the prior decision to be bad law; but that they are not law."[38] Horwitz concludes that "Swift then came as close as any jurist of the age to maintaining that law is what the courts say it is."[39] It is clear, however, that this characterization of precedent was a highly conventional one, and referred to judicial authority to construe precedent collectively and to decline to follow a judicial pronouncement deviating from the weight of authority. In short, it was a traditional view of common law *method* regarding the construction of a general rule from previous cases, and not a claim to modify clear rules because of some judicial policy at odds with them. The judicial technique Swift described was addressed to the *clarity* of the previous case technique, not to the weight which might be given a case which *accurately* represents the rule.

As Blackstone had remarked about three decades earlier in the context of a discussion of the method of rendering a series of judicial pronouncements internally consistent in their description of the common law rule: "For if it be found that this former decision is manifestly absurd or unjust, it is declared, not that such a sentence was *bad law*, but that it was not law."[40]

As other writers have recognized, the discretion permitted by this procedure entailed the identification and elimination of inconsistencies in the judicial record of common law rules, and not the rejection on policy grounds of a clearly evidenced law.[41] If a line of relevant cases contained some judicial

---

originating in *de facto* popular consent. As Sir Frederick Pollock observed, "the elements of reason and custom have been recognized by the highest authorities as inseparable and strengthening one another." F. POLLOCK. ESSAYS ON THE LAW 64 (1922).

[38] HORWITZ, *supra* note 1, at 25, *citing* SWIFT, A SYSTEM OF THE LAWS OF THE STATE OF CONNECTICUT 41, 46 (1975).

[39] *Id.*

[40] ST. G. TUCKER, BLACKSTONE'S COMMENTARIES (1803) [hereinafter cited as TUCKER]. Indeed the entire discussion in Blackstone concerns preventing judicial deviation from the "authentic record" of fixed customarily and consensually derived standards of conduct, rather than the judicial ability to say what the law is. What Swift referred to, and what Blackstone and older commentators were referring to, was the necessity for a particular "reasonable" decision in terms of congruity with the entire judicial record of precedent, rather than according to some general conception of "reasonableness." *See also* M. HALE, THE HISTORY OF THE COMMON LAW OF ENGLAND 45 (C. Gray ed. (1973)).

[41] Indeed, it has long been observed that the use of the terms "reasonableness" or "inconvenience" had their origins in the judicial attempt to achieve some conformity between the particular principles of the common law and the overriding conditions of the "natural law" by excercising judicial discretion in a quite limited fashion, and not according to some general power of "judicial legislation." See Winfield, *Public Policy in the English Common Law*, 45 HARV. L. REV. 76, 79-82 (1928) [hereinafter cited as Winfield]. As Winfield remarked, it is obvious that

pronouncements which were at variance with the rule articulated by the majority of them, it would of course be foolish to follow those decisions. A series of decisions which purport to collectively state the existing legal principles must of course raise problems of construction in litigation when a court attempts to derive the rules of law from them and determine what they mean to a new state of facts. Horwitz thus mistakes the inevitable lack of absolute consistency in the judicial treatment of legal rules over the course of time, and the method developed by the common law for dealing with this inconsistency, with some creative power to legislate.

These examples should adequately illustrate the Horwitz methodology: the highly selective use of artificially circumscribed and oversimplified evidence in representing the *old* legal process, so as to exaggerate the sense of change and novelty associated with the *new* process.[42] Moreover, these are intended *only* as illustrative examples, for an real insight into Horwitz's method will require a somewhat more extended analytical apparatus. This will be necessary because Horwitz not only subjects particular legal principles to his method, but does so with whole areas of the law and the legal system; therefore, before any meaningful evaluation of Horwitz's thesis is possible, an alternative context for each significant legal principle used by Horwitz will have to be presented. Only in this fashion can we test the claims for novelty of any given element of evidence and turn the thesis for novel conception of law which in Horwitz's opinion these elements demonstrate. This necessitates a closer look at the cornerstones of Horwitz's case for the transformation of American law.

13

THE COMMON LAW PROCESS, THE GENERAL COMMERCIAL LAW AND CONFLICT OF LAWS

Since Professor Horwitz relies heavily upon his interpretation of the "general commercial law" in the federal courts, particularly its treatment by

---

when "the founders of our common law spoke of 'reason', 'the law of reason,' 'the law of nature,' they doubtless had a vision of some abstraction and wished to make the law harmonize with that" *Id.* at 99. The fact that these ideal conditions were at times identified with "the postulated eternal immutable law of nature", rather than taking the form of the "classical creative natural law of the seventeenth century" should not deceive the observer of the common law into believing in some continuous, prerevolutionary "discovery" monolith employed to rationalize judicial discretion. The older authorities reveal a system much more complex than this, and the classical texts in the nature of the law, much as ST. GERMAIN'S DOCTOR AND STUDENT, *supra* note 28, were in reality expressions of what most lawyers and jurists "felt and practiced." See *id.* at 77. See R. POUND. LAW AND MORALS 36 (1923), quoted in Winfield, *supra* at 84 n.46. Winfield has observed the interesting fact that two quite different books, DOCTOR AND STUDENT with its theoretical description of the "vital spirit" of the English legal system, and Fitzherbert's incredibly complex NEW NATURA BREVIUM (1534), were both recommended by Matthew Hale to aspiring students of English law. See Winfield, *supra* at 79. *See generally* Knight, *Public Policy in English Law,* 38 L.Q.R. 207 (1922).

[42]"Amazingly, sometimes Horwitz actually splits the elements of the old or traditional common law system and calls one "old" and the other "new." Two integrally related principles in the

the Supreme Court, and since this issue implicates an important part of William Crosskey's debated thesis on the subject, it will be useful to address both the common law process and the general commercial law at some length.

The Common Law Process

First, an important distinction must be drawn between the common law process and common law rules.[42] Though the two are related, the failure to distinguish these two elements in the analysis of the common law system has accounted for much confusion. The most fundamental element in understanding both the *system* of rules and *process* which produces such rules is an understanding that the way in which the process places limits upon judicial discretion in the classical system is not in the "making" of law as that process is currently understood, but rather in the application of certain general principles in the construction of presumptively binding legal rules contained in precedent, so as to augment and extend the precedent to new situations. Under these decisional rules as they were conceived and articulated in the eighteenth century, the judicial decisions comprising precedent or authority in a particular legal point were commonly said to be "evidence" of what the governing legal rule actually was.[44]

This characterization, though often derided as a fictional rationale and justification for judicial legislation, actually was a part of the general recognition that the common law process was comprised of several very distinct phases.[45] These phases may be most generally described as a process of evolu-

---

common law process are labelled as distinct because varying emphasis may be found on one element as opposed to another in previous judicial opinion, and thus the illusion of change is created by asserting a chronology for the appearance of each element of proof which in fact did not exist. This feat of legerdemain is one of Horwitz's finest.

[43]Differing emphasis upon these two facets of the overall process-rule content and decisional technique—has long been a part of discussions on the common law, and has accounted for a great deal of the confusion about the role of the common law in the post-revolutionary American system. It is interesting that this emphasis is a natural result of the overall process of maturation in the common law system which produces various degrees of specificity and completeness among different subject matter areas.

[44]*See* TUCKER *supra* note 40, at 68-73. This of course is the conventional terminology which was embraced in the general commercial law decisions and which has often been confused with some "discovery" or "brooding omnipresence" characterization of the common law. Actually the phrase was descriptive of the relationship between precedent and law, rather than descriptive of a general legal theory alone. The way in which the rules which the precedent evidenced were in fact circumscribed under the common law system (for example, according to locality) contradicts the characterization of such phraseology as a mere endorsement of some unfettered judicial authority to discover correct or reasonable general uniform rules de novo in each case. *Compare* Horwitz, *supra* note 1, at 245 and his erroneous characterization of Swift v. Tyson, 42 U.S. (16 Pet.) 1 (1842) *with* notes 72-77 *infra* & text accompanying. *See also* M. HALE, THE HISTORY OF THE COMMON LAW OF ENGLAND 45-46 (C. Gray ed. 1971); L. Lewis, *The History of Judicial Precedent* (pt. II), 46 L.Q.R. 341, 353-55 (1930).

[45]Significantly, some modern writers have seen that the focus on one particular phase of the common law process to the partial exclusion of others has in fact accounted for much disagree-

tion from a judicial inquiry into autonomous fact—for example, the fact of a certain general and long standing standard of party behavior, that is, a custom—to a state in which the factual inquiry has produced in the "authentic records" of the common law a sufficiently precise and inclusive description of the rules of conduct that the primary factual inquiry has disclosed.[46]

At each stage in which a question of a similar nature occurs, the necessity to make factual inquiry of the same type as in the original case is lessened because the court has already created in the form of a precedent a useful, though partial, description of the governing standard.[47] The basic

---

ment and confusion in the literature. As Larry Arnhart has recently pointed out, the scholarly analysis of whether or not and how the English common law was "received" or incorporated into the American judicial system has often been colored by this selective characterization. In discussing the conflict between the opinions of Justice Joseph Story and Professor Crosskey on the nature of the common law in America, Arnhart remarks that "Crosskey quotes the passages in *Swift v. Tyson* where Story refers to Cicero's description of a law that is the same everywhere, but Crosskey denies that Story's decision rests on anything beyond the positive law." that is the rules of decision actually in force. "Hence, while Story can explain the reception of the common law as the transmission to America of those general principles of natural justice that had been a part of the English common law, Crosskey has to demonstrate that the English common law was formally adopted in America as positive law." Arnhart, *William Crosskey and the Common Law*, 9 LOY. L.A.L. REV. 545, 553 (1976). Thus the measurement of the status of the common law is conducted by the differing standards of rule content as opposed to similarity of *general* principles in the decisional process. The problem with the Story-Crosskey conflict stems from a differing emphasis on the content of precedent as opposed to the principles of the decisional function. Really, the conflict stems from the effect of the purely positivistic rationale for legal rules on the analysis of the common law system, as opposed to a system of though less insistent on identifying the rule content with a sovereign command. See *id.* at 593-94; note 73 *infra* & text accompanying.

15

[46]The following general description or model should be borne in mind when considering the particular evidence of the common law process discussed later in this section. To the degree to which the abstract description is a valid generalization for the process, and to which the American decisions of the nineteenth century actually conform to it, the claim for revolutionary transformation in the common law system will be refuted. As Arnold Toynbee remarked:

> The operation of constructing a model is different from the operation of testing whether it fits the phenomena. But, so far from its being proper to dissociate the two operations from each other, it would seem to be impossible to obtain sure results from either of them if they are not carried out in conjunction. The model has to be constructed out of only a fraction of the total body of data, or we should never be able to mount it for use in investigating the remainder. But, just on this account, the structure will remain tentative and provisional until it has been tested by application to all the rest of the data within our knowledge. Conversely, our picture of the data as a whole will remain chaotic until we have found a model that brings out in them a pattern of specimens of a species.

A. TOYNBEE, A STUDY OF HISTORY 53 (rev. ed. 1972). It is this precise task that we now have preceded Horwitz's selective inferences from isolated data. Until this is done we are unable to "tell whether the items in a particular conglomeration of data that we have picked out of the chaos, like a child picking spillikins out of a heap, have hung together accidentally." *Id. See also* F. HAYEK, LAW, LEGISLATION AND LIBERTY 29-30 (1973).

[47]For examples from the English system where a rule produced by earlier factual inquiry attained sufficient definition so as to remove the need for further proof of custom, and to allow the rule to be finally classified as a rule of law, see Magadara v. Hoit, 89 Eng. Ref. 597 (1691); Bramwich v. Lloyd, 125 Eng. Ref. 870 (1699).

The degree to which a common law rule could be deemed "settled" by a congruous series of judicial decisions was critical also in the treatment of state rules of decision by the federal courts, especially in diversity cases. This was, however, merely a function of the established common law

philosophical conception behind this process is that the ultimate source of the standard is not the court, which only reflects or evidences the standard on the occasion when its intervention is necessary, but rather the vast universe of private activiry which achieves "reciprocal orientation" of individual action by voluntarily assuming certain modes or patterns of behavior or custom. The *actual rule* is nowhere personified or ever perfectly circumscribed into an inflexible definition, because the permutations in the custom or standard as practiced follow progressively changing patterns as society itself changes. The "blackletter rule of law," although it constitutes the fond dream of most law students, is at best an imperfectly articulated representation of the ongoing process of limited judicial intervention. As many commentators have pointed out, this "primacy of the abstract"[48] is a traditional element in the whole common law process, and stereotyped renderings of a particular rule of law, though known, do not themselves eliminate the necessity to understand the application of the abstracted rule through the search for precedent.[49] In debating the application of case law to a particular state of facts, the debate is thereby actually focused upon the degree to which party behavior may be said to conform to the general standard of which the abstract rule in the cases is evidence.[50]

16

---

function of deriving articulate precedent from a course of judicial decisions and therefore pertained to state as well as federal cases. See the cases collected in R. POUND, READINGS ON THE HISTORY AND SYSTEM OF THE COMMON LAW, 227 (1913). Just as Professor Horwitz mistakes federal cases performing an ordinary "rule construction" function or common law resolution of an extraterritorial case with overt deviations from presumptively applicable state law, see HORWITZ, *supra* note 1, 211, he also fails to appreciate the degree to which any individual case represents a particular phase within the common law process of rule settlement. For example, at one point Horwitz remarks that "one looks in vain for any general observations on the nature and limits of the binding authority of commercial custom." *Id.* at 189. Yet the cases contained *built in* limitations which emerged as the judicial acknowledgement of common law rules progressed to the stage where the statements of positive law contained in the cases was thoroughly settled. For example, The Reeside, 20 F. Cas. 458 (C.C.D. Mass. 1837) (No. 11,657), which Horwitz cites on another point, HORWITZ, *supra* note 1, at 197, represents the characteristic decline in judicial willingness to liberally admit factual proof of the content of custom after the contours of the positive rule had fully emerged in previous cases. See 20 F. Cas. at 459.

    [48]F. HAYEK, LAW, LEGISLATION AND LIBERTY 30 (1973). Significantly, Professor Horwitz treats evidence of the abstract quality of common law rules as a postrevolutionary novelty. *Horwitz, supra* note 1, at 144. *See* J. Story, *A Report of the Commissioners Appointed to Consider and Report Upon the Practicability and Expediency of Reducing to a Written and Legitimate Code the Common Law of Massachusetts, or any Part Thereof; Made to His Excellency the Governor, January, 1837,* in THE MISCELLANEOUS WRITINGS OF JOSEPH STORY 698, 701 (1951) [hereinafter cited as Story].

    [49]*See generally* Stimson & Smith, *State Statute and Common Law,* 2 POLITICAL SCI. Q. 105 (1887).

    [50]Moreover, the forces external to unfettered judicial discretion of the sort envisioned by Hobbes and his school set qualifying standards, or over-all tests for utility and "convenience", on each individual decision since its success was largely dependent upon successful integration over a wide variety of decisions spanning a long period of time. M. HALE, THE HISTORY OF THE COMMON LAW OF ENGLAND xxxii-xxxiii, 45 (C. Gray ed. 1971). This feature of the common law process is ignored by Horwitz's argument for a high level of authority in each individual judge. Among courts without authority to bind other courts—*i.e.*, among courts whose authority was *inter se* persuasive—the degree of unanimity of opinion which would have been required for the unified

The common law process itself has this essential capacity to reach ever more mature stanges of development in two essential respects. First, the process matures in the degree to which accumulated judicial references to a given standard have produced an effectively inclusive or complete articulation of the standards. This causes the need for further factual inquiry to be lessened. The process of accumulating related precedent on like or similar cases is the obvious example. Secondly, the process mature to the degree to which the factual inquiry and gradually evolving complex evidence of the rule is extended to more and different subject matter areas. The common law when considered from the standpoint of rule content has thus achieved a state of definition and sophistication similar to a *corpus juris* on some subjects, though it is relatively incomplete as to others.[51] The various levels of maturation according to subject matter area should be born constantly in mind in assessing the evidence which follows herein. Relatedly, the potential differences in rules among different places which, in some but not all respects, are governed by the same *general* principles can also be accounted for in the common law process. This aspect of the growth of the common law produced the familiar distinctions between so-called "general" and "particular" or "local" customs or laws. This multiphase process was often recognized and articulated by the jurists of the nineteenth century in a manner strikingly parallel to the functional descriptions of the common law precedent in the eighteenth century. As Justice Redfield of the Vermont Supreme Court remarked in a commercial law case in 1854:

17

> [U]ntil such rules became necessarily settled by practice, they have to be treated as matters of fact, to be passed upon by juries; and when the rule acquires the quality of conformity and the character of general acceptance, it is then regarded as a matter of law. It is thus that the commercial law has from time to time grown up.[52]

Thus, the common law process ultimately reached a state of maturation in which the "authentic record" of the positive rule is to be found in the case law.[53] Obviously this created a problem with the movement of the rules themselves along the lines of autonomous party behavior since the transactions litigated will be tested against the judicial record and not according to a

---

alliance with the commercial "elite" to work is of course obvious. It is the limited nature of common law intervention, however, and the wide variety of judicial opinion forming the collective prevailing law which makes the conspiracy which Horwitz envisions unlikely.

[51] STORY, *supra* note 48, at 706, where the feasibility of codifying the common law is described as dependent to the degree to which any particular subject where judicial decisions have made the legal principles capable of "distinct enunciation." *See also id.*, at 729-30 for a reference to distinct subject matter areas within the common law which have reached to a "distinct" phase of "enunciation."

[52] Atkinson v. Brooks, 26 Vt. 569 (1854). *See also* STORY, *supra* note 48, at 698, 701 (1951). *Id.* at 702-03. *Compare* M. HALE, THE HISTORY OF THE COMMON LAW OF ENGLAND 45-46 (C. Gray ed. 1971).

[53] See F. HAYEK, LAW LEGISLATION AND LIBERTY 100 (1973).

factual inquiry upon a clean slate. How does the system change? How is the same progressive consensual private authority shared among various individuals and groups in society allowed to continue its influence on the formulation of the rules? This of course was one of *the* most critical questions in the common law process and was in part treated under the conception of "disuetude" or the discontinuance of a general custom by disuse or contrary usage replacing it. This function of the process called upon the judges to evalute claims for the irrelevance of custom or its discontinuation in fact, and their task in so doing greatly resembled evaluation of evidence of a particular custom allegedly displacing a general one — that is, evidence of a peculiar local rule which constitutes a variation in the otherwise applicable general rule. It is here that the exercise of judicial discretion was most critical, for naturally the burden of displacing a well recorded positive rule either by demonstrating its general or local invalidity was greater and much different than the task of demonstrating the *initial* existence and content of the rule.[44] The judges were, in short, called upon to evaluate the relationship between the *record* of autonomous party behavior — or custom — as opposed to new and unrecorded evidence of a general or local standard deviating from that record.

It is in the performance of this critical task that much of the evidence Horwitz mistakes as a new conception of law was produced. It is, however, absolutely essential to bear in mind that the exercise of judicial discretion in this fashion was vastly different than an unfettered instrumental authority to compose rules out of the judges' conception of good social or economic policy. For in the case of the actual common law process, the record as evidence of the fact of a rule and new and contrary unrecorded facts were the objects of judicial inquiry, and always tied judicial activity and discretion to autonomous behavioral phenomena described in the old books under the head of customary law. The most fundamentally significant implication of this process is that it did *not* comprehend an all inclusive design or set of social policies for the society to which it applied; it was largely based upon the continuous recognition of an ongoing order of actions which judicial action only touched upon intermittently, and in a fashion supportive of the ongoing order rather than in a fashion designed to manipulate or wholly reform it. In intervening, the role of the judge was to apply the extant

---

[44] Similarly, the basic expectations supported by a particular rule may require some changes in the applications of the rule as facts change. This function resembles the judicial acknowledgment of changes in customary practices and allows those changes to be reflected in precedent. For example, if the raison d'etre of a property law rule was the protection of certain expectations which private parties have about the use, enjoyment, or development of property, the common law would permit judicial acknowledgement of changes in those expectations as the technological possibilities for use and development made them possible. It required no transformation of legal theory to transform the precedent in any given area. For example, consider the judicial reaction to new development demands on the use of water in the riparian rights cases, described in HORWITZ, *supra* note 1, at 34, *et seq.*

"authentic record" of these   autonomous standards, if any, in conjunction
with an empirical investigation of their evolving use in actual practice so as to
cause the resolution of a dispute by judicial action to conform as near as
possible to the legitimate expectations of parties as determined by external
common standards of conduct. This interstitial method of dispute resolution
was often heralded by the older writers in their discussions of the "convenience" of the common law, as compared with legislation. As Sir John Davies
remarked, the common law

> doth far excell our written Laws, namely our statutes of Acts of Parliament:
> which is manifest in this, that when our Parliaments have altered and chang-
> ed any fundamental points of the Common Law, those alterations have been
> fund by experience to be so inconvenient for the Commonwealth, as the
> Common law has in effect been restored again. . .[45]

In short, the classical model for common law adjudication roughly sketched above is based upon an entirely different set of assumptions about the
relationship between law and judicial action on the one hand and the actions
of the individual and society on the other. It keyed the evalutation of judicial
action to the level of maturity, the rule content aspect, of the common law
according to various subject matters, and the degree to which autonomous
behavior provided a reliable guide to the formulation or exigesis of rules of
decision. Not all subjects were able to satisfy these traditional tests with equal
success, as might be expected. The point that must be borne in mind is that
highly traditional criteria may very well account for what might appear to be
a judicial "unwillingness" to follow a particular alleged rule of common law,
rather than some instrumental design to make new and better law,
unrestricted by any forces external to the judicial process.[46]

19

---

[45] *Davies Report* 5 (1615).

[46] On the compatability of this theoretical description of the common law system and that
existing in eighteenth century England and American, see TUCKER, *supra* note 40, at 67-79 (footnotes omitted); Nolan, *Sir William Blackstone and the New American Republic: A Study of Intellectual Impact* 51 POLITICAL SCI. REVIEWER 731 (1976). As Professor Nolan points out, though
the commentaries were not often used so much as authority to dispose of a particular legal question as to illuminate a particular issue or legal area, its impact upon the American judiciary was
nonetheless profound as a lucid description of the English legal system. As Justice Joseph Story
remarked it was "a work of such singular exactness and perspicacity, of such finished purity of
style, and of such varied research, and learned disquisition, and constitutional accuracy, that, as
a textbook, it probably stands unrivaled in the literature of any other language." Story, *The
Value and Importance of Legal Studies*, in MISCELLANEOUS WRITINGS OF JOSEPH STORY 503, 547
(W. Story ed. 1852).

It is clear that the various phases in the common law system and the varying degrees of
judicial discretion required to facilitate it were very much in the minds of eighteenth century
judges and jurists. The judicial functions of applying a relevant precedent to novel facts by extending its general principle to cover them included: the construction of the general rule from a
collection of somewhat inconsistent case law in order to assess whether any given case contained a
"reasonable"—that is accurate—statement of the governing rule, the required sensitivity to proof
of new custom, or the decline and abandonment of old custom, the geographic limitations
signified by the distinction between "general" customs and "particular" or local customs, the

The basic question is, is the above model an accurate generalization of the conception of the common law system extant during the late eighteenth century and more importantly, if it is, how much did the adaption of this form familiar to the American system after the revolution result in a transformation of the process and its underlying premises? To successfully demonstrate a change in the total conception of law and judicial action, writers such as Professor Horwitz must demonstrate not merely a change in *precedent*, which is a phenomenon distinct from the source of legal obligation, but also demonstrate that whatever changes occurred did so in a manner *not* in conformity with an accurate model of the older conception of this common law process.

An understanding of the origins and mechanics of judicially applied rules during the early federal period is essential to a correct understanding of the judicial role. The fundamental error in Horwitz's analysis lies in confusing the terms "precedent" and "law," and a consequent failure logically to pursue the ramifications of maintaining a once well-understood distinction between the two in analyzing early cases. It is this fundamental distinction in the common law decisional process which accounts for at least some of Professor Horwitz's

20

---

limitations of precedent to the sovereign from which it originated, the harmonizing of different and potentially conflicting rules according to an extraterritorial custom, or private international law. All these were comprehended in a complex, highly flexible evolutionary system. The resultant ability to distinguish the source of the law, the legitimizing principles behind it, and precedent or case law which it produced enabled the common law to grow both widely and quickly. Despite Blackstone's insistence on the great age of custom which would be enforced by the courts, Tucker stated in a footnote in his American edition of Blackstone's COMMENTARIES that:

> It may be therefore doubted whether any custom can be established in the United States of America. For, Time of memory hath been ascertained by the Law to commence from the reign of Richard I, and any custom, in England, may be destroyed by evidence of its non-existence, at any subsequent period. Now, the settlement of North American by the English did not take place 'till the reign of Queen Elizabeth, near four hundred years afterwards. TUCKER *supra* note 40, at 76 n.7. Moreover, the same adaptability had existed a century before he wrote.

See Goebel, *King's Law and Local Custom in Seventeenth Century New England*, in ESSAYS IN THE HISTORY OF EARLY AMERICAN LAW 83 (D. Flaherty ed. 1969). As Goebel described the conditions in the New England colonies, "Each colony had, of course, its peculiar characteristics, but in the seventeenth century before the Leviathan common law had been set in motion, the basic factor was the transplantation of local institutions and customary law." *Id.* at 119-120. Others, of course, have also recognized the long standing practice of analogical extension of customary roles within the common law process. *See* 1 F. POLLOCK & F. MAITLAND, THE HISTORY OF ENGLAND LAW 183 (2d ed. reissued 1968) (footnotes omitted) [hereinafter cited as POLLOCK & MAITLAND]. *See also* J. CARTER, LAW 69-71 (DeCapo ed. 1974) [hereinafter cited as CARTER].

The ratio descedendi of the system was not the enforcement of judicially created, class oriented rules, but the preservation of a wide range of private expectations by adjusting the judicial record of the rules to autonomous party behavior. This theory of the common law system could of course permit great expansion and change in the common law *rules*. Thus a critical question becomes whether the inherent flexibility of the traditional system, rather than the appearance of a revolutionary new "instrumental" one accounted for the doctrinal growth during the period considered. The conclusion of this writer is that a lack of familiarity with the decisional mechanics of the English common law system has caused Professor Horwitz to mistake their use in America with judicial inventiveness and novelty.

confusion about the indicia of changes in the "law," that is the basic theory, as opposed to doctrinal change within an existing theory.[17]

Indeed, Professor William Nelson in an excellent study of the operation of the pre-revolutionary legal system in Massachusetts has concluded that English common law and local custom played a role in the administration of justice in that "colony."[18] Suggesting at least the possibility that a conventional adaptation of the common law system could have accounted for the variety of new legal rules produced by the judicial process there, Nelson describes the authority of the jury in Massachusetts to find the law as enacted in regard to a disputed fact in a case as "virtually unlimited," which gave the "representatives of local communities assembled as jurors . . . effective power to control the content of the province's substantive law."[19] Because of the power of juries, the legal system Nelson describes could not serve as an instrument for the enforcement of coherent social policies formulated by political authorities, either legislative or executive, whether in Boston or in local communities, when those policies were unacceptable to the men who happened to be serving on a particular jury. The ultimate power of juries thus raises the question whether the judgments rendered in the courts on a day-to-day basis were a reflection more of law set out in statute books and in English judicial precedents or of custom of local communities.[20] Professor Nelson concludes

21

---

[17]An understanding of the possibilities for expanding legal rules under the prerevolutionary judicial system as it was then understood in England and America (certainly the understanding of the system may vary from place to place in some respects) is essential to determining whether new precedent equals new legal theory, as Horwitz claims. We cannot otherwise assess the real novelty of each bit of evidence Horwitz adduces for the supposed transformation. For example, Horwitz alleges that it is part of the "new" view of the law to allow private parties to calculate in advance consequences of particular courses of conduct." HORWITZ, *supra* note 1, at 26. However, this allegation of novelty arguably concerns an element in the common law process that was absolutely essential to the "old" conception, and was one of the results of the interstitial, empirical process of evolving law from autonomous fact that made the common law so "convenient," even in the eyes of commentators two hundred years before the American Revolution.

[18]W. NELSON, AMERICANIZATION OF THE COMMON LAW 28-29 (1975) [hereinafter cited as NELSON].

[19]*Id.*

[20]It would be wrong, however, to conclude that community custom was the sole source of prerevolutionary law. In most reported cases, lawyers called the attention of jurors not to rules laid down by custom but to rules of common law . . . . The usual function of custom was only to fill in interstices in statute or common law . . . . The unceasing efforts of counsel to find the rules of common law and to argue those rules to juries suggests . . . that juries were swayed by those rules, that they generally decided cases in accordance with them, and hence that the common law of England rather than local custom was the usual basis of the law. But the fact remains that in every case they decided juries possessed the power to reject the common law and that juries as well as judges and even legislators did on occasion permit local custom to prevail over clear common law. In short, the communities of prerevolutionary Massachusetts freely received the common law of England as the basis of their jurisprudence but simultaneously reserved the unfettered right to reject whatever parts of that law were inconsistent with their own views of justice and morality or with their own needs and circumstances.
Id. at 30.

that both local custom and the English common law were applied by the jury in prerevolutionary Massachusetts, and his explanation of this indicates that, with the possible exception of the scope of the law finding function of the jury, the Massachusetts system resembled the typical common law process.[61] The interaction between the "received" common law of England and the articulation of local deviations, is, of course, suggestive of the frequently made distinction between the common law as a body of rules, and the common law as a continuous process of adjusting such rules according to new factual inquiry and the exegesis of extant rules.[62]

The appearance in Massachusetts of a flexible and adaptive common law system in which local opinion about presiding custom interacted with the judicially originated statements of common law rules is revealing. It demonstrates that prerevolutionary lawyers and jurists did not view the common law as a monolithic body of rules, the departure from which entailed a revolution in legal theory, but rather viewed it as also entailing a process by which the positive rules could change. Now the exact placement of the discretion to depart from precedent as between this jury and judge is of course critical. But the varying emphasis on judge as opposed to jury had for centuries been critical to the adaptability of the common law process, and the decision about when to "let in" new custom or practice to modify the effects of a given common law rule had occurred before the revolution. Christopher St. Germain's account of the differing authority to determine general as opposed to local custom was one example,[63] but so were the perennial outcries about the variation between a previously acknowledged common law rule and current practice,[64] a phenomenon common to the centuries both preceeding and following the American Revolution.[65] For this *not* to have been so, the adjustment of rule to practice in the common law process, that is such things as discretion and the proof of new or local custom, would have to have been self executing. They were not, but rather called for some judicial discretion, albeit prompted by the urgings of private parties and their advocates. But the main point is that the Horwitz thesis so understates and ignores the discretionary dynamics of the conventional or traditional system that he mistakes the ordinary for the revolutionary.[66] Thus a number of features in the

---

[61] Tucker, *supra* note 40, at 68-76.

[62] Jones, *The Common Law in the United States: English Themes and American Variations,* in Political Separation and Legal Continuity 92, 134 (H. Jones ed. 1976).

[63] *See* note 65 *infra.*

[64] *Id.*

[65] Compare the reaction to Lord Holt's reliance on rules at variance with the prevailing practice, in C. Fifoot, Lord Mansfield 15-17 (1936) and the complaints of the commercial community against the common law courts in the nineteenth century discussed in Chorley, *The Conflict of Law and Commerce,* 48 L.Q.R. 51 (1932). *See also* 1. Plucknett, A Concise History of the Common Law, 342-50 (5th ed. 1956).

[66] Indeed, Nelson provides further evidence of this awareness in the concluding chapter of his work, in which he describes how juries were brought under control of the courts, and the entire Massachusetts system first rigidified, when judges followed precedent closely, and then, by

prerevolutionary common law process relate directly to judicial discretion, and comprise the traditional dynamics of judicial action by the common law system which modern writers mistakenly regard as novel. First was the conception of legal obligation and the source of rules as distinct from precedent. Change in the former simply cannot be proven by pointing to change in the latter. Next was the process of "rule settlement," whereby the judicial inquiry into the application of a formerly recognized principle provided a good deal of discretion. Unless previous cases spoke intelligibly about litigated factual situation, some relatively more independent judgment by the judiciary was necessary in order to resolve the case.[67] Similarly, the necessary decision about the accuracy with which any given opinion in a larger number of opinions reflected the rule which cases sought to collectively articulate often provided a degree of judicial discretion.[68] As Blackstone described the process, the general adherence to particular precedent admitted "of exception where the former determination is most evidently contrary to reason . . . . ."[69] This was not a license to reject any given law for policy reasons. Judges "do not pretend to make a new law, but to vindicate an old one from misrepresentation."[70]

Thus, in the process of "rule settlement" the effective limits of individual judicial descretion are largely set by the coherency of the judicial declarations taken as a whole and compared with any one such pronouncement. As Sir

---

the 1820's relaxed, when judges began to accept the "propriety" of departure from precedent. NELSON, *supra* note 58, at 167-74. Nelson describes the reasons for this "shift in attitude" as being the transfer of law-finding power from juries to judges, which threatened to "impose a straitjacket on future legal development" and the fact that judicially administered legal change had become "an abiding and unavoidable feature of the legal system," by the early nineteenth century, which in turn resulted in a situation whereby if "judges [had] said that they were merely applying precedent in bringing about such change" they would have been ignoring reality. *Id.* at 171. Apparently, Professor Nelson means that the "shift in attitude" by the judges was toward a view that they could make law, or, in his words, "that the direction of change was a matter of choice from competing policies rather than deduction from first shared principles." However, the early nineteenth century system he describes is perfectly compatible with the traditional common law system, leading one to suspect that Professor Nelson may be confusing an ongoing evolution of custom, and a consequent expansion or refinement of the precedent designed to evidence custom, with a mere departure from or "overruling" of precedent.

Nelson identifies certain contemporary statements about the common law with what he feels is a totally novel recognition of a new sort of judicial authority. For example, Chief Justice Parker's remark that the "principles of common law . . . . [would] undoubtedly apply" coupled with the observation that the *application* of those principles would vary from age to age, was taken by Nelson as an insight which the judges in the prerevolutionary era failed to have. *Id.* at 172. But again what indicates the *novelty* of those observations? Similarly, the absence of any real cohesive "procommercial elite" in the sense of a monolithic and unified force, pushing the development of precedent entirely in one direction suggests the process for change rested on influences which were much more diffuse than Horwitz suggests. See the discussion of this point in Presser, Book Review, *Revising the Conservative Tradition, Towards a New American Legal History* 52 N.Y.U.L. REV. 700, 706 (1977).

[67] TUCKER, *supra* note 40, at 69.
[68] *Id.* at 69-71.
[69] *Id.* See also POLLACK & MAITLAND, *supra* note 56, at 184-85.
[70] *Id.* at 70.

Matthew Hale put it, the "consonancy and congruity" of decisions was in the, long run an effective guide to their correctiness and weight, and it was this standard, and not individual judicial perceptions which measured the "reasonableness" of a particular pronouncement.[71] When carefully considered, this is of course one of Professor Horwitz's more extreme oversimplifications of the process, though admittedly oversimplification is more acceptable than selective, misleading and incomplete use of data. For clearly no such judge or group of judges could escape the matrix of rules being observed by the greater number, or the forces which operate upon the exercise of judicial discretion, such as the metamorphosis of autonomous practice along which the adjustments of precedential record in the common law process gradually, if roughly, followed. The conspiratorial antics of the great mass of the American judiciary, glancing sidelong at one another as they step in unison to gratify big business by consciously overthrowing the private law of the country is somehow a spectacle which one finds difficult to accept without some real proof. Simplifying the complex forces working a change of precedent so that they fit some linear *neo-Marxian* model explaining all such phenomena as manifestations of class interests is of course a handy way of dispensing with most data beyond the change in precedent.

Additionally, the geographically limited application of some governing rules—represented by the distinction between general and local laws—entailed the judicial evaluation of evidence establishing deviations from the previously acknowledged common law rules. As will be shortly demonstrated, many cases dealing with this ordinary process of assigning certain weight to both localized peculiarities and to allegedly general deviations from a rule which had become relatively settled in previous precedent, have been mistaken by Horwitz as shifts in and out of entirely different conceptions of law. The case law, however, made it clear that once a customary rule, such as a rule of private international law of a commercial nature, had universally established itself and become judicially recognized in precedent among a variety of states and nations, naturally the burden of proving as a matter of fact that the weighty record of party behavior should be called into question, in particular places or generally, was quite high. This was only a method of establishing stability through the use of a reasonable presumption given to evidence of the widespread utility and universal approval of a particular way of doing things; it did not foreclose an inquiry into the facts of autonomous party behavior in future cases.

Lastly the integration of this decisional system with the American Federal Constitution provided still more jurisdictional complications and controversy surrounding the relative authority among different sovereignties.

It will now be useful to take this collection of decisional principles and employ them to test the Horwitz thesis. The degree to which their presence in

---

[71]M. HALE, THE HISTORY OF THE COMMON LAW OF ENGLAND 45-46 (C. Gray ed. 1971).

the case law relied on by Horwitz accounts for precedential change will hopefully enable us to more reliably assess the "transformation" thesis.

The General Commercial Law and Conflict of Laws

As Professor Horwitz correctly observes, "One of the most interesting and puzzling developments in all of American legal history is the appearance of the Supreme Court's decision in *Swift v. Tyson* in 1842."[7] As a case brought under the diversity of citizenship jurisdiction, *Swift* raised questions about the effect of local or state common law rules and, should state law be in applicable, the content of potentially alternative rules of decision. Horwitz attempts to analyse both the independence of the federal judiciary from peculiar "localized" rules of commercial law, which would have in the absence of diversity jurisdiction been applied by state courts, and the *apparent* variations in the opinions of the Supreme Court about the status and content of the general commercial law. However, he does so within the "transformation" dialetic applied to state cases. Further, this shift from purely state cases to the federal opinions involves a set of totally new relationships between the federal and state governments and, in the context of the diversity jurisdiction, among the states themselves—a point either generally unknown to or ignored by Professor Horwitz. He did, however, sufficiently recognize that *something* in the universe of legal relationships with which law dealt had changed in the shift to federal case law, so that he felt compelled to call on William Crosskey for help, albeit to employ one of the weakest aspects of Crosskey's general theseis.[8] In the context of Horwitz' thesis, the basic issue is

25

---

[7]HORWITZ, *supra* note 1, at 245; Swift v. Tyson, 41 U.S. (16 Pet.) 1 (1842).

[8]Horwitz argues, "As Professor Crosskey saw, 'the now prevailing conflicts-of-laws technique ha[d] little application in the eighteenth century and was the slow development of a later time,' roughly after 1820. The shift to a 'conflicts' approach reflected the erosion of the orthodox view that, since judicial decisions were mere 'evidence' of a 'true' legal rule, a conflict of decisions inevitably meant that one of those rules was simply mistaken. The field of conflicts of laws, then, arose to express the novel view that incompatible legal rules could be traced to differing social policies and that the problem of resolving legal conflicts by assuming the existence of only one correct rule from which all deviation represented simple error." HORWITZ, *supra* note 1, at 246. Two basic errors are contained in Horwitz' interpretation of Crosskey: First, the notion that a belief in the natural law foundation of legal rules entailed the assumption that all *particular* rules of law would of necessity be identical is entirely false, since the structure of the natural or eternal law argument entailed the use of those more abstract notions of the legitimacy of legal rules as theoretical and philosophical justifications for *particular* rules that admittedly differed from place to place, or nation to nation. The *positive* laws among nations were justified by the theorems of natural and eternal laws but their precise *content* was not required by this theory to be identical, whatever the different epistomotogical views of the natural law philosophies throughout history may have been. *See* HALE, CONSIDERATIONS TOUCHING THE AMENDMENT OR ALTERATION OF LAWS, in I. HARGRAVE, A COLLECTION OF TRACTS RELATIVE TO THE LAW OF ENGLAND, 269-70 (1787). Compare the various forms of law and ultimate source of legal rules in T. AQUINAS, SUMMA THEOLOGICA, Pars Secunda Q. 91 Arts. I-V, with Germain, supra note 28, at 4. Human laws or positive laws were generally treated as "particular determinations" which though possessing a good deal of variety, simply conformed to certain "other essential conditions" of a general nature for their validity. T. AQUINAS, SUMMA THEOLOGICA, Pars Secunda Q. 91, Art.

this: was there a growing body of transcendent legal rules known as the "general commercial law" which was acknowledged by the federal courts and which would literally supercede otherwise applicable state rules of law, and if this is so, is this evidence of a willingness of the federal courts, like their state bretheren, to engage in self conscious, interest-oriented judicial legislation?

a. *Obligatory "Local" Law in the Federal Courts*

In order to deal with this dual question it is necessary to first consider the true scope of the federal power in regard to diversity jurisdication. In *Swift v. Tyson*,[14] Mr. Justice Story construed § 34 of the Judiciary Act of 1789 to make certain local laws obligatory in the federal courts, but to exclude certain kinds of laws from its operation. Justice Story regarded as obligatory "the positive statutes of the state . . ." and state cases construing them, and laws pertaining "to things having a permanent locality," such as real estate, *and* other "matters . . . intraterritorial in their nature."[15] Contrariwise, nothing required the federal courts to follow state laws applicable "to questions of a more general nature."[16] Furthermore, Story clearly did not make the distinction between statutes and case law determinative of what was obligatory, but rather included both within the scope of the obligation to follow local law. The obligation was determined by the nature of the question and not by the nature of the legal pronouncement.[17]

In the first place, Story referred not only to statutes as obligatory but also as "established local customs having the force of laws."[18] Further it was clear that there was a distinct interplay between extraterritorial matters and local customs, which could become sufficiently developed and certain to counteract the general principles, in which case they would control.[19] Additionally, commercial cases arising under the diversity jurisdiction were by definition extraterritorial to the sovereignty of any single state. Clearly Justice Story recognized that this implicated a pool of case law including but not limited to

---

III. Horwitz's implicit contention that the underlying belief in the system would require the rules of negotiability, for example, to be literally the same among various states or nations is rather absurd. However there are even more profound objections to his statement. In the manner in which private international law and conflict of laws rules actually developed and were employed in America after the Revolution, clearly no such requirement of literal rule conformity was ever thought necessary. See text *infra* in this section. Secondly, Horowitz's statement of the meaning and Crosskey's quote is mistaken and misleading. W. CROSSKEY, POLITICS AND THE CONSTITUTION IN THE HISTORY OF THE UNITED STATES 563 (1953).

[14] 41 U.S. (16 Pet.) 1 (1842).

[15] *Id.* at 18-19.

[16] *Id.* at 18.

[17] *Id.* See the erroneous conclusion in this point drawn by Professor Gray in J. GRAY, THE NATURE AND SOURCES OF THE LAW 254-56 (2d rev. ed. 1972).

[18] 41 U.S. (16 Pet.) 1, 18 (1842).

[19] *Cf.* Bliven v. New England Screw Co., 64 U.S. (23 How.) 420, 433 (1859); Hazard's Adm'r v. New English Marine Ins. Co., 33 U.S. (8 Pet.) 557 (1834).

that of any given states, and called for an independent judgment on the part
of the federal courts. In such cases "the state tribunals are called upon to
perform the like function as ourselves, that is, to ascertain upon general
reasoning and legal analogies, what is the true exposition of the contract of
instrument, or what is the just rule furnished by the principles of commercial
law to govern the case."[80] To have done otherwise would have been to abdicate their primary function in diversity cases—to insure impartial justice
between citizens of different states.

Equally important, however, was the recognition of a variety of subject
matters which were or could be "localized" by a state, so that the local rule
could be obligatory on the federal courts. Most importantly, "localization" required a *particular form* of local pronouncement about the legal issue in
question *and* a congruity between the commercial and private international
law conflict principles. A body of interstate common law rules dictated when
and under what circumstances one state could localize a transaction *vis a vis*
another. The case law taken as a whole reveals that federal courts would
defer to localization, by statute or judicial decison, only in accordance with
general conflict of laws principles. This was, moreover, a practice in accord
with conceptions of sovereignty inherent in *both* the federal and state cases.[81]
Under these conceptions, sufficiently clear local laws—either statutes or decisions—would be obligatory when they pertained to matters local per se, such
as real property within the state, and where they pertained to certain features
of commercial transactions as well.[82] The federal case law makes it clear that
the judges were concerned with determining which set of potentially relevant
rules the private parties may legitimately have assumed were relevant to their
transaction. In cases where an articulate localization had taken place, even if
the rule thereby promulgated differed from the general rules of the law mer-

27

---

[80]41 U.S. (16 Pet.) 1, 19 (1842).

[81]Even so, the cases would have to speak to a differing fact situations, and speak with sufficient clearity about the legal rule. Otherwise the federal courts would have to engage in a construction of whatever authority there was, even if the local laws were statutory in form, or took
the form of unclear judicial pronouncements construing statutes.

See, *e.g.*, Richardson v. Curtis, 20 F. Cas. 707 (C.C.S.D. N.Y. 1855) (No. 11,781). *See also*
Townsend v. Todd, 91 U.S. 452, 453 (1875): "The question depends upon the recording acts of
the State of Connecticut; and we are bound to follow the decision of the state in their construction of those acts, *if there has been a uniform course of decisions among them.*" (emphasis added). The point in the text is closely related also the the practice of the federal courts to
disregard state decisions in diversity cases when the parties had entered into their transaction,
etc. under a prior course of decisions. The federal courts would, however, be reluctant to construe local statutes, since any construction of ambiguous language might be at variance with the
meaning ultimately ascribed to it by the state cases. *See* Coates v. Muse, 5 F. Cas. 1116
(C.C.D.Va. 1822) (No. 2,917). Thus, construction of statues unaided by state judicial decision
was, according to Chief Justice Marshall, therefore, a matter of necessity, to be entered into only
reluctantly; and the reason was that the "exposition of the acts of every legislature . . . the
peculiar and appropriate duty of the tribunals, created by that legislature." *Id.* at 1117.

[82]19 F. Cas. 1270 (W.D.Va. 1846) (No. 11, 383), *aff'd on other grounds*, 29 U.S. (18 How.)
470 (1850).

chant, and the shared extraterritorial rules of sovereignty—the conflict of laws rules—pointed to the state where the localization had occured, the rule would be followed, but not otherwise.[33] Thus, rather than the "either-or" conflict between the transcendent and instrumental general law and applicable local law, the pattern that *actually* emerged was one in which parties to commercial transactions were obligated under the conflict of laws principles which controlled commercial cases to look to the appropriate state, in order to determine whether there had been a localization by statute or custom, of the relevant controlling law. If none was found, it could be presumed that the general custom prevailing in the commercial world would be applied, at least in the federal courts in cases within the diversity jurisdiction. This did not, of course, eliminate all uncertainty from interstate commercial dealings; but it did provide a regularized, relatively coherent system within which the expectations of the parties to various commercial transactions could be generally preserved intact. Moreover, it provided ample space for local variations from general commercial jurisprudence, enforceable in both state and federal courts, thus securing the only important state and party interests in the application of local rules.[34]

Not only would the common pursuit of rules limiting state sovereignty be conducted by the federal and state courts, but also both sets of courts consistently observed further limitations on common law authority, which were designed to better serve private expectations. For example, the federal courts would not follow local decisions, even where they were clear, in cases where the decisions had become settled only after the transaction litigated had occurred.[35] Thus the timing of the state precedent with respect to the disputed

---

[33]*Id.* at 1272. There were of course many commercial cases, like *Prentice*, in which the federal courts routinely adhered to state decisions construing state statutes, construing such statutes independently when no state authority was available to assist them. *See, e.g.,* Oates v. National Bank, 100 U.S. 239 (1879); Townsend v. Todd, 91 U.S. 452 (1875); Sumer v. Hicks, 67 U.S. (2 Black) 532 (1862); Henshaw v. Miller, 58 U.S. (17 How.) 212 (1854); Brasher v. West, 32 U.S. (7 Pet.) 608 (1833); Beach v. Viles, 27 U.S. (2 Pet.) 675 (1829); DeWolf v. Rabaud, 26 U.S. (1 Pet.) 476 (1828); Bell v. Morrison, 26 U.S. (1 Pet.) (1828); Paine v. Wright, 18 F. Cas. 1010 (C.C.D. Ind. 1855) (No. 10,676); Greene v. James, 10 F. Cas. 1151 (C.C.D.R.I. 1854) (No. 5,766); Cleveland P. & A.R. Co. v. Franklin Canal Co., 5 F. Cas. 1044 (C.C.W.D. Penn. 1853) (No. 2,890), Betton v. Valentine, 3 F. Cas. 311 (C.C.D.R. 1852) (No. 1, 370); Boyle v. Arledge, 3 F. Cas. 1108 (C.C.D.Ark. 1849) (No. 1,758); Bennett v. Boggs, 3 F. Cas. 221 (C.C.D.N.J. 1830) (No. 1,319).

[34]A full development of all the cases wherein the federal courts would differ to local authority, as opposed to presuming that private parties had acted under the expectation that extraterritorial rules were relevant to their conduct, is beyond the scope of this work. For a more complete description of the shared common law rules governing the choice between state and extraterritorial authority, see R. BRIDWELL & R. WHITTEN, THE CONSTITUTION AND THE COMMON LAW, THE DECLINE OF THE DOCTRINES OF SEPARATION OF POWERS AND FEDERALISM. (1977).

[35]This was especially true when the retroactive enforcement of a common law rule would have placed a disproportionately heavy burden on nonresidents, whose expectations were central to the diversity jurisdiction. *Compare* Groves v. Slaughter, 40 U.S. (15 Pet.) 449 (1841) and Rowan v. Runnels, 46 U.S. (5 How.) 134 (1847) *with* Nesmith v. Sheldon, 48 U.S. 17 (7 How.) 812 (1849). It is interesting to note that in the former two cases wherein the Supreme Court

transaction, and a decisional principle disfavoring retroactivity under certain conditions, plus the required correspondence between sovereignty-limiting rules of interstate common law, plus the rule construction function which often required an independent judgment about the content of local law, all served to provide a context for the diversity cases infinitely more complex than the "transcedant instrumental law v. local law" dichotomy supporting the transformation thesis.[44] An examination of the early federal cases involving more than one state illustrates a complicated judicial function which is not adequately explained by Horwitz.

b. *Single State v. Multistate Elements in the Common Law*

In finding that the federal courts indulged in self conscious, interest oriented judicial legislation creating a general commercial law, Proffessor Horwitz discusses several early federal cases and the celebrated *Swift* opinion. For example in *Mandeville v. Riddle* (1803),[47] Justice Marshall speaking for the Court reversed a lower court opinion in a diversity case which had held that, despite a Virginia rule against the negotiability of promissory notes, which would have been necessary to permit assignees of such notes to sue remote assignors in a claim of assignment, the assignee could sue anyway, a result apparently contrary to the state rule. In reversing, Marshall (according to Horwitz) held that a state statute would have been necessary to confer assignability or negotiability upon such notes. Absent this, the federal court should not allow recovery. As Horwitz saw the significance of the decision, "Most important of all in terms of the much debated issue of whether the early federal judiciary enforced a general commercial law, Marshall treated the question as simply one of applying Virgina law, offering not the slightest suggestion that the federal courts had any independent power to establish

29

refused to give retroactive impact to state court decisions which would have disallowed transactions apparently legal when consummated, the burden of the state decision would be felt primarily by nonresident holders of negotiable instruments taken by exchange for slaves sold within the state in question. In *Nesmith*, however, wherein the court followed local law which affected transactions apparently legal when consummated, the burden of complying with the decision fell equally upon residents and nonresidents alike, which of course helped to dispel the suggestion of bias present in *Groves and Rowan*.

[44]For other cases discussing the limits imposed in the operation of state law in diversity cases, consider Union Bank v. Jolly's Adm'rs, 59 U.S. (18 How.) 503 507 (1855); Watson v. Tarpley, 59 U.S. (18 How.) 517 (1855) referring to the necessity for imposing the limitations on the operation of local law described in the text so that local laws would not "affect, either by enlargement or diminution, the jurisdiction of the courts of the United States as vested and prescribed by the constitution and laws of the United States . . ." *Id.* at 520. Professor Horwitz sees Watson as further evidence of an "instrumental" conception of law, HORWITZ. *supra* note 1, at 225 n.57, but it appears from the facts of the case that conventional private international law conflict rules would not have subjected the plaintiff to the Mississippi statute, that is this would *not* be a case where Mississippi could "localize" the rule of decision under these facts. The Watson opinion regarded the Mississippi rule as "a violation of the commercial law, which a state woud have no power to impose." *Id.*

[47]5 U.S. (3 Cranch) 290 (1803). HORWITZ. *supra* note 1, at 220.

rules of commercial law."[88] This significant case was brought up a second time six years later, resulting in what Horwitz claimed to be a reversal of Marshall's original position.[89] The Chief Justice, "despite the contrary view of the Virginia judges," held "out of the blue" that the endorsee could sue a remote endorser.[90] This result, according to Horwitz, meant the "Marshall's own conception of the underlying source of negotiability had radically shifted from the position that it arose only through legislative command to the view that it was founded on 'the general understanding' of the nature of the contract itself."[91]

The implicit assumption relied upon by Horwitz is that the law of Virginia was applicable to the case, absent some federal rule which might displace it. This assumption alone renders Horwitz explanation deficient because the issue was not exclusively the effect of the "legislative command" of Virginia upon the parties' contract, but rather it included the relevance of the laws of other states, as well as principles of law common to more than one state in a multi-state transaction. The form of the local rule was not so important to the outcome of a case under diversity jurisdiction as was the limitation on the effect of the local law, however manifest, upon a multistate transaction. The federal courts' general understanding of the conflict of laws rules set limits on the effect of any loal law and a federal court could depart from it by adverting to a common multistate rule or the rule of some other state involved in the transaction without displacing the local rule with a federal one. Horwitz's presumption of the applicability of the rule taken from the state where the federal court is sitting is a corollary of his "either-or, instrumental v. local" dialectic, but unfortunately belies an ignorance of the principles of federalism observed by the federal courts.[92]

Horwitz treats these and other apparently commercial law decisions,[93] and the subsequent *Swift* opinion by Joseph Story as an endorsement of a

---

[88] HORWITZ. *supra* note 1, at 221.

[89] Riddle v. Mandeville, 9 U.S. (5 Cranch) 322 (1809).

[90] HORWITZ. *supra* note 1, at 223.

[91] *Id.* at 221.

[92] The diversity jurisdiction upon which the original suit was based necessarily raised issues other than the abstract relationship between the federal courts and the single state of Virginia. The extraterritorial form of the transaction in question—a note ultimately endorsed to a citizen of another state—potentially implicated the rules of the foreign state and consequently the rules of private international law which would be relevant to differences among the legal rules of states implicated in the transaction. This result was necessarily tied to the question of the degree to which the federal courts were bound by the local view of *Virginia alone*. In short, Horwitz has provided no analysis of the degree to which non-federal rules of law obligatory on federal courts sitting in diversity cases *included interstate rules*, which set the limits on the ability of individual states *inter sese*, to "localize" legal rules for multistate transactions. Since interstate relations in the private law area were involved in such diversity cases along with federal-state relations, the role of private international law, including conflict of laws rules, was a critical question in diversity litigation and the resolution of these issues explains the superficially dissimilar results of the federal case law. However, Horwitz merely treats the dissimilarities in the holdings as battle over the acceptance of transcendent commercial law in federal courts.

[93] See his treatment of Withers v. Greene, 50 U.S. (9 How.) 213 (1850) in HORWITZ. *supra* note 1, at 224.

30

general commercial body of law and related judicial authority to "discover" its contents, subject to the important limitation that state rules in a statutory form, unlike "discovered" common law rules, are obligatory on the federal courts in diversity cases.[14] The issue is thus simply put: Will the federal courts abide by local rules or, in an ultra-traditional reversion to the natural law "discovery" model as described by Howitz, will they rather follow their own abstract concept of the general law?[15] *Swift* was thus a return to the "pure" natural law discovery model of judicial decisions to vindicate the new partisan, interest-oriented "instrumental conception" of law. Further Horwitz argues that, ironically, the efficacy of the *Swift* opinion itself was eroded by the rise of the "conflicts approach" pursuant to which a federal court could selectively opt out of the otherwise binding local state rules. Though the conflict of laws principles employed by the federal courts were an assault on the natural law theory used in *Swift* to avoid undesirable local rules of law, the conflicts approach itself served the same instrumental ends. All this is just about as wrong as it could be.

31

Critical to the understanding of the actual significance of the general commercial law and conflict of laws principles as employed by the federal judiciary and their relationship to the source of legal obligation is an understanding of the relationship between these subjects and the law of na-

---

[14]HORWITZ. *supra* note 1, at 225, where Horwitz erroneously asserts that Watson v. Tarpley, 59 U.S. (18 How.) 517 (1855) was retreat from the natural law thesis of *Swift*. *Watson* is discussed later in this section.

[15]See HORWITZ, *supra*, note 1, at 245-46. The status of the "general law" dealt with in Swift v. Tyson is in typical fashion treated by Horwitz in terms of the "declaratory" theory, which would permit freedom from judicial pronouncements of the states since these were undifferentiated "evidence" of actual laws, and require only the observance of state statutes by federal courts. See *id.* at 245. The positivistic view of law, classifying even judicial decisions as sovereign pronouncements, and the "discovery" theory which would not so classify them, were made to seem in conflict. This misleading characterization of the "old" view has produced a misleading characterization of *Swift* itself.

Thus, by this point, the discrete views of the state courts and jurists, those of the federal judiciary, the complex questions of interstate relations and federalism involved in diversity cases, and the role of private international law rules in settling these issues in both the federal and state courts, are all subsumed under the natural law v. positivism dialectic that is the heart of the "transformation" theme. As Horwitz remarks:

> The jurisprudence of the treatise on *Conflicts* [by Justice Story] shows no trace of the view that differing [legal] rules of commercial law can be reconciled by reference to one overriding general law. Indeed, the treaties is written precisely because such a view of law can no longer satisfactorily explain the existence of a growing number of conflicting legal rules. In short, the conception of law put forth by Mr. Justice Story in *Swift v. Tyson* stands sharply opposed to the jurisprudence of his treatise on *Conflict of Laws* written just eight years before.

HORWITZ. *supra* note 1, at 248-49. The essentially narrow description of the natural law tradition and the *alleged* incompatability between divergent legal rules (or the acceptance of them as fact) and the continuation of the former natural law basis for rules has again produced the impression of profound change, and of a massive change of mind affecting nearly every one over the span of a few years. However, the method by which the rules of private international law including the "general commercial law" were integrated with the diversity jurisdiction through traditional common law processes reveals that the *Swift v. Tyson* approach was *perfectly* compatible with the approach in Story's treatise on Conflict of Laws.

tions generally. Just as the law of nations must deal with multinational transactions, the creation of a federal government in the United States required a
means of dealing with multistate transactions. The means employed were not
novel in that they followed the pattern set by international law, and followed
a pattern of judicial decision-making which repeated the earlier incorporation
of multinational principles in the English common law.[96] In understanding
the role of commercial law as a part of the law of nations, it is important to
recognize that there was originally no sharp distinction drawn between civil
admiralty and maritime jurisprudence and commercial law. They were one
and the same jurisprudence, and only after the passage of time did they
become thought of as separate parts of international law.[97] Consequently,
because commercial law was originally customary law, and because it was also
a branch of private international law, it was dealt with in the same fashion
by the courts as cases within the general customary system of common law
adjudication.[98]

32

---

[96]Sack, *Conflict of Laws in the History of English Law*, in 3 LAW, A CENTURY OF PROGRESS
342 (1937) [hereinafter cited as Sack].

[97]G. GILMORE & C. BLACK, THE LAW OF ADMIRALTY 5 (2d ed. 1975). *See also* T.
PLUCKNETT, A CONCISE HISTORY OF THE COMMON LAW 657-59 (5th ed. 1956); Scrutton, *General
Survey of the History of the Law Merchant*, in 3 SELECT ESSAYS IN ANGLO-AMERICAN LEGAL
HISTORY 7-8, 11-12 (1909) [hereinafter cited as Scrutton]. *See also*, Adler, *Business
Jurisprudence*, 28 HARV. L. REV. 135 (1914); Burdick, *What is the Law Merchant?*, 2 COLUM. L.
REV. 470 (1902); Ewart, *What is the Law Merchant?*, 3 COLUM. L. REV. 135 (1903); Kerr, *The
Origin and Development of the Law Merchant*, 15 VA. L. REV. 350 (1929); Thayer, *Comparative
Law and the Law Merchant*; 6 BROOKLYN L. REV. 139 (1936); Tudsbery, *Law Merchant and the
Common Law*, 34 LAW Q. REV. 392 (1918). See CROSSKEY, *supra* note 73 at 568:

"Hence, [in the eighteenth century] it was considered that there was, in such cases, a
complete defect of applicable local law; and the natural law, modified by international
custom, was again regarded, in the rather rare cases in which such questions arose, as
the appropriate rule of decision. But it was a natural law, and customs, as to what to
do when such foreign local matters were involved."

[98]STORY, *supra* note 48 at 698, 705 (1851). *See also* the extensive reporter's note to
Mandeville v. Riddle, 5 U.S. (1 Cranch) 290 (1803), found at *id.* 367. The note contains an excellent description of how the commerical law was received by the federal courts, and seems
strongly to indicate that the process was one of deriving law from custom, rather than any in-
trumental process. *See* especially *id.* at 374. Moreover, there were numerous state cases in which
the same view was taken of the international customary character of the commercial law process.
Perhaps the most enlightening state case expanding upon the concept that commerical custom
and usage were part of the law-of nations was Atkinson v. Books, 26 Vt. 569 (1854). Judge Redfield, in an eloquent opinion, dealt with an issue similar to that which had confronted Story in
Swift v. Tyson: whether a bona fide holder, who had accepted the note as collateral security for
a preexisting debt, was indeed a holder for value. He then referred "to the English law, and the
general commercial law." According to

the general commercial usuage, there is, then, no essential difference in principle,
whether a current note or bill is taken in payment, or as collateral security for a prior
debt, provided the note is, in both cases, truly and unqualifiedly negotiated, so as to
impose upon the holder the obligation to conform to the general rules of the law merchant in enforcing payment.

Id. at 574.

For other state cases, accepting the general rule of *Swift*, whether extended to include
holders for collateral security of merely for payment, or whether decided before or after *Swift*
itself, *see* Petrie v. Clarke, 11 Serg. & Rawl 377 (Pa. 1824); Steinmetz v. Currie, 1 Dall. 269 (Pa.

Similarly there was eventually a clear identity of function between substantive commercial law rules and conflict of laws rules which governed their application. It was thus quite appropriate for eminent writers on these subjects to describe conflict of laws doctrine as but a "branch of commercial law."[99] The conflict of laws rules designed to serve legitimate party expectations and intentions by making it universally obvious which of the potentially involved substantive rules applied to any given case. The commercial law rules interacted with the conflict of laws rules to serve this end. This was possible because of the increasingly regular, sterotyped forms which the commercial law had in many of its aspects assumed. It had become, as it were, a sort of international or interstate language, which enabled the parties to engage in "reciprocal orientation of their actions" across state lines.[100]

For example, it was clear to parties in commerce from the facts of a transaction, particularly the forms by which it was conducted, whether or not it pertained to an extrateritorial as opposed to a purely municipal or local set of governing rules. Various sets of rules, including customary ones both recorded and unrecorded in precedent, were present to govern or control most any transaction, and the conflict of laws principles when logically applied to a given transaction revealed whether it was confined to a particular sovereign or not. Thus, in creating a negotiable bill of exchange, certain commonly recognized features were necessary before the instrument became negotiable, a quality considered to be the very essence of such an instrument, and to constitute "its true character."[101] Such terms as "or order" and "or bearer" were, according to the general or extraterritorial methods of commerce, essential to negotiability. The form which the transaction assumed according to the common multi-state language of commerce determined whether its consequences were to be measured by one set of rules or another, that is by particular, or local, as opposed to general, or multistate rules.

It is of course quite tempting to view the conflicts approach as the real antithesis of the general commercial law in that the latter signifies an identical substantive rule shared by various sovereigns while the former signifies a set of

33

1788). *See also* Carlisle v. Wishort, 11 Ohio 173, 192 (1842). *See generally* Story, *Growth of the Commercial Law,* in W. STORY, THE MISCELLANEOUS WRITINGS OF JOSEPH STORY 262 (1852). It is clear that *both* federal and state courts were acutely aware of the disutility of extensive departure from the rules of general commercial law. See Aud v. Magruder, 10 Cal. 282 (1858), where the California Supreme Court discusses this issue at length.

[99]J. STORY, COMMENTARIES ON THE LAW OF BILLS OF EXCHANGE 156 n.3 (4th ed. 1860) [hereinafter cited as STORY, BILLS OF EXCHANGE].

[101]J. STORY, COMMENTARIES ON THE LAW OF PROMISSORY NOTES 184-84 (6th ed. 1868) [hereinafter cited as STORY, PROMISSORY NOTES]. *Compare* STORY, BILLS OF EXCHANGE, *supra* note 99 at 156 *et seq.,* with STORY, PROMISSORY NOTES *supra* at 176 *et seq.,* and STORY, BILLS OF EXCHANGE, *supra* note 99 at 175 *et seq.,* 183-85, 216, *with* STORY, COMMENTARIES ON THE CONFLICT OF LAWS at 575 *et seq.,* 598 (3d ed. 1946), respectively, for another illustration of the integral relationship in the textual treatment of commercial law and conflict of laws.

[101]STORY, BILLS OF EXCHANGE, *supra* note 99, § 3. *See generally id.* §§ 32-69, at 41 *et seq.* on the requisites of a negotiable bill and the characteristics it assumes by becoming negotiable. *See* C. TIEDEMAN, A TREATISE ON THE LAW OF COMMERCIAL PAPER §§ 1-9, at 1-24 (1889).

independent rules which determines which of various different sovereign rules prevail at the expense of others. This is the antitethical characterization made by Professor Horwitz: but what if several sovereigns who would be implicated in a multistate transaction have different rules on the substantive principle at issue (for example the requisites of negotiation, or the effects of receiving negotiable paper as collateral security, or the particular terms of restrictive endorsement) but would, on the other hand, all choose the same sovereign as the source of the applicable rule? Are identical conflict of laws principles themselves a part of the general commercial law even though they sometimes result in the application of a substantive rule observed by only one of several implicated sovereigns? Naturally the problem of classification was somewhat ambiguous, and unless one placed so much emphasis on the technicalities of rule selection in multistate transactions so as to insist that *true* general commercial law includes only *substantive* commercial rules but not other legal rules, then the relationship between choice of law or conflict of laws rules and the substantive rules themselves becomes obvious[101] Indeed, the employment

34

[101]Professor Horwitz's observation that the process of selecting among admittedly different governing standards, as opposed to applying a "universal" or "general" law was per se a repudiation of the "natural law theory" which could contemplate only one "true rule" is unsupportable. Actually many early cases *within* England acknowledged the difference between various local customs and formulated a sort of "intranational" choice of law approach dependent upon a classification of the cases resembling the continental distinction between "personal" and "real" statutes or laws. *See* Rutter v. Rutter, 23 Eng. Rep. 400 (ch. 1685); Chomley v. Chomley, 23 Eng. Rep. 663 (ch. 1688); Webb v. Webb, 23 Eng. Rep. 680 (ch. 1689). Likewise the acknowledgment of these distinct customs, the acknowledgment of the content of the "general" law, or law merchant, *and* the content of a possible deviant local foreign law, were all dealt with the initial, factual inquiry stage of the common law process. On the "general law" *see* Vanheath v. Turner, 124 Eng. Rep. 20 (C.P. 1621); Pierson v. Pounteys, 80 Eng. Rep. 91 (K.B. 1609). On the acknowledgment of foreign rules, see particularly Holman v. Johnson, 98 Eng. Rep. 1120 (KIB. 1775); Mostyn v. Fabrigas, 98 Eng. Rep. 1021 (K.B. 1774). The "shift" to an adjustment of a case with extraterritorial features according to a foreign rule differing from English common municipal law as opposed to a general common rule was not a shift in legal theory, but both really resulted from the inevitable divergence of legal rules among municipal laws, even in the case of once common or general rules. *See* Sack, *supra* note 96, at 349-50, 376-77. Moreover, the *lex loci* approach was often consciously evaluated in terms of the traditional common law function of supporting party expectations. For example counsel in the *Mostyn* case argued as the use of foreign law: "For it [the action] must be determined by the law of the country, or by the law of the place where the act was done. If by our law it would be the highest injustice, by making a man who has regulated his conduct by one law, amenable to another totally opposite." *Id.* at 1024.

Indeed, the way in which Professor Horwitz creates the impression of novelty by assigning new and entirely subjective motives to highly conventional processes is strikingly revealed in his discussion of the treatment given the law merchant in the American state courts. Horwitz notes the use of the "struck jury", a practice which he asserts is a manifestation of "mercantile control over the rules of commercial law", and the eventual decline of the expert merchant jury to enunciate governing rules "under the pretext of fact finding"; HORWITZ, *supra*, note 1 at 155, 157. The eventual decline of the process is seen by Horwitz as representing a growing "pattern of judicial hostility to competing sources of legal authority," and as such constituting another novel postrevolutionary trend indicative of the overall transformation of the legal system. *Id.* at 159. Actually, Horwitz fails to appreciate how closely this development in America paralleled that which occurred in England about two centuries earlier, and the fact that this development there occurred entirely *within* highly conventional common law processes. The phenomenon which

of common rules either implicitly or explicitly observed by all concerned sovereigns to mitigate the inevitable differences in the substantive rules and their application among different nations and states, was essential to the successful settlement of multistate problems. The form in which a particular multistate transaction was conducted would in the contemplation of *both* the state and federal courts implicate a body of law which no state alone was constitutionally competent to supply because of the limiting conception of sovereign authority embodied in private international law rules.

This will, if properly understood, explain why the various state cases were not thought to be in direct conflict with some obligatory pronouncement

---

Horwitz characteristically mistakes as revolutionary *actually* concerned the relative weight to be assigned to precedent which represented various stages of maturation within the common law process. The "pattern" was merely one of the typical and gradual judicial acknowledgements of customary rules in which increasingly dispositive weight was given to these judicial acknowledgements as they became more precisely "settled," or relatedly extended themselves to new and different applications of a rule of decision. For example, after a series of internal changes in which the common law courts began to exercise jurisdiction *within* England over cases technically arising within counties other than that in which suit was laid, the courts in the early seventeenth century extended their jurisdiction to cases wherein a truly *international* as opposed to *intranational* choice of law question might arise. In so doing, the courts began a long process by which common, international customary rules were incorporated into the common law by treating their existence initially as fact questions, and later as legal or precedential matters. *See* Sack, *supra* note 96, at 342. As Sack describes the process

> [T]he common law courts appear to have treated the law merchant not as a law but as a custom. The rules of the law merchant had to be pleaded specially, and proved, each time, as a fact.
> . . . The rules of that law gradually ceased to be treated as questions of fact. In 1699, Judge Treby declared, with reference to bills of exchange, that there no longer was any need to allege and prove the custom.

And so gradually, the law merchant became 'part of the Common law.' *Id.*, at 376-77. For cases illustrating the movement toward the recognition of positive rules of the *lex mercatoria* in the common law process, see Martin v. Boure, 79 Eng. Rep. 6 (K.B. 1603) (first *common law* case dealing with a foreign bill of exchange), Pierson v. Pounteys, 80 Eng. Rep. 91 (K.B. 1609). Vanheath v. Turner, 124 Eng. Rep. 20 (C.P. 1621), Magadara v. Hoit, 89 Eng. Rep. 597 (K.B. 1691), Bromwich v. Lloyd, 125 Eng. Rep. 870 (C.P. 1699).

As the various exegesis of the common *lex mercatoria* became "municipalized" local variations were treated the same way internal variations in the English common law system had initially been treated—as factual questions which were addressed by reference to a common *choice of law* rule. The function of the choice of law rule was the same as the initial general law rule, and was incorporated into the initial "fact-finding" stage of the common law process in the same manner as the general law. The conflict or choice of law rule ultimately developed a very efficient interplay with the general law rules themselves in the American federal system, a fact largely ignored by our legal scholars. *See generally* Sack, *supra* note 96. The old "natural law" theory thus neither commanded absolute uniformity in the rule content of positive law, nor any particular method of addressing deviations from identical rules.

If the judges' "unwillingness any longer to recognize competing lawmakers" is a product of an increasingly instrumental "vision of law" as Horwitz claims, it is an "instrumental vision" established in our "received" common law system almost synchronous with the initial settlement of our country. A "continuation" rather than a "transformation" thus apty describes such precedential development in post-revolutionary America—at least in terms of basic common law processes—whether or not what was being done is labelled as "instrumental." If all that is being said is that we *inherited* and "instrumental vision" of law, then the most that can be said of Horwitz's research is that, like many before him, he has "discovered" the common law.

35

about the correct rule of general commercial law by a federal diversity court
and why most state decisions were not in any case obligatory on the federal
diversity courts. Professor Horwitz's "Federal Court v. Local Rule" metaphor
is, it will be observed, entirely inaccurate.[103] To fully understand the litigation in the early federal cases, it must be understood that the ability to
discern in advance which body of rules and usages would be deemed relevant
to a trasaction was the key to understanding the early commercial decisions.
It was here that a decisional technique, which was the legacy of a customary
system attentive to autonomous part behavior, was felt the strongest. Most
importantly the mature system of mercantile law and the mechanisms for
selecting and acting according to given sets fo particular or general usages
was evident not only to parties, but to courts, and was critical in assessing the
degree to which any particular judicial decision could be though to represent
the pretensions of a sovereign *to exclusive dominion over an issue*, as opposed
to an *interpretation* of extraterritorial, general law.

    This was largely possible because the commercial law had in many
areas—for example, negotiable paper—assumed a certain generally recognized formality through the dealings of private parties. As one writer decribed
the character of commercial practices relating to negotiable paper, "The
rules of law on the subject of negotiable paper are more exact and technical
than those of any other department of Mercantile Law.;"[104] The certainty of
the rules meant certainty of consequences through the use of particular forms
prescribed by international custom. It was through the use of these forms of
commercial dealing that it was made evident to parties and to courts that the
backdrop of usage, so important in fulfilling the aims sough by the parties,
would at times be usages among states, and common to many, rather than
peculiar to any one of them. The use of these forms, or failure to do so,
would in many cases be a clear indicator of which sort of customs—municipal
or local, as opposed to extraterritorial—would be applicable to the transaction. It is of utmost significance that *both* the federal and state courts would
identify the appropriate or governing precedent according to the formalities
of the transaction, and judge the consequences to the litigants according to
whichever body of rules their behavior had implicated—extraterritorial or intraterritorial ones. Did an agruably relevant state precedent *purport* to be (or
not to be) in accordance with extraterritorial rules, as opposed to local ones?
That was a question. The answer to it dictated the body of case law with
which the state case was to be compared.

    The value of a judicial decision as precedent in extraterritorial cases was
determined with reference to a wider field of data and by different standards
than was the case with purely municipal rules, and this was so without affec-

---

[103]See Horwitz's characterization of the conflict of laws rules in HORWITZ, TRANSFORMATION,
supra note, at 246, and the discussion of MANDEVILLE at notes 57-61 *supra* & text accompanying.
    [104]T. PARSONS, LAWS OF BUSINESS FOR ALL THE STATES OF THE UNION, WITH FORMS AND DIREC-
TIONS FOR ALL TRANSACTIONS 156 (1869).

ting any considerations of federalism whatsoever. It is enough for our present purpose to note the implication of prevailing extraterritorial custom through the use of well understood transactional forms and the role this played in judicial settlement of private disputes. Quite naturally the federal court sitting in a diversity case which *per se* involved *some* multistate elements (and usually in the commercial law cases actually involved an interstate or multistate transaction) would have to determine what the appropriate source of the governing rule was, and by adverting to the presumptively applicable multi-state rules of a customary origin in such cases should not be confused with a pretension to "make" the governing law by blatantly ignoring a local state rule. Further, in deciding controversies within the context of this mulitstate customary system, state judges would thus resort to extraterritorial considerations, and in so doing they did not manifest the act of a sovereign "freezing" a rule within its geographical power to do so, but rather acted in a cooperative fashion in an area over which they could not pretend absolute authority. The originally non-sovereign origin of commercial rules in the common law process, of course, accounts for the fact that judicial opinions were not referred to as laws but only as evidence of the law, and this aphorism was even more apt in the state cases admittedly dealing with transactions over which the state involved could not pretend any absolute authority, that is in cases involving extraterritorial or multistate rules. Thus, if a large portion of the common law rules involved "interstate common law," then federal judicial exegesis of the principles contained in these rules posed no direct conflict with state sovereignty at all. And more to the point, such cases cannot be construed as examples of judicial creativity in conflict with presumptively applicable state rules, because under such an interpretation the conflict is absent. At least no more of a conflict or deviation from state case law would be represented than is present in the *ordinary* common law process of construing precedent which takes place *within* the state. The ultimate results in applying the general rules may vary from court to court as may opinions about their true content, but this of course proves nothing about any novel or instrumental variety of judicial power.

37

Under this view of the commercial law as originally customary law, and as subject to the common law process, the nature of diversity jurisdiction in commercial cases should be apparent. In a customary law system in which the purpose of a grant of subject matter jurisdiction is to protect nonresidents form local bias, it would be essential that the intentions and expectations of the parties to every dispute be determined by a tribunal independent of the apprehended local prejudice. The law applied would be determined by the exercise of independent judgment by the impartial tribunal, just as factual disputes between the parties would be resolved by a presumptively unbiased trier of fact. Neither function, law determining or fact finding, would be dispensable to the achievement of the jurisdictional objectives. Indeed, abrogation of the law determining function in a customary law system would have certainly defeated the purposes of the jurisdictional grant, since by hypothesis law was being created or adopted *not* by a particular sovereign, but by the private actions of the parties over a long course of time. Thus, failure of the federal courts to exercise independent judgment on the controlling elements of law in commercial cases would have *violated* the doctrine of separation of powers, because it would have involved a disregard by them of the congressional command embodied in the diversity jurisdiction to provide impartial justice in disputes between citizens of different states.

For example, in the *Mandeville* case, the basic problem was defining the content of the multistate or extraterritorial rule to which the parties adverted by using a particular transactional form—a note. The rule content on the particular legal issue involved—the negotiability of a promissory note—was a matter of much debate. The duty to follow the rule once identified was not debatable however, nor was the effect of an attempted localization of the legal rule in a manner contrary to the limitations on state sovereignty provided by the conflict of laws rules, that is by the interstate common law.[105]

In viewing the federal case law of the early nineteenth century as a whole, it is striking to observe how the general conceptions of sovereign authority—particularly rules of private international law—correlated with judicial choice of relevant precedent. The common law process in both the federal and state courts evolved a set of commonly accepted general rules which dictated when the courts of any particular sovereign would be looked to as authority. The inventiveness or instrumental character of any given judicial decision would have to be assessed against the background of precedent that all courts concerned would have regarded as relevant. The interaction of the substantive rules and the conflict rules dictated to the common law courts *which* precedents were relevant. Unless the cases from the state where a diversity court happened to be sitting were automatically accepted as authoritative, then federal cases appearing to depart from them are not germane to the degree of judicial discretion being exercised. That is, if the state cases *themselves* are addressed to subjects or situations over which the state has no absolute authority, then the body of judicial data which other courts, including federal ones, may evaluate to resolve a dispute is *not* confined to the state cases. Departure from a state precedent under this assumption thus may be nothing more than a departure from any precedent which inaccurately states the rule revealed as the whole body of relevant cases. Once the question of federal v. state sovereignty drops out, all that remains are federal and state cases which must be viewed collectively as part of the common law process shared by both federal and state courts, rather than as clashing exponents of "local v. instrumental" law. The degree to which the common law process was amenable to the incorporation of rules of private international

---

[105]R. BRIDWELL & R. WHITTEN, THE CONSTITUTION AND THE COMMON LAW 175, n.79 (1977).

law by which both the state and federal courts would measure the correlative position of the states as sources of law for multistate disputes, and the resultant degree to which judges conceived of such rules as a part of the common law process is therefore crucial to the "instrumental" thesis. This is so because it is critical to the presumed applicability of the state precedent *where* the federal court happened to be sitting. The resolution of this question will destroy the impression of tension existing exclusively between the federal and the state common law rules from the state wherein the federal court sits, which is so critical to the Horwitz thesis. For it is true that the integration of private international law rules into the English common law system had proceeded apace for over a century before the American Revolution, and continued in both the American federal and state courts thereafter.[106]

In summary, the Horwitz thesis proceeds from an artifically narrowed conception of the common law process, based on evidence taken from the larger context. This conception is transferred to the American federal system without any analysis of the subtle but observable constitutional and jurisdictional changes which the system entailed. Federal and state cases are thus equally subject to the over-simplifying transformation dialectic, with the result that federal cases are judged against the background of a narrow pool of case authority which Horwitz regards as exclusively applicable—the state cases where the federal courts are sitting. Thus any arguable departure from *those* cases is taken as more evidence of the new instrumentalism.

If one accepts the foregoing hypothesis about a more complex system of rules governing sovereignty having been integrated into the common law system, however, the pool of authority relevant to the federal court would include other state cases as well as federal cases in situations involving matters beyond the exclusive authority of any one state, and yet not committed to federal authority. The "rule construction" function alone would thus account for an apparent departure from the state cases from the state in which the federal court sat, simply because the pool of relevant case data is *ex hypothesi* much larger than just the cases of that state.

C. *Conflict of Laws and Interstate Common Law*

It is clear that the conflict of laws scheme in private international law was integrated into the common law process in the federal courts in order to accommodate the operation of the local laws of the coequal states and to insure the necessary protection, under the diversity jurisdiction, of the expectations of noncitizens and foreigners.[107] The diversity jurisdiction operating under the merely declaratory injunction of the Rules of Decision Act was

39

---

[106]Sack, *supra* note 96, at 376.

[107]*See* Brown v. Van Braam, 3 U.S. (3 Dall.) 344 (1797). *Compare* Warren, *New Light on the History of the Federal Judiciary Act of 1780*, 37 HARV. L. REV. 49, 88 n.84 (1923), *and* Crosskey, *supra* note, at 822-24.

naturally not taken by the federal courts to require unconditional obedience to local laws (a presumption essential to create the illusion of contrast in Horwitz's use of the apparently deviant federal case law to prove the "instrumental thesis). Rather, the coequal sovereign status of the states in a federal system made apparent "some limitation on the operation" of the Rules of Decision Act's directive, and it was a limitation which arose "whenever the subject matter of the suit is extraterritiorial."[108] To have blindly imitated local rules would "clearly defeat nearly all objects for which the Constitution has provided a-national court."[109]

The application of the Rules of Decision Act in accordance with private international law conflict of laws principles is in fact the quite logical outcome of the transfer of the conventional common law approach to the federal system. Viewed in this light, the activities of the federal courts during the early nineteenth century appear as quite a conventional adaptation of the jurisprudential and decisional norms of English law to the American federal system. Clearly *Swift v. Tyson*,[110] long the controversial symbol of illegitimate judicial creativeness, cannot be adequately explained by Horwitz's oversimplified and crude "discovery" or "natural law" model. Though the decisions of the New York courts were unsettled on the basic point of law involved in *Swift*,[111] Justice Story assumed *arguendo* that they *were* settled and rested his decision upon the non-obigatory nature of the local decisions under the facts of the case.[112] Story's initial explanation for this is essential to an understanding of what was going on in *Swift*. He stated: "It is observable that the Courts of New York do not found their decisions upon this point upon any local statute, or positive, fixed, or ancient local usage: but they deduce the doctrine from the general principles of commercial law."[113] In other

---

[108]Van Reimsdyk v. Kane, 28 F. Cas. 1062 (C.C.D.R.I. 1812) (No. 16871), at 1065, *rev'd on other grounds sub nom.* Clark v. Van Reinsdyk, 13 U.S. (9 Cranch) 53 (1815).

It has long been recognized that implicit limitations on the sovereign authority of coequal states were judicially enforceable by the federal courts, even when a judgment of a state court was involved. The Law of Nations then played a role as an implicit element in the Supreme Courts view of the full faith and credit clause, U.S. CONST. art. IV, § 1, and a fortiori played a large role in their view of the extraterritorial effect of state laws. *See* Rheinstein, *The Constitutional Basis of Jurisdiction*, 22 U. CHI. L. REV. 775, 791-96, 802 (1955). Compare Nussbaum, *Rise and Decline of the Law of Nations Doctrine in Conflict of Laws*, 42 U. COLO. L. REV. 189 (1942).

[109]Van Reimsdyk v. Kane, 28 F. Cas. 1062, 1065 (C.C.D.R.I. 1812) (No. 16871).

[110]41 U.S. (16 Pet.) 1 (1842). Swift v. Tyson involved the legal issue of whether or not a preexisting debt was valuable consideration for a negotiable instrument, and thus sufficient to give the holder immunity from defenses existing between the endorser and the obligor. Since it was a diversity case, the question of which body of rules could be used to answer this question naturally arose. Justice Story's opinion in *Swift*, declining to be bound by the judicial opinions of the New York courts, has been characteristically interpreted by Horwitz as an "instrumental" attempt to impose procommercial national legal rules, invented by the federal judges, upon unwilling state judges. HORWITZ, *supra* note, at 245-52. This essay presents a different view.

[111]41 U.S. (16 Pet.) at 16-18.

[112]*Id.* at 18-19.

[113]*Id.* at 18. *See also* Gloucester Ins. Co. v. Younger, 10 F. Cas. 495, 500-01 (C.C.D. Mass. 1855) (No. 5, 487).

words, there had been no "localization" of the rule of commercial law involved since the Courts of *New York themselves* purported to follow the general
commercial law, not to deviate from it by establishing a rule derived from
some "positive, fixed, or ancient local usage." Once the importance of this
fact is understood as to *Swift* and all similar cases within the ambit of the
general commercial law, the justification for the federal courts making an independent judgment about the applicable rule of law becomes clear. Appreciating the significance of this fact within the context of the unique
jurisdictional and constitutional status of the federal courts and within the
context of the commercial and conflict rules relevant to that unique status, is
absolutely essential to reading the real meaning of *Swift* and similar cases.

It also becomes clear why § 34 of the Judiciary Act did not bind the federal
court to follow state courts decisions in general comercial cases—*i.e.* why
state decisions were not "laws,", but only "evidence of . . . laws,"[114]

When the state courts of a particular state *themselves* purport to follow
the general commercial law in particular cases, they create a set of expectations on the part of nonresidents who deal with the citizens of that state. The
expectations are that the general customs of the commercial world will
operate to control transactions entered into with citizens of the state, or
within the state, and the nonresidents can act accordingly in their dealings by
ignoring the possibilíty that their transactions will be controlled by some
other rules. This does not, of course, mean that the subjective state of mind
of the nonresident will be examined to determine whether he was aware of
local deviations from the general commercial practice in a given locality.
Rather, it means that when a state encourages its citizens to act in accordance
with stereotyped general commercial practice, rather than *formally* localizing
a practice by statute, or by explicit recognition in a judicial decision that the
state in given transactions is *not* following general commercial law, it creates
expectations on the part of outsiders that those stereotyped forms mean the
same thing in the state that they mean everywhere else. If, therefore, a noncitizen relies on these implicit representations in his dealings with residents of
a state, and if the state subsequently applies a rule to the dealings which
deviates from the general practice, the expectations of the noncitizen have
been defeated. He has, in short, been misled by the state's apparent approval
of general commercial law.

Just as the common law courts characteristically had to determine which
universe of general or particular customs and positive rules derived from
customs a particular transaction implicated, so the federal courts in performing their decisional function would pursue the inquiry into the content of the
governing rule in the same manner as the state courts, that is to discern the
content and application of the correct general, extraterritorial rule. In this
sense, and not in some vague "discovery" sense the federal courts were perfor-

41

---

[114]Swift v. Tyson, 41 U.S. (16 Pet.) 1, 18 (1842).

ming a "like function" as the state courts. The necessity for both sets of courts to engage in the exegesis of extraterritorial rules was the product of the fact that, unlike England, the United States was not a unitary system wherein judicial *enforcement* (as opposed to promulgation) of common law rules could proceed unaffected by the limitations on the general legal authority of coequal sovereigns.

If one asks the question, what would one *expect* to happen under the adaptation of conventional common law judicial techniques in dealing with the consequences of federalism, what *actually* happened makes a good deal more sense, and the novelty thesis of the current revisionists such as Horwitz suffer by being thus placed in an historical context they would rather ignore. Consequently, the federal court, to protect the expectations of the noncitizen, had to make its own independent judgment about the general commercial principles, rather than relying on the decisions of any given state, since those decisions were only "evidence" of what the general commercial practice was, rather than "law."

In the above example reference to the fact that the "maker used terms of negotiability in his contract" is an implicit reference to a set of principles which would give the words chosen that effect. In describing the parties' choice of form in just this way, the primary significance of the acknowledgment of such principles by the parties and the fact that the principles transcended state boundaries and thus state sovereign authority is made clear. Otherwise such words should not have the capability of "binding him [the maker] to the endorsee" at all if they would not have that effect under the law of the place where the note was made. The predictable implication of general customary rules from the use of particular transactional forms is thus perhaps the most consistent feature in the analysis of these multistate problems, and is the key to understanding the authority of judicial decisions about them.

Swift v. Tyson itself is a prime example of how the diversity jurisdiction operated to preserve the intentions and expectations of the parties when their dealings had taken place against the assumed background of general commercial practice.[118] Thus everything practical encouraged states to leave general commercial custom intact as they found it, rather than to attempt to "localize" general rules of commerce in accordance with some supposed state policy. It is the conformity of such commercial law opinions as *Swift v. Tyson* to an extremely broad international constituency, and the support found for such decisions in the customary paractices of innumerable private parties pur-

---

[118]It is difficult to imagine any real expectations Mr. Tyson might have had being defeated by the *Swift* decision. He employed an instrument clearly subject to negotiation in foreign states, or to persons therein, according to usages or rules generally observed. It is interesting to note the reliance on party expectations in many of the more modern discussions of conflict of laws. See A. Shapira, *'Grasp All-Loose All': On Restraint and Moderation in the Reformulation of Choice of Law Policy*, 77 COL. L. REV. 248, 265-68 (1977).

42

suing their own autonomous commercial dealings, that best illustrates the fictional quality of "instrumentalist" views of judicial decision making as a distinctly early nineteenth century phenomenon. Such a characterization merely shifts the description of a perfectly traditional judicial function from the gradual recognition of widely held and objectively provable practices to a subjective evaluation of judicial behavior. This creates the impression that something quite ordinary is in fact new.

It seems illogical to assert the supposed novelty of "instrumentalism" in judicial activity, the engineering of social and economic policy according to judicial perceptions, when in fact the supposedly instrumentalist decisions reflect the views and practices of the majority of the commercial world. Historically speaking, cause and effect are thus reversed, and the judicial role is described as one of creating rather than recognizing. We may of course admit to a degree of discretion in employing the processes of reasoning and analogy in the common law decisional process, but the question which plagues historians of the period concerns the basic assumptions from which judicial decision making begins. For if, as appears to be the case, the proponents of instrumentalism and their interpreters base their opinion that judges came in the early nineteenth century to "view their role" as lending support to economic maximization by departure from precedent or upon some other novelty in the judicial opinions, their proof seems to fail.[116] As has already been shown, departure from precedent does not necessarily signify any change at all in the judicial view of the source of law, and the highly traditional nature of opinions now viewed as examples of judicial inventiveness seems to undermine the basic theory. The insistence in viewing judicial activity in purely positivistic terms has created the impression of conflict and novelty where none existed in fact. The subtle aspects of the decisional process have been conveniently characterized from time to time as "glittering generalities."

The current acquiescence to a positivistic legislative model in analyzing judicial activity has created a distorted impression of the legal history of the early national period. Deviations from precedent or the articulated purposes of an announced rule in early cases have been viewed by the standards of expediency and convenience thought to be relevant to the wise legislator, and the notion that judicial pronouncements were in fact reactions to a universe of changing customary practices and expectations has been discounted. The "invisible hand" has become a favorite target of critics anxious to explode the notion that legitimate philosphical and practical differences separated the judges and the legislator. Judicial as opposed to legislative function is a "fiction which "nobody believes."[117] However, the starting point for the judicial

43

---

[116]See generally Priest, The Common Law Process and the Selection of Efficient Rules, 6 J. LEGAL STUD. 65 (1977); Rubin, Why Is the Common Law Efficient? 6 J. LEGAL STUD. 51 (1977).

[117]See Stimson & Smith, State Statute and Common Law, 2 POLITICAL SCI. Q. 105, 106 (1887).

function and its necessarily limited interference with the vast bulk of human activity which typifies the early nineteenth century case law, particularly in the admittedly significant commercial law area, indicates that the "innovative" judicial work was accomplished without a revolution in the theory of legal obligation. It is, moreover, the breadth of the constituency supporting the rules of private commercial law which makes the characterization of judicial activity in this area questionable. The social intercourse which produced the mature *lex mercatoria* is grossly simplified by the positivistic model. In fact, early commentators explicitly recognized the diffuse source of the rules of law and the resultant relative inability to mold them according to economic or class preferences.[118]

The nonpreemptive character of federal decisions on local matters, and the general acknowledgment of "like function" performed by both state and federal courts in extraterritorial matters,[119] all dispel the specter of powerful federal intervention of an "instrumental sort." The utterance of the sovereign was simply not regarded as being quite as important in resolving private matters as it is today.

44

CONCLUSION

Ironically, it is the "common law context," the common law system, which more than anything else Horwitz seeks to illuminate while it is that feature of Anglo-American legal history he has apparently explored the least. The use of suggestive intellectual constructs such as "the will theory" of law and various bits of evidence taken out of context as suggestive of some novel conception, such as the "consensual" descriptions of the common law process, reveal one of the greatest apparent weaknesses of our current so-called "intellectual history." Precisely, the "intellectual" developments sought to be proved actually are the *a priori* assertion with which the author *begins* rather

---

See Holt, *Now and Then: The Uncertain State of Nineteenth Century American Legal History*, 7 IND. L. REV. 615 (1974). The author notes the process by which these sweeping theories such as instrumentalism are based upon slight evidence.

"Horwitz's support for his views seems somewhat weak and will require some sublateral monographic aid, but the thesis is convincing." *Id.* mat 632. However it is quite possible that the emphasis upon the positivistic creative, legislative model in analyzing early case law causes the significance of isolated and slight evidence to be overstated. The case law must be evaluated in whole units—for example private commercial law adjudications in specific courts or jurisdictions.

[118]See 1 I. PARSONS, A TREATISE ON THE LAW OF SHIPPING AND THE LAW AND PRACTICE OF ADMIRALTY 4-5 (1869), where Parsons notes that commercial law rules, being "founded as they were upon the necessities, and the usages of the merchants generally" are by their general acceptance in an extensive commercial community are "seldom, if ever, materially affected by the rights and prejudices of caste or class." Indeed, one interpretive theme which seems to divide legal historians is the question of whether or not judicial action in America has taken place within a broad social consensus. Contrary to Horwitz' view, James Willard Hurst has consistently emphasized broad popular support for legal change in America. See J. HURST, LAW AND SOCIAL OORDER IN THE UNITED STATES 226 (1977). My own view of the period is more in agreement with Hurst.

[119]Atkinson v. Brooks, 26 Vt. 569, 582 (1854).

than demonstrates. "Intellectual history" of the sort necessarily employs arbitrarily selected evidence judged by its superficial conformity to a "theme" rather than its relationship to elements in a real context. Forgetting the injunctions of many past analysts of legal theory,[120] extrapolations from evidence selected for its compatability with a preconceived theme obscure what people to any given time actually thought. A disembodied chain of extrapolations emerges which in reality is only consistent with itself, and the real devotees of the preconceived theme are hardly ever worried about the fact that adherence to it requires us to believe that the characters whose thoughts we seek to know often to constantly vascillate in their most basic ideas.[121]

In short, almost everything is measured by these gross extrapolations from incomplete data—such as Horwitz's fantastical explanation of the use of conflict of laws principles as a repudiation of natural law's one "true rule," making this subject area convincing evidence of the changed theory of law. The point is that "conceptual" assertions with no regard at all for the *legal* context in which the evidence occurred appear to be insufficient as a basis for "intellectual history." This legal context is in reality as important an ingredient as the construction of our intellectual, legal part as any other data. It is as if Professor Horwitz sought to carefully exclude from consideration the *holdings* of all the case data he analyzed, and rely exclusively on *dicta*. But the conceptions and rules of construction which shaped the meaning of judicial pronouncements were (and are) themselves an important part of the historical and intellectual context of the data used. The overall pattern of the case law and the structured meaning which the cases collectively had for lawyers and jurists simply will not permit the use of apparent deviations in outcome among cases plus selective dicta to successfully carry off the "transformation" thesis.

The intellectual apparatus which lawyers *then* employed to illustrate the conformity of superficial outcome differences with consistent general principles strongly suggests that the meaning Professor Horwitz ascribes to their actions its false. Not only would the application of some quite familiar techniques for analysis of legal data enable Professor Horwitz to derive a more

45

---

[120]"To lurk under shifting ambiguities and equivocations in matters of principal weight is childish." *R. Hooker, The Laws of Ecclesiastical Polit*, Bk. VIII, ch. 1, § 2 p. _____ , in THE WORKS OF RICHARD HOOKER, J. Kemble, ed (   ).

[121]Practically everyone in Professor Horwitz's scenario changes his mind incessantly. Chief Justice Marshall regularly has "radical shifts" in his understanding of basic legal questions, HORWITZ, *supra* note 1, at 223, and Justice Story "sharply opposes" his own recently held views with regularity. *Id.* at 248-49. While theories of law appear, vanish and then reappear like some ghostly shade. See *id.* at 196, where the "theory of preexisting custom" having died, rematerializes briefly and then vanished again (or does it?). This passage is particularly worth a second reading. Surely people do change their minds, and ideas come and go, but certainly one would think that a chosen theme which converts the mass of evidence about our legal past into such a chaos would be at least initially scrutinized in light of explanations which would accord some of the principal characters at least a degree of consistency.

defensible and more accurate meaning from it, but to do so would have illuminated the milieu of our early law according to intellectual techniques which those living then employed. But serious analysis of intellectual change in legal history has come to repudiate its less fashionable intellectual apparatus, with at least the lay reading public probably none the wiser. A simple consideration of implicit principles common to a wide variety of case data would have disclosed certain general consistent "theories" in the case law itself, which would in turn explain what specifically appears to be "transformation." Selective use of outcome differences plus dicta in the case data hardly measures up to the traditional composite analysis and search for underlying "thematic" principles common to the lawyer's art.

Such books are of course written for people, perhaps by people, who already fervently believe what they seek to prove. Thus, the "intellectual history" at its apparent finest ironically turns out to be the most unmitigated form of "consensus history," an even more formidable and counter productive variety than the "old" consensus history because it relies more on the *a priori* structure of its arguments and initial preconceptions and less on empiricism, which is easier to deal with analytically and therefore more to be avoided in this new "intellectual history." The postulation of these intellectual constructs has a way of becoming an effective substitute for serious inquiry into intellectual change. The inefficacy and weakness of the new potent revisionist *genre* are, however, better concealed than former purely doctrinaire methodology, because it effectively assumes all the popularized hallmarks and trappings of respectability, replete with declaration after declaration that what is being revealed is "consciousness" and other "emerging" things. An abstract litany of soothing, comforting, largely apparitional theorems with a false though convincing appearance of novelty emerges, and this in turn lulls us into an increasingly comfortable indifference to naive assumptions that the contemporaries of the eighteenth century *really* meant what they said, and knew themselves as well as we know them. In fact, a sort of protective coloration asserts itself, an effective scholastic camouflage, whereby the more empirical and evidence-oriented writing can be rejected as a sort of "advocate's brief," and crabbed "arid formalism," as having too much "detail" and not enough proof. Amazingly, some who opt for the broader themes without proof, or with half-proof, acknowledge the lack of support for such thesis as those of Horwitz, but find that the "thesis is convincing" anyway.[122] How we are to be convinced without proof is hard to say. Perhaps half-proof of correctness is though to equal proof of half-correctness, so that the proponents of thesis without proof assume the thematic writers such as Horwitz must be at least half right in what they say.

Likewise by contrast, the more conventional empiricism, which in the unlikely event it appears at all in the face of unchallenged orthodoxy, ap-

---

[122]*See* Holt, *Now and Then: The Uncertain State of Nineteenth Century American Legal History* 7 IND. L. REV. 615, 639 (1974); L. FRIEDMAN, A HISTORY OF AMERICAN LAW 1-7 (1973).

pears more and more to be really "not with it." A general plea has been made for a good deal less of the "lawyer's detail" and for more emphasis on broader interpretive themes, and surely what this represents is on the whole good. But, on the other hand, hopefully this essay has at least provided a plausible argument for some close scrutiny of the work product that purports to satisfy this demand, and has provided some evidence of the dangers of the popular aversion for the "adversaries' brief" or the art of "narrowing cases to fit their facts." As Frederick Maitland observed, lawyers usually don't make good historians, but to be a good *legal* histroian, being a lawyer helps, and the classical function of lawyers plays a large part—albeit a technical and often forbidding part—of understanding our legal past with any degree of accuracy.[128] The ascent to the ambitious observation of broad themes runs the strong risk of loosing a precise and indispensable knowledge of the various important strands in the whole theme, and the rush to turn a beacon on the whole of the law and its fundamental meaning may shed more light on the observer than on the subject.

47

Admittedly, phenomena such as "judicial discretion" are not easily quantified. The relationship between extant precedent, judicial discretion and precedential change resulting from a mixture of these two common law elements is difficult to define precisely. The ability of a prevalent decisional technique to accomplish extensive and profound doctrinal change and still remain the same technique or constitutional common law process is an exceedingly complex phenomenon to understand, as is the point at which thoroughgoing precedential change is a fact attributable to a wholly new conception rather than being an extension of the old. Horwitz's book adds little to our understanding of this process, and at most presents largely unsupported conclusions with a mere description of doctrinal change, sometimes stated inaccurately.

This is apparently a rather critical stage in the research and writing of American legal history. This book and similar ones illustrate one of the more serious problems in this critical phase. Particularly, the promising and necessary emphasis on theme is quite likely to turn out to be a set of blinders, rather than enlarging our vision as it should. Once the blinders are removed and our vision is in fact expanded, the original theme which the blinders produced quickly evaporates. The delicate construction of the evidence outside of any extended context and the weakness of the arguments when the context is supplied indicates that this praticular book, like any overly doctrinaire approach to a complex subject, actually superimposes the final result on artifically constructed evidence, rather than developing it from the historical data. Even more interesting is the intellectual process which may employed to undermine Professor Horwitz's transformation theme at almost every turn, for

---

[128]F. Maitland, *Why the History of English Law Was Never Written*, in FREDERICK WILLIAM MAITLAND, HISTORIAN 132, 140 (R. Schuyler ed. 1960).

it boils down to one of the more elemental analytical tools of the lawyer: the comparison of a good deal of data, primarily from case law, in order to discover if some implicit pattern in the data can illuminate it, and assist in its whole comprehension. The pattern is, when articulated, a useful model in the search for the more important, if less overt, fundamental legal processes at work and is one of the vital intellectual tools employed to expand knowledge beyond the suggestive impressions conveyed by mere doctrine. In seriously investigating legal change, it must form *at least* a competing role in the analytical process. The by-products of the complete separation of thematic or intellectual history, from the more formal, albeit "arid," process of case analysis on a vast scale can be most countrproductive, as Horwitz's book demonstrates. The merging of both federal and state cases, which in fact represented extremely different constitutional and jurisdictional contexts, and evolved under different influences and considerations, within the simple "transformation" dialectic really obscures much that is relevant. We should then cautiously refrain from the "lawyers formalism v. thematic or intellectual history" dichotomy and thereby better avoid thoroughly confusing either of the forms with reality, and confusing pretensions of proof in an agreeable disguise with actual proof. The intellectual apparatus of the profession should not be the handmaiden of fashion, which seems to be a result more possible than many of us would like to believe. In short, the "Theme" may be quite expansive, and the understanding it permits quite narrow.

Naturally it would be a mistake to conclude that the alternative interpretation offered here—of a largely self ordering system supportive of autonomous individual behavior and experiment, adjusting itself with the aid of limited judicial intervention that does not effectively elevate the narrow interests of "caste or class"—is a whole or complete picture of reality. As an historian of science once remarked: "If there is a lesson in our story it is that the manipulation, according to strictly self-consistent rules, of a set of symbols representing one single aspect of the phenomena may produce correct, verifiable predictions, and yet completely ignore all other aspects whose ensemble constitutes reality."[184] But the doctrinaire insistence on a narrow "strictly self-consistent" theme hides the richness of the whole ensemble with its widely varied judicial personalities, complex and various jurisdictional and constitutional considerations, and astonishingly diversified array of private interests (many of which respond to their legal environment without leaving any litigational record). It states a claim for law upon life which is, I think, a bit overstated and too self-important, and is a theme which inverts the position of the individual *vis a vis* the law as it was understood during the early national period, at least as I read it. The emphasis upon a simple theme which calls our attention to this richness and complexity, if only by burying it under a doctrinaire plot, may be Horwitz's greatest service to our understanding of Amercian legal history, and for this he should certainly be praised.

---

[184] A. KOESTLER, THE SLEEPWALKERS A HISTORY OF MAN'S CHANGING VISION OF THE UNIVERSE 533 (1959).

LEGAL REALISM AND HISTORICAL METHOD: J. WILLARD HURST AND AMERICAN LEGAL HISTORY

*Stephen Diamond**

LAW AND SOCIAL ORDER IN THE UNITED STATES. By *James Willard Hurst*. Ithaca, New York. Cornell University Press. 1977. Pp. 318. $17.50.

For many years, J. Willard Hurst has been the dominant figure in American legal history. He is one of the few legal historians whose work has been enthusiastically received both by professional historians and by lawyers. Historians have traditionally insisted upon a research monograph as an entrance credential into their community and Hurst has produced a massive and impressive example of such a work.[1] Hurst and his students have analyzed in detail the interaction between law and particular economic activities in nineteenth-century Wisconsin.[2]

Lawyers, on the other hand, have typically applauded histories of their subject that are broad in scope, believing that without great effort (and thus usually with little attention to primary materials), they can grasp the main themes in the evolution of their discipline. Such synoptic overviews have frequently been presented first as a series of lectures, among the most notable being works by Holmes, by Pound, and by Gilmore.[3]

Hurst has himself contributed greatly to this tradition. In *Law and the Conditions of Freedom in the Nineteenth Century United States* (1956) he summed up a century of legal development in the phrase, "the release of energy"—a theme now familiar even to those who have not read Hurst's book. In *Law and Social Process in United States History* (1960) the scope was even broader—the entire national period of American history—as was his task understanding the role of law in America. Hurst's most

---

* Assistant Professor of Law, Benjamin Cardozo School of Law, Yeshiva University. B.A. 1967, Swarthmore College; M.A. 1968, J.D., Ph.D. 1976, Harvard University.

1. J. HURST, LAW AND ECONOMIC GROWTH: THE LEGAL HISTORY OF THE WISCONSIN LUMBER INDUSTRY (1964) [hereinafter cited as LAW AND ECONOMIC GROWTH].

2. The list of such works includes L. FRIEDMAN, CONTRACT LAW IN AMERICA (1965); R. HUNT, LAW AND LOCOMOTIVES (1958); S. KIMBALL, INSURANCE AND PUBLIC POLICY (1960); G. KUEHNL, THE WISCONSIN BUSINESS CORPORATION (1959); AND J. LAKE, LAW AND MINERAL WEALTH: THE LEGAL PROFILE OF THE WISCONSIN MINING INDUSTRY (1962).

3. O. HOLMES, THE COMMON LAW (1881); R. POUND, THE FORMATIVE ERA OF AMERICAN LAW (1938); G. GILMORE, THE AGES OF AMERICAN LAW (1977).

recent book, *Law and Social Order in the United States,*[4] is an equally ambitious effort. Not surprisingly, much of it is a recapitulation and condensation of his earlier works, which are frequently cited in the footnotes.

Since Hurst has so significantly determined the direction and shaped the structure of recent writing about American legal history, it is perhaps somewhat difficult to remember that he too was the product of a certain time, of certain attitudes and interests, in American legal studies. Hurst is in many ways the product of legal realism, loosely defined. Like the realists, he has emphasized the relationship between law and society; legal history could not simply chronicle the emergence and development of legal doctrines, nor treat them largely as intellectual insights divorced from the actual world in which they occurred. Hurst, like the realists, minimizes the autonomy of law; law rather reflects changes in society, most often or most critically, changes in the economy. With realism, "Cases & Materials on . . ." replaced "Cases on . . ." as the standard law textbook title. This often, however, meant only the inclusion of descriptions of the legislative or administrative process. This approach broadened the scope of legal research, but preserved, as the domain of legal academics, law as a subject distinct from the social sciences in general.

Much like the realists, Hurst, even as he insists that law be seen in a larger social context, devotes himself almost entirely to an analysis of legal materials. He examines trial court results, statutory materials, and executive actions, particularly those taken by administrative agencies as well as appellate opinions. In doing so he at least implicitly adopts Roscoe Pound's rather formal definition of law as the product of just such governmental institutions, as the systematic application of force by politically organized society. Hurst calls this "the operation of distinctive . . . legal agencies."[5]

Hurst similarly reflects the realist denigration of the importance of courts, as against other branches of government, in the creation of law.[6] This attitude described both the real and the ideal to many liberal academics in the 1930s, as it was a conclusion which supported opposition to judicial interference with legislative decisions. Hurst somewhat anachronistically continues to insist that the courts are relatively unimportant in spite of the clear evidence of the growing influence of federal courts over more

---

4. J. HURST, LAW AND SOCIAL ORDER IN THE UNITED STATES (1977) [hereinafter cited as LAW AND SOCIAL ORDER].

5. *Id.* at 25.

6. *Id.* at 38, 100, 132-43, 186-87.

and more aspects of contemporary American society.[7]

Hurst again reflects the realist tradition in his emphasis upon the relationship between law and the market and his relative lack of interest in other social institutions. Although Hurst has written at length about the American commitment to individualism, particularly as it relates to economic behavior, he has almost entirely ignored the family and religion, both institutions whose study would test the depth and breadth of this commitment. Hurst assumes that, after 1800, the market was the sole object of interest for Americans, apparently because, in the nineteenth century, they concentrated entirely upon accumulating wealth, and in the twentieth century upon enjoying what it brought.[8]

Other issues, however, did hold the attention of Americans. The nature and role of government was still problematic, and the frequent state constitutional conventions attest to strong yet divided opinions about government beyond its effect on the market.[9] Suffrage, apportionment, slavery, prohibition, and civil rights were all at various times issues of great moment, and ones to which Hurst devotes little attention. It has been noted that Hurst's focus upon the relation between law and the market —a subject on which he has shaped the structure of subsequent research and analysis—minimizes any harmful consequences of his failure to use extra-legal materials.[10] The legal materials themselves present a relatively clear picture of economic behavior—despite the cautioning of realists and their descendants that contract law in the abstract is often a poor guide to business behavior. The relation between law and the family, a social institution still relatively less influenced by and described in legal materials, could not be so studied without greater recourse to extra-legal sources.

Law and the Social Order recapitulates the sequence of Hurst's publications. The book is divided into four chapters. The first presents a strategy for legal history; the second records the development of legal agencies in America; the last two chapters

51

---

7. *See* G. GILMORE, *supra* note 3, at 15. It is not unfair to emphasize here the recent influence of federal courts because Hurst focuses his presentation of twentieth-century developments on national, rather than state, law.

8. LAW AND SOCIAL ORDER, *supra* note 4, at 125. *See* Scheiber, *At the Borderland of Law and Economic History: The Contributions of Willard Hurst*, 75 AM. HIST. REV. 744, 752 (1970).

9. Scheiber, *supra* note 8, at 752-53.

10. *See* Gordon, *J. Willard Hurst and the Common Law Tradition in American Legal Historiography*, 10 LAW & SOCY. REV. 9, 52-53 (1975).

finally turn to the substance of legal doctrine. Hurst first published "Legal History: A Research Program";[11] he next wrote *The Growth of American Law; The Law Makers* (1950), a lengthy history of the development of the branches of government; and then in *Law and Economic Growth* and, in a more discursive form, in *Law and the Conditions of Freedom* (1956), he examined legal decisions themselves rather than the bodies that made them.

In Chapter I, in which Hurst attempts to define the subject of legal history, his adoption of Pound's approach to law as the product of governmental institutions has the merit of limiting the scope of the legal historian's enterprise. It does, however, confine a scholar who insists that law be examined in relation to society in general. Hurst recognizes this, and thus, includes a section in this chapter entitled, "Although the operation of legal agencies provided the core of legal history, realism requires also a history of law's relation to other institutions and ideas." Hurst here avoids the pitfalls of an unduly restrictive definition of his subject, but does so at a level of abstraction that leaves little content to the generalizations that remain.

There are other instances in which Hurst presents a broad principle and then qualifies it with its negation. He reiterates his view that the principle underlying much nineteenth-century law was the "release of energy," a belief in individualism and in entrepreneurial activity as the basis of economic growth. But he does not conclude with such a sweeping overstatement. He also finds in nineteenth-century law the principle of constitutionalism, "a stubbornly persistent demand that all organized power be accountable to others than the immediate powerholders for the quality of the ends and means of using power."[12] This principle, which emerged as a limitation on governmental power, was also applied to private power. Hurst has thus provided a principle and a counter-principle. Individual activity is to be encouraged, but it is to be evaluated by social norms. The analysis thus retains subtlety, but at the cost of indeterminacy. Content can be given to the operation of these two principles only by a more precise examination of their applicability in a particular context.

In Chapter II, Hurst describes legal decision-makers with a realist's emphasis upon legislatures and administrative agencies. In Chapter III, he turns his attention to the substance of legal

52

---

11. Hurst, *Legal History: A Research Program*, 1942 Wis. L. Rev. 323.
12. Law and Social Order, *supra* note 4, at 45.

decisions, in particular to the relationship between science and technology and the law. The choice of this topic—the relationship between man and his environment—to introduce the treatment of substantive law itself recapitulates the evolution of Hurst's publications.[13] This approach generally emphasizes the technical and technological rather than the political content of the problems legal agencies face.

Hurst in general thinks that bad decisions are not caused by favoritism or political preference, so much as by a lack of information and foresight. For him, the opposite of consensus is drift and inertia; the opposite of agreement is not disagreement, but ignorance and confusion. He criticizes courts because they easily lose sight of affected interests not represented by the opposing parties, and he criticizes legislatures for not gathering information as well as they could.

Hurst is most critical of nineteenth-century law for its failure to overcome a contemporary tendency to favor short-run results at the expense of long-run interests, an attitude he describes as "bastard pragmatism." Law is not autonomous; its task is not to make society's choices but, in a role similar to that given economics by many of its modern practitioners, it is at least to make society aware of the true costs involved in its choices.[14] If, as Hurst argues, law is a method for the national exploitation of the physical environment, difficult problems of distributional choice can be avoided as long as productivity is increased. Hurst finds this technique has typified American law in general; it is an approach of which he apparently approves.[15] To the extent that social conflicts—the confrontation of groups—erupt, they are implicit generational ones, as bastard pragmatists with a short-run view impose costs upon their descendants; they are not contemporaneous social divisions, which are explicit and articulated.

In its first three chapters, *Law and Social Order* clearly tracks Hurst's earlier work, presenting it in summary form. In the

53

---

13. In LAW AND ECONOMIC GROWTH, *supra* note 1, Hurst analyzed in detail the effect of law on the exploitation of Wisconsin's timber resources in the nineteenth century.

14. Here, again, Hurst reflects his realist heritage. For the realists, it was easy to announce that law should reflect contemporary values when the Supreme Court was, in some celebrated cases, rejecting such values as expressed in legislative decisions and instead enacting "Mr. Herbert Spencer's *Social Statics.*" The extent to which law could be used to initiate change, not to reflect a social consensus, but to create one, was a subject on which realists remained ambiguous and tentative.

15. In this context Hart and Sacks discuss the fallacy of the static pie. On the relation between Hurst and what loosely can be called the legal-process school, see Tushnet, *Lumber and the Legal Process*, 1972 WIS. L. REV. 114, 115 n.7.

final chapter, "Consensus and Conflict," Hurst looks not at the relationship between man and his environment, but at relations between groups of men. The emphasis, of necessity, is less on technology and more on politics. This is new, a substitution of consensus-conflict for the consensus-inertia polarity that Hurst employed in the past. There is at least now the suggestion that profound disagreement rather than haste, inadvertence, or ignorance might sometimes explain the failure to consider what Hurst would deem all of the relevant factors in reaching a decision.

This chapter appears to be Hurst's response to criticism that he has exaggerated the element of consensus in American history, that he has written the victors' view of history, and failed to consider contemporary opposition to the nineteenth-century use of law to facilitate market capitalism and generate economic growth. Hurst may in particular have been reacting to Morton Horwitz's *The Transformation of American Law, 1780-1860* (1977).[16] Horwitz explores much of the same ground as Hurst—the relation between law and the economy in the nineteenth century—but appears to offer a very different interpretation, one which, according to Hurst, stresses conflict rather than consensus.[17]

While Hurst has now formally recognized conflict as a possible explanation of various aspects of American society and of its law, he is actually much more confident in and comfortable with a consensus approach. It is not simply that Hurst believes that American development has been dominated by a consensus on middle-class values.[18] That is a substantive conclusion which may well be justified; it is, at any rate, one that is shared by many others. Hurst, however, goes further; his very definition of "consensus" almost inevitably leads to the conclusion that consensus has dominated the American experience. Consensus, as used by Hurst, included situations in which there is disagreement, or no agreement; it can comprehend near-unanimity of sentiment and the absence of strong disagreement. Given Hurst's terminology, there appears to be no issue so divisive it cannot be described as demonstrating a consensus of a sort. When discussing state abandonment of corporate regulation in the late nine-

---

16. While both books were published in 1977, many chapters of Horwitz's book had earlier appeared in various journals and the thrust of his argument was certainly well-known to Hurst at the time he delivered the lectures at Cornell, in April 1976, which later became Law and Social Order, *supra* note 4.

17. *See* Hurst, Book Review, 21 Am. J. Legal Hist. 175 (1977).

18. *See* Law and Social Order, *supra* note 4, at 43-44, 64.

teenth century and interstate rivalry, especially between Delaware and New Jersey to be corporate refuges, Hurst refers to an "evident prevailing consensus" on this issue.[19] He apparently cannot fully accept the existence of a widely shared confidence in unrestrained corporate activity. There is, after all, well-known nonlegal muckraking and trust-busting literature that clearly suggests disagreement on the issue of corporate power. The actions of the federal government also suggest that state laws did not reflect a unanimity of approach.[20]

Although Hurst seems more comfortable focusing upon consensus, he does maintain that many situations in American law reflected varying degrees of both consensus and conflict. Laws to regulate hunting emerged, he suggests, from the pressures exerted by hunters and in the absence of any clear expression of view by those not directly concerned.[21] In effect, hunting laws exemplified what Hurst has generally called inertia and drift. Hurst then presents the case of competition between railroad and trucking interests, as the former attempted to thwart the latter's requests for authorization to carry larger loads. There were clear adversaries here and it was thus less likely that a decision would result from drift, from a failure to have its possible adverse consequences clearly articulated. What conflicts existed, however, were between two parties competing in a game, the rules of which they both accepted. They did not criticize the game itself. Hurst describes this as a situation in which there were adversarial interests, but a consensus that the legal processes should resolve the issue. Any litigation would, by this standard, apparently reflect both conflict and consensus.

Hurst writes of antitrust law at greater length. There, the acceptance of the rules of the game is more problematic. He describes the alteration in American policy between efforts to maximize competition and to increase economic stability. He refers also to the strong political component, which feared the accumulation of power in private hands, in some antitrust sentiment. He

55

---

19. *Id.* at 242.

20. Hurst suggests that consensus is demonstrated by the fact that all states abandoned regulatory efforts. The absence of regulation in any one state, however, (in an application, in effect, of Gresham's law to this subject) made such regulation impossible in any other state. Moreover, even if the abandonment of regulation was a truly independent decision in each state, this does not mean that, within each state, there was not still significant opposition. Hurst sometimes suggests that continuity demonstrates consensus, and, at other times, admits the fact of power and the possibility of a consensus only among the victors. *Id.* at 220.

21. *Id.* at 215.

states that these political, "balance-of-power" views were "not rejected in a clear-cut debate between political and economic priorities, but rather [were] lost to sight in an opportunistic, unplanned course of action by those charged with enforcing the antitrust laws."[22] Here, again, what appears to be "conflict" turns out to be "inertia." Hurst concludes that forty years of antitrust law failed to evolve into a "reasonably definite and coherent set of ideas with a firm base in popular understanding and acceptance."[23] The consensus was "ambiguous."[24] It may be simply a matter of point of view whether one describes a glass as half empty or half full; Hurst, at any rate, prefers to find, not disagreement, but the failure to reach agreement.

Hurst prefers to discuss issues in which the question of redistribution is muted and can be avoided by a strategy of enlarging the pie rather than redividing the shares; he avoids those issues which, in a zero-sum world, must have both winners and losers. He devotes almost no attention to labor law, finding little of it in the nineteenth century because "the times had to ripen for effective legal intervention,"[25] an explanation that obviously skirts the issues of power and class conflict. What conflict existed Hurst sees as part of a larger consensus; twentieth-century labor law enforced collective bargaining, reflecting, he feels, a consensus in favor of "limited, generally peaceful conflict."[26] Hurst also has almost nothing to say in this chapter about taxation; elsewhere in the book, he does briefly describe conflict over the extent to which taxation should redistribute wealth. Here, again, the conflict is part of a larger consensus. "[C]onflict seems to be over the extent and conditions of such transfer payments, not over the legitimacy of government use of its resource-allocating authority to some extent to increase the life options of individuals of small means."[27]

Every legal doctrine, every institutional statement or pattern of behavior can be viewed as expressing consensus, a shared belief, either a homogeneous response or a conscious compromise. It can, on the other hand, be seen as mediating an underlying

---

22. *Id.* at 265.
23. *Id.* at 257.
24. *Id.* at 263.
25. *Id.* at 46.
26. *Id.* at 236.
27. *Id.* at 122. Hurst ignores issues like suffrage, apportionment, and prohibition, on which disagreement was fundamental and no solution could satisfy everyone. *See* Scheiber, *supra* note 8, at 752-53.

contradiction, as attempting to reconcile or hide a potential conflict.

Hurst believes that one of law's primary purposes is to provide society with the information necessary for informed choice, to force it, for instance, to consider its long-run as well as its immediate interests. Law in Wisconsin failed, as Hurst so thoroughly explained in *Law and Economic Growth,* when it let the lumber industry destroy itself by thoughtless overcutting. Implicit in Hurst's criticism of law's failure in this regard is the belief that, when the costs of activities are revealed, a consensus responsive to the additional considerations will evolve. But conflict may be more deep-seated, based not on misinformation, but on well-founded perceptions of opposed interests. At such a time, a choice between the opposed groups must be made; in such a circumstance, law's task in reducing social conflict may become not to reveal where the possible sources of conflict lie, but rather to hide these social seams, to submerge group conflict, letting groups and individuals live comfortably with others and with themselves, without resolving apparently irreconcilable, but not fatal, conflicts of-interest or contradictions in ideology.[28]

57

Whether American law reflects consensus or conflict is a question whose answer may very well reveal more about the author than the subject. Consensus and conflict are as likely to be approaches to a topic as descriptions of it. Hurst's present interest in consensus and conflict, and his influence within the discipline, suggest that there is a danger that American legal historians, perhaps with Hurst and Horwitz as the standard-bearers, will now debate the relative merits of these two paradigms.

It will be particularly easy to be adversarial since American historians have relatively recently engaged in just such a controversy. For several decades, they disputed the merits of consensus and conflict as descriptions of the American experience.[29] "Progressive historians" and their progeny discovered repeated conflict between classes and masses, between the special interests of property and the principles of egalitarian democracy. They have portrayed the Jeffersonians, the Populists, the Progressives, and the New Dealers as recurrent challengers to the asserted privileges of the propertied. For such scholars, American history has been discontinuous, as one side or the other, justifying itself

---

28. This point has been made by Gordon, *supra* note 10, at 53, among others.
29. *See,* J. HIGHAM, HISTORY 171-232 (1965).

on ideological grounds, seized power in what were called revolutions:[30] the War for Independence, the Constitutional Convention, Jacksonian Democracy, the Civil War, and the New Deal, among others.

"Consensus historians," on the other hand, have emphasized continuity and stability in the American experience. They have seen American politics, not as the battleground in a struggle between the propertied and the masses, but as an expression of middle-class values which were shared by most of the population. Disputes were pragmatic, not ideological; outsiders demanded equal opportunity, but not a restructuring of society.

It would be particularly unfortunate for legal historians to recreate this debate. It obscures, by the rhetorical excesses it generates, the similarity between Hurst and Horwitz. For both historians, the major achievement of nineteenth-century law was the creation of a system of market capitalism. While Horwitz is more explicitly critical of this result, Hurst does not accord it unqualified approval: "bastard pragmatism" is, after all, hardly a term of approbation. And while Hurst does not claim that what happened was good for everyone, Horwitz does not actually accuse law-makers of disingenuousness in appealing to the public good as a criterion of decision. Much of the divergence between them reflects differing evaluations of the extent of ideological opposition to the prevailing ethos. Both, moreover, generally limit their researches to legal materials. Hurst does not look to literature, or to sermons, for instance, to see if they reveal attitudes about individualism or economic growth similar to those expressed in legal materials, an investigation which might help corroborate his claim that law in these regards simply reflected popular values. Horwitz does not examine the hard economic data that might demonstrate the extent to which law did affect economic growth or the distribution of wealth.[31]

With so much of American legal history still unexplored, it is tempting to over-generalize: to assume the representative na-

58

---

30. These might just as easily be called "transformations." This is the kind of conflict that Horwitz describes, but Hurst rejects.

31. *See* Williams, Book Review, 25 UCLA L. Rev. 1187, 1210-14 (1978). Both Hurst and Horwitz also tend to use regional materials to make generalizations about the entire nation. In his review of Horwitz, (Hurst, *supra* note 17, at 176), Hurst notes that Horwitz focuses on the eastern seaboard, especially the middle and New England states. Hurst himself has been criticized for taking Wisconsin, especially considering that state's refusal to undertake internal improvements directly, as representative of the United States in general. *See* Scheiber, *supra* note 8, at 753.

ture of a relatively narrow body of primary materials or to support large abstractions on a fragile base.

A debate over consensus and conflict is particularly vulnerable to such over-generalization because the legal historian can too easily borrow an already developed rhetoric. Consensus and conflict are certainly not inappropriate categories of analysis and it may even be that one or the other best describes the character of American legal history, but much careful and particularized research is needed to confirm such a judgment. Moreover, consensus and conflict are only appropriate categories; they are not the only categories and it would be unfortunate to ignore the possibility of different theoretical structures. Hurst himself concludes that consensus and conflict are both present in most situations and implies that efforts would better be spent examining agreement, conflict, compromise, and inertia in particular [59] circumstances. Such exhortations for future research are useful, but are needed less than is the research itself, the kind that Hurst has in the past so impressively produced.

An Approach to American History: Willard Hurst as Legal Historian

by DAVID H. FLAHERTY*

I

James Willard Hurst is a distinguished gentleman in his late fifties, who for more than thirty years has been a member of the law faculty at the University of Wisconsin.[1] Willard Hurst is also the foremost historian of American law. Yet despite his authorship of five books on American legal history, Professor Hurst is almost unknown among historians, who have long bemoaned the narrowness and technicality of this subject. The resistance of the historical profession to the study of legal history can best be overcome through the vehicle of Hurst's writings.

At the beginning of his academic career in the late 1930's, Willard Hurst began to write of the significance of American legal history when approached in a meaningful fashion. The outlines of his later writings and major conceptions concerning legal history appeared in book reviews and articles in the early 1940's.[2] Hurst has since devoted a scholarly lifetime to the elucidation of these ideas.[3] His output has spanned the spectrum between highly theoretical expositions that enter the field of jurisprudence, and complex explications of his basic premises in volumes on substantial subjects.

The primary purpose of this paper is to demonstrate and explain Hurst's importance on the contemporary historical scene. By

60

University of Virginia.

1. This introductory guide to the writings of Willard Hurst on American legal history was originally presented to a joint session of the American Historical Association and the American Society for Legal History in New York City, December 29, 1968.

2. Review of Charles Fairman, *Mr. Justice Miller and the Supreme Court, 1862-1890* (1939), in 40 *Col. L. Rev.* 564-71 (1940); Hurst, "Legal History: A Research Program," *Wis. L. Rev.*, 323-33 (1942); Hurst, "Uses of Law in Four 'Colonial' States of the American Union," *ibid.*, 577-92 (1945).

3. In addition to the articles and volumes by Hurst noted below, see "Treason in the United States," 58 *Harv. L. Rev.*, 226-72, 395-444, 806-857 (1945), "Law and the Balance of Power in the Community," 22 *Okla. B. A. J.*, 1223-34 (1951); "Perspectives upon Research into the Legal Order," *Wis. L. Rev.*, 356-67 (1961); "Legal Profession," *ibid.*, 969-79 (1966); "Changing Responsibilities of the Law School, 1868-1968," *ibid.*, 336-44 (1968).

identifying law as a crucial focal point for the understanding of American society, Hurst has opened up broad new vistas to be examined. In proceeding to write the *social* history of law, Hurst has set out to answer questions of significant magnitude and complexity. This paper will examine Hurst's conception of legal history, his approach to the writing of legal history, and some of the possible limitations of his ideas on this subject. Given the scope of Hurst's accomplishments it will be difficult for this paper not to trumpet his virtues and do injustice to the brilliance of his conceptions in the course of summary. In simplifying for purposes of generalization, one must reduce some highly intricate and sophisticated work to an almost commonplace level and run the risk of exposing the author to unjust criticism.

One should be aware that Hurst's interests in legal history extend beyond the development of a scholarly discipline. He employs legal history, "the logic of experience," as a vehicle for ventures into jurisprudential writing, and is gradually being recognized as a major figure in American jurisprudence.[4] This recognition has come slowly because Hurst has masqueraded as a legal historian. This dual aim helps account for the historian's occasional bewilderment while following Hurst through an involved and highly philosophical line of argument. At the same time Hurst shares the desire of some law professors to make legal history a more significant part of contemporary legal education. In fact, if legal history does stage a renaissance in the law school curriculum, Hurst's own works will have done much to make the subject meaningful again.

Some sense of the scope of Hurst's accomplishments can be conveyed by a brief comment on his major publications. In 1950 Hurst published *The Growth of American Law: the Law Makers,* which treated the growth of the principal agencies of law in the United States between 1790 and 1940. Although masked in an institutional framework, with successive sections on the legislature, the courts, the bar, the constitution makers, and the executive, *The Growth of American Law* demonstrated a pathbreaking approach to the study of legal history. This is the best single introduction to modern American legal history. Hurst's repeated focus on the social functions of the legislature or one of his other institutional subjects is the most original contribution of the volume. *The Growth of American Law* plainly suggests the directions of Hurst's thinking about legal history, yet only dimly foreshadows the magnitude of his later accomplishments.

61

---

4. See Russell E. Brooks, "The Jurisprudence of Willard Hurst," 18 *J. Legal Ed.,* 257-73 (1966); also Earl Finbar Murphy, "The Jurisprudence of Legal History: Willard Hurst as a Legal Historian," 39 *NYU L. Rev.,* 900-43 (1964).

Hurst's next work *Law and the Conditions of Freedom in the Nineteenth Century United States*, published in 1956, revealed that the author was engaged in "a long-term program of research in the history of the interplay of law and other social institutions in the growth of the United States." This slender volume sought "to define some key values and attitudes out of which men consciously shaped their uses of law in this society." [5] The two volumes which Hurst added within the next decade pursued his search for hypotheses concerning the role of law in United States history in an even more philosophical mode. *Law and Social Process in United States History*, which appeared in 1960, initially discusses the subject matter of legal history in broad and penetrating fashion. The three subsequent essays concern "ways in which law exercised or might have exercised direct influence on conditions of social stability and change in United States history." [6] Hurst's 1964 volume, *Justice Holmes on Legal History* is an argument for the relevance of legal history to the modern lawyer. Since historians accept the premises that Hurst is arguing for, there is less need for the historical profession to consult this particular volume.

Hurst's most important work to date, *Law and Economic Growth: The Legal History of the Lumber Industry in Wisconsin, 1836-1915* was published in 1964. This volume lends meaning and substance to some of Hurst's earlier philosophical explorations. If his three previous volumes are viewed as commonplace books in which the author could work out his basic conceptions and approaches to legal history, *Law and Economic Growth* has fulfilled the most critical expectations of those who awaited a full-scale demonstration of Hurst's ideas in action. This volume is an incredible feat of scholarship, the work of a lifetime, and an achievement that ranks with other major studies of American history.

II

The importance of Hurst's approach to the study of American legal history can only be appreciated in the first instance against the backdrop of the generally sorry state of this field. Even the history of early American law, traditionally the most flourishing part of American legal history writing, has shared certain basic inadequacies.[7] Legal history has not been integrated with the general

---

5. J. W. Hurst, *Law and Economic Growth: The Legal History of the Lumber Industry in Wisconsin, 1836-1915 VII* (1964).

6. *Law and Social Process in United States History* 28 (1960).

7. See David H. Flaherty, "An Introduction to Early American Legal History," in Flaherty, ed., *Essays in the History of Early American Law* pp. 32-38 (1969).

history of the United States, and has often been written not as *history*, but rather as law. The focus of legal historians has too consistently been on studies of origins or narrowly institutional approaches.[8] In particular, legal historians have not begun their work by posing broadly conceived questions, but have followed narrowly circumscribed paths.

Hurst himself has written in sympathetic fashion of the plight of the legal historian. "The study of United States legal history will come of age when its practitioners give as much effort to framing questions as to assembling answers. . . . Because the historian's job preoccupies him with concrete particularities, he incurs occupational hazards which may rob his work of meaning. Immersed in detail, he may be diverted into the collectors' mania, and wind up an antiquarian. The passing days make him painfully aware how time-costly it is to uncover the full dimension of events. Harassed by the calendar, he begrudges time taken from collecting data in order to shape and test the theoretical framework of his inquiries. So he is tempted into a naive empiricism—using his research simply to document the unexamined assumptions and prejudices of common sense or tradition, or behaving as if he believed that meaning could be squeezed out of data by the sheer weight of their accumulation."[9]

63

Hurst has described in even more specific detail the limitations of some legal history writing. There has been too much attention to courts and activities related to litigation, too much work on colonial legal history and not enough follow through into later periods; too little on the social functions of law. To illustrate one of these points, Hurst has written that "the broader the reach of our hypotheses and the deeper our concern to study the social functions of legal order, the more we will learn to respect the relative influence of inertia and drift in affairs. The most realistic view of all aspects of man's history leads to the conclusion that most of what has happened to men has happened without their wanting it or striving for it or opposing it or—more important—without their being aware of the meaning of trends until patterns of structure and force have developed past points of revoking. This general judgment seems no less true of legal history in this country."[10] Where many of us

---

8. See Calvin Woodard, "History, Legal History and Legal Education," 53 *Va. L. Rev.*, 89-121 (1967).

9. Hurst, "Themes in United States Legal History," in Wallace Mendelson, ed., *Felix Frankfurter: A Tribute* pp. 199-200 (1964).

10. Hurst, "The Law in United States History," 104 American Philosophical Society, *Proceedings*, 523 (1960). His critique of American Legal History is on pp. 521-23. This article is the best single introduction to Hurst's writings.

work at legal history with little seeming concern for why we are doing it. Hurst has devoted a considerable portion of his efforts to understanding why and how American legal history should be studied.

The major inadequacy of American legal history has been the absence of a working philosophy. According to Hurst, the legal historian must develop a general theory of United States legal history and thereby approach the study of his subject on the basis of hypotheses. The proper study of legal history presupposes organizing ideas and modes of analysis. The goal should be "to understand the law not so much as it may appear to philosophers, but more as it had meaning for workaday people and was shaped by them to their wants and vision." [11] The historian must study the role of law in American society and seek to define the working principles behind this use of law. Thus the role and functions of law in the development and shaping of American society is the governing concern in the Hurst conception of legal history. At the outset this creates the need to look at law in terms of the total situation, on the assumption that at any given period law has been one of the crucial dimensions in the shaping of American society.

One of Hurst's central assumptions is that back of every legal determination by either a court or a legislature "lay some dynamic, confidently accepted, validating principle." In the matter of franchises for stream improvements in nineteenth century Wisconsin, for example, "There was a dynamic consensus of value behind the bold use of law in this area. This moving principle was the common belief . . . that it was common sense, and it was good, to use law to multiply the productive power of the economy. Productivity was the central test and validating canon." [12] Thus the Hurst approach to legal history involves a constant search for the identification and explication of working principles that underlay the use of law in society at any particular era.

Legal history must be concerned with the history of law in the life of a society. Legal history (as well as law itself) has meaning only in the logic and setting of experience. The principles of law that are recognized in any particular era are the product of experience. That is why legal history is important, to emphasize an idea that Hurst holds in common with Justice Holmes. [13] The law follows and embodies the wishes, desires, and ambitions of the populace, it does not lead. Law is thereby an entrée to the history of ideas and attitudes that have given character to life in the United

64

---

11. *Law and the Conditions of Freedom in the Nineteenth Century United States* 5 (1956).

12. *Law and Economic Growth, op. cit. supra.* note 5, at pp. 171-172.

13. See *Justice Holmes on Legal History* Chap. 1 (1964).

States. Law has "yielded the largest single body of articulated values and value-oriented contrivances in society." Hurst argues that in the nineteenth century the law was more important than the church and the school in "defining choices and directions implicit in developing large patterns of social relations." [14] The central principle of the American legal order is that "law exists for the benefit of people and not people for the benefit of law." [15] It follows that a "full-dimensioned legal history must tell of the shaping force exercised upon the law from outside it, by what people wanted, by the functional needs of other institutions, and by the mindless weight of circumstances." [16] In fact Hurst would argue that the social history of law is at the center of change in a society. "Law offers special insights into the growth of this North American society because so many forces for stability and change came into focus at points of legal action." [17]

Hurst has evolved a number of major hypotheses concerning the use and functions of law in American history, and particularly the nineteenth century. These working principles appear time and again in Hurst's writing in cumulative fashion. A principle first enunciated in *Law and the Conditions of Freedom* has become highly involved and sophisticated by the time it reappears in *Law and Economic Growth*, where the scholar who has now completed research can reassert the same with increased confidence. Hurst's major insights revolve around his argument that the release of creative human energy was the governing principle in all aspects of nineteenth century American law, as embodied for example in such major areas of early nineteenth century innovation as contract law and the law of negotiable instruments.[18] Land should be made as transferable as possible, and completed contracts should be as binding as possible. "The substance of what business wanted from law was the provision for ordinary use of an organization through which entrepreneurs could better mobilize and release economic energy . . . it is characteristic of the nineteenth century that there was here also a demand for positive help from the law. Merely to be let alone to combine capital was not the substance of the entrepreneurs' desire." [19] Law had to provide the entrepreneur with positive advantages and keep open the channels of change. Hurst is quick to

65

---

14. *Law and Social Process, op. cit. supra* note 6, at pp. 11-13.
15. *Law and the Conditions of Freedom, op. cit. supra* note 11, at p. 5.
16. *Law and Social Process, op. cit. supra* note 6, at p. 10.
17. *Law and Social Process, op. cit. supra* note 6, at p. 17.
18. This is the theme of part 1 of *Law and the Conditions of Freedom, op. cit. supra* note 11.
19. *Law and the Conditions of Freedom, op. cit. supra* note 11, at p. 17.

defend his sketch of "the release-of-energy policy almost entirely in terms of the relation of law to the economy. This accords with the emphasis which the times gave this policy. It was a century which put all the energy and attention it could into economic interests." [20]

Hurst ascribes certain distinctive social roles to law in the history of this country, and the elaboration of these themes again forms a consistent focus of his writings. Law has exercised the legitimate monopoly of force in this society and superintended the total distribution of power in the community. Law has expressed the constitutional ideal and provided regular procedures for defining and choosing values. It has been the major instrument for allocating scarce resources in the course of shaping American economic development. To enunciate these themes is to give some sense of the importance of law in American history, and at the same time to run the risk of making Hurst's ideas seem mundane and indeed almost trivial. Such limitations are the direct product of an attempt to reduce a sophisticated literature to the confines of a short, introductory paper. Hurst has to be read to be appreciated, and my ultimate goal is to encourage historians to do that.

66

III

If Hurst has evolved new conceptions and hypotheses concerning the role of law in the history of American society, how has he set about implementing these working principles through historical studies? Far from imitating the example of his innumerable predecessors who filled the reviews with laments about the sorry state of American legal history, and rarely proceeded to do much more about it than this, Hurst has devoted considerable efforts to the development and carrying out of a research methodology. *Law and Economic Growth* is the leading example of the Hurst method, but in all his works Hurst devotes much time to an account of what he is attempting and how he plans to go about it.

This Hurst method has a number of important characteristics. In line with his emphasis on hypotheses and working principles, meaningful generalization about the logic of legal experience is an essential goal of Hurst's research. This is the eventual justification for immersion in specifics. A chapter normally begins with broadly conceived questions and proceeds to generalization by means of an analytical approach and immersion in the total picture. All of Hurst's volumes illustrate his own extraordinary talent for asking the right questions.

20. *Law and the Conditions of Freedom, op. cit. supra* note 11, at p. 29, see also pp. 18 and 27.

Law must be studied in all the dimensions of its total role in a society. One of the major distinctions between such an approach to legal history and those of the past is Hurst's focus on the role of legislatures in policy making. Since the legislature was the dominant force shaping public policy through its statutory enactments, a comprehension of the principles that were distilled in the process of lawmaking is a major interest of the legal historian. The legislatures, not the courts, were the major influences on nineteenth century law. Hurst is much less concerned with the role and influence of individual judges and lawyers or of dramatic or colorful episodes. Broad social forces shape the law. Legal history must be written from the products of state legislation and the basic areas of contract, property, and tort laws. "It is harder to write history out of these everyday staples; yet, the fact that they are everyday staples demands that legal history find organizing ideas and modes of analysis which will make such materials yield up their meanings for the tough-fibered, sustained life of society. . . ." [21]

67

The Hurst method initially demands exposure to such a substantial volume of materials that the scholar might justifiably be frightened away from the notion of studying legal history. After all, Hurst utilized close to one thousand pages, including three hundred pages of finely printed footnotes, to write the legal history of the Wisconsin lumber industry between 1836 and 1915. A mass of individual cases at the appellate level had to be examined. While Hurst would emphasize the need to study all of the relevant materials, so that law could be pictured in its total role in an aspect of society, one can defend the incredible size of *Law and Economic Growth* on additional grounds. This was a seminal work, and now that Hurst has provided a model, the task of research in legal history in the future may be of less Gargantuan proportions. Nevertheless the mass of materials studied over a period of time is absolutely essential if the scholar is to uncover the underlying principles, and, more importantly, be able to see and recognize important changes in the role of law.

The Hurst method is predicated upon carrying out intensive studies on the state level as the first requirement in the revivification of American legal history. Analysis, the formulation of hypotheses, depth research, and the broad time span should all be applied at the state level in the first instance. As Hurst wrote in this pertinent example, the experience of Wisconsin, the primary stamping ground to date of the Hurst school of legal historians, was "a typical demonstration within a small theater, that our ultimate policy was to use the law to provide facilities of exchange." [22] "In

---

21. *Law and Economic Growth, op. cit. supra* note 5, at p. XII.
22. *Law and the Conditions of Freedom, op. cit. supra* note 11, at p. 58.

due time comparative analysis will be in order. But it must wait upon more knowledge of particular units." [23]

IV

An historian can scarcely quarrel with the goals and enlightened methodology of the Hurst approach to legal history, but he can suggest some of the possible limitations of the studies to date. Given the breadth of Hurst's achievements, criticisms can take on a carping quality, or be based on an inability to recognize what the author has attempted in a particular instance. Hurst's work is incredibly learned—the five hundred and sixty-five footnotes in chapter three of *Law and Economic Growth* cover one hundred and twenty pages of fine print. The judgments in the latter volume betray the sensitivity and maturity of a scholar with great insight into the human personality and condition. At one point or another in his many volumes Hurst has also anticipated most of the criticisms that can be levelled against his work.

Willard Hurst's writings have suffered most from their apparent neglect by the legal and historical professions. His interpretations have not been subjected to enough serious criticism. Historians in particular need to test out Hurst's basic ideas on the history of law in America. By almost ignoring Hurst's work, both historians and the legal profession have deprived Hurst of that sharpening of insight that can be achieved by the exchange of ideas. While the limitations of Hurst's writings are in no way a paramount characteristic, certain traits do come to the surface. He occasionally makes generalizations which are embarrassingly vague and almost commonplace. The search for underlying or working principles becomes highly artificial or obvious at times. While Hurst's style often approaches heights of perception and clarity, he does not fully share Maitland's ability to convey difficult material in highly comprehensible terms. There is a tendency to overwrite in his books, and one often has the feeling that nothing has been excluded, particularly from *Law and Economic Growth*. While most of Hurst's major insights are extremely important, their frequent repetition in a given volume and in subsequent works can be tedious. But given the inattention his volumes have too often met with, Hurst should perhaps be forgiven the urge to repeat basic ideas in the expectation that this time they might encounter more fertile soil.

There is a more substantive side to this lack of criticism of Hurst's writings on American legal history; his volumes have necessarily involved endless interpretation of statutes, court records, and political decisions. Specialists in varied parts of Hurst's topics need

---

23. *Law and Economic Growth, op. cit. supra* note 5, at p. X.

to review and criticize his judgments. In the course of discovering basic principles one senses that Hurst occasionally comes close to overreading and overinterpretation of a statute or text. In volumes of such breadth there are obviously a number of instances, both of a factual and interpretative kind, where scholars would quarrel with Hurst. Unfortunately little serious criticism of Hurst has been published. Professor Calvin Woodard of the University of Virginia Law School has been one of the few to criticize an aspect of Hurst's work, focusing on the latter's notions of the myth of laissez faire in *Law and the Conditions of Freedom*. [24] Some of Hurst's most important interpretations need such criticism. One wonders whether Hurst, for example, has not exaggerated the impact of drift and default in the nineteenth century? Perhaps there was more self-conscious philosophizing and planning with greater impact than Hurst has recognized.

Hurst is of course aware of the serious lack of a comparative aspect in his work and that of his disciples. [25] While one can hardly fault Hurst himself for such a deficiency, this does not remove the problem. Some of his generalizations about the role of law in the nineteenth century, for example, are in doubt because of this limitation. He is perhaps too assertive of the validity of his working principles given the limitations of the Wisconsin experience. Wisconsin law on the lumber industry may have grown primarily out of Wisconsin experience and Wisconsin precedent, but is this true or does it apply in other geographical and legal areas? Hurst's major theses seem more suited to nineteenth century frontier areas in the midwest than to the states of the eastern seaboard. Drift and inertia seem less apparent influences on legal developments in some of the more established areas. In Massachusetts Chief Justice Lemuel Shaw certainly contributed mightily to shaping the role law played in Massachusetts society. [26] The study of the legal history of one of the eastern states may thus involve substantially different problems and require different approaches. The lack of a colonial legal history in Wisconsin also limits the applicability of some of Hurst's generalizations to other parts of the United States. In fact,

69

---

24. See Woodard, *Review*, 19 *La. L. Rev.*, 560-73 (1959).

25. "Until we know our legal history better, we may fairly go on the hypothesis that there have been dominant trends toward uniformity in the growth of law in the United States, being ready at the same time to see that as we learn more we are likely to find more and more important local and regional variations." Hurst, *The Growth of American Law. The Law Makers* 19 (1950).

26. See Leonard W. Levy, *The Law of the Commonwealth and Chief Justice Shaw. The Evolution of American Law, 1830-1860* (Harper Torchbook edition, 1967).

Hurst seems to have a negative attitude towards exploiting the history of early American law as an important dimension of the American legal experience.

The major interest of Hurst and his associates has revolved around the theme of law and economic growth, which they argue is peculiarly appropriate to their interest in nineteenth century America. Some of this writing on occasion reveals flashes of the approach to history of the progressive historians, although Hurst is much too sophisticated to be an economic determinist. The problem may arise in transposing Hurst's conceptions of legal history and his methodology to other areas of interest to the legal historian. Hurst is certainly not oblivious to these other areas. "There is valid ground for criticism if legal history develops no hyphenate interests, as in legal-economic, or legal-religious, or legal-social relations." In North America "we have woven law into a wide range of living." [27] One can envision other industries in addition to the important lumber industry, such as cotton manufacturing and the railroads, for which one could write a legal history. Hurst might profitably devote some of his time to published speculations about the applicability of his ideas to the study of criminal law or the law of slavery, for example. Again, what was the impact of industrialization on American law in the ante bellum period? The ability to transfer the Hurst approach to additional areas of legal history will be an important issue in ultimately drawing a balanced assessment of Hurst's importance as a legal historian.

Lest this essay should have conveyed an opposite impression, one should note that Hurst himself has no desire to overemphasize the role of law in United States history. "Legal history should not yield to the vanity of exaggerating its own importance." [28] He adds that "in the interaction of law and American life the law was passive, acted upon by other social forces, more often than acting upon them." [29] "An adequate history of law's roles must relate legal order to social order generally. Of course this does not mean that legal history overlaps all social history. Plainly law played a larger role in some aspects of United States history and a much more limited role in others." [30] It fits Hurst's own emphasis to argue that while law was directly involved in economic growth, its participation in such matters as the family and education was indirect.

27. *Law and Social Process, op. cit. supra* note 6, at p. 6.
28. *Law and Social Process, op. cit. supra* note 6, at p. 92.
29. *Growth of American Law, op. cit. supra* note 25, at p. 4, see also pp. 6 and 19.
30. *Law and Social Process, op. cit. supra* note 6, at p. 8.

V

Despite the perhaps obvious pertinence of Willard Hurst's studies in American legal history to the historian, it may be valuable to spell out this importance in more specific and summary terms. His great achievement has been the redirection of the study of American legal history, not only in terms that we have spelled out, but with comparative reference to the kinds of studies that have too often alienated the critical historian from legal history. Through his dedication to the orderly development of the subject, Hurst has practically created the field of modern American legal history in both a theoretical and practical fashion. His hypotheses have brought order to the field. The magnitude of his achievement perhaps escapes his fellow scholars, because his work is now available and in the libraries. If it were in the planning stages, the doubters might have turned even Hurst from his self-appointed task.

Not much more could be asked of any historian than Hurst has produced, and his scholarly career is far from through. He asks the right questions, has an eye for the pertinent and the relevant, and has carried his ideas through to concrete form. His ultimate significance may well be in the kinds of questions that the legal historian of the future will be forced to ask. Hurst has shown the way, and no historian can ignore his hypotheses and models with impunity. Hurst will certainly not be the last word on American legal history, but he is the first man that anyone now aspiring to write legal history must grapple with.

In the process of writing legal history in his own way, Hurst has put forward a major interpretation of American history in terms of the central role of law in the development of our society. Where historians have ignored law for all practical purposes because of its technical nature, Hurst's broad approach has made the subject comprehensible. His works also serve as a primer through which the historian can learn much about the ways of the law in relatively painless fashion. Hurst's powers of generalization and his desire to do so have meant that any section or subsection of his major works begins at the most elementary level. Such qualities give his volumes broader significance and greater educational value than their titles imply. Extraordinary insights into the historical development of the United States are hidden between the covers of a history of the Wisconsin lumbering industry, for example. Hurst himself has noted that "the legal history of the Wisconsin Lumber industry embodies issues and materials of broad reach in the general history of the United States." [31] This makes his many volumes a gold mine for political, economic, and social historians. In fact despite

71

---

31. *Law and Economic Growth, op. cit. supra* note 5, at p. XIV.

the titles of some of his books, and despite the superstructure of legal history, significant parts of Hurst's writings are almost pure political and economic history. In short, his legal history is meaningful and comprehensible for all historians.

Where American legal history could once be ignored by American historians with a certain justification, such an excuse is no longer tenable. Hurst has written the kind of legal history that has relevance to all of our interests. Hurst has freed legal history from the narrow concerns of the past. In many ways Hurst's liberation of legal history remains to be accomplished in ordinary historical writing, for his work is the equivalent of the best in present day avant-garde historical interpretation.

72

AMERICAN LEGAL HISTORY: THE HURST APPROACH †

JOHN P. FRANK*

T HIS is the most significant work on legal history ever produced in the United States. It is no disservice to the many first-class studies in the field to say this; the plain fact is that only Charles Warren's *Supreme Court in United States History* rates very close to it.

Fundamentally, Hurst's book is a study of evolution in law. It would indeed be a cheap novelty to note that law grows and changes; by now even the schoolboys perceive this. But precisely how it grows and changes is another matter. Growth has been studied episodically often enough—the "From Old Deal to New Deal" kind of useful history in constitutional law, for example. But it has not previously been studied comprehensively.

73

Comprehensive study—a truly total wringing out of all humans can know about their past—necessarily means a narrow study. It has taken the best efforts of Professor Hurst, our most skilled and diligent legal historian, over twenty years to write his book. That the study is narrow in topic is a positive plus; a complete study in the field of evolution is necessarily so. Professor Hurst has found good scope by taking the almost closed circle of Wisconsin lumber industry from its origin in 1836 to its near end by 1915.

This stupendous work—about 350,000 words of text and almost as much in notes—has a kaleidoscope quality; what the viewer sees depends on how he looks at it. Three possible vantage points are the book viewed (a) as a source of information on its subject matter; (b) as a study in historical method; and (c) as a study in ideas, whether on social criticism or on legal and historical philosophy.

I

Hurst chose the Wisconsin pine forest as the place to build. Territorial (pre-1848) Wisconsin had timber on 30 million of its 35 million acres. There were 129 billion board feet of white pine in the forest in 1830. This was reduced to 17 billion board feet by 1898, and one billion

† LAW AND ECONOMIC GROWTH: THE LEGAL HISTORY OF THE LUMBER INDUSTRY IN WISCONSIN, 1836–1915. By James Willard Hurst. Washington, Belknap Press of Howard Univ. Press, 1964. Pp. xv, 946. $17.50.

* Member of the Arizona Bar.

by the 1920's.[1] Over 26 billion board feet had been wasted, mostly burned.

When the land was being stripped, men supposed it could still be used —the timber was supposed to be "an extra bonus to be reaped in the course of 'improving' land for its normal use for farms and towns."[2] But it has not proved so; the land left is largely wasted, very little of it fit for general agriculture.

The Nineteenth Century State never very seriously thought to preserve its assets; by the time of the great conservation fight of the Theodore Roosevelt-Taft years, Wisconsin was cut over. Hurst traces every stirring of public concern,[3] but concern came too late. The "facts of law and economics—government's possession of the public domain, industry's sharp-felt lack of fluid capital, and the need of special franchises in the provision of essential transport—created an extraordinary opportunity for law to exercise leverage on the situation."[4] But the law was too inexperienced, undermanned, and unmotivated; its role was to serve up the firewood for the Great Barbecue of a national asset, and no more. Individuals saw the hazards of waste,[5] but "as it was, men confronted large issues with little leisure or experience to season their judgment."[6]

Hurst is an historian, not a judge; and he is not writing to praise or condemn. For those struggling with great problems, his tone is more sympathetic than censorious. This is an objectivity hard to maintain for one who, like this reviewer, can remember the end of the timbering in the 20's, and has seen the utterly ruined, burned over lands. Had the Huns or the Goths passed through Northern Wisconsin, the destruction would not have been so bad. And all this to surprisingly little effect. Hurst peaks the direct employment in lumbering at about 20,000 persons in 1890;[7] there were some adjunct industries, and a few tycoons were made. Weyerhaeuser is almost the only name Hurst mentions still greatly prominent on the business scene.

This stupendous exploitation has in it every thread of legal history, and Hurst finds them all. Taking as his central theme "the study of the law's role in defining and sanctioning the allocation of decision-making power over the use of the forest, and in contributing to intelligent,

---

[1] Pp. 2–3.

[2] P. 94.

[3] See, e. g., pp. 100–06 on the theory of disposal.

[4] P. 11.

[5] See, e. g., the message of Governor Harvey, p. 22.

[6] P. 23.

[7] P. 4.

willed direction of the course of events," [8] he begins with the law of property.[9] The first topic relates timberland policy to the general public land policy of the United States. By 1890, most of the timberland was in private ownership; all the problems of acquiring land, protecting it from others, using it, and paying or avoiding taxes on it, are detailed here.

But getting the land, and the equipment and crews to cut it over, and protecting it would be as nothing without transportation of the timber. A tree standing upright in North Central Wisconsin or a log on ground in the same place is valueless; its value lies in getting it to a mill.[10] This was not usually a task for trains;[11] most logs floated to the saw. "Access to bulk transport spelled life or death for particular lumber ventures."[12] This led to the growth of transport corporations, to the grant of franchises to develop and use the rivers. We are thus dealing with important origins of corporate and public utility law, and of legislation on each. Hurst analyzes 802 special statutory franchises for the use of Wisconsin waters and 158 inland stream cases in the State Supreme Court.[13] He discusses common law theories of riparian ownership, problems of nuisance and reasonable use (consider the problem of the riparian owner who suddenly discovers a thousand tons of logs beached on his land), and the interplay of legislation and common law in dealing with the problems of stream use.[14] This also involved price control in the utmost detail; for example, the Chippewa River boom company franchise provided that the company might charge for its services only 12½ cents a thousand for shingles, 10 cents a twelve foot log, 20 cents a thousand feet of sawed timber for up to twenty days storage behind the company's boom.[15]

The law of property and of public utilities required innovation to meet lumber needs. This was less so in the "substantial role of law" to "provide an assured framework of contract doctrine and administration with-

75

8 P. 5.

9 " 'Property' in law means the legitimate power to initiate decisions on the use of economic assets." P. 9.

10 Hurst weighs transport as 40 to 75 per cent of the cost of getting lumber to market. P. 145.

11 See pp. 270–81 for exposition; and see p. 145.

12 P. 144.

13 Pp. 152 et seq.

14 See, e. g., pp. 537–50.

15 P. 550. Hurst nobly escapes the sin of excessive particularism of detail; I suspect he threw away as much material as he used. However, p. 551 does tell me more about particular storage prices in 1870 than I would have thought it necessary to know.

in which private arrangements might work themselves out." [16]   Of 700 lumber industry contract cases in the Wisconsin Supreme Court, "They are almost all contract-law cases first, and lumber-industry cases second." [17]   "The body of lumber-contract case law made its most distinctive adaptation to the peculiarities of the industry insofar as it admitted evidence of trade custom in interpreting agreements, and evidence of trade facts in applying contract terms, to decide whether there was adequate performance or a material breach;" [18] but this was a simple law merchant adaptation.   For the most part, contract law simply adapted, as in "the recognition that standing timber was a saleable item, apart from the title to the land on which it grew." [19]   A minor new property interest was created in timber "minutes," descriptive notes on timber quantity and quality sold by the number of acres covered.   New arrangements for financing exploitation were necessary for this money-tight economy; the means of swapping credit for woods knowledge and skill are fully described. [20]

In the lumber economy, labor was also a resource to be fully used. Recruitment, company store problems, and "dockage" are all reported. Consider, for example, the case of "Peter Larson" who " 'got killed in the woods while in the company's employ. His wages were docked 20 per cent for not working his time out.' " [21]   As Hurst politely puts it, "Legitimate management needs were being pressed through contract in the context of inequalities of bargaining power too great for the market to adjust." [22]

The failure of any regulation to govern the forest exploitation resulted partly from sheer inability; Nineteenth Century man had not yet learned how to create and manage a legal system to preserve a resource. [23]   But this "was part of the environment of policy derived from sweeping delegation of social functions to the market." [24]   Partly this was because "we lacked knowledge or interest about forestry practice which would manage timber stands for continuing yield. We did not have cost-ac-

---

[16] P. 289.

[17] *Ibid.*

[18] P. 290.

[19] The consequences of this, on such matters as the statute of frauds, are considered at pp. 298 *et seq.*

[20] Pp. 312 *et seq.*

[21] P. 485.

[22] P. 486.

[23] On general theory of Nineteenth Century regulations, Hurst is much indebted to LOUIS HARTZ, ECONOMIC POLICY AND DEMOCRATIC THOUGHT (1948).

[24] P. 125.

counting concepts which would at least define the issue of competition between present and future yields." [25] The lacks were state and federal; there was a "total lack of a program specifically adapted to disposal of federal forest lands in Wisconsin through the decades that counted." [26] What little policy there was lacked enforcement machinery,[27] and concern with the excesses of Nineteenth Century legislative bounty with what might have been Twentieth Century assets did not sharply occur until the Twentieth Century.[28] Uses of the investigative power occasionally served as a "crude makeshift" for more substantial policy.[29] Regulation began to have some purpose, if not much effect, in fire control legislation; some modern foresters believe that with even fair fire prevention and fire fighting, the forests might have been preserved.[30]

The real "policy" of Wisconsin in the Nineteenth Century was drift, the policy of no policy, of extemporization. This was the common state of the public law of the time. The legal story is very largely that of "the force which the prevailing drift obtains when there is no agency equipped to give sustained attention to exploring policy." [31]

77

II

In its most superficial sense, this is a book on the history of the lumber industry in one state in a by-gone time. But no one supposes that this, by itself, is a proper life work for our foremost historian. Details, if isolated, are for Ph.D. candidates.[32]

The book hits a more important level as an exemplar of historical method. The general design, under its headings of property, contract, police power, and public policy widely stretch those hum-drum labels. The concepts used here can be applied not only to any natural resource, but to any area of humanity's experience. For example, the estimable Louis Mumford doing his next volume on cities could do a better book by considering the Hurst concepts of the growing community, as distinguished from the Hurst details.

[25] *Ibid.*

[26] P. 64.

[27] See pp. 245–46.

[28] For illustrations, see p. 260; and for Hurst's vindication of Nineteenth Century legislatures as fairly reflecting contemporary values, p. 261.

[29] P. 442.

[30] See pp. 456 *et seq.*, 505.

[31] P. 507.

[32] "More time cost was invested in this project than would be warranted at a more developed stage of legal history research, when more knowledge should make it safe to cut corners." P. *x.*

Part of the Hurst method is new ideas of what to look for. Part is incredible thoroughness. For illustration, consider a sentence of text referring to the general pattern of Nineteenth Century economic theory, in which lumber economies must be set. The note not merely cites but uses some dozen different works to lay solid foundation for a seemingly casual observation.[33] The notes together run some 300 pages. They contain whole subsidiary chapters, such as a discussion of the conflict between lumber transportation and local industrial needs.[34]

There were some 700 contract cases concerning the lumber industry in the Wisconsin Supreme Court, almost all of them between 1860 and 1909. Hurst has studied them all, breaking them out into the problems of logging, transportation, milling, and other categories.[35] 137 accident cases receive similar close attention.[36] All the grants of eminent domain power in stream use special franchises are analyzed, as are special dam franchises, special stream use franchises, all of the vetoes of stream franchise bills, all of the special charters, and special subsidiary analyses of the accident cases in terms of types of accidents and types of defenses.[37]

The bedrock Hurstian element, then, is thoroughness: thoroughness so complete as to put a new dimension on the word. The thoroughness of course must be to a purpose, and the second half of the method is the formulation of far-ranging concepts about law and human affairs which the accumulated facts may prove or disprove. Here is so full a bushel basket of ideas that they will be taken up separately. Hurst believes that [38]

if we would know the history of law in the life of a society, search cannot stop with formal procedures. Especially when we study the history of policy made within a constitutional legal order, we must attempt to measure the impact of law's formal operations relative to men's informal behavior (both within and outside of legal institutions), and also relative to the formal and informal works of other institutions with which law interacts. So far as the issue is the shaping of overt action—which is typically the purpose of using law—form has significance only if it affects substance, however else the situation may be in art, where the issue is to shape perception and feeling as an end in itself.

[33] See p. 43 and p. 643 n. 37.

[34] See note 505, pp. 799–802.

[35] P. 293.

[36] P. 492.

[37] See p. 736 n. 148; p. 741 n. 170; p. 754 n. 217; p. 784 n. 412; p. 861 n. 103; p. 885 n. 36.

[38] Pp. 204–05.

In reaching substance, he treats of law both as a master and as a servant of events; for in the grip of the acquisitive urge, "men made fresh, complex demands upon law." [39] His task thus has become to determine what those demands were, how they were served, how the system in fact worked out. From his study he concludes: [40]

Nineteenth-century lawmaking was narrowly operational by choice, moved by compulsions of feeling and will derived from men's reaction to the experience of opening a new continent. Prevailing opinion was impatient with lawmaking; men wanted to put their prime energies into the challenges they saw in the market. Both in market and in public policy, prevailing opinion was impatient with plans or decisions which looked very far ahead in time or very far abroad in current calculations; when there was obviously so much to do, and such frustrating scarcity of mobile capital with which to realize opportunities, men felt overwhelming impulsion toward improvisation, opportunism, and the quick return. The same temper which set the tone of dealings with public lands moved through dealings with public waters. Lawmakers surrendered to this temper of the times with enough awareness to be uneasy, yet in response to such deep undercurrents of attitude that their imagination could not or would not break free into bolder generalization of policy.

79

An analysis of a few-page fragment illustrates the method. The Wisconsin of the lumber boom was money short, energy long, and resource very long. The central problem was how to harness money and energy to cash in on the resource. This leads to a ten-page discussion of "bootstrap finance." [41] Hurst begins with Tocqueville as he is regularly likely to do; this is the ancient sage of the new history. Tocqueville had been astonished at the number of small enterprises in the United States. Hurst begins by giving the statistics of capital investment throughout the lumber period, showing the transition from small capital to major investment. A couple of sentences give the transition. But throughout, "the financing of smaller operators depended on the procedures made available by contract law."

A sampling of the specific cases shows how contract related dollars and energy, showing how the system worked for "men with cash and loggers without it." He illustrates with a case in which the Wisconsin Supreme Court found that "labor and skill were contributed to the business on one side, and capital on the other. There was necessarily a communion of profit and loss." We get into the details of the transactions,

39 P. 145.
40 P. 206.
41 Pp. 309–21.

of how the operator undertook to cut and haul "all the pine timber suitable for saw logs." This the operator was to mark "with the log mark J*MX, and as soon as the stage of water will admit in the spring or summer of 1876, he will drive all said logs into the St. Croix boom and deliver" them.[42] Pay was slow and the operator "traded this bill to Kelly for a horse. It is hard to say whether he was a pretty good horse. Some might consider him a good horse and some wouldn't. I would just call him a middling horse." Firmly mounted on this middling horse, Hurst canters on to the statute of frauds which the Wisconsin court was called upon to interpret in such fashion as would facilitate lumber operations.

Hurst traces out into the actual transactions the various wrinkles of contract adjustment which made the exploitation of the forest possible. These were frequently simple transactions of simple people: "McArthur had some teams, cattle, horses, and sleds, and he was to put in such proportion of his stuff as was required, and to log them off, and we were to cut them, or sell them in the market, as the case might be." [43] When the operator had nothing to put up for security, his only possession being his energy, the capitalist necessarily made his advances on hope secured by withholdings. If the operator had something else, such as timber title, to offer, different arrangements could be made, and they are all explored. When we are done, we know about all of the security interests in land which could be used to facilitate its development, and we know how the law grew in this period to serve this need. The development of the lumber lien law is compactly described.

This whole system of energizing dollars which Hurst calls bootstrap financing was a vital element of the lumber industry. The question remains, just how vital, and where? Hurst finds "that the pinch of cash scarcity was felt the more sharply the closer operations were to the woods." The great stack of case statistics is re-sorted to show that the money shortage was most clearly felt in the logging itself the closer the product came to the mill or to sale, the more readily conventional financial arrangements could operate; but in the woods "a significant function of contract law was not merely to supply the parties with a formal frame for dealing, but to contribute mobility to fixed capital and give leverage for productive effort." [44]

An essential part of the Hurst presentation is a fluent, easy style. This mountain of information could be impossible to climb. The possibility

[42] P. 313.
[43] P. 315.
[44] P. 321.

80

of sinking into a mass of particularist details is very great. The opposite hazard of seeking to link details with impossibly obscure abstractions could have clouded the material in hopeless obscurity.   Hurst escapes these hazards and presents this story in a good clean line from beginning to its distant end.[45]

III

The information and the method are but the platform of Hurst's thoughts both in social criticism and in legal philosophy.   The intellectual abundance makes the harvest too great even seriously to open in a review. A thumb on any page will pull out a plum of an idea.

As I have said, Hurst has not written a book to deplore the rape of a forest; this is no polemic. Indeed, the record is too disheartening to need epithets and is all the starker if coolly described, as when a summary tells us that the federal and state governments "offered the industry a subsidy in fixed capital, minimized its working capital needs, held down operating costs by foregoing any attempt to impose minimum standards of efficient forest use, and relieved the industry of any obligation to create depletion reserves against the costs of a substitute economy for the cut-over region." [46]

The era operated "with uncritical enthusiasms for growth as a self-evident good," [47] and as a 1916 Wisconsin Attorney General observed of stream use charters, "there was no thought then of uniform flow, of fisheries, of public health, of highways, of hydroelectric power, of navigation, or of 'performing the public duty imposed.' " [48]

This, as Hurst emphasizes, does not warrant particular criticism of Nineteenth Century lawmakers or Nineteenth Century lumber barons; conservation and the multi-purpose project are Twentieth Century ideas and there is neither justice nor profit in criticizing an earlier generation for failure to know what we have learned. Indeed, our lesson is in large part the product of their experience.[49]

And yet it is hard to resist a sorrowful backward glance. The girl who follows promiscuity with virtue may be complimented on her new estate, but nothing can restore the virgin whether she be female or forest.

---

45 Hurst gives credit to a Harvard University Press Editor, Mrs. Dorothy W. Whitney, for skilled work on the manuscript, which I suspect is richly deserved.

46 P. 502.

47 P. 560.

48 P. 260.

49 P. 261.

As Hurst says, "passing moral judgments on ancestors warms the ego." [50] This is an indulgence which he denies himself while noting that conservation came to Wisconsin too late to make any difference; by the time of Theodore Roosevelt, "the Wisconsin forest industry had passed its peak of activity." [51] But he does narrate the story of the rear-guard action, telling how, even though late, the Wisconsin Legislature sought to save the remnant; and he tells how the State Supreme Court knocked out the program. The Court's conclusion, we are told, "cannot be justified; it can only be explained." [52] In the middle of the discussion of the Court's decision is a contemporary picture of a cut-over area which could not look much more a monument to man's ruin of earth than if an atomic bomb had struck.[53]

All else is merely tributary to the central theme of the volume: "the study of the law's role in defining and sanctioning the allocation of decision-making power over the use of the forest, and in contributing to intelligent, willed direction of the course of events. As in all social history of the law, the allocation of power and the channeling of change are here the essence of the story." [54] The government's possession of the land, industry's lack of funds, and the need of special franchises for transportation "created an extraordinary opportunity for law to exercise leverage on the situation." [55] By 1860 it was clear that our ancestors "believed in using law affirmatively to shape certain basic social and economic—as well as political—conditions of our life. . . . We used law not so much to hold things steady as to direct change, not to maintain ordered status but to encourage mobility, to give scope to private decision making through private property, but also to make public investment of substantial resources to promote the quality of political and social power, and to create facilities that might multiply private production." [56]

Nineteenth Century law was not an instrument of repression or control, but rather a tool to facilitate the exploitation of natural resources and of expanding population and markets. The prime purpose of this law was not to keep the serf on his fief but rather to serve the accumulation of riches by reach and take. 1892 timber cutting is the logical consequence of 1492 exploration and is simply a natural resource form of

82

---

[50] P. 429.

[51] *Ibid.*

[52] P. 583.

[53] P. 580. The book's most ruinous pictures are those at p. 452. Others of the numerous pictures range from ox sleds to log mark records to a 1907 cook shack.

[54] P. 5.

[55] P. 11.

[56] P. 20.

Cortez and the gold of Montezuma. The cutting of the forests is of a piece with the killing of the buffalo, the turning of the topsoil of the plains, the mining of the gold and silver of the Far West. Social philosophy, and with it legal philosophy, was more the philosophy of the get than the philosophy of the keep, and Hurst's largest attention is to the role of law in this taking function.

The ultimate form of acquisitiveness is plain theft and Hurst has studied closely the ineffective attempts of the law to control it. The inability to control any theft from public lands, made more acute by strong public sentiment in the areas involved in favor of timber trespass, accentuated the pressures for sale. Law was so helpless that private interests probably could protect the forest lands better than the government itself.[57] This portion of the story, illustrating the total incapacity of legal tools to serve the public interest, is contrasted with developments in the Twentieth Century when better controls have been devised. The actual facts of timber trespass again illustrate Hurst's recurrent theme of the relation of form to substance, for there is no greater contrast between law's formal pretentions and "men's informal behavior."

Among agencies of law making, the legislature was frequently the central instrument, and this is particularly true on stream use. From Hurst's analysis of the failures of the Wisconsin Legislature in the 1850's and 60's, we can learn a good deal which can contribute to the improvement of the legislatures today. As he says, to make policy "men must (1) perceive problems, (2) find facts relevant to workable comprehension and resolution of the problems (whether the finding be by fresh investigation, by draft upon present knowledge, or simply by assumption), and (3) choose among limited means and ends . . . "[58] He notes that the best of legislatures are not well suited for original research and that they need effective committees and staff. The Wisconsin Legislature for the lumber years had nothing but clerks. It had no standing committees equipped to deal with waterways policy, no staff for studies and reports. For all the river franchises the Legislature gave, there is not one single committee study or report on the common problems of stream management.[59] Any contemporary legislature must struggle to avoid making the same mistakes over again.[60]

---

57 Pp. 97 et seq.

58 P. 248.

59 P. 251.

60 It is sad to observe in my own state of Arizona in 1965 legislative conditions of overwork, underpay, and understaffing directly parallel to those Hurst illustrates. The principal difference is the shift away from a giveaway philosophy toward natural resources protection in the interim.

83

Because Hurst deals with every facet of law use and law making, he shifts the focus away from court decisions which are the conventional stuff of legal history. He recognizes that most of the cases which get to a state supreme court involve "marginal phenomena," cases in which the clarity of law breaks down sufficiently that controversy could exist.[61] The general change factor in law was legislation, and the greatest single force of law was not its change but its tradition which enabled people to do business within a contract framework which pre-existed lumber. Not all legal history is change, and Hurst speaks of the stability and applicability of law as much as of its growth. Yet change is always in Hurst's focus, and particularly when he speaks of the police power:[62]

A working society means relationships which must be kept in some minimum balance, and requires fulfillment of some minimum functions of reciprocity and mutual restraint. The order which law helps create and keep is not a static condition. It is a moving equilibrium, product of continuous adjustment to diverse pressures and to the constant press of changed circumstance. The police power refers to the role of law in effecting these adjustments.

Man's ability to regulate his own conduct has improved considerably since the Nineteenth Century, and yet, as current and rising mid-Twentieth Century crime statistics show, the task of social regulation—of the police power—is far from completed. This is illustrated by contrasting figures from the lumber industry. Hurst estimates that two-thirds of all the timber cut in Northern Wisconsin was wasted, that not over 40 per cent of the timber available reached the sawmills, that fire loss exceeded the cut in some areas, and that inefficient saws cost a billion of board feet of pine in Wisconsin between 1872 and 1905. On the other hand, as Hurst notes, "it chastens our judgments on the nineteenth-century industry to learn that in the 1940's about 30 per cent of the total annual drain on the country's forest resources was preventable waste, that half of the timber cut for lumber was wasted in the process, and that losses by fire, disease, pests, and storms accounted for about 11 per cent of the annual decrease in stock."[63] Our legal system makes progress slowly. A Wisconsin report in 1867 dealt with the "Disastrous Effects of the Destruction of Forest Trees Now Going on so Rapidly in the State of Wisconsin."[64] How much better will our legal machinery be in 1967?

[61] P. 297.

[62] P. 427.

[63] P. 431.

[64] P. 447.

Hurst reiterates and illustrates the theme that the police power, to be effective, must be administration as well as policy formulation; it was here that Nineteenth Century law broke down. "Just enough happened of a positive character to show that although the nineteenth-century state government was not wholly incapable of glimpsing relevant general policy, its processes were usually incapable of translating particular insights into firm and general form." [65] To be of any effectiveness at all, the police power had to move to reach an all-planning by government which required "the emergence of strong legislative and administrative leadership in affairs," contributed by the progressive movement of Theodore Roosevelt and Robert M. LaFollette.[66] In this respect the police power as it related to the lumber industry had to grow toward administrative effectiveness in every other phase of public affairs as well and this is a course which clearly is yet far from run.

Hurst's method of perceiving fact and relating it to perceptions about law is illustrated in a few pages on river transportation. He notes that the law makes "value choices when, to promote creative release of men's wills, it treated some activity as lawful in the absence of positive regulation or prohibition, but required the law's explicit license as a condition for other action" [67]; thus he illustrates that it was lawful for a man to cut the timber on his own land without needing special authorization, but on the other hand he could not build a dam on the stream to control the float of his logs to market without express public authority. The law has thus, whether deliberately or not, ranked interests, giving one a preference over the other.

From this Hurst takes as his problem a discussion of interest-ranking in law. This requires first an analysis of the procedures by which interests are recognized in law; second an analysis of the social functions served by particular legal devices; and third an inventory of particular valuations made among the interests involved. Discussing each of these three,[68] he leads to the hierarchy of interests recognized in stream franchise policy. If the categories seem abstract, the talk is extremely practical. Hurst notes that "always, someone must bear the costs (in time and energy if not in money) of making law and putting it in motion; always, those who found law moving against their interests must submit, or lay out their own costs to satisfy it or turn it aside." [69]

85

---

65 P. 528.

66 P. 586.

67 P. 207.

68 Pp. 207-25.

69 P. 210.

Thus someone who wanted a bill risks the possibility that he might not get it; his money for drafting, for lobbying, his energy in the cause—all might be wasted. The law made a choice in imposing this risk when the Wisconsin Supreme Court determined that it was a nuisance to build a dam on a navigable stream without legislative authorization; at that point anyone wishing to build a dam had to bear the cost of initiating legislation, while anyone who wished to use the flowing water for simpler navigation had the benefit of the rule. He who wished to move a boat on the stream could stand pat; he who wished to hold and control the flow of logs could not. At this point the law had advanced the boatman's interest at the expense of the loggers'.

On the other hand, court decisions later modified this rule to eliminate the requirement of a special bill as to some kinds of dams on some kinds of streams with some kinds of passageways. At this point the law had altered the hierarchy of interests; it had shifted the balance back to the logger and away from the boatman.

Much such close analysis leads to Hurst's conclusions. Early stream policy showed no concern for aesthetic or recreational values; "rather, it attended almost exclusively to those economic values which the market could translate into a dollar calculus." [70] There was no concern for public health or safety. The law bent its back to aid big dollar returns as against smaller ones, so that transport and water power was given a high preference over riparian land use. An illustration of this preference is the delegation of the eminent domain power to dam builders. So also is the legislative authorization to log owners to go on private property to get logs which had floated ashore. [71] Fisheries were given little value. Navigation had a preference over power. Within any category, the first to claim a particular stream use might well be favored in enjoying it.

IV

The big question about this book is its value to those who don't really care about the details of the Wisconsin lumber industry in the 1800's but who are interested in questions of the growth of law to meet new demands made by new forms of organization and institutions, and a rapidly expanding extractive-base economy. Does this work mean that only through extremely detailed studies of this sort is it possible to explore questions relating to the legal process in this connection? Or is there some other way by which sufficient source material may be gathered to support a more generalized kind of analysis? Does Hurst's method,

[70] P. 220.

[71] The preference given to the owners of wandering cattle in the West is analogous.

if the only valid one, impose a prohibitive limitation on meaningful discussions of the legal process?

Clearly this book cannot be a model for legal historical research. The number of persons who would have the time and the talent to match it is too small. Certainly the book is not too long, for since the themes are the central themes of all North American legal-economic-growth relations in the Nineteenth Century, the sweep is big enough to require a big book.

Those following in such studies will never have to do as large a job as Hurst has done because he has done it. The transatlantic flight and the four-minute mile both were easier the second time. Hurst had to fumble to discover what areas to explore; the next scholar can follow his lead. Hurst used foundation grant help. The next scholar can reasonably expect to have more of it. But most important of all, Hurst gives those who follow new ideas about law-society relationships which can now be had for the taking.

Hurst gives renewed demonstration that Nineteenth Century law was a law of growth and change whose hierarchy of values was not static. For illustration, in the lumber years, the Legislature preferred transport to power. In the early Twentieth Century, as the lumber industry died off and the electric power industry expanded, the Legislature veered toward favoring power use of the streams. "Time, thus, was patently an important dimension of policy." [72]

V

Time has also been an important dimension of Hurst's work. Because this is a major work on legal evolution, it reminds one of Darwin's *Origin of Species*. Charles Darwin got long mileage on the back of a Galapagos tortoise, but the process was slow—his tortoise was whizzing along at 360 yards an hour.[73] Darwin himself noted in his introduction that [74]

when on board H.M.S. "Beagle," as naturalist, I was much struck with certain facts and the distribution of the organic beings inhabiting South America, and in the geological relations of the present to the past inhabitants of that continent. These facts, as will be seen in the latter chapters of this volume, seemed to throw some light on the origin of species—that mystery of mysteries, as it has been called by one of our

[72] P. 225.

[73] At least on the ride of October 8, 1835 on James Island; see 6 GAVIN DeBEER, CHARLES DARWIN 51 (1964).

[74] CHARLES DARWIN, ON THE ORIGIN OF SPECIES 1 (1859).

87

greatest philosophers. On my return home, it occurred to me, in 1837, that something might perhaps be made out on this question that by patiently accumulating and reflecting on all sorts of facts which could possibly have any bearing on it.

Professor Hurst has made the Northern Wisconsin forest the terrain for his voyage of the "Beagle." He has patiently accumulated and reflected on all sorts of facts. What he has produced is the most original work yet written on the nature, function, and growth of law in the life of the people of the United States; and this will do as a "mystery of mysteries," for those whose deepest interest is in either law or history.

88

Reviews

Heart Against Head: Perry Miller and the Legal Mind

Lawrence M. Friedman†

The Life of the Mind in America, From the Revolution to the Civil War. By Perry Miller. *New York: Harcourt, Brace & World, 1965. Pp. 338. $7.50.*

I.

When Perry Miller, the great intellectual historian, died suddenly in 1963 at the age of 58, he left behind him fragments of a massive, comprehensive study of the American mind from the Revolution to the outbreak of the Civil War. Of nine projected parts, two and a portion of the third have been published in one volume.[1] Book II of this volume, *The Legal Mentality*, contains Professor Miller's judgment on the intellectual life of American law. Publication of an essay on the intellectual side of the law by an author of high prestige is a major —and rare—event in American legal historiography. On the whole, however, this is a disappointing work. It has a certain grandeur of design, a certain beauty of style, but it is disfigured by many errors of fact[2] and more significantly by its strained and strange view of American law and the legal profession. Some errors would no doubt have been corrected had the author lived. Others, however, are more fundamental errors in deep-seated premises, errors that infuse the entire

---

† Professor of Law, University of Wisconsin. B.A. 1948, J D. 1951, LL.M. 1953, University of Chicago.

1. P. MILLER, THE LIFE OF THE MIND IN AMERICA, FROM THE REVOLUTION TO THE CIVIL WAR (1965) [hereinafter cited as THE LIFE OF THE MIND].

2. For example, a discussion of equity, *id.* 171-182, consistently confuses the various senses in which this complex legal word is used. Professor Miller also states that "[i]n the colonies, such controversies as in mid-eighteenth century England were finding their way to Chancery usually had to be adjudicated, if at all, by the legislatures." *Id.* 171. This ignores the fact that some colonies (such as South Carolina) had fully-developed Chancery courts; moreover, some jurisdictions enforced in their ordinary courts what would be elsewhere labeled equitable claims.

work. I shall attempt to set forth Professor Miller's approach to American legal history, to state frankly why I think it is wrong, and then to suggest alternative ways of looking at the same field.

II.

Professor Miller, of course, is an intellectual historian. The actual content of the legal system is not his concern; his subject, rather is the development of legal ideas and their relationship to other aspects of American intellectual life.[3] He finds the substance of American legal thought in works of formal jurisprudence and in the speeches and treatises of important lawyers. Professor Miller, however, was not a lawyer. His vast erudition did not extend to such technical legal material as case reports and statutes. His research was generally limited to the study of formal texts of leading or archetypical jurists; on these he bases his generalizations. He then compares his jurisprudential findings with other data, drawn in the same manner from formal writings in other fields, such as religion and literature. His findings are further compared with his conceptions of the "American character" or the "American mind," which is in turn a composite of or an abstraction from the legal mind, the literary mind, the revivalist mind, and the scientific mind.

Any scholar must be granted the right to choose his own subject, and the intellectual historian has the right to deal solely with products of the intellect if he desires. He may treat his subject in relative isolation; though society is a seamless web, it is neither necessary, nor even possible, to take fully into account the railroad and the cotton gin in dealing with Emerson and Poe. But it is another thing entirely when an intellectual (or social, or economic) historian claims for *his* subject matter and his concepts that they alone explain what makes and moves the world.[4] To blame Auschwitz and Buchenwald exclusively or even largely on Nietzsche or Wagner would be blatantly untrue to the science of society. Judgments of causation are slippery at best. Many slight or invisible ropes bind and loose the social order; present knowledge of causation is too embryonic to unravel them.

3. THE LEGAL MIND IN AMERICA, FROM INDEPENDENCE TO THE CIVIL WAR 11 (Miller ed., 1962). This was a collection of documents edited by Professor Miller, with brief essays introducing each selection.

4. John Higham wrote, almost prophetically, in 1951 that Miller seemed "chiefly concerned with estimating the force of ideas themselves. There are dangers in this enterprise —dangers of assuming the autonomy of ideas and losing oneself in abstractions." Higham, *The Rise of American Intellectual History*, 56 AM. HIST. REV. 470 (1951).

90

Whether the Civil War was in essence a culture conflict, a moral crusade, the working out of blind economic forces, or all of these in some specific mix, or something entirely different, is beyond our capacity to determine.

Professor Miller can and does contribute to understanding when he confines himself to the intellectual life of his society, considered as a set of circles of literary effort which overlap or surround each other and are in turn collectively enclosed in one grand circle of American thought. Unfortunately, however, he goes further. Throughout the section on the legal mind, he makes assertions which are, explicitly or not, assertions of causal connections between intellectual developments and socio-economic events. These go beyond his data and frequently offend against common sense. Moreover, his boldest leaps are concealed by a highly metaphoric style, so that the reader is apt to follow along, dazzled into agreement, unless he stops to analyze each phrase.

91

III.

Let us first take an example of the kind of general argument that Professor Miller makes. The "mass of the People," he says, distrusted the law in the post-revolutionary period. This was because law was "by its very nature sophisticated, whereas the American people" were "natural, reasonable, equitable."[5] The lawyers' "real controversy with their society was that they stood for the Head against the Heart."[6] Though great courtroom "romantics" appeared later on in the century, American legal thought remained intellectually committed to the forces of cold reason. The legal profession bent every effort to the pursuit of reason and to the creating, out of its rude past, of an intellectual profession and a rational system of law. The mind of the lawyers differed from the revivalist mind (the subject of Book I of the volume), which dreamed of creating in America "a distinct, unique millenial utopia." The lawyers sought rather to "subject the society to a rule of universality," that is, to the dominance of the (supranational) common law.[7] Partly because of this basic intellectual posture, the lawyers—exemplified by such men as James Kent, Joseph Story, and John Marshall—constituted a highly conservative element in society. They fought to preserve the property qualification; they fought against the elective

5. THE LIFE OF THE MIND 104.
6. Id.
7. Id. 133.

judiciary. The "conservative" bar, we are told, "trembled" at the equation of the elective principle with democracy.[8] To them, elected judges meant the rule of the mob, the dethronement of reason, the triumph of "instinct."

The reader will note that the molding of opinion on specific, concrete policies (appointive judgeships, the property qualification) is explained by the logical relationship between these positions and a more general intellectual position. That, for example, certain lawyers might want to preserve the rule of the rich because they themselves were relatively rich seems not to have entered Professor Miller's mind. Moreover, Professor Miller thinks it makes sense to speak of the legal profession as a whole. To him, the profession represents a distinct stratum of society, with a distinctive frame of mind. That frame of mind, of course, is the one he senses peering out of the pages of formal legal texts. At least he is consistent; he generalizes no less glibly about society as a whole:

> The populace in general, however, were strongly of the opinion that if there were to be lawyers at all, those who worked by instinct were the most tolerable.[9]

Neither here nor, of course, anywhere else does Professor Miller tell us how he knows what the "populace in general" thought about this or any other subject. The passage is based on evidence drawn solely from the writings of some articulate portion of the public. Thus there are two weaknesses in the argument: first, a sort of intellectual determinism; second, the drawing of conclusions that go far beyond the data.

Not that the methodological puzzle is easily solved. It may seem plausible to assume that most lawyers objected to the elective principle for judges and the broadening of the suffrage. But how can we prove it? There is no historical equivalent of the Gallup poll. We must settle for the best available evidence. But how shall we gather it? How much weight shall we place on a speech by Chancellor Kent? Was he a leader? Who listened to him? How many prominent leaders spoke on the other side? Who listened to them? Is there any way of finding out what less prominent lawyers thought? Of course these are hard questions, perhaps even impossible ones. But a historian of opinion owes his audience some rigor, some attention to methodology. Professor Miller's book not only fails to solve these problems, it seems barren of any awareness that the problems exist.

8. *Id.* 234.
9. *Id.* 110.

We could forgive a lack of journeyman's rigor if instead we gained
flashes of insight that no dull empiricism could hope for. And there
are such flashes of insight, here and there. Unfortunately, we also find
great expanses of vague metaphor, papering over a basic hollowness of
argument. For example, in one passage, dealing with the appointment
of Joseph Story to a chair at Harvard Law School, we read that when
Story

> joined to the crushing burden of his work . . . the labor of teach-
> ing at Harvard, his prestige made the Law School a national insti-
> tution. From this point on may be dated the rapid growth . . . of
> law schools, so that by mid-century the time when a youth could
> set up as a lawyer merely by reading Blackstone in the office of
> the local practitioner was fast becoming a thing of what seemed a
> distant past. . . .[10]

What do we learn here? No doubt, Story's prestige was important to
Harvard (let us leave aside what it means to say that his prestige "made"
the Law School a "national institution"). According to Miller there
seems to have been some connection between the growing prestige of
Harvard and the decline of the apprenticeship method. Plausible perhaps: but precisely what was the connection? Professor Miller does
not quite *say* that there was a connection, or of what sort; he merely
says that the new development "may be dated" from the appointment
of Story to his professorship—a baffling ambiguity. What is the mechanism which made Story's appointment crucial for Harvard and made
the rise of Harvard a crucial factor in inducing radical change in the
aims and methods of American legal education? One might guess that
legal training and admission to the bar were affected by changes in the
economics and social status of the bar, that these changes were connected with general trends in the professionalization of American occupational groups, and that these trends were in turn connected with
gross changes in the economy, population, and society of the United
States. Not a word, or a hint of these factors is to be found in *The Life
of the Mind*. The passage on Story, typically, takes us to some distant
realm where only disembodied thought exists. And even in that sphere
the argument moves by poetry and allusion. On close inspection, the
bones of the argument turn to water. Nor can we save the argument
by calling Story's appointment not a cause but a landmark or symbol
—an occurrence which may be taken as a dramatic outward manifes-

93

---

10. *Id.* 142. Story was appointed to a professorship established at Harvard by Nathan
Dane in 1829. 1 C. WARREN, HISTORY OF THE HARVARD LAW SCHOOL 415-18 (1908).

tation, an external stigma of deep silent forces or events, The trouble is that Professor Miller does not treat it as such; at best he equivocates between the symbolic and causal planes. And his metaphors serve not to illuminate, but to hide the vacillation between these two levels of analysis.

The same vacillation recurs throughout the text. One page away from the passage about Story is an even more blatant example. Theophilus Parsons, we are told, "sadly" noted in 1852 two great streams of opinion in the bar—one, that legal scholars must turn to specialization, the other, that law, "like all true sciences, springs from a few simple principles which can readily be acquired."[11] It made Parsons "melancholy" to realize that the specialist view was on the rise. Professor Miller here adds his own view:

> The behemoths of legal scholarship had overreached themselves. They had created so massive an engine of rational erudition that the intellects of ordinary American students could not keep up with it.[12]

94

Now the historical problem under discussion is what was the origin of specialization in the study and practice of law. Are we really to believe that this phenomenon owes anything—let alone everything—to "behemoths of legal scholarship" who created an "engine of rational erudition" too "massive" for the "intellects of ordinary American students?" Is specialization in medicine, the sciences, and history to be blamed on "behemoths" who "overreached themselves" in their philosophical writings? The increasing *bulk* of American law was due more to population growth, economic development, and social diversity than to "behemoths." If anything, "legal scholarship" was struggling to reduce the enormous burden of raw legal matter to practical, manageable form. This bulk was one reason why Parsons longed for a skeleton key of simple principles. Professor Miller speaks as if scholars *created* specialization at the bar by pushing legal erudition past the point of easy grasp. There is a grain of truth in the argument, but only a grain. No lawyer could grasp the whole of the legal system because the system became simply too big. Its size, however, owed nothing to Story and Kent and everything to social and economic events which Professor

---

11. The reader will be immediately reminded here of Langdell's famous passage: "Law, considered as a science, consists of certain principles or doctrines. . . . [T]he number of fundamental legal doctrines is much less than is commonly supposed." C. LANG-DELL, CASES ON CONTRACTS vi (1871).
12. THE LIFE OF THE MIND 142-143.

Miller entirely ignores. Moreover, professional specialization is a response to market demands. There is a patent bar and a tax bar because these are needed; nobody wants a bailments bar.

By ignoring the world in which the legal profession worked, Professor Miller constantly misses the point, even in the *intellectual* history of law. Here is a prime example:

> . . . the accumulated weight of . . . tomes . . . rolled through the decades before the Civil War like a juggernaut. Hoffman's lectures and the volumes of Kent and Story were reinforced by other classics of what Roscoe Pound calls "doctrinal writings:" Reve's *Baron and Feme* (1816), Gould's *Pleading* (1832), Greenleaf's *Evidence* (1842-1843), Parson's *Contracts* (1853-1855), Washburn's *Real Property* (1860-1862), to mention only the most ponderous. Against the whimpering protests of beginners who felt that all they need know was American statute, such overpowering figures as Thomas Sergeant of Philadelphia patiently explained that these treatises were indispensable. . . . [T]hey shed upon the law a light of order.[13]

95

The first thing we notice about the passage is its maddening imprecision: what, if anything, does it mean to say that the accumulated weight of these "tomes . . . rolled through the decades . . . like a juggernaut?" In what respect were the treatises mentioned the "most ponderous" of pre-Civil War treatises? Professor Miller has probably never really read these books and compared them with others which he found less "ponderous." In what respect was Thomas Sergeant an "overpowering figure"? Few readers will have heard of this minor figure in American legal history.[14] In the second place, the passage is sublimely innocent of law and life. Legal neophytes, whether of the whimpering sort or not, surely had heard of the common law. They surely knew that statutes were not the whole of the law. A naive student might have thought the matter was the other way around. Moreover, there is the innuendo, quite characteristic of Professor Miller's thought, that the "ponderous" tomes were exercises in pure legal logic and that they were somehow imposed on the helpless young, mesmerizing them despite their "whimpering" complaints. Nothing could be more fanciful. The simple fact is that these treatises were written to make money. Nathan Dane financed Story's chair at Harvard out of the proceeds of his multi-volume

---

13. *Id.* 156-7.
14. Thomas Sergeant (1782-1860) is probably remembered, if at all, for his reports of cases decided by the Pennsylvania Supreme Court, which he edited in collaboration with William Rawle. He also served as a justice on that court from 1834 to 1846, and wrote a number of treatises. 16 DICTIONARY OF AMERICAN BIOGRAPHY 590 (1935).

pot-boiler.[15] Lawyers were hungry for plain, useful texts. They did not buy these books for philosophy. The books indeed contained no philosophy, but only a thin soup of borrowed notions served up with the meat and potatoes of law. Lawyers bought these books for the same reason then that they buy them today: to help them in study or practice. The "light of order" shed by these books was pragmatic in conception and execution. Some of them were as severely practical as a form-book; others discussed the "principles" underlying particular rules of law and made some attempt to harmonize cases and isolate exceptions to the rules.[16] In general, the impact of legal treatises on the intellectual life of their readers (Kent and Story were perhaps partial exceptions) was probably not much more than the intellectual impact of the Sears Roebuck catalog on farmers.

IV.

96

In short, Professor Miller constantly romanticizes and exaggerates the impact of formal intellect on the habits and achievements of the law. The "sublimity" of legal literature—such as it was—probably meant next to nothing in the life of the average lawyer. In the absence of more hard facts, one may also gently doubt whether the jurisprudential elites had quite as much and as baneful an influence on American politics as Professor Miller seems to suggest. As we have seen, he equates his post-revolutionary lawyers with classical rationalism, with Head rather than Heart, and with conservatism and revulsion against democracy. To him the work of the lawyers was "negative." They inherited and cherished an ancient system of law, which had been decisively formed in a struggle against the power of the English crown. Well into the era of independence, the lawyers continued to be deeply suspicious of power. They were fearful of government—particularly a government ruled by the mob. America, a "hard-working, pushing society," "appeared headed for catastrophe" in its race to achieve popular democracy.[17] The lawyers fought manfully against the evils of their

---

15. *See* 1 C. WARREN, HISTORY OF THE HARVARD LAW SCHOOL 415 (1908).

16. Here is an example from Tapping Reeve's *Baron and Feme*, one of Professor Miller's "ponderous" tomes: "Sons-in-law are not obliged to maintain the pauper parents of their wives. This case is an exception to the rule [that husbands can be compelled to perform duties incumbent on the wife prior to her marriage]; for before marriage the wives were obliged by law (if they were of sufficient ability) to maintain their necessitous parents. It is not very easy to discover the principle which governs this exception to the general rule. Perhaps it consists in an anxious desire to preserve domestic tranquility, which might be endangered by the operation of the general rule." T. REEVE, BARON AND FEME 75 (1816).

17. THE LIFE OF THE MIND 215.

times. Professor Miller thinks it is "fair" to say that the "tremendous concern of the legal generation of 1820 to 1850 for the imposition of negatives upon the emerging society is largely responsible for the great esteem the principle has subsequently enjoyed."[18]

Much of this argument is more or less plausible. But the final hypothesis is far too sweeping. No doubt there is *some* connection between doctrines and tactics employed by appellate courts before the Civil War (*Dred Scott* is a hideous example) and the conservatism of the due process cases in the late nineteenth century.[19] Cooley, Tiedeman, and the other postwar theorists of constitutional limitations used prewar case law and theory in constructing their manifestoes against popular democracy.[20] But movements generate manifestoes; manifestoes do not make movements. The "great esteem" enjoyed in this country by principles of limitation on the power of the government is not a matter of esthetic tastes and only partly a matter of ideological conviction. Limitations on government cannot be fully understood without reference to specific economic and social struggles in which principles of limitation were asserted. They cannot be summed up in so pat a formula as Professor Miller suggests, and they cannot be treated as a closed system of theories explainable as dialectic developments from earlier ideas and dialectic ancestors of later ones. The "negatives" imposed on a Populist legislature, on King George III, on the Congress of the nineteenth century, and on a white supremacist city council today are not the same either in theory or in context, and it is wrong to treat them as the same.

The point about negativism is all glitter and no gold in another sense, too. Here is Professor Miller again: "Oddly enough, all Marshall's great decisions were aimed at striking something down, whether a state or the administration. Whatever may have been his inward dreams of empire, what he most notably did as a jurist was to prevent people from acting."[21] A curious way to characterize this great and varied career! Moreover, every time Marshall prevented one side in a law suit from acting, by the same token he allowed the other side to have its way. Every lawsuit is a clash of interests; no lawsuit can have purely negative results. Perhaps Professor Miller is speaking of some

97

---

18. *Id.* 216.
19. *See* CLYDE JACOBS, LAW WRITERS AND THE COURT (1954).
20. T. COOLEY, A TREATISE ON THE CONSTITUTIONAL LIMITATIONS WHICH REST UPON THE LEGISLATIVE POWER OF THE STATES OF THE AMERICAN UNION (1868); C. TIEDEMAN, LIMITATIONS OF POLICE POWER (1886).
21. THE LIFE OF THE MIND 219.

specific kind of negation or "prevention"—but what is it? Restrictions on state government meant more freedom for the federal government or for the entrepreneur. In a new government, institutional boundaries needed definition; economic and political consequences flowed from jurisdictional decisions. The courts mapped borders of authority between the states, between state and federal governments, between private citizens and various levels of government, between competing interest groups, and between the judiciary and other branches of government. This work was as much positive and creative as it was negative and restrictive. As Professor Miller elsewhere concedes, American law and government in all its branches served the cause of rapid, unfettered economic development, which nineteenth century policy-makers felt was the best road to the common good, and which seemed to serve best the interests of that broad class of literate freeholders who mattered in society. Thus the aim of law and policy was the release of economic energy, as Hurst has argued;[22] not negation, but the creation of a framework of order that might maximize desirable economic growth. And this goal of growth was not held merely by an intellectual elite (law and layman) but widely shared among the mass of the people, insofar as can be judged by their habits, expressions, and work.

V.

But perhaps enough has been said about Professor Miller's data, methods, and general point of view. He has at least raised a question about the character of American legal thought in the post-revolutionary period; and the influence of that thought on the legal system. His general verdict is highly laudatory: though conservative, American jurists producd a powerful system of legal thought. For this reason, and despite some conspicuous failures and omissions, a brilliantly adaptive legal system developed.

Another less laudatory view of American jurisprudence and law can be plausibly advanced. As to jurisprudence in the strict sense, most scholars would agree that precious little in the post-revolutionary period was worthy of the name. Kent's *Commentaries*, for example, were modeled on Blackstone's; like Blackstone's, they were extremely useful to American lawyers,[23] were clearly organized, well written and imbued

22. J. Hurst, Law and the Conditions of Freedom in the Nineteenth-Century United States (1956).
23. James Kent's *Commentaries on American Law* were first published in 4 volumes from 1826 to 1830, were enormously successful, and went through many editions. The standard biography of Kent is J. Horton, James Kent, A Story in Conservatism (1939).

with much good sense. But Kent was not a great systematic thinker, and he did not pretend to be. Nor is there any depth or system to the rather pedantic prose of Joseph Story. There was political genius in America; the Federalist papers are proof of that. But the reason, system, and logic that Professor Miller somehow sees in windy prefaces and orations hardly seem worthy of his praise. Perhaps after years of reading sermons, even the prose of the lawyers appeared profound.

There is no reason for surprise in the lack of a great jurisprudential school in the early days of the republic. In the common law system, systematic legal thought does not serve as an authoritative guide to legal action. Cases and enactments make law; scholars do not, or, if they try to, they hide the fact. Therefore there was no *need* for a system of jurisprudence, and none sprang up. The common law countries were weak in philosophy of law. Legal writing was abundant, and abundantly welcomed, to be sure; but only because of the need for practical guides and shortcuts toward mastery of the empirical tools of the trade. The great value of Kent and Story was that they helped lawyers function in their jobs. Story's erudition, his civil law learning, his quotations from French and Latin jurists—these were of secondary value if not a downright nuisance. They lent tone to the works and did not unduly detract from the practical merits. But the utility of Story lay in the fact that he provided arguments, raw materials, models, guides —often in fields of law that had been poorly explored or were in process of rapid growth. His was merely a higher form of an art exemplified also in the hundreds of manuals and practice-books which were published or circulated in manuscript.

99

This is not to say that a formal jurisprudential system serves no function in a common-law jurisdiction. Such a system shows that a profession is mature and worthy of honor; that it is not a lowly trade, but is founded rather upon a body of independent non-self-evident principles. The layman must undergo specialized training before he can grasp the meaning of the science, let alone practice the art. Skills and learning therefore legitimize the claim of the profession to a monopoly of the work within the field of professional competence. The development of an occupational group, clearly demarcated from the lay public, and concerned with professional status, may be a likely prerequisite to the development of a school of formal jurisprudential thought. This does not mean that lawyers, in any culture, consciously sit down to create a formal jurisprudence to be used as a weapon in their struggle for legitimacy and economic power; but it does mean that the development of a jurisprudence is most likely to occur under such conditions.

Is the "sublime" then to be looked for, not in the literature of law, but in the law itself—in the creation of a sound legal order, well-suited to the American condition? Such a claim would have a surface plausibility. The claim would be that the practical work of judges like Kent, John Marshall, Lemuel Shaw, John Gibson, and hundreds of well-known and anonymous members of the bar produced a craftsmanlike American law. A proper assessment of such a claim would require close attention to precisely those source materials which Professor Miller omits: the case law, statute law, and working lawyers' files of the day. Moreover, though research would illuminate all sorts of dark pages in our legal history, it could not tell us whether or not our law was exceptionally adaptive. Against what criterion is adaptability to be measured? Can we agree upon the identity of other, maladaptive legal systems?

In general, a system of law suitable to the condition of its own society is no novelty in human history; it is, if anything, a constant. A legal system *must* respond to the needs of its time and its society. When one speaks of a legal system as out of tune with its society, one is usually referring to quite a different phenomenon: a conflict between parts of society or specific interest groups in which the legal system, or some specialized institution, responds to or reflects some interests but not others. To state, for example, that judges of the late nineteenth century who issued labor injunctions and voided welfare legislation were out of step with their society or unresponsive to social needs is simply to take the victor's view of history. These judges were out of step with a growing, powerful social movement; but their decisions were enunciated in cases brought or defended by real litigants with real economic and social interests.[24] A decision is an act of taking sides; one side may be ethically preferable to the other, but both sides represent social interests of *some* kind. A highly ritualized system of procedure—the medieval common law may be an example—might more plausibly be accused of disharmony with all social needs (other than those of legal professionals). But even here one must ask why society could and did tolerate what other societies, both "primitive" and "advanced," have found and do find utterly intolerable.

If it is sublime, therefore, to manufacture a working system of law, then *any* process is sublime—the development of American slang, or the decline of barge traffic when the railroads were built. Of course

24. For this thesis, *see* Friedman and Ladinsky, *Social Change and the Law of Industrial Accidents*, 67 COLUM. L. REV. 50, 72-77 (1967).

the legal system had capacity for growth. All legal systems that are worthy of the name do. Legal systems do not "atrophy," except in the eyes of scholars who are watching closely the decline of one part or institution while another part or institution grows. Courts and legislatures may atrophy, but if their society continues to survive, some other institutions must carry on the functions they once performed. The work of social control *must* go on. A legal system is "great" if its society is great or if it takes a form such that other societies find it useful for *their* own purposes. The common law system is great chiefly in the former sense. It is the system that pertains to a major society. It is the system that governs legal relations in a number of countries which have become rich, populous, and powerful—the countries of the British Commonwealth and the United States. This fact is its chief claim to greatness, just as the chief claim of the English language to greatness is its vast utility in a world where millions óf people—and members of dominant cultures—speak English. Of course English vocabulary is richer than that of, say, Icelandic or Manx. But this richness is a consequence of the numerical, political, and cultural strength of the speakers of English, and not vice versa. A Shakespeare is statistically more probable in a major population group. Or if a Shakespeare arises in what is or turns out to be a major society, he is that much more likely to be recognized as such. A great Nepali or Samoyed poet, if one exists, is not likely to ever get his due. And the major cultures define the standards of greatness.

A legal system acts in much the same way. As its society develops, it develops too; like language, it is a tool of culture, and it is static or dynamic when its culture is. There was nothing sublime or particularly praiseworthy in the development of railroad law in the United States. Railroads bring on railroad law, in one way or another, just as they bring on a railroad vocabulary. The new law may be borrowed from outside, made up of existing native materials, or enacted relatively fresh; it may take the form of case law evolution, executive decree, ratification of private arrangements by governmental authority, administrative manipulation, or any or all of these—all depending upon the nature and state of the legal culture. But in any event railroad law *must* come to be. If some institutions (such as the courts) prove incapable of handling the emerging functions of railroad law, then legitimized private arrangements, or statute law, or administrative law will fill the gap.

American legal institutions were, moreover, quite accustomed to the process of the adaptation of law to changed conditions; complex

101

methods of new ordering for old arrangements had been systematically explored during the Colonial period. The sudden flowering of American law in the early nineteenth century—Roscoe Pound's "formative period"—is a myth, or at best a gross exaggeration, as Stanley Katz has recently pointed out.[25] The Revolutionary War did not bring about total disruption of the legal system, nor necessitate a wholly new start. Colonial law was a long, rich process of adaptation of old law to new ends, and invention of new law to suit colonial conditions.[26] The process of adaptation continued, unabated, after the Revolution.

VI.

Something remains to be said about the legal profession, the possessor of that "mind" which has so preoccupied Professor Miller. As we have mentioned, Professor Miller draws his data almost exclusively from the literary remains of a small group of eminent jurists. The same names constantly recur in the book—notably Joseph Story, James Kent, David Hoffman. That the writings of these men reflect the "mind" of the profession requires a bold evidentiary leap, especially in the light of the extraordinary diversity and range of the profession. For one thing, there were no significant barriers to entry into the profession. Very little training was required of a man who decided to set himself up as a lawyer. The "training" of such eminent men as John Marshall, Alexander Hamilton, Abraham Lincoln—and of thousands of others less eminent—was brief, almost perfunctory.[27] Young lawyers started out their careers with nothing more than a few months spent with Blackstone, some exposure to copy-work in a law office, and perhaps some few months of practical training under a senior member of the bar. Nowhere did the state, the courts, or the organized bar succeed in making rigorous training a prerequisite to practice, or set up meaningful threshold examinations to control the quality or quantity of men entering the bar.[28] In general, American lawyers did not form a cohesive self-governing occupational group, and nobody governed

102

25. S. Katz, Book Review, 33 U. Chi. L. Rev. 867 (1966).
26. Some notion of the range of current scholarly opinion on colonial law can be gathered from Law and Authority in Colonial America (G. Billias ed., 1965).
27. On Marshall, who read Blackstone and attended law lectures at William and Mary College, see 1 A. Beveridge, Life of John Marshall 154, 161, 174-76 (1929); on Hamilton, see 1 The Law Practice of Alexander Hamilton 47-49 (J. Goebel ed. 1964); on Lincoln, see J. Duff, A. Lincoln, Prairie Lawyer 3-34 (1960).
28. See generally A. Reed, Training for the Public Profession of the Law (1921), still the best treatment of legal education and controls over admission to the bar in the nineteenth century.

them from above. Professional organizations hardly existed before the Civil War; the New York City Bar Association was founded in 1870, the American Bar Association in 1878.[29] Until the organized bar gradually gained strength and succeeded in imposing standards on the profession and in the law schools, the profession was enormously fluid and open-ended.

Precisely because it was so easy to pass oneself off as a lawyer in the early nineteenth century, the conventional picture of an unstratified, homogenous bar must be regarded with suspicion. Lawyers were professionally a less diversified lot than they are today, of course, but the bar was stratified nonetheless. The professional life of a man like Alexander Hamilton at the height of his career was fundamentally different from that of a struggling small-town lawyer, in exactly the ways in which one might expect. Hamilton had rich clients, who brought him complex and lucrative matters. The small-town lawyer had petty clients; he collected debts, searched titles, handled minor contract and criminal litigation; perhaps he dabbled in real estate or ran for local office. Before the Civil War virtually all lawyers had courtroom experience—a record which today's bar could scarcely claim; yet most of these lawyers practiced before local courts, while only a famous few argued great cases before the United States Supreme Court. Cases of ocean trade went to sophisticated seaport lawyers; small lawyers of the plains replevied cows.[30]

Along with business, land speculation, and politics, the practice of law was an avenue to social mobility. Anybody with intelligence and ambition could aspire to become a lawyer. Young men with nerve and energy often tried their hand at the law; many failed and drifted out into other lines of work. Others stayed on and made money, or used law as a stepping-stone to political or business success. Towns on the frontier of settlements attracted swarms of young lawyers on the make. Some were ignorant charlatans; others were men of ability and even of culture.[31] The bar was diverse in talent and crowded with fortune-seekers because the door to the bar was wide open.

103

29. On the founding of the American Bar Association, see E. SUNDERLAND, HISTORY OF THE AMERICAN BAR ASSOCIATION AND ITS WORK 3ff. (1953); on the founding of the Bar Association of the City of New York, see H. TAFT, A CENTURY AND A HALF AT THE NEW YORK BAR 147-50 (1938).

30. Compare the description of the career of R. M. Blatchford, in 1 R. SWAINE, THE CRAVATH FIRM AND ITS PREDECESSORS 1819-1947, at 14-15 (1946), with the description of Lincoln's early practice in Duff, supra note 28, at 62ff.

31. For a vigorous picture of the charlatans of the frontier bar see J. BALDWIN, FLUSH TIMES OF ALABAMA AND MISSISSIPPI (1853). For more balanced, if less entertaining pictures see W. ENGLISH, THE PIONEER LAWYER AND JURIST IN MISSOURI (1947); W. HAMILTON, AN-GLO-AMERICAN LAW OF THE FRONTIER: THOMAS RODNEY AND HIS TERRITORIAL CASES (1953).

In the United States, an enormous number of people had a voice in the social order as owners of capital, voters, churchgoers, citizens, shapers and snarers of significant opinion. A broad-based middle-class society was evolving—and it was paralleled by a broad-based middle-class legal profession. Freedom of entry meant a great quantity of lawyers, some good, some bad, some cheap, and some expensive. Many jobs that lawyers were willing to perform could have been performed by other occupational groups, had the bar been a smaller, more guild-like occupation. Law would then have been a learned profession in the narrow sense, with the boundaries of its competence sharply defined. A small, proud, skillful—and expensive—profession, perhaps on the order of English barristers, would have grown up. As things turned out, however, a somewhat crudely trained, mobile bar and a broad-based middle-class society emerged at the same time, with important consequences for each other and for the law. Both lawyer and layman, for example, demanded radical simplification of those aspects of the legal system which came within their everyday experience. In a society where thousands of ordinary citizens dealt in land, and thousands of half-trained men were their land lawyers, the rococo excesses of British land law were not tolerable. Perhaps one reason why American procedure was successfully reformed was that the public could not trust its lawyers to maneuver through the classical arts of pleading.

At the same time, of course, the law was growing vastly more complex; but its complexity was a consequence of complexity in the economic sphere. This complexity gave rise to an urge for clarity and pragmatic order in legal literature, and that was the impetus that sent some lawyers rushing to their desks to write treatises. But the state of the profession did not provide a climate conducive to the development of formal jurisprudence. Nor did the bustling economy and its demands on the legal profession lead to a radical, consistent difference between the mind of the lawyer and that of the layman of similar income and locale. The lawyer was very much a man enmeshed in everyday affairs. It is likely that a complete study of the lawyers of 1800, 1830, or 1860 would show far fewer differences between the opinions of lawyers and laymen than Professor Miller seems to think. A thorough study would also have to abandon the notion of a monolithic legal mind and recognize instead a set of minds, divided by region (perhaps), by class (more likely), and probably also by size of town and nature of practice. Or it would give up the notion of a legal mind altogether, and choose instead to study the profession in context, admitting into evidence the work of the lawyers in courtrooms, offices, and in the streets, along with their higher flights of thought.

104

NOTES TOWARD A HISTORY OF AMERICAN JUSTICE*

LAWRENCE M. FRIEDMAN**

In Kent County, Delaware, in 1703, Adam Latham, a laborer, and Joan Mills, wife of a laborer named Andrew Mills, were brought before the county court. The grand jury presented Joan Mills for adultery. She pleaded guilty to the charge. For punishment, the court ordered her to be publicly'whipped—21 lashes on her bare back, well applied; and she was also sentenced to prison, at hard labor, for one year. Adam Latham was convicted of fornication. He was sentenced to receive 20 lashes on his bare back, well laid on, in full public view. He was also accused of stealing Isaac Freeland's dark brown gelding, worth 2 pounds 10 shillings. Adam pleaded guilty; for this crime he was sentenced to another four lashes, and was further required to pay for the gelding. Adam had been in trouble over Joan Mills before, charged with "the Sin of Incontinency and fornication." At that time, he was acquitted, but the court ordered him to post bond guaranteeing "good behavior." He had broken his word. Now he was ordered to "weare a Roman T on his left arme on the Outside of his uppermost garment . . . for the space of six months next."[1] These were typical crimes and punishments in colonial America. Published colonial records show hundreds of similar examples.[2]

105

We note the tremendous stress on visibility. The whipping post, pillory, and stocks stood in the public square. They did not gather dust. Countless men and women felt the whip, or stood in the stocks.

---

*This article is adapted from the Mitchell Lecture delivered by the author at the State University of New York at Buffalo School of Law on October 17, 1973. The author wishes to thank Professor Marc Galanter of the Buffalo School of Law for his helpful criticisms.

**Professor of Law, Stanford University, Stanford, California. J.D., University of Chicago, 1951; M.LL., 1953.

1. COURT RECORDS OF KENT COUNTY, DELAWARE 1680-1705, at 234-35, 270-71 (L. de Valinger ed. 1959).

2. The trial of Joan Mills and Adam Latham did deviate somewhat from the norm in that a prison sentence was imposed. Colonial society did not, in general, make use of prisons in this way. Society needed workers; a man in jail was not a productive hand. The colonists used jails to detain people waiting for trial or for sentence, or to hold those who did not pay their debts. Whipping, branding, fines, and the stocks were far more common. D. ROTHMAN, THE DISCOVERY OF THE ASYLUM 53 (1971).

When Christopher Lawson, of York County, Maine, came into court "unsevelly," with a "turbilent beheaviouer," in July, 1669, he was forthwith "comited to sitt on ower in the stockes."[3] In the same volume of records we read about Sarah Morgan, who struck her husband, horror of horrors, and was given the choice of paying a fine or standing for a half hour at Kittery, at a public town meeting, with a gag in her mouth and "the cause of her offence writt upon her forhead."[4] The law made common use of brands and badges of shame. A burglar, under the Laws and Liberties of Massachusetts (1648), was to be "branded on the forehead with the letter (B)." A second offender would be "branded as before," and whipped. The third offender would be "put to death, as being incorrigible."[5] Colonies made liberal use of devices such as the bilbo, the cucking stool, and, for military offenders, the wooden horse—all of which carried stigma and shame.

It is commonplace that social forces produce law, directly and indirectly. It follows that different cultures will make law in different ways. In every society there are the rulers and the ruled; some individuals, groups and strata have more power or influence than others; the law that any society makes will reflect the interests of those on top, to the extent of their superior might. But power and influence do not directly act on law. Law—statutes, doctrines, legal behavior in general—comes about only when individuals and groups make *demands* on the system. *Demands* then, rather than interests, are the proximate causes of law. The structure of demands is a cultural factor; no doubt its shape always reveals the powerful pull of long-term pressures, deriving from those with influence and power. But one cannot deduce the catalog of demands current in society directly from a knowledge of the real, objective needs of those with power, actual and potential. Every society rests on a set of implicit bargains about the legitimate limits of law; in every society a set of important attitudes support these bargains.

In every era, we want to ask: what forces had power, real and potential; what were their interests; and what were their demands? These demands need not be solely economic in nature. Power is not

---

3. 2 Province and Court Records of Maine 174 (C. Libby ed. 1931).
4. *Id.* at 224.
5. Laws and Liberties of Massachusetts 4 (1929).

solely economic. Distinct and important are the demands for the maintenance of *moral* hegemony—demands for a monopoly of respectability, in short, for legitimacy.

We will analyze, in a much oversimplified scheme, three periods of American history in terms of these simple propositions. The three periods are: colonial America, the first two-thirds of the 19th century, and the period from about 1870 to the present. There is nothing neat about these "periods." They do seem, however, to reflect differences in prevailing frames of mind.

We began with colonial America. We cannot sum this period up, of course, in a single glib formula. There were more than a dozen separate "colonies," and the colonial "era" spanned a century and a half. But for much of this period the rulers, particularly in New England, had a clear idea of what crime meant. Crime was a kind of sin. Society's leaders did not easily abandon hope for the sinner. These were, in the main, small societies; they believed, rightly or wrongly, in repentence and rehabilitation. Except for the most hardened and abandoned cases, it was thought that men could respond to pressure and improve their way of life if they were instructed in proper behavior, punished for wrong conduct, subjected to shame and derision from their neighbors, and stigmatized when they strayed from the straight and narrow path. This is the reason why punishment was so open, so public. The man who was whipped in view of everyone was receiving physical punishment; but far more important, perhaps he felt on his back the invisible whip of public opinion. Colonial society hoped to reform the sinner by invoking the mockery and scorn of his neighbors. Of course, everyone knew that a certain hard core would not respond. These people were, first, clearly labeled as the damned; and then, in the most aggravated cases, banished or put to death. Kai Erickson has pointed out that branding marked a person "with the permanent emblem of his station in life." Branding thus made it difficult to restore the offender to a normal social role.[6] Only serious offenders then, or repeaters, suffered this penalty. The death penalty was infrequently used, but it also was an instrument of education. Hanging was as public as whipping. The world could observe the wages of sin.

The records of Kent County identified Andrew Mills and Adam

107

---

6. K. ERIKSON, WAYWARD PURITANS 197 (1966).

Latham as laborers. Colonial society was nowhere democratic; indeed, no colonial society even pretended to such an ideal. Society was stratified and hierarchical. To be sure, compared to England, great numbers of people owned property and, therefore, made use of common law institutions and the political process. James A. Henretta, in a study of colonial Boston, found 1,036 individuals in 1687 who paid taxes on real estate or on their income from trade.[7] The population of Boston was then roughly 6,000. Since children could hardly be expected to own property and most wives were effectively outside the economic system, landowners and tradesmen clearly constituted a sizeable percentage of the people of colonial Boston and, therefore, were customers for the tools and techniques of formal law.

108

At the bottom of the social pyramid were the landless laborers, indentured servants, and, in the South, the mass of blacks held in slavery. What the records make clear is that the weight of colonial social control bore down most heavily upon this underclass. It was not the merchant, landowner, or minister who was whipped in public, branded and set in the stocks. These were punishments for servants, laborers, and apprentices. The people who owned property, the leaders and their willing followers defined what was the correct morality. The criminal law enforced this code, upholding a moral regime that the upper classes no doubt considered universal, but which strained the human nature of their servants. Whatever its ethical base, the code had a cold-blooded function. It aimed to maintain control over a work force on whose labor and obedience the community depended.

From the standpoint of the 20th century, crime and punishment in the American colonies is remarkable because of its emphasis on crimes against morality—particularly what we would now call victimless crimes. But to the colonists every crime had a victim: society. In colonial Massachusetts, the man who blasphemed God, who was idle, who failed to attend church, or who slept with a servant girl was a criminal—and a sinner. He had to be punished in order to preserve the moral order. The argument that these acts hurt nobody would have puzzled and annoyed the good citizens of Massachusetts Bay. The moral order *was* society; injury to one was injury to both.

7. Henretta, *Economic Development and Social Structure in Colonial Boston*, in 1 NEW PERSPECTIVES ON THE AMERICAN PAST 83, 96 table 1 (S. Katz & S. Kutler eds. 1969).

Colonial social control was by no means unique in this regard. Law and order take a similar form in small, face-to-face communities which have clear lines of authority—explicit notions of who is on top and who is on the bottom. Discipline in Massachusetts Bay was not unlike discipline among schoolchildren. We note, for example, Wylie's study of a village in France, where the usual way to punish a school-child was through shame—isolating him, and pitting the rest of society against him. Teachers in the village consistently used "mocking criticism" to bring children into line. Sometimes they made a child kneel at the wall, pressing his forehead against it, his hands folded on top of his head. Or they made a child spend recess walking in a circle in the schoolground, hands folded on his head, while other childern mocked.[8] Derision, of course, is a common form of punishment; and, in stateless societies an almost inevitable one.[9] The criminal law of colonial society used a common technique, then, when it invoked public opinion to enforce the rules of moral order. These rules were a paramount concern of that small closely knit community.

109

The civil side of the law in colonial society also fit the needs and demands of that particular social order. Colonial justice was open and cheap. People did not hesitate to bring disputes to court, even for rather petty claims. In 1639-40, in the Pynchon Court Record of Western Massachusetts, we read of an "action of the Case for 3 boards;"[10] and an action of debt for 2s 6d.[11] In these small communities everyone knew who the judges were and where they could be found. In colonial records we find thousands of small wills processed, thousands of petty complaints, and thousands of local disputes. These show how low the threshold of access to court was, at least in some colonies and in some periods of time. In this regard, too, colonial courts were like the courts of preliterate societies or, in some ways, like the neighborhood courts of Cuba and other socialist countries.[12] In colonial society courts were inexpensive and at

---

8. L. Wylie & A. Bégué, Village in the Vaucluse 84, 86 (rev. ed. 1969).

9. See, e.g., J. Reid, A Law of Blood 242-45 (1970); G. Van den Steenhoven, Leadership and Law Among the Eskimos of the Keewatin District 91 (1919).

10. Colonial Justice in Western Massachusetts 204 (J. Smith ed. 1961).

11. Id. at 209.

12. For a discussion of communist law as "parental" and "educational," see H. Berman, Justice in the U.S.S.R. 277-84 (1963); Berman, The Cuban Popular Tribunals, 69 Colum. L. Rev. 1317 (1969).

everybody's door step. No affair was too petty for scrutiny. It was a gossipy, ingrown society. People regularly brought disputes before the courts. The courts settled them—admonishing, governing and teaching. These traits differed, of course, from colony to colony. They were probably most pronounced in the early period and in the Puritan theocratic colonies. In these, law was bossy, parental, and moralistic; but (on the civil side) it was cheap and open of access as well.

In the 19th century the legal system changed dramatically. To be sure, much of the *formal* criminal law was carried over from colonial days. The statute books kept the old moral laws. Fornication, adultery, and blasphemy were still crimes after the Revolution, as they had been before. But this is only the surface; in reality, these laws soon fell out of use. William E. Nelson studied criminal prosecutions in seven Massachusetts counties, between 1760 and 1774, at the very end of the colonial period. He counted 2,784 prosecutions; no less than 38 percent of these (an astonishing percentage) charged sexual offenses, mostly fornication. Another 13 percent, 359 in all, were for religious offenses—blasphemy, profanity and nonattendance at church.[13] These figures confirm that the statutes were part of the living law of the colony. But in the early 19th century, without major change in the statutory base, the rate of prosecution for these crimes declined almost to nothing. Criminal justice turned its attention to crimes against property: crimes such as burglary and theft.

There is evidence that this lack of interest in crimes against morality was generally felt. Francis Laurent carefully sifted the court records of Chippewa County, Wisconsin. Between 1855 and 1894 he found a total of five cases of incest, nine of adultery, four of fornication, and one of lewd and lascivious behavior—not much of a harvest of sin.[14] Jack Williams studied crime and punishment in pre-Civil War South Carolina, hardly a society without sinners; he found few prosecutions for crimes against morality. Indictments for bastardy ran

---

13. W. Nelson, The Americanization of the Common Law During the Revolutionary Era 126-27, 1971 (unpublished thesis), *as cited in* L. FRIEDMAN, A HISTORY OF AMERICAN LAW 63 (1973). In every fornication case except one (and 95 percent of the sex cases were for fornication), the defendant was the mother of an illegitimate child. Yet Nelson rejects the argument that fornication was punished merely because it burdened towns with support of illegitimate children. He points out that prosecutions were brought even against mothers who had married their partners, and in cases where there was no economic motive at all.

14. F. LAURENT, THE BUSINESS OF A TRIAL COURT 122 (1959).

to about two percent of the total, but many of them were really cases of nonsupport. Incest, bigamy, sodomy, and adultery hardly appeared in court records.[15]

One is welcome to believe, of course, that actual rates of fornication and blasphemy declined in this country in the 19th century. This may be; but such dramatic declines are unlikely. What changed, then, must have been a social factor, which affected the *demand* for prosecution of victimless crimes, and which altered the system of criminal justice. The secular, instrumental men of the 19th century were less interested in the moral code as such, so long as infractions wore a low profile. Colonial magistrates had wanted to build an ideal, godly society. But in the 19th century wealth and opportunity were recurrent themes in the writings (and presumably the thoughts) of the elite and articulate. The task of law was to foster what J. Willard Hurst has called "the release of individual creative energy."[16] People had "sighted the promise of a steeply rising curve of material productivity as the dynamic of a new kind of society";[17] they had a "deep faith in the social benefits to flow from a rapid increase in productivity."[18] Consequently, the main emphasis of the law shifted to the encouragement of economic activity, rather than enforcement of the ideal moral code.

In any event the cozy colonial system of social control was no longer possible. Society was larger, more mobile and transient; it was busy with commercial affairs; rapid technological growth brought constant novelty and complexity. Society was less able to entrust its safety to stigma, shame, and the opinion of neighbors, particularly in the industrial North. Hence, reformers of the 19th century no longer saw society as cleansing and educating, as a hammer of reform and retribution, or as the teacher and parent of men. Rather, as David Rothman has argued, they saw society in a much more questionable role. The peer group was, if anything, corrupting. Bad company, idleness and vice were ever present in society. A rotten environment was ruinous to man. Everyone was "under siege . . . . Once, observers be-

111

---

15. J. WILLIAMS, VOGUES IN VILLAINY 55-58 (1959).
16. J. HURST, LAW AND THE CONDITIONS OF FREEDOM IN THE NINETEENTH CENTURY UNITED STATES 6 (1956).
17. *Id.*
18. *Id.* at 7.

lieved, neighbors had disciplined neighbors. Now, it seemed that rowdies corrupted rowdies."[19]

This was the age in which a new institution, the penitentiary, was devised. In it, the deviant would be *removed* from society, to be reshaped in a monastic, protected environment. Of course, the whipping post did not vanish overnight. It continued to be used, particularly in the South. Many states, such as South Carolina, still hung incorrigibles in public; and people flocked on foot, on horseback, sometimes even on special trains, to see the spectacle.[20] But more and more, imprisonment became the standard punishment for serious crimes.

The old style jails had been dirty, insecure and loosely run. The new prison was radically different. To work reform, prisons had to be redesigned. The two most famous of the early penitentiaries, Auburn in New York and Cherry Hill in Pennsylvania, were both based on the principles of solitude and silence. In Auburn (1821), the prisoners slept alone at night in their cells. During the daytime they worked together in a workshop, but were not allowed to talk to each other, or even to look at their fellow inmates. Cherry Hill (1829) tried to achieve even more radical isolation. Prisoners ate, worked and slept in individual cells. Sometimes they wore masks. They listened to religious services through peepholes. They were utterly silent, utterly alone.

The new penology burst like a bombshell in the world of social thought. Foreign visitors, such as Beaumont and de Tocqueville, came to study the penitentiary in its native habitat. On the whole, the two Frenchmen were impressed by its rigor, its efficiency.[21] Charles Dickens, who came a bit later, visited Cherry Hill and found it horrible: the prisoners seemed to him like men who were buried alive. Isolation, he felt, was a mental torture worse than any "torture of the body."[22] Apparently, few of his peers saw things his way. Certainly contemporaries endlessly argued the merits of the two systems,

112

---

19. D. ROTHMAN, *supra* note 2, at 71.
20. J. WILLIAMS, *supra* note 15, at 101.
21. *See* G. DE BEAUMONT & A. DE TOCQUEVILLE, ON THE PENITENTIARY SYSTEM IN THE UNITED STATES AND ITS APPLICATION IN FRANCE (1833).
22. C. DICKENS, AMERICAN NOTES 109 (1900); *see* L. FRIEDMAN, A HISTORY OF AMERICAN LAW 259-60 (1973).

which to us today are as alike as Tweedledum and Tweedledee. But all over the country, legislatures eagerly copied the one or the other.[23]

In its pure state, the silent system could not and did not last. To keep one man to a cell, in solitude, cost a good deal of money; and the money was simply not forthcoming. Penitentiaries gradually became mere prisons; the solitude and silence were surrendered except as a special punishment for troublemakers. By the time of the Civil War even the famous penitentiaries, which had led the way, often slept more than one man to a cell; and only a handful of wardens still made a serious effort to enforce the regulation of silence.[24]

But the basic idea of the penitentiary flourished. Reformers believed that strict regimens, sermons, piety, loneliness and quiet would regenerate a shattered soul. The average man probably rejected the advanced views of the reformers, while agreeing that hard work, regimentation, a spartan life and long sentences were appropriate punishment for crime. Criminals were dangerous to society. They could not be cured through stigma and shame. They, therefore, had to be removed from normal life. Those who were not to be hung or imprisoned forever would hopefully be cured of their tendencies. If not, the prisoner was at least out of harm's way.

113

Victorian society has a reputation for prudery and sexual intolerance. American society was as prudish in language and official behavior as the corresponding circles in England. Yet, as we saw, apparently nowhere did the law take seriously the job of enforcing the sexual code. The law of divorce also illustrates the complex interaction between official morals and unofficial behavior. Divorce had always been difficult to get, rare and expensive. Absolute divorce was not available at all in England, except through act of Parliament;[25] and in some Southern states before the Civil War divorce was equally difficult and uncommon.[26] Yet in the North, a group of states dramatically relaxed their divorce laws. In Maine, by a law of 1849, any justice of the supreme judicial court could grant a divorce if he felt it was "reasonable and proper, conducive to domestic harmony and

---

23. C. DICKENS, *supra* note 22, at 108.
24. D. ROTHMAN, *supra* note 2, at 242.
25. *See* Mueller, *Inquiry into the State of a Divorceless Society*, 18 U. PITT. L. REV. 545 (1957).
26. *See generally* N. BLAKE, THE ROAD TO RENO (1962).

peace, and consistent with the peace and morality of society." Connecticut, too, had an easy divorce law.[27] The divorce rate was very low by modern standards, but some contemporaries still found it alarming that there should. be divorce at all or that divorce rates should rise.

Divorce, however, unlike adultery or blasphemy, could not be allowed to exist in a kind of moral underworld. There was a genuine demand for it for social and economic reasons. For the sake of the legitimacy of children, for security of property rights, for the right to live *legally* with a second consort, divorce was an absolute necessity. Hence, the attack on easy divorce ultimately failed. But the easy *laws* were repealed. They were replaced with tougher, more "moral" laws—laws with a strong, healthy ethical surface—but the collusive divorce and the Nevada divorce mills made the situation one of extreme and blatant hypocrisy.[28]

Yet the 19th century seemed to prefer, even to welcome, this hypocrisy. By all accounts, throughout the century, particularly after the first quarter of the century, there was a great deal of crime, brawling, drunkenness, gambling, and general hell-raising, just as one would expect of normal human flesh. But a rather sharp line was drawn between that which was officially allowed and that which was unofficially tolerated. This is the key, perhaps, to the strange fact already noted: that the state stopped punishing fornication and other crimes against morality, but never repealed the laws against these acts. This may be the very heart of Victorian attitudes toward moral behavior. What had to be preserved at all costs was the *official* code of strict morality. What went on underneath was deplorable, but inevitable, and in a curious way almost acceptable.

Evidence of the dark underbelly of Victorian life[29] throws this hypocrisy into high relief. Victorians on both sides of the Atlantic published and read dirty books, cavorted with prostitutes, engaged in buggery and every form of vice. They drank and gambled to excess. But they seemed to take care not to sin in such a way as to threaten the moral norms publically. A society can tolerate a great deal of deviance, so long as the deviants do not attack the norms themselves, but remain hidden in the woodwork. When deviants become what

114

---

27. *Id.* at 60-61.
28. *Id.* at 130-51.
29. *See* S. MARCUS, THE OTHER VICTORIANS (1966); R. PEARSALL, THE WORM IN THE BUD (1969).

Joseph Gusfield has called "enemy deviants,"[30] that is, when they attack the norms themselves and try to overthrow them, they represent a greater (or at any rate a different) danger; and those who benefit from the normative status quo, economically or spiritually, will react repressively.

One such group of enemy deviants was the body of the Mormon faithful, who insisted on practicing polygamy. Many people all over the country were polygamists in fact if not in law. Yet, the Mormons were open, defiant polygamists. A crusade against polygamy followed whose savagery and shrillness can barely be imagined today.[31]

A kind of Victorian hypocrisy also characterized the whole of the criminal law. On paper, every man was entitled to elaborate procedural safeguards. He came to trial wearing the armor of the Bill of Rights; he had a claim to a fair and speedy trial before a jury of his peers, and scrupulous observance of the rules of the game. But during the century, the sheer volume of trials overwhelmed these rights. Society became more serious about catching and trying thieves and murderers. Instead of amateur, haphazard methods of patrolling cities, after 1830 many cities turned to full-time professional police.[32] The police themselves often ignored formal law and fought violence with its own weapons. Masses of people were arrested and treated routinely, almost cavalierly, in court. Rights were never *formally* relaxed. Upper courts zealously combed the records of lower courts looking for errors. The state renounced terror and torture as means to control the lower classes. But, as far as we can tell, the lower courts and the enforcers, particularly in the cities, ignored many of the formal rights. The population never accepted as an absolute good the official legal code. The vigilantes in the West, lynch mobs in the South, and police brutality in the cities all demonstrate over and over that, when the chips were down and the situation serious enough, men inside and outside the system were willing to take the law into their hands.

There was a similar hypocrisy in the civil part of law. American law affected the work and welfare of great masses of people. In the United States, land law was not a remote, aristocratic concern; mil-

115

---

30. Gusfield, *Moral Passage: The Symbolic Process in Public Designations of Deviance*, 15 SOCIAL PROB. 175 (1968).

31. *See* T. O'DEA, THE MORMONS 41-75 (1957).

32. For an account of the origins and early years of two municipal police forces, see R. LANE, POLICING THE CITY, BOSTON 1822-1885 (1967); J. RICHARDSON, THE NEW YORK POLICE 23-51 (1970).

lions dealt in the market, buying and selling land, moving about, getting and giving deeds, using mortgages, drawing up wills. Many borrowed money, or lent it out at interest; it was common to make, endorse, or accept bills and notes. Perhaps, compared to old Massachusetts, a rather lower percentage of the people directly confronted the law. But, if commercial and land law did not touch the life and interest of everyone, they did affect the life and interest of the vast middle class.

To accommodate this mob of "consumers," to release latent economic energy, to maximize opportunity, society developed its law in such a way as to make transactions both safe and efficient, that is, routine. The documents in use were redesigned to become simple, streamlined, and standard. Deeds shrank in size. Businessmen developed form contracts to sell goods on the installment plan. These forms depended, in a way, on the courts. The courts ratified the devices that businessmen developed—devices such as conditional sales, garnishments, and chattel mortgages—and began to process them swiftly and efficiently. At the same time, society seemed to feel that in a market economy the legal system could not both promote efficiency and do strict, careful justice between individual parties. Courts turned their back on what in most societies is their primary and ordinary function—the settlement of disputes. They abandoned people to their own institutions and devices. The law of a mass economy avoids individualization. It reduces transactions to the typical, to the routine; it slices up some small segment of reality and handles it in a standardized way. Behaviors are converted to legally relevant forms. A person pays his debts by check—a piece of paper fixed in form and in legal meaning. Routinization makes a good deal of sense. The work of society could not proceed if judges had to stop to examine each little dispute in a compulsive thoroughgoing way.

It is dangerous, of course, to attempt to read the minds of past generations and generalize about what "society" thought. Yet one senses in the 19th century a widely-held belief that it would be best if people stayed out of court, tending their own affairs. Through law, society established a basic framework, ensuring security to property and contract. Inside this framework people were to do their jobs, getting and spending, making the wealth of the country grow. In American law and, so far as we can tell, in Western law in general, courts gradually withdrew from the basic task of settling everyday disputes.

116

One bit of evidence is the startling fact, suggested by data from a number of countries, that formal litigation tends not to keep pace with population growth in the industrial nations. During an initial period of expansion (perhaps because of the removal of restrictions left over from the medieval past), the caseload rises; but with mature industrialization, the number of cases per 1,000 population turns static or even declines. In England, where judicial statistics after 1850 are relatively good, the number of cases filed in court rose throughout the 19th century—perhaps less, however, than one might expect. In the 20th century, the trend reversed itself.[33]

In the long run, cost was an important monitor of the case loads of courts. Litigation seems to have become more and more expensive. High costs raise the threshold at which it makes sense for a person to funnel disputes into court. Colonials litigated over pennies. Many matters got to court or were appealed that could appear today, if at all, only in a small claims court.

Costs of litigation defy precise measurement, especially in the past. The largest element, for example, is the lawyer's fee; but this does not show on the face of the record. This fact itself is an interesting historical footnote. American courts do not award attorney's fees to the winner of a lawsuit, as do the English. The American rule seems to date from around 1850.[34] Supposedly, this rule was an historical accident, but if so, it was a suspiciously convenient one. What the rule does, of course, is raise the threshold of suit. Even a winning party loses, unless damages cover the attorney's fee and then some. The natural result of the American rule is to discourage small claims and noneconomic causes of action.

Delays and overcrowding also raise the price of a lawsuit. Colonial courts did their business quickly. They had no backlogs. Of course, these were not mass societies. Great delays occur when judges and staffs are inundated by the volume of cases. This happens in a society with a huge population. But when one considers how economical it is to run a system of justice, compared to schools, hospitals, highways, or armies, one wonders why society was never willing to spend a few

117

---

33. *See* Civil Judicial Statistics 19 (1972) (Comparative Table: Courts of First Instance—Proceedings). An unpublished study of litigation rates in Spain by Jose Juan Toharia shows similar results for recent decades, a period of rapid economic growth in that country.

34. *See* Ehrenzweig, *Reimbursement of Counsel Fees and the Great Society*, 54 Calif. L. Rev. 72 (1966).

dollars more in order to expand the system and meet growing needs. One senses a feeling, implicit no doubt, that a logjam in court is not all to the bad. It discourages litigation. Then too, the country has allowed its lawyers to unionize (as it were), raising standards and fees; it has refused to subsidize litigation, and it has made, until recently, only feeble attempts to provide cheap justice for the poor.[35]

Most important of all, perhaps, is the nature of law itself. Legal rules and procedures are impersonal and remote, dryly technical, forbidding. Law in the urban, industrial countries is very different from law in small societies. Legal and social norms are much the same in small societies; everybody knows a lot of law since it is nothing special to know.[36] Colonial law had some smattering of this aspect. The law was technical in detail, but in broad outline it spoke an everyday language.[37] A high degree of technicality will inevitably discourage litigation. If justice is mysterious, if law resembles a lottery, people will be unwilling to take a chance even if they feel morally secure in their cause. An unpredictable outcome is a high cost, high risk result.

All these factors create a zone of behavior which one might call a "zone of reciprocal immunity."[38] Landlord and tenant sign a lease agreement. The tenant promises not to play his radio loud or late at night. The landlord promises to keep the outside stairway in repair. Each violates a little. Because litigation is costly, because there is no neighborhood court, because justice is risky, far-off, and expensive, each is in a way immune from legal attack, at least for these minor infractions. They must settle the matter themselves.

On the whole, a system of reciprocal immunities may be quite functional in a society of our type. We do not want people running to court at the drop of a hat. But this sort of system produces severe and dangerous side effects. Compared with other societies and other periods, Western legal systems have removed the bulk of the population from any voluntary contact with the courts. The system of immunities on the whole favored business over private citizens; it was,

---

35. *See, e.g.,* J. Carlin, J. Howard & S. Messinger, Civil Justice and the Poor (1967).
36. *See, e.g.,* S. Schlegel, Tiruray Justice 163 (1970).
37. On this point, see W. Nelson, *supra* note 13.
38. Friedman, *Legal Rules and the Process of Social Change,* 19 Stan. L. Rev. 786, 806 (1967); *see* M. Galanter, Why the Haves Come Out Ahead 17 n.29, August, 1973 (unpublished paper on file at the *Buffalo Law Review* office).

therefore, itself a device of allocation. The 19th century, practically speaking, denied justice to the poor and the powerless. Redress of grievances through law was distinctly abnormal. There may have been, in absolute terms, a tremendous volume of litigation. But the man in the street did not use courts to adjust his problems or settle his disputes. The average man was left alone, separated from whatever wisdom, understanding, and justice may inhere in the formal principles of law.

Nor was the situation of the lower middle class much better. The courts did not and could not reach out for the business of the common man even if he were an entrepreneur of sorts. It may be that courts in urban, market societies simply cannot play the role that a tribal or village court plays. American courts, however, never tried, though a certain number of schemes helped patch the system up, helped mitigate some of the most severe defects of justice.

119

Many scholars, looking at the legal system in the first part of the 19th century, have come away impressed with a sense of economic optimism. Obviously, many things were palpably wrong with the country. A gigantic failure to solve problems of region and race brought on the great Civil War. Cycles of boom and bust destroyed thousands of homes, businesses, farms, and fortunes. Yet overall, people believed that America was a land of opportunity, that in the long run economic horizons would constantly expand, that the stock of national wealth would grow larger and larger. Here, then, was a second period of American justice—a period of rapid growth in society and rapid change in law. Criminal justice and civil justice alike ceased to be concerned with the individual as such. Rather, they became responsive to the socioeconomic needs of the society (as courts and legislatures interpreted these) through routinization of transactions on the civil side, and through routinization and professionalization of law enforcement, the penitentiary system, and the stressing of the protection of property rather than morality on the criminal side.

The age of optimism did not last forever. By the end of the 19th century it seemed to have come to an end, and a new, third period can be said to have begun. A sense of crisis, a kind of darkening of mood, seemed to seize the country. Concrete social change underlay this shift in the climate of opinion. Much of the population lived in big cities, which seemed more and more rotten, filthy, crime-ridden, ugly, crowded, and corrupt. People deserted the wholesome life of farms and small towns for the dreary life of factories and slums. New inventions and techniques made life healthier, but somehow complicated it beyond the grasp of the average man. The frontier passed away. There was no more free land at the end of the rainbow. Never mind the question of how real the frontier had been, how much of an outlet it was for American energies. It was the symbol of unlimited opportunity, and by 1890 or 1900 it was gone. By this time many in the middle class felt that something vital had disappeared from American life. There was no longer room in the economy for everyone; social life was a struggle for survival. What one gained, another lost. The economy could not expand forever. The spectre of class struggle hung over the nation. Interest groups jockeyed for power and position, more blatantly than before.[39]

120

A certain paranoia set in on the subject of race. This was the period of lynch law and the furor over the so-called yellow peril. At one time the country had welcomed immigrants. The country wanted settlers and workers. Immigrants would create a demand for land and commodities; land values would rise and the economy would gain. Of course, people had in mind only a certain kind of immigrant. When others took the welcome sign too literally, nativist reaction developed. The debates over the Chinese at the California Convention of 1878-79 make hair-raising reading: one speaker denounced the Chinese as "moon-eyed lepers"; speaker after speaker expressed fear of cheap coolie labor. The Chinese would destroy white civilization and pauperize the people of California: "If clover and hay be planted upon the same soil, the clover will ruin the hay, because clover lives upon less than the hay; and so it is in this struggle between the races. The Mongolian race will live and run the Caucasian race out."[40] John R. Commons felt that immigrants from northwestern Europe—Germans and Scandinavians—were from the start the model farmers of America; they had qualities of thrift and self-reliance and pursued intensive agriculture.[41] The Jewish immigrant on the other hand was "unfitted for the life of a pioneer."[42] Commons drew a line between the "thrifty, hard-working and intelligent American or Teutonic

---

39. L. FRIEDMAN, *supra* note 22, at 295-99.
40. 2 DEBATES AND PROCEEDINGS OF THE CONSTITUTIONAL CONVENTION OF THE STATE OF CALIFORNIA 700, 704 (1881).
41. J. COMMONS, RACES AND IMMIGRANTS IN AMERICA 133 (1913).
42. *Id.*

farmer," and the "backward, thriftless and unintelligent races," who worked best "in gangs in large estates."[43] "Races wholly incompetent as pioneers and independent proprietors are able to find a place when once manufactures, mines and railroads have sprung into being, with their captains of industry to guide and supervise their semi-intelligent work."[44] Attitudes such as these helped mold a body of immigration law that became more and more restrictive and complex. The first step was to exclude the Chinese. Ultimately, the federal government put sharp limits on entry and adopted a quota system in 1924. The quotas discriminated, of course, against the "incompetent races."[45]

It is particularly interesting to note in the history of immigration law how fear of the effect of immigrants on the economy is mingled with moral or cultural horror. Both motives were behind the movement to exclude the less-favored immigrants. Perhaps the economic mood caused the moral mood; perhaps the lines of causality ran the other way around. At any rate, by the turn of the century millions were displeased with the national prospects. Industrialism was a monster that had run amuck. The mobs of "incompetent races" who flooded the country only stimulated the growth of this monster and, in the process, drove down the wage rate. Tremendous industrial combines were forming. Small businessmen, farmers and merchants trembled in fear of their power. Today, fear of the "trusts" seems as overwrought as fear of Chinese workers. But in the days of the Sherman Act, passed in 1890,[46] the fears were certainly real and in deadly earnest.[47]

Naturally, each major concern bred a mass of new law. In the struggle for existence, the power of the state was one of the most useful of weapons. In the late 19th century, economic interest groups multiplied in number. The urge to organize stemmed, at least in part, from the natural feeling that in union there was additional strength; and strength was sorely needed in difficult times. The interest groups fought each other in the marketplace and occasionally on the streets, but primarily in the halls of the legislatures. Unions, for example,

121

---

43. *Id.* at 132.
44. *Id.* at 133-34.
45. *See* G. STEPHENSON, A HISTORY OF AMERICAN IMMIGRATION 1820-1924, at 170-92 (1926).
46. Act of July 2, 1890, ch. 647, 26 Stat. 209 (codified at 15 U.S.C. §§ 1-7 (1973)).
47. *See* W. LETWIN, LAW AND ECONOMIC POLICY IN AMERICA 54-71 (1965).

wanted legitimacy for their tactics; and when those tactics failed, they wanted to win through law what they could not gain through bargaining and fighting with management.

This was only one instance of the use of law to achieve organizational aims. Occupational licensing was another. Doctors, lawyers, barbers, plumbers, nurses and accountants lobbied for licensing laws. Licensing was a way to give control of a trade group to itself, along with the power to keep out the marginals and support the prices and prestige of the members. A whole array of occupations, ministering human wants from cradle to grave (from midwives to morticians and embalmers), asked for and got the right to be licensed. Even coal miners were briefly licensed in Illinois.[48] The form was novel, the concept was not. In general, workers joined unions, farmers joined farm organizations, businesses belonged to trade associations and formed combines. The middle class trades licensed themselves.[49]

Along with the economic struggle raged a fight for normative domination. The Victorian solution slowly broke down. Deviant minorities burst into public view, bringing uneasiness and pain to the moral majorities. The process was, and is, slow and complex. Frequently, the moral majorities fought back. When deviants openly defied them, they had no choice but to repress—or else surrender their claims to moral superiority. Consequently, after a long period of relative quiet, a number of dead moral laws seemed to spring into life, and new laws on similar subjects were passed. Sometimes the motives seemed mainly economic. Toward the end of the century, the Sunday laws were the focus of enforcement campaigns in many cities. Labor strongly supported these laws. They wanted to win a shorter work week for their members, and Sunday laws were a useful means to that end.[50] But ministers and preachers were their willing accomplices; labor and religion formed an odd but understandable coalition. Arguably, Sunday laws were all show and hypocrisy—economic laws masquerading as moral legislation. But probably the moral disguise which the economic motives wore was not wholly lacking in meaning. If the

48. Act of June 1, 1908, [1908] Laws of Ill. 90.
49. Friedman, *Freedom of Contract and Occupational Licensing 1890-1900*, 53 CALIF. L. REV. 487 (1965).
50. L. FRIEDMAN, *supra* note 22, at 511-12; *see, e.g.*, Act of May 25, 1897, ch. 188, [1897] Laws of Conn. 883. Of course, Sunday laws had been enforced off and on throughout the century. For some glimpses of this complex history, see W. JOHNS, DATELINE SUNDAY, U.S.A. (1967).

concept of a Sunday full of harmony and rest had had no power of persuasion, the unions could not have put together a coalition with the religious.

Many other signs of a resurgent moral militancy appeared at the end of the 19th century. The federal government crushed interstate traffic in lotteries in 1895.[51] The temperance movement became stronger and ultimately achieved a disastrous success. Joseph Gusfield, for one, interprets the temperance struggle as a struggle for normative dominance, a struggle to show the "superior power and prestige of the old middle class in American society."[52] In the early 20th century, some states even tried to ban the cigarette. One of these states was Arkansas, which, in 1907, made it a crime to make, sell or give away cigarettes or cigarette papers to anyone, child or adult.[53] In the same year, Arkansas prohibited betting on horse races[54] and passed a law against malicious disturbance of church congregations by "profanely swearing, or using indecent gestures," violence, or any "language" or act which would "disquiet, insult or interrupt said congregation."[55] This period too had the honor of ushering in a crusade against drugs and addiction. Arthur Conan Doyle described how Sherlock Holmes, as one author has put it, "relaxed at the Baker Street flat after his bouts with Professor Moriarity by summoning Dr. Watson to prepare him a needle."[56] There was little or no opprobrium attached. Troy Duster has written that in 1900, "[a]nyone could go to his corner druggist and buy grams of morphine or heroin for just a few pennies. There was no need to have a prescription . . . no moral stigma attached to such narcotics use."[57] Within 20 years, the law savagely proscribed the addict, who was now labeled a dope fiend; severe federal and state sanctions were imposed, and the country embarked on the dubious adventure of trying to stamp out drug use through repressive measures. Finally, in 1910, another nightmare or fantasy of a beleagured moral

123

---

51. Act of March 2, 1895, ch. 191, 28 Stat. 963 (codified, *as amended*, at 18 U.S.C. § 1301 (1970)). Lotteries, common in the early part of the century, were outlawed in many states. *See* J. EZELL, FORTUNE'S MERRY WHEEL (1960).

52. J. GUSFIELD, THE SYMBOLIC CRUSADE 122 (1963). *See generally* D. PIVAR, PURITY CRUSADE (1973).

53. Act of May 8, 1907, No. 280, [1907] Acts of Ark. 653.

54. Act of February 27, 1907, No. 55, [1907] Acts of Ark. 134.

55. Act of May 9, 1907, No. 287, [1907] Acts of Ark. 682.

56. R. KING, THE DRUG HANG-UP 17 (1972).

57. T. DUSTER, THE LEGISLATION OF MORALITY 3 (1969).

majority gave rise to the Mann Act, which outlawed "white slavery."[58]

We are paying a heavy price for some of these nightmares. Arguably, prohibition created a generation of lawbreakers, unwittingly vested immense power in gangsters, corrupted officials, and distorted the administration of justice.[59] Similar charges are leveled at the modern enforcement of drug laws.

More hopeful and productive was another breach of the Victorian compromise. This was the revolt of the underdogs themselves—the refusal of the downtrodden to accept their labels. It included the insistence of moral minorities on the right to their own view of life, not secretly, but *de jure,* right up front. This revolution is quite recent. It has been influenced strongly by the example of the civil rights movement, which is in one sense as old as slavery, but in another sense distinctly a product of the 20th century. Some might think that to put under one roof the civil rights movement and the revolt against moral taboos (obscenity, blasphemy, and non-Biblical behavior in bed) trivializes the struggle for racial equality. But this much is held in common: unwillingness to abide by Victorian arrangements. These were arrangements made with the expectation that the lower orders —"lower" in the social, economic, and also the moral sense—would more or less stay in their place.

Numerous devices fastened down the Victorian arrangements, and convenient ideologies and myths buttressed them. It is not the purpose of this paper to examine this subject in detail. However, some of the myths and ideologies might be mentioned. One was equality before the law. Obviously inequality was rife, not to mention corruption, but a system of beliefs justified or excused inequalities. Among these was the belief that the United States was a country of great social mobility. Most influential was the notion that nothing much could be done to redistribute power and wealth without ruining the country— that is, nothing which was radical or required active state action. Economists and their popular spokesmen told the country that only disaster could result from interference with natural laws. No one believed this entirely, but enough people believed it enough to keep the country politically calm—at least for a while. But faith in the invisible hand lasted only as long as the optimism of the formative

---

58. Act of June 25, 1910, ch. 395, 36 Stat. 825 (codified, *as amended,* at 18 U.S.C. § 2421 (1966)).

59. A. SINCLAIR, ERA OF EXCESS 178-219 (1964).

period. When the hand dealt bad cards, the players began to cheat. This ushered in the age of the pressure groups.

Whatever the causes, 20th-century man seems less inclined to accept the social order as a given and his place within it as fixed. He demands for himself, his interests, and his aspirations, recognition and legitimacy, as well as practical achievement. There is, consequently, a massive demand to close the gap between the official surface of the law and the reality. Already in the late 19th century, devices to improve the administration of justice and access to the law had developed; the pace of these changes quickened in the 20th century.

The law of obscenity provides us an excellent example. Pornography itself was centuries old. The first amendment to the Constitution —and a rather strong national tradition—protects freedom of speech. Yet no one in the 19th century imagined for a moment that "free speech" included hard core pornography. Pictures and descriptions of sex were taboo, except for medical and scientific purposes, or behind a screen of euphemism. Nudity on the stage or in live sex shows was out of the question. There was no demand for these entertainments, no test cases; the idea was simply unthinkable. The United States Supreme Court did not decide an obscenity case until after the Second World War.[60] This first case dealt with Edmund Wilson's novel, *Memoirs of Hecate County*. The Court divided equally. Not even a Bible-belt schoolmarm would blink at the book today, with the *Kama Sutra* and *Lady Chatterly* in every drug store, to mention only the mildest examples. Since 1948, the law has amazingly expanded the public zone of sexual expression—what can be said, seen, touched, felt, and done in the open. Whether there is a similar explosion of sexual behavior is much less clear. No doubt behavior has changed and will change further, but the initial and more dramatic change is in the balance between licit and illicit, between what is flaunted and what is hidden. Indeed, one of the best examples of the new permissiveness is John Cleland's book, *Memoirs of a Lady of Pleasure,* commonly called *Fanny Hill*, written in the late 18th century but safely underground until about 10 years ago. The question whether *Fanny Hill* is obscene

125

---

60. Doubleday & Co. v. New York, 335 U.S. 848 (1948) (per curiam), *aff'g* 297 N.Y. 687, 77 N.E.2d 6 (1947). The next obscenity case did not come before the Court until almost 10 years later. Roth v. United States, 354 U.S. 476 (1957).

has been adjudicated by the United States Supreme Court itself;[61] it goes without saying that never before in its two hundred years would this book have dared show its face in public. Yet a market for pornography existed in 1800, 1850, and 1900. There were people who wanted to read *Fanny Hill*, and who were willing to pay for a copy. What was lacking was an appreciable demand on the law to legitimate that market. People were content to remain underground in their lechery, or resigned to this fate. There were deviants, but not enemy deviants.

What does this history suggest? Law, we have said, is a kind of map of interests and demands. Its structure and substance betray current conceptions of law and current concepts of the legitimate limits of law. Law reflects the agenda of controversy—the things that are in actual dispute. It also gives strong negative evidence about which issues are *not* in dispute, the things that nobody questions. The issues in dispute are demands and counterdemands. When we speak of a crisis in law, civil or criminal, we mean a crisis in demands. Clearly, in the third and present period, which began roughly a century ago, two distinct pressures on law have produced such a "crisis." First, the oppressed and the deviant have demanded legitimization; second, counterpressure has developed from the old majorities, whose moral and economic dominance has been threatened.

The current agitation about law and order—crime in the streets— is a meeting ground or battlefield of these two armies, pushing against the legal structure from opposite sides. Most people assume that crime is rampant in the cities; a walk in the streets after dark is perilous. Also widespread is the idea that life in the cities is rotten and corrupt, and getting worse. This, of course, is not a new idea. The bad reputation of the cities is centuries old. But there seems to be an increase now, a stridency in the fears and demands of broad masses of people.

Yet in the face of this clamor, some scholars flatly proclaim that the crime wave is a myth. Over the long haul, they say, violent crime has, if anything, declined in the cities.[62] Urban crime may have jumped, but only in the last few years, and even that is disputed. New

61. A Book Named "John Cleland's Memoirs of a Woman of Pleasure" v. Attorney General, 383 U.S. 413 (1966).
62. *See* D. BELL, THE END OF IDEOLOGY 151 (1962); Lane, *Urbanization and Criminal Violence in the 19th Century*, in VIOLENCE IN AMERICA 468, 469 (H. Graham & T. Gurr eds. 1969).

York and other big cities, it is argued, were hot beds of crime in 1870 to a much greater extent than today.

If so, then what is the crisis in crime? First of all, it is possible that something real *has* happened to the crime rate. People care less about raw numbers of crimes than about the kinds of crime, who commits what acts, in what places, how, and to whom. It is one thing for crime to run rampant where the middle class never penetrates, in places it cares nothing about; but it is quite another thing for those same crimes to be committed in a city in which everyone is interdependent and within striking distance of one another. This is the condition of cities in a mass society, with mass mobility, and in which slums gird the core of the city. The "dangerous classes"[63] once lived in tight districts, out of sight and almost out of mind. Now no place is safe. The paths of those who live in the slums cross the paths of the rich on their way to work, theaters, restaurants, and banks.[64]

127

Much violence in the past took place outside the cities. In a raw frontier community, a Dodge City let us say, grown men committed violent crimes—many of them on other grown men. What horrifies people today is violence committed on the helpless and the innocent. When an addict murders an 80-year-old widow, the statistic is the same as when one gunfighter shoots down another. Socially, however, the two crimes are quite different. In one case victim and killer stand on an equal footing. Both entered a violent world, more or less of their own free will. In the other case, the relationship is involuntary— a relationship of predator and prey.

Even so, the crisis in law is a crisis of demand. Whether or not conditions have gotten worse in the outside world, the tolerance level has certainly declined, and correlatively, the level of demand that something be done has risen. The demand for an attack on crime is a demand for sterner police measures, tougher prisons, less "permissiveness." It is tied—not logically but emotionally—to fear and hatred of the moral minorities and of the unruly and political factions of the underprivileged. The demands of *these* people have brought about great improvements in access to law and in the administration of justice. Demand now meets counterdemand of equal or almost equal

---

63. *See* C. Brace, The Dangerous Classes of New York, and Twenty Years Work Among Them (3d ed. 1880).

64. *See generally* Silver, *The Demand for Order in Civil Society,* in The Police: Six Sociological Essays 1-24 (D. Bordua ed. 1967).

strength. There is no obvious short-run solution to the clash of these sets of demands.

The third period, then—our period—is a period of conflict and struggle in the two specific areas we have stressed. There has always been conflict and struggle, but the current forms seem particularly nasty and sharp. This is because the moral world appears to have lost some of its classical shock absorbers. The unshakeable faith of the colonial elites is gone. The 19th century was fortified by faith in economic growth and a basic stock of moral principles. Now old compromises and accommodations have lost much of their strength. Opposing forces are struggling, not only for power, but also for legitimacy; and legitimacy is not easy to share. No doubt there will be new accommodations and new compromises; but their shapes and sizes, at least for now, are not visible to the naked eye.

128

COLUMBIA LAW REVIEW

VOL. XXXVIII   APRIL, 1938   NO. 4

CONSTITUTIONAL HISTORY AND CONSTITUTIONAL LAW*

A certain amount of history is implicit in the study of constitutional law, although this quantum tends to shrink in ratio to emphasis upon systematic analysis. The adoption of the subject in law school curricula has tended toward the abandonment of the historical element, partly because the cases excite the dialectic urge, and partly because current term calendars have exerted large influence upon what phases of constitutional law are important for purposes of instruction. Before the relentless advance of the glacial jurisprudence of interstate commerce, taxation and substantive due process, the erstwhile leading cases with their gaudy background have one by one vanished from the casebooks.[1] What need can there now be to rekindle the ardours of long settled political battles, when the fires of contemporary conflict are lit by balance sheets, valuation charts and the profundities of economic theory?

129

---

* This article was read at the annual meeting of the American Law School Association in December, 1937.

[1] The mold for casebooks in constitutional law appears to have been set by THAYER, the first edition of whose CASES ON CONSTITUTIONAL LAW appeared in 1895. THAYER declared his intention of promoting a "genetic" method. So, while he described his subject as a "body of *law*—of law in the strict sense," he adhered to the view that the study of law "was ennobled by an alliance with history." Further, he regarded the subject as allied with statecraft, so that one gains the impression he conceived that an adequate view of the sweep of constitutional development would enable the student to cope with new problems that might arise in the future. In general the later casebooks of McCLAIN (1909), HALL (1913) and EVANS (1916) conformed to the notions expressed by THAYER. More recently the focus in these books of instruction has swung from the past to the modern age. In some instances points of doctrine are illustrated by nearly contemporary cases alone; in others an early "first statement" case is followed by a collection of recent decisions with little or nothing to bridge the gap of years. One compiler has explained to the writer that discussion of intervening cases by a court in a recent decision is supposed to do the bridging—a disguised acceptance of the textbook method, *viz.* what someone says about a source instead of the source itself. This is objectionable on another score—the substitution of judge-written history for scientific study.

Why there has been so radical a change in the casebooks is a question that can hardly be answered from the editors' introductions. DODD (1932) is concerned with justifying the wide scope of problems covered and so suggests that "the functional approach" is best served by emphasizing the function of the written constitution in our legal system. He does not consider what may be the implications of this "functional approach" in respect to a "genetic" selection. He admittedly preserves lead-

It is probably true that even the most legalistic expositor of constitutional law is aware of the volatile political base of his distillations. If he writes a book he can relegate such matter to footnotes whence it can rarely rise to bemuddle his system. If he is a teacher he can, as usually he must, assume that the student comes armed with at least a citizen's knowledge of American government and history. This is a supposition quite unsupported in fact, but it has acquired the force of an irrebuttable presumption of law. Conveniently enough it enables the teacher to maintain his propositions of doctrine in appropriate aloofness and detachment from political history, while a semblance of juristic quality is preserved by allusive reference to procedure, torts or contracts. Thus drained of historical significance the constitutional cases may the more easily be manipulated as so many capsules of legal essence. To be sure it is possible to master and comprehend the law in the dreary passages of White, C. J., in *Standard Oil v. United States*,[2] without the added burden of Ida Tarbell's history or an understanding of the noisy trust busting of T. Roosevelt. But overemphasis on single or groups of legal concepts inevitably destroys the element of tradition which in any system of law is its source of vitality. If this is too long persisted in you may one day find the black lettering of your hornbook, no longer over the measured periods of John Marshall, but over the colossal dullness of *Das Kapital*.

The technique of approaching constitutional problems as problems of law has become so neatly ditched and scoured that it amounts at least to an encroachment to suggest that some attention be paid to the recurrent tides of political circumstance. As long as the bulk of contemporary Supreme Court business is taken as the base of discussion it is, indeed, arguable that understanding is hardly improved by attempts to assess precedents in terms of the political past. It is always possible to trim old cases to the size of a gloss and to treat as wastage the historical implications that loom so large when the cases are left intact. Command

ing cases which "a lawyer should know" and indicates where the student can learn history. McGovney (1928-30) uses what he describes as an historical method for the development of a few doctrines to give the student "broad training." He does not explain why this method is not pursued throughout, beyond stating that he seeks to offer "variety of treatment." Dowling (1937), being concerned chiefly with the regulatory powers of government, and emphasizing the teacher's task of instructing the student in what is the "lawyer's job" in presenting constitutional questions, offers the best apology for the lavish use of "new" material. Rothschaefer (1932) avers that he selected cases which involved modern applications of old principles. He believes the approach of modern judges is different from that of their predecessors, indicating thus a belief that contemporary matter furnishes a better basis for prediction than old cases. I submit that even in a course of limited content historical orientation of the student is a problem which ought not be perfunctorily dismissed.

² 221 U. S. 1 (1910).

130

of constitutional history is not essential to an understanding of the due process problems of *Old Dearborn v. Seagram Distilleries*,[3] or the *Pep Boys, Manny, Moe & Jack v. The Pyroil Sales Co.*[4] On the other hand it is not to be denied that even if one minimizes the historical approach and cleaves to a legalistic up-to-the-minute view of constitutional law, there are certain situations arising at even this late date where mere dialectic acumen is unavailing. It is unavailing because in these cases the Supreme Court itself has employed the method of historical enquiry with a steadfastness which makes recourse to history an inescapable burden upon counsel. I am not referring to the cases where out of pure intellectual exuberance some learnéd justice festoons his opinion with a baroque of plea roll or yearbook citations.[5] I have in mind that important branch of constitutional law, somewhat redundantly described as procedural due process, where problems arising under the so-called Bill of Rights and even the Fourteenth Amendment are still dealt with in terms of tradition.

131

For eighty years the Supreme Court has maintained the general position that in determining whether a given procedure satisfies the due process guarantees, it is necessary to inquire into English common law and American colonial practice. It was not until 1855, in the case of *Murray v. Hoboken*,[6] that this rule of interpretation was for the first time made explicit in respect of the Fifth Amendment. Yet there is no question but that for two generations previously recourse to common law standards had been consistently had in the solution of constitutional problems as well in the federal as in the state courts.[7] This was a tradi-

---

[3] 299 U. S., 183 (1936).

[4] 299 U. S., 198 (1936).

[5] *E.g.* Holmes, J., in The Blackheath, 195 U. S., 361 (1904); Brandeis, J., in Red Cross Line v. Atlantic Fruit Co., 264 U. S., 109, 122 (1924); Taft, C. J., in *Ex Parte* Grossman, 267 U. S., 87 (1925); Stone, J., in Hudson v. U. S., 272 U. S., 451 (1926); Sutherland, J., in Atlantic Cleaners and Dyers v. U. S., 286 U. S., 427 (1932).

[6] Den. *ex dem.* Murray v. Hoboken, 18 Howard 272 (U. S. 1856). The approach of Curtis, J., in this case is already clearly forecast in his decision in Greene v. Briggs, 1 Curtis 311 (C. C. 1852).

[7] The following are typical.

U. S.: Vanhorne v. Dorrance, 2 Dall. 304 (1795).

New York: In the Matter of John and Cherry Street, 19 Wend. 659, 676 (Su. Ct. 1839); Taylor v. Porter, 4 Hill. 140, 146 (Su. Ct. 1843); Gardner v. Newburgh, 2 John. Ch. 162 (1816); People v. Ruggles, 8 John. 290 (Su. Ct. 1811).

North Carolina: Hoke v. Henderson, 4 Dev. 1, 15 (1833); Den ex Dem Trustees v. Foy, 1 Murph. 58 (N. C. 1805).

New Hampshire: Dartmouth Coll. v. Woodward, 1 N. H. 111, 129 (1817); Hutchins v. Edson, 1 N. H. 139 (1817).

Tenn.: Bank v. Cooper, 2 Yerg. 599, 605 (Tenn. 1831); Jones' Heirs v. Perry, 10 Yerg. 59, 71 (Tenn. 1836).

Conn.: State v. Danforth, 3 Conn. 112 (1819).

Mass.: Comm. v. Davis, 11 Pick. 432 (1831); Comm. v. Phillips, 16 Pick. 211 (1834); Fisher v. McGirr, 1 Gray 1, 29, 37, 45 (1854).

tion that can be traced directly to the debates over the ratification of the Constitution and would scarcely have had to be made explicit but for the fact that the middle of the century was experiencing revolutionary changes in the structure of the common law remedies.[8]

The canons of *Murray v. Hoboken* were carried over by the Supreme Court to the interpretation of "procedural due process" under the Fourteenth Amendment. In *Hurtado v. California*[9] there was a gleam of what the rationalists would regard as a possibly more enlightened view. But it was a false dawn. The cases that have been decided since that date even where they have coursed the familiar ground— whether the general due process clause includes or excludes the particular guarantees such as jury trial, etc.—have rested on the assumption that the historical tests of *Murray v. Hoboken* must be made.

What all this has to do with constitutional history is not immediately apparent, for the conventional image of English constitutional history is a firmament dotted with magna cartas, petitions of rights, or acts of settlement, and the picture of colonial American constitutional history is not dissimilar. I submit, however, that these conventional images being the product of a literary tradition fostered by laymen are mere illusions. Except for such occasional high lights as the Magna Carta, the Act of Supremacy or the Bill of Rights, the details of English constitutional history are only to be found in the common law and the

132

---

[8] This seems to be in the background of the thinking of Curtis. At an early date he expressed his views on the trend toward "codification" of the common law. In a letter to Ticknor, Feb. 21, 1836 [1 CURTIS, A MEMOIR OF B. R. CURTIS (1879) 74-5] he wrote: "Perhaps, however, there will be no Common Law when you come back; for among other wild theories with which the Legislature now in session are bitten is an idea of codifying the Common Law. You remember that the Statute Law of the Commonwealth was undergoing revision when you left Massachusetts. Having got well through with that, the Legislature are so much encouraged that many of them imagine that the whole body of the law may now be reduced to a pocket volume, so that any man may carry about with him his own lawyer. It does not occur to them that a good system of law must be at the same time so extensive as to apply to and govern all the existing relations between men in society; so stable and fixed in all important principles, as to furnish *a certain* guide; and so flexible as to be capable of adaptation to the ever-changing forms into which property is thrown by the unwearied enterprise and all-absorbing love of gain which distinguish our people. With the exception of this scheme, I think matters are going on well in Massachusetts."

Again in 1851 as a member of a commission to revise the proceedings in courts of Justice of Massachusetts, Curtis signed a report condemning the previous statutory "reforms" of common law pleading and advocating the general approach of the common law. "Our earnest endeavor, therefore, has been to take what we now have . . . and amend and build upon it . . . as far as possible with old materials and after old fashions calling things by their old names whenever they can be applied." 2 *ibid.*, 149, 155, 159. *Cf.* also 1 KENT, COMMENTARIES (1848) 473 n. (a) where is mentioned "the rage for bold reckless and presumptuous innovation, so prevalent at this day acting in contempt of the usage and wisdom of the common law. . . ." This statement appears first in Kent's last revision (6 ed. 1848).

[9] 110 U. S. 516 (1883). *Cf.* also Davidson v. New Orleans, 96 U. S. 97 (1877).

activities of the common law courts. In short, as Dicey long ago observed, English constitutional history is inextricably a part of common law history at large.[10] In England "before the emigration of our ancestors," there was no concept of separation of powers and no such title as public law.[11] In consequence every litigated issue of constitutional right was primarily a question of private law, was raised by private law procedure, and was settled not as an affair of state but as a matter of general law.[12] I would not except from this generalization even cases arising by *quo warranto* or *scire facias,* for it was only during the course of the 17th century that king and crown become discrete

---

[10] Dicey, Introduction to the Study of the Law of the Constitution (8 ed. 1920) 191: "We may say that the constitution is pervaded by the rule of law on the ground that the general principles of the constitution . . . are with us the result of judicial decisions determining the rights of private persons in particular cases brought before the Courts. . . ." ". . . some polities, and among them the English constitution, have not been created at one stroke and far from being the result of legislation in the ordinary sense of the term, are the fruit of contests carried on in the courts on behalf of the rights of individuals." (*ibid.*, 192).

[11] It was hardly possible to develop a doctrine of separation of powers when the crown functioned as executive, as legislator (with its wide powers of enactment by writ or proclamation), as judge in parliament, in council or, in theory, in King's Bench. The parliament is both court and legislative body. The courts perform judicial functions and administrative functions as, *e.g.* in the visitation of eleemosynary corporations. In the sixteenth century the lawyers theorize about the English polity in terms of their common law doctrine of corporations. So Y. B. 14 Hy. VIII, Mich., pl. 2, p. 3 (1523) "Auxy est corporacion per le common ley come le parliament du Roy et seigneurs et les comuns sont une corporacion." This is picked up again in Plowden, 234 (Willion v. Berkley [1561]); and is adopted by Coke, Fourth Institute, 2. The significance of this mode of thought lies in the fact that so far as one can read implications of political theory into such statements, such implications can be amplified only out of the fantastic body of yearbook learning on corporations—*viz.* common law doctrine. There is a discussion of trends toward a theory of separation of powers in Klimowsky, Die Englische Gewaltenteilungslehre bis zu Montesquieu (1927).

The absence of any such category as "public law" in the thinking of common lawyers during the 16th (*cf.* here Pickthorn, Early Tudor Government: Henry VII [1934], 159) and certainly the early 17th century may be attributed to the pervasiveness of the current classifications. While the abridgements get no further than a alphabetical arrangement of doctrine, St. Germain, Doctor and Student (1523), I, c. iv; II, c. ii, offers an analysis of the law which precludes any division of public and private; this analysis is in the main followed by Blackstone, Commentaries, Intro. § 3 and remains standard into the nineteenth century. The only instance we have observed where the distinction between public and private was applied to common law doctrine occurs in Lambard, Eirenarcha (1592 ed.) Bk. 2; c. 7, in reference to felonies: "By Publicke Felonies, I doe here in this Table meane those offences that do not so much touch any particular (or private) person, as the universall Commonwealth itself: either in the head thereof (which is the queene) or in the body, which is framed of all the Subjects within the Realme: Between which twaine, there is such a neere Sympathie and mutuall feeling, that whensoeuer the one is offended, the other is also hurt, and doth suffer with it."

It should be observed that here the distinction is made with reference to the corporate doctrine mentioned above.

[12] The point is discussed by 1 Vinogradov, Collected Papers (1928) 192 (*Constitutional History and the Yearbooks*).

133

juristic entities, and consequently in issues so raised the medieval king was essentially but a super-privileged individual.[13]

It must not be supposed that during the Middle Ages when our procedural forms were evolved, the judges were conscious of the constitutional aspects of their activities. This period was characterized by certain dominant ideas—the supremacy of the law, the essential unity of the law, the integrity of the procedural structure—and judicial thinking was conditioned by these notions. In consequence, even where the courts had to wrestle with some basic change by statute in the structure of remedies or rights, they do not speak as if they were cognizant of constitutional change, but they appear concerned chiefly with the matter of integration, a task at which they were so adept that they frequently seem to have regarded these changes as mere matters of form.[14] Thus the law which they were sworn to preserve absorbed change with so little effort that, if our knowledge of English constitutional history were

134

---

[13] 3 MAITLAND, COLLECTED PAPERS (1911) 253 *et seq.*, In the 16th century the courts are wrestling with the problem of disassociating the body natural of the king from his body politic [Case of the Duchy of Lancaster, 1 Plowden, 213 (1562)]; this was but the first step toward isolating the office from the person.

[14] The posture of medieval courts toward acts of Parliament has been discussed chiefly in rather large terms—"common law versus statute" etc. (McIlwain, *Magna Carta and Common Law*, MAGNA CARTA COMMEMORATION ESSAYS [1917] 122 *et seq.*) or in respect of the expressed rules of interpretation (PLUCKNETT, STATUTES AND THEIR INTERPRETATION IN THE FIRST HALF OF THE FOURTEENTH CENTURY [1922]). The problem cannot at all be solved by matching passages which use the word "statute" against the passages that use the expression "common law," nor can it be completely elucidated by instances where the courts become articulate on their canons of interpretation. Until a thorough examination has been made of the courts' dealing in all its ramifications with particular statutes generalizations are misleading. In the period of which Mr. Plucknett writes, the courts did not regard a statute introducing a new remedy to have abolished common law (*supra* at 131), they were reluctant to admit modification (*supra* at 134), and by the middle of the century they were committed to a policy of strict interpretation (*supra* at 90, 169). The courts during the 15th century exercised a vast discretion over the enforcement of statutes by the evolution of an artful series of classifications, *viz.* statutes in the affirmative and statutes in the negative (*e.g.*, Y. B. B. 10 Edw. IV, Pasc. pl. 18 (1470); 4 Hy. VII, Trin. pl. 6 (1489)); statutes general and statutes particular (Y. B. B. 34 Hy. VI, Pasc. pl. 1 (1456); 37 Hy. VI, Hil. pl. 5 (1459)) with the crowning subtlety of a statute "particular in a generality" (Y. B. 13 Edw. IV, Pasc. pl. 4 (1473)). Some notion of the scope of scholastic achievement here can be observed in Holland's Case, 4 Co. Rep. 75 (1597) and Foster's Case, 11 Co. Rep. 56b, 61a (1614).

It should be noted that when the first of the great Edwardian statutes is enacted the core of the common law is that which had grown up about the writs, and judicial thinking in civil causes is dominated by the schematic proprieties of the form of action concept. In consequence the major intellectual problem of the courts is the adjustment of statutory changes or additions to this existing structure. An example of how a statute giving a right is implemented by the courts arguing from common law precedents and so absorbed into the common law scheme is the case Y. B. 35 Hy. VI, Mich. fol. 6, pl. 9 (1457). Sometimes a statute is integrated only to the extent that it exists as an alternative to common law (Y. B. 10 Edw. IV, Pasc. pl. 18 (1470)). Compare further 43 Lib. Ass., pl. 9, and the rule respecting Stat. West. II, c. 9, FITZHERBERT, NATURA BREVIUM, 137 A (1794 Ed.); COKE, SECOND INST. 372.

derived from plea rolls and yearbooks alone, we would gain little feeling of the impact of those abrupt and sometimes sanguinary crises which slowly brought the realm closer to its modern institutional structure.

An example of the almost lethargic state of judicial doctrine is the plethora of material on the king's prerogative. This body of dogma is the heart of what we would describe as medieval constitutional law, just as it is the heart of what little political theory comes out of medieval England. If you start with Bracton and proceed to read the so-called Statute *de Prerogativa Regis*[15] and then thumb through every crown case in the two great 16th century abridgements, you will come out with just two basic generalizations: that the king is under the law, but that to the courts the ceiling of this law is so lofty that the king can move about most comfortably and often soar to dizzy and to us tyrannical heights. About new detail you will find much. But you will find over three hundred years practically no fundamental disturbance of anything very basic.[16] And how could it be otherwise—there was but one law and the king in the medieval phrase the *principium unitatis*.

But if the medieval judges were themselves hardly if at all aware that they were building constitutional law into the common law edifice, the 17th century judges and lawyers who lived in a period of acrid political conflict were intensely conscious of it. One has only to observe the skill with which Sir Edward Coke underlined the constitutional implications of one yearbook case after another in cases which he reported or in which he sat as judge. Moreover, the method by which this pointing of constitutional ideas is accomplished is still in the medieval tradition. It is almost invariably some question of property or procedure that is in issue and forms the occasion of a more or less pointed digression. Consider for example the case of the *Postnati* that starts as an assize of novel disseisin, and the defendants plead in bar the plaintiff's alienage.[17] The Exchequer Chamber decides that Scotch born Robert Calvin is a subject of James I—an issue of the greatest immediate and future constitutional import—but in the course of its discussion

---

[15] 1 STAT. REALM 226; cf. on this Maitland, *Praerogativa Regis* (1891) 6 ENG. HIST. REV. 367.

[16] CHRIMES, ENGLISH CONSTITUTIONAL IDEAS OF THE FIFTEENTH CENTURY (1936) 61 indicates how legal theory of that century remains substantially what it was in the earlier period. For the early Tudor period cf. PICKTHORN, *op. cit. supra* note 11 at 157-62.

A point of considerable significance in relation to the conservative views of the bar at large is the fact that STAUNFORD, EXPOSITION OF THE KING'S PREROGATIVE (1568) compiled out of the yearbooks follows the chapters of the Statute *de Praerogativa Regis*. This work was published in 1568 and was the leading treatise into the seventeenth century. It was printed six times by Tottel. The Company of Stationers printed an edition in 1607.

[17] Calvin's Case, 7 Co. Rep. 1 (1609).

brings into focus a staggering amount of medieval judicial precedent respecting not only the matter of alienage, but allegiance in general, and more pertinent still, for the future colonial policy, the matter of right in overseas demesnes. Again in the *Earl of Shrewsbury's* case,[18] the nature of various offices is analyzed. In the case of *Sutton's Hospital*,[19] the power of the crown in respect of incorporation is set forth at length, and in the array of copyhold cases the rights of a considerable and downtrodden body of farmers are placed upon a firm footing of common law procedural right.[20]

It is impossible to review at length the remarkable bulk of petty constitutional detail on which Coke expressed his views, whether or not they were necessary to the case reported. One thing, however, is clear, (whether the attentive reader resorts to Coke, Bulstrode or Hobart) that in the early 17th century reports, common law and constitution are synonymous to the point that whatever remedies the former afford are *eo ipso* the basis of constitutional right. Moreover, even the most skilled of pleaders will be hard put to disentangle from procedural precedents the substantive matter involved. This is the ore from which common law due process must be reduced.

It follows from the peculiar character of the English constitution, from the fact that precedents on forms are at once precedents of common law procedure and of constitutional right, that any contemporary judicial enquiry into English common law due process should embrace all facets of the matter examined. True, we are prone to read our own distinctions into old cases, to set off statutes against judicial pronouncement, to fuss about dictum and decision;[21] but in the end, since such enquiry is itself made to determine instant constitutional issues, our courts are in fact proceeding along paths trodden by the long procession of long dead judges of long dead kings. This is inevitable, for although modern scholars can point triumphantly to the fact that the phrase "due process" occurs for the first time in the statute 28 Edward III c. 3,[22]

---

[18] 9 Co. Rep., 46b (1613).

[19] 10 Co. Rep., 1 (1613).

[20] In particular, Margaret Podgers's Case, 9 Co. Rep. 104 (1613); Combes's Case, 9 Co. Rep. 75b (1614); Swayne's Case, 8 Co. Rep. 63 (1609). It is not without significance that Coke reported a variety of cases from the reign of Elizabeth dealing with copyholds that were basic to the subsequent protection of copyholders *viz.* Brown's Case, 4 Co. Rep. 21 (1581); Melwich v. Luter, 4 Co. Rep. 26 (1588); Hobert v. Hammond, 4 Co. Rep. 27b (1600). On the development of the common law *cf.* TAWNEY, AGRARIAN PROBLEM IN THE SIXTEENTH CENTURY (1912) 288 *et seq.*

[21] *Cf.* the characterization of Coke's methods in 5 HOLDSWORTH, HIST. ENG. LAW, 462 *et seq.* (1924).

[22] *Viz.* Corwin, The Doctrine of Due Process of Law before the Civil War (1911) 24 HARV. L. REV. 366. "The phrase 'due process of law' comes from Chapter 3 of 28 EDW. III . . ." Accord, MOTT, DUE PROCESS OF LAW (1926), 4. Mr.

136

the notion itself is older than the Norman Conquest[23] and has ever since been basic in the thinking of English speaking peoples.[24]

It is the tradition of Coke's time that passes over to the American colonies, for it is upon the methods and constitutional views of Coke that the colonial lawyers were nurtured.[25] Once American law passes

---

Corwin is categorical when he should be genealogical. The expression is used earlier, *e.g.* Y. B. 13 Edw. III, 101 (1339) [R. S.]—"le roi ne deit mes recorder mes par due processe"—and is approximated in the act exiling the Despensers, 15 Edw. II (1321), 1 Stat. Realm 183—"sauntz due proces selonc ley de terre."

[23] For example as early as the year 991 we find the principle laid down that a man was entitled to property of which he had been disseised before he could be required to plead (19 Mansi, Concilia, 122-3). The same point is made by the bishop of Durham at his trial in 1088 (Symeon of Durham, 1 Historia Eccl. Dur. [R. S.], 171-2). It appears as a rule in *Leges Henrici*, 61, 21 "et nemo placitet dissaisiatus." (1 Liebermann, Gesetze der Angelsachsen (1903), 582). *Cf. Leg. Hen.* 5, 3; 29, 2a; 53, 5. This rule lies at the basis of the later rules respecting process and surety for appearance.

[24] While the eventual identification of "due process of law" with "per legem terrae" of Magna Carta (c. 39) was to be of considerable significance in American constitutional development, it is clear that for better than a century after Runnymede procedural rights or expectations are urged in terms of the common law at large and not in terms of the collateral security of the Great Charter. This is obvious from the most cursory view of the cases in the Placitorum Abbreviatio (1811) where in unending detail the picture of what is proper procedure stands forth: *e.g.* if a man is not summoned properly he can recover damages for irregular amercement (p. 273, rot. 4); a grand assize does not lie for land in ancient demesne (p. 117, rot. 9); no one need answer in England for trespasses done without the realm (p. 201, rot. 53); judgment must be delivered in court and not *extra bancum* (p. 226, rot. 49).

In the cases collected in Ryley, Pleadings in Parliament (1661) (and *cf.* 1 Rotuli Parliamentorum) the recurrent formula *temp.* Edward I "nec est juri consonum vel hactenus in curia ista usitatum" (Ryley, *supra* at 43) suggests clearly enough the notion that bad procedure is not law of the land. Coke has been consistently berated by modern scholars for identifying (Second Institutes, 50-51) the *per legem terrae* of Magna Carta with due process of law (*Cf.* Mc-Kechnie, Magna Carta [2 ed. 1914] 381; Vernon-Harcourt, His Grace the Steward and Trial of Peers [1907] 215; Mott, Due Process of Law [1926] 77; Corwin, *Doctrine of Due Process of Law before the Civil War* (1911) 24 Harv. L. Rev. 366, 368). In Coke's day there was available a great array of precedent establishing what was in law good or bad procedure. Since Coke was familiar with these precedents he could hardly fail to be aware that the sum of these detailed common law rules added up to a notion of due process and that this notion was basic to the whole common law system. That he should, none the less, have desired a grounding in the Great Charter is to be deduced from his recurrent remarks respecting the binding effect of the Charter upon the crown. One can brush away this use of Magna Carta as bad history, but one cannot impeach the testimony of the medieval precedents.

[25] Professor Radin has recently suggested that the common law "throughout the colonial period remained a subsidiary supplementary law" and intimates that it is misleading to emphasize the writings of Coke. Radin, *The Rivalry of Common Law and Civil Law Ideas in the American Colonies*, in 2 Law: a Century of Progress 1835-1935 [1937], 404, 421, 427. These appear to the writer to be dangerous generalizations. As far as the status of the common law is concerned the characteristics of the seventeenth century are very different from those of the eighteenth (*cf.* 3 Flick, History of the State of New York [1933], 35; Goebel, Cases and Materials on the Development of Legal Institutions [4th ed. 1937], 382, 708) and the law as practiced in local courts differs greatly from that in the higher provincial tribunals. If, for example, one compares practice in the

out of the phase of rude imitation of local court practice and assumes the semblance of a cultivated jurisprudence, this tradition begins to have its effect. In America one may observe two trends. On the one hand, the colonial courts proceed to deal with occasional constitutional issues, entirely in the tradition of the medieval English courts. They are treated not as constitutional questions *per se*, but as questions of law at large.[26] On the other hand, there is what may be called the polit-

---

Virginia County Courts such as Lancaster or Accomac with the Reports of Randolph in the same period, or the Common Pleas records of Orange county, New York, with the Mayor's Court of the metropolis, the degree of the variation is obvious. As far as the superior courts are concerned, however, there is no reason whatever to doubt that by 1750 the common law was dominant. This is clearly indicated by the character of the authorities cited in court. It is true that works on natural law were in vogue but a document relating to the training of lawyers in New York (circa 1750) leaves no doubt but that the natural law is the subsidiary, the common law the basic study. (Mss. Wm. Smith Junior Papers Miscellanea A, New York Public Library.)

With respect to the diffusion and use of Coke's Institutes and Reports, the writer, having examined the court minute books and the papers of all the various New York counties settled before 1776, as well as the papers of leading eighteenth century New York lawyers, is convinced that Coke was by all odds the writer most used and cited. There are many indications that this was true in other provinces. Already in 1687 "'the men of Massachusetts did much quote Lord Coke'." (1 BANCROFT, HISTORY OF THE UNITED STATES [1886 ed], 586.) In 1705 Sewall recounts having cited him (Sewall's Diary, Mass. Hist. Soc. Coll., series 5, vol. 6, p. 149) and Coke's reports and Institutes are constantly cited in the arguments of counsel set forth in Quincy's Reports. *Cf.* further the well known pamphlet of OTIS, RIGHTS OF THE BRITISH COLONIES (2 ed. Boston and London, n. d.), 67 *et seq.*, 85, 89, 93, 106. Compare further for Maryland; DULANEY, THE RIGHT OF THE INHABITANTS OF MARYLAND TO THE BENEFIT OF ENGLISH LAW (1728) reprinted in 21 JOHNS HOPKINS UNIVERSITY STUDIES IN HISTORY AND POLITICAL SCIENCE [1903], 541 *et seq.*; 1 HARRIS AND McHENRY'S REPORTS (1656-1776) *passim*. For Virginia consult the reports of Randolph and Barradall 1728-41 in 1 and 2 VIRGINIA COLONIAL DECISIONS, and for later the cases in JEFFERSON, REPORTS (1730-1772). For Pennsylvania consult the pre-revolutionary cases in 1 DALLAS, REPORTS.

[26] We mean, of course, the type of "public law" question which, as in England, is settled collaterally to some private law issue. For example in New York in 1702 in the Matter of the estate of Onzel van Swieten letters of sequestration issued. The will was subsequently proved but a sister of the decedent obtained letters of administration from the Archbishop of Canterbury and brought trover against the administrator *cum test. annexo.* In the Supreme court, *held,* on demurrer that the Archbishop was without jurisdiction. H. R. SURR. OFFICE, Ms. WILLS, Liber 7, pp. 1, 52, 521. Again in 1729 the applicability of St. 12 GEO. II, c. 29 is argued on the basis of Calvin's Case, etc. McCullogh v. Murphy, Ms. MIN. MAYOR'S COURT, July 1729-October 1734. And note also the preliminary manoeuvres against the judge's commission in the Zenger case. TRIAL OF JOHN PETER ZENGER (1745) 6-8. See further Gray v. Paxton (1761) Quincy (Mass.) 541 and the arguments of counsel *ibid.*, 541; Maxwell v. Lloyd. 1 Harris and McHenry 212 (Md. 1763) involving the power to vacate patents.

That questions of the type indicated above are conceived of by common lawyers as constitutional questions appears explicitly in the brief of the appellants in a Rhode Island case (Holmes v. Freebody) taken to the Privy council on appeal. In this case the Rhode Island assembly had granted a new trial after the appeal had been taken. The respondents argued that this was colonial usage. De Grey and Dunning for the appellants argued that the General Assembly was not a court of judicature and ought not to interpose or hinder the common course of justice and

ical tradition that had become attached to the 17th century jurisprudence as it appears in the reports. This runs its course in the legislative and public debates and in the colonists' contests with royal officers. These move quite in early 17th century grooves chiefly because they take the form of attacks upon the royal prerogative which, as to colonists, was still in *statu quo* Jac. I. In form a battle for common law rights, it is in substance a demand for the English statutory modifications of crown authority. The claim to have a bench by tenure of good behavior as in England under the Act of Settlement, is an example.[27]

How devoutly the colonists' faith was pinned to the common law during the early phases of revolutionary agitation has been considerably obscured by the fact that debates very rapidly mounted to the more airy and less palpable realm of natural law.[28] Specific rights which could be grounded upon Magna Carta or identified as basic common law policies, were soon transmuted into inalienable rights.[29] One need only

139

---

that the granting of new trials by the assembly "is novel, unwarrantable and manifestly tending to injustice and is a power the assembly have no legal or constitutional right to exert." Indorsed on the brief in a contemporary hand is the note: "Chief Justice Wilmot totally denied the Right of the General Assembly to grant new trials and said it was an illegal and usurped jurisdiction to which he would give no countenance . . ." (April 7, 1770).

[27] The persistence in the colonies during the 18th century of political issues that had been settled in England at the end of the 17th century, explains somewhat the pervasive use of the munitions which had served earlier in the homeland. This is clear in the battle over the tenure of judges following the Board of Trade's attempts in 1752 to tighten control over the colonial administration. *Cf.* 4 ACTS OF THE PRIVY COUNCIL, 216; 6 *ibid.*, no. 538; 6 DOC. REL. COL. HIST. OF NEW YORK, 755, 760, 788, 947 *et seq.* In Pennsylvania, an act providing for tenure during good behavior was disallowed. 5 PENNSYLVANIA STATUTES AT LARGE, 722. In New Jersey, the governor who ignored his instructions because the assembly withheld salaries was recalled. 9 NEW JERSEY ARCHIVES, 349, 379 *et seq.* In New York, the lieutenant Governor signed an appropriation bill providing salaries only if the judges accepted commissions during good behavior. The new chief justice appeared with a royal warrant directing the governor to issue a commission at pleasure. He received no salary and the Board of Trade ordered he be paid from direct crown revenue. 7 DOC. REL. COL. HIST. NEW YORK, 506. The provincial judges had protested the new form of compression [N. Y. STATE LIBRARY, MSS. COUNCIL MIN. vol. 25 p. 378, 396] but finally accepted commissions at pleasure. 7 DOC. REL. COL. HIST. NEW YORK, 797. The New York Statute was disallowed by the Crown. RUSSELL, REVIEW OF AMERICAL COLONIAL LEGISLATION BY THE KING IN COUNCIL (1915) 190. To the colonists these manifestations of the royal prerogative were in the disgraceful Stuart tradition. The subsequent turmoil over Townshend's "civil list" scheme directed to the same control of the judiciary is familiar history.

[28] The bridge between the initial viewpoint and that after 1776 is suggested in a letter of Jefferson to Judge Tyler (6 WRITINGS OF THOS. JEFFERSON [Washington Ed. 1855] 65, June 17, 1812): "I deride with you the ordinary doctrine that we brought with us from England the common law rights. This narrow notion was a favorite in the first moment of rallying to our rights against Great Britain. But it was that of men who felt their rights before they had thought of their explanation. The truth is we brought with us the rights of men, of expatriated men."

[29] The extent to which the Magna Carta literature had permeated the colonies before 1774 is worth a careful study. In addition to the widespread use of COKE'S

compare several resolves in the Continental Congress' *Declaration of Rights* (1774),[30] and in particular the blunt claim of title to the common law of England, with the Declaration of Independence of 1776 to observe the lapse from legalism to the inflammatory imprecision of contemporary political theory. It is interesting to observe, however, that although the political objectives of the colonists moved away from the earthy limitations of English law, the specific design of securing the common law was effected in nearly every colony by statute or constitution.[31] These reception statutes vary considerably in form, but they possess one feature in common, that, so far in fact adopted and not repugnant to the new instruments of government and so far as adaptable to local circumstances, the common law was the law of the particular jurisdiction. Then, as if this were not enough, the constitution makers proceed to spell out in terms the several safeguards of the individual hardly won by the common law courts over a period of 500 years: jury trial, due process, etc. Here was created a corpus of presumably indefeasible right.

140

While one may regard these reception statutes as no more than a

INSTITUTES, the little work of CARE, ENGLISH LIBERTIES OR THE FREEBORN SUBJECTS INHERITANCE (16—) enjoyed great vogue. There appear to have been 6 English editions published before the Revolution. An American edition was printed in 1721 (Boston) and in 1774 (Providence).

In this relation it should be noted how the Magna Carta tradition was related to the Declaration of Rights in the contemporary mind. The original print of the Proceedings of the Congress bears a colophon—twelve hands grasping a column on a pedestal labelled "Magna Carta. (1 JOURNALS OF THE CONTINENTAL CONGRESS (Ford ed. 1904), 102; 6 WINSOR, NARRATIVE AND CRITICAL HISTORY OF AMERICA (1887), 100).

Note further on the point in the text the letters of Adams regarding judicial tenure in 3 ADAMS, WORKS (1773) 519-28. The argument is on common law grounds with liberal citations of Coke.

[30] 1 JOURNALS OF THE CONTINENTAL CONGRESS, 63 *et seq.* "Resolved N. C. D. 5. That the respective colonies are entitled to the common law of England and more especially to the great and inestimable privilege of being tried by their peers of the vicinage, according to the course of that law." (*Ibid.*, 69.)

[31] *Connecticut:* The Act of 1776 continued the charter of 1662 as the organic law. The charter contains the usual provision regarding concurrence of the colonial law with the law of England. *Cf.* POORE, FEDERAL AND STATE CONSTITUTIONS (1878) 257 and the introduction in ROOT's REPORTS (1798). *Delaware:* Constitution of 1776, Art. 25; *id.* at 277. *Georgia:* Act of 1784. PRINCE, DIGEST OF THE LAW OF THE STATE (1822) 310. *Maryland;* Constitution of 1776, Decl. of Rights III. POORE, *supra* at 817. *Massachusetts:* Const. of 1780, c. vi, art. vi. *New Hampshire:* Const. of 1792, Sec. 90. POORE, *supra* at 1306. *New Jersey:* Const. of 1776, c. XXII. POORE, *supra* at 1313. *New York:* Const. of 1777, Arts. 35 (1 New York Laws [Kent Radcliffe Rev. 1813], 15). *North Carolina:* Acts of 1778, c. 5 (Public Acts of the General Assembly of North Carolina [1804] 252). *South Carolina:* Act of 1712 (Public law 99 in 1 BREVARD, DIGEST OF PUBLIC LAWS OF SOUTH CAROLINA [1808] tit. 44) affirmed in Const. of 1776, c. 29. POORE, *supra* at 1620. *Cf.* Smith v. McCall, 1 McCord 220 (S. C. 1821). *Virginia:* Ordinance of Convention 1776 c. V § 6, 9 Hening, 126. Provisions like that in Massachusetts or New Hampshire or South Carolina providing the law in force shall remain in force are *pro tanto* reception statutes.

sensible provision for the perpetuation of extant legal systems,[32] they are in a sense an achievement of revolution, a view made colorable by the insistence upon specific detail like *habeas corpus* or jury trial to which all the libertarian traditions of centuries attached. The citizens, erstwhile subjects, were suspicious of government as a colt of the bridle. The certainties of the common law were preferable to the vagaries of politicians.[33]

To comprehend how generally the common law was regarded as a foundation to which the new instruments of government were cemented, it is necessary to realize that for well over a century legislative activity in the colonies had been subject to the test of conformity with English law. Thus, the common law system had itself served as a standard of right, in a sense as a sort of constitution.[34] It is this experience (plus the fact that in all questions of law arising under the new constitutions the courts were largely and for some time cast upon English authorities alone) that sustained at once the organic relation of constitution and common law and of English and American jurisprudence. Only when by statute the face of the old law is radically altered does it become necessary to recall that due process must be tested by common law tradition.

During the first half of the 19th century, at least, enquiry into pro-

141

---

[32] This was the view of Hamilton who wrote (Federalist no. 84) respecting the New York reception provision "The only use of the declaration was to recognize ancient law, and to remove doubts which might have been occasioned by the Revolution."

[33] As far as one can judge from available printed matter the enthusiasm for the common law was at its height between 1774-1776. After the revolution libertarian doctrine has its effect, and when the citizenry discovered that the common law meant actions for debt as well as *habeas corpus* there appears a decided hostility toward law and lawyers among the population at large. *Cf.* the episodes recounted in 1 McMaster, History of the People of the United States (1900), 254, 303-6, 344, 348, 350.

[34] It was theoretically made so in the charters which provided that laws were not to be repugnant to, or were to be agreeable to the law of England. Prior to the establishment of the Lords of Trade and Plantations in 1675 the efforts to assure conformity were desultory and ineffective. The movement for vacating the charters in the last years of Charles II and after James II's accession was to some extent prompted by the matter of non-conformity. The control became over legislation and judicial decision absolute if not entirely effective after the establishment of the Board of Trade. (*Cf.* Russell, Review of American Colonial Legislation by the King in Council [1915] *passim*, and Washburne, Imperial Control of the Administration of Justice in the Thirteen American Colonies, 1684-1776 [1923], *passim*.)

It should be observed, further, on the point of the common law serving as a standard to which legislation must conform that in the eighteenth century it was a well established rule that the by-law powers of corporations must be exercised in conformity with the common law. *Cf.* here Chamberlain of London's Case, 5 Co. Rep., 62b (1592); Clarke's Case, 5 Co. Rep. 64a (1596); Case of the Tailors of Ipswich, 11 Co. Rep. 53 (1615); Ms. Min. Supreme Court of New York, 1732-35, an information (Oct. 23, 1735) against the city of New York for a by-law as being unreasonable and against law.

cedural questions was conducted with a rather clear apprehension of the broad implications of such problems and generally with a competent historical search (by contemporary lights). While it is true that from time to time judicial consciences have been salved by a little perfunctory thumbing of Blackstone,[35] it is plain in cases like *Ownbey v. Morgan,*[36] *Powell v. Alabama,*[37] and *U. S. v. Wood,*[38] that the old methods if not all the old skill still prevail. Since the courts' search of the common law is generally governed by the usual caveat, "is it applicable to our conditions," they do not commit the blunder of asserting that historical tests are conclusive on a point of due process. On the other hand, they appear to have been unwilling to apply so-called tests of reason until they were clear what the range and meaning of past experience had been. It is this body of data and not some abstract idea about what is fair that must serve as a premise for reasoning about new procedure. I say *must,* for there can hardly be any question but that the due process provisions in the Federal bill of rights were intended to maintain the individual's expectations regarding procedure and, in particular, the few safeguards against arbitrary action that the common law had evolved.[39]

142

---

[35] The legitimation of this method dates from the year 1903 when Brewer J. remarked: "Blackstone's Commentaries are accepted as the most satisfactory exposition of the common law of England. At the time of the adoption of the Federal Constitution it had been published about twenty years, and it has been said that more copies of the work had been sold in this country than in England, so that undoubtedly the framers of the Constitution were familiar with it." Schick v. United States, 195 U. S. 65, 69 (1904). Contemporary testimony is competent here: *cf.* Jefferson's letter cited *supra* note 28 "A student finds there [Blackstone] a smattering of everything and his indolence easily persuades him that if he understands that book he is master of the whole body of law. The distinction between these and those who have drawn their stores from the deep and rich mines of Coke Littleton seems well understood even by the unlettered common people, who apply the appellation of Blackstone lawyers to these ephemeral insects of the law."

[36] 256 U. S. 94 (1921).

[37] 287 U. S. 45 (1932).

[38] 299 U. S. 123 (1936).

[39] From a study of the debates in the several state conventions held for the ratification of the federal constitution it appears a strong sentiment existed that it was desirable that the peripheral powers of government implicit even in an instrument of expressed powers be confined within the bounds of what anciently and still was deemed to be common law due process—and this we understand to embrace any of the procedural safeguards of the individual. The state of feeling can be gauged in the arguments both for and against a bill of rights. *Cf.* for Massachusetts, 2 Elliot, Debates (1876) 111 *et seq.,* 153; Maryland, *id.* at 550; New York, *id.* at 398; Pennsylvania, *id.* at 435 *et seq.,* 457; North Carolina, 4 *id.* at 143, 148, 155, 165; South Carolina, *id.* at 300, 307, 337; Virginia, 3 *id.* at 446, 450, 468, 470, 512. The impression gained from a study of these debates suggests that the advocates of a bill of rights desired not only explicit assurance respecting such matters as jury trial, search and seizures etc. but the added guarantee of a blanket law of land or due process clause. It is clear from Coke's exposition (Second Institutes, 50) as well as from such works as Care, *op. cit. supra* note 29, that the due process clause was understood to comprehend both particular as well

It is easy to underestimate how important is the maintenance of the common law tradition in dealing with procedural matter because it is not obvious how potent and extensible a technique this is. We are accustomed to regard enquiry into procedure as primarily a scrutiny of forms having little to do with the merits of a litigation. This is true where a procedural device is discussed merely in ·terms of what technical purpose it serves in the particular array of devices used in a specific litigation. A due process enquiry, however, conducted in what I have called the common law tradition may involve a broader consideration of function. Being essentially a comparative study it must be settled what in general a time honored device accomplished, to make its preservation vital to the litigant's interest. Only then is it possible to ascertain whether or not the procedure complained of is equivalent to or defeats established practice. The more broadly a court considers the office of procedural forms the more it will incline to view them as matters of substance. The objection, "it cannot be done in this manner," if sustained, may become an insuperable obstacle to do it at all. It needs but a revival of the flexible notion of "jurisdiction" as it prevailed for so long in the English courts in the discussion of procedural points, to extend the reach of this type of due process inquest. The doctrine of "fundamental or jurisdictional facts" set forth in *Crowell v. Benson*[40] suggests that such a revival may be imminent. It is because of these functional implications that one may venture to suppose, if the time ever comes when by Senator Borah's proposed amendment courts are divested of their power to deal with "substantive due process" in cases arising under the Fourteenth Amendment, that the benefits of exhaustive inquiry into the remedial phases of the common law will become manifest. The method first laid down in *Murray v. Hoboken* has served the

143

---

as general guarantees. Since the decision in Powell v. Alabama this question has acquired some contemporary importance in respect of the Fourteenth Amendment. *Cf.* Note (1931) 31 COLUMBIA LAW REV. 468; and the Note in DOWLING, CASES ON AMERICAN CONSTITUTIONAL LAW (1937) 632.

The arguments of the opponents of a bill of rights are set forth best in Hamilton's paper in the FEDERALIST (No. 84). In his view the bills of rights were essentially contractual arrangements between crown and subjects, "abridgements of prerogative in favor of privilege, reservations of right not surrendered to the prince." He emphasizes the political character of such instruments and implies that certain matters are not to be protected since there was no grant of authority over them. In the WILSON Mss. (Pennsylvania Historical Society) vol. 2, fo. 44 in the Notes on Convention (Dec. 8, 1787) occurs the following: "What occasion for a Bill of Rights when only delegated powers are given? One possessed of 1000 a. conveys 250 is it necessary to reserve 750?" *Cf.* further the jeering comments regarding the inefficacy of the bill of rights by Gouverneur Morris in 1811, 2 DIARY AND LETTERS OF GOUVERNEUR MORRIS (1888) 529. Note finally Jefferson's comments on the need for a bill of rights in a letter of Dec. 20, 1787, 5 WRITINGS [Ford Ed. (1892-9)] 370.

[40] 285 U. S. 22 (1932).

narrow purpose of determining the propriety of a particular procedural device. To a judge with a clear historical perspective, the justification of a form by reference to past experience of necessity includes some regard of its function. As a mere matter of tradition the court would be on nearly unassailable ground. This was precisely the method used by Coke again and again: the commission of the Welsh and Northern council is tested by the possibility of pleading to the jurisdiction;[41] the commission of the High Commission is tested by the statutory and common law restrictions on ecclesiastical sanctions;[42] the admiralty's commercial jurisdiction is obliquely ousted by applying old rules respecting record.[43] And Coke was virtually unassailable because he was upholding the law of the land by knowing more, or at least by being able to prove more, regarding every procedural detail than any other Englishman.

But if a hearty knowledge of common law materials can readily be made to conserve the extant jurisdiction of the Supreme Court in "substantive" due process matters it should also be pointed out that it equally can be made to pervert the fundamentals of our political structure. There can be no question but that the radicals of the late 18th century were desirous of maintaining the benefits and rejecting what they regarded as the detriments of the common law. The people were conceived to have succeeded to the royal prerogative and where certain aspects of this prerogative underlay the performance of some important social function, the extant or pre-revolutionary delegation was not disturbed, or was adjusted to meet the exigencies created by the general acceptance of the separation of powers. Certain procedural forms that were in England associated with prerogatives were still employed in America, insofar as they were indispensible to the administration of the law, and were justified in terms of the political theories which underlay the new sovereignties. Some prerogative rights simply fell into abeyance.[44] Now the significant phase of this is that there were a variety of

---

[41] Case of the Lords Presidents of Wales and York, 12 Co. Rep., 50 (1608).

[42] Fuller's Case, 12 Co. Rep. 41 (1607) and compare also the similar technique in Commissions of Inquiry, 12 Co. Rep., 31 (1607).

[43] Tomlinson's Case, 12 Co. Rep. 104 (1604).

[44] In many instances rules that were in England specifically justified as exercises of royal prerogative are dealt with in America without reference to this justification as general common law practice, e.g. Stoughton v. Baker, 4 Mass. 522 (1808). In the early decades of the republic there are a great number of cases where the problem of prerogative occurs. Without attempting to make an exhaustive catalogue the following cases may be regarded as typical of different points of view. Atty. General v. Utica Insurance Co., 2 Johns. Ch. 371, 388 (1817); People v. Thurman, 3 Cowen 16 (Sup. Ct. 1824); Jackson v. Fitzsimmons, 10 Wend., 9 (Sup. Ct. 1832); Fairfax v. Hunter's Lessee, 7 Cranch 603, 631 (U. S. 1812); Kendall v. United States, 12 Pet. 524 (U. S. 1838); The Emulous, 1 Gall. 563, 580 C. C. Mass. (1813); U. S. v. Hoar, 2 Mason 311, 315 (1821); Crawford v. Comm., 1 Watts 480 (Pa. 1833); Martin v. Comm., 1 Mass. 347 (1805); Vaux v. Nesbit, 1 McCord Eq. 352 (S. C. 1825).

procedural powers and devices, all unquestionably part of the English common law or equity systems, that were not employed here after 1776, chiefly because they were associated with monarchical government. Their future availability, since they are by every common law test due process, rests actually upon a shift in emphasis in our political thinking, a shift which every increase in central authority and every diminution in local authority brings nearer. The further we drift from the inhibitions of 18th century federal theory toward the unitary ideas now current, the more likely is the shift. It is more usual today to talk of public interest instead of the people's interest, and the public interest can with little trouble become the State. There are already perceptible some signs of this transition.

In *U. S. v. Curtis Wright Corporation*[45] Mr. Justice Sutherland remarked, "As a result of the separation from Great Britain by the colonies acting as a unit the power of external sovereignty passed from the crown not to the colonies severally but to the colonies in their collective and corporate character as the United States of America."[46] "In this vast external realm with its important, complicated, delicate and manifold problems the President alone has the

145

---

[45] 299 U. S. 304 (1936).
[46] 299 U. S. 304, 316 (1936). The court cites Penhallow v. Doane's Adm., 3 Dall. 54, 80-1 (U. S. 1795). There is nothing in the passages cited to support the explicit statement of Sutherland, J. The furthest Patterson, J. goes is to remark: "The truth is that the States individually were not known or recognized as sovereign by foreign nations nor are they now: the states collectively under Congress as the connecting point, or head, were acknowledged by sovereign powers as sovereign. . . ." Note further Iredell, J.'s words (*id.* at 91) regarding the *status quo* before the Articles of Confederation: ". . . previously thereto they [the Congress] did exercise with the acquiescence of the states high powers of what I may perhaps with propriety for distinction call external sovereignty. . . ." Again (at 92) "If Congress previous to the articles of confederation possessed any authority it was an authority as I have shown derived from the people of each province in the first instance." Compare also Chase, J.'s opinion in Ware v. Hylton, 3 Dall. 199, 231-232 (U. S. 1796). *Cf.* also McIlvaine v. Coxe's Lessees, 4 Cranch 209, 212 (U. S. 1808).
It is certainly open to doubt whether or not the treaty with Great Britain (September 3, 1783) "gave practical application" to the "passing" of sovereignty from Great Britain to the Union. (299 U. S. at 317.) In Article I His Britainic Majesty acknowledges the "said United States *vis.* New Hampshire, Massachusetts Bay, Rhode Island etc. to be free sovereign and independent States." 1 MALLOY, TREATIES, CONVENTIONS ETC. OF THE U. S. (1910) 587. This form of acknowledgement was necessary owing to the anterior corporate identity of each colony as a matter of English law. In point of form it recalls the first international act entered into by the rebels, the treaty of amity and commerce with France (Feb. 6, 1775). Here the contracting parties are the most Christian King and the "Thirteen United States of North America to wit New Hampshire Massachusetts Bay . . ." etc. (1 MALLOY, TREATIES, CONVENTIONS ETC. OF THE U. S. [1910] 468). It is reasonably certain that at the time of the conclusion of the treaty of peace with Great Britain, the states regarded themselves as a unit in foreign relations because of the Articles of Confederation. *Cf.* the resolution of Congress, May 7, 1784: "That these United States be considered in all such treaties in every case rising

power to speak or listen as a representative of the nation."[47]   To one familiar with the panoply of procedural devices which the English crown possessed in respect of its prerogative in foreign affairs, the learned justice's manipulation of the political scientists' classification of sovereignty and his averment that external sovereignty passed from the crown to the Union is fraught with future consequence. It is so because the novel idea that external sovereignty passed from king to the Union implies a transfer of the common law powers connected therewith, especially since Mr. Justice Sutherland states that "the powers of external sovereignty do not depend upon affirmative grants of the constitution." Mr. Justice Sutherland ignores the theory of control over foreign affairs both before and under the Confederation[48] and the fact that in 1787 the grant to the president of a share in the treaty making power was regarded as a matter requiring explanation and justification.[49] He chose instead to frame an opinion in language closely parallel to the description of royal prerogative in foreign affairs

146

---

under them as one nation, upon the principles of the Federal Constitution." 6 WHARTON, REVOLUTIONARY DIPLOMATIC CORRESPONDENCE (1889), 802.

Sutherland, J.'s view of sovereignty passing from the British crown to the union appears to be a perversion of the dictum of Jay, C. J. in Chisholm's Executors v. Georgia, 3 Dall. 419, 470 (U. S. 1799) to the effect that sovereignty passed from the crown to the people. Under the theories prevailing in the early years of the republic this was a notion basically different from Justice Sutherland's.

[48] "He *makes* treaties with the advice and consent of the Senate; but he alone negotiates. Into the field of negotiation the Senate cannot intrude." 299 U. S. at 319. This seems a somewhat misleading description of presidential authority in foreign affairs. During Washington's administration the Senate was frequently consulted before negotiations, 5 MOORE, DIGEST OF INTERNATIONAL LAW (1906) 196 and this has been done occasionally since, CRANDALL, TREATIES, THEIR MAKING AND ENFORCEMENT (1904) 51-61. The power of the Senate to advise and consent has been wielded as an effective condition precedent of amending negotiations. Furthermore, the power of Congress over appropriations is a possible means of affecting negotiations. There can be no question of the restrictive effect upon the negotiating power in extant legislation: as witness the copyright laws.

[49] Discussed in 1 WHARTON, *op. cit. supra* note 46, §§ 103, 210. *Cf.* also the letter addressed to the states April 13, 1787 in 32 JOURNALS OF CONT. CONGRESS 176. If the Union's original sovereignty was as plenary as Mr. Justice Sutherland avers, it is difficult to explain the weak-kneed language of Article VI of the Articles of Confederation respecting the powers of states to send Embassies, make treaties, make war etc. *Cf.* Hamilton at the New York convention to ratify the constitution: "Under the old Confederation the important powers of declaring war, making peace etc. can be exercised by nine states," 2 ELLIOT, DEBATES 263.

[*] The discussions in the FEDERALIST (Ford ed. 1898) are in terms of joint or concurrent power in respect of treaties when Hamilton is writing (no. 66; no. 69; no. 75). Jay, in no. 64 emphasizes particularly the role of the Senate. Parts of these passages are embodied in the discussion of Story in 3 COMMENTARIES ON THE CONSTITUTION (1833) 354 *et seq.* They are mentioned here because Sutherland, J., making an appeal to history by quoting Marshall's remarks of March 7, 1800 in support of his own views, is attempting to establish an historical justification for his thesis regarding "the plenary and exclusive power of the president as the sole organ of the federal government in the field of international relations." 299 U. S. 320. The remarks in the FEDERALIST suggest that the views of Sutherland, J., lack a comprehensive historical foundation.

in the *Ship Money Case.*[50]   The parallel is so close indeed as to suggest
at once that an embargo statute can be enforced by the due process of
ne exeat.[51] And it also suggests that once we recommit to our sovereign
this writ we recommit the full and nearly untrammelled rights over the
subjects' movements that prevailed in 1607.

---

[50] Rex v. Hampden (1637) in 3 HOWELL, STATE TRIALS 825 *et seq.*
St. John for the defendant (*id.* at 860) :

"My lords, by the Law the king is *pater-familias,* which by the Law of
OEconomick is, not only to keep peace at home, but to protect his wife and
children, and whole family from abroad.   It is his vigilancy and watchfulness
that discovers who are our friends, and who are our foes; and that after such
discovery first warns us of them; for he only hath power to make war and
peace."
Littleton, for the crown (*id.* at 930) :
"Again it is a Droit Royal to meddle with war and peace, subjects have
nothing to do with it.   Sometimes dangers are fit to be communicated to the
people, and sometimes not.   The king should best know what is done abroad,
who hath his close council of war; he knows what is done abroad, what can
the people tell of these things? and it is very fit that preparation be made
before-hand. . . ."
Berkley, J. (*id.* at 1098) :
"There are two maxims of the law of England, which plainly disprove
Mr. Holborne's supposed policy.   The first is, 'That the king is a person trusted
with the state of the commonwealth.'   The second of these maxims is, 'That the
king cannot do wrong.'   Upon these two maxims, the 'Jura summae majestatis'
are grounded, with which none but the king himself (not his high court of
parliament without leave) hath to meddle, as, namely, war and peace, value
of coin, parliament at pleasure, power to dispense with penal laws, and divers
others; amongst which I range these also, of regal power to command provision (in case of necessity) of means from the subjects, to be adjoined to the
king's own means for the defence of the commonwealth, for the preservation
of the 'salus reip.'   Otherwise I do not understand how the king's majesty may
be said to have the majestical right, and power of a free monarch."
Hutton, J. (*id.* at 1194) :
"I confess there are some inseparable prerogatives belonging to the crown,
such as the parliament cannot sever from it . . . such is the care for the defence of the kingdom, which belongeth inseparably to the crown, as head and
supreme protector of the kingdom: So that if an act of parliament should
enact that he should not defend the kingdom, or that the king should have no
aid from his subjects to defend the kingdom, these acts would not bind, because
they would be against natural reason. . . ."
[51] This writ has been styled a "prerogative writ."   It is commonly called *ne
exeat regno* although the title in 1 FITZHERBERT, NATURA BREVIUM (9th ed. 1794)
85 is "de Securitate inveniendo quod se non divertat ad Partes exteras, sine Licentia
Regis."   Fitzherbert prefaces his discussion by averring that at common law a man
might go out of the realm for whatever purpose he pleased, but because he was
bound to defend the king and realm, the crown at its pleasure could order a
man to remain at home.   The writ was addressed either to the individual or to the sheriff or justices of the peace.   In the latter case the officer was
ordered to compel the individual to find security.   There is no doubt of the great
antiquity of royal prerogative to forbid subjects to leave the country.   COKE,
THIRD INSTITUTE 178 suggests it is derived from the restrictions upon the movement of clerks dating from the Constitutions of Clarendon (1164).   The Magna
Carta of 1215 contained a provision (c. 42) respecting the subjects' freedom of
movement, not contained in the confirmation of 1217.   There are entries in the
extant fine and close rolls of John's reign indicating the connection of the *ne exeat*
with both war power and a general supervision of exportation (*e.g.* Rot. Lit. Clause
94, 118, 120, 133, 137, 148b).   The entry *id.* at 91 (1207) is worded to indicate the

147

Less than a year after the *Curtis Wright* case was decided the Congress enacted a statute which permits the Attorney General to intervene as a party in private litigation where a constitutional issue is raised and to take an appeal directly to the Supreme Court.[52] Obviously it is possible to excuse such intervention as a matter of theory on the general ground that the people have an interest in having the actions of their agents, the legislators, upheld. The new enactment is, however, so sharply reminiscent of the right possessed by the crown at common law to have proceedings stayed when its interests were involved until it could intervene (the *non procedendo rege inconsulto*)[53] and have the

---

rule of license to depart is general. See also *id.* at 355 (2 Hy. III). There are many entries in the letters close of Henry III to indicate the crown continued to enjoin passage abroad. (*Cf.* Fleta 383 s. 1, 2; Britton, c. 123.) By statute 5 Ric. II c. 2 s. 6, 7, which was aimed at embargoing the exportation of precious metals and jewels, the restriction is made general excepting great lords, soldiers and notable merchants. This statute was repealed by 4 Jac. I c. 1. This repeal does not appear to have affected old prerogatives for in BACON'S ORDINANCES (15 SPEDDING, WORKS OF BACON 369) no. 89 it is stated that the writ is granted "in respect of attempts prejudicial to the king and state" upon the prayer of any of the principal secretaries without causes showing. The history is discussed in BEAMES, BRIEF VIEW OF THE WRIT NE EXEAT (Am. Ed. 1821) c. 1. Various cases relating to the writ are there collected. It should also be observed that a phase of the same prerogative right was to order the return of an absent subject, and upon failure to appear, the subject's property could be taken in to the king's hand. Dyer 168; Cater's Case, 1 Leonard 8.

[52] Pub. L. No. 352, 75 Cong. 1 Sess. *Cf.* on this Legis. (1938) 38 COLUMBIA LAW REV. 153.

[53] The history of this writ is yet to be written. Examples of forms used in REGISTRUM BREVIUM (1687) 220. The writ takes its origin apparently in part from the recognized prerogative of the crown in early times in difficult matters concerning the administration of justice (*e.g.* NORTHUMBERLAND ASSIZE ROLLS [88 SURTEES SOC.] 85, 111; SELECT PLEAS OF THE CROWN [SELDEN SOC.] pl. 113; 2 MADOX, HISTORY OF THE EXCHEQUER (2d ed. 1769) 116; in part from the position of the crown as suzerain in matters respecting tenure; and in part from the extensive jurisdiction over franchise rights. Most of the Yearbook cases have to do with questions connected with these two latter phases of royal interest. The most comprehensive and incisive discussion of the writ and its use is Bacon's argument in the case of Brownlow v. Cox and Michell, Moore 842 (1616); 3 Bulstrode 32 (1616). This argument is published in 1 HARGRAVE, COLLECTANEA JURIDICA (1791) 168 *et seq.*; 15 SPEDDING, *op. cit. supra* note 51 at 257. There is some modern discussion of the growth of the rule that no plea involving the king's interest could be proceeded with by royal justice without the king's command in EHRLICH, PROCEEDINGS AGAINST THE CROWN (1216-1377) [6 OXFORD STUDIES 1921], 144-5, 152, 155.

As Bacon expressed it "The efficient of this writ is that same *primogenita pars legis* which we call the king's prerogative; and, namely that branch of it which is the king's prerogative in suits. . . ." The effect of the *non procedendo* is to make the crown a party to the litigation, and the seventeenth century procedure establishes that the Attorney General appeared to argue the allowance. The king being made a party, the practice was for the case to be removed to Chancery which proceeded on the common law or Latin Side. This rule was founded upon the notion that a cause must go where the king's interest was most favored, although this idea was later expressed in terms of hastening the king's business. Sir Edward Coke's Case, Godbolt 291 (1624). After the Restoration there is authority to show that the Exchequer was employed as the forum to which cases involving the king's interest were removed. Rex v. Cotton, Parker 112 (1751);

case removed to Chancery that, we may confidently predict, no due process argument will prevail against the constitutional validity of this statute.[54]

If what I have suggested respecting the implications of due process seems fanciful, it may be sobering to reflect for a moment upon the process of Exchequer. Long ago Mr. Justice Curtis brandished the *extent* as an historical justification for the use of distress warrants to collect taxes. In his day there was small need for the imitation of a process as elaborate and vicious as that of the English Exchequer. But with the fantastic expansion of government credit, the spawning of infinite lending agencies, it is not unreasonable to assume that with the ancient benison of the Supreme Bench the revival of the *extendi facias* will strengthen the sinews of state.[55]

Anon., 1 Anstruther 205 (1793). The last case suggests that by the end of the eighteenth century, injunction rather than the old fashioned *non procedendo* was employed.

The modern lawyer may have difficulty in discerning the parallel suggested in the text. It should be remarked, however, that in the English common law even where the matter in issue concerned a question of property, if the crown's interest was in any way involved, since this trenched upon the prerogative, the issue was also a question of state, a constitutional matter. Note finally, the cogent argument of Bacon that where new offices are created if these be drawn in question the writ lies (SPEDDING, *supra* at 204). The appointive power is conceived at once as a prerogative and as a perquisite having property value.

[54] The problem presented by the language of Article III of the Constitution rests on a different historical foundation.

[55] American courts have exhibited a certain bias favoring the reception of royal fiscal prerogatives, *cf.* South Philadelphia Banks Insolvency, 295 Pa. 433, 145 Atl. 520 (1929); U. S. Fidelity and Guaranty Co. v. Carter, 161 Va. 381, 170 S. E., 764 (1933); *contra* Fidelity and Deposit Co. of Maryland v. Brucker, 205 Ind. 273, 183 N. E. 668 (1933) but compare the array of cases there cited; Crane, *A Royal Prerogative in the United States* (1928) 34 W. VA. L. Q. 317. There is actually little accurate information available in these opinions respecting the nature and scope of Exchequer process, the most drastic of which became the *extendi facias*.

The extent procedure is sketched by Curtis, J. in Murray v. Hoboken, *supra*, n. 6. There are detailed accounts in WEST, A TREATISE ON THE LAW AND PRACTICE OF EXTENTS (1817); CHITTY, PRACTICE ON THE LAW OF THE PREROGATIVES OF THE CROWN (1820) 262 *et seq.*; PRICE, TREATISE ON THE LAW AND PRACTICE OF THE EXCHEQUER (1830) 162, 233, Ch. XIV *passim*.

Forms of the writ are in BROWN, COMPENDIUM OF THE SEVERAL BRANCHES OF PRACTICE IN THE COURT OF EXCHEQUER (1688) 412 *et seq.*; WEST, *supra* App. 16.

There is some question at what date the *extendi facias* became crown process of execution against debtors. The writ is founded on the theory that "at the common law the body, the land and the goods of the accountant, or the king's debtor were liable to the king's execution." Harbert's Case, 3 Co. Rep., 11b (1584). The *extendi facias* as it was used after STAT. 33 Hy. VIII c. 39 permits execution simultaneously against all. On the authority of Sir Thomas Cecil's Case 7 Co. Rep. 18b (1599) it is usually averred that the STAT. 33 Hy. VIII c. 39 created the remedy for the crown. WEST, *supra* at 2; BROWN, *supra* at 3. Although American courts are not prone to distinguish sharply between common law remedies and those established before 1800 by Act of Parliament, it is obvious this line of distinction is not without significance in any due process inquiry, the more so here as the exact status of Exchequer precedents outside the Exchequer itself was still mooted in

149

All of this is pretty grim. And I have no doubt that counsel for the respondent in *U. S. v. Wood* felt much the same way when their objections to federal employees upon the jury were mowed down by the solicitor-general's barrage of yearbook cases. We have got this mode of due process interpretation and what I have suggested comes to this—

---

the 16th century: Case of Mines, 1 Plowden 310 (1568) ; Lane's Case, 2 Co. Rep. 1621 (1596). It is further to be noted that our courts are not disposed to go behind Coke's expositions of the crown's fiscal rights as set forth in his REPORTS and INSTITUTES. But even a casual survey of available data regarding exchequer practice discloses that Coke's basic proposition regarding the liability of the king's debtor must be subject to much qualification. Apart from the fact that the words "at common law" beg all questions of historical evolution, Coke's formula ignores certain basic distinctions both in respect of liability and mode of execution that governed administrative policy in the Middle Ages. In the first place there were distinctions as to the manner in which the debt arose, *viz.*; fine, tallage, oblates, feudal due. Secondly, there were distinctions based upon status whether official or social-tenurial. That these distinctions obtained as early as the reign of Henry II is evident from the DIALOGUE OF THE EXCHEQUER (II, iii, xiii, xiv) and they prevailed well into the fourteenth century. 2 MADOX, HISTORY OF THE EXCHEQUER [1769 ed] c. 23. They determine both what assets are liable to execution as well as the order of liability.

It is difficult to make any generalization about the situation of crown debtors for the period between the DIALOGUE (*ca.* 1178) and 1215 partly because norm cannot readily be distinguished from aberration at a time when any favor was for sale, and partly because a fiscal representative usually stands between the exchequer and the debtor. Moreover, when any direct debt is contracted some security is exacted on which the entries are rarely specific. (But *cf.* ROT. DE OBLATIS [Hardy Ed.] 108, 192). On the point of the order of liability of assets it appears that although the Dialogue shows chattels are first in the order of execution, in John's reign the debtor's land was taken, *cf.* ROT. DE OBLATIS, 103; ROT. LITT. CLAUS. 56; 85; EARLIEST LINCOLNSHIRE ASSIZE ROLL (Stenton Ed.) no. 1143; 6 CURIA REGIS ROLLS, 49, and note the case 3 CURIA REGIS ROLLS, 287, where the son of the debtor holds lands at farm until discharge. The disseisin of lands by the crown followed as of course in cases of offences, *e.g.* ROT. LITT. CLAUS. 87b, 91b. In the later rolls of John's reign there are indications of wholesale disseisins but little or nothing to show if these were for debts, although a situation must have existed which warranted Article 9 of Magna Carta whereby the crown bound itself to proceed in the first instance against a debtor's chattels. It is to be observed, however, that while article 9 is an implicit recognition of the ultimate liability of lands, it may be taken as establishing a basic rule respecting precedent liability of chattels over land on crown execution. This is reflected in the later statutes, the so-called Statute of Rhuddlan (1 STAT. OF REALM 69) and the *De Districtione Scaccarii* (1 STAT. OF THE REALM 197).

These general rules did not affect the case of the sheriff who in the 13th century was bound by an oath in broad terms (2 MADOX, *supra* at 147), and a recognizance (3 RED BOOK OF THE EXCHEQUER [R. S.] cccx). Against such defaulters a single process for chattels, lands and body might issue. 2 MADOX, *supra* at 237-8. The scope of these precepts corresponds with the later *extendi facias* and raises the question whether or not the process for defaulting sheriffs may have been adapted for use against ordinary debtors.

There is little to indicate what was the normal course of Exchequer process during the 13th—16th centuries, the *extendi facias* appears first in the Close Rolls of John. I ROT. LITT. CLAUS., 4, 5b. From the wording of the early writs it must even then (1204) have been established practice to extend *viz.* to survey and value lands coming into the king's hands by way of escheat (*ibid.*, 7b). The function of these early writs appears primarily to make a record although an order to seize some third party of all or a portion of the lands extended is often included (*cf. ibid.*, 8b and 12b; 13b). An entry in the fine rolls of 1204 regarding an extent to settle the terms of a ferm indicates clearly enough that the matter of

150

that we had best gird our young men to deal competently with it. For if, in Coke's phrase, good pleading is the heartstring of the common law, it can be likewise the bowstring of constitutional right.

JULIUS GOEBEL, JR.

COLUMBIA UNIVERSITY SCHOOL OF LAW.

---

record is the real purpose of the writ. ROT. DE OBLATIS, 212. This can be further established by the collation of cases (*temp.* Henry III) in the CALENDAR OF IN-QUISITIONS MISCELLANEOUS with close roll entries respecting the same tenements. The proper place of return for these writs was the Exchequer. The Ordinance 16 EDW. II (1323) provides that the king's Remembrancer had custody of extents concerning the crown, 3 RED BOOK OF THE EXCHEQUER, 857.

While there is no doubt that the crown could, during the 13th century, proceed against the lands of debtors either by way of distraint or final process the printed records are provokingly silent on the form of process. Since by the Statute of Merchants (1283) 13 EDW. I, st. 3, and the Statute of Westminster II (1285) c. 18 a right of execution on lands was given to private parties and extent was stipulated, it seems probable that the crown was already using this remedy against debtors. The orthodox learning is that the remedies of these statutes derived from practice respecting the Jewry, 3 HOLDSWORTH, HISTORY OF ENGLISH LAW, 131. The alternative avenue of approach here indicated deserves further investigation, particularly as the extent procedure becomes used for the assessment of sequestered franchises (FOWLER, ROLLS FROM THE OFFICE OF THE SHERIFF OF BEDS, AND BUCKS 1332-34 [1929] 39) and for inquest into violations of mortmain statutes.

As the rule respecting the liability of debtor's lands became cast in general form (*e.g.* Y. B. 43 EDW. III pl. 27, f. 98) it is possible that process tended to become more uniform than it seems to have been in earlier times.

With regard to crown debtor's liability to arrest the available sources have never been analyzed. The distinctions already spoken of obtained during the 12th-13th centuries. The *Statute of Marlborough* (1267) 1 STAT. REALM 19 which allowed a capias in actions of account can be interpreted to include the crown. On the other hand the statute *de Districtione Scacc.* 1 STAT. REALM 197 leaves open the question as to how an absent debtor with neither chattels nor lands could be dealt with. This was not settled until 19 EDW. II when the ordinances established that the crown had the common law remedy of account, 3 RED BOOK OF THE EXCHEQUER 944. By the Statute of Westminster II, c. 77 process here would proceed to the exigent. This Exchequer rule was no limitation upon the crown as witness CAL. PAT. ROLLS 1345-48, 32, where collectors of tenths and fifteenths are authorized to arrest and imprison at the king's pleasure persons failing to pay.

As the foregoing fugitive observations may suggest the question of Exchequer process is considerably more complicated than one would assume from *Harbert's Case* and the remarks in later textbooks. It deserves painstaking study particularly in view of the posture of American courts toward the matter of reception of fiscal prerogatives.

151

INTRODUCTION:

J. WILLARD HURST AND THE COMMON LAW TRADITION IN AMERICAN LEGAL HISTORIOGRAPHY*

ROBERT W. GORDON

State University of New York at Buffalo

In 1963 the Italian historiographer Arnaldo Momigliano told an assembly of legal historians that they were gathered to celebrate "a historical event of some importance, the end of history of law as an autonomous branch of historical research." At least in the historiography of ancient law, he said, "the elimination of history of law as independent history now seems to me to be settled."

> Nor is it important to debate whether it was Max Weber or the French school of sociology or the teaching of Marx and Engels or, finally, the influence of Marc Bloch that precipitated this solution. It is inherent in the general recognition that law, as a systematization of social relations at a given level, cannot be understood without an analysis of the sexual orientations, the moral and religious beliefs, the economic production and the military forces that characterize a given society at a given moment, and are expressed in associations of individuals and in conflicts. It is conceivable today that history of literature, history of art, history of science, and history of religion can each retain some sort of autonomy, inasmuch as each is concerned with a specific activity of man. But what is no longer conceivable is that history of law should be autonomous; for by its very nature it is a formulation of human relations rooted in manifold human activities. And if, in some civilizations, there is a class of jurisconsults with special rules of conduct and of reasoning, this too is a social phenomenon to be interpreted.[1]

In the historiography of American law, the process Momigliano thus described as completed is only just beginning, for American legal historians have usually worked on the assumption that, at least for the purpose of dividing academic labor, it makes sense to identify a sphere of "legal" phenomena in society, and to write about how these have changed over time. It has never, of course, been possible to mark off the precise boundaries of such a field, but as a practical matter it almost inevitably turns out that they are drawn around the institutions,

---

* This essay owes much to conversations with Paul R. Duggan, Marc Galanter, David Hollinger, Stewart Macaulay, John Henry Schlegel, David Trubek and Mark Tushnet, and to the members of the Faculty Seminar on Law and Development of the SUNY at Buffalo Law School, who heard and criticized an earlier version. They do not by any means all share the views reported here; and are not responsible for errors and distortions.

1. A.D. Momigliano, "The Consequences of New Trends in the History of Ancient Law," in Momigliano, *Studies in Historiography* 239, 240-241 (1966).

the occupations, the ideas and the procedures that have the appearance at any one time of being *distinctively legal*.[2] One might crudely represent this way of looking at law in society as follows:

input ———→ "law" ———→ output

Inside the box is "the law," whatever appears autonomous about the legal order—courts, equitable maxims, motions for summary judgment; outside lies "society," the wide realm of the nonlegal, the political, economic, religious, social; the "inputs" are social influences upon the shape of the mass of things inside the law-box, the "outputs" the effects, or impact, of the mass upon society. Within the structure of this crude model there is, of course, a great range of possible theories of law, from a theory asserting that law derives its shape almost wholly from sources within the box (i.e. that it is really autonomous as well as seeming so), to one claiming that the box is really empty, the apparent distinctiveness of its contents illusory, since they are all the product of external social forces. Yet even those who incline to the latter view[3] take the contents of the box, epiphenomenal

153

---

2. This would seem to imply that no one could write the legal history of a society that had no notion of "law" as a bundle of specialized activities distinct from, and to some extent autonomous of, other social phenomena—e.g., a society that did not distinguish between legal and religious norms. Legal historians usually solve this problem by treating of the aspects of such societies that appear to serve counterpart social functions to those of the relatively autonomous legal systems. For example, courts perform certain dispute settlement functions in modern Western societies which might, in other societies of the past, have been performed by councils of warriors or village elders. The warriors or elders will therefore be treated in the legal history of the other society. Yet though dispute settlement may be done by warriors or elders in modern Western societies also, that is not "law" and is therefore usually of no interest to legal historians This somewhat curious manner of defining the field of specialization is partly responsible for the fact that focus abruptly shifts (and narrows) whenever a society exhibits traces of an autonomous legal order. On this point, see text at notes 29-31, 40-44, *infra*. On the emergence of "autonomous" legal orders in modern societies, see *Max Weber on Law and Economy in Society* (Rheinstein ed. 1954), especially chs. 7-9, 11; for a brilliant recent reinterpretation, Roberto Mangabeira Unger, *Law in Modern Society* (forthcoming, 1976), especially at 52ff.

3. Lawrence M. Friedman probably inclines as far as anyone. See e.g., his *History of American Law* (1973):
   This book treats American law . . . not as a kingdom unto itself, not as a set of rules and concepts, not as the province of lawyers alone, but as a mirror of society. It takes nothing as historical accident, nothing as autonomous, everything as relative and molded by economy and society. . . . The [legal] system works like a blind, insensate machine. It does the bidding of those whose hands are on the controls. . . . [T]he strongest ingredient in American law, at any given time, is the present: current emotions, real economic interests, concrete political groups.

though they may be, as the main subject-matter of concern to the legal historian. Not that this is the only way of treating law historically, as Momigliano's words make clear;[4] but it probably *is* the only way for someone who defines himself as a "legal" historian; he has no choice.

Where he does have a choice, and an important one, is between writing internal and external legal history.[5] The internal legal historian stays as much as possible within the box of distinctive-appearing legal things; his sources are legal, and so are the basic matters he wants to describe or explain, such as changes in pleading rules, in the jurisdiction of a court, the texts assigned to beginning law students, or the doctrine of contributory negligence. The external historian writes about the interaction between the boxful of legal things and the wider society of which they are a part, in particular to explore the social context of law and its social effects, and he is usually looking for conclusions about those effects.

154

Up until very recently, and with few exceptions, American legal history has been of the internal kind. From time to time the few proponents of external history would direct an exasperated complaint against this situation, without much altering it.[6]

Id. at 10, 14. Professor Friedman acknowledges the existence of legal phenomena that are purely "internal" or "formal"—technical aspects of the system that can be altered or adjusted without affecting much (if at all) the outside society. See his "Law Reform in Historical Perspective," 13 *St. Louis U.L.J.* 351 (1969). He also recognizes that people living in some societies may perceive their legal order to be autonomous and to associate autonomy with legitimacy; he would classify such beliefs as part of a society's "legal culture"— "values and attitudes which . . . determine the place of the legal system in the culture of the society as a whole." See his "Legal Culture and Social Development," 4 *L. & Soc'y. Rev.* 29, 34 (1969).

4. Some scholars would go further than Momigliano; see, e.g., Richard L. Abel, "A Comparative Theory of Dispute Institutions in Society," 8 *L. & Soc'y Rev.* 217, 221-224 (1973), for the views of a legal anthropologist who has given up on "law" altogether as a useful organizing concept in social research.

5. These terms are borrowed from T.S. Kuhn's treatments of (remarkably similar!) problems in the historiography of science. See especially his "Relations between History and History of Science," 100 *Daedalus* 271, 279 (1971). "External history" seems to me a better label than "social" history because it is more inclusive; specifically, it includes intellectual and cultural history.

6. The best of these are, I think, Daniel J. Boorstin, "Tradition and Method in Legal History," 54 *Harv. L. Rev.* 424 (1951); George L. Haskins, "Law and Colonial Society," 9 *Am. Q.* 354 (1957); Stanley N. Katz, "Looking Backward: The Early History of American Law," 33 *U. Chi. L. Rev.* 867 (1966); Lawrence M. Friedman, "Some Problems and Possibilities of American Legal History," in *The State of American History* 3 (Bass ed. 1970); Morton J. Horwitz, "The Conservative Tradition in the Writing of American Legal History," 17 *Am. J. Leg. Hist.* 275 (1973); Herbert Alan Johnson, "American Colonial Legal History: A Historiographical Interpretation," in *Perspectives on Early American History* 250 (Vaughan & Billias eds. 1973), hereinafter Johnson, "Colonial Legal History"; and the many

As it happens, I tend to sympathize with most of these complaints, but writing another one is not my present purpose, since others have already said trenchantly what needed to be said; and in any case the situation is rapidly improving and there is no need for one. At this point it is more interesting to ask how the tradition of internal historiography got itself established, how it managed to last so long, and what the consequences of its ascendancy were for historical writing about American law. With that kind of perspective it might be possible adequately to assess the achievement of James Willard Hurst, the legal historian who broke decisively with the main tradition over thirty years ago, and who has since become the leading exponent and practitioner of an external historiography.

With the purpose of attempting that assessment in mind, the brief essay that follows tries to sketch the broad outlines of the paths taken by American legal historians since the beginnings of their discipline in the 1880's.[7] As I see it, there was a Classical Period from about 1880 to 1900, followed by a long slump lasting until about 1930; a First Revival of interest and activity in legal-historical studies from the 1930's through the early 1960's; then a Second Revival starting around 1970 and still going strong.[8]

155

---

historiographical contributions of Willard Hurst, of which the most comprehensive, as well as the most recent, is "Legal Elements in United States History," in *Law in American History* 3 (Fleming & Bailyn eds. 1971), hereinafter Hurst, "Legal Elements." Much acerbic and astute criticism of the state of the art has appeared over the years in the *Annual Survey of American Law's* "Legal History" sections written by John Phillip Reid (1962-66); Reid and William E. Nelson (1969-70); and Nelson (1967-69; 1973-present). I am very indebted to all the articles cited here. One of the many ironies connected with American legal history is that its shortcomings have called forth so useful a historiographical literature.

7. See Calvin Woodard, "History, Legal History, and Legal Education," 53 *Va. L. Rev.* 89 (1967) for a similar sketch arriving at somewhat different conclusions.

8. Some readers may find my idea of what constitutes "American legal history" idiosyncratic—both too inclusive and too exclusive. It includes studies in *English* legal history in the 1880s and 90s, but then drops these; and excludes constitutional, administrative, and other plausible candidates for the category of American legal history throughout. Let me try to justify this. Hardly anything one could call American legal history was written in the 1880s and 90s, but one has to say something about the legal history that was written (English, mostly), because it exerted such a strong influence on what came later. After that I try to stick to the American side, including in the "legal history" field whatever contemporaries were likely to include, which until recently meant the history of "private law" subjects and not much else except perhaps constitutional history, which I do not feel competent to discuss, but which I gather has suffered from comparable if considerably less severe limitations. See the bibliographical note, and sources there cited, in Harold M. Hyman, *A More Perfect Union* 557-560 (1973). Notions of what legal history is about are, of course, rapidly changing (as witness the essays in this issue) thanks in large part to the work of Willard Hurst and his school. See text at notes 132-135, *infra*.

Some hedges and qualifications are in order. I do not try here to provide a comprehensive bibliographical survey; there are several excellent ones available.[9] I shall have very little to say about the literature of the Second Revival, contemporary historiography, since I plan to write about that on another occasion. And I can't do here what really ought some day to be done: a full-blooded social history of legal historiography in this country, showing the relationship of attempts to reconstruct the legal past to changes in the situation of lawyers generally, not only in the schools but in practice and in politics; and to intellectual developments outside the law, especially in philosophy and the social sciences.[10] In other words, this story is properly a minor subtheme of a much larger one—which remains untold because its telling has had to wait upon the development of an external legal historiography.[11] In this piece there are

156

---

9. See, e.g., Reid & Nelson, *Ann. Survey Am. L., supra,* note 6; Friedman, *History of American Law, supra,* note 3, at 596-621; Friedman *supra,* note 6; Johnson, "Colonial Legal History"; David H. Flaherty, "An Introduction to Early American Legal History," in *Essays in the History of Early American Law* (Flaherty ed. 1969); Wythe Holt, "Now and Then: The Uncertain State of Nineteenth Century American Legal History," 7 *Ind. L. Rev.* 615 (1974); and Harry N. Scheiber, "Federalism and the American Economic Order," 10 *L. & Soc'y Rev.* 57 (1975) (in this issue, *infra*).

10. For an example of the exciting possibilities of a historiography relating law and lawyers to a wider culture, see William J. Bouwsma, "Lawyers and Early Modern Culture," 73 *Am. Hist. Rev.* 303 (1973) and the contributions already made to such a history cited in *id.* at 304 n.4.

11. Friedman, *History, supra,* note 13, at 567-595 sketches a provocative brief outline of 20th century American legal history. The best general secondary treatment of the history of the American bar remains, 25 years later, Willard Hurst, *The Growth of American Law: The Lawmakers* [hereinafter Hurst, *Lawmakers*] 249-375 (1950), a circumstance that probably gives the author little satisfaction. The history of legal education has been well treated recently in Robert Stevens, "Two Cheers for 1870: the American Law School," in *Law in American History* 405, *supra,* note 6; Jerold S. Auerbach, "Equity and Amity: Law Teachers and Practitioners, 1900-1922," *Id.* at 551; and William Twining, *Karl Llewellyn and the Realist Movement* (1973). Two books are especially successful at relating legal to philosophical thought in the 20th century: Morton White, *Social Thought in America: The Revolt Against Formalism* (2d ed. 1957) and David A. Hollinger, *Morris R. Cohen and the Scientific Ideal* (1975). There are several studies of Realism: among them Wilfrid E. Rumble, Jr., *American Legal Realism: Skepticism, Reform, and the Judicial Process* (1968); Calvin Woodard, "The Limits of Legal Realism; an Historical Perspective," 54 *Va. L. Rev.* 689 (1968); Twining, *supra,* this note; Edward A. Purcell, Jr., *The Crisis of Democratic Theory* (1971); and G. Edward White, "From Sociological Jurisprudence to Realism: Jurisprudence and Social Change in Early Twentieth Century America," 58 *Va. L. Rev.* 999 (1972). This literature on Realism, though interesting and useful, still leaves one with the feeling that something important has been left out. Except for Twining, the authors tend to treat the Realists as (rather inept) legal philosophers, quoting from their more speculative work and from their debates on the nature of law with critics like Roscoe Pound and Morris Cohen. What gets slighted in the process is most of the stuff that the Realists themselves considered their most important work: their studies of subjects like procedure and commercial law. Research

hints and whispers about the important relationships, but nothing more.

I

At the beginning of professional legal historiography in the United States which, for convenience, may be taken to be the publication by Henry Adams and his students of their *Essays in Anglo-Saxon Law* in 1876, nobody would have drawn a distinction between legal history and any other kind. For the first generation of professional historians in this country borrowed from Germany not only the name and method of "scientific" historiography, but also the idea of the proper subject-matter of that science: the development of political institutions from their remotest origins to the present. In the hands of the leading professionals in England like Freeman and Stubbs, and in America like Herbert Baxter Adams and John W. Burgess, this turned out to mean that virtually all history was to be legal and constitutional history: they were going to do for Anglo-American political forms what their German models had done for the Roman. Thus there was nothing eccentric about the young Henry Adams's choice of Anglo-Saxon law as his Harvard seminar project in medieval history, or about the young O.W. Holmes's decision to study first Roman law and then the early forms of common law: the most exciting intellectual problems of the day were problems concerning origins of present political and legal forms, and the hottest debates over whether these origins were Roman or Teutonic.[12]

157

This preoccupation with origins resulted, of course, from the subscription of 19th century historians to various kinds of evolutionary assumptions about the development of political institutions. These assumptions varied greatly in their particulars and patrimony from historian to historian: some learned an idealist historical jurisprudence from Savigny; others picked up Freeman's idea of history as the gradual unfolding of political liberty; still others borrowed metaphors from anthropology or comparative philology. At the common core of these theories were the assumptions that all societies undergo comparable processes of development from the simple to the complex, the

---

now being done by John Henry Schlegel should help to correct this. Jerold S. Auerbach, *Unequal Justice: Lawyers and Social Change in Modern America* (1976) appeared too late to be consulted for this essay.

12. On the significance of Henry Adams' seminar, see Helen M. Cam, *Law Finders and Law-Makers* 176-182 (1962); on the influence of German writers on Holmes, Mark DeWolfe Howe, *Justice Oliver Wendell Holmes: The Proving Years, 1870-1882*, ch. 5 (1963).

primitive to the civilized; that these processes are continuous and progressive; and that the business of scientists was to discover, through the comparative study of developed and undeveloped peoples, the laws governing the growth of civilizations.[13] The particular business of historians was to trace the development of customs and ideals of already developed civilizations back to their ancient beginnings. For the extremely influential historians H.B. Adams and Burgess, who were especially impressed by German conceptions of history as the science of the state, this program dictated studying the development of political institutions, in their legal and constitutional forms.[14] National and racial ethnocentrism then combined to make Anglo-American civilization the focus of study; and this in turn made of the historiography of North America simply the study of the most recent stages of a long, continuous process beginning in the ancient Teutonic forests.[15]

158

Institutional-evolutionary studies in legal history flourished in the law schools too in the 1880s and 90s, especially at Harvard it was under the influence of this school (to varying degrees that Holmes, Bigelow, Thayer and Ames made their contribution to the study of early English law.[16] The point of dwelling on the assumptions of the historical school is not to depreciate the achievement of these men, who were among the few people Maitland found it worthwhile to correspond with on professional subjects;[17] it is that these assumptions have continued to linger around the law schools to the present day, like radio-active matter with an abnormally long half-life. Professional histor

---

13. J.W. Burrow, *Evolution and Society, A Study in Victorian Soci Theory* (1966) emphasizes the variety of 19th century evolutionar theories; Robert A. Nisbet, *Social Change and History* 166-1 (1968), their similarity.

14. See especially Jurgen Herbst, *The German Historical School American Scholarship* 112-116 (1965); and John Higham, *Histor Professional Scholarship in America* 158-161 (1965). Out of 15 hi tory courses given at Harvard in 1890-91, "twelve were wholly partly concerned with constitutional development." Cam, *sup* note 12, at 182.

15. The titles of some of H.B. Adams' articles will convey the flav of some of his scholarship: "The Germanic Origin of New Engla Towns," *Johns Hopkins Studies in History and Political Scien* (ser. 1, no. 2, 1882); "Saxon Tithing-Men in America," id. (ser. no. 4, 1882); "Norman Constables in America," id. (ser. 1, no. 1883).

16. James Barr Ames, *Lectures on Legal History and Miscellaneous I gal Essays* (1913); Melville M. Bigelow, *Placita Anglo-Normann* (1879) and *History of Procedure in England from the Norman Co quest* (1880); O.W. Holmes, Jr., *The Common Law* (1881); Jam Bradley Thayer, *A Preliminary Treatise on Evidence at the Comm Law* (1898).

17. See C.H.S. Fifoot, *Frederick William Maitland: A Life*, at viii, (70, 75-76, 80 (1971).

ians—helped and sometimes led by the legal historians—soon repudiated the simpler tenets of this school, such as the theories of a unilinear evolutionary development and of the Teutonic origins of Anglo-Saxon civilization; and most of them went on to shake off its influence almost entirely. What we have to account for is the survival of 19th century evolutionary theory not only in amateur legal writing—the brief "historical introductions" to textbook or article—but in various indirect ways in monographic legal history as well.[18]

The solution to the puzzle lies, I think, in the reasons that the new law schools were so hospitable to legal-historical studies in the first place: their faculties (at least initially) perceived no conflict between historical research and the strictly professional ambitions of the schools. To be sure, the founding generation of law teachers defined a role for themselves in the profession differing from the practitioner's. The legal scholar was not simply to train his students in the law as it was, but to ascertain the principles truly underlying the law through scientific research, to the end of reforming existing law by bringing it into conformity with those principles.[19] History was supposed to be the primary field of research. But ultimately the results of research were to be grist for the judicial mill. Ames, for example, thought of historiography simply as one of the useful lawyer's tasks that the professor, because of his freedom from the press of business, could attend to with the greater efficiency that comes from specialization of function. What was wanted was:

> a high order of treatises on all the important branches of the law, exhibiting the historical development of the subject and containing sound conclusions based on scientific analysis. . . . Too often the just expectations of men are thwarted by the action of the courts, a result largely due to taking a partial view of the subject, or to a failure to grasp the original development and true significance of the rule which is made the basis of the decision.

As an instance he cites the rule denying enforceability to creditor's agreement to release debtors on part payment of the debt: this "unfortunate rule", says Ames, "is the result of misunderstanding a *dictum* of Coke. In truth Coke, in an overlooked case, declared in unmistakable terms the legal validity of the creditor's agreement."[20]

159

---

18. See text at notes 23-27, 32-44, *infra.*
19. See Auerbach, "Equity and Amity," *supra,* note 11 at 553-72.
20. James Barr Ames, "The Vocation of the Law Professor," in Ames, *supra,* note 16 at 366. [The reference is clearly to Foakes v. Beer, 9 App. Cas. 605 (1884), *citing* Pinnel's Case, 5 Co. Rep. 117a (1602).]

If only historians had earlier brought to light Coke's other case! Ames, plainly, felt none of Maitland's skepticism about the results of mixing legal dogma and legal history. Maitland said: "The lawyer must be orthodox otherwise he is no lawyer; an orthodox history seems to me a contradiction in terms."[21] Like most of his colleagues, Ames did not see the contradiction. He hoped to subordinate the development of dogma to historical science. In fact, things turned out exactly the opposite: legal history was subordinated to legal technique, the immediate needs of the profession to keep current dogma rationalized in line with past authority. The historical school's view of law as the continuous development of institutional forms lent itself beautifully to these needs, since that view made it easy to confuse the history of law with the "common law tradition"—the fictional continuity that each generation of common lawyers imposes, in its own fashion and for its own ends, on the development of judicial doctrine.[22]

160

Institutional-evolutionary studies prospered in the law schools because they had something to offer the profession: documentation of the unbroken chain of connection between living lawyers and an ancient tradition. The successors in historiographical fashion to the historical school, however, could offer nothing of the kind. The second generation of American institutional historians, C.M. Andrews and H.L. Osgood in particular, rejected the idea of universal and necessary legal development; and picked up from the research of Maine, Brunner, Maitland,

---

Ames also saw a role for the law professor as an "expart counselor in legislation," by which he meant advisor on technical law reform. *Id.* at 367-68.

21. "Why the History of Law Is Not Written," *Collected Papers,* I, 480, 493 (1911).

22. Horwitz, *supra,* note 6 at 282-83, calls attention to the "incredibly striking" parallels between lawyer's legal history and scientists' history of science, quoting T.S. Kuhn, *The Structure of Scientific Revolutions* 137-38 (2d ed. 1970):

Textbooks . . . begin by truncating the scientist's sense of his discipline's history and then proceed to supply a substitute for what they have eliminated. Characteristically, textbooks of science contain just a bit of history, either in an introductory chapter or, more often, in scattered references to the great heroes of an earlier age. From such references both students and professionals come to feel like participants in a long-standing historical tradition. Yet the textbook tradition in which scientists come to sense their participation is one that, in fact, never existed . . . [S]cience textbooks . . . refer only to that part of the work of past scientists that can easily be viewed as contributions to the statement and solution of the text's paradigm problems. . . . No wonder that textbooks and the historical tradition they imply have to be rewritten after each scientific revolution. And no wonder that, as they are rewritten, science once again comes to seem largely cumulative.

and Vinogradoff (among others) the program of studying the effects upon legal forms of specific and local variations in social environment.[23]   Meanwhile the New, or Progressive historians led by Turner and Beard were carrying off much of the historical profession in their challenge to the primacy of the study of the development of political institutions, insisting that legal and constitutional forms were only secondary derivatives of economic and social forces.   Beard was of course the most influential proponent of a revised notion of law as the expression, not of the evolving ethical ideals of the Anglo-Saxon race, but of economic interests pursued through factional politics.[24]

The law schools had small use for either of these modes of practising history, even though Holmes and Pound, both law teachers, had been instrumental in promoting them.   Very little American history of any distinction in the institutional vein of Andrews and Osgood was written in the law schools between 1900 and the revival of legal-historical studies in the 1930's; this is probably because history, like liberal learning generally in that period, fell victim to the case method's exclusive claim on the undergraduate law curriculum.   Moreover the institutional approach demanded long and patient study in primary materials, time taken away from, and not yielding any particularly valuable results in aid of, treatise and case-book writing.[25]   As for Pro-

161

23. On the new institutional (or "imperial") historians, see Higham, *supra*, note 14 at 162-166; Johnson, "Colonial Legal History." Maine is usually thought of as an evolutionist; but Kenneth E. Bock has persuasively argued that he was an opponent of the theory of a unilinear evolutionary development, and not interested in hunting for origins among primitive peoples, but instead was concerned to study law in relation to the entire surrounding culture, including its "relatively recent history." (I.e., Maine was disposed to explain ancient law by ancient history, but not modern law.)   "Comparison of Histories: The Contribution of Henry Maine," 16 *Comp. Stud. in Soc'y & Hist.* 232, 247 (1974).

24. On the Progressives, see Richard Hofstadter, *The Progressive Historians* (1968), especially 181-218; and Higham, *supra*, note 14 at 171-182.

25. The case method, in Langdell's original conception a way of getting across the basic principles of legal science, rapidly acquired its present-day justification as a pedagogic vehicle for the teaching of legal method.   Thus justified, it became the device for teaching every undergraduate law course, tending to drive out subjects (such as legal philosophy and history) not suited to being so taught.   See Stevens, *supra*, note 11 at 435-449.   In 1960, commenting bitterly on the anti-intellectualism accompanying the spread of the Harvard method in the late 19th and early 20th centuries, Karl Llewellyn recounted that when

[William A.] Keener was called to Columbia in 1890 to put that law school on a footing worthy of a great University, he brought with him two policies: (1) "The" case-system . . . (2) All that noise which is not "law" must go out; a "law" curriculum must cast out Ishmael.   Columbia . . . had therefore to amputate from any official "law"-connection what became the Department of Political Science.   Thus the Roman Law Perspective of a Munroe Smith, the scholarship

gressive history, it was simply anathema. When the Progressives took over American constitutional history they pretty well wiped out internal—doctrinal and intellectual—approaches among the historians, leaving these to be cultivated (with great distinction, as it turned out) by political scientists like Corwin and McIlwain.[26] They could obviously not have converted many lawyers to their method in the early part of this century, since in its extreme forms it denied the existence of any autonomous content to law, and hence any meaning to legal historiography as traditionally practiced. The Progessives did not themselves produce (at least, until Willard Hurst began to write) any significant body of work on private law; but their hostility helped effectively to split off legal history from the main action in American scholarship and to isolate it in the law schools.[27]

162

Confined to the law faculties, reduced to the status of auxiliary service for strictly professional tasks, and written for the most part by amateurs, legal historiography suffered a rapid narrowing of scope. The old historical school had held out the promise of connecting the history of law and of society. In the study of medieval English law, that promise was being fulfilled. In America it was cut short, and legal history was reduced to internal history.

In part this happened because the historical school's organic theory of culture paradoxically encouraged scholars to disregard the social context of law, just as the "comparative method," by generalizing patterns of development in a single civilization to

---

and vision of a [Frank J.] Goodnow, the power and range of our greatest international lawyer, John Bassett Moore [who trained, among others, Julius Goebel, Jr.], flourished not within the law curriculum, nor for it, but across the barbarian border . . . . In 1915, when, already our foremost jurisprude, [Roscoe Pound] became Dean at Harvard Law School, he deliberately took his own Jurisprudence course *out of the undergraduate curriculum.* He kept it out, lest his bulk of graduates be distracted—or contaminated.
Llewellyn, "The Study of Law as a Liberal Art," in *Jurisprudence* 375, 377-78 (1962). [Italics Llewellyn's; interpolations mine.]

26. See generally, Herman Belz, "The Realist Critique of Constitutionalism in the Era of Reform," 15 *Am. J. Leg. Hist.* 288 (1971); Paul L. Murphy, "Time to Reclaim: The Current Challenge of American Constitutional History," 69 *Am. Hist. Rev.* 64 (1963).

27. It is not always appreciated how wide the split was. One can get some sense of it from casual remarks made recently by non-lawyer historians who have become interested in law. For example: (a) Eugene Genovese: "[T]he fashionable relegation of law to the rank of a superstructural and derivative phenomenon obscures the degree of autonomy it creates for itself." *Roll, Jordan, Roll* 25 (1974). (b) Harry N. Scheiber, speaking of recent developments in economic history, refers to "*new* lines of inquiry that stress institutional and doctrinal development in American law . . ." "Government and the Economy: Studies of the 'Commonwealth' Policy in Nineteenth Century America," 3 *J. Interdisc. Hist.* 135, 151 n. 44 (1972) [Italics added]. Historians are discovering law, lawyers society.

all others, in fact justified ethnocentricity. James Coolidge Carter, Savigny's chief popularizer in this country, give the game away when he said that the field of research for judges trying to locate the true or just rule of law for a case by the historical method was "the habits, customs, business and manners of the people, *and those previously declared rules which have sprung out of previous similar inquiries into habits, customs, business, and manners.*"[28]   This was certainly a convenient method for legal scholars: it meant that in practice they carried no greater research burden than would any legal positivist, for whom legal history was only the history of past state commands, rather than the history of an entire culture.

But of course the main reason lawyer's history became, and remained, internal—confined to the boxful of distinctively legal things—is that it was written from inside the box, was itself a "form of professional activity within the legal system—like adjudication, or advocacy, or counseling."[29]   As long as the common law tradition was a source of normative authority, the doing of legal history was conceived to be a professional task; as long as it was a professional task it was bound to be internal. Legal scholars not only took the boxful of legal things as their exclusive subject-matter, but whenever possible adduced as factors explaining the development of legal things only *other* legal things.   The rule seemed to be: stay inside the box; the most common application of the rule was explanation of current case-law doctrine by means of prior case-law doctrine.

This is why, long after the discrediting of evolutionary theories of history, legal history was still so frequently written as if these theories still held sway.   For the historian who restricts his sources to the strictly legal, there often is no explanation available other than the genetic.   Suppose one wanted to explain the use of the "fellow-servant" rule to limit liability of employers for the costs of industrial accidents in the 19th century, and one's search were confined to the rule's predecessors in form.   One would learn a good deal about the common law of master and servant and the writ of trespass on the case, but

163

---

28. *The Ideal and the Actual in Law* 10-11 (1890).
29. This is how Richard L. Abel describes a "law book," a "study [that] identifies, defines, organizes the rules [that legal institutions apply] by means of criteria proper to the legal system—it *rationalizes* them in Weber's sense."   He contrasts such a "law book" to a "book about law," which is a "mode of *reflection* upon the legal system".   "Law Books and Books About Law," 26 *Stan. L. Rev.* 175, 176 (1973) [Italics Abel's].   This is another (and very effective) way of stating Maitland's distinction between legal history and legal dogma, text at note 21, *supra*.

nothing about the 19th century industry, however useful such knowledge might be.[30]

Limitations of method thus kept driving American lawyers backwards in search of the ancestors of current legal categories in early English forms. When they got there they found a historiography that was often extremely technical, but not internal; the further back one went, the more one found law connected to social structure, economic organization, agricultural method, administrative practice, currents of religious and philosophical speculation. The great researchers of the classical period and their successors had given medieval law a context. But as one approached more recent times, legal history started to thin out to the distinctively "legal" again, and explanations for the shape of legal things to revert to the genetic.

164

Around 1900 then, at the point serious work in legal history slumped in American law schools, scholarly convention in the field suggested it was all right to try to account for old law by external circumstance, but not new law. This way of looking at things matched nicely with the contemporary jurisprudential theory that the common law, though it had started out derived from Custom, had come, as its administration was brought under a professional judiciary, to be based upon Reason.[31] It is tempting to suggest that the law schools were not interested in developments in historiography that would tend to controvert this theory. At any rate, the configurations that legal-historical

---

30. The late Professor Goebel employed his gift for Latinate astringency to characterize this method as treating

> the growth of doctrine as something projected on a horizontal plane of rational manipulation unmindful of its perpendicular support in time or circumstance. In expositions of the doctrine of consideration, the judgments of his majesty's judges in the seventeenth century rub shoulders with those from the American backwoods two hundred years later. To legitimate the control of business, Tudor sumptuary statutes are forcibly wedded to the legislative indiscretions of the seventy-third Congress . . .
>
> That so fantastic a conception of history should prevail as a convention in the bulk of our legal literature is attributable in some degree to the intellectual tyranny which the judicial opinion exerts. It is a truism that to know the common law its history must be known. Our courts, however, seek enlightenment on the past chiefly in the judgments of their predecessors. These judgments are rarely treated as single but complex assessable facts, for the mass of relevant data of which they are merely parts is usually ignored. In consequence, the antecedent judicial opinion is elevated to a status of preposterous importance as a source. . .

Julius Goebel, Jr., *Felony and Misdemeanor* xvii–xviii (1937).

31. Beale was expounding this theory to Harvard law students in 1909, according to notes taken by Robert Lee Hale of his lectures on jurisprudence in that year. These notes are published, with an introduction, in Warren J. Samuels, "Joseph Henry Beale's Lectures on Jurisprudence, 1909," 29 *U. Miami L. Rev.* 260 (1975). See *id.* at 288–293.

scholarship achieved by 1900 were decisive for the future shape of the field—especially in American legal history.

Look for example at the Association of American Law Schools' *Select Essays in Anglo-American Legal History* (1907), which purported to collect in three volumes the cream of current scholarship in the field.[32] This includes some wonderful stuff— e.g. Maitland's famous essay on "English Law and the Renaissance"—but is mostly interesting now for the subjects it includes. Most of the essays (after the traditional start with Teutonic Law) have to do with English law; after some broad surveys, the essays tend to be organized by type of court (Chancery, Admiralty, etc.) and doctrinal field (assumpsit, agency, trover, defamation, etc.). The stress is on the common law, though equity receives seven essays in all, and there are brief treatments of canon law, admiralty, and the law merchant. With very few exceptions, the essays are concerned with tracing the early forms of modern practice categories—"The Historical Development of Code Pleading"—"Early Forms of Partnership"—"The Early History of Negotiable Instruments"—and the exceptions are the essays set in early English history and unabashedly making no pretence at current relevance.

The American entries are of most interest. They cluster around colonial legal history and are primarily devoted to exploring the extent to which colonial law was influenced or determined by English models. Then there are treatments of 19th century attempts at procedural reform in the common law, dealing with proposals to simplify pleading and the organization of courts and with the fate of schemes to codify the common law in whole or in part, from Bentham to David Dudley Field. Lacking (as yet) only the addition of something on the reception of English law after the Revolution, the basic canon of American legal history was fixed—and fixed almost before any work had been done!—upon transplantation to America of the common law and the subsequent challenge and defeat, save for partial accommodation in the form of Code Pleading, of the common law's arch rival, codification. Even to the present, general surveys and collections of materials on American legal history are faithful to the broad outlines of this canon. This is a wonderful example of the survival of form beyond its inspiring context, for these

165

---

32. And did so in fact. Its nearest rival was a compilation of essays in American legal history put out by members of the Yale Law School faculty, *Two Centuries' Growth of American law, 1701-1901* (1901), sketching the antecedents of some 18 fields of contemporary practice, and now interesting mostly as revealing how little access even learned lawyers had to their own past.

subjects are the vital ones of American experience only within a theory such as the old historical school's—by which American history simply records the later stages of the common law's triumphant struggle for continuous development through Anglo-Saxon civilization.

There were two jarring notes in this collection. One was the famous attempt by Reinsch, a disciple of Turner's at Wisconsin, to demonstrate the domination of colonial law not by English models but the primitive law of the frontier.[33] Oddly enough this environmental (and later proved erroneous[34]) explanation was absorbed along with the rest of the 1907 collection into the orthodox view of the American past. The assumption of the continuity of Anglo-American legal development was neatly rescued despite the Reinsch theory by Roscoe Pound, who simply moved up the period of "reception" of English law in America to a "formative era" after the Revolution.[35] The other oddity in the collection was the presence of contributions by Simeon Baldwin and the young Samuel Williston on early corporation law.[36] Corporation law too was to find a niche in the permanent canon of appropriate subjects, either as a subspecies of commercial law or on its own. These particular articles, like the others, tended to emphasize the most formal aspects of corporations and the earliest forms at that; there was nothing here like Maitland's speculations on the social functions of different forms of group legal personality.[37] Nonetheless, corporation law had so obviously responded to political and economic pressure in recent history that the inclusion of it in the standard canon was prophetic. Sooner or later, it would be the most promising candidate for external historiographical treatment; and so it eventually proved to be.[38]

---

33. Paul Samuel Reinsch, "English Common Law in the Early American Colonies," *Select Essays in Anglo-American Legal History*, I, 367 (1907).

34. By the work of Goebel, Morris, and Haskins in particular. See Johnson, "Colonial Legal History," and the essays collected in Flaherty, *supra*, note 9.

35. Pound, *The Spirit of the Common Law* 113-118 (1921); *The Formative Era of American Law* 6-12, *et passim* (1938). For an account of Pound's "enormous influence on the study of American law" with these two books, see Michael G. Kammen, "Colonial Court Records and the Study of Early American History: A Bibliographical Review," 70 *Am. Hist. Rev.* 732, 738 (1965); and Katz, *supra*, note 6.

36. Baldwin, "History of the Law of Private Corporations in the Colonies and States," in *Select Essays, supra*, note 33, at III, 236; Williston, "The History of the Law of Business Corporations before 1800," *id.* at III, 195.

37. Maitland's essays on trusts, corporations, and unincorporated bodies are all collected in *Maitland: Selected Essays* (Hazeltine, Lapsley & Winfield eds. 1936), as well as in Maitland, *supra*, note 21.

38. There is a fuller literature on the history of the American corporation

166

Anyone who is skeptical about the extraordinary persistence through our time of this late 19th century view of the proper scope of legal history should pick up any of the standard history texts published for law students.[39] Or he might look at the historical section of any recent law review article. I am looking at one now, chosen because it is near at hand and because it is one of the best things of its kind, not one of the worst: an excellent synthesis of anthropological and historical literature about contract law.[40] The article is explicitly evolutionary; it begins with economic transactions in "primitive" societies and ends with 20th century American contracts; in between lie ancient Rome, England from medieval to modern times, and 19th century America. The sections on primitive society are rich in detail about the relation of forms of transactions to social life— to kinship systems, religion, land tenure, warfare.[41] Even by the time he reaches medieval England, the author is still interested in externals: we learn for example something about theological views of contract.[42] But from the moment the common law courts get into the picture, the focus of the narrative shifts almost exclusively to institutional and doctrinal forms: case, assumpsit, indebitatus assumpsit, consideration, up to Slade's Case in 1602, whereupon, saving a brief "Epilogue", the article ends![43] It ends presumably because the story of doctrinal developments is now complete; the Epilogue treats summarily of the high point of "freedom of contract" in the 19th century and of the tendency in the 20th to limit this freedom by legislation.[44] Except for passing references to the work of Weber, Hurst, and Lawrence Friedman, there is scarcely a word on the tremendous changes that have taken place in the nature of economic exchange relationships between the 17th century and the present, no allusion even to the standard economic histories of Europe and America for that time. It would be absurd to

167

---

than on any other subject that plausibly belongs in the field of American legal history. See the bibliography in Willard Hurst, *The Legitimacy of the Business Corporation in the Law of the United States, 1780-1970* at 165 (1970).

39. See, e.g., William F. Walsh, *A History of Anglo-American Law* [Bobbs-Merrill] (2d ed. 1932); Max Radin, *Handbook of Anglo-American Legal History* [West Hornbook Series] (1936); Frederick G. Kempin, Jr., *Historical Introduction to Anglo-American Law in a Nutshell* [West Nutshell Series] (1973). Of course these vary greatly in quality: Radin's is the outstanding one.

40. E. Allan Farnsworth, "The Past of Promise: An Historical Introduction to Contract," 69 *Colum. L. Rev.* 576 (1969).

41. *Id.* at 578-88.

42. *Id.* at 591.

43. *Id.* at 592-99.

44. *Id.* at 599-607.

blame this situation on the author, who is a scholar of distinction; he was working with materials that are at hand to tell the story that has commonly been thought the one worth telling. The point is to show how deeply ingrained in the consciousness of the modern lawyer is the late 19th century's subordination of legal history to the common law tradition.

II

American legal historiography began to revive in the late 1920's. It is not clear why this happened. Perhaps in part it was simply because the students whom Andrews and Osgood had interested in the study of primary source material on British imperial administration were starting to turn out their own work; in part because some of the younger law teachers, especially at Columbia, were trying to break down the hedges that had grown up between other university departments and the law schools. In 1930 the American Historical Association organized a conference of lawyers and historians to draw up a program to publish American legal source materials: this resulted in the American Legal Records series.[45] In the same year, private and foundation gifts established the Foundation for Research in Legal History at Columbia Law School, under the direction of Julius Goebel, Jr., which underwrote research and publication expenses of new secondary work.[46]

For the purposes of this essay, the most interesting aspect of this period of revival, which lasted through the mid-1960's (and is perhaps still going on—these periodizations never work out very neatly), is that its scholarship did not bring about any very substantial redefinition of the field of legal history. (There were exceptions, which will be noted). On the face of it, this is rather surprising. The period was dominated by work in colonial law done by historians of formidable talent—Goebel, George L. Haskins, Mark DeWolfe Howe, Richard B. Morris, Joseph H. Smith. None of these historians believed that law develops primarily according to the logic of an internal dynamic, independently of surrounding political, social, and economic con-

---

45. The committee consisted of Charles McLean Andrews, Carroll T. Bond (Chief Judge of the Maryland Court of Appeals and editor of the first volume in the series), John Dickinson, the ubiquitous Felix Frankfurter, Evarts B. Greene, and Richard B. Morris. See Evarts B. Greene, "Foreword" to *Proceedings of the Maryland Court of Appeals, 1695-1729* (American Legal Records, I; Bond ed. 1933). Greene acknowledged "the encouragement, given at an early stage of the development of this project, by Mr. Justice Brandeis . . ." *Id.* For a list of publications in the series, see Kammen, *supra*, note 35 at 733.

46. See Goebel, *supra*, note 30 at ix.

168

ditions; indeed each thought that belief one of the failings of the amateur historiography of the early 20th century, for among other errors it propagated the theory of the process of reception and development of English law taking place in a uniform manner and rate across all of early America. Though some members of this fresh group of colonial historians, notably Morris,[47] were eventually again to emphasize similarities among colonial legal patterns, all of them recognized that any generalizations would have to be based upon archival study of local materials in individual colonies.

Yet though a conviction of the importance of the influence of social surroundings on law was what drove historians of this period to research in local sources in the first place, it did not carry most of them so far as to write external legal history. They stayed chiefly within the orthodox canon of subjects— the reception of English common law in America and its 19th century rivalry with "codification"—and continued to take their materials from the box of distinctively legal things. Their teaching materials, enriched by the results of their research in primary sources, were enormously more sophisticated than similar products of the old institutional-evolutionary school; but they were organized by the same categories as the old school's (reception, codification, corporations, etc.), and the detail filling the old categories, though new, was all *legal* detail.[48] Symbolically, the most important collective effort of professional American legal historians at the end of the period was of the same kind as at the beginning—publication of colonial legal records.[49]

169

One must point out immediately that there were significant exceptions to this pattern; and that historians of this period did make major contributions to an external legal historiography. Daniel Boorstin's study of Blackstone's *Commentaries* and Mark

---

47. See his *Studies in the History of American Law* (1958); and Johnson, "Colonial Legal History" at 258-261.

48. See, e.g., Julius Goebel, Jr., *Cases and Materials on the Development of Legal Institutions* (2d ed. 1937) [but *see* Ch. 3 of this book, on "Social, Economic and Intellectual Factors Conditioning Legal Development," which mostly accords with tradition in confining discussion of such factors to the earlier English law, but not entirely: cf. *id.* at 620-626 on American corporations]; Mark DeWolfe Howe, *Readings in American Legal History* (1949); and Joseph H. Smith, *Cases and Materials on the Development of Legal Institutions* (1965).

49. The William Nelson Cromwell Foundation underwrote in whole or in part: *Colonial Justice in Western Massachusetts (1639-1702): The Pyncheon Court Record* (Smith ed. 1961); *Legal Papers of John Adams* (Wroth & Zobel eds. 1965); and *The Law Practice of Alexander Hamilton* (Goebel et al., eds. 1964-   ). I am not complaining about this; these volumes are superbly edited, and if there is one place where lavish spreading of technical detail is surely justified, it is in the edition of a primary text.

DeWolfe Howe's of Holmes's *Common Law* both succeeded in connecting law books to wider regions of the thought of their time.[50] After a series of monographs written in a more cautious mode, George L. Haskins built a new framework for colonial legal studies by taking as his subject not the specialized concerns of lawyers, but the whole governmental and clerical apparatus of social control in 17th century Massachusetts.[51]

But these, like the work of Hurst and his followers to be discussed later, were exceptions. The main business of the period was to make a start at giving American law historicity, localizing it to specific times and places. Under the spell of evolutionism and professional habit, the earlier school of lawyer-historians had ransacked the past for ancestors of their own day's categories, though these categories might have possessed no significance, or a very different one, for the previous generations back through whom they were traced. The researchers of the 1930's and onward corrected this by showing us colonial law through the eyes of contemporaries—but usually through the eyes of contemporary lawyers, and abnormally bookish lawyers at that. Research that adopted a different perspective was not likely to be considered "legal" history at all, even if it relied primarily on legal sources as evidence—e.g. Richard Morris's great study of colonial labor conditions and regulation[52] or the studies of 19th century "public policy" in the states.[53]

What can account for the almost unrelenting preoccupation with internals? Daniel Boorstin and Calvin Woodard, who at different times both called for a more catholic vision of the scope of legal history, both attributed its unsatisfactory state in part to the pragmatic temper of legal studies since the 1930's. Boortin said: "[N]early every American contribution to legal history which ought to be considered a classic was made *before* the movement [to integrate law and the social sciences]"; he blamed the law schools' fads for policy science, social science, and clinical education.[54] Woodard reproached legal scholars "somewhat intoxicated with the delusion of complete freedom from the past" for promoting among students the view that law

170

---

50. Boorstin, *The Mysterious Science of the Law* (1941); Howe, *supra*, note 12.
51. Haskins, *Law and Authority in Early Massachusetts* (1960). The influence of this approach may be detected in the range (as well as the title) of a recent collection of essays, *Law and Authority in Colonial America* (Billias ed. 1965).
52. *Government and Labor in Early America* (1946).
53. See Scheiber, *supra*, note 27.
54. "The Humane Study of Law," 57 *Yale L.J.* 960, 963-64 (1948).

is merely "engineering," or "the vector of so many mid-20th century social forces rationalized in accordance with the personal preference of so many contemporary judges and legislators."[55]

The trouble with this explanation is that it was precisely those people who took the most pragmatic view of present law that tended to urge the study of the past—urged it, indeed, partly for the sake of ridding the present of the deadwood of irrelevant survivals. Maitland took this view, for example;[56] so did Holmes, the founder of American pragmatic legal thought.[57] In fact a very large number of lawyers associated with the pragmatic movement[58] took more than a passing interest in legal history. Pound's lectures on the "formative era of American law" influenced several generations of historians;[59] Frankfurter was not only instrumental in obtaining research funding for legal history, but also wrote histories of the Commerce Clause, and (with others) of federal jurisdiction and labor injunctions;[60] Karl Llewellyn, Jerome Hall, Walton Hamilton, Walter Nelles, and Hessel Yntema, all Realists, all did some of their own work in history[61] and followed closely what was done by others.

171

---

55. Woodard, *supra,* note 7 at 110-114.
56. See, e.g., Maitland writing to Dicey in 1896 (cited in Fifoot, *supra,* note 17 at 143):
    > The only direct utility of legal history (I say nothing of its thrilling interest) lies in the lesson that each generation has an enormous power of shaping its own law. I don't think that the study of legal history would make men fatalists; I doubt it would make them conservatives. I am sure it would free them from superstitions and teach them that they have free hands.
57. See, e.g., "Law in Science and Science in Law [1899]", in Holmes, *Collected Legal Papers* 210, 225 (1920):
    > From a practical point of view, [the use of history] is mainly negative and skeptical . . . [I]ts chief good is to burst inflated explanations. Everyone instinctively recognizes that in these days the justification of a law cannot be found in the fact that our fathers have always followed it. It must be found in some help which the law brings toward reaching a social end which the governing power of the community has made up its mind that it wants . . . [H]istory is the means by which we measure the power which the past has had to govern the present in spite of ourselves, so to speak, by imposing traditions which no longer meet their original end.
58. This phrase seems broad enough to encompass Holmes's pragmatism, Pound's sociological jurisprudence, and the many varieties of legal Realism.
59. See note 35, *supra.*
60. Frankfurter, *The Commerce Clause under Marshall, Taney, and Waite* (1937); Frankfurter and James M. Landis, *The Business of the Supreme Court, A Study in the Federal Judicial System* (1928); Frankfurter and Nathan Greene, *The Labor Injunction* (1930).
61. Llewellyn: "On Warranty of Quality and Society," (Pts. 1 & 2) 36 *Colum. L. Rev.* 699 (1936), 37 *Colum. L. Rev.* 341 (1937); "Across Sales on Horseback," 52 *Harv. L. Rev.* 725 (1939); "The First Struggle to Unhorse Sales," 52 *Harv. L. Rev.* 874 (1939). (This superb quartet on the history of sales law may be Llewellyn's most

Pragmatic legal studies were at their height during the revival of professional legal historiography in the 1930's; Goebel was one of the young Turks at the Columbia Law School; Howe was a clerk to Holmes and protégé of Frankfurter's; Haskins was inspired by Pound's theory of interests; and —as will be seen— Hurst's work is written out of an explicitly pragmatic theory of law. The failure of the period of revival to develop an extensive external historiography of law does not stem from pragmatic thinking, but—I am persuaded—from loss of nerve in the face of the implications of that thinking; not from reckless disregard of the common law tradition, but from an anxious solicitude to preserve it.

The program set forth by pragmatists like Holmes and Pound for development of a science of law called for reconnecting legal

172

---

durable work. Yet he said [of "Warranty of Quality," Pt. 1, *supra* this note at 699 n.*] he was not writing "history, . . . [but] an appeal for history. It is a sad commentary on our dogmatics that sales cases over a hundred and fifty years and more than fifty jurisdictions have been treated as if they floated free of time, place and person. Whereas it is time, place, person and circumstance which give them meaning. A few major trends are here presented. But not as history. History calls for detailed knowledge, for detailed background, and for discrimination even more detailed.")

Hall: *Theft, Law and Society* (1935).

Hamilton: "The Ancient Maxim *Caveat Emptor*", 40 *Yale L.J.* 1133 (1931).

Nelles: "*Commonwealth v. Hunt*," 32 *Colum. L. Rev.* 1128 (1932); "Towards Legal Understanding," (Pts. 1 & 2), 34 *Colum. L. Rev.* 862, 1041 (1934).

Yntema: *Sourcebook on Roman Law* (1929) (with A. Arthur Schiller).

But see Grant Gilmore, Book Review, 21 *The Law School Record* (Chicago) 38 (Summer, 1975):
When I studied law at Yale in the early 1940's there was no suggestion, in any of the instruction which I received, that there was any point in thinking about law as a historical process. The implicit philosophical or jurisprudential bias which the entire law faculty seemed to share was that law was a sort of mystical absolute waiting to be discovered, described, catalogued, mapped out, so to say, reduced to possession. [Gilmore adds that his instructors included some noted Realists.] It was not until considerably later—if we must have a date, 1960 will do as well as any—that a historical approach to law seemed, almost overnight, to become fashionable, at least among academic theorists.
The absence of a historical approach at Yale in the 1940's does not surprise me; the intellectually curious and innovative phase of legal pragmatism was by then over. I am somewhat perplexed by the reference to a new fashion for history starting about 1960. In 1963 Edward Re surveyed law school curricula to find legal history courses other than "development of Anglo-American legal institutions" (often shortened to DLI) virtually non-existent; and even DLI was rare. (DLI was sometimes real history camouflaged as evolutionism, as in John P. Dawson's splendid Harvard Law School version; more often [to judge from course descriptions cited in Re] simply orthodox evolutionism.) Of course this is not necessarily inconsistent with Gilmore's recollection; "a historical approach to law" does not have to mean legal history courses. But legal history courses provide some evidence of the seriousness of commitment to the approach. See Re, "Legal History Courses in American Law Schools," 13 *Am. Univ. L. Rev.* 45 (1963).

to social history, since the contribution of historical study to the program was to liberate the present from law that had arisen out of entirely different social contexts and modes of thought and was not, as a consequence, necessarily suited to modern needs. This was potentially quite a radical view, since it repudiated the whole concept of tradition. Scholars like Langdell (and to a lesser extent Ames) tended to equate historical method and legal science: accurate tracing of the historical development of rules would reveal their immanent principles. Holmes and Pound said that since the end of law was the efficient adjustment of conflicting social interests, *real* legal science consisted in accurate measurement of those interests. The role of history was the important but auxiliary one of clearing away the rubbish of pointless old law.[62]

Outside the law schools these ideas had considerable influence on historians, especially constitutional historians, among whom the impact of economic, social and political factors upon judicial decision-making was a commonplace idea well before the ascendancy of legal Realism.[63] Yet among the lawyers the pragmatic prescription for legal science, assisted by a historiography devoted to destroying instead of beatifying the common law tradition, perhaps not surprisingly failed to make complete converts even of its chief proselytizers. Without knowing for sure what cut short the pragmatic movement as a whole, it is hard to tell what happened to the minor appendage of a program for an external historiography. But here are some ideas.

Training in the common law tradition was what gave a significant elite of the American bar its sense of identity as a mandarinate of masters of an ancient technique; the tradition associated law with both science and high culture, and justified

173

62. See Pound, *Interpretations of Legal History* 152 and Ch. 7 *passim* (1923); Holmes, "The Path of the Law [1897]," in *supra*, note 57 at 167, 191-195. The difference between Holmes's and Ames's views on tradition and function in law is really only one of emphasis: in practice they often arrived at the same conclusion. Ames believed that traditional authority, accurately interpreted by means of scientific historiography, would also produce the socially functional results he thought desirable. Holmes rejected, of course, the idea that the past could supply "correct" legal doctrine, but argued nonetheless for judicial conservatism towards reforming traditional doctrine—". . . because I believe the claim of our especial code to respect is simply that it exists, that it is the one to which we have become accustomed . . ." "Law in Science," *supra*, note 57 at 239.

63. See Herman Belz, *supra*, note 26 and "The Constitution in the Gilded Age: The Beginnings of Constitutional Realism in American Scholarship," 13 *Am. J. Leg. Hist.* 110 (1969); Richard Hofstadter, *The Progressive Historians* 200-202 (1968). Charles Beard acknowledged Holmes, Pound and Goodnow as forerunners in *An Economic Interpretation of the Constitution of the United States* 9 (1913).

the prestige and power of its practitioners.[64] Law was authoritative because autonomous; and its autonomy derived from two sources, its formality (or technicality) and its antiquity. An evolutionary and internal legal historiography contributed, like legal scholarship generally, to reinforcing the tradition.[65] To deprive lawyers of the tradition entirely, as the pragmatists apparently (but, as will be seen, only apparently) proposed to do, was to make orphans of them. It was a threatened professionalism, among other things, that squashed legal pragmatism in the end.

This professionalism more likely arose from within than without the law schools. I doubt that the common law tradition had much mythic significance for the great majority of American lawyers, who probably were content to think of themselves as technicians rather than mandarins.[66] Even among the elite practitioners there can have been few who knew or cared much about the kind of legal history that was being done at the law schools; though if they had known it is entirely possible that they would have favored inculcation of the text-

---

64. Beale: "[L]aw is a traditional manner of thought about right behavior; the lawyers and judges are experts in it." *A Treatise on the Conflict of Laws* xiii (2d ed. 1935). He developed the idea in his 1909 lectures (Samuels, *supra*, note 31 at 292-93):

    [The principal characteristic of the common law] is that it requires a scientific knowledge on the part of a legal caste, thus coming back to a characteristic of the most ancient times, where it was in the knowledge of a priestly caste. . . .
    How can you tell what is the law of Massachusetts today? You can of course ask the judges, as special experts; but they will not say unless a case is brought before them. The law of Massachusetts is what the body of the Massachusetts bar thinks it is.

    I use Beale to stand for orthodoxy because the Realists, especially Frank, did so; and Beale did not seem to mind. How seriously members of the bar took the image of a priesthood is another question, which would require much more research to answer.

65. The point is forcefully made by Horwitz, *supra*, note 6, "The Conservative Tradition in the Writing of American Legal History," that preoccupation with formality and technique in legal history is ideological, in that it serves the interests of the profession to write about law as if it were autonomous from politics and inaccessible to the uninitiated. I think this is right but in some need of qualification and elaboration, which the text following this note tries to supply.

66. See Maxwell Bloomfield, "Law v. Politics: The Self-Image of the American Bar (1830-1860)," 12 *Am. J. Leg. Hist.* 306 (1968), a study of 19th century lawyers suggesting that most of them disavowed intellectual pretensions and presented themselves as practical businessmen and skilled craftsmen. Jerome Carlin's study of individual practitioners found that "[t]hese lawyers although generally handling matters that require little in the way of technical legal skill, still have fairly frequent contact with the courts and are thereby able to find a link with the most commonly accepted image of a lawyer . . . [T]he big firm lawyer, in their view, has not only lost his identity as a real lawyer by virtue of his more infrequent contact with the courts . . . but his independence as well." *Lawyers on Their Own* 187 (1962). In short, their identification is with the image of the trial lawyer, not with the more mandarin image of the appellate judge.

book view of Anglo-American legal "development" which still permeates legal rhetoric.[67]   But law teachers too think of themselves as lawyers as much as professors, and usually more so;[68] it was the professional identities of the legal pragmatists themselves that the tendencies of their movement most threatened. As Leslie Stephen said of Gibbon: "Insects who are eating the heart out of an old tree are not generally gratified, it may be supposed, by the crash and thunder of the fall."[69]

The intellectual currents that eventually converged in Realism, one of which was the proposal for a legal historiography relativized to social and economic surroundings, challenged the professional viewpoint in several ways.   (1) Pragmatism promoted research into non-legal materials.   The amateur legal historians had stuck to the case reports; their professional successors had added legal manuscript sources of all kinds; but pragmatic legal history would apparently require the historian to step outside the box of distinctively legal things entirely. How far outside one could venture and remain a *legal* scholar? (2) Ames's conception of the legal-scholar-scientist gave him an inside role in the legal system, expert confidant to the judge (and in the extreme case where some statutory adjustment might be required) to the legislature.   Pragmatic legal science offered at best a "negative and skeptical" role to the legal historian in present-day practice, whose relation to the judge would be the relatively indirect one of pointing out the irrelevance of the past to the solution of current problems—the role of an outsider, and a critical outsider at that.   (3) The proposed field of research not only promised to transform legal scholars into some kind of subspecies of social scientist, but also to displace the judge from the center of the intellectual universe.   The judge is of course the key figure in studies of the common law tradition, since he

175

---

67. See, e.g., William D. Guthrie, *Magna Carta and Other Addresses* (1916) and Elihu Root, *Addresses on Government and Citizenship* (1916), for a view of Anglo-American history as the progressive realization of the principle of individual liberty against the state. Guthrie and Root were the two leading Wall St. practitioners of their time.   But it is dangerous to generalize too far.   Some Wall St. men belong, now as then, to the quasi-acadmic bar, which restates the law in the American Law Institute, serves on law reform commissions and the Cromwell Foundation, takes an active and informed interest in the curricula of the schools, and is familiar with scholars' legal history.   It is worth remembering that there are several elites of lawyers—a municipal bond elite, a trial elite, etc.—and that they are not much like one another.

68. I have no authority for this beyond my own observation of teachers and colleagues.

69. *History of English Thought in the Eighteenth Century*, I, 379 (1876). Stephen thought Gibbon's skeptical views had helped to bring about the French Revolution which horrified him.

is the carrier of the tradition. The pragmatic view of law—that it arises out of social needs and is to be evaluated by the efficiency with which it serves social functions—merges law into administration; the judge becomes simply one kind of official among many, and often not the most important. (4) Finally, and inevitably, the program of studying law in its social context opened up for discussion the whole explosive issue of the relationship between the inside and the outside of the law-box; of how far legal decisions are determined, or influenced by external pressures and how far by internal criteria; in short, of the reality of the idea of an autonomous legal order in modern society.

176

Social research in law along pragmatic lines was a quagmire for legal method and legal ideology. The program of investigating the social contexts and effects of law, to the end of discovering how efficiently it performed its social functions, made potentially relevant to legal study the entire universe of experience outside the law box. Some of those who ventured into that universe to gain broader perspectives on law never came back—Daniel Boorstin and David Riesman, for example. For others immersion in social research brought about something close to religious conversion: the story is told of Underhill Moore that he was found one day in his office,

> pulling drawers from his filing cabinets and dumping the contents into wastebaskets, cursing meanwhile most frightfully. The student inquired what was going on. "It's my life work," said Moore, "all the notes I have taken in a lifetime of research and it's all wrong." Moore had decided to discard everything he had ever done [he was an authority on Bills and Notes] and start over again, devoting the rest of his life to the experiments needed to work out a scientific theory of legal control in terms of behavioristic psychology.[70]

This episode took place at Columbia Law School in the 1920's, where Moore and others who were to form the core of the Realist movement made the first real attempt to institutionalize the "functional" study of law-in-society in a law school. This famous attempt failed; what is especially instructive about it for our purposes is that it began with the strictly professional purpose of reforming the curriculum to prepare students better for "the actual work in modern law practice";[71] and ended with many of its backers convinced that social research in law could not be performed in a professional setting at all.[72] (Some of

---

70. Julius Goebel, Jr. et al., A History of the School of Law, Columbia University 251 (1955).
71. Stevens, supra, note 11 at 472 n. 28.
72. For the Columbia experiment, see especially Twining, supra, note 11, ch. 4 (and the annotations to that chapter at 399-402, which con-

them went off to found the short-lived Johns Hopkins Institute.) But most of the Columbia reformers—those who went off to Yale as well as those who stayed on—avoided falling into the quagmire by fashioning lifelines of limiting principles on the scope of their legal research, which kept them connected to traditional professional identities.

One such lifeline, for example, was the notion that the purpose of social research in law was to explore the gap between "law on the books and law in action," or the "limits of effective legal action." (Both these famous slogans were, of course, coined by Pound, who pioneered not only the pragmatic movement in law but the later retreat from it.[73]) This program solved two problems at one stroke. It gave the study of extralegal "action" a restricted scope symmetrically co-extensive with that of the law-box itself: one looked for the counterpart in "reality" of a law in the "book." It also annexed social research to a respectable professional and ideological purpose, i.e. closing the gap, making legal action more effective.[74] After the burst of empirical studies done at Yale in the 1930's, research in this mode largely vanished from the law schools. It never did much influence legal history, though it produced a large body of "impact research" in sociology and political science.[75]

The pragmatic lawyers soon found a lifeline that was stronger and more enduring. This was simply to revive Ames's conception of the law professor as a scholar who helps the judge ensure the sound development of case law, and thus to limit research to such social facts as were potentially relevant to judicial decision-making. To be sure, they expected such research to range farther afield than traditional research, because the judge, to be properly advised, would need to know much more than traditional research could tell him.[76] Julius Goebel,

177

---

tain some useful warnings against generalizing about the Realists too broadly).

73. See text at notes 88-96, *infra*.

74. For the preoccupation of social-legal research with the gap between law on the books and law in action, see Abel, *supra*, note 29 at 185-89 and Marc Galanter, "Notes on the Future of Social Research On Law" (unpublished ms. on file with the *Law & Society Review*).

75. For discussions of these impact studies, see Stephen L. Wasby, *The Impact of the United States Supreme Court: Some Perspectives* (1970); Richard Lempert, "Strategies of Research Design in the Legal Impact Study: The Control of Plausible Rival Hypotheses," 1 *L. & Soc'y Rev.* 111 (1966); Martin Shapiro, "The Impact of the Supreme Court," 23 *J. Leg. Ed.* 77 (1971).

76. This position probably came easiest to the teachers of commercial law, a field in which facts of business practice had been supposed to have some relevance to adjudication since Mansfield's time.

for example, thought the judge ought to have an immensely detailed acquaintance with 18th century criminal procedure.

> Our law is one of the few occupations where history is of direct and specific utility. Traditionally it is by an inquiry into what the law was or has been that the solution of present perplexities is sought. The further back in time this quest is pressed, the more difficult is the finding, and it is then that the aid of the legal historian is sought. Where such a historian, therefore, undertakes to speak of the past, since it is something a future court may need and use, he assumes a responsibility not lightly to be dismissed. This is a moral obligation the implications of which are far-reaching, for not only must the judge put trust in his word, but the parties-litigant whose rights and whose fortunes will be affected by it . . .[77]

This was all the more astonishing as it came from someone who certainly could not have been accused of writing practitioner's history, and who was one of the fiercest critics of textbook legal history. Yet he was even more hostile to laymen's trespasses on law; for he felt himself to be first and foremost a lawyer. His work locates colonial law in its full political context of imperial administration and shows how much its forms owed to that context; yet the relation of lawyer's detail is so thorough and minute that it tends to occupy almost the whole foreground—presumably because it is the lawyer's detail that will most interest the 20th century judge.[78]

The instance of Goebel may seem unique, and in a way it is—no one had a greater command of the legal sources or delighted more in flourishing them in the faces of the ignorant[79] —but the strategy for saving professional identity was entirely typical. The persisting case-law centeredness of legal scholarship hardly needs documentation, but it is worth noting that all those commonly named as principals in the revolt against formalism—Holmes, Gray, Pound, Frank and Llewellyn—contributed to it;[80]

178

---

77. Goebel & T.R. Naughton, *Law Enforcement in Colonial New York* xxxiii-xxxiv (1944).

78. Goebel's legal history materials are the first to stress extralegal influences on law (*supra*, note 48); as director of the Foundation for Research in Legal History he sponsored the publication of studies of the history of corporations that were the most ambitious attempts yet to relate modern law to social and economic context [Armand DuBois, *English Business Companies after the Bubble Act* (1933); Shaw Livermore, *Early American Land Companies* (1939)]; and his background essays in *The Law Practice of Alexander Hamilton*, *supra*, note 49, especially those on "The Law and the Judicial Scene," *id.* at I, 1 and "The Economy in Hamilton's New York," *id.* at II, 29, reveal a grasp on extra-legal detail as sure as on the law. It is especially striking that someone with so much range should have deliberately unbalanced so much of his work towards the internal.

79. See, e.g. "*Ex parte Clio*," 54 *Colum. L. Rev.* 450 (1954), reviewing W.W. Crosskey, *Politics and the Constitution* (1953).

80. Frank did try to direct attention away from appellate and toward trial courts in *Courts on Trial* (1949). Llewellyn, in his general work in legal sociology, notably "What Price Contract —An Essay

and before long I hope a history of American legal pragmatism will properly stress its conservatism in this respect as
much as its iconoclasm in others.   Pound's life (1870-1964)
spanned the entire period.   His biographer has related how his
professionalism, his dislike (heightened by the New Deal) of
administrative regulation, and his increasingly uncritical admiration of the judiciary steadily narrowed his interests to the point
where, in the late 1940's, the prophet of "sociological jurisprudence" stopped reading social science altogether in order to give
his full time to Anglo-American case reports.[81]   Pound had been
one of the first to venture outside the law-box.   After a while
he did not like what he saw, so he went back in and slammed
the door.

This was an extreme version of a common process of
withdrawal.   It is once again necessary to emphasize that this
limitation of scope to gathering fodder for the judge, even the
fantastically erudite and open-minded judge of the legal pragmatists' imagination, was, in view of their general intellectual
program, almost completely arbitrary.   They undertook to look
at law from the point of view of the functions it performed in
society: this led them to the position that for the purpose of
organizing research, it was useful to think of law as a system
of social control, or as what officials do about disputes, or
lawyers do for a living.   By any of these standards litigation
in courts (especially litigation to appeal) was only a fragment
of diverse complex processes, and through the 20th century a
rapidly shrinking one; few of the graduates of the schools
where the legal pragmatists taught were ever likely to have
much contact with it.[82]   Yet the continuing preoccupation of
legal research, including legal history, with the work of judges
is so taken for granted that its extraordinary perversity is rarely
even noticed.

Why this should have happened remains something of a
mystery.   Undoubtedly the great success of the case method as
a teaching device had something to do with it: practically the
whole curriculum has been organized around criticizing the work
of the appellate bench and this has carried over to research

179

---

in Perspective," 40 *Yale L.J.* 704 (1931), showed he was perfectly
aware of the limits of the case-lawyers' view—which makes it all
the more interesting that he settled down into that view in *The Common Law Tradition: Deciding Appeals* (1960). See text at notes
97-99, *infra.*

81.   David Wigdor, *Roscoe Pound, Philosopher of Law* 207-81 (1974).

82.   On changes in the role of courts and types of law practice, see Hurst,
Lawmakers 85-87, 301-305; Robert T. Swaine, *The Cravath Firm and
its Predecessors,* II, 461-66 *et passim* (1948).

because law professors tend to direct their research towards ultimate incorporation in teaching materials. But by itself this explanation will not serve. Judicial opinions cannot, for instance, be *that* much better teaching tools than administrative opinions, yet courses in Administrative Law tend to be about judicial review of administrative action. That is probably because judges have something administrators do not have: the capacity to represent the learned and cultivated side of law practice,[83] immunity from at least the more obvious kinds of client or constituent pressure, and the ideal of the law-giver who derives his authority from sources independent of the dominant forces in society. Yet the learning, immunity, and authority that judges were supposed to symbolize all followed from their expertise in the common law tradition, which the legal pragmatists had spent two decades deriding.[84] That was all right when their basic pro-

180

---

83. See the extraordinary elegy of Julius Goebel, Jr., "Learning and Style in the Law—An Historian's Lament," 61 *Colum. L. Rev.* 1393 (1961), in which the author calls up the classical learning of great past judges ("Diversion . . . was on a level almost incomprehensible to us. I cannot picture Holt, or Hardwicke, or Mansfield viewing a so-called 'better' program on television, or, if trapped into so doing, esteeming what they had looked upon to be a fit subject of conversation." *Id.* at 1395-96.); and contrasts it invidiously with the present situation:

> A reasoned opinion that rests upon impeccable authority and that carries conviction by reason of this and of its inner logic, unquestionably is difficult to compose. Fortunate it is that there are so many written. Such are, alas, much outnumbered by those patchworks of cases stated, passages from cyclopedias and snippets from a *Restatement*. This is a style highly esteemed in some trans-Appalachian jurisdictions . . . [This has been accompanied by] the descresence of allusive and epigrammatic writing, which so conduces to elegance . . .
> Surely the law must lose something of majesty if its oracles think of their pronouncements in terms of threading a pipe or of contriving a passable mitre joint. Let us leave such ideas to the legislators. To judges and lawyers the past calls out that we should cherish writing as the exercise of art. This let us not forget.

Id. at 1398-1400.

84. David Riesman pointed this out in 1951:

> To be sure, most lawyers today recognize that their most important work is done in the office, not in the courtroom; the elaborate masked ritual of the courtroom holds attraction only for the neophyte and the layman. Yet it is astonishing how strongly the image of the judge stands as the image of the lawyer-hero. While at the better law schools at least one and often nearly three years are spent in debunking upper-court opinions, in showing their largely derivative quality, their endless fallacies, their interminable self-confusion as to what they are "actually" deciding (as against what they say they are deciding), the better products of the better law schools want nothing more exciting when they get out than a chance to serve as clerk [as I did] to an appellate judge—the "upperer" the better. And as members of the bar they will move heaven and earth to get on the bench themselves (which is the source of much dirt in our political system, since many congressmen have partners who itch to be judges), although they know from prac-

gram was critical, e.g., revealing the personal and class bases of Supreme Court decisions invalidating social legislation, or the confusions and contradictions of Langdellian method. When the Court switched directions in 1937, the growth of executive power in the New Deal seemed to some lawyers to portend administrative tyranny unless checked by the courts; and when the Germans reduced their courts to tools of the Nazi Party, even the most skeptical lawyers felt compelled to reassert the idea of legal autonomy.[85] Under this compulsion, perhaps because no better substitute had been found in the meantime, perhaps no better could be found, the notion of the common law tradition revived.[86]

The revival took several forms, all the way from Catholic natural law theory and Hutchins' and Adler's neo-Artistotelianism to Thurman Arnold's view that the idea of neutral and wisely applied law above men is a myth, but one whose general acceptance (by powerholders as well as others) is necessary to civilized society.[87] Two forms that were especially significant for legal historiography found their archetypes in the work of Pound and Llewellyn.

181

---

tical experience how little power the judge has under the American system and how skilled lawyers are in emasculating that little.

"Towards an Anthropological Science of Law and the Legal Profession," in Riesman, *Individualism Reconsidered* 440-41 (1954). See also *id.* at 462-63.

85. I am uttering here what is rapidly becoming the standard social-political explanation for the decline of Realism. See Edward A. Purcell, Jr., "American Legal Realism Between the Wars: Legal Realism and the Crisis of Democratic Theory," 75 *Am. Hist. Rev.* 424 (1969); G. Edward White, "The Evolution of Reasoned Elaboration: Jurisprudential Criticism and Social Change," 59 *Va. L. Rev.* 279, 281-285 (1973); both of which stress the attacks associating the positivism and skepticism of the Realist movement with fascism, and later with communism.

And yet I wonder. One might have thought that the rise of Nazism and Stalinism would as likely have promoted social research in law as put an end to it, would have encouraged Americans to investigate the sociological bases of the rule of law rather than simply to assert its autonomy from social conditions. This is the sort of work that C.J. Friedrich, Franz Neumann, and Friedrich Hayek all did (from rather different perspectives); was there similar work going on in the law schools? I am not sure, but I think the answer is not much even among the émigré lawyers. *The Journal of Legal & Political Sociology*, started in 1942, began to address these issues (Karl Llewellyn and David Riesman were among the first contributors), but it petered out after a few numbers. The retreat from external social perspectives on law in the late 1930s and 40s is only just beginning to be explained. We need to know a lot more about the politics of law teachers, their attitudes towards the New Deal, towards communism and civil liberties in the 1950s; more also about the contribution of the émigré scholars, about how they altered (and failed to alter) our perspectives on study of the legal system.

86. Or perhaps simply survived; it may never have been abandoned.

87. On the Catholic natural lawyers and Hutchins and Adler, see Purcell, *supra*, note 11; on Arnold, see his *Symbols of Government* (1962); Rumble, *supra*, note 11 at 217-220.

Pound's contribution was his famous idea of a "taught legal tradition." He began to develop this idea well before the general crisis of pragmatic thought in the 1930's (as has been mentioned already, his was one of the earliest retreats from pragmatism), as a method of attacking the "economic interpretation" of legal history, the domesticated and vulgarized Marxism of the historians who assumed law to be nothing more than an instrument for realizing the self-interest of a dominant class, wielded by judicial members of that class.[88] Proponents of this interpretation were most vulnerable when they were most specific, as when they tried to explain results in individual cases by reference to the class position of the winning party or the judge.[89] Pound was able to run rings around them, showing that contemporary judges with the same backgrounds had reached opposite conclusions on the same issues; and that big economic interests had sometimes won in the courts and sometimes lost.[90] It was a completely sterile debate, since both sides assumed that decisions in the appellate courts accurately represent the extent to which the legal system responds to the claims of economic interests[91] (even if this were valid the case samples were too thin to prove anything either way). The interesting aspect of the debate was that when it provoked Pound into insistence upon a degree of autonomy for law, this is what he came up with:

182

> Tenacity of a taught tradition is much more significant in our legal history than the economic conditions of time and place. These conditions have by no means been uniform, while the course of decision has been characteristically steady and uniform, hewing to common-law lines through five generations of rapid political, economic, and social change, and bringing about a *communis opinio* over the country as a whole on the over-

88. For an early American version, see Brooks Adams, *Centralization and the Law* (1906). The "economic interpretation" was most effective in the robust muckraking and debunking histories of the Supreme Court: notably Gustavus Myers, *History of the Supreme Court of the United States* (1918) and Louis B. Boudin, *Government by Judiciary* (1932). Other reductionist theories of law prevalent in the 1930's, such as Watsonian behavioristic psychology, apparently failed to influence historical writing.

89. Francis H. Bohlen, "The Rule in *Rylands v. Fletcher*," 59 *U. Pa. L. Rev.* 298 (1911); Walter Nelles, "*Commonwealth v. Hunt*," *supra*, note 61.

90. Pound's attacks on the "economic interpretation" may be found in "Political and Economic Interpretations of Legal History," *Proc. Am. Polit. Sci. Ass'n* 95 (1912); *Interpretations of Legal History*, ch. 5 (1923); *The Formative Era of American Law, supra*, note 35; "The Economic Interpretation and the Law of Torts," 53 *Harv. L. Rev.* 365 (1940).

91. For example, Pound concluded from the fact that interpretations of corporate and partnership law restricted businessmen's choice of forms of doing business and of ways of operating across state lines that "capitalists" (whom he conceded were the dominant class at the end of the 19th century) had suffered as much from courts' hanging on to traditional forms as had "laborers." See his *Interpretations of Legal History, supra*, note 90, at 111-112.

whelming majority of legal questions, despite the most divergent geographical, political, economic, social and even racial conditions . . . Economic and political conditions of time and place have led to legislative abrogations and alterations of rules and even at times to attempts to alter the course of the taught tradition. But such changes are fitted into the traditional system in their interpretation and application, and affect slowly or very little the principles, conceptions and doctrines which are the enduring law. The outstanding phenomenon is the extent to which a taught tradition, in the hands of judges drawn from any class one will, and chosen as one will, so they have been trained in the tradition, has stoood out against all manner of economically or politically powerful interests.[92]

Have we seen this before? Of course: it is our old friend, the common law tradition, the continuous, uniform development of law over time by masters of a method. The obviously political part of law, legislation, is "fitted into the traditional system" by interpretation, without much affecting it.[93] Otherwise, the only role for economic and social factors is that of supplying problems for the aloof inhabitants of the law-box to resolve by resort to their learned technique.[94]

183

The "economic interpretation" refused to concede any autonomy to law: your law-box, its authors said, is really empty. Pound rightly denied this, but when pressed to say what was in it, fell back on the old identification of legal autonomy with formal doctrinal development. This had two bad effects: it prevented the leading advocate of a sociological legal history (and most of the legal historians who followed him) from seeing how much American law *could* quite satisfactorily be explained as the outcome of organized economic interest-group pressure.[95] It

---

92. Pound, *Formative Era, supra,* note 35, at 83-84.

93. Pound explained the vulnerability of legislators to economic pressures by their lack of training in the tradition: "The legislator . . . has no settled habits of applying an authoritative technique to authoritatively given materials." "Economic Interpretation," *supra,* note 90, at 366. A colleague to whom I showed this passage suggested that since many judges are legislators who have failed of re-election, the critical training experience might be the crucible of failure.

94. The "taught tradition" idea seems particularly hard to square with Pound's historical account of various theories he supposed had influenced American judicial decision-making in the 19th century (law-of-nature theory, analytic and historical theories, etc.) or with his frequent criticisms (especially in his earlier years) of late 19th century courts on the grounds that they had prevented necessary adaptations to social and economic needs, including adaptations sought to be accomplished by legislation. He worked himself into the position of saying that the taught tradition, apparently proof against "all manner of economically or politically powerful interests," fell victim to the influence of any jurisprudential scribbler who happened to be in the neighborhood; and also that the autonomy of courts consisted in their being perpetually out of tune with modern needs—the very quality for which he had once attacked them.

95. For fine recent examples of what might be called a "neo-Progressive" approach, see Lawrence M. Friedman, "The Usury Laws of

also prevented them from inquiring further into what could not—into the ways in which the specialized activities inside the law-box might be variables independent of and directing, channelling, diverting or obstructing those pressures. If there was one thing that the realists had made clear, and left as their enduring legacy, it was that the autonomous element in law was *not*—at least not necessarily, not always—its surface formality; that indeed such formality was most likely to mask the unexamined (or at any rate unacknowledged) presence of outside political or economic influences. But if it wasn't that, what was it? Pound's regression to the "taught tradition" discouraged any attempt to find out.[96]

184

The other contribution that the pragmatic movement made to the eleventh-hour revival of the idea of tradition in law was given its best and fullest expression in the work of Llewellyn. He saw the "common law tradition" not as a continuously developing body of doctrine but as historically diverse methods ("craft-styles") of judicial decision-making:

> the general and pervasive manner over the country at large, at any given time, of going about the job, the general outlook, the ways of professional knowledge, the kinds of thing the men of the law are sensitive to and strive for, the tone and flavor of the working and of the results. [Craft-style] is well described as a "period-style"; it corrresponds to what we have long known as period-style in architecture or the graphic arts or furniture or music or drama.[97]

There were thus several traditions, each specific to a period; the period 1820-1860 having been dominated by a "grand style," 1880-1910 by a "formal style;" the period from 1930 onwards, Llewellyn believed, by a renaissance of the "grand style." (It is hopeless to explain Llewellyn's typology properly in a short space, but for those unfamiliar with it, here are the basics: a grand-style judge is concerned not only to harmonize his decisions, wherever feasible, with past case-law, but to justify them as functional; he tries to work out over time general approaches to handling recurrent types of dispute situations, approaches that will "make sense" to people in the disputants' positions. The formal-style judge, by contrast, cares only about making sure that each decision logically fits into a pre-existing doctrinal

---

Wisconsin: A Study in Legal and Social History," 1963 *Wisc. L. Rev.* 515; Robert S. Hunt, *Law and Locomotives* (1958).

96. I don't wish to imply that the *net* effect of Pound's influence on legal historiography was baneful. In this field as in so many others, he called attention to the right problems and pointed to suggestive lines of inquiry; and the fact that the Dean of the Harvard Law School uttered phrases like "sociological jurisprudence" gave social research in law respectability it could have acquired in no other way.

97. Llewellyn, *Common Law Tradition, supra,* note 80 at 36.

scheme: "the rules of law are to decide the cases; policy is for the legislature, not the courts."[98]) This was the most ingenious reconciliation yet of tradition and function in law. It did not turn its back on the idea of law as pragmatic method, social engineering; neither did it reject the work of past judges: it married the two in the tradition of the grand style. Tradition was preserved, but as exemplary rather than authoritative. Whatever its merits as jurisprudence,[99] this way of looking at law had incidental benefits for legal history. It encouraged the study of grand-style judges from the point of view of what made them exemplary, since the historian working in an age of unabashedly "policy-oriented" jurisprudence will try to bring out, rather than suppress as unfortunate or irrelevant, past judges' view of their society and of what law is needed for it. It is possible to see the two best judicial biographies of recent times, Levy's of Shaw and Reid's of Doe,[100] both grand-style judges, as reflecting the influence of pragmatic legal thought in treating their subjects as architects of bodies of socially serviceable case-law. Llewellyn also taught legal scholars to read judicial opinions more carefully, for rhetoric as well as result, for sources of analogy and authority, for facts used and facts ignored, and above all for the characterization of implications for future cases. (His own excursions into history are probably the best examples of the deployment of the method.)[101] Finally, the concept of period-style (though ahistorical in one of its premises, i.e., that present-day judges were recapturing the reasoning modes of 19th century ancestors fundamentally different in mental outlook)[102] suggested possibilities for historical-sociological theories of legal reasoning styles along the lines of Max Weber's, possibilities that are beginning to be realized in the work of Friedman, Horwitz, Nelson and Tushnet.[103]

185

---

98. *Id.* at 39. The most effective statement of the concept of craft-style is in Llewellyn, "On the Good, the True, the Beautiful in Law [1942]", in Llewellyn, *supra*, note 25 at 167.

99. For effective criticisms from differing perspectives, see Charles E. Clark & David Trubek, "The Creative Role of the Judge: Restraint and Freedom in the Common Law Tradition," 71 *Yale L.J.* 255 (1961); Duncan Kennedy, "Legal Formality", 2 *J. Legal Studies* 351 (1973).

100. Leonard W. Levy, *The Law of the Commonwealth and Chief Justice Shaw* (1957); John Phillip Reid, *Chief Justice: The Judicial World Of Charles Doe* (1967). Howe's biography of Holmes, *supra*, note 12, doesn't count as "judicial" biography because it ends before Holmes goes on the bench.

101. See Llewellyn articles cited *supra*, note 61.

102. Though perhaps not so different in their aspects with which Llewellyn was particularly concerned, as judges in commercial cases.

103. Lawrence M. Friedman, "On Legalistic Reasoning—A Footnote to Weber," 1966 *Wisc. L. Rev.* 148; Morton J. Horwitz, "The Emergence

Yet though Llewellyn's concept of tradition, unlike Pound's, pointed towards a more expansive historiography, it maintained the insider's perspective on law, specifically that of insider-as-advisor-to-the-judge. And there are disadvantages to the perspective even of the most social-context-conscious, cosmopolitan insider: everything gets filtered through the lens of professional working concerns and categories. This may have any or all of the following consequences.

(1) The insider's categories to which even extra-legal detail tends to be assimilated may, while rendering it familiar and manageable to lawyers, seriously distort it in other ways. A good illustration from our legal history is the category of "codification," under which has been subsumed a vast diversity of behavior: evangelical antilegalism; backwoods resistance to debt-collection; merchant creditors' pressure for more efficient debt-collection; anglophobe propaganda; small legal practitioners' complaints about pleading complexities; aesthetic distaste for the disordliness, and democratic distaste for the feudal origins, of the common law; Jefferson's, Bentham's, and Field's plans for codes; the Massachusetts Laws and Liberties of 1648, Field's procedural code, the Federal Rules of Civil Procedure, and the Uniform Commercial Code, not to mention the Law of the Twelve Tables and the BGB. There are few purposes indeed for which it makes any sense at all to lump all this stuff together; yet our historiography to a greater or lesser degree repeatedly did so, combining most of it into a single prolonged "codification movement" that supposedly lasted throughout the 19th century and achieved its greatest successes in the 20th.[104] Scholarship

---

of an Instrumental Conception of Law," 5 *Perspectives in Am. History* 287 (1971); William E. Nelson, "The Impact of the Antislavery Movement upon Styles of Judicial Reasoning in Nineteenth Century America," 87 *Harv. L. Rev.* 513 (1974); Mark Tushnet, "The American Law of Slavery 1810-1860: A Study in the Persistence of Legal Autonomy," 10 *L. & Soc'y Rev.* 119, *infra*. So far as I know, nobody has taken up Llewellyn's hint that it might be valuable to apply methods of art or architectural history to law.

104. The codification theme can be tracked from Charles M. Hepburn, "The Historical Development of Code Pleading in America and England," in *Select Essays, supra*, note 33 at II, 643; through Charles Warren, *A History of the American Bar*, Ch. 19 (1911), Alison Reppy, "The Field Codification Concept," in *David Dudley Field Centenary Essays* (Reppy ed. 1949); Pound, *Formative Era, supra*, note 35; and Howe, *supra*, note 48. The theme was picked up by Perry Miller in *The Life of the Mind in America* (1965) (Book 2, "The Legal Mentality"); and has recently been sounded again in Carl B. Swisher, *The Taney Period, 1836-64* at 339-56 (Oliver Wendell Holmes Devise History of the U.S. Supreme Court, V, 1974). One reason for what must be described as the obsession of our legal historians with this theme is that 19th century American lawyers were obsessed with it also; "codification" was the staple topic of their occasional essays, articles in law periodicals, and orations at bar dinners and memorials. They had as great a capacity to as-

is only recently beginning to break this "movement" up into its component parts.[105]

(2)   Appellate case-law comes to stand for the whole "legal system." This would be troublesome if only for the obvious reasons that it limits research to the legal business that happens to flow into the appellate courts; prevents institutional comparisons showing how alike courts are to other parts of the system, and how different, and how power and business are allocated among the various parts. (Prevailing jurisprudential theories of appropriate institutional jurisdiction or competence are likely seriously to misrepresent historical actualities in these matters.) It can also lead to a tendency to overintellectualize, to see the law as a complex body of attempted judicial and academic solutions to a set of philosophic puzzles. Obviously an extremely elaborate jurisprudential literature is an important cultural product, worth studying on its own terms; but as an *exclusive* approach to legal history, this can result in a perception of law as an elevated activity engaged in for its own sake by the lawyers and their clients, and thus fundamentally betray the nature of the subject.

(3)   Perhaps most important, history from the lawyer's perspective, if it pays any attention to the world outside the law-box, is bound to focus more closely on inputs than on outputs, and mostly on those inputs that the insiders consciously employ as materials of their craft. This is bound to leave out of consideration major (it is not necessary to argue primary) determinants of the shape and content of the law-box—the reasons for there being any law-box in the first place—i.e., what it is that people in society demand, or expect, of their legal order.

III

The readers of Willard Hurst's first major work, *The Growth*

---

similate everything to their own categories as we do. Even the great Haskins may have been somewhat taken in by the appeal of the "codification" category: compare his "Codification of Law in Colonial Massachussetts: A Study in Comparative Law," 30 *Indiana L.J.* 1 (1954) (Massachusetts Law and Liberties of 1648 is the first modern law code in the West) with Ronald G. Walters, 'New England Society and the Laws and Liberties of Massachusetts", 106 *Essex Inst. Hist. Colls.* 145 (1970) (the "Laws" is not "basically a code of law but rather something more mundane: a handbook for justices, an instrument for the use of a public and a body of magistrates likely to be of uncertain and conflicting knowledge." *Id.* at 167).

105.   See especially Richard E. Ellis, *The Jeffersonian Crisis* (1971); William E. Nelson, *Americanization of the Common Law*, ch. 5 (1975); Friedman, "Law Reform," *supra*, note 3; Maxwell Bloomfield," William Sampson and the Codifiers: The Roots of American Legal Reform, 1820-1830," 11 *Am. J. Leg. Hist.* 234 (1967); Gerald W. Gawalt, "Sources of Anti-Lawyer Sentiment in Massachusetts, 1740-1840," 14 *Am. J. Leg. Hist.* 283 (1970).

187

of American Law (1950), could tell from the first few pages that although the book purported only to synthesize existing second- ary materials, the synthesis represented something new in Amer- ican legal history. This was a history of law-making agencies— not only courts, but constitutional conventions, chief executives, administrative agencies, and the bar—inquiring into the social functions these agencies had served since the founding of the Republic. Though described with an insider's understanding and grasp of detail, its perspective on the operations of the legal sys- tem was that of an outsider: it was a critical Inspector General's report on how legal institutions had served the society that supported them. Hurst had formulated and announced his pro- gram of defection from the main line of legal historiography as early as 1942.[106] *The Growth of American Law* was the corner- stone for the imposing body of external legal history that he, and the Wisconsin school of legal studies he founded,[107] have been writing since, and are still adding to.

188

This essay has advanced the argument that the actualization of pragmatic legal theory in historical writing was stunted and sometimes choked off entirely by the reluctance of legal scholars to shake off their old roles of interpreters of the common law tradition. But in Hurst's work pragmatic legal theory reached full flowering, probably unexcelled anywhere else in American legal scholarship. Others have appraised,[108] some of them brilli- antly,[109] his work in general: my concern here is only to try to show how his ways of thinking about law dissolved the con- straints most legal historians had felt upon taking an external approach.

For this purpose, it is useful to consider Hurst's work as an effort to apply the general insights of pragmatic theory, espe- cially as formulated by John Dewey,[110] to the study of the

---

106. "Legal History: A Research Program," 1942 *Wisc. L. Rev.* 319.
107. The works of this school on Wisconsin legal history are: Lawrence M. Friedman, *Contract Law in America* (1965); Hunt, *supra*, note 95; Spencer Kimball, *Insurance and Public Policy* (1960); George J. Kuehnl, *The Wisconsin Business Corporation* (1959); James A. Lake, *Law and Mineral Wealth: The Legal Profile of the Wisconsin Mining Industry* (1962); Francis W. Laurent, *The Business of a Trial Court, 100 Years of Cases* (1959); Samuel Mermin, *Jurisprudence and Statecraft: The Wisconsin Development Authority and its Implications* (1963); Earl F. Murphy, *Water Purity* (1961).
108. See the "Bibliography", *infra*, this issue, § V.
109. The outstanding ones are both, as it happens, by contributors to this volume: Harry N. Scheiber, "At the Borderland of Law and Economic History: The Contributions of Willard Hurst," 75 *Am. Hist. Rev.* 744 (1969), and Mark Tushnet, "Lumber and the Legal Process," 1972 *Wisc. L. Rev.* 114.
110. There are other significant influences detectable in Hurst's work, notably Max Weber's; but as a factor shaping Hurst's external per-

specific historical phenomenon of American law in the 19th and 20th centuries. "Law" is here a general label for several species of applied social intelligence, which may be understood only by reference to the conditions out of which they are generated and by the consequences to which they give rise. The basic function of law, as of any other form of social intelligence, is to increase men's ability to achieve rational control over social change in order to liberate their natural capacity for growth. Men achieve rational control through experimental method, which expands their empirical appreciation of the consequences of their conduct; expanded awareness of consequences enlarges their ideas of what is desirable as well as of the most efficient means of attaining it; and this leads to growth in the range and quality of life experience, especially emotional experience, for "reason probably finds justification ultimately as an instrument by which men achieve more subtle, more varied and more shared emotion."[111]

189

The special focus of Hurst's attention is governmental activity, the work of agencies and of those who interpret and apply it; Hurst calls this "law." (It is not a definition of law, since Hurst does not try to define law; it is a term of convenience without any precise boundaries.) His reason for concentrating on official action is that the state possesses special characteristics that impart to the exercise of directive intelligence through its agencies an exceptional social significance. Of all associations in society, it is the public organized in the state, acting through the legal order, that stands the best chance of increasing rational control over social change. This is not to say that American law has lived up to its potential in this respect. Far from it: one of Hurst's main themes is that social change has usually been permitted to take place by "drift," "default," or "inertia," by which is meant experience transmuted into social action without the intervention of reflective intelligence. The consciousness from which people draw their desires and preferred means of satisfying them tends to be imprisoned in habitual modes and forms,[112] but old forms are continually coming up against and mixing with one another, in different combinations, thus con-

---

spective, American pragmatic thought seems to me to have been more significant.

111. Hurst, "The Law in United States History," 105 *Proc. Am. Phil. Soc.* 518, 519 (1960). For Dewey on the same themes, see, e.g., *Experience and Nature*, ch. 10 (2d ed. 1929).

112. For Hurst on drift, see *Law and Social Process in United States History* (1960), especially at 66-75; cf. Dewey on habit, *Human Nature and Conduct*, Pt. 1 (1922).

tinually producing a new social environment.[113] Acted upon by new conditions, the old forms will of course yield new consequences. Men's failure to subject new conditions to experimental evaluations means that they are constantly being surprised and baffled by experience, instead of being able to achieve some mastery over it in the interests of human growth.

For Hurst, as for American Progressives generally, the most conspicuous example of "drift" is the persistence through the late 19th and early 20th centuries of the habitual consciousness of private-market-and-business-oriented individualism.[114] In the early 19th century this had been a mode of thinking more functional for growth: it had released human talents and energies for the purpose of settling a continent and fulfilling the basic economic conditions for community existence. But at the same time it had defined business as the main arena for the exercise of talent, so that instrumental intelligence was rarely directed toward the elaboration of any but the most short-term economic consequences of social action. Private economic interests had thus in time come to overwhelm social life, with the results that: (1) men's consciousness of the desirable and how to reach it came to take account only of immediate economic costs and benefits (a method of thought Hurst calls "bastard pragmatism") and not of longer-run consequences for more various modes of growth; and (2) men had lost the talent for politics, that is, for organizing to promote, through the legal agencies of the state, ideas of the general good of their communities less parochial than purely economic interest.[115]

Hurst thus follows the main tradition of Progressive thought in relating the exercise of social intelligence to conditions of social organization: its effectiveness depends upon the wide dispersal of power among diverse solidary communities of shared values. Thus rational policy-making, dispersal of power, and community solidarity are all conditions of one another's existence; and all three are conditions of social growth.[116] The

190

---

113. This phrase tries very clumsily to give a brief impression of Hurst's intricate theoretical account of how imprisonment in habit produces social drift. For this account in its most developed form in Hurst's work, see his *Justice Holmes on Legal History* 11-13 *et passim* (1964).

114. For typical descriptions of this consciousness, see Hurst, *id.* at 39-50; *Law and Social Process, supra*, note 112 at 54-55.

115. Hurst's most powerful expression of these ideas remains that in the final chapter of his *Lawmakers, supra*, note 11, at 439-446 *et passim*; see also *Law and the Conditions of Freedom in the Nineteenth Century United States* (1967). Here the allegiance to Dewey is especially strong: see *The Public and its Problems* (1927).

116. Hurst, "Legal Elements," *supra*, note 6 at 88-89; see Dewey, *id.*, especially at chs. 5-6. There is an excellent discussion of this aspect

importance of law in society (though Hurst keeps insisting that like other forms of rational planning law can never have more than a marginal directive impact on social change) is that it has special equipment to help nudge these conditions into being. In particular, as the monopolist of legitimate force, the state has authority to hold private power accountable to the general welfare and in extreme cases to adjust its distribution in society, either by breaking up power centers or balancing them with countervailing powers. But perhaps the most important feature of state action is that it is normatively rational, is supposed to operate through forms and procedures designed to encourage deliberate, informed, and accountable decision-making. More than any other association the government is subject to expectations that its decisions will not be habitual reflexes, but will be mediated through careful reflection upon long-run consequences; and it has extraordinary resources (e.g. the ability to call upon a wide range of expert opinion representing diverse interests in legislative investigation, administrative rule-making, etc.) to generate the appropriate laboratory conditions for the operations of experimental intelligence. In other words, the norms of American constitutionalism ought to provide an especially favorable environment for pragmatic method.[117]

191

The legal historian's task, as Hurst sees it, is to measure the actual past performance of government against this potential. It takes a historian to do this, because only a perspective on several generations can reveal the habitual modes that have conditioned decision-making as well as the long-run consequences of the actual decisions. The present generation of lawyers needs to know, and needs history to inform it, which circumstances promote, and which prevent, intelligent direction of society in favor of growth. Hurst's rebellion against the dominant tradition in legal scholarship was not made in the name of disinterested reconstruction of the past; he is an intensely committed moralist, for whom the past is full of dreadful warnings.

But for the purpose of this essay, I want to look at these issues exactly backwards from the way Hurst does. He is always

---

of Progressive thought in David E. Price, "Community and Control: Critical Democratic Theory in the Progressive Period," 68 *Am. Polit. Sci. Rev.* 1663, 1672 (1974).

117. For a representative passage on the constitutional ideal, see Hurst, "Legal Elements", at 3-7. Hurst never goes quite so far as to equate constitutionalism and his own normative pragmatic method (though he is not entirely innocent of sometimes confusing them in his discourse), since the constitutional ideal has held officials and private holders accountable to serve *individual* life, but not (at least not consistently) to serve social or community life. See *Law and Social Process, supra,* note 112 at 3.

concerned to see how history can contribute to the living lawyer's exercise of pragmatic method in the public interest; but it is also worthwhile to ask how his vision of pragmatic method contributes to his work as a historian. I think the answer is that, while the general theoretical apparatus outlined above creates some troublesome problems of its own in Hurst's work, it is effective in freeing that work from the limitations of the insider's perspective.

For one thing, Hurst does not feel out of place or pulled apart by being an historian in a law school; he sees no opposition between social research in law and lawyer's business. His view is in keeping not only with Dewey's insistence on the unity of thought and action but with the "Wisconsin idea"—that social science research in the university should lead to social reform through legislation. Historical research and legislative drafting are just specialized aspects of the operations of instrumental intelligence. His paradigm example of law's working the way it should work is the development of workmen's compensation in Wisconsin in the early 20th century: John Commons's university research seminars helped Charles McCarthy's legislative research department develop the legislation; and advisory committees of employers, unions, insurance companies, and the public helped administer it.[118] In fact, if one had to sum up in a phrase Hurst's deviation from the mainstream of legal historiography, it would be that his allegiances are to the Wisconsin Progressive tradition of lawmaking instead of the common law tradition.[119]

This has important consequences for his work. His first book made clear that he had no interest in linking law practice to the authority and complexity of common law tradition, since he

192

---

118. Hurst, *Law and Social Process, supra,* note 112 at 37-41.
119. But it would be misleading to conclude that Hurst simply carried on a going tradition at the Wisconsin Law School, since the Law School was only really brought into the Wisconsin tradition after World War II. In the heyday of the Wisconsin idea before World War I, the faculty consisted mostly of part-time practitioners; after World War I, "the faculty's major service contribution related not to legislation, but to law in the courts," i.e., work on the Restatements. John E. Conway, "The Law School: Service to the State and Nation," 1968 *Wisc. L. Rev.* 345, 346. The "law-and-society" approach that now distinguishes the Wisconsin Law School was pioneered after World War II by men recruited to the faculty by Dean Lloyd K. Garrison just before it: notably Jacob H. Beuscher and Willard Hurst. See W. Scottt Van Alstyne, Jr., "The University of Wisconsin Law School 1868-1968: An Outline History," *id.* at 321, 330-31; and Fran Thomas, *Law in Action: Legal Frontiers for Natural Resources Planning—The Work of Professsor Jacob H. Beuscher* (Land Economics Monographs No. 4, 1972).
    Hurst therefore had to cut all his own trails. But of course it is not likely that his enterprise could have prospered anywhere else as well as in Madison.

thought that a stubborn clinging to traditional images of the profession was in part responsible for the bar's failure since 1870 to realize its possibilities for exercising social leadership: there were too many lawyers who were just technicians with no sense of the larger social effects of their jobs.[120]   (The bar's contributions to "law reform" with Restatements, uniform laws, and the like don't count; the Wisconsin Progressive wants social reform through law, not technical law reform.[121])   Nor does he need to preserve the centrality of courts in legal study for their symbolic capacity to legitimate the legal order as a whole through their claims to autonomy derived from the distinctiveness of their doctrines and procedures: since far from thinking law achieves its capacity for control over social change from its distinctive forms, he believes one of the common causes of "drift" is mindless adherence to such forms.[122]   Like Llewellyn, he replaces tradition-as-doctrine with pragmatic method as the source of what little directive influence law is ever likely to achieve—you don't achieve control by denying you're part of society but by recognizing how much you are a part of it—but does not go on to equate pragmatic method with case-law craftsmanship; because although courts continue to have an important public role as protectors of liberties against arbitrary state action, their pre-Civil War careers as major planners and coordinators of state policy have long since ended.[123]

193

The great strength that his historical work derives from his pragmatist's vision is the outsider's perspective: everything is to be examined for what it tells us about law's capacity to overcome the heavy odds in favor of social drift.   Hurst's masterwork, the huge study of the legal history of the Wisconsin lumber industry,[124] responds to a single accusing question: how did it come about that the legal system so failed in its job of providing rational processes to increase awareness of long-run consequences that it permitted Wisconsin lumbermen to cut 30 million acres of forest to exhaustion?[125]   Answering this leads him

---

120. See Hurst, *Lawmakers* at 370.
121. For an illuminating discussion of the distinction, see Friedman, "Law Reform," *supra*, note 3.
122. See, e.g., *Law and Economic Growth: The Legal History of the Lumber Industry in Wisconsin, 1836-1915* (1964) [hereinafter, Hurst, *Law & Lumber*] at 99, 298.
123. See Hurst, *supra* note 82; and *Law & Lumber* 249-50 (on built-in institutional limitations of common law litigation as decisionmaking method).
124. *Law & Lumber.*
125. I do not mean that this book is accusing in tone; on the contrary it is a model of scholarly neutrality, full of warnings against applying the criteria of the present age to the 19th century. (The earlier

into (a) an account of the basic social and cultural conditions (scarcity of working capital, abundance of land, an aggressive manipulativeness towards nature, etc.) that engendered the consciousness of 19th century Wisconsin policy-makers; (b) a decription of the consciousness itself ("bastard pragmatism," measurement of benefits by short-term money yields); and (c) an analysis of the results of the applications of this consciousness to legal policy towards the lumber industry (fragmentation of decision-making into one-at-a-time resolution of strictly local problems; great ingenuity in promoting—finding non-monetary subsidies for, allocating power and resources in favor of, inventing financing devices to benefit—those interests believed most capable of getting timber cut, transported, and marketed; also complete failure to bring to awareness, and hence to deal with, problems like depletion of the forest or the conditions of lumber labor).

194

By his choice to organize his work around the concept of "law", Hurst has committed himself to a version of the box model of the legal order in society, but it is a wonderfully different box from those of the standard legal histories. It is much larger, of course, since it includes all official activity: its contents are the habitual modes and forms of official thought—dialect variations, as it were, of the dominant consciousness of the surrounding culture—such as a legislative disposition to protect working men through labor liens but not through state accident insurance. The dialects are significant data for Hurst if and only if they are likely to be consequential for a society's growth; this means that although his work is rich in detail, it is all detail accumulated towards generalization about its social function. As a result—

(1) It tends to be what we might call democratic detail. Legal historians have favored aristocratic detail, worked into intricate tapestries by jurisconsults out of the appellate case law; Hurst's concern is with the system's routine business. This is partly because the effectiveness of law as an instrument of growth has to be assessed by its impact on the ordinary people in society[126] but also because habitual consciousness is formed

Lawmakers is much more overtly didactic.) But it is a grim and passionate book all the same, the more impressively so for its outward reserve.

126. Cf. Hurst's very Brandeisian early statement of this position:
  Emphasizing the economic setting, [a legal history course] would deal [in part] with the security and values of individual personality in a world increasingly marked by centralized, large-scale power arrangements. The emphasis

out of the cumulation of tiny decisions. The study of big decisions fundamentally misleads, since it is only by tracking long sequences that it is possible to sketch the dynamics of drift.

(2) A remarkably small proportion of Hurst's detail consists of the technical stuff of doctrine and procedure beloved of internal legal historians. At least in 19th century Wisconsin law related to lumber, on which Hurst has read *everything*, and reported everything he thinks significant, the particular forms of lawyer's law simply do not seem to have possessed much social significance.[127] The legal variables that *do* matter by his criteria tend to be broader institutional or conceptual traits of the system—e.g. adversary process in litigation as a means of organizing facts and bringing them to the awareness of decision-makers; or the survival into new contexts of thought-patterns formed in old ones, such as the fee simple as the desirable mode of conveying timberland, or the English practice of treating standing timber as an ordinary commodity of trade.[128] And Hurst always makes it clear that peculiar dialect-forms of the legal order survive and flourish in part *because* of outside social conditions, not (as Pound's "taught tradition" theory holds) despite them; thus, for example, the 700 lumber-industry contract cases Hurst studies have autonomous characteristics (are "contract-law cases first, and lumber industry cases second" and doctrinally stable over the industry's lifetime) because the abstraction of contract doctrine met the industry's immediate needs for security of market dealings; and the lumbermen's modes of thought did not encourage them to seek anything beyond those needs.[129]

(3) Hurst's organization around the concept of social function encourages comparison among official institutions, and between official and unofficial institutions.

It must be added that Hurst's theory also has some disadvantages for his history.[130] Two of a general nature might be mentioned here:

(1) The theory associates normatively adequate exercise of pragmatic method, or instrumental intelligence, with growth, and

195

---

would be on the small man—laborer, white-collar worker, farmer, small business man. Hurst, *supra*, note 106, at 331.

127. See, for one of the rare instances in which Hurst cites a pleading form as significant, *Law & Lumber* 354-55 (where he also points out that it wasn't *very* significant).

128. See citations to *Law & Lumber, supra,* notes 122, 123.

129. *Law & Lumber* 289-90.

130. For other criticisms (in the course of generally appreciative treatments) of Hurst's work as theory and history, see the articles by Scheiber and Tushnet, *supra,* note 109; Julius Stone, Book Review, 78 *Harv. L. Rev.* 1687 (1965); and Richard B. Abrams, Book Review, 24 *Stan. L. Rev.* 765 (1972).

failure adequately to exercise it with inertia and drift. This makes it hard to deal with historical situations in which, in retrospect, it appears that heightened awareness of consequences would have been dysfunctional for growth (as Hurst conceives it) and a relative lack of awareness functional. This is most likely to happen when people's interests are in fundamental opposition, but at least one side doesn't know that: and Hurst himself suggests this situation has been a common one:

> [O]n the whole contemporary community values supported, acquiesced in, or were indifferent or unseeing toward most of what private interest sought and obtained from law concerning exploitation of the Wisconsin forest. Undoubtedly there would have been more conflict, and more skulduggery, had contemporary attitudes and energies existed to bring more of these matters to explicit issue. . . . [But in this history] the limitations of men's perception, imagination, and will were more significant than their purposes.[131]

196   To the extent that a condition of growth is the accommodation of conflicting interests, it may be more functional for the legal system to obscure consequences rather than to reveal them,[131] to legitimate social change by pretending that it all accords with comfortable old forms. I am perhaps suggesting here that Hurst's normative view of the decision-making process may somewhat blunt a sense of historical irony.

(2) Hurst's history relies upon a model of the interaction of law and society drawn chiefly from the peculiar context of 19th century American state promotion and regulation of economic enterprise, which may be difficult to apply outside that context. In a way, Hurst has got hold of the easiest case: (a) the social actors to whom legal regulation is addressed may be counted on to look to extract short-term economic advantage from every decision; (b) they have relatively clear access to legal decision-makers (legislature and courts); (c) the decision-makers pretty much share their views of what is generally desirable for the society; they are really part of the same subculture of entrepreneurs; (d) the rest of society shares or passively accepts the same norms as they do; (e) regulation is almost all promotional and facilitative, rather than adversary; so that there are few significant problems of enforcement.

One could go on, but the point is that these particular conditions all combine to minimize the terrible problems of method faced by those who would practice an external historiography. They make it possible to infer social conditions and consequences

---

131. Tushnet, *supra*, note 109 at 125-26 points out in this connection (citing Albert Hirschman on unbalanced growth) that economic development may sometimes *depend* upon concealment of externalities.

to a large extent from the legal materials themselves:[132] which in other contexts, involving groups whose norms are alien to those of the decision-makers, or whose access is limited, or who seek symbolic legitimacy for themselves and condemnation of others rather than economic gain from the legal system, or seek nothing from it because they can get what they need outside it, or who resist compliance with its decisions, one cannot safely do.

But even for the study of contexts differing from those out of which he developed his theory, Hurst's milking of legal detail for every ounce of social significance has contributed not only a theoretical account of the social function of law, but some extremely refined techniques for what might be called the intellectual history of government action: how the state, through legal process, expresses social values; the devices by which it ratifies and legitimates certain values and ranks them in relation to others. These techniques—which enable the reader to discover basic notions about prevailing views of favored economic interests, the nature of property rights, or the appropriate role of government from such clues as how a statute allocates burdens of proof—are useful in their own right, whether or not the context also permits inferences as to the actual effects of law on social behavior.

197

Hurst's main contribution has been to expose the hitherto invisible ways in which the apparently most commonplace incidents of a legal order illuminate social values. By so doing he managed, almost single-handed, to lower from inside the drawbridge over the moat isolating American legal from general historiography.

Others had been bridging the moat from the outside—with studies of 19th century public policy and corporations, of public lands, and of administrative history[133]—but it required an in-

---

132. Tushnet, *id.* at 122, says that purely legal materials cannot adequately test even Hurst's theory, and that his "law centeredness seeems totally ingenuous." This is unfair. Hurst is acutely aware of the problems of law-centered research, and repeatedly qualifies the inferences he thinks permissible to draw from it. See, e.g., "Legal Elements" at 21-22; *Law & Lumber* at 225-227 (where Hurst also makes it clear he did not use business records because none existed). But *some* inferences about the effects of law on extralegal behavior can be drawn from the legal sources: e.g., the output of the legal system may be supposed to be important, or at least to be thought important, to people who resort frequently to it (seek amending acts in the legislature, litigate in the courts); and less important to those who could use it but do not (like the big lumber companies that tended to refrain from litigation). *Law & Lumber* 200, 226, 321 *et passim.*

133. See Scheiber, "Federalism and the American Economic Order," *infra* at 57.

sider with unassailable lawyer's as well as historian's credentials
to throw open the gates. For a time, Hurst's work was about
the only view law students obtained on the social context of the
history of their law.[134] But since what I have called the Second
Revival of American legal history started a few years ago, his
perspective is becoming the dominant one.[135] One of the events
signifying the revival was the devotion of an issue of *Perspectives in American History* to legal history. That was a joint
effort by lawyers and historians; and of course the leading article was written by Willard Hurst.[136]

I believe the present collection will also show how busily
the traffic has been humming across the drawbridge between law
and history. I think it best to let these essays, written by people
trained in law, in history, and in both fields, speak to the reader
for themselves, unmediated by any attempt on my part to generalize factitiously upon the relationships and resemblances among
them. I am only sorry that in the nature of the case this
collection could not include another contribution to the external
historiography of American law by the field's most distinguished,
most prolific and most active practitioner.

198

---

134. See Re, *supra*, note 61.
135. See, e.g., the large number of respondents stressing the necessity of
    an external approach to legal history (and taking such an approach
    in their courses and publications) in Joseph H. Smith, *Report on
    the Teaching of Legal History in American Law Schools* (AALS
    Legal History Section; Nov. 1973).
136. This is his "Legal Elements," *supra*, note 6.

MORTON HORWITZ AND THE TRANSFORMATION OF AMERICAN LEGAL HISTORY

WYTHE HOLT*

I. INTRODUCTION

The publication in 1977 of Morton Horwitz's *The Transformation of American Law 1780-1860*[1] was a signal event for American legal historians. Prefigured by the appearance of some of its chapters in the preceding several years[2]—chapters whose promise "dazzled"[3] many of us who were entering the field during that time—and culminating what appeared to be a burst of energy and enthusiasm in an area previously arid, antiquarian, oriented toward the colonial era, and relatively unpopulated with sound scholars, the book seemed at long last to herald a fresh and progressive "field theory"[4] with which to approach the study of American legal

* Professor of Law, University of Alabama. B.A., Amherst College; J.D., Ph.D., University of Virginia. An earlier version of this essay was read at a faculty seminar at Osgoode Hall Law School, York University, on March 12, 1979. Several of my colleagues and friends generously have given criticism and moral support indispensable for the completion of this essay: Peter d'Errico, Jay Feinman, Harry Glasbeek, Fred Konefsky, L.H. LaRue, Michael Mandel, Jack Schlegel, and especially Karl Klare. Partial financial support in the form of unresticted summer research grants has come from Dean Thomas Christopher and the University of Alabama School of Law. This essay is dedicated to the memory of *Marxist Perspectives* and to the spirit of its spirit, Eugene Genovese.

1. M. HORWITZ, THE TRANSFORMATION OF AMERICAN LAW, 1780-1860 (1977).

2. Chapter I originally appeared as Horwitz, *The Emergence of an Instrumental Conception of American Law, 1780-1820*, in 5 PERSPECTIVES IN AMERICAN HISTORY 287 (D. Fleming & B. Bailyn eds. 1971); chapter II originally appeared as Horwitz, *The Transformation in the Conception of Property in American Law, 1780-1860*, 40 U. CHI. L. REV. 248 (1973); a large portion of chapter VI originally appeared as Horwitz, *The Historical Foundations of Modern Contract Law*, 87 HARV. L. REV. 917 (1974); and chapter VIII originally appeared as Horwitz, *The Rise of Legal Formalism*, 19 AM. J. LEGAL HIST. 251 (1975). Slight changes in each have occurred through their reappearance in book form, but nothing essential was revised.

3. Used pejoratively by John Phillip Reid to describe my reaction to Horwitz's early work. Reid, *A Plot Too Doctrinaire* (Book Review), 55 TEX. L. REV. 1307, 1310 (1977). While I admit that my views have matured on these matters over the past few years, this essay will demonstrate the extent to which I am still dazzled by Horwitz.

4. The phrase is my own. *See* Holt, *Now and Then: The Uncertain State of Nineteenth-Century American Legal History*, 7 IND. L. REV. 615, 625 (1974). By using the phrase, I

history.

More than a tinge of freshness and progressivism was expected because of Horwitz's trenchant criticism of many of his predecessors in the field. Three general characteristics of the work of those predecessors drew Horwitz's ire. "[O]rthodox lawyer's legal history," by emphasizing timelessness, continuity, technique, professionalism, doctrine, and "logic,"—Horwitz noted in a fiery review essay—has been "part of a politically conservative ideology of legalism" which has deliberately separated and ignored the influences of politics and economics upon the law and which has paid no attention to "political struggle," in order "to pervert the real function of history by reducing it to the pathetic role of justifying the world as it is."[5] Thus, Horwitz concluded, much of what has been done previously in legal history was actively conservative and almost consciously anti-democratic.

Second, too much emphasis had been placed by others on constitutional law. Not only are "constitutional cases . . . unrepresenta-

200

---

meant that "[r]esearch and writing should be based upon solid philosophical grounds and should be devoted to the argumentation and explication of broad but definite sociophilosophical points of view," Holt, *Preface* to ESSAYS IN NINETEENTH-CENTURY AMERICAN LEGAL HISTORY at xiii (W. Holt ed. 1976), by those who operate "from the assumption that legal doctrine grows and changes only to meet certain social needs," in the desire to demonstrate the ways in which "[l]aw and legal institutions have proven to be crucial in American history. . . . To grapple with such material, only a broad and deep theoretical approach will suffice." Holt, *Now and Then, supra,* at 616-17 (footnote omitted).

A few others seem to have seen the primal necessity of working from and within a comprehensive field theory. *See, e.g.,* Presser, *Revising the Conservative Tradition: Towards a New American Legal History* (Book Review), 52 N.Y.U. L. REV. 700, 711 (1977). While I reject any idealistic conclusions that might be drawn from these statements—neither theories nor ideas nor laws will bring about necessary social change by themselves; nor can theory usefully be completely abstracted from history or practice—a theoretical and scientific understanding of history and law remains a *sine qua non* for useful legal history. As the rest of this essay will make clear, I believe that the best theoretical perspective on modern social life is provided by the works of Karl Marx, as amplified and extended by the work of many other people who write from the standpoint of the political left.

5. Horwitz, *The Conservative Tradition in the Writing of American Legal History,* 17 AM. J. LEGAL HIST. 275, 276, 283, 281 (1973). Using the excellent example of the writing of Roscoe Pound, Horwitz accurately characterized the political thrust of these writers as "anti-Marxist," who never tell us about "the growth of democracy or, indeed, of the emergence of socialism," and who dismiss seemingly democratic trends in the law, such as the codification movement during the Jacksonian Era, "either as the political goal of a lunatic fringe led by a demagogic leader or, when all else is lost, as an unwholesome and untrustworthy democratic force." *Id.* at 277, 280, 281.

tive either as intellectual history or as examples of social control,"
Horwitz felt, but also "the excessive equation of constitutional law
with 'law' . . . focuses historians on the nay-saying function of law
and, more specifically, on the rather special circumstances of judicial intervention into statutory control." A useful enterprise would
be, Horwitz asserted, "to study the relationship between private
law (tort, contract, property, commercial law) and economic
change," in order to eliminate the distortions of special circumstances and to study the manner in which judges acted positively
to aid social change.[6]

Finally, Horwitz noted that a large group of nearly-contempora-
neous legal historians, who eschewed both the simplistic and ethereal neutralism of the orthodox conservatives and the distorted focus of the constitutionalists, nevertheless were to be criticized for
their adherence to a "consensus view" of American history. In a
massive and relatively successful attempt to buttress the governmental activism of the New Deal by demonstrating that "laissez-
faire" was the aberration and not the norm with respect to economic intervention and direction by government in the United
States' past, these historians "were much more concerned with
finding evidence of governmental intervention than they were in
asking in whose interest" the interventions were had. Thus, "the
historical writing of the last generation [has] tended to ignore all
questions about the effects of governmental activity on the distribution of wealth and power in American society."[7]

Horwitz promised to show that, despite the best efforts of generations of legal historians to hide the fact, law was and is politics,
actively made by lawmakers, judicial as well as legislative; and that
a thorough study would exemplify the consistent trends of favoritism towards certain elements of society in the legal-history record.
It was indeed quite a dazzling prospect for those of us who had
partially and varyingly grasped the truths toward which we now
hoped and expected to be led. Also, many legal historians who did
not agree with these goals awaited the demonstration that they
were apologists for an economically biased but neutrally disguised
political order.

---

6. M. HORWITZ, *supra* note 1, at xii.
7. *Id.* at xiii-xiv.

The complete book now has been available for more than five years. It has received a good deal of critical attention, both from the left[8] and from the right.[9] Its general provocative excellence was recognized by its having been awarded the Bancroft Prize, emblematic of the best volume or volumes of history published in a given year. Unfortunately but not unexpectedly, scholarly criticism has focused on *Transformation*'s weaknesses rather than its strengths, obscuring or even denying its important contributions with a volley of quibbles, distortions, misunderstandings, and even in some cases open refusals to accept the evidence Horwitz has so painstakingly gathered. Only four attempts have been made to discredit Horwitz's reading of the evidence from the nineteenth century, however.[10] Even radical commentators, while generally more

202

8. *See, e.g.*, Foner, *"Get a Lawyer!"* (Book Review), N.Y. REV. BOOKS, Apr. 14, 1977, at 37-39; Genovese, Book Review, 91 HARV. L. REV. 726 (1978); Tushnet, *A Marxist Analysis of American Law*, 1 MARXIST PERSPECTIVES 96, 106-08 (1978); Sugarman, Book Review, 7 BRIT. J.L. & SOC'Y 297 (1980); Sugarman, *Theory and Practice in History: a Prologue to the Study of the Relationship between Law and Economy from a Socio-historical Perspective*, in LAW, STATE AND SOCIETY 70, 74-80 (B. Fryer et al. eds. 1981) [hereinafter cited as Sugarman, *Theory and Practice*].

9. *See, e.g.*, Bridwell, *Theme v. Reality in American Legal History: A Commentary on Horwitz*, The Transformation of American Law, 1780-1860, *and on the Common Law in America*, 53 IND. L.J. 449 (1978); McClain, *Legal Change and Class Interests: A Review Essay on Morton Horwitz's* The Transformation of American Law, 68 CAL. L. REV. 382 (1980); Simpson, *The Horwitz Thesis and the History of Contracts*, 46 U. CHI. L. REV. 533 (1979); Teachout, *Light in Ashes: The Problem of "Respect for the Rule of Law" in American Legal History* (Book Review), 53 N.Y.U. L. REV. 241 *passim* (1978); Arnold, Book Review, 126 U. PA. L. REV. 241 (1977); Bloomfield, Book Review, 30 VAND. L. REV. 1102 (1977); Gilmore, *From Tort to Contract: Industrialization and the Law* (Book Review), 86 YALE L.J. 788 (1977); Hurst, Book Review, 21 AM. J. LEGAL HIST. 175 (1977); Kettner, Book Review, 8 J. INTERDISCIPLINARY HIST. 390 (1977); Presser, *supra* note 4; Reid, *supra* note 3; Scheiber, *Back to "the Legal Mind"? Doctrinal Analysis and the History of Law* (Book Review), 5 REV. AM. HIST. 458 (1977); Williams, Book Review, 25 U.C.L.A. L. REV. 1187 (1978); Winship, Book Review, 31 SW. L.J. 751 (1977).

10. See Bridwell, *supra* note 9; Williams, *supra* note 9; and Simpson, *supra* note 9, all discussed in part III.D. of this Article.

As this essay was going to press, a major critique of Horwitz's treatment of nineteenth-century tort law became available. *See* Schwartz, *Tort Law and the Economy in Nineteenth-Century America: A Reinterpretation*, 90 YALE L.J. 1717 (1981) [hereinafter cited as *Reinterpretation*]. In a thoroughly-documented and well-written if acerbic fashion, Gary Schwartz argues that Horwitz (and others mentioned herein, such as Lawrence Friedman and Robert Gordon) have failed to show either that negligence succeeded strict liability at the beginning of this time period or that negligence law provided a subsidy for the development of industry and entrepreneurship (except in the specific instance of work-related injury). Schwartz attempts to demonstrate that the notion that liability should follow fault

favorable and more enthusiastic, have neither placed strong enough emphasis on the book's significant breakthrough nor focused sufficiently thorough theoretical attention upon its flaws.[11]

It is the purpose of this essay to demonstrate that *The Transformation of American Law* is a significant and important contribution both to history and to historiography. Horwitz has shattered

---

has always been the norm in Anglo-American tort law, and that, at least in the nineteenth-century United States, negligence law was not discriminatory: plaintiffs won much of the time when they sued industry and entrepreneurs. *See also* Schwartz, *The Vitality of Negligence and the Ethics of Strict Liability*, 15 GA. L. REV. 963 (1981) [hereinafter cited as *Vitality*].

I have neither the time nor the expertise necessary to assess the validity of Schwartz's claims, at this juncture. A few preliminary and tentative observations are, however, possible. First, Schwartz deals chiefly with New Hampshire and California cases, attempting to refute only three interpretations of cases made by Horwitz and otherwise not coming to grips with the historic social and economic context presented by Horwitz. Second, while Schwartz finds not "a single New Hampshire tort opinion that bears the stamp of the dynamic, utilitarian reasoning that Horwitz believes was characteristic of that period's judiciary," *Reinterpretation, supra*, at 1731, the instrumentalist thesis of *Transformation* is hardly disturbed. Horwitz does not claim that instrumentalism was characteristic of each and every opinion.

Third, Schwartz may be right that "strict liability" is an erroneous reading of the pre-1800 tort cases, but he is right for the wrong reasons. Schwartz's work is founded upon an ahistoric view that some "common-sense" notion of fault, apparently roughly defined just as the core idea of negligence is defined today, *see Vitality, supra*, at 991-92, 993, 995, 999, has always been "there" in Anglo-American jurisprudence. This ignores class, status, and the realities of differentials in political power and access to the courts. Robert Rabin is likely much closer to the mark when he takes into account "a conservative judiciary" and "traditional notions of class privilege, social custom, and commercial usage" to underpin his argument that "fault liability emerged out of a world-view dominated largely by no-liability thinking." Rabin, *The Historical Development of the Fault Principle: A Reinterpretation*, 15 GA. L. REV. 925, 960, 928 (1981). That is, nineteenth-century tort theory allowed more plaintiffs to think they would be able to sue, but probably not nearly so many actually to recover.

Fourth, Schwartz criticizes from the right. He finds Richard Posner's law-and-economics maxims "delightfully audacious," *Reinterpretation, supra*, at 1722 n.31, but has only harsh words for Horwitz when all other torts law historians of whom he treats receive at least modicums of praise. In time-honored particularistic and stridently individualistic fashion, he twists the focus knob so as to bring into view only "*A vs. B*," ignoring social context and the broader questions about the social meaning of "fault." Most importantly, from the standpoint of this essay, Schwartz believes in the unmitigated existence of "the public morality" and "community attitudes," *Vitality, supra*, at 1003, 1004—in short, in consensus, a notion which will be called into question by the thrust of my essay.

11. The two pieces by Sugarman, *supra* note 8, give a judiciously balanced appraisal of Horwitz, to which I am much indebted, but unfortunately do not treat their subject at sufficiently great length. Sugarman's promised paper, *Horwitz, Simpson, Atiyah and the Transformation of Anglo-American Law*, infra note 127, should supply some of this deficiency and should complement most of the conclusions reached herein.

203

the grip of conventional legal history upon the past, making it now impossible for the old apolitical, deterministic or idealistic categories to seem so powerful, so convincing, or so useful. The many who continue to practice the older necromancy will be unable to avoid peeking guiltily over their shoulders, while the rest of us have an example of a critical approach to legal history, one which by its emphasis upon political, economic, and social interaction recommends the study of legal practice and adjudication as *praxis*—as world-creating, meaning-endowing, value-full, living human activity.[12] Horwitz has opened a whole new universe for us, the real universe of the past and present.

Transformation does, however, contain significant problems of content, attitude, and explicit theoretical perspective, problems which allow it only to point towards a useful "field theory" rather than to contain and demonstrate it. The book lies suspended between the old and the new, deeply ambiguous and troubled about the proper manner in which to treat a world both flawed and chaotic and yet so full of promise, looking to the future while unable to rid itself of much of those intellectual modes of the past it so correctly condemns. In all this it is perhaps a mirror of our times. Marxists following Gramsci[13] have rejected a Leninesque determinism,[14] finding it crucial to deal with artifacts such as law and the state, but without widespread agreement upon the proper theoretical treatment to be accorded such "superstructure" elements.[15] A

---

12. *Cf.* Klare, *Law-Making as Praxis*, 40 TELOS 123 (1979).

13. *See* A. GRAMSCI, SELECTIONS FROM THE PRISON NOTEBOOKS (Q. Hoare & G. Smith eds. 1971).

14. Determinists emphasize "structure" in interpreting the following fundamental observation by Marx, giving "superstructure" an insufficient amount of attention:

> The totality of these relations of production constitutes the economic structure of society, the real foundation, on which arises a legal and political superstructure and to which correspond definite forms of social consciousness. The mode of production conditions [sometimes translated as "determines"] the general process of social, political and intellectual life. It is not the consciousness of men that determines their existence, but their social existence that determines their consciousness.

K. MARX, A CONTRIBUTION TO THE CRITIQUE OF POLITICAL ECONOMY 20-21 (M. Dodd ed. Moscow 1970) (1st ed. 1859). "Law [in a class society] has been characterized in orthodox Marxism (particularly in the writings of Lenin) as nothing more than the direct embodiment of the interests of the dominant economic classes in society." Sugarman, *Theory and Practice, supra* note 8, at 81.

15. Important recent contributions to this debate, in English, include G. COHEN, KARL

part of their difficulty may be understood as similar to that of Horwitz: a continuation of the use of bourgeois categorization.[16] Horwitz cannot be sharply faulted for failure to resolve such a deep-seated problem. That so many committed and thoughtful Marxists have remained enmeshed in the coils of an essentially bourgeois determinism is ample demonstration of the sheer, overpowering difficulty of breaking with the culture of an existing mode of production absent systemic economic changes.

The increasingly chaotic and warlike circumstances of everyday life for us all[17] render it increasingly more imperative that we find ways to change the future, in part by understanding the past, in part by coming to recognize the differences between bourgeois culture and socialist culture. Horwitz has moved legal history forward from *Transformation*,[18] but a thorough critique of that work will, it is hoped, help forward movement accelerate. This essay first will attempt to summarize the main thrusts of Horwitz's argument in

205

MARX'S THEORY OF HISTORY: A DEFENCE (1978); T. SKOCPOL, STATES AND SOCIAL REVOLUTIONS (1979); E. THOMPSON, THE POVERTY OF THEORY AND OTHER ESSAYS (1978); R. WILLIAMS, MARXISM AND LITERATURE (1977); Anderson, *The Antinomies of Antonio Gramsci*, NEW LEFT REV., Nov. 1976-Jan. 1977, at 5-78.

16. "By deciding to work with capitalist categories, Proudhon, according to Marx, cannot completely disassociate himself from the 'truths' which these categories contain." B. OLLMAN, ALIENATION: MARX'S CONCEPTION OF MAN IN CAPITALIST SOCIETY 13 (2d ed. 1976) [hereinafter cited as B. OLLMAN, ALIENATION]. The first portion of Ollman's important book demonstrates the necessity of using Marx's dialectical mode of reasoning and speaking. *Id.* at 3-69. *See also* Ollman, *On Teaching Marxism*, in SOCIAL AND SEXUAL REVOLUTION: ESSAYS ON MARX AND REICH 126 (1979) [hereinafter cited as Ollman, *Teaching Marxism*].

17. For a thorough and apt description of much of the chaos of modern life, see C. LASCH, THE CULTURE OF NARCISSISM; AMERICAN LIFE IN AN AGE OF DIMINISHING EXPECTATIONS (1978). *See also, e.g.*, B. OLLMAN, ALIENATION, *supra* note 16, at 131-233; H. BRAVERMAN, LABOR AND MONOPOLY CAPITAL: THE DEGRADATION OF WORK IN THE TWENTIETH CENTURY (1974). For a theoretical perspective on the interpretation of ruling class and working class consciousnesses, creating leeway for a greater understanding of disaffecting circumstances in the "middle classes," see E. WRIGHT, CLASS, CRISIS AND THE STATE 30-110 (1978).

18. See, for example, his masterful (if overly condensed) treatment of the law-and-economics movement: Horwitz, *Law and Economics: Science or Politics?*, 8 HOFSTRA L. REV. 905 (1980) [hereinafter cited as Horwitz, *Law and Economics*]. *Cf.* Horwitz, *The Historical Contingency of the Role of History*, 90 YALE L.J. 1057 (1981) [hereinafter cited as Horwitz, *History*]. Many of the articles in the *Yale Law Journal Symposium on Legal Scholarship* (of which this latter article is a part) demonstrate the manner in which others are beginning to join Horwitz on the path toward a radical legal scholarship, and it may be seen that no contributor (save Tushnet) has gone as far as Horwitz. *See* Kennedy, *Cost-Reduction Theory as Legitimation*, 90 YALE L.J. 1275 (1981).

Transformation. His essential radicalism[19] will be demonstrated by contrasting his views with the arguments of those who have criticized the book from the right. The essay will conclude with a discussion of what may be learned from *Transformation*'s flaws.

II. THE ACHIEVEMENT IN *Transformation*

Horwitz's thesis is that basic rules in important segments of "private law" were consciously altered or repudiated by common law judges in order to aid, legitimize, and mystify the transformation of the American economy into an entrepreneurial-capitalist one, during the period between the Revolution and the Civil War.[20] At the time of the Revolution, Horwitz claims, American law mir-

---

19. For purposes of this essay, radicals are those who see the systemic nature of the contemporaneous organization of society and who understand that the system is at the root of social problems. Marxists are radicals who understand precisely "how this system gives rise to these problems. . . . Marxists analyze the workings of capitalism to make sense of the patterns that radicals only see and liberals still have to learn about." Ollman, *Teaching Marxism, supra* note 16, at 131. Three different words, "liberal," "capitalist," and "bourgeois," each give some sense of the ethos and culture surrounding this contemporaneous organization of society; they will be used interchangeably in this Article to refer to that society and those who defend it (whether consciously or not). The interlocking, contradictory, and complex nature of liberal thought is depicted and criticized in R. UNGER, KNOWLEDGE AND POLITICS (1975).

It must be noted that contemporaneous political usage, which finds great differences between "liberals" and "conservatives," is not followed here; both of these groups are included with all of the supporters and defenders of capitalism. *See* Tushnet, *Dia-Tribe* (Book Review), 78 MICH. L. REV. 694 (1980): "The politics of liberalism . . . are inherently conservative. They assume that contemporary American society approximates a just society . . . . They also, and concomitantly, deny the need for massive and therefore probably violent changes in the structure of the society." *Id.* at 709.

Richard Hofstadter long ago recognized the essential unity of America's supposed political divisions:

> [T]he range of vision embraced by the primary contestants in the major parties has always been bounded by the horizons of property and enterprise. However much at odds, on specific issues, the major political traditions have shared a belief in the rights of property, the philosophy of competition; they have accepted the economic virtues of capitalist culture as the necessary qualities of man. . . . The business of politics—so the creed runs—is to protect this competitive world, to foster it on occasion, to patch up its incidental abuses but not to cripple it with a plan for common collective action.

R. HOFSTADTER, THE AMERICAN POLITICAL TRADITION at viii (1948).

20. As will be seen by a comparison, this section of the essay is deeply indebted to the summaries of *Transformation* in Foner, *supra* note 8; Gilmore, *supra* note 9, at 788-89; Presser, *supra* note 4, at 701-10; Sugarman, *Theory and Practice, supra* note 8, at 74-76.

rored English law in its promotion of calm and stability, its emphasis on protection of existing landed property rights, its focus on strict liability for invasions of person or property, and its lack of attention to the solution of typical commercial transactions. The economic realities of life in the new nation soon began a change—slowly at first, and then ever more rapidly and disjunctively—as commodities markets and futures markets came into being and as entrepreneurs, factory-builders, land-speculators, and corporation-founders replaced petty merchants and the landed gentry in positions of economic importance. American law changed also, Horwitz demonstrates, in ways that were overtly intended to aid capital growth and those who benefited from it, at the expense of other segments of society. "[S]ubsidisation through technical legal doctrine mystified the underlying political choices," avoiding "the more open public discussion and scrutiny that would have resulted if development had been encouraged by direct taxation."[21]

The major change in law can be described as the advent of a "contractarian" or will theory. Grant Gilmore has succinctly summarized Horwitz's argument:

> Property interests lost their sacrosanct status as the ideas of economic growth and competition came to have a more compelling charm for the 19th-century mind than the older ideas of stability and monopoly. For strict liability and the wide protection afforded existing interests in property, there was substituted the much narrower concept of liability based on carelessness, fault, or negligence . . . . [E]merging "contractarian" theories . . . purported to base liability on will, consent, or "meeting of the minds," rather than on status or vested property rights.[22]

Law now seemed to focus on the individual, or on individual units in society, and emphasized their independence, their ability to act and interact more or less as they chose, and their ability both to amass and to use economic power to solve and resolve the problems of daily life, rather than any need to rely upon group, communal, or civil aid. As noted by Marx (who came to these conclusions essentially during the time period of which Horwitz writes), the individualistic ethos of contractarian legalism plays a

---

21. Sugarman, *Theory and Practice, supra* note 8, at 75.
22. Gilmore, *supra* note 9, at 789.

necessarily central role in the growth and stability of a society based upon commodities, exchange, profit, and the supposedly bargained-for appropriation of the power of workers by employers.[23] Horwitz capably demonstrates the truth of Marx's insight: contract (as we know it today) was both new and central to the period.

Contractarianism, as broadly defined above, became suffused throughout American law, and in several thorough chapters Horwitz carefully delineates these changes in important areas of law.[24] In contract (strictly defined), the eighteenth-century emphasis on "just price" and fairness in interpersonal dealings gave way to assumptions of equality of bargaining power and a focus on what the parties "intended." The old "objective theory," which allowed bargains to be judged by external standards of fairness and value, was replaced by a new "subjective theory," in which *caveat emptor,* express contractual language, and refusal to investigate duress or inadequacy of "consideration" became the standard approach.

Soon, however, commercial needs for predictability caused the introduction of another "objective theory," as the actual, expressed "will" of the parties gave way in many crucial situations to judgment based on standards derived from commercial practices. The market now reigned supreme, having replaced "the outlook of a society in which social and moral obligations were considered superior to economic ones, and in which making the highest possible profit was not the principal motive shaping human behavior."[25]

---

23. 1 K. MARX, CAPITAL: A CRITIQUE OF POLITICAL ECONOMY 84, 87, 170, 176, 271, 398-99, 540, 574, 583-84, 624 (Int'l Pub. ed. New York 1967) (1st ed. 1867) [hereinafter cited as K. MARX, CAPITAL). Max Weber is commonly held to have come to an apparently similar conclusion, "that law played an indispensable role in guaranteeing the security and certainty that capitalism required." Sugarman, however, concludes that the latter's

> position seems to have been that, whilst the theoretical implications of the law's coercive power to guarantee certainty and predictability would lead one to assume that the law was essential to market capitalism, in practice this was not always the case. . . . Weber contended that whilst today "economic exchange is quite overwhelmingly guaranteed by the threat of legal coercion," from "the purely theoretical point of view legal guarantee by the state is not indispensable to any basic economic phenomenon."

Sugarman, *Theory and Practice, supra* note 8, at 72-73.

24. Horwitz deals with contract and commercial law in chapters V and VI of *Transformation,* with property and competition in chapters II and IV, and with tort and damages law in chapter III.

25. Foner, *supra* note 8, at 37.

Not so incidentally, the labor of working people came to be viewed judicially as a commodity like any other.

In property law, the "natural flow" doctrine, which barred riparian owners from interrupting the flow of a stream to other users and enjoyers, was replaced, legislatively by mill acts which gave the owners of economically "beneficial" mills an almost unimpeded right to flood the lands of others, and judicially by doctrines of "prior appropriation" and "prescription," encouraging further mill construction by permitting the first miller on a stream to interrupt the flow and to prevent other mill construction thereby. The potential for stanching further development inherent in these rules then helped persuade judges to overthrow the rules in favor of "reasonable use" doctrines, wherein conflicting uses could be balanced and new, if competing, uses allowed. Established businesses of a public nature could in the eighteenth century enjoin competition, but Horwitz shows that early in the nineteenth century judges began granting such injunctions on the theory that exclusive franchises would promote growth. This notion was in turn discarded when it became evident that exclusivity would hamper further development; the landmark *Charles River Bridge* case[26] "represented the last great contest in America between two different models of economic development,"[27] holding against privileged exclusivity and in favor of a "free, active, and enterprising [country where] . . . new channels of communication are daily found necessary."[28] Property, inventiveness, even industry itself came to be understood within the contractarian viewpoint.

209

Notions of strict legal accountability for "private" activity gave way to restricted liability which allowed considerable interference with others as long as one's conduct adhered to judicially established "reasonable" standards of care. New "consequential" rules of damages further limited the liability of actors such as steam locomotives, whose owners might not have to pay for fires caused by spewing sparks. Just as in other areas of law, "[t]he move from nuisance to negligence was accomplished in fits and starts,"[29] not

---

26. Charles River Bridge v. Warren Bridge, 36 U.S. (11 Pet.) 341 (1837), *aff'g* 24 Mass. (7 Pick.) 344 (1829).

27. M. HORWITZ, *supra* note 1, at 134.

28. 36 U.S. at 547.

29. Presser, *supra* note 4, at 704.

in a smooth and logical development of doctrine, as successive waves of entrepreneurs seized upon various and sometimes contradictory theories of law to justify first their entry into the market and then their retention of a competitive position. These contradictions were only apparent from up close, however; overall, Horwitz successfully demonstrates that American private law moved towards a contractarian, individualistic, competitive philosophical underpinning.

As can be seen, Horwitz believes that most of "the rewriting of liability law was . . . accomplished on the judicial . . . level."[30] In theory judges were not supposed to make law, but in the late eighteenth century a revolutionary, activist self-conception of the judge's role appeared, mushrooming in the first part of the nineteenth century into a widely-accepted "instrumentalist" approach whereby judges undertook to change or invent doctrine according to their own notions of what was useful for society, rather than attempting to adhere to old rules or to fit developments into precedent and tradition. Horwitz asserts that the instrumentalist view was necessary, as the emergence of rapid economic growth mandated the use of concepts and rules which had little or no precedent, and the communitarian ideological foundations of the older society had to be dispensed with. The notion of instrumentalism implies that activist judges understood their goals, and indeed Horwitz shows that in many instances doctrine was altered for specific developmental reasons. However, the cause-and-effect relationships were not always so simple; new rules often emerged "before new or special economic or technological pressure for change" was applied.[31]

Instrumentalism is a dangerous theory, relying for its socioeconomically consistent application upon mechanisms for selection of the judiciary which are not always available in a democracy. "The open-endedness of debate, the irreverence for the past, the passionate advocacy of fundamental change . . . must be suppressed in the name of the new consensus."[32] Just as instrumental-

210

---

30. Gilmore, *supra* note 9, at 789.
31. M. HORWITZ, *supra* note 1, at 3. *See also, e.g., id.* at 89 (negligence).
32. Gilmore, *supra* note 9, at 790. Eugene Genovese elaborates upon this point:
   However much sentimentalists and utopians may rail at the monotonous recurrence of a positive theory of law whenever revolutionaries settle down to re-

ism was attaining its heyday in the 1820's, Horwitz finds, notions of formalism—the neutrality of law, the political impartiality of judges, seemingly blind adherence to precedent, and the like—began to seep back into private law from the realm of public law, where they had always been predominant. Horwitz concludes that by the 1860's formalism once again had become the pervasive mode of judicial exegesis.

"The reformulation of substantive law by the judges went hand in hand with a systematic reduction of the role of the civil jury."[33] The eighteenth-century power of juries, usually comprised, as Eric Foner points out, of small property owners,[34] to award damages according to their own sense of the equities of the situation, was severely limited by the new theories of restricted liability in a contractarian world. The jury's function of "finding" both the law and the facts—allowing jurors in essence to be the source of applicable law—was reduced to only a fragment of the latter role, as judges both issued definitive and restrictive instructions about rules of law and combined the realm of facts with other rules which essentially converted many factual issues into issues of law. Jurisdictions which had never used juries—admiralty and equity—were greatly expanded during the period.

Horwitz also depicts the role of lawyers in helping to bring about this transformation.[35] Those with commercial interests had, before about 1800, consistently shunned lawyers and the common-law courts by taking their disputes to arbitrators or to special commer-

211

---

build the world they have shattered, any other course would be doomed to failure. . . . [A]ll modern ruling classes have much in common in their attitude toward the law, for each must confront the problem of coercion in such a way as to minimize the necessity for its use, and each must disguise the extent to which state power does not so much rest on force as represent its actuality. Even Marxian theory, therefore, must end with the assertion of a positive theory of law and judge natural-law and "higher-law" doctrines to be tactical devices in the extralegal struggle.

E. GENOVESE, ROLL, JORDAN, ROLL: THE WORLD THE SLAVES MADE 26 (1974) (Vintage ed. 1976). As will be discussed at more length in part IV of this Article, see text accompanying notes 164-167 infra, positivism seems to take one of two legal forms, the instrumental mode or the formal mode, each containing inner tensions and contradictions which, when squeezed by socioeconomic reality, tend to force elite legal theorists to turn to the other.

33. Gilmore, supra note 9, at 790.

34. Foner, supra note 8, at 37.

35. See especially chapter V of M. HORWITZ, supra note 1.

cial courts where commercial law, more to their liking, was applied, or by using penal bonds (eliminating the issues of liability and damages) of special "struck" (*i.e.*, all-merchant) juries in many instances in which they did resort to the common law. The law and the lawyers reciprocated this pre-1800 separation, Horwitz finds, by essentially being occupied with the problems of property owners. As commercial interests began to oppose each other—merchants versus their insurors being the instance Horwitz finds paradigmatic—and as the instrumental mode of judicial lawmaking developed simultaneously with a bench more understanding of and devoted to the ethos of entrepreneurial growth, litigation before the regular courts became more useful and more palatable. The limits placed on jury discretion further "enhanced the prospects for certainty and predictability,"[36] while courts' emerging hostility to the enforcement of arbitration awards and to struck juries in commercial cases tended to force commercial disputes to become lawsuits. Lawyers cast off their previous primary allegiance to landed interests and "became the enthusiastic allies—or perhaps the willing servants—of the new masters."[37]

Transformation is not a book simply about lawyers, or doctrine, or even law. As Foner has said:

> [F]or Horwitz, law . . . is a way of interpreting the world . . . . The relation between law and society is a reciprocal one; law both reflects and influences social change . . . . The modifications of law which constitute the subject of this book are elements of what Karl Polanyi called the "great transformation" from a pre-market society, a historical process which affected entire ways of life, human relations, and, of course, the law.[38]

The rise of market relations, and the corresponding rise to predominance of a market-oriented class emphasizing exchange, profits, and (eventually) the use of factories and large masses of hired workers to produce commodities, were accompanied by the gradual emergence into general social consciousness of a market ethos characterized in part by certain typical modes of thought which

212

---

36. Presser, *supra* note 4, at 707.
37. Gilmore, *supra* note 9, at 789.
38. Foner, *supra* note 8, at 37; K. POLANYI, THE GREAT TRANSFORMATION: THE POLITICAL AND ECONOMIC ORIGINS OF OUR TIME (1944).

were reflective of, supportive of, and derived from the new ways in which the relations of production were organized. Legal notions and relationships were a quite important part of this new capitalist culture. While Horwitz's chief occupation is in the telling of the story of the emergence of liberal rules of law in the American context, there is also evidence in many parts of *Transformation* of the advent of typically liberal elements of philosophy and belief: for example, the death of a communal and corporatistic view of society, and its replacement by a particularistic, atomistic, individualistic view;[39] the emergence of revulsion against investigating questions involving substantive justice and against accepting social definitions of value;[40] and the appearance of a tendency to substitute assumptions of equality and similarity for observations of inequality and difference.[41]

Most important, however, is the emergence of the false neutrality with which most realities of capitalist life begin to be disguised when they are described in liberal language. It probably would be fatal for the social support (or, at least the docility) needed by the dominant elements of the system, and perhaps for the self-esteem of many members of those elites, if the actual inequalities and real, political influences of capitalism were openly reflected in the manner and means by which capitalism is described to the world. The disguises, however, were not and are not adopted consciously by elites, but arise organically as an integral part of the mystification inherent in a market ethos.[42] Thus, the formal, apolitical mode of decision writing overtakes the instrumental, activist mode. Horwitz demonstrates that phrases such as "commercial uniformity" and "legal certainty and predictability" are not neutrally descriptive but mask political values of and political victories by certain elements of the population, values and victories that were resisted and opposed by many who did not want, or did not reap many immediate or large benefits from, the new market of social ordering.[43]

Despite the lack of evidence presented by Horwitz, there is a

213

---

39. M. HORWITZ, *supra* note 1, at 104, 111.
40. *Id.* at 161, 181-82.
41. *Id.* at 240.
42. *See* text accompanying notes 135-137 *infra*.
43. M. HORWITZ, *supra* note 1, at 212.

strong sense in *Transformation* that many people opposed the new ideas and economic organization and that many people were hurt or ruined thereby. Further, Horwitz finds manipulation of the law by the merchants and entrepreneurs, and their allies on the bench and at the bar, for the benefit of those elements which had come to dominate American society. Not only was "law . . . thought of as . . . simply reflective of the existing organization of economic and political power":[44]

> By the middle of the nineteenth century the legal system had been reshaped to the advantage of men of commerce and indus-try at the expense of farmers, workers, consumers, and other less powerful groups within the society. . . . [L]egal doctrines . . . maintained the new distribution of economic and political power . . . [and law] actively promoted a legal redistribution of wealth against the weakest groups in the society.[45]

214

Most of Horwitz's research into changing legal doctrine demonstrates that the new rules attempted to favor entrepreneurs, businessmen, and capitalist growth-oriented interests by altering traditional notions of liability so as apparently to reallocate much of the costs of enterprise to others—to workers, to consumers, to the landed gentry, to those caught up in or injured by the dangerous consequences of growth. He concludes that instrumentalism and the new rules subsidized growth, and that an alternative and potentially more egalitarian, less open form of subsidy—taxation—was not turned to.[46]

At the heart of the various previous approaches to legal history criticized by Horwitz were devices whose effect has been to ignore or obscure both the manipulation of law by elites and the fact that American history has been a continuous social struggle, some groups winning, while other groups, containing much larger numbers, lost. While the conservative school has assumed the law is always neutral, ethereal, and apolitical, with lawyers and judges being professionalistically unconcerned in the results of legal dis-

---

44. *Id.* at 253.

45. *Id.* at 253-54.

46. "[T]he law had come simply to ratify those forms of inequality that the market system produced." *Id.* at 210. For the discussion of taxation as an alternative not taken, see *id.* at 99-101, 260.

putes, Horwitz has demonstrated that judges and lawyers during the early modern period of American history took sides motivated by politics and economics. While the constitutionalists deflected attention from the socioeconomic nitty-gritty by studying decisions whose language was neutrally formal and whose chief concerns seemed to be in the ideological realm of fundamental principles, Horwitz uses a study of everyday legal doctrines to hold the reader's feet to the fire of real problems. And while the consensus historians "assumed that nineteenth-century law reflected the underlying consensus of a society united in its commitment to economic growth and entrepreneurial activity, Horwitz sees the legal system as ridden with deep social and ideological conflicts . . . [that] reflected far-reaching divisions in a society undergoing rapid economic transformation."[47]

The initial breakthrough promised by Horwitz has, in *Transformation,* been realized. No one can put down the book without having had shaken to the core basic assumptions about the neutrality of law and the calm, efficient, majority-approved nature of economic growth and American history. Whatever its deficiencies, *Transformation* has turned a corner in American legal historiography by drawing aside the curtain of fuzziness, mystique, and neutrality that has until now cloaked the history of law and attempted to keep us from seeing naked its political, biased reality.[48] Law is but an element—if a crucial one—in the continuing social struggle. Morton Horwitz in *The Transformation of American Law* has at the least demonstrated that primary fact.

215

III.   THE FAILURE OF HORWITZ'S CRITICS

The best measures of Horwitz's success and superiority have been given by his mainstream critics. Each has retained those characteristics of conservatism and adherence to legalistic catego-

---

47. Foner, *supra* note 8, at 37.

48. Some radicals apparently have concluded that demystification constitutes the whole of the radical task. *See* Davis, *Critical Jurisprudence: An Essay on the Legal Theory of Robert Burt's Taking Care of Strangers,* 1981 WIS. L. REV. 419, esp. 436 n.42; Freeman, *Truth and Mystification in Legal Scholarship,* 90 YALE L.J. 1229 (1981). While demystification is certainly essential, a program for change informed by materialistic social theory is concomitantly necessary in order to avoid social chaos.

ries which Horwitz pointed out and condemned,[49] and the utility of which he refuted in *Transformation*. None has been able to assimilate or appreciate any part of the fundamental truth he demonstrated—that law is a socioeconomic phenomenon, its principles biased towards socioeconomic elites. Only three 'attempts have been made to dispute his interpretation of the nineteenth-century cases, and none of these has been successful. Shocked, amazed, bemused, bewildered, urbanely smug, or thoroughly rattled, these scholars have either politely applauded and then ignored Horwitz's central thesis, or have gotten angry in various scholarly ways, but none has yet successfully refuted him.

216

All three of the trends in writing conservative American legal history identified by Horwitz are represented among those who have criticized Horwitz from the right. Some scholars fall into more than one of the categories used,[50] which is not anomalous (though it may result in internal contradiction) since all of these schools are basically bourgeois,[51] supportive of the existing system in ways that a thorough understanding of that system would lead one to predict and identify.[52] The first three sections of this part will describe Horwitz's critics using the three categories he developed, while the fourth will deal briefly with the three attempts to call his substantive interpretation into question.

---

49. Note 5 & accompanying text *supra*.

50. For example, while Gilmore's review of Horwitz is deterministic, *see* text accompanying note 55 *infra*, his book THE DEATH OF CONTRACT (1974) follows a quite orthodox idealism; some of the reviewers of Horwitz exhibit characteristics of each of the three trends, *see, e.g.*, Bloomfield, *supra* note 9; Winship, *supra* note 9. *Cf.* Tushnet, Book Review, 45 U. CHI. L. REV. 906 (1978).

51. For a definition of the use of "bourgeois" in this essay, see note 19 *supra*; for a thorough treatment of bourgeois and other critiques of contemporary legal scholarship, see Gordon, *Historicism in Legal Scholarship*, 90 YALE L.J. 1017 (1981); Tushnet, *Legal Scholarship: Its Causes and Cure*, 90 YALE L.J. 1205 (1981). Both of these articles are critiqued in Freeman, *supra* note 48.

52. *Accord*, Tushnet, *supra* note 50, at 906-07; Mensch, *Freedom of Contract as Ideology*, 33 STAN. L. REV. 753, 754-55 (1981):

> [P.S. Atiyah's history of freedom of contract in England] blends an active instrumental model (law as promoting or facilitating the needs and values of a changing society) with a reflective, passive one (law as depicting through its forms an otherwise intact social reality). This vague model . . . allows him to maintain a balanced, liberal viewpoint throughout the book.

A. *The Consensus Critique*

The "consensus" approach essentially derives from Charles Beard and the Progressives, Legal Realists, and New Dealers who, believing themselves to be located upon the left of American politics, supported governmental intervention to chastise and restrain business, to stabilize the economy, and to assure that disadvantaged groups receive at least minimal moral and economic support in their struggle to approximate the American dream. Consensus historians accept the primacy of economics and economic interest groups in politics (assuming their benevolence), and have little regard for the motivating importance of individuals or ideas upon history.

A restrained and unemotional branch of consensus thought adopts a rigid determinism, whereby law and other structures of thought always directly reflect patterns of social and economic organization. Lawrence Friedman's *A History of American Law*, for example,

217

> treats American law . . . not as a kingdom unto itself, not as a set of rules and concepts, not as the province of lawyers alone, but as a mirror of society. It takes nothing as historical accident, nothing as autonomous, everything as relative and molded by economy and society. . . .[53] The [legal] system works like a blind, insensate machine. It does the bidding of those whose hands are on the controls. The laws . . . reflect the goals and policies of those who call the tune.[54]

Thus, Grant Gilmore praises Horwitz's book because "it focuses on the process by which the precapitalist law of the 18th century was, as it had to be, metamorphosed. . . . Professor Horwitz has gathered a rich harvest for any reader who is interested in the process by which a system of law is transformed in response to fundamen-

---

53. L. FRIEDMAN, A HISTORY OF AMERICAN LAW 10 (1973).

54. *Id.* at 14. In a penetrating essay, Mark Tushnet has demonstrated the inability of Friedman's deterministic approach to provide a useful analysis of legal history, *see* Tushnet, *Perspectives on the Development of American Law: A Critical Review of Friedman's "A History of American Law,"* 1977 WIS. L. REV. 81, but in many ways Tushnet's criticism does not extend to the breadth and depth of Friedman's liberalism, and I believe it can be usefully supplemented by remarks made herein.

tal changes in the society which the law reflects."[55]

Another, more optimistic and ebullient branch of the consensus school, while deterministic, is not so rigidly so, admitting of more autonomy for historic actors and ideas at intermediate levels of analysis, finding limits of the human capacity to plan and to understand located in dark and mystical notions of "drift and default" surrounding human history.[56] Thus, Harry Scheiber allows that "none of the evidence" his review of Horwitz has brought forward "suggests that 'the weakest groups in the society' were not exploited through the law by the 'strongest.' But the form that opposition did take, in reacting to dominant trends, deserves attention."[57]

218

Both branches unite, however, in extending praise to those portions of *Transformation* which seem to underscore the emphasis which this group of scholars has always placed upon "pragmatism" ("Horwitz's . . . instrumentalism . . . advances under a new label what [Willard] Hurst called, simply 'pragmatism' ")[58] arguing that most of the book repeats points they have been making for years: "[T]he essentials of the argument—Professor Horwitz would, I am sure, agree—are not all that novel; they have been current for 30 or 40 years."[59]

Consensus legal historians and other Progressives and New Dealers have always emphasized the interplay of economics and pressure groups in the formulation of law—John Dawson comes immediately to mind—and the Legal Realists such as Karl Llewellyn (contrasting the Grand Style with the Formal Style of adjudication) and Jerome Frank were characterized by a common insight that judges made law. Horwitz owes these scholars a great debt—one which Gilmore is correct in presuming Horwitz readily

---

55. Gilmore, *supra* note 9, at 792, 793 (footnote omitted).

56. Scheiber, *supra* note 9, at 464. For an early, somewhat idealistic analysis of "drift" in the work of the foremost member of this branch of the consensus school (Willard Hurst), see Holt, Book Review, 1971 WIS. L. REV. 982, 987-90. For an apt critique, see Gordon, *supra* note 51, at 1036-37.

57. Scheiber, *supra* note 9, at 464.

58. *Id.* at 465.

59. Gilmore, *supra* note 9, at 791. Scheiber is a bit harsher on this point: "[T]his work . . . would have been . . . much richer . . . had it . . . been less concerned with wrapping some well-established ideas in the drapery of new rhetoric." Scheiber, *supra* note 9, at 459-60.

would acknowledge—but his failure to cite them as his intellectual forebears in *Transformation* is a way of underscoring that he has radically gone beyond and broken with their work. Economic pressure groups, as seen by the consensus thinkers, do not cleave into two main classes, one powerful, small, and in·control, the other large, weak, and always fighting for control; and the Legal Realists never came to a coherent explanation of how or why judges made law because the Realists refused to acknowledge the existence of these two fundamental competing social forces.[60] According to the consensus historians society runs essentially harmoniously thanks to the existence of a basic social consensus growing out of competition among assumedly equal interest groups, all for the better since this agreed-upon economic growth is asserted to benefit everyone. Consensus historian Charles McClain concludes:

> Seen from this perspective many of the changes in the common law described by Horwitz . . . seem salutary. Rather than constituting evidence of a conspiracy to gut the law of its humane core, these changes appear to reflect the legal order's responsiveness to changed social conditions and its ability to evolve in the direction of greater flexibility, greater maturity, and, indeed, greater plain common sense.[61]

219

The arguments presented by Horwitz, reflecting a society torn between groups in struggle, not mediated by any underlying consensus, are ignored.

The chief criticism advanced by the consensus advocates is that Horwitz fails to emphasize the shifting pluralistic diversity of America and the interest groups which contend in it. "In many specific cases [analyzed by Horwitz]," asserts Scheiber, "paradoxically the litigants on both sides were often indistinguishable as to wealth and social class."[62] "Nor is it possible, without gross oversimplification," argues Gilmore, "to reduce the emerging rules in such commercial specialities as sales and negotiable instruments to

---

60. This argument about the Legal Realists is elaborated upon in Holt, *Why American Law Schools Cannot Teach Justice*, 3 ALSA F., Sept. 1978, at 5; Tushnet, *supra* note 51, at 1207, 1210.

61. McClain, *supra* note 9, at 396-97 (footnote omitted).

62. Scheiber, *supra* note 9, at 463; *accord*, McClain, *supra* note 9, at 395.

the simple paradigm of capitalists exploiting consumers."[63]

While on the surface of events interests and causative patterns seem many and varied, a sophisticated class analysis which gets beneath the surface to hidden interconnections among groups, events, and interests in order to demonstrate cultural and ideological patterns and influences (an analysis which, unfortunately, is not developed by Horwitz, as will be argued in part IV of this essay) can demonstrate that, for example, cases involving solely upper class litigants yet serve upper class purposes. Taking a definition of "economics" and a notion of causation which are both entirely too narrow and constricted,[64] the determinists of the consensus school focus too closely, expecting to find a direct, immediate, one-to-one correspondence in *every* instance. When their expectations are not met they conclude that division of the world into two classes is too simple, and that society's story is really the interaction of a kaleidoscope of variously defined and shifting, relatively equal interest groups.[65] Willard Hurst insists that, because "there was a substantial consensus on the social utility of the market," much of nineteenth-century conflict was between members of the "upwardly mobile middle class" for whom "class attitudes and aspirations were blurred."[66] Stephen Presser carries this argument to extremes:

220

> While most private law doctrines that were litigated in the appellate courts support Horwitz's thesis of merchant and entrepreneurial ascendancy in the law, there must have been many other legal developments in the nineteenth century that had little to do with these groups. . . . [A]ction by state legislatures [other than that occasionally hinted at by Horwitz] may have had a significant social impact on American life in realms apart from economics. . . .
>
> . . . For all we know, most of the consumers and farmers, in

---

63. Gilmore, *supra* note 9, at 795.

64. *See generally* B. OLLMAN, ALIENATION, *supra* note 16, at 5-40.

65. A diversity in regional development is another favorite argument. *See, e.g.,* Bloomfield, *supra* note 9, at 1106; Hurst, *supra* note 9, at 176.

The point is not whether regional variations exist but whether our inquiry for an explanation of legal variants should end when we discover regional origins for them. A better theoretical focus always will impel one behind geography to economics.

66. Hurst, *supra* note 9, at 178. Scheiber also expresses continued adherence to this consensus view, giving no justification. Scheiber, *supra* note 9, at 463.

absolute terms, were better off after the nineteenth-century legal changes than before.[67]

This substitution of wishful thinking for analysis demonstrates both how unsettling Horwitz's views are and how strongly a cherished viewpoint lingers even when its holder suspects how little evidence he has for it. The possibility that "economics" might be defined quite broadly as a *primary social factor,* one which has pervasive influence upon most other "realms" of life, and the possibility that "legal developments" concerning which no commercial interests were directly represented nevertheless might be influenced significantly by social forces favorable to the overall economic interests of capitalists, are somehow never visualized.

The tendency of liberal thought to particularism makes it easy for members of the consensus school to focus on specific events without looking for deeper connections, and thus to produce evidence of variety; however, the kind of evidence of a struggle between competing interests and the concomitant lack of an underlying social consensus brought forward by Horwitz should at least give scholars pause. This is not to say that the interests of competing classes are not expressed in a variety of ways, with a variety of intensities, and indeed sometimes contradictorily, depending primarily upon one's time-period of historical focus and one's level of analysis; it *is* to argue that Horwitz's analysis implies a more pow-

221

---

67. Presser, *supra* note 4, at 720-21. Presser concludes by denying the possibility of a class analysis, while simultaneously suggesting that factors of class in the law made the burst of entrepreneurial growth possible:

> Perhaps in nineteenth-century America, particularly in the West, people moved so freely from one occupational group to another that attempts to draw sharp distinctions between "farmers" and "merchants" distort social reality. . . .

> Horwitz's work is most impressive not because it demonstrates the ascendance of any particular group in the law, but because it suggests that the development of American law reflects a continuing struggle between competing economic and social interests. . . .

> In the limited sense that the law may have provided equal economic opportunity for those willing and able to learn the techniques of commerce and for those able to employ native intelligence, inventiveness, and shrewdness, the law may have been much more democratic than Horwitz suggests.

Id. at 721-22. What an immense amount of economic restraint can be captured by and hidden in the single word "able" in that passage! Who was "able," and why? Horwitz's theory of law can tell us; Presser's cannot.

erful explanation than that of the consensus thinkers because it is willing to take into account conflict and struggle in American history, thereby dispensing with the need for false and mystifying masks, such as the theory of an underlying consensus, and thereby attempting to explain the sources of bias which permeate American law. Horwitz's analysis does not ignore the plight of millions by assuming that growth and abundance benefited everyone to a greater extent "than before," whatever that is.

B. *The Constitutionalist Critique*

The school of constitutionalists has a few representatives among those teaching in law schools but is larger amongst "purer" historians. This school has arisen since the Second World War essentially in reaction to New Deal-consensus thought and to the latter's emphasis on the importance of economics. Its adherents are usually middle-of-the-road to somewhat-tight-lipped-conservative in their politics; they usually disavow economic determinism in favor of an openly idealistic approach to the interpretation of history. Following Bernard Bailyn[68] and Gordon Wood,[69] constitutionalist scholars find the chief motivating factor in the American experience to be ideas, particularly great constitutional principles; their pivot in history is the American colonial experience culminating in the Revolution, whence derived "those moral values that are embodied in the fundamental principles of legality, . . . a deep respect for the fundamental worth and dignity of all persons, and . . . a central commitment to the ideals of equality, fairness, justice, and freedom from arbitrary control."[70] Unleashed by these powerful ideas, constitutionalists assert that the Revolution unleashed many new ideas and created many new conditions.[71]

---

68. *See, e.g.,* B. BAILYN, THE IDEOLOGICAL ORIGINS OF THE AMERICAN REVOLUTION (1967).

69. *See* G. WOOD, THE CREATION OF THE AMERICAN REPUBLIC, 1776-1787 (1969).

70. Teachout, *supra* note 9, at 287.

71. Principles and ideas are so important to some constitutionalists that they find it difficult to accept any notion of "instrumental" activity by judges. John Phillip Reid, for example, takes an article by Scheiber, which argued (contrary to Horwitz) that the instrumental mode persisted long beyond the Civil War, *see* Scheiber, *Instrumentalism and Property Rights: A Reconsideration of American "Styles of Judicial Reasoning" in the 19th Century,* 1975 WIS. L. REV. 1, 10 n.43, 12, as demonstrating that the concept of instrumentalism itself was "questionable." Reid then criticizes Horwitz for "continu[ing] to believe there was an era of instrumentalism." Reid, *supra* note 3, at 1310. For Reid's adherence to the Bailyn

Thus, according to John Phillip Reid's critical review, "[t]he transformation of American law about which Professor Horwitz writes . . . [arose] out of the related transformation of the American economy produced by independence from Great Britain and the concurrent industrial revolution,"[72] the latter factor treated by Reid as subordinate and determined by other factors. Reid says at another point:

> The great burst of judicial energy that characterized the pre-Civil War decades was due . . . to the fact that a new nation needed new law, or because it was an epoch when questions were for the first time being asked and, by the very nature of things, many innovative decisions were certain to be made.[73]

The principled motivations of those who made their marks as actors in history are also quite important to the constitutionalists, as therein lies the evidence of the importance of fundamentals. Never mind that this approach limits us by and large to that small segment of the population that was literate, had the leisure and the inclination to record their feelings, and was fortunate enough to have had succeeding generations recognize that what they had done was important enough to have preserved those remains. Never mind that they may have had conscious or subconscious reasons for putting down less than or more than what actually happened. Never mind that each actor in history has only a partial and biased view of events no matter how important he or she may have been. "It is, of course, asking too much of the new legal historians that they take men at their own word," Reid expostulates.[74] Thus, he agrees with Horwitz that

223

> many who thought in the Hamiltonian tradition preferred to have questions about private property and vested rights settled not by the legislature but by the judiciary, [but] their reasons

---

analysis, see J. REID, IN A DEFIANT STANCE: THE CONDITIONS OF LAW IN MASSACHUSETTS BAY, THE IRISH COMPARISON, AND THE COMING OF THE AMERICAN REVOLUTION (1977); Holt, "We Are All Latent Tories"? (Book Review), 3 ALSA F., May 1978, at 45-51.

72. Reid, supra note 3, at 1312. I have transposed Reid's negatively phrased construction here, and in the text accompanying the next footnote, to a positive construction without, I think, changing his meaning.

73. Id. at 1310.

74. Id. at 1314 n.17.

were due to legal ideology, not the fear that property might be redistributed. . . . It was the doctrine—the idea—not the implementation that troubled conservative lawyers.[75]

Ideological determinism, using principles derived from the Revolutionary experience, constitutes the answer to historical puzzles:

> The demise of employer paternalism may have been due as much to the rise of urbanism as to the scheming friends of business who sat on nineteenth-century courts. It may also have been due to . . . the stress by the courts upon individual freedom, a legal doctrine then attributed to the winning of independence from Great Britain. Employing only evidence available in this book, it is possible to argue that even . . . the fellow-servant doctrine . . . followed inevitably from the principles of the American Revolution. . . . [N]ow the individual, free to enter or to reject a perilous employment, was made responsible for his own decisions.[76]

224

The constitutionalists do not, of course, see themselves so narrowly. They accuse Horwitz of doctrinairely marching to the tune of "a single set of ideological coordinates," while they see themselves as "constantly judging and discriminating, . . . responding . . . to the whole of human experience."[77] Anyone who wishes to point to factors other than ideological, however, is a victim of "Horwitzian determinism," or rather is "a neomarxist on the scent of an economic explanation."[78] Economic determinism is evil, while neutrality (meaning the well-principled intentions of historical actors) is unquestionably good. "There is no neutrality in the legal history of Horwitz. Economics determines all issues, conspiracy explains most events."[79]

A "conspiracy" exists when a group attempts to influence events because of evil (meaning economic) motivations. But it is neither conspiratorial nor deterministic, apparently, for Reid to assert that

---

75. *Id.* at 1314.
76. *Id.* at 1317 (footnote omitted).
77. Teachout, *supra* note 9, at 246.
78. Reid, *supra* note 3, at 1313, 1317.
79. *Id.* at 1315. "It is this 'neutrality,' 'comprehensiveness,' and 'breadth of sympathy' . . . that we expect and need from historical writing. And it is precisely this quality that, because of its ideological preconceptions, new school historiography [*i.e.*, Horwitz] fails to provide." Teachout, *supra* note 9, at 280 n.131.

the courts were . . . opening opportunity to a wider class of citizens. If the new law encouraged individuals to employ their intelligence and inventiveness unencumbered by restraints previously protective of those possessing vested privileges or lacking in venturesomeness, the purpose of that new law can be as fairly labelled "democratic" as "Machiavellian."[80]

The constitutionalists cannot accept that new shackles for large numbers of people might have been substituted by the new order in place of the old restraints, or that the new "contractarian" notions of "individual freedom" might have been shams in practice for many without the means or luck to employ them. Problems of class struggle, if they ever existed on this side of the Atlantic and above the Caribbean, were for constitutionalists whisked away by a Revolution that saw most Americans united against their British oppressors on matters of principle which transcended and obliterated most petty economic grievances. Americans were blessed with liberty, justice, and rights under a benign rule of law (and a duly restrained government with fragmented power), which represented the actuality of existence for most people.[81] Beginning from such a principled consensus,

225

> the changes that Horwitz traces in pre-Civil War law, . . . taken individually, . . . can only be interpreted as efforts to free the economy from legal restrictions no longer relevant to American society. Surely at the time they seemed to promise neutral results. . . .
> Who can say that contemporaries expected that these changes in law would result in the "subsidization" of a commercial class and the economic domination by a favored few? Far more likely it was contemplated that everyone would, to some extent, be a "winner."[82]

Individual motivations and constitutional principles remain, to the end, the only salient factors involved in history. The constitutionalists' ideologically deterministic explanations are, as a result,

---

80. Reid, *supra* note 3, at 1318.

81. "It is a simple empirical truth," the constitutionalist Teachout apparently believes, "that where there is genuine respect for the rule of law and the principles that underlie it, brutality and oppression cannot survive." Teachout, *supra* note 9, at 280.

82. Reid, *supra* note 3, at 1319-20.

quite hollow, and their "Who would've guessed?" theory of the advent of vast economic disparities, political control exerted by a "favored few," and social degradation and misery for countless people is unconvincing.

It is significant that these constitutionalists make no attempt to prove or suggest that the kinds of changes which Horwitz demonstrates to have occurred in private law did not occur, or occurred in some other fashion for different reasons than those advanced by Horwitz, and with nonredistributive results. The constitutionalists, like most idealists, operate with their heads in the sand, ridiculing the notion of deep social division and conflict because their frame of understanding does not admit of its possibility. Their complacency rests upon twin unproven hopes, or, shall we say, predictions about the past. First, and most important, they posit, life in the United States existed as a matter of everyday fact for the overwhelming majority of its citizens under the operation of a rule of law, implying that a fair and neutral governmental structure harmoniously presided over the distribution of substantial justice and guaranteed to them the rights and liberties which the Revolution supposedly was fought over. Second, and in part as a result of the first, the vast majority of citizens actually received some of the fruits of abundance and growth, while most of those who attempted to exercise their "intelligence and inventiveness" were rewarded with larger pieces of the pie; further, the amounts of these dividends increased with the economy. Thus, the constitutionalists conclude, there could have been no reason for any social division of great magnitude to have occurred.

After the 1970's, perhaps the twilight of legitimacy for the American government, the failure of both of these prongs of the American dream has become evident. "The rule of law" has been demonstrated to have been a myth;[83] fairness and justice do not characterize the workings of the system at least in this century;[84]

226

---

83. *See, e.g.*, G. GILMORE, THE AGES OF AMERICAN LAW *passim*, esp. 105 (1977); R. UNGER, *supra* note 19.

84. *See, e.g.*, J. AUERBACH, UNEQUAL JUSTICE: LAWYERS AND SOCIAL CHANGE IN MODERN AMERICA (1976); R. HARRIS, FREEDOM SPENT: TALES OF TYRANNY IN AMERICA (1976); LAW AGAINST THE PEOPLE: ESSAYS TO DEMYSTIFY LAW, ORDER AND THE COURTS (R. Lefcourt ed. 1971) [hereinafter cited as LAW AGAINST THE PEOPLE]; M. LEVINE, POLITICAL HYSTERIA IN AMERICA: THE DEMOCRATIC CAPACITY FOR REPRESSION (1971); R. KLUGER, SIMPLE JUSTICE:

the existence of deep social divisions has begun to be noticed by scholars working in the Revolutionary,[85] "middle,"[86] Reconstruction,[87] and Progressive[88] periods of American history; and the pie which we supposedly have been given larger pieces of has proven to be plastic, poisonous, and increasingly devoid of any nourishing content.[89] The theory of Horwitz, which takes conflict into account and which explains the existence of bias in the law, provides a much more convincing account than does constitutionalism.

C. The Orthodox Critique

The orthodox school, typified usually by the writings of Roscoe Pound, originated in the period of the rise of lawyers to organized professional status (and the rise of law teaching to a separate profession) in the last decade of the nineteenth century and the first two decades of the twentieth. Having few adherents today (but perhaps growing rapidly), it shares the idealism of the constitutionalists, differing from them only in that it focuses on the common law as its central idea rather than on those constitutional principles which came to flower because of the Revolution. The history of humans is, to the orthodox, essentially a history of the development of ideas and clusters of ideas. If not timeless, these ideas certainly are understood to have a life of their own somehow

227

THE HISTORY OF BROWN V. BOARD OF EDUCATION AND BLACK AMERICA'S STRUGGLE FOR EQUALITY (1975).

85. See, e.g., D. SZATMARY, SHAYS' REBELLION (1980); D. HOERDER, CROWD ACTION IN REVOLUTIONARY MASSACHUSETTS, 1765-1780 (1977); S. LYND, CLASS CONFLICT, SLAVERY AND THE AMERICAN CONSTITUTION (1967); E. FONER, TOM PAINE AND REVOLUTIONARY AMERICA (1976); THE AMERICAN REVOLUTION: EXPLORATIONS IN THE HISTORY OF AMERICAN RADICALISM (A. Young ed. 1976).

86. See, e.g., E. GENOVESE, supra note 32; A. DAWLEY, CLASS AND COMMUNITY: THE INDUSTRIAL REVOLUTION IN LYNN (1976); H. GUTMAN, WORK, CULTURE AND SOCIETY IN INDUSTRIALIZING AMERICA (1976) (also deals with the Reconstruction period).

87. See, e.g., M. SCHWARTZ, RADICAL PROTEST AND SOCIAL STRUCTURE: THE SOUTHERN TENANT FARMERS' ALLIANCE AND COTTON TENANCY, 1880-1890 (1976); J. MANDLE, THE ROOTS OF BLACK POVERTY: THE SOUTHERN PLANTATION ECONOMY AFTER THE CIVIL WAR (1978); M. DUBOFSKY, INDUSTRIALISM AND THE AMERICAN WORKER, 1865-1920 (1975); J. WIENER, SOCIAL ORIGINS OF THE NEW SOUTH: ALABAMA 1860-1885 (1978).

88. See, e.g., G. KOLKO, THE TRIUMPH OF CONSERVATISM: A REINTERPRETATION OF AMERICAN HISTORY, 1900-1916 (1963); M. DUBOFSKY, WE SHALL BE ALL: A HISTORY OF THE INDUSTRIAL WORKERS OF THE WORLD (1969). See also W. WILLIAMS, THE GREAT EVASION (1974).

89. See C. LASCH, supra note 17, and other works cited there.

independent of and above society and human actors. Such concepts motivate and impel human action, as humans adapt themselves to and attempt to complete the concepts.

Concepts such as the common law are thought by the orthodox to be neutral and to grow (influenced at a great remove by slow and widely-shared changes in human custom) according to their own internal needs on a course charted by logic and reason, which are "assumed to be [themselves] governed by historically unchanging criteria."[90] When legal historians assert that changes in the law are a product of social forces rather than the result of logic and reason, they begin "to undermine the indispensable premise . . . that its characteristic modes of reasoning and its underlying substantive doctrines may not be universal or necessary, but rather particular and contingent."[91]

228

Randall Bridwell denies both that judges made law and that contemporary socioeconomic conditions or interest groups had much of an effect on the law. He conceives of the law as "a largely self ordering system supportive of autonomous individual behavior and experiment, adjusting itself with the aid of limited judicial intervention that does not effectively elevate the narrow interests of 'caste or class.' "[92] "Autonomous individual behavior" is custom, the "vast universe of private activity" which assumes "modes or patterns" that change "as society itself changes."[93] The judicial discretion permitted by the law "entailed the identification and elimination of inconsistencies in the judicial record,"[94] that is to say only the weeding out of mistakes, a technique whose use would be compelled to cease when "the contours of the positive rule . . . fully emerged [from] previous cases."[95] Bridwell points out, how-

90. Horwitz, *supra* note 5, at 278.

91. *Id.* at 281.

92. Bridwell, *supra* note 9, at 496. *See also* Gordon, *supra* note 51, at 1028-36.

93. Bridwell, *supra* note 9, at 464. Bridwell allows that "new custom" could be proved as such, *id.* at 470, but does not tell us how common law judges could discern true custom from temporary aberration.

94. *Id.* at 460.

95. *Id.* at 464 n.47. In the same note Bridwell explains that·"the cases contained *built in* limitations which emerged as the judicial acknowledgement of common law rules progressed to the state where the statements of positive law contained in the case was [sic] thoroughly settled." *Id.* Neither of these statements, nor any other that I can find in Bridwell's long article, answers the question of where the *first* cases and rules came from; cases, rules, and

ever, that "[t]he *actual rule* is nowhere personified or ever perfectly circumscribed into an inflexible definition."[96] Thus, while "the common law process" has the "essential capacity to reach ever more mature stages of development" by producing an increasingly "effectively inclusive or complete articulation of the standards" and by extending rules to other subject-matter areas, this process is limited by custom and existing precedent and was "largely based upon the continuous recognition of an ongoing order of actions which judicial action only touched upon intermittently, and in a fashion supportive of the ongoing order."[97] Rules are separate entities which define themselves to be complete; inconsistencies are obvious because of the law's internal logic; and the whole "process" is "supportive of the ongoing order." In Bridwell's view, Horwitz mistakes the ordinary limited discretion of the common-law process for "instrumentalism" because he has not studied sufficiently deeply to understand the continuities involved and to see how already developed principles were merely being extended and adapted to new evidence of custom.

229

Bridwell's theory that judges act only or primarily to flesh out, to apply, or to extend legal rules because of the very existence of the rules and of an "ongoing order" fails to convince on two accounts. First, the underlying assumption that society is an essentially harmonious and consensus-oriented entity whose history extends immemorially into the past directly ignores the possibility of social disruption and disharmony. Second, judges do not seem to act in the fashion he postulates. In *Transformation* Horwitz presents evidence contrary to both of Bridwell's assumptions. In the crucible, Bridwell is able in a forty-five page article to present

---

the law are assumed by the orthodox to exist. Bridwell does acknowledge that the narrow range of discretion was necessary "for the adjustment of rule to practice," but his extraordinary idealism is demonstated by his conception of what would have existed in the absence of discretion: this necessary "adjustment . . . would have to have been self-executing." *Id.* at 470. Ideas would correct themselves, without human intervention, and judges would be reduced to mere mouthpieces for the law!

96. *Id.* at 464. For the orthodox, rules are not only hard to pin down; they obey something like the Heisenberg principle, in that the very attempt to measure them is disturbing to them. "[A]lmost any attempt to isolate legal or Constitutional phenonmena [sic] rends the 'seamless webb' [sic] of history and to some degree inevitably distorts the truth." *Id.* at 451 n.8.

97. *Id.* at 465, 466.

no convincing evidence that Horwitz is wrong.[98] The best he can do
is to tell us that the job is difficult:

> Admittedly, phenomena such as "judicial discretion" are not
> easily quantified. . . . The ability of a prevalent decisional tech-
> nique to accomplish extensive and profound doctrinal change
> and still remain the same technique or constitutional common
> law process is an exceedingly complex phenomenon to under-
> stand . . . . Horwitz's book adds little to our understanding of
> this process, and at most presents largely unsupported conclu-
> sions with a mere description of doctrinal change, sometimes
> stated inaccurately.[[99]]
> [T]he application of some quite familiar techniques for analysis
> of legal data [would] enable Professor Horwitz to derive a more
> defensible and more accurate meaning from it. . . . A simple
> consideration of implicit principles common to a wide variety of
> case data would have disclosed certain general consistent "theo-
> ries" in the case law itself, which would in turn explain what
> specifically appears to be "transformation."[100]

230

Bridwell cites no substantive cases and gives no "general consistent theories" to refute Horwitz's massively presented documentation of legal change over an eighty-year period in several major
subject-matter areas. His orthodox ideological-deterministic argument is merely asserted.

Ironically, it is Bridwell who castigates Horwitz for selective use
of the material,[101] and the empty irony of the orthodox critique is
compounded by the following remarkable charge: "The conspiratorial antics of the great mass of the American judiciary, glancing
sidelong at one another as they step in unison to gratify big business by consciously overthrowing the private law of the country is
somehow a spectacle which one finds difficult to accept without
some real proof."[102] Why are not the actions of judges (robbed of
any independent use of their intelligence, it is true) who adhere to

---

98. Bridwell does spend 20 tedious pages on one attempt at disproof, which will be
treated in the succeeding section of this essay; his convoluted and difficult argument is not
very convincing.

99. *Id.* at 495.

100. *Id.* at 493-94.

101. These castigations occur frequently. *See, e.g., id.* at 494.

102. *Id.* at 472.

custom and precedent in the common-law process equally "conspiratorial?" Do not Bridwell's judges "step in unison," only to a different tune? Immediately preceding the passage last quoted, Bridwell notes that the common-law judges rode herd on each other—"no judge or group of judges could escape the matrix of rules being observed by the greater number";[103] are these not "sidelong glances" of people "consciously" in lock-step? Conspiracy is not conspiracy when it is a consensus, apparently.

A variant of the orthodox argument, smugly produced by law-and-economist Stephen Williams, supplies a large gap in Bridwell's scheme by identifying the mode by which custom is taken into account by common-law judges. No conspiracy indeed, it is all a matter of utilitarian efficiency, which, Williams is sure, is timeless and neutral, not an approach invented in the late eighteenth century as a way of justifying contemporary value judgments. The "thread of utilitarianism stretches back into the remotest reaches of Anglo-American law,"[104] he asserts, utilitarian language coming more into use post Bentham, "seep[ing] into judicial opinions . . . thereafter."[105] Effortlessly ignoring Horwitz's identification of instrumentalism with bias and partiality, Williams transmogrifies the overt attempt of the judges to stimulate growth into a neutral, natural application of standards of efficiency. Courts are *supposed* to aid growth: "The central problem is one of assuring that rights be readily *marketable*—a prerequisite if private rights in property are to allocate resources efficiently."[106] Indeed, courts always did, though they may have been ignorant of what they were doing:

> [W]e may note some general reasons for skepticism about the idea that pre-"transformation" law was innocent of utilitarian goals. . . . [I]t seems scarcely credible that society could long exist without viewing a goal of maximizing aggregate utility . . . as at least *relevant to a substantial* number of cases. . . .
>
>   . . . [S]o many legal justifications preceding utilitarian analysis are patently tautological . . . [that] it seems natural to suppose that the utility of the rule, rather than the tautological

231

---

103. *Id.*
104. Williams, *supra* note 9, at 1187.
105. *Id.* at 1201.
106. *Id.* at 1198.

mumbo-jumbo, was the true source of the judicial decision.[107]

Utilitarian efficiency itself has here become the timeless central idea of orthodoxy, which, since it "seems natural," is assumed not to be partial or economically biased.

The members of orthodoxy want to shut out from their consciousness any possibility that law might be partisan, produced by political efforts to achieve the interests of this or that segment of the social whole.[108] They ignore the desires and demands of any segment of the population that is not "supportive of the ongoing order," and elevate the partisan results of social interaction and coercive governmental behavior into immemorial custom or utilitarian efficiency supposedly understood and voluntarily adhered to by all. Ideas enable the orthodox to ignore the realities of discord and social struggle, but, like all liberals, they bottom their understanding and approach upon an assumed consensus.[109] They too

232

---

107. *Id.* at 1202.

108. The *Maitre de ballet* of law-and-economics has recently "come out of the closet" of scientistic neutrality, arguing in two recent articles that utilitarian efficiency is utilized by courts to maximize the wealth of the wealthy. *See* Posner, *The Ethical and Political Basis of the Efficiency Norm in Common Law Adjudication,* 8 Hofstra L. Rev. 487 (1980); Posner, *Utilitarianism, Economics, and Legal Theory,* 8 J. Legal Stud. 103 (1979), criticized aptly in Horwitz, *Law and Economics, supra* note 18 (the "closet" quote is from *id.* at 912). It will be interesting to see whether this radical shift from neutralism to ideology will, as Horwitz predicts, split apart the law-and-economics movement, but the event does provide additional evidence for the thesis that the Rule of Law is rapidly crumbling. *See generally* Holt, The Future of the Rule of Law: Notes on Post-Liberal Jurisprudence (1981) (unpublished manuscript).

The connection between Bridwell and the patriarch of the modern legal utilitarians, Friedrich von Hayek, is noted by Sugarman, *Theory and Practice, supra* note 8, at 99 n.26.

109. Thus, Bridwell finds himself "more in agreement with Hurst" despite the latter's determinism because, "contrary to Horwitz's view, . . . Hurst has consistently emphasized broad popular support for legal change in America." Bridwell, *supra* note 9, at 492 n.118. Reid, also representing an idealist school, similarly bridges the putatively immense chasm between himself and the economic determinists: "In the legal history of Professor Hurst, economic interests struggled against other economic interests. . . . The courts acted as neutral referees . . . . Hurst attributes the transformation . . . to drift and inertia . . . ." Reid, *supra* note 3, at 1321. The primary factor in the analysis of all these superficially diverse scholars is not their scholarly findings, not the theoretical framework (emphasizing ideas of economics) within which those findings are located, but their aversion to the very mention of social discord and divisions. Bridwell and Reid accuse Horwitz of tailoring his evidence to fit preconceived theories, Reid, *supra* note 3, at 1317; Bridwell, *supra* note 9, at 492-93, but it is evident that liberal scholars tailor their evidence to fit their theories too. Their work is just as political as is the law they strive to see as neutral.

have been unable to present any convincing arguments that the doctrines of law which Horwitz demonstrates to have emerged in the early national period of our history were not produced in an "instrumental" fashion to serve partisan purposes, attempting to aid certain segments of American society at the expense of others.

D. The Failure of Substantive Critiques

Three attempts have been made to gainsay Horwitz's reading of the evidence from the nineteenth century. Two of these, by Randall Bridwell and Stephen Williams of the orthodox school, are quite unconvincing. Bridwell fails to come to grips with the substance of *Transformation,* that is, Horwitz's thorough survey of the basic areas of common-law adjudication to cull evidence of judicial attempts to aid economic development. Bridwell essentially snipes at flanks, choosing the adjective area of conflict of laws for the burden of his refutation, and fighting on the territory of *Swift v. Tyson,*[110] a decision which Horwitz does not proclaim to be openly instrumental (since it was not). Rather, in a short discussion which has met with the approval of other reviewers,[111] Horwitz argues that Justice Story disguised a prodevelopmental decision in neutralistic, already outdated natural law theory, requiring federal diversity courts to apply general commercial rules favoring negotiability rather than the peculiar New York rule which Tyson thought applied, one which would have stanched negotiability.

Although it is hidden in a confused flurry of criticism and deprecation,[112] Bridwell's agreement with the prodevelopmental nature both of *Swift* and of the general doctrines of commercial law emerges from a close reading. "[E]verything practical encouraged states to leave general commercial custom intact as they found it,"

233

---

110. 41 U.S. (16 Pet.) 1 (1842).

111. The eight-page discussion of Swift (out of Horwitz's 348 pages), M. HORWITZ, *supra* note 1, at 245-52, 345-46, has been noted with approval by Horwitz critics Gilmore, *supra* note 9, at 789-90, and Scheiber, *supra* note 9, at 461.

112. Bridwell variously accuses Horwitz of misunderstanding general commercial law prevalent before the Civil War, misunderstanding the content and role of the conflicts rules of the time, misinterpretation of the federal system of courts *and* of contemporary ideas of federalism, oversimplification, selective use of evidence, and crudity of presentation; he concludes, "All this is just about as wrong as it could be." Bridwell, *supra* note 9, at 473-92, 479.

because such was supported by "the customary practices of innumerable private parties pursuing their own autonomous commercial dealings."[113] Bridwell even finds it "quite ordinary" that judges would undertake "the gradual recognition of widely held and objectively provable practices."[114] It is surprisingly unsurprising to him that "decisions reflect the views and practices of the majority of the commercial world."[115] The world has become "the commercial world," and only a "majority" of that; the only relevant people are those with sufficient resources to pursue "autonomous commercial dealings." Bridwell's consensus underpinnings, however, preclude his recognition of the partiality and bias of his beliefs. His argument reduces to the naked assertion that Horwitz must be wrong in attributing overt class bias to judges because it is only natural for them to have followed "widely held" commercial practices—and Bridwell makes this argument, significantly, with regard to a case which does not contain the kind of openly developmental language Horwitz demonstrates in many other instances.

234

Williams attempts to show that the law in three areas—negligence, nuisance, and riparian rights—did not change as drastically as Horwitz claims it did. In each instance his attempted proof falls far short of being persuasive. Horwitz argues that the advent of entrepreneurial capitalism persuaded many judges to introduce an element of fault into torts, thus altering that field's theoretical basis from strict liability to negligence. The argument is not new, but Charles O. Gregory had urged that 1850 was the turning point,[116] whereas Horwitz wishes to move the date back a half century. Williams agrees with the contrary, idealistic argument of E.F. Roberts that strict liability was never the rule, fault being required in accidental injury cases long before 1800.[117] Williams finds comfort in several early English cases,[118] but Horwitz had at-

---

113. *Id.* at 490-91. Mr. Tyson, who presumably was pursuing his own autonomous commercial dealing, was apparently as wrong-headed as Horwitz was to prove to be: "It is difficult to imagine any real expectations Mr. Tyson might have had being defeated by the *Swift* decision." *Id.* at 490 n.115.

114. *Id.* at 491.

115. *Id.*

116. Gregory, *Trespass to Negligence to Absolute Liability*, 37 VA. L. REV. 359 (1951).

117. Roberts, *Negligence: Blackstone to Shaw to ? An Intellectual Escapade in a Tory Vein*, 50 CORNELL L.Q. 191 (1965).

118. Williams, *supra* note 9, at 1190, 1215-18.

tempted to reject the Roberts argument solely on the basis of American cases.[119] Williams cites no *American* cases to refute Horwitz's claim that the American and British developments were different, quibbles with Horwitz's reading of several admittedly obscure and difficult decisions, and concludes weakly and idealistically that, "[a]fter looking at his core authorities, one emerges suspecting that American law contained vast empty reaches waiting to be filled."[120] The assertion that decisions which dealt with contemporary problems in contemporary if obscure terms are meaningless and "empty" not only fulfills the historian's task poorly but also fails to convince that Horwitz is wrong. Rather, one is moved to reject Williams's arguments instead.

One has seen Williams's strongest point by this time. He advances several arguments that might constitute exceptions to Horwitz's view of nuisance law, but admits that "it is hard to ascertain the extent to which [these exceptions] may have commanded judicial adherence at any given moment," and again fails to cite a single American decision to refute Horwitz.[121] Williams notes that there are not a lot of cases to back up Horwitz's claim that riparian law changed from a concept of natural flow to one of reasonable use, in order to allow courts to interrupt stream flow for developmental reasons, but again he cannot find much with which to dispute Horwitz either, coming to rest on the assertion that "for all their talk of 'balancing,' courts have very rarely denied relief to an established user whose interests were substantially interfered with by a newcomer."[122] The reason for Williams's production of popguns when cannons were announced is not long in evidencing itself: he agrees with development and, like Bridwell, finds it natural for courts to promote economic growth. "Surely the public purpose is making possible the production that would have been foreclosed if every adversely affected riparian owner were allowed an injunctive remedy."[123] If "maximizing aggregate utility" is the goal of all sane judges, as Williams thinks it is,[124] then one ought to

235

---

119. M. HORWITZ, *supra* note 1, at 91 & n.156.
120. Williams, *supra* note 9, at 1193.
121. *Id.* at 1196.
122. *Id.* at 1199.
123. *Id.* at 1200.
124. *Id.* at 1202, discussed in text accompanying note 107 *supra*.

expect very little substantive difference between Williams and Horwitz with regard to the nineteenth century cases, and that is what one finds.

The third criticism seems more formidable. In an urbane essay, one of the doyens of contemporary English contractual legal history, A.W.B. Simpson, has disputed Horwitz on many significant points in *Transformation's* study of contract law.[125] While it has proved beyond my competence to investigate the charges made, it appears that Simpson's critique is not very forceful either. First, Simpson lines himself up with the developmental idealism of Bridwell and Williams: "many of the doctrines that [Horwitz] identifies as characteristic of the transformation were common in the eighteenth century."[126]

Second, the British legal historian David Sugarman has investigated some of the competing claims made by Horwitz and Simpson about the history of contract law. Sugarman finds several substantive and methodological flaws in Simpson's work which partially undercut the force of Simpson's critique. If Sugarman is correct, Simpson's criticisms carry significantly less force in important respects than would otherwise be the case. Sugarman's work[127] should be published soon, but, given my sympathy with his previous conclusions,[128] I assume the correctness of his judgment in this instance.

Third and most important, Betty Mensch has concluded that the recent, massively detailed history of modern English contract law (written by Oxford University Professor P.S. Atiyah, the other doyen of English contractual legal history) "provides detailed and convincing evidence that Horwitz was right"[129] in his analysis of doctrinal change, as distinct from the social and economic conclusions to be drawn therefrom. Indeed, Atiyah acknowledges his debt to Horwitz.[130] Atiyah's undoubted orthodoxy on social and eco-

236

---

125. Simpson, *supra* note 9.

126. *Id.* at 542.

127. Sugarman, *Horwitz, Simpson, Atiyah and the Transformation of Anglo-American Law*, in LAW AND ECONOMY: ESSAYS IN THE HISTORY OF ENGLISH LAW 1750-1914 (forthcoming 1982).

128. *See* note 11 *supra*.

129. Mensch, *supra* note 52, at 756 n.9; *see id.* at 756-58, *passim*.

130. *See, e.g.*, P. ATIYAH, THE RISE AND FALL OF FREEDOM OF CONTRACT 566 n.5 (1979).

nomic matters,[131] plus his detailed doctrinal conclusions, confirm both that Horwitz is essentially correct (at least in the realm of contract law) and that *Transformation* cannot be dismissed as the product of sheer prejudice or bias. Neither Simpson nor Williams nor Bridwell has managed substantially to refute Horwitz's reading of the nineteenth-century American cases.

E. *Conclusion*

The comparison of *Transformation* to the work of those who have criticized it from the right has put into even starker, more favorable contrast the signal achievement of Horwitz. He is willing to accept that there might have been deep social and economic divisions in the American polity during the period 1780-1860, with certain interest groups consistently getting the greater share of the spoils from the struggle. He argues that this was both reflected in and enhanced by changes in major doctrines of law, and that judges and lawyers, far from being professionally neutral, allied themselves with those who benefited, the rising entrepreneurial and industrial capitalists. All legal historians of the three liberal schools in current vogue, in their theories and in their research, unquestioningly accept an underlying social consensus as a fundamental axiom. Some conventional legal historians are idealists, who ignore or submerge economic and social factors; others are determinists, who elevate economic factors to the front of analysis but understand them only on the surface, failing to look beneath them for the hidden interconnections and influences which demonstrate deep tensions and conflicts of interests. All, however, as has been shown, rest on consensus.[132]

237

A materialist view of history, carefully utilizing Marx's dialectical methodology,[133] describes the past and present very differ-

---

131. *Id.* at 220-24, 389-90 (carefully adopting an orthodox political position).

132. *Cf.* Freeman, *supra* note 48, at 1233-34, 1236.

133. One cannot repeat too often that Marx's dialectical approach involves the rejection of a familiar bourgeois way of looking at the world in favor of the development of a more comprehensive, qualitative, substantive approach wh.ch, among other things, disavows the liberal fact/value distinction and the liberal mode of definition-by-isolation. *See* B. OLLMAN, ALIENATION, *supra* note 16, at 5-40, *passim;* notes :6, 64 & accompanying text *supra;* Ollman, *Teaching Marxism, supra* note 16, at 125, 126, 136:

[U]ndoubtedly the major hurdle in presenting Marxism . . . is the bourgeois

ently.[134] It discovers that humans have been in fundamental conflict in all of recorded history over the means available to reproduce their daily lives in a physical sense ("the means of production"), and that these conflicts take place between social groups identifiable by their access to control of the means of production. Those in control exploit the others, who must toil for the controllers. Those who do not have control wish to escape the oppressiveness of being subordinated to others and the deprivation of the products of their labor, in order to satisfy their own needs. Chief among these needs is to retain and fulfill the basic attributes of humanity, to attain "the full and free development of every individual."[135]

Different "modes" of production, or methods of extracting labor from workers, have existed at different times. The present epoch is one of capitalism; the workers create and donate surplus value to capitalists essentially through a process of mystification rather than one involving brute force or fear. Workers consent to the system because they are supposedly free to contract with employers · for their labor-time, inequalities of bargaining power being success-

---

ideology, the systematic biases and blind spots, which even the most radical
bring with them. . . . Underpinning and providing a framework for all [bour-
geois biases and blind spots] is an undialectical, factoral mode of thinking that
separates events from their conditions, people from their real alternatives and
human potential, social problems from one another, and the present from the
past and the future. The organizing and predisposing power of this mode of
thought is such that any attempt to . . . present a Marxist analysis of any
event is doomed to distortion and failure unless accompanied by an equally
strenuous effort to impart the dialectical mode of reasoning. . . . It is important . . . [to] see that formal education in America is in large part training in
how to think undialectically.

134. Marx was especially careful to oppose idealism:
My dialectic method is not only different from the Hegelian, but its direct
opposite. To Hegel, the life-process of the human brain, i.e., the process of
thinking, which under the name of "the Idea," he even transforms into an independent subject, is the demiurgos of the real world, and the real world is
only the external, phenomenal form of "the Idea." With me, on the contrary,
the ideal is nothing else than the material world reflected by the human mind,
and translated into forms of thought.
1 K. MARX, CAPITAL, supra note 23, at 19. While this quote may be taken to reinforce a
deterministic version of the "structure"-"superstructure" dichotomy, see note 14 & accompanying text supra, it appears to me that Marx is linking together the mind and the material world rather than disjoining them.

135. Id. at 592.

fully hidden behind the appearance of fairness and freedom. The mystification resonates throughout the culture of the capitalist social system. Inequalities in access to power are successfully hidden within structures of liberal democracy, constitutionalism, and the rule of law.[136] Inequalities in access to satisfaction of needs are successfully hidden within a flood of consumer products, the availability of stock ownership, welfare supports and other governmental redistributive schemes, and belief in freedom of opportunity. Class lines are blurred, and struggle is defused or deflected, as most people are unable fully to sense their own objective interests resulting from their objective economic situation.[137] Ideologues, such as historians, reproduce the mystification by investigating only the appearances, accepting without question such fundamental liberal notions as consensus when the existence of consensus is what they should be questioning scientifically.

Horwitz has radically broken with liberal legal history and its mystifying categories and assumptions. He has demonstrated the bias of law and law-people in the period 1780-1860, destroying the myth of the neutrality of law and opening the way for the study of law as an active element of human socioeconomic history in the manner of E.P. Thompson,[138] Eugene Genovese,[139] Douglas Hay,[140] and Staughton Lynd,[141] among others.[142] *Transformation* ranks

239

---

136. *Cf.* Tushnet, *Truth, Justice, and the American Way: An Interpretation of Public Law Scholarship in the Seventies,* 57 TEX. L. REV. 1307, 1347-50 (1979).

137. The two-class model used by Marx may be better understood, to the extent it might be thought to be descriptive of contemporary social formations, as a metaphor rather than as an objective reality. Marx wrote during a time when capital and labor stood blankly opposed to each other, snarling across a rather clearly defined abyss. Proletarian conditions today form a part of almost everyone's objective experience. *See* works cited in note 17 *supra.*

138. *See* E. THOMPSON, WHIGS AND HUNTERS, esp. 245-69 (1975).

139. *See* E. GENOVESE, *supra* note 32, esp. 25-49.

140. *See* Hay, *Property, Authority and the Criminal Law,* in D. HAY et al., ALBION'S FATAL TREE 17-63 (1975). Hay is critiqued in Sugarman, *Theory and Society, supra* note 8, *passim.*

141. *See, e.g.,* Lynd, *Government Without Rights: The Labor Law Vision of Archibald Cox,* 4 INDUS. REL. L.J. 483 (1981); Lynd, *Investment Decisions and the Quid Pro Quo Myth,* 29 CASE W. RES. L. REV. 396 (1979); Lynd, *The Right to Engage in Concerted Activity After Union Recognition: A Study of Legislative History,* 50 IND. L.J. 720 (1975).

142. *See, e.g.,* LAW AGAINST THE PEOPLE, *supra* note 84; Glasbeek & Rowland, *Are Injuring and Killing at Work Crimes?,* 17 OSGOODE HALL L.J. 506 (1979); Klare, *Judicial Deradicalization of the Wagner Act and the Origins of Modern Legal Consciousness, 1937-1941,*

(with Mark Tushnet's recent book *The American Law of Slavery*[143]) as the most suggestive, comprehensive, and sustained work to be produced by the critical legal theory movement of aware legal scholars which has emerged in the past five years.[144] The product of a slow but steady disaffection with bourgeois historiography and politics, it is and should remain a model for us all and a monument to the struggle toward demystification which most of us must go through.

Nevertheless, problems remain with *Transformation* as an exemplar of materialist history. In much of his methodology, in most of his explicit efforts at summary and analysis, and in many of the attitudes he exhibits, Horwitz did not effect the same radical break with the premises of liberal legal history as do the impact and approach of the volume as a whole. While, as noted before,[145] many of the aspects of materialist historiography are subjects of considerable debate and part of the problem can be attributed to a similar retention of aspects of liberal ways of thinking, the attempt to delineate some of these problems may help to reduce the occurrence of similar confusion and, thus, to accelerate the advance of materialist scholarship.

240

IV.   THE PROBLEMS WITH *Transformation*

A.   *The History of Capitalism*

Two common misconceptions about the past mar *Transformation*. One may be called the "golden era" error, and the other con-

---

62 MINN. L. REV. 265 (1978); Ravitz, *Reflections of a Radical Judge: Beyond the Courtroom,* in VERDICTS ON LAWYERS 255, 255-68 (R. Nader & M. Green eds. 1976); Wexler, *Practicing Law for Poor People,* 79 YALE L.J. 1049 (1970); P. Gabel, The Social Psychology of Law and Legal Process (1981) (unpublished doctoral dissertation).

143. M. TUSHNET, THE AMERICAN LAW OF SLAVERY 1810-1860: CONSIDERATIONS OF HUMANITY AND INTEREST (1981).

144. A Conference on Critical Legal Studies was organized in 1977, when few of its members were Marxists. A majority of the participants in the 1982 meeting of the Conference in Cambridge appeared to be Marxists. Many of its members, and some others, consider themselves to be a part of a critical legal theory movement. *See* Kennedy, *supra* note 18, at 1275; Freeman, *supra* note 48. While *Business Week*'s estimate of 10,000 Marxists now teaching at the college level or above is obviously overdrawn, there has been a significant growth of materialist membership on university faculties and particularly in law schools in very recent times. *See* U.S. NEWS & WORLD REPORT, Jan. 25, 1982, at 42-45.

145. *See* notes 13-16 & accompanying text *supra.*

cerns the dating of the advent of capitalism. Many historians who perceive conflict and social tension in a given period will conclude that it represents a declension from a previous time when harmony prevailed.[146] At points, Horwitz describes· life in colonial America as though a real consensus existed then, in a socially undifferentiated world free from class struggle. "[V]iolations of the tort law were [then] universally regarded as unjustified and antisocial acts," he says; "[l]aw [was] once conceived of as protective, regulative, paternalistic and, above all, a paramount expression of the moral sense of the community, . . . [of] the legal and ethical culture of the small town, of the farmer, and of the small trader."[147] The reader is led to conclude that capitalism reared its ugliness only with the advent of an outburst of entrepreneurship in the 1790's.

At other points in *Transformation*, however, there are overtones of a different analysis, where colonial law is said to reflect the interests of "[t]he great English gentry, who had played a central role" in shaping it.[148] As Simpson observes:

> A Marxist might have argued that the English commercial bourgeoisie, linked with elements of the landed classes, forged an equitable theory of contract in the eighteenth century as a weapon in their struggle with a law reflecting earlier, less commercial times; and that once it triumphed, the new order cut back on the dangerous legal doctrines it had used against the old.[149]

McClain is in accord: "the class which created the common law and was most protected by it was the class at the top of the hierarchy—the English landed aristocracy."[150] As Genovese has noted, "Historically, private property has meant bourgeois property . . . . The early advance of capitalism may, therefore, be measured by the doctrinal advance of 'absolute' property, most notably in land."[151] Rather than the advent of capitalism, *Transformation* concerns a change from one form of it to another. Eric Foner sums

241

---

146. *See, e.g.,* J. AUERBACH, *supra* note 84.

147. M. HORWITZ, *supra* note 1, at 81, 253, 186.

148. *Id.* at 36.

149. Simpson, *supra* note 9, at 535-36.

150. McClain, *supra* note 9, at 396; *accord, e.g.,* Gilmore *supra* note 9, at 794; Winship, *supra* note 9, at 754; Bloomfield, *supra* note 9, at 1107.

151. Genovese, *supra* note 8, at 732 (footnote omitted).

it up: "what Horwitz is describing is precisely a change from what [C.B.] Macpherson calls 'possessive individualism,' in which property is valued primarily as a guarantee of individual autonomy, to a market view of property as a means to economic development and capital accumulation."[152]

Marx insisted that "the modern history of capital dates from the creation in the 16th century of a world-embracing commerce and a world-embracing market,"[153] with "the first beginnings of capitalist production as early as the 14th or 15th century."[154] England led the way. The British North American colonies were settled as "colonies," and were treated as such by the mother country. While much of the settlement had an enduring frontier quality, there eventually developed major cities where many people engaged in commerce (and even banking), and *The Legal Papers of John Adams*, among other sources, make clear that emerging elitist and professionalistic groups of lawyers in the urban centers were beginning to devote themselves at least in part to the affairs of businessmen long before 1800.[155] Poverty and wretchedness existed both in the countryside and in the cities, and increasingly after 1700 inflation was a major problem, particularly during the crises which led to the Revolution.[156] Social historian Edward Pessen's recent conclusions deserve quotation at length:

> A dramatic inequality of condition long antedated Tocqueville's visit to America. . . . In the century prior to the American Revolution, colonies in every geographical section of British North America witnessed the emergence of families possessed of substantial real and personal property. . . . American communi-

242

---

152. Foner, *supra* note 8, at 38; C. MACPHERSON, THE POLITICAL THEORY OF POSSESSIVE INDIVIDUALISM: HOBBES TO LOCKE (1962); *cf.* 1 K. MARX, CAPITAL, *supra* note 23, at 89:
    Man has often made man himself, under the form of slaves, serve as the primitive material of money, but has never used land for that purpose. Such an idea could only spring up in a bourgeois society already well developed. It dates from the last third of the 17th century . . . .

153. *Id.* at 146.

154. *Id.* at 715. *See also* S. COHN, THE LABORING CLASSES IN RENAISSANCE FLORENCE (1980).

155. *See generally, e.g.,* THE LEGAL PAPERS OF JOHN ADAMS (3 vols., L. Wroth & H. Zobel eds. 1965); Klein, *The Rise of the New York Bar: The Legal Career of William Livingston,* in ESSAYS IN THE HISTORY OF EARLY AMERICAN LAW 392 (D. Flaherty ed. 1969); G. NASH, THE URBAN CRUCIBLE (1979).

156. *See* D. HOERDER, *supra* note 85, *passim.*

ties without exception witnessed increasing concentration or maldistribution of wealth with the passage of time. . . . [I]n almost every colony a small, wealthy ruling class "dominated the local political machinery [and] filled all or nearly all the important local offices". . . . It is a fair summary that over the course of the colonial era several thousand families, constituting less than one percent of the American population, had amassed great riches based on diverse sources, lofty social prestige and a near monopoly of influence and power which they appear to have regarded both as a fitting recognition of their possessions and eminence and as a means of promoting their own personal interests and those of their class.[157]

The Salem witch craze, the "Regulator" movements in backcountry Carolina before the Revolution, and the rebellions, such as Shays', that flared up in the 1780's and 1790's against the new regime, demonstrate the potential for social unrest and class division.[158] While capitalism may have entered a period of rapid entrepreneurial growth in the United States with the advent of nationhood, it was the dominant mode of sociopolitical relations long before 1800, with concomitant crises, social struggle, and the biased use of law to aid elites. There was no "golden" colonial era, except in Pessen's sense.

243

B. *The Organic Nature of Capitalist Culture*

Capitalism is a way of life, not merely a set of economic relationships. The particular mode of production of any epoch infuses and is infused by a concomitant organic culture, an interrelated, possibly internally contradictory, but characteristic complex of institutions, feelings, habits, beliefs, interpretations, morals, and

---

157. Pessen, *Wealth in America Before 1865*, in WEALTH AND THE WEALTHY IN THE MODERN WORLD 167, 168, 169, 170, 172, 174-75 (W. Rubenstein ed. 1980).

158. For the Salem witch craze, see P. BOYER & S. NISSENBAUM, SALEM POSSESSED: THE SOCIAL ORIGINS OF WITCHCRAFT (1974); D. KONIG, LAW AND SOCIETY IN PURITAN MASSACHUSETTS: ESSEX COUNTY, 1629-1692, at 3-34, 158-91 (1979). *See generally* M. HARRIS, COWS, PIGS, WARS AND WITCHES (1974). For the Regulator movement, see M. Kay, The Institutional Background to the Regulation in North Carolina (1962) (unpublished doctoral dissertation, University of Minnesota), M. KAY, THE NORTH CAROLINA REGULATORS, 1766-1776 (forthcoming), and J. Whittenburg, Backwoods Revolutionaries: Social Context and Constitutional Theories of the North Carolina Regulators, 1765-1771 (1974) (unpublished doctoral dissertation, University of Georgia). For Shays' Rebellion, see D. SZATMARY, *supra* note 85.

doctrines:

> According to Marx, social conditions determine character, both
> directly, through their effect on the individual's powers and
> needs, and indirectly, through the creation of interests which he
> then strives to satisfy . . . . The visible result is a psychological
> and ideological superstructure which is practically the same for
> all men caught up in a given set of material relations.[159]

For most people, the result is internalized and is only partially
consciously perceived to be a peculiar, historically specific phenomenon; during the heyday of capitalism, most people feel that the
capitalist ethos is "natural." It is not a surface, intellectual brush
with ideas; an individual's whole approach to and appreciation of
the world—his or her emotions, perceptions, speech, and
thought—are influenced and formed by the underlying material relations. They are the way she or he understands reality.[160]

Horwitz notes that the instrumental mode of decisionmaking reshaped some rules "before new or special economic or technological
pressure for change in the law . . . emerged."[161] He explains this

244

---

159. B. OLLMAN, ALIENATION, *supra* note 16, at 120. Marx stated this truth as follows:
Upon the different forms of property, upon the social conditions of existence,
rises an entire superstructure of distinct and peculiarly formed sentiments, illusions, modes of thought and views of life. The entire class creates and forms
them out of its material foundations and out of the corresponding social relations. The single individual, who derives them through tradition and upbring-
ing, may imagine that they form the real motives and the starting point of his
activity. . . . [A]s in private life one differentiates between what a man thinks
and says of himself and what he really is and does, so in historical struggles
one must distinguish still more the phrases and fancies of parties from their
real organism and their real interests, their conception of themselves, from
their reality.
K. MARX, THE EIGHTEENTH BRUMAIRE OF LOUIS BONAPARTE 47 (Int'l Pub. ed. New York
1963) (1st ed. 1852) [hereinafter cited as K. MARX, EIGHTEENTH BRUMAIRE]. Closely related
to this is the "structure"-"superstructure" problem. *See* note 14, & text accompanying notes
13-16 & 145 *supra*.

160. Christopher Lasch reaffirms that "social patterns reproduce themselves in personality." C. LASCH, *supra* note 17, at 50-51. Mark Tushnet terms this a "psychology of ideology
which . . . has been neglected by prominent Marxist scholars until recently[:] . . . people
must interpret the material conditions of their existence in ways that make their experience
coherent. . . . [T]he primary, though not exclusive, material conditions that shape interpretations of the world are the material social relations of production." M. TUSHNET, *supra*
note 143, at 31-32.

161. M. HORWITZ, *supra* note 1, at 3.

apparent cause-effect anomaly by postulating autonomous economic interests peculiar to judges, lawyers, and "the law," unconnected with the interests of entrepreneurial capitalism, which produced the changes before they were "necessary." As has been seen, however, capitalism had been dominant in American social relations for a long time; it was "in the air." Judges, lawyers, and legal commentators, formed psychologically and intellectually by and caught up in the ethos of capitalism, would have some feeling for "the way things ought to be," and could have in effect invented solutions for problems which might not have yet occurred.[162] Economics and law, as ideological phenomena, interact not in a linear, simple, one cause-one effect way, but in a complex, interrelated, organic fashion.[163]

Another, more important consequence of the organic nature of capitalism is a deeper perspective on the notion of "instrumentalism." Horwitz has argued in a linear cause-and-effect mode: "instrumentalism" rises to "dominance" after about 1820, being phased out in favor of a newly-dominant "formalism" around 1860.

245

---

162. Organicism is *not* idealism in disguise; it *is*, however, the materialist posture of the same perceptual mode. Idealists reify to abstraction, attempting (whether consciously or not) to isolate the perceived phenomenon from its socioeconomic context. Materialists also reify, but they refuse to disconnect their perceptions from each other and from the historic social and economic matrix within which their origins, meanings, and consequences lie. Much of the confusion at the heart of Davis, *supra* note 48, lies in its idealistic failure to grasp this distinction. While phenomena persist after their matrix of genesis has subsided, due to the collective existence of human mental capabilities such as memory, K. MARX, EIGHTEENTH BRUMAIRE, *supra* note 159, at 15, and while humans strive not only to reproduce themselves but also to escape the realm of "necessity and mundane considerations" for the purpose of developing "human energy as an end in itself," 3 K. MARX, CAPITAL, *supra* note 23, at 820, both of which render socioeconomic determination mediate rather than immediate in many instances and produce "relative autonomy," the human situation is nevertheless still best understood materially, since "the true realm of freedom . . . can blossom forth only with th[e] realm of necessity as its basis." *Id.*

163. The victory of economic subjectivism at law enormously strengthened its supporters within the economics profession itself. The ideological struggle [over the nature of contracts] within the legal profession may well have had as great an impact upon economic thought as vice versa—economic thought appealing to the newly prevailing subjectivism of legal doctrine as if all opposition had been swept from the field, and legal thought increasingly resting its pretension to science upon an economic reality perceived as pure market mechanism, but in fact partly a result of the very legal intervention sanctioned by the economic theory to which it was now appealing in the name of scientific objectivity. Genovese, *supra* note 8, at 731-32.

Since *Transformation* focuses almost exclusively on decisions from the northeastern United States,[164] that is, upon the region rapidly undergoing capitalist development, variations from, or negations of, the prescribed rise-dominance-fall pattern on some other regional (or perhaps temporal) basis could be used as a solid argument for rejecting the Horwitz theory.

An organic approach might observe that the legal aspect of the ethos of capitalism is positivism, and that legal positivism usually has been expressed in one of two modes of judicial reasoning—instrumentalism or formalism—as demanded by material conditions and the job to be accomplished. "Instrumentalism" is a useful legal-positivist mode when a fundamental attack must be made upon a received legal tradition, or where frontier conditions exist. Thus, "instrumentalism" probably lasted long past 1860 on the frontier and in frontier conditions or frontier areas of law,[165] and it was as useful in firming the foundations of emerging monopoly capital in the first four decades of this century (by a generation of Legal Realists) as it had been in establishing the foundations of entrepreneurial capital a hundred years before. Formalism, on the other hand, as Horwitz says, never disappeared. It was always the mode used—by the *same* judges—in public law and especially in the constitutional law field.[166] We should not be surprised if both coexisted,[167] perhaps sometimes being evidenced side by side in the same opinion. In fact, while instrumentalism has enjoyed periods

246

---

164. As noted by, for example, Scheiber, *supra* note 9, at 462; Bloomfield, *supra* note 9, at 1106.

165. *See* Presser, *supra* note 4, at 721 n.69; Bloomfield, *supra* note 9, at 1106, 1107. *See generally* Scheiber, *supra* note 71, esp. pp. 8, 10, 12, 13-17.

Compare the supporting view of periods of formalism and instrumentalism in Anglo-American jurisprudence in Siegel, *The Aristotelian Basis of English Law 1450-1800,* 56 N.Y.U. L. REV. 18 (1981); S. Siegel, Perpetuities: A Study of the Substantive Impact of Jurisprudential Thought 25-26 (to be published in 1982 in the *Miami Law Review*).

166. M. HORWITZ, *supra* note 1, at 253-56. That the same judges were involved was noted by Bloomfield, *supra* note 9, at 1104.

167. *See* Scheiber, *supra* note 71, at 5 (footnotes omitted):

[Although] American judges frequently rejected or modified common-law doctrines and precedent, . . . [they also] bent far . . . to acknowledge the basic validity of . . . "ancient English and American authorities". . . . American judges felt constrained to cast emergent riparian law in the traditional framework. . . . In the closely related field of eminent domain law, . . . judges continued to honor formalistic precedents that had relied upon higher-law notions of inalienable property rights.

of prominence, formalism was (and is) probably the "dominant" mode, if such judgments be useful, because it provides the better mystification within which economic interests can maneuver. An organic culture can contain contradictory notions existing side by side, both of which serve the dominant economic interests but in very different ways.

Further, the "formalistic"-"instrumental" dichotomy is too sharp, seeming to separate phenomena which actually perform some similar functions. "Formalism" is instrumental, if by that term we mean "activist," because it too allows judges leeway to manipulate rules to achieve desired results. Scheiber points out that "even when they posited formalist doctrines of higher law and inalienable rights, post-1865 due process decisions favored" business and economic growth.[168] Moreover, "instrumentalism" is formalistic, if by that term we mean "false," since the biased nature of judicial manipulation is still hidden. No instrumentalist judge openly stated that his action was taken to benefit a small segment of the population. Instrumental opinions are infused with something like the idea of consensus: economic growth is for the good of all, and all really desire it. The judicial display of naked bias toward any small, elitist interest group is incompatible with the security and legitimacy of the capitalist system of government. No instrumentalist decision overstepped these bounds.[169] An organic conception of society avoids the particularism inherent in liberal culture.

The way in which neutralist formalism and "consensus" instrumentalism disguise the partisan purposes and uses of law is an example of the ideological function of law. In addition to its two more obvious tasks—the repressive function, exemplified by the criminal law and similar methods of "legitimately" exerting force, and the facilitative function (overemphasized by Horwitz) of rendering matters easier for the elites—"law must discipline the ruling class and guide and educate the masses."[170] Discipline becomes necessary because the ruling class is fractured and divided against itself, and its overall interests do not always coincide with the

---

168. *Id.* at 12; *accord*, Gilmore, *supra* note 9, at 797.
169. *Cf.* Bloomfield, *supra* note 9, at 1105.
170. E. GENOVESE, *supra* note 32, at 27.

desires of this or that segment. (Law is not the only institutional form used for such a purpose.) Perhaps the most important function of law is, however, educational and cooptative, to achieve for the dominant elites what has become known as "hegemony." The juridical system is one of the instruments "by which . . . the ruling class imposes its viewpoint upon . . . the wider society."[171]

The ideology of the ruling class is not simply a falsification of the facts; it is a *distortion* which focuses too narrowly and partially, from an angle favorable to the elites. The supposedly neutral or "consensus" nature of law is such a distortion, since law does not represent a consensus of the interests of all in society; rather, it represents the interests of some disguised as the interests of all.[172] The central relationship in capitalism, that of worker to capitalist, also is distorted in such a fashion. The worker appears to sell her labor-power freely to the capitalist, when in fact most workers have no alternative other than to starve.[173] "Freedom of contract" is thus a way in which law is ideology.

248

A major criticism of *Transformation,* and of Marxist scholarship in general, has noted a focus on the facilitative function of law, to the exclusion of consideration of its ideological function. Horwitz has provided evidence for this criticism by arguing forcefully that the effect of instrumental decisions was redistributive. Charles McClain, for example, notes that Horwitz has failed to show the redistributive effects.[174] Stewart Macauley, in the same vein, has for years been documenting the argument that the fundamental rules of contract law are essentially irrelevant to the conduct of capitalist business.[175] Robert Gordon helps to redirect the focus:

> Morton Horwitz' much-criticized thesis that 19th century judges fiddled the liability rules in part to help transportation and industrial enterprises externalize their costs . . . seems to me perfectly correct if taken as a proposition about judicial ideology: it's what the judges repeatedly said they wanted to do. Whether

171. *Id. See also* M. TUSHNET, *supra* note 143.
172. *See* K. MARX & F. ENGELS, THE GERMAN IDEOLOGY 64-68 (Int'l Pub. ed. 1970) (written in 1845-46).
173. *See generally* Mensch, *supra* note 52, at 767 n.43.
174. McClain, *supra* note 9, at 394-95.
175. Macauley, *Non-Contractual Relations in Business: A Preliminary Study,* 28 AM. SOC. REV. 55 (1963).

the rules had any such effect is a totally different question, not resolvable by doctrinal history and possibly not resolvable at all.[176]

Although it is likely that contract and liability law were in fact more facilitative than Macauley and Gordon give them credit for, an organic perspective on law in capitalist society would not fail to take into account law's ideological function. Mark Tushnet has analyzed the ways in which law serves such a function: first, he says,

> [L]egal doctrines appear as evidence of the dominant consciousness, which by justifying the institutions of a society to its members serves to support those institutions. . . . A coherent body of doctrine may [also] demonstrate [to lawyers] how rules of law that in fact perpetuate domination are nonetheless consistent with [important ethical] traditions. . . . [Finally,] legal doctrine may serve to reconcile people in the wider society to the conditions of their existence. . . . [T]he details of doctrine . . . derive from fundamental structures of legal thought which penetrate society and help justify its arrangements.[177]

249

In other words, the apparent economic relations in society are reinforced by laws that appear to be based upon them; as social institutions with the appearance of fairness and common consent, and as the only apparent legitimate social ordering devices, the laws are persuasive and useful. Private law was supremely ideological in establishing social tone, social boundaries, and a pattern for belief in the way things were supposed to be.

Horwitz has overlooked the ideological significance of constitutional law by his refusal to include it within his purview. The ideology of constitutionalism was crucial to "acceptance" of the new private-law doctrines by many whose real interests in fact conflicted with those of the entrepreneurs, and was thus essential to the creation of the appearance of a social consensus. A major, perhaps the major, means of reconciliation with and indoctrination of the lower orders by the leaders of society after their triumphs in

---

176. Gordon, Book Review, 94 HARV. L. REV. 903, 907 n.17 (1981).

177. Tushnet, *supra* note 8, at 98-100; *cf.* Balbus, *Commodity Form and Legal Form: An Essay on the "Relative Autonomy" of the Law,* 11 L. & SOC'Y REV. 571 (1977); B. OLLMAN, ALIENATION, *supra* note 16, at 196-98; 1 K. MARX, CAPITAL, *supra* note 23, at 71-83; 3 *id.* at 831.

the Revolution and in the Constitutional Convention was the diffusion throughout American culture of the liberal-democratic ideology of fundamental rights and principles. The notion of government under a rule of law always has been a powerful civilizing factor,[178] and now it was coupled with the appearance, and with more than a little of the reality, of civil freedom guaranteed by open, debated, fundamental public documents which apparently severely limited governmental power and gave much of the populace the apparent power to have some effect upon that government.

Whether or not these were real advances, and I am inclined to conclude that despite the many shortcomings and failures of bourgeois democracy exhibited from the outset[179] the changes had much that was progressive about them,[180] the ideological nature of law made them appear to be very real. Many people came to believe that they had won a large measure of individual and collective freedom by independence from Great Britain and by the establishment of democratic government under law, and American governments and much of the elite went to enormous lengths to reinforce those beliefs.[181]

As a result, the new government became "legitimate," and the culture of entrepreneurial capitalism became the ethos of American democracy, excluding and crushing all competing visions of democratic life. Genovese accurately concludes that "with the legal system rooted in an ostensibly democratic polity, [a challenge to established authority] had the poorest possible prospects."[182]

---

178. *See* E. THOMPSON, *supra* note 138, at 258-69 (1975); Holt, *supra* note 108.

179. *See, e.g.,* L. LEVY, JEFFERSON AND CIVIL LIBERTIES: THE DARKER SIDE (1963); R. ELLIS, THE JEFFERSONIAN CRISIS: COURTS AND POLITICS IN THE YOUNG REPUBLIC (1971).

180. *Accord,* Tushnet, *supra* note 136, at 1350.

181. E. GENOVESE, *supra* note 32, at 608; Genovese, *supra* note 8, at 735.

182. Genovese, *supra* note 8, at 735-36. Perhaps Genovese expects both a too well articulated class consciousness and a too modern tone and substance for contemporaneously-held concepts of the solutions to economic difficulties when he also concludes that "even [nineteenth-century] workers and farmers (at least the increasing portion oriented toward the market) accepted a developmental perspective while having as yet no model of their own." *Id.* at 736. Marx predicted that most preproletarian classes, and especially peasants and the petty bourgeoisie, would be conservative in their protest goals, and that a full class consciousness on the part of the oppressed could only occur under the conditions of fully developed capitalism:

The lower middle class, the small manufacturer, the shopkeeper, the artisan,

Many protests by dissident elements within American society were made, but they were weak, diffuse, unsuccessful, and ignored. The hegemony of constitutional ideology helped to diffuse and destabilize social protest, making possible widespread acceptance of judicial instrumentalism and lawyerly elitism, and ensuring acceptance of the changes in substantive law which Horwitz details.

C. Determinism

The tendency in liberal historiography toward determinism has already been noted.[183] An unsophisticated linear notion of cause-and-effect relationships expects direct connections at all points between economics or economic interests and events or ideology, rather than the complicated analysis involving multiple interactions between material "structure" and political, psychological, and other "superstructure" elements which Marx actually used.

251

> When dealing with real situations, Marx does not offer the development of technology or any other version of the economic factor as self-generating, but as the result of a cluster of factors coming from every walk of life and from every level of social analysis. Likewise, when concerned with actual events, Marx does not treat political and cultural progress as an automatic response to changes in technology; his explanation is invariably complex, and it is not always economic factors which play the leading role.[184]

Such a sophisticated methodology is to be expected from the organic nature of capitalism and the holistic dialectic which Marx used to understand and describe it, points which were not apparent to many early Marxists, sparking a "structure"-"superstructure" debate which endures.[185]

Throughout *Transformation* Horwitz unfortunately emphasizes

---

the peasant, all these fight against the bourgeoisie, to save from extinction their existence as fractions of the middle class. They are therefore not revolutionary, but conservative. Nay more, they are reactionary, for they try to roll back the wheel of history.

K. MARX & F. ENGELS, THE COMMUNIST MANIFESTO 19 (Int'l Pub. ed. New York 1948) (1st ed. 1848).

183. *See* notes 50-56 & accompanying text *supra.*

184. B. OLLMAN, ALIENATION, *supra* note 16, at 8.

185. *See* note 14 & accompanying text *supra.*

the primacy of economics and economic motivations in the narrow, liberal sense, and both radicals[186] and liberals such as Bloomfield have noted his determinism:

> [Horwitz] never makes clear, for example, why judges favored one entrepreneurial group over another, or what kind of special relationship existed between the bench and the marketplace. At times he posits an effective collaboration between elite lawyers, big businessmen, and sympathetic judges. At other times he credits judges alone with anticipating economic trends, and occasionally he identifies legal change with the workings of an impersonal Zeitgeist.[187]

We still need a description of the mechanics of legal change in nineteenth-century America which will demonstrate that all three, and more, of these mechanisms or linkages were operative, and will explain why each type of linkage was appropriate in certain instances. Struggle existed both within the elites and between classes; history, tradition, custom, precedent—all the ways that results of past struggles have persisted—played important parts; entrepreneurs themselves likely attempted to influence the outcome of some litigation; and we need to know much more about the social backgrounds and interactions of specific lawyers, judges, and other legal actors.[188] These categories represent different kinds of linkage.

The modes of the expression of economic interests are many, varied, and constantly interacting. To understand history requires that the variety of linkage mechanisms be explained, especially so that "economics" comes to be understood, not as a concatenation of impersonal forces that emanate mysteriously from goods, money, greed, and the invisible hand, but as the extensive variety of ways in which humans in social, work-related groups attempt through interaction to satisfy their needs and desires, *plus* the ways in which those interactions (including the reified remains of

---

186. *See* Tushnet, *supra* note 8, at 105-07; Genovese, *supra* note 8, at 729.

187. Bloomfield, *supra* note 9, at 1105. This criticism has been made, although somewhat less elegantly, by many of those who have reviewed *Transformation* from the right. *See, e.g.,* Winship, *supra* note 9, at 755.

188. On this last point see K. HALL, THE POLITICS OF JUSTICE (1979), which is reviewed by Konefsky, *On the Early History of Lower Federal Courts, Judges, and the Rule of Law*, 79 MICH. L. REV. 645 (1981). *See also* Mensch, *supra* note 52, at 757 n.10.

past interactions[189]) act as boundaries or limits to each other.[190]

D. *Class and Class Struggle*

The most important weakness in *Transformation* is Horwitz's narrow and limited formulation of class and class conflict. He has demonstrated a willingness to write history in terms of a struggle between business or commercial interests, on the one hand, and a vaguely defined group of losers, on the other, and he presents some good evidence thereof. Horwitz does not, however, exhibit a rigorous theoretical grasp of the nature of the struggles or even of the participants therein. At times it appears that the groups engaged in conflict were self-defining; at times, the groups seem to be defined by their occupations; at times there is a liberal concept of classes as defined by social position or status; and finally it sometimes appears that membership in the groups depended upon the outcome of phases of the struggles. *Transformation* can be put down or dismissed as hokery on grounds that Horwitz has failed to define the winners and the losers in the battles he depicts, and it has been.[191]

253

Materialists understand "class" to refer to the way in which groups of people, within a given mode of production, have access to the means of production. In an emerging capitalist society there are two primary ways in which persons can be so described: laborers, who must sell their labor-power and have no real access, and capitalists, who buy labor-power to extract surplus value therefrom and have control of the access. There may be subsidiary classes, most notably peasants and the petty bourgeoisie, who have been created by a previous mode of production and who are in the pro-

---

189. *See* K. MARX, EIGHTEENTH BRUMAIRE, *supra* note 159, *passim,* esp. 15-18; E. WRIGHT, *supra* note 17.

190. [W]hen a Marxist analyzes a particular event or . . . specific doctrines, he or she must not pretend that the structural determinants of a dominant ideology operate directly to produce those doctrines [or the event]. Rather, transient political forces, the influences of intermediary groups, and the need . . . to present law as a neutral force, all intervene to produce what has come to be called a specific conjecture inserted into the general structure of capitalist society.

Tushnet, *supra* note 136, at 1348.

191. Presser, *supra* note 4, at 719-24; Reid, *supra* note 3, at 1318-20; Scheiber, *supra* note 9, at 463-64.

cess of being dissolved by the forces of capitalism into the working class. If one focuses more closely, each of the two main classes is fractured into lesser groups. Struggle is the definition of the relationship between the two central classes in capitalism because of their inherent mutual antagonism over access to the means of production. It is not merely a sometime thing involving a few visible battles spread over time, after each of which genuine harmony prevails—although, in large part due to the mystification generated by capitalism and in no small part due to powerlessness of the workers, open and violent conflict breaks out only from time to time. "Class" and "struggle" are thus terms descriptive of economic relationships. Categories of kinship or occupation or social status are not determinative of membership in a class (though each is important).

254

Horwitz variously identifies the winners as entrepreneurs, commercial interests, or businessmen, rather than as capitalists. At points he talks about struggles within this group, for instance between speculators and improvers of land,[192] or between business enterprises and their insurors,[193] but Horwitz has no theoretically clear position that, although the elite has a single interest in maintaining its dominance over the lower classes, antagonism between various groups inside the elite is naturally a part of the war of all against all for a bigger share of the market. His imprecision allows his critics to conclude that occupational fluidity, a characteristic of the nineteenth century, contradicts any assertion of the existence of a single ruling class. The liberal critics also can define the insurors to be underdogs (rather than capitalists), since they had less power than the entrepreneurs they insured, which, since they apparently won their battle, means that the "ruling class" did not always come out ahead.[194]

Whether it is useful to view the ruling class as a whole or as an externally united set of internally warring interests depends upon the purposes of the inquiry and the level of abstraction. Marx in *Capital,* and Marx and Engels in the *Manifesto,* generally took the broadest analytical perspective, discussing social struggle at the

---

192. M. HORWITZ, *supra* note 1, at 61 & n.153.

193. *Id.* at 154, 228-29.

194. *See* Reid, *supra* note 3, at 1318; Presser, *supra* note 4, at 723.

level of capital versus labor; but in *The Eighteenth Brumaire,* Marx focused in much more closely upon class struggle in France during the period 1848-1852 and made clear his understanding that many different factions and interests made up the ruling class.[195] Erik Olin Wright has recently emphasized the necessity of understanding whether one is utilizing the analytical level of "capital in general" or that of "many capitals."[196] Genovese accurately notes that *Transformation* is primarily a description of "a struggle within the bourgeoisie and only secondarily between the bourgeoisie as a whole and other classes."[197] Use of Wright's suggested analytical level of "many capitals" would have sharpened the description while avoiding giving the impression that the volume deals primarily with the conflict between capital and labor. Theoretical rigor also would have prevented Horwitz from seeming to describe history in terms of clashes between discrete interest groups, whose membership is fluid and who shift positions and opponents easily. Class forces are not interest groups, but are intricately and intimately related both in internal struggle and in interclass struggle. The relations and the struggle need to be depicted plainly in order that the nature of the winners can be delineated.

255

More important is Horwitz's failure to tell us who the losers were. The book appears, to many liberal critics, to have been an attempt to accomplish just that, but in fact throughout Horwitz pays little attention to those who presumably paid the price of development and whose interests did not in fact coincide with the emerging liberal "consensus." At one point he notes "strong elements in American society opposed to the expanding values of a market economy" who reflected "a still dominant precommercial consciousness of rural and religious America."[198] At another point he concludes that "the legal system had been reshaped . . . at the expense of farmers, workers, consumers, and other less powerful groups within the society."[199] At still others he notes how those

---

195. K. Marx, Eighteenth Brumaire, *supra* note 159, at 23, 27-28, 36-37, 46-48, 90, 95, 102-03, 107, 122.

196. E. Wright, *supra* note 17, at 122 & n.13. *See also id.* at 48 n.37, 73 n.66, 188 n.13.

197. Genovese, *supra* note 8, at 732.

198. M. Horwitz, *supra* note 1, at 211.

199. *Id.* at 253-54.

with land—the gentry—lost much ground to the entrepreneurs.[200] Horwitz has lumped together groups that ought to remain analytically separate: the old winners (gentry), those outside the immediate mainstream of growth who must still have suffered (farmers, shopkeepers), and those who were most intimately involved in the rapid changes in the organization of production (workers, artisans, immigrants, consumers).

As Genovese and Scheiber note, much more attention should have been paid by Horwitz to the political battles of the period.[201] Who opposed corporations, and why? Who advocated more taxation, and why? What about protests specifically raised by workers, or slaves, or rural elements? What sorts of changes occurred after important economic events such as the Panic of 1837, and why? To what extent were regional conditions important? What sorts of alliances did various lower segments of American society form, with each other and with elite groups, and why?

We need to know who really lost what during the emergence of entrepreneurial capitalism, if only to still the insensitive and upper-class-oriented arguments of liberals who persist in asserting that some groups got a "free ride" (that is, they supposedly received benefits they were contemporaneously unaware of, which presumably cancelled out burdens they *were* aware of[202]), or that the losers were always the immoral, the lazy, and the undeserving,[203] or that, because of occupational fluidity and the trickle-down effect of emerging abundance, nobody really lost.[204] It is likely that such studies collectively will show that real wages and income diminished for many American workers and that degrading working conditions increased; that concomitant ills beset other lower segments of northern and western American society (as Genovese has demonstrated for slaves in the South[205]); that, in short, proletarian-like conditions began to emerge for many, all concomitant with (if not directly caused by) the changes in substantive law detailed in *Transformation*. Horwitz's history unfor-

---

200. *Id.* at 140-41, 146.
201. Genovese, *supra* note 8, at 734-36; Scheiber, *supra* note 9, at 463-64.
202. *See* Presser, *supra* note 4, at 721.
203. *See* Reid, *supra* note 3, at 1317.
204. *See* Presser, *supra* note 4, at 722.
205. E. GENOVESE, *supra* note 32, and other works by Genovese.

tunately does not tell us much about the losers, and by its obscurity in use of loose liberal interest-group characterization it can reinforce a notion that nothing was really lost.

Case law is likely to have little to do directly with workers or their conditions, but Horwitz omits most areas of law which did take the interests of workers into account. A three-page discussion of "the application of the will theory of contract to labor contracts"[206] adverts to a branch of the law that must have been directly important to working class interests, but beyond the notation that certain doctrinal inconsistencies in early labor law "seem . . . to be an important example of class bias,"[207] the investigation is disappointingly legalistic, doctrinal, and free from overtones of economic consequences. The focus of most of the book is from the top down, concerned with the ways in which elite tools were used during elite interactions to serve essentially elite purposes.

A central example concerns the alternative to unbridled economic growth: Horwitz uses the term "redistribution" without elaboration of other social changes that would inevitably be entailed.[208] Deterministic—that is, it assumes that the "mere" rearrangement of social wealth-holding would have solved the most pressing and difficult of social problems—the term "redistribution" connotes a focus on narrowly defined "economic" interests rather than humane ones, seeming to ignore the difficulty of achieving a systemic solution which would eliminate social oppression. The real interests of those who attempted to refuse to go along with the nineteenth-century ethos of capitalism lay in achieving an entirely different egalitarian ethos emphasizing genuine freedom and social cooperation,[209] and did not stop abruptly at demands for a larger

257

---

206. M. HORWITZ, *supra* note 1, at 186; *see id.* at 186-88.

207. *Id.* at 188.

208. *Id.* at 66, 101, 255.

209. [T]he realm of freedom actually begins only where labor which is determined by necessity and mundane considerations ceases; thus in the very nature of things it lies beyond the sphere of actual material production. Just as the savage must wrestle with Nature to satisfy his wants, to maintain and reproduce life, so must civilized man, and he must do so in all social formations and under all possible modes of production. With his development this realm of physical necessity expands as a result of his wants; but, at the same time, the forces of production which satisfy these wants also increase. Freedom in this field can only consist in socialized man, the associated producers, rationally

or more equal share of the pie. What the *upper* classes feared was "redistribution."

By focusing on elites, *Transformation* subliminally reinforces the view we are supposed to have that only the rich, the powerful, and the important are crucial or interesting. It admits of the possibility of class struggle but then shies away from the ways in which legal interactions might have demonstrated the ugly reality of class conflict and class bias. To Horwitz's gentleness, compassion, and outrage—to his break with the liberals—must be added the strength of a materialist analysis of history. Horwitz's story must be taken further, expanded, drawn from the standpoint of the losers; succeeding works in radical legal history must deal with class and class struggle.

V. CONCLUSION

258

Despite its shortcomings, which can be remedied by Marxist historiography, *Transformation* stands as a monumental achievement. Bourgeois historians and bourgeois historiography have been demonstrated to be what they are, biased and partial rather than neutral and timeless. The "consensus" assumptions underpinning all schools of mainstream American legal history have been shown to be partisan, and partisan from the standpoint of the elite. The way has been cleared for legal historians to place the focus where it belongs, on socioeconomic evidence of class conflict. Law now will be viewed as an element of *praxis*, that is, meaning-creating human activity.[210] Also, since law is a fundamental ideological phenomenon,[211] important contributions to the "structure"-"superstructure" debate can be expected, aiding the resolution of central Marxist theoretical problems as we continue to come to grips with

---

> regulating their interchange with Nature, bringing it under their common control, instead of being ruled by it as by the blind forces of Nature; and achieving this with the least expenditure of energy and under conditions most favorable to, and worthy of, their human nature. But it nevertheless still remains a realm of necessity. Beyond it begins that development of human energy which is an end in itself, the true realm of freedom, which, however, can blossom forth only with this realm of necessity as its basis.

3 K. MARX, CAPITAL, *supra* note 23, at 820.

210. *See* note 12 & accompanying text *supra*.

211. *See* note 14 *supra*.

our rejection of the bourgeois radical disjunction between subject and object, between consciousness and actuality, and as we continue to develop a socialist culture.

LEGAL ELEMENTS IN
UNITED STATES HISTORY

AN IDEAL of constitutionalism has been central in the traditions by which we have related law and life in the United States. Recognizing that a humanly satisfying life must be lived in society, this ideal yet asserts that service to individual life is the ultimate measure of the moral legitimacy of all organized, public or private power.[1] The ideal often failed of realization. But awareness of the failures and controversy over them attested to the existence of the ideal as a living factor in this legal order.

Constitutionalism found expression in demands that all organized power be responsible by measures of utility and of justice. Power might be legitimated by being functional to a socially acceptable end; for example, public policy accepted increasingly liberal law for incorporating business firms, as serviceable to productivity.[2] Power must be legitimated by procedures for making powerholders accountable to others than themselves, and by criteria other than those they alone defined, both for the ends they chose and the means they adopted to pursue those ends; for example, legislative control of the public purse provided surveillance of the executive branch of government, and both legislative and executive authority might be put under constitutional challenge in

1. A classic expression of the constitutional ideal is in the declaration of the Fifth and Fourteenth Amendments of the United States Constitution, that "no person shall be deprived of life, liberty, or property, without due process of law," at the hands of government. *Cf.* Tancy, C.J., in Proprietors of the Charles River Bridge v. Proprietors of the Warren Bridge, 11 Pet. 420, 547–548 (U.S. 1837); Shaw, C.J., in Commonwealth v. Alger, 7 Cush. 53, 84–85 (Mass. 1851); Howard Jay Graham, *Everyman's Constitution* (Madison, 1968), chaps. iv, v, and vii.

2. Wilber G. Katz, "The Philosophy of Midcentury Corporation Statutes," *Law and Contemporary Problems*, 23 (1958), 177.

the courts.[3] The law of contract and tort, as well as the law of public utilities and an increasing range of laws regulating conduct in the market, expressed the judgment that private, as well as public power must be responsible.[4] Both in the public and private spheres, the two ideas of responsibility—utility and justice—sometimes had separate, sometimes mingled expression, but both continued to figure in the growth of public policy.[5]

The constitutional ideal required satisfaction both of rational and of emotional demands. That organized power should be legitimated by utility to acceptable ends was a demand primarily that policy-makers operate according to reasonable ideas of cause and effect, and on reasonable calculations of gain and cost.[6] But rationality could serve purposes hostile to a humane concept of individual life—could serve unacceptable, though rationally arranged, legal segregation of races, for example. Translation of the ideal of responsible power into the just use of power rested partly on reason, but in the end on emotion.[7] Thus, the history of this constitutional legal order must take account of both rational and emotional components of the culture in which law operated. In such classic policy battles as those over the Second Bank of the United States in the 1830's, or over roles of law in adjusting management-labor relations in the 1930's, feeling played a larger role than rational calculation.[8]

Legal history must, also, take account of the fact that the tap roots of the constitutional ideal ran outside as well as within the law. Our ideas of the public interest stemmed from experience of

261

3. Richard F. Fenno, Jr., *The Power of the Purse* (Boston, 1966), chaps. vi, vii, and xi; Robert G. McCloskey, *The American Supreme Court* (Chicago, 1960), chap. vii.

4. Oliver Wendell Holmes, Jr., *The Common Law* (Boston, 1881), chaps. iii, iv, and vii; Ernst Freund, *Standards of American Legislation* (Chicago, 1917), chaps. i and iii; Hughes, C. J., in Appalachian Coals, Inc. v. United States, 288 U.S. 344, 359 (1933).

5. Charles Bunn, "Bank Collection under the Uniform Commercial Code," *Wisconsin Law Review* (1964), 278; Arthur H. Dean, "Twenty-five Years of Federal Securities Regulation by the Securities and Exchange Commission," *Columbia Law Review*, 59 (1959), 697, 698–706.

6. O'Gorman & Young, Inc. v. Hartford Fire Insurance Co., 282 U.S. 251 (1931).

7. Griswold v. Connecticut, 381 U.S. 479 (1965).

8. Foster Rhea Dulles, *Labor in America* (New York, 1949), pp. 274, 276; Marvin Meyers, *The Jacksonian Persuasion* (Stanford, 1957), pp. 6–7, 18–19.

the commonwealth in the Greek city states. We drew our conviction that power must be legitimated by its service to individual life partly from the concept of Roman citizenship, partly from the medieval church's care of souls. The English inheritance from the spirit of the commercial and industrial revolutions as well as from the Parliamentary revolution made particularly important contributions to the constitutional ideal—including emphasis on the desirability of broadly dispersed power, on the primacy of a popularly elected legislature, and on the availability of the courts to redress individual grievances against either official or private oppression. These were ideas given ready hospitality in the circumstances of community growth in North America, particularly from about 1750 on. The break with England, the consequent need to attend to formal organization of authority in the original states and then in the growing number of new states, and the novel problems of devising a federal structure, launched the people into uncommon concern with issues of the legitimacy of official power, so that the constitutional ideal was woven broadly into patterns of life in the United States.[9]

262

Within the constitutional ideal we used law for certain functions distinctively identified with legal process, and which reached so pervasively into community life as to forbid a narrow definition of legal history.

1. Law claimed the legitimate monopoly of force, and, as a corollary, the right to appraise the legitimacy of all private forms of power. Whenever organized private power made itself felt, law was likely to become involved in some degree, whether to promote the utility of organized effort, or to set standards of fairness in its use.

2. Public policy emphasized regular and rational procedures in using law to determine social ends and means and to make particular application of general policy. Inherent in this stress on rational procedure was an insistence, also, on some level of rationality in the substance of public policy. Law pursued values of rationality

9. *Cf.* James Willard Hurst, *Law and Social Process in United States History* (Ann Arbor, 1960), pp. 68, 107, 112–114, 119, 121.

most closely as to its own operations. Our tradition valued dispersion of decision-making power, and we therefore tended to limit the law's intervention in private organization of affairs. Nonetheless, law sought to apply measures of rationality to private as well as to public power, as when in tort it measured liability by the test of the conduct to be expected of reasonable and prudent men.

3. We used law more and more to allocate scarce economic resources. Indeed, law came to be the principal instrument of resource allocation, next to the market and the family. Law allocated resources by taxing, and by spending tax-derived money. It allocated resources indirectly through public borrowing, and also by the standards by which it regulated behavior (as when, by setting sanitary standards for marketing food, it required a certain level of capital investment by food dealers). This resource-allocation role involved law in a wide range of individual and group concerns outside law—in the conditions of occupations, health, education, and science and technology.[10]

263

We failed often in realizing the constitutional ideal. Conflicts of interest produced waste, or injustice, which law did not prevent. Of as great, if not greater impact was the influence of uncalculated drift and inertia in human affairs. The constitutional ideal implies relying on law—as on other institutions of social order—to combat not only wasteful or unjust products of conflicts of interests, but also to help men enlarge the meaningful content of life against the threat of formless experience. A full-dimensional legal history needs take realistic account of the law's relation both to conflict and to drift in men's affairs.[11]

To appraise the law in the context of the constitutional ideal and of our failures to realize that ideal is to make us more sharply aware of unfortunate limitations in the existing literature on legal history.

1. Work in legal history has tended to focus too much on courts, and with unfortunate limitations even within that range. The United States Supreme Court has captured too much attention, at the expense of the state courts (which, for example, have had at

10. *Ibid.*, pp. 5–17.
11. *Ibid.*, chap. ii.

least as important roles in developing public policy on corporations, franchises, taxation, and social capital investment). Students have identified the law too much with the work of appellate courts, state and federal, at the expense of properly weighting the impress of trial courts on public policy. Emphasis on judge-made law does not necessarily mean, but in practice has meant, want of due attention to the legislative process, to rule-making and precedent-building by executive and administrative offices, and to the great body of operating public policy created by the ways in which lawyers and their clients, and laymen working without benefit of counsel shape affairs with more or less use, avoidance, or evasion of the law emanating from official agencies. Thus, the legal history of contract should not become fascinated with the evolution of judges' formulae on consideration and ignore the growth of statutory and administrative prescriptions for the practical content of agreements in one specialized field of transactions after another, as in insurance, labor relations, public utility service, corporate securities, negotiable instruments, and urban residential leases. Nor can a realistic history of contract look simply at the breakdown of relationships which produces lawsuits, and ignore the creative contributions made by inventions and adjustments of businessmen and their lawyers in negotiating, drafting, and administering the great bodies of transactions which do not break down.[12]

2. Research in legal history has tended to exaggerate attention to judge-made constitutional law, as the prime type of legal contribution to social structure. Great parts of constitutional law itself consist in lines of authority marked out mainly by legislative and executive debate, practice, and decision. Most of the purse power has been so defined, with most of the law of legislative and executive privilege, and most demarcations of roles of central and local government within the states. Moreover, measured by continuity and impact upon distribution of functions basic to social life, much law has been constitutive which does not fit the conventional historical

---

12. Lawrence M. Friedman, *Contract Law in America: A Social and Economic Case Study* (Madison, 1965), chap. iv; Stewart Macaulay, *Law and the Balance of Power* (New York, 1966), pp. 202–207.

preoccupation with formal constitutional law. Given the constitutive roles in this society of the market, the business corporation, public utilities, the church, trade associations, trade unions, public and private educational organizations, and welfare and research foundations, aspects of law related to the legitimation and distribution of practical power within and among such institutions must be taken to be parts of the functional history of the law. To be specific: with the emergence of the large-scale business corporation, the course of public policy on the relations of investors and corporate management should be reckoned a relevant part of the history of law bearing on the basic structure of power. Again: given the growth in social impact of developments in scientific and technical knowledge, the effects of the law on evolving roles of government-determined and government-supported research compared with research directed or aided by private foundations belong to a realistically broad concept of the "constitutional" roles of law.[13]

265

3. Legal history studied within a legal tradition which puts as much stress as ours does on separation of powers among formal legal agencies and on the procedures of such agencies tends to give inadequate attention to the substantive content of public policy. In giving form and content to wants and needs and means of pursuing them, the law entered into a wide range of men's concerns extending beyond the law's own operations. Thus legal processes affected conditions of mutual trust (in standardizing agreements, or in attacking fraud or duress), security of expectations (in protecting against breach of contract or loss from personal injury), biological integrity (in public health and sanitation laws, or in laws regarding the natural environment), and the range of options open to will (through the law affecting education, research, communication, and association). The beginning of wisdom is to recognize that the law typically operated only in marginal areas or with mar-

13. Adolph A. Berle, Jr., *The 20th Century Capitalist Revolution* (New York, 1954), chaps. i, iii; Harold M. Kelle, "Note on Congressional Investigations," *American Bar Association Journal*, 40 (1954), 154; Marion R. Fremont-Smith, *Foundations and Government: State and Federal Law and Supervision* (New York, 1965), *passim*; Warren Weaver, *U.S. Philanthropic Foundations* (New York, 1967), chaps. ix, xiv.

ginal effects upon such broad human concerns. Yet even a quick inventory of statute books teaches that these marginal operations grew to affect large sectors of life.[14]

4. So far as it ventured outside the study of separation-of-powers and agency-procedure issues, legal history tended to identify the history of public policy too much with regulation (setting and enforcing legal standards or rules of behavior, in the relations of individuals and groups with the government, or with each other). This emphasis ignored or underplayed the impress which law made by allocating scarce economic resources. Law allocated resources directly by taxing and spending and transferring public property (selling public lands, granting radio or TV franchises to use public air waves). It allocated resources indirectly through tax exemptions (as to churches), or tax deductions (as to promote private investment by depreciation allowances), or indeed by regulatory laws which worked to shift economic burdens (as when workmen's compensation acts transfer some of the cost of industrial accidents from the injured workers to the consumers of the product). Emphasis on regulation likewise tended to ignore or underplay the law's effects in legitimating forms of conduct to implement private choices—as in offering the privilege of incorporation under terms which left large discretion to private draftsmen in fixing the corporate structure, or providing standardized but optional terms for certain kinds of contracts or property titles. To point up such uses of the law is to note that legal history must be broad enough to include the considerable effects law had by indirect as well as direct compulsion (as when we seek results by taxing and spending instead of invoking the policeman), by structuring general situations as well as acting on specific relationships (as when we build and operate public recreational facilities as well as providing juvenile courts to contain the exploring energies of youth), and by channeling conduct for ends of utility or justice by providing convenient legal services or instruments as well as by providing penalties (as when we provided a reliable coinage by creating a public mint, without formally outlawing privately made metal tokens,

14. Julius Stone, *Social Dimensions of Law and Justice* (Stanford, 1966), chaps. v, vi.

while we used the criminal law to protect public coins against counterfeiters). The prevailing attitudes which insisted that the law help in making social organization useful and just—that is, constitutional—embodied demands inherently too far-reaching to be met simply by legal Thou Shalts or Thou Shalt Nots. Legal history should match the range of uses of the law.[15]

5. Related to exaggeration of direct legal regulation as compared with uses of the law for indirect compulsion or situation structuring was a tendency to exaggerate areas of combat in examining substantive public policy. Emphasis on overt clashes of interests comes naturally in studying an institution which prominently creates forums for resolving ordered conflict, whether in legislative halls, administrative hearing rooms, or courthouses. But legal history should recognize that law was involved also in the continuities of such social institutions as the market, that the content of public policy was made in large part by flows of uncontested legal administration (for example, in the day-in, day-out regular operation of tax laws or laws providing social security payments), and that a great part (indeed probably the greater part) of men's social experience in which the law was involved entailed neither combat nor consent, but merely the mindless cumulation of unperceived, unplanned, unchosen events. Precisely because the constitutional ideal made heavy demands for directed use of law, a realistic legal history must take due account of the full pervasiveness of law as it operated consciously in other-than-combat situations, and its involvement in the undirected drift which challenged constitutionalism in ways more potent and subtle than those presented by conflict of interests.[16]

267

There are substantial scholarly contributions to legal history which do not so style themselves. We learn about the roles of law from historians of politics and politicians who, like Dumas Malone

15. James M. Buchanan, *Public Finance in Democratic Process* (Chapel Hill, 1967), chaps. iii, iv; Cornelius P. Cotter, *Government and Private Enterprise* (New York, 1960), chaps. i, ii, xv; K. William Kapp, *The Social Costs of Private Enterprise* (Cambridge, 1950), chap. xvi; Walz v. Tax Commission of the City of New York, 90 S. Ct. 1409 (1970).

16. Robert A. Dahl and Charles E. Lindblom, *Politics, Economics and Welfare* (New York, 1953), chaps. iii, iv; note 10, above.

in his biography of Jefferson, describe not only the internal life of parties but also the interplay of partisan maneuvers with formal public policy and the structure and traditions of legal agencies. Historical studies in public administration, such as Leonard White's volumes on the federal executive branch or those of George Galloway on Congress, tell parts of legal history. So do monographs on economic history which emphasize the uses of law in structuring economic activity (for example, the Handlins' examination of law and economic growth in Massachusetts, the similar Hartz inquiry into Pennsylvania policy before the Civil War, and Scheiber's history of Ohio's venture in building and operating a canal system in the early-nineteenth century).[17] Even within this broader bibliography, however, familiar limitations appear. Political historians and political scientists have given more attention to processes than to the content of public policy. Disproportionate attention is given to contested situations, at the expense of due attention either to institutional continuities or to institutional drift. With honorable exceptions, too much emphasis has been placed on federal lawmaking without a balancing study of the history of state and local government, especially in the nineteenth century. The disappointing character of the literature lies not so much in what has been published—for that includes much helpful work—as in what has not been. Thus we lack sufficient studies of the law's roles concerning race and social class in United States society, the functional structure and changing resource-allocations roles of markets, the use of the natural environment, and the course of scientific and technical knowledge. These deficiencies are specially marked for the nineteenth century, in decades which set the terms of important twentieth-century problems.[18]

268

17. George B. Galloway, *History of the House of Representatives* (New York, 1961); Oscar and Mary Flug Handlin, *Commonwealth: A Study of the Role of Government in the American Economy: Massachusetts, 1774–1861* (Cambridge, 1969); Louis Hartz, *Economic Policy and Democratic Thought: Pennsylvania, 1776–1860* (Cambridge, 1948); Dumas Malone, *Jefferson: The President* (Boston, 1970); Harry N. Scheiber, *Ohio Canal Era* (Athens, Ohio, 1969); Leonard D. White, *The Federalists: A Study in Administrative History* (New York, 1948).

18. *Cf.* Willard Hurst, "Perspectives upon Research into Legal Order," *Wisconsin Law Review* (1961), 356.

Apart from such limitations of subject matter, researchers without some specialized training often fail to realize the possibilities in
legal source materials. They tend to take judges' words too much
at face value—readily accept the invocation of "police power" as
an explanation rather than merely a statement of a result. They
tend to watch only the star acts under the spotlights of political
controversy, and to neglect substantial issues implicit in what seem
colorless, routine affairs. For example, scholars have been slow to
see that the technical details of property rights have often served
to affect the incidence of economic benefits and costs among economic interests, and not merely to regularize titles or relations between parties to particular transactions.[19] Students not specially
trained to handle legal sources have largely neglected the evidence
afforded by such sources of what people have believed, or how
they have perceived or experienced life. Thus, for historians of
ideas there is evidence of applied theories of human nature in the
law of negligence and contributory negligence, as in the law of
master and servant, or the rules of evidence, or in the law demar-
cating private and public morality.[20] Finally, the student who has
not become specially adept in squeezing out of legal sources all the
juice he can will probably fall short of realizing their possibilities
for helping to identify and to weigh growth, change, stability, and
inertia in wants, needs, functions, gains, and costs in men's social
experience. Because of the sobering costs of using legal processes,
and because compared with other modes of social adjustment law
yields an uncommon amount of formally defined choices and decisions, legal sources present to a knowledgeable reader a specially
reliable means to identify continuities and discontinuities or changes
of direction in social relations. Trends in the statute books, for
example, can help to identify, to place in time, and to measure the
substantial shift from an almost wholly producer orientation of
public policy to more and more of a consumer orientation in the

269

19. Edwin W. Patterson, *Jurisprudence: Men and Ideas of the Law* (Brooklyn, 1953),
pp. 95, 103, 520–522, 524.
20. Edmond N. Cahn, *The Sense of Injustice* (New York, 1949), pp. 56–92, 124–132,
148–150; Julius Cohen, Reginald A. H. Robson and Alan Bates, *Parental Authority: The
Community and the Law* (New Brunswick, 1958), *passim*.

hundred years since 1870. To use the statute books so, however, means using them in more detail, with more attention to their technical content over substantial periods of time, than general historians have been accustomed to do.[21]

These last comments should not be read to imply that specialist legal historians have developed the range of topics or possible uses of legal sources which non-specialists have fallen short of exploiting. Work in legal history in all quarters adds up to a very limited accomplishment. Nor should criticism of non-specialists' handling of legal sources be taken to imply that fruitful work with such materials is the sole prerogative of lawyers. The scholar does not need a law degree to extract all he can from legal sources. He does need some substantial introduction to legal language and to the operation of legal processes. He also needs enough work in mastering some particular areas of legal doctrine so that he learns how to read statutes, court opinions, and administrative rules and orders with an eye to defining precisely what is being done or decided, to detecting fictions or question-begging, or loose or slippery concepts, to identifying overt or unacknowledged judicial notice of facts underlying rules of law, and to marking the presence of pattern, trend, or jumble, as the case may be, in the course of legal action.[22] A capable student should be able to acquire a good launching facility in these commonsense skills with the equivalent of a year or at most three semesters of law study. The field needs capable work from more lawyer scholars. But its proper development will lag if it is left to depend on these alone.

270

21. Frank E. Horack, Jr., "The Common Law of Legislation," *Iowa Law Review*, 23 (1937), 41.

22. Edward H. Levi, *An Introduction to Legal Reasoning* (Chicago, 1949); Karl N. Llewellyn, *The Common Law Tradition: Deciding Appeals* (Boston, 1960).

1. Handling the Materials of Legal History

THE constitutional ideal—the responsibility of organized power to be useful and to be just—together with its opposing
aspects (the conflicts of interest which work to defeat it, as well as
the forces of inertia which mock its claims to achieve meaning)
offer a framework within which to spell out more particular content for legal history. However, another kind of consideration is in
order before we move to further definition of subject matter. Our
tradition makes larger-than-life demands on the law: not only that
law should seek utility and justice, but also that it should control
force within and without the law, promote rational procedures to
adjust social relations, and share with the market the job of resource
allocation. These demands are impossible of full satisfaction. Moreover, they involve law in a complicated interplay with other social
institutions. These are reasons why we need realistically to assess
what we can expect to learn about legal order as part of general
social order. Because of the pervasive demands our tradition made
on law, the potential content of legal history is dismayingly broad
in scope and dense in detail. Thus it is wise to inquire into the
strengths and limitations of the evidence available for studying legal history before we commit ourselves to any particular definitions
of its subject matter.

271

ACTION OUTSIDE OF PRESCRIBED LEGAL FORMS

We should acknowledge the most difficult problems first. Recognizing them, we can more realistically define the matters with
which we can hope to do better. The greatest difficulties for legal
history lie in relating the formal operations of law—passing statutes, deciding cases, making administrative orders or rules—to the
life that flowed outside the legal forms. The basic organizing ideas
of this legal order will not let us escape this effort. When prevailing
values insist that the law, along with other institutions, be useful
and just, we must ask about law's relations to other-than-legal institutions, and about relations of formal operations of legal pro-

cesses to the total behavior of those who worked or used those processes. Criteria of utility and justice require that legal history must, first, include hyphenate legal history: legal-economic history, legal-religious history, legal-class-and-caste history. For so far as criteria of utility and justice figure in our social experience, legal history cannot look at law as a self-contained institution; by these measures, the life of law consists in its relations to the rest of life. Second, these criteria demand full-dimensioned knowledge of legal operations themselves; utility and justice are ideals for performance and not of mere ritual; so far as the outcomes of legal processes include ends and means or behavior not adequately represented in the law's formal operations, legal history should take account of such informal elements.

272

Defining legal history in hyphenates (legal-economic history, for example), multiplies the historian's normal difficulties of juggling variables. Under such a definition he must reckon with cause and effect in more than one field of experience. A history of antitrust law proper might stick to the Sherman and Clayton Acts and rulings of the courts and the Federal Trade Commission. But a history of the law's relations to market structure and procedures and of the results for resource allocation must invoke some economic theory and economic history, as well as materials from political science and sociology.[23]

Focusing on law in relation to some other institutional area highlights a second problem—whether resort to law has been innovative or declarative, relative to the other-than-legal field of values or actions. The development of federal public land law through various pre-emption acts to the Homestead Act showed a strong policy favoring widely dispersed private ownership, improvement, and marketing of land. In the social context this trend primarily declared values developed outside the law, concerning the relative roles of public and private control in the economy and the place of

23. Donald Dewey, "Competitive Policy and National Goals: The Doubtful Relevance of Antitrust," in Almarin Phillips, ed., *Perspectives on Antitrust Policy* (Princeton, 1965), p. 62; Willard F. Mueller, *The Celler-Kefauver Act: Sixteen Years of Enforcement: A Staff Report to the Antitrust Subcommittee of the Committee on the Judiciary of the House of Representatives* (90 Cong., 1 Sess., House Committee Print, Washington, 1967).

fee simple ownership in political and class structure. On the other hand, imposing the federal land survey on patterns of land disposition was an influential innovation by the law in the whole land picture, as were, later, the special provisions by law for grazing, mineral, timber and waterpower rights in the semi-arid and mountain parts of the country. It is hard to measure the innovative impact of law compared with other institutions. Even subtler problems arise in appraising the impact of law which mainly declares or ratifies values derived outside of legal processes. The law punishing classic crimes against person or property—murder, rape, armed robbery, theft—expressed common morality rather than new moral judgments. Yet the record cautions against writing off such declarative law as of no distinctive effect. The effects may be plus or minus. Declarative law may add to social inertia which works against adjusting prevailing morality to new experience or hampers desirable diversity of life styles; for example, in various respects the law on sex badly lagged behind changes in attitudes and values in the middle-twentieth century with results not good either for respect for law or for individual happiness. Law may declare general objectives whose vitality stands already established from forces outside law, and yet the law may be innovative in particulars which materially affect conduct. At its core the law of public utilities simply reflected community perception that some businesses put their customers under such fundamental dependence that their conduct might not be left to ordinary private bargaining; yet the law's particular regulations of rates and services injected into the economy elements which the law largely determined (for example, legally enforced standards and rules on allowances for depreciation, affecting the nature and timing of capital investment).[24]

273

A third problem posed by hyphenate legal history, corollary to the first two, is the frequent need to follow events in and outside the law within different spans of time. Consider, for example, the

24. Marion Clawson, *Uncle Sam's Acres* (New York, 1951), pp. 43–47, 58, 61, 62, 64; Morris R. Cohen, "Moral Aspects of the Criminal Law," *Yale Law Journal*, 49 (1940), 987, 988–990, 1005–1007, 1012–1016; Felix Frankfurter, *The Public and Its Government* (New Haven, 1930); Roy Marvin Robbins, *Our Landed Heritage: The Public Domain, 1776–1936* (Princeton, 1942).

different time periods which are significant, respectively, for the development of the legislative branch of government, and of public policy toward banking. Legislative organization and practice took certain influential directions in a formative period from about 1776 to 1820, in which two chambers became the normal structure, and the legislature turned detailed work over to select or *ad hoc* committees, and fell into a pattern of narrowly pragmatic approach to problems. The years from about 1830 to 1900 saw fresh developments, particularly the shift to standing committees and major resort to the legislature's powers to create franchises as means for promoting and to some extent regulating private activity. From 1900 into the 1920's there were major but usually *ad hoc* innovations in the legislative determination of standards and rules of behavior (the regulatory or police power), and in legislation broadening the reach of law by delegation to administrative bodies. An overlapping span from about 1887 to 1940 launched a massive increase in the relative policy roles of Congress as compared with state legislative authority, as well as a significant development of the purse power in both states and nation. The years after 1940 witnessed an increase in policy leadership by the executive, especially on the national scene, uncertain development in the potentially great legislative powers of investigation, and over-all a relative decline in statutory contributions to the whole content of public policy, except for still greater impact through taxing and spending. Over the years from 1781 (with the incorporation of the Bank of North America) to 1970 the law concerning banks provided important themes of policy on the money supply, the supply of working and investment capital, the growth of markets, the response to the business cycle, and the distribution of wealth and political and social power in the United States. The structural and procedural capacities and limitations of the legislative process materially affected the content of policy on banking over this whole span. But the growth of banking business and of banking law moved in different time spans from the history of the legislative branch. These differences in period affected outcomes in both fields. Significant in the banking picture were a short period of

274

exploration of special bank charters (1781 to about 1820); two experiments with central banking of national scope (1791–1811,
1816–1836); the multiplication of state bank charters carrying note-
issuing franchises under free-banking (general incorporation) acts
beginning in the 1830's; creation of a rather rigid system of national free banking laws and the grant of a monopoly of banknote
currency to those banks, 1863–1865; fragmented and often inefficient regulation of banking coupled with inadequate reliance on
private organization to deal with cyclical problems from about
1870 to 1913; gradual development of central banking under the
Federal Reserve System after 1913; and growth of a shifting balance of functions among Congress, the Presidency (including the
Treasury), and the Federal Reserve concerning contracyclical monetary and fiscal measures from the middle 1930's on. Compared
with the high functional importance which money supply policy
had for this market-oriented society, the record was one of great
fumbling and delay in aligning public policy with economic and
social needs. No small part of the reason for inefficient policy-
making lay in the discrepant periods which, on the one hand, mark
the course of policy concerning legislative structure and procedures, and, on the other, the course of substantive policy about
banking. Policy suffered in particular because the timing of banking growth did not match the development of legislative experience and confidence in setting broad goals and making proper
delegations to adequately equipped, specialized administrators.[25]

There are no easy answers to the complexities introduced by
trying to relate the interplay of law with other institutions or with
ends and means derived largely from other-than-legal experience.
One who works in hyphenate legal history must acquire at least a
learned amateur's status in other men's disciplines; often the best
estimates the historian may be able to make of the likely impact of
law among various cross currents will rest on prophecies from economic, sociological, or statistical theory. Hyphenate legal history

25. *Cf.* James Willard Hurst, *The Growth of American Law: The Law Makers* (Boston,
1950), chaps. ii, iii, and Paul B. Trescott, *Financing American Enterprise: The Story of
Commercial Banking* (New York, 1963), chaps. ii, iii, vii, xii.

probably requires more linking of particular topics as they run together in given periods of time than would be necessary for the narrower enterprises of relating the history of particular courts or legal procedures or particular lines of legal doctrine. Concern with the law's relation to other social institutions emphasizes the need for distinguishing innovative from declarative roles of law. In a degree legal history can lift itself by its bootstraps while it contributes to a more sophisticated knowledge of social organization and processes, by learning more about how law exercises leverage on events through instruments peculiar to itself. For example, it seems likely that law has been most innovative through its procedures, and most declarative in defining general values or goals.[26]

What we have so far spoken of are difficulties of theory and evidence posed by the need to study the history of law in relation to that of other institutions. Another source of trouble affects the study of legal as well as of other social processes. This is the fact that great parts of experience relevant to values and procedures formally defined in law escape, avoid, or flout the law's formal processes. To appraise realistically what the law does through its regular, defined operations, we should put this activity into proper perspective relative to a great, environing body of informal, if not often formless, activity. Yet in its nature this informal behavior within and outside legal agencies resists demonstration, and all the more so in proportion to the investigation of greater reaches of time.

Various styles of action by public officers reduce the relevance or reliability of formal records of what they do. Judgments of trial courts, and orders of executive or administrative officers, stand on the books mostly without printed records of their underpinnings in fact-findings or doctrine. Much executive or administrative action, and a good deal of trial-court action, invoke standards of delegated power so broad that they do not reveal the particular ideas of cause and effect or values on which they rest. Examples

26. Holmes, *The Common Law*, p. 253; Frederick William Maitland, *The Forms of Action at Common Law* ed. 7, A. H. Chaytor and W. J. Wittaker (Cambridge, Eng., 1941), p. 1.

would be actions taken under sweeping statutory admonitions to welfare officials or to judges to act for "the best interest" of a child, or the varying severity or leniency with which different courts impose penal sentences. Under some regulatory laws what is at stake for the regulated persons is so great as to give public officials vast bargaining power beyond the range of any well-defined mandate from superior authority—as is true, at one end of the social class spectrum, with welfare officers' judgments on allowances to welfare clients, or, at the other, with the terms that may be bargained out in a consent decree between the Department of Justice and businessmen charged with antitrust violations. Again, when for some reason official misconduct blossoms into sufficient controversy to provoke a formal investigation, we learn that the realities of legal order include some illegal official conduct which in ordinary course escapes the formal record. In such ways we become uneasily aware what large expanses of informal official behavior surround or permeate the official conduct which produces formal evidence.[27]

277

This reality is of even greater weight when we consider private action relevant to legal order. An important distinction our legal tradition draws between what is public and what is private is precisely that most private activity requires no particular formal record defined by a legal agency. This is more than a matter of fact; to a large extent it is the result of constitutional principle. This principle favors privacy. It favors legal legitimation and protection of broad areas of activity which persons outside the official apparatus may engage in without having to publicize the activity or conform to any patterns set by public officers. Thus there is a vast amount of private action taken within bounds only generally set by law, and subject in case of sufficient challenge or breakdown to the law's ultimate scrutiny, which is reduced to no preserved public legal form, and at most may be embodied in formal documents of more or less legal effect held in private files, like the bulk of pri-

27. Kenneth Culp Davis, *Discretionary Justice* (Baton Rouge, 1969), pp. 221–233; Francis W. Laurent, *The Business of a Trial Court: 100 Years of Cases* (Madison, 1959), pp. vii–x.

vate contracts. In addition to this great body of private action not cast in forms imposed or produced by official agencies, much private action escapes the bounds of formal legal records for less justifiable reasons. Some private action is done within forms generally legitimated by law but for the purposes of which the conventional form gives little clue or gives only ambiguous clues—as with trusts created to avoid taxes. By design, heedlessness, or ignorance lawbreakers engage in much activity which leaves no formal legal record, yet provides part of the social context which determines the reality of law.[28]

Legal historians face hard and perhaps often insoluble problems of proof in establishing relations between the formal and informal dimensions of law in society. Could they get at the evidence of informal behavior touching the law, its volume would threaten to swamp understanding—as with oral bargains, or the face-to-face, unrecorded dealings of public officers and private persons. So far as an answer lies in sampling, by hypothesis the only reliable evidence from which to draw a sample of activity which does not leave a formal record will usually be evidence contemporary with the researcher. Apart from volume, the absence of preserved records of any sort will handicap the full-dimensioned study of much public and private action related to law. So far as an answer lies in disciplined field observation, this is practically limited to what is going on in the researcher's own time. There are suggestive materials to be gleaned from memoirs, letters, diaries, and the like—for example, the letter-file evidence of nineteenth-century railroad management decisions gleaned by Thomas Cochran—but most of such evidence will not provide means by which we can confidently measure how representative it is.[29] In addition to problems of volume or want of reliably representative evidence there are problems of access to evidence of informal behavior affecting legal order. So far as individual testimony is needed, time will have blot-

28. Lawrence M. Friedman and Stewart Macaulay, *Law and the Behavioral Sciences* (Indianapolis, 1969), pp. 145–164, 427–470.

29. Thomas C. Cochran, *Railroad Leaders, 1845–1890: The Business Mind in Action* (Cambridge, 1953); *cf.* Francis X. Sutton, Seymour Harris, Carl Kaysen and James Tobin, *The American Business Creed* (Cambridge, 1956).

ted it out once the story moves any distance into the past. So far as informal record evidence exists, there are great time costs in locating and collating it, together with obstacles raised by interests which individuals, business firms, and other groups are likely to have in maintaining their privacy against the scholar's curiosity. These difficulties of fact are compounded if the legal historian wants to use evidence in lawyers' files, where professional scruples are likely to raise the lawyer-client privilege, even though clients may be long dead or associations dissolved, or transactions may be routine, innocent, or praiseworthy. This last difficulty is peculiarly costly to historical inquiry, for lawyers' files—of letters, office memoranda, draft documents—potentially offer the richest, most orderly sources of evidence of much of the informal context of law, notably affecting the economy. Because of the collision here between research needs and professional ethics, the problem is unlikely to be solved by negotiation between individual researchers and law firms, but only by compact between scholars and custodians of the canons of legal ethics.[30]

279

Meantime, in the current flow of legal-historical scholarship, how do we cope with the realities of the informal dimensions of law in society? The beginning of wisdom is the lesson of the legal realist movement in the late 1920's and 1930's: to cultivate a lively awareness of the existence of the informal context of formal legal operations. In proportion as scholars are sensitive to this context, they are more likely to enlarge their evidence of it. Further, legal history research should foster and contribute to contemporary field studies and sampling of data which can be given some reliable reach back from the present moment. Work in legal history has been subtly constricted by a bias which identifies history only with what is relatively quite old. If we get more used to seeing that today and yesterday belong to history along with the day before yesterday, we are more likely to build up the stock of evidence of informal behavior by more disciplined study of activity that is open to our

30. Emily P. Dodge, "Evolution of a City Law Office: Part II: Office Flow of Business," *Wisconsin Law Review* (1956), 35, 36–37; Erwin O. Smigel, *The Wall Street Lawyer* (New York, 1964), pp. 18–21.

inquiry. A third point: the formal character of records of legal operations does not mean that such records may not offer some evidence of the informal context. Formal legal action includes sustained trends in policy-making, where judicial decisions, statutes, or administrative orders and rules turn the law's energies in one direction rather than another. Given the inertia and the interest conflicts which must be overcome to produce formal legal action, such trends are likely to offer circumstantial evidence of patterns of informal behavior preceding and environing them. Thus movements in twentieth-century public policy toward more emphasis on consumer protection, conservation of natural resources, standards of hours, labor, and safety in employment, and protection of business competition imply substantial evidence of things that were found wanting in the operational effects of the nineteenth-century use of the law of contract, property, and tort. Again: in proportion as formal legal action produces defined choices of ends or means, the action carries implicit—sometimes explicit—evidence of the immediately preceding informal situation; thus creation of the Clayton Act and the Federal Trade Commission Act generated both explicit and circumstantial evidence of working defects in prior antitrust policy. And finally, where legal processes involve adversary contests, combat induces men to produce claims and evidence which often reveal a good deal about the general circumstances of the time, apart from the matters immediately in issue, especially where the contest goes on via legislative or administrative investigations.[31]

The sum of these considerations teaches modest estimates of how much of the legal-social history we can hope to capture. The constitutional tradition means that we cannot properly appraise law as a self-contained institution. True, law has fallen far short of the constitutional ideals of utility and justice, but these ideals have had enough working reality to provide basic organizing ideas for understanding the reality of law in United States history. Thus, as

31. Friedman and Macaulay, *Law and Behavioral Sciences*, pp. 198–508; Eugene V. Rostow, *Planning for Freedom: The Public Law of American Capitalism* (New Haven, 1959), chap. xiv; Wilfred E. Rumble, Jr., *American Legal Realism* (Ithaca, 1968), chap. iii.

criteria of legal order the constitutional ideals of utility and justice require that we identify and assess all relevant dimensions of experience, to the extent that we can. It is hard enough merely to identify areas where behavior not contained within regular legal forms affects the roles of law in society. It is even harder to trace lines of cause and effect and measure the relative impact of legal and other-than-legal factors in the informal relations of law and other institutions. But, however great and perhaps in some measure insuperable the difficulties, honesty requires that we acknowledge that the full dimensions of the social history of law include great areas of behavior of which we have no evidence produced by the regular operations of legal processes. These areas are no less real, though we may not be able adequately to chart them. Their felt presence should at least induce a realistic estimate of the evidence which we do find available, and a realistic skepticism about the fullness of the legal history we tell.

ACTION RECORDED IN PRESCRIBED LEGAL FORMS

The difficulties of piecing together the social history of law out of informal evidence of practices, attitudes, and interests point up the distinctive importance of legal processes in producing formal records of public policy. Among social institutions probably only organized science and technology have generated as great a flow of controlled, supervised records as has the law. This aspect of legal order creates a potential as yet little realized for contribution by legal history to general history.

There is a great range in the formal records of social relations produced with the law's encouragement or fiat. Such records may be made by official or private actors or by related action of both. On the official side, legislatures produce statutes and a variety of auxiliary material including published legislative hearings, committee reports, and debates; courts produce judgments, decrees, and orders, along with opinions explaining their grounds of decision; executive and administrative agencies produce generalized rules and particularized orders within the scope of statutory delegations of authority. Private persons produce great quantities of records which they deliberately cast into more or less stylized forms because the form is functional to some assurance or result they want from the legal order. Thus private dealers produce bills of sale or deeds or leases to regularize transfer of titles, draw checks or promissory notes to put credit to use in situations where they want the benefits of legal negotiability, issue bonds or shares of stock of largely standardized content to muster capital, file applications for licenses and make returns of taxes according to terms set by statutes or administrative rules. In the variety of situations with which the law deals many gradations emerge between formality and informality in records produced incident to legal operations. This is true both of official and private actors. The attorney general of a state issues opinions advisory to state agencies; some of these are stated in the measured analysis of a judicial opinion and are published in official volumes to become part of the governing legal precedent of the jurisdiction; some of them are rendered simply by letters to local district attorneys or corporation counsel, stay in the officials' letter files, but nonetheless govern official action. Private dealers may cast a loan of money in the shape of a negotiable instrument every term of which is part of a pattern firmly established in law as to its consequences for the immediate parties and third persons as well; or they may arrange their loan in a non-negotiable contract the terms of which may be highly special to their circumstances, and yet fall within law-defined concepts of what will make a binding agreement. At some point relations are so little reduced to any defined, regularized legal form that their study presents the problems noted in the preceding section of this essay. Thus an attorney general's opinions are part of the formal record evidence generated by the law whether they exist in published volumes or in the attorney general's letter files; when an assistant attorney general gives an opinion over the telephone, on the basis of which a local prosecutor decides how he will proceed in a given matter, the incident is no less a part of the working legal order, but it is part of that great informal domain of the law's activity which is peculiarly hard to chart.[32]

282

32. Robin M. Williams, Jr., *American Society* (New York, 1951), pp. 140, 144–146, 214, 230–231, 232, 484–486, 501–511.

Another way to appreciate the range of formal legal records is to note the various functions in the legal order which may lead to formally recorded activity. Some records are created preparatory to obtaining some legal effect, as court records of testimony, lawyer's briefs, legislative history materials, data presented in license applications, or reports made for tax purposes. Some records constitute enabling acts or enabling uses of law. Enabling action may be by officials, as when a legislature or an executive officer under statutory delegation grants a charter of incorporation or a franchise for some special activity, or when a court enters a declaration or decree as to status, as in a divorce. Many privately initiated actions produce deliberately formal enabling documents, as with contracts, deeds, wills, or trust instruments. A great body of official action generates records of disposition or adjustment of scarce assets or satisfactions. This is the nature of legislation or judge-made law setting standards or rules of behavior—what we ordinarily call regulation. This is the nature of formal allocations of economic resources by legal grant, disposing of public lands, or appropriating public money to provide public services or to subsidize private activities deemed of public interest. Of a mixed regulatory and allocations character are the law's grants of exclusive or restricted franchises; as to the grantees, these charters serve primarily an enabling function, but as to all those excluded from the grants they operate as imposed regulations or allocations of resources. Finally —apart from records of a preparatory, enabling, or dispositive character—some formal legal records are created to justify or offer checks on the propriety of uses of law, as with judicial or administrative opinions accompanying judgments or orders, or legislative committee reports or statute preambles setting out findings of fact and value judgments as underpinnings of legislation.

283

Law, thus, fosters or requires an uncommon production of formal records. The historical utility of these records must not be discounted just because they are formal, though common speech often exalts "substance" over "form." Values which give good content to life exist not only in the substance but also in the forms of experience. Perception, and thought or feeling based on perception, require forms to organize experience. These forms can degenerate into objects of narrow vested interest or functionless habit. But to channel experience into regular forms can create high values both of a rational kind (for example, to promote such security of expectations as is needed to foster continuities of action and commitment essential to a full life), and of an emotional kind (for example, to insist that social order be implemented only by means consistent with regard for individual worth and dignity).[33]

As evidence of substantial reality in social relations, formal records are not inherently inferior in reliability to informal evidence. In a given context, formal-record evidence may be hollow, or fictitious, or marginal to the life areas it touches; the reality which we perceive from evidence of informal behavior cautions us to learn sophistication in appraising how much formal records show of the whole story. Sophistication learned from close study of legal processes will also tell us, however, that too much energy goes into their working and too much cost is paid for the outcomes formally declared by the law to make it plausible that there is not great substance represented by the formal records. Moreover, the formal records reflect more continuity of effort, contest, and decision than is consistent with charades. For example, the long-term trend to expand the judge-made law of negligence to protect consumers and to enlarge the statutory-administrative law on public health bears the stamp of reality in the cumulative direction it shows in committing law's resources. Sophistication does counsel that we heed the limitations which form imposes. But this caution does not mean a wholesale discounting of formal records. Rather it simply enjoins, for example, that we note that normally all we can learn from a court judgment is who won the lawsuit and to what relief he is entitled, and that to explain why he won is the business of the court's opinion.

The law's processes are typically used to foster effective choices of some sort (whether for action or no action, for stability or for change, for one alignment of values or another). Hence, the formal records yielded by legal processes have special relevance to under-

33. Hurst, *Law and Social Process*, pp. 83, 106, 131–150.

standing the course of social life. So viewed, law stands out as one of our prime inventions for creating meaning in experience. That legal processes exist has tended to encourage men to bring facts into focus, and to translate into formal records wants, needs, and tensions which otherwise might be hard to identify or measure at all. We can see, for one thing, that law has exerted a kind of magnetic attraction by offering possibilities of benefit; that a legislature sits, equipped with authority to tax and spend, to grant franchises, and to declare standards or rules of behavior, has meant that men have been drawn to formulate demands or petitions and muster energy to pursue them. Law also has attracted men to organize their experience by offering them reassuring security of expectations by regularizing commitments, in standard forms of property title, for example, or of contract or status (as in marriage). The law's compulsions have pressed men to bring problems in their relationship to one another into awareness, calculation and resolution; if one interest proposes legislation, the threat of legislative action prompts a counter interest better to express itself.[34]

285

To make a case for the utility of formal legal records as historical evidence is not to adopt a pseudo-scientific approach such as that taken by Dean Langdell when he said that the law is a science and all the available materials for its study are contained in printed books. Langdell saw law as a self-contained body of principles and procedures set out in the decisions and opinions of courts, to which the rest of life must conform. Plainly, this essay does not focus on formal legal records out of any such concept. A realistic history of law in the United States will be a social history of law, taking law as man-made, and as the product of both deliberation and drift, but not of any immanent superior order of reality. The law's formal records gain importance as tools of historical inquiry precisely because of what they reflect of law's relations to wants, needs, and currents of action and inaction embodied also in other-than-legal

34. *Ibid.*, pp. 102, 137, 158. *Cf.* Stephen K. Bailey, *Congress Makes a Law* (New York, 1950), chap. xii; Freund, *Standards of American Legislation*, chap. iii; Bertram M. Gross, *The Legislative Struggle* (New York, 1953), Part II; Theodore J. Lowi, *The End of Liberalism* (New York, 1969), chaps. iv, x.

institutions, and because they reflect law as a prime instrument for extracting meaning from what always threatens to be chaotic experience.[35]

The uses and functional character of formal legal processes give a number of special utilities to formal legal records as evidence of the social history of law.

1. Forms of legal action help to identify a wide range of social phenomena including (a) wants (expressed in the competing claims advanced by legislative lobbies and in lawsuits); (b) functional requisites of other-than-legal institutions aided by law (as law helps sustain broader, impersonal markets by its doctrines of negotiability, bona fide purchaser, and principal and agent); (c) functional requisites of individual life in society (reflected in law's provisions concerning family solidarity, education, access to jobs, care of health); (d) the social context of situations relevant to legal operations (as when stated grounds of applications for franchises reflect conditions of the licensed business); (e) the comparative operation of calculated and uncalculated factors in social relations (reflected, for example, in fumbling public policy toward the automobile, treating it first only as another commodity in the market except as road building subsidized expansion of its market, then belatedly moving into concern with its bearing on public safety, on land use, and on public health). In addition to helping define such particular aspects of life in society, the wide range of matters brought to law means that formal legal records help show these elements as a total context; from the whole flow of business through legislatures and courts we can get a better sense of what wants, needs, and tensions made themselves felt together or successively, in what hierarchies of attention and valuation men ranked these co-existent or successive objects of concern, and what relationships in experience were brought into some workable adjustment and what were not. Thus the statute books from 1870 to 1970 reflect shifts in the structure of

286

35. On Langdell, compare Charles Warren, *History of the Harvard Law School* (New York, 1908), II, 360–361, with *Holmes–Pollock Letters: The Correspondence of Mr. Justice Holmes and Sir Frederick Pollock, 1874–1932*, ed., Mark DeWolfe Howe (Cambridge, 1941), I, 17.

markets and of private and public organized power, through inter-
weaving changes in the law concerning corporations, public utilities, antitrust, unfair competition, investment channels, collective
bargaining, and administrative agencies. This utility of formal legal
records for identifying social currents is basic because the beginnings of historical wisdom lie in perception, and awareness becomes more and more difficult in a society marked by great range
and pace of change and increased complexity of cause and effect.
The utility of formal legal records is broad because of the uses this
society has made of law. Because our legal tradition would bring
all forms of organized power under legal scrutiny, emphasizes rational procedures to define and resolve values, and makes law a
major instrument to allocate scarce resources, it insures that the
law's formal output will bring into focus a wide range of social   287
relations.[36]

2. Formal records of legal action offer specially tested evidence
of the felt reality of social relations brought under law, and of the
intensity of response to those relations. This utility of legal records
arises because legal processes usually require investing substantial
attention, will, and energy to put them in motion. To some extent
this required investment is enforced by public policy. A litigant
must show standing (focused, factual impact on him of the issue he
wants decided) to persuade a court to act. It takes the agreement of
two legislative chambers, and usually also that of a chief executive,
to create a statute. Beyond requirements of regular legal procedures, facts of life raise a threshold of effort and commitment over
which those must step who would get some product from legal
process. That law works so much through formal procedures itself
imposes psychological costs. It is easier to accept situational pressures toward drift or inertia than to labor to formulate issues and
muster support of interested parties to get a bill drawn and pressed
to passage. Legal procedures are specialized and technical; hence
there is social distance to overcome between the inexpert laymen
and the expert operators of the system, and someone must meet the
costs of overcoming that distance. Legal processes do not always

36. James Willard Hurst, *Justice Holmes on Legal History* (New York, 1964), chap. i.

operate through conflict of interests, but they often do. Whether proposed action in law is taken or is not taken, if conflict determines the outcome, the legal disposition of the matter will represent some substantial spending of time, money, and will to attest that what was at issue in fact mattered to someone. Modern attitude research works to fashion more sophisticated techniques for determining what people truly experience as meaningful issues and how intensely they hold their declared responses to those issues. We don't have such techniques to probe the reality or felt intensity of people's exposure to most public policy questions of the past. But because of the threshold requirements for invoking law, records of legal action offer some substitute.[37]

3. The principal legal processes—legislation, litigation, administrative rule-making and adjudication—provide standardized, continuingly available means to define, deliberate, and decide social relations choices or issues; a key characteristic of this legal order has been that it has not required *ad hoc* creation of means to deal with each situation. This continuing availability of legal processes means that formal records of legal operations are a specially important body of evidence to witness the existence of facts which come into being only by virtue of sustained sequences of attitude or action. Such facts are not only important in history; they have their being only in history, since their continuity makes their existence. An institutional example is the market, which could not exist without a security of expectations to which legal order in the United States made varied contributions, in the law of contract, property, and tort, as also through constitutional doctrine developed under the contracts clause and the due process and equal protection clauses. A market-related example of a particular policy is the emergence of the law's favor toward diffusing costs through the insurance principle (as in workmen's compensation, bank deposit insurance, broad doctrines of manufacturers' products liability which invite insurance, or government subsidy of private credit for housing or foreign trade through government insurance against loss). The

37. James M. Buchanan and Gordon Tullock, *The Calculus of Consent* (Ann Arbor, 1962), chaps. viii, xx.

market as a working institution and the insurance principle as a proved technique for adjusting social relations did not spring into being at any particular date or by virtue of any particular invention or enactment. They were constituted by sustained sequences of ideas and action in which uses of the law figured to a large extent.[38] The records of formal legal action provide prime evidence of such facts which exist only in long-term sequence, because the standardized continuity of legal processes builds law into the existence of such facts. Our categories overlap here. Formal legal records help to identify these facts and to measure their reality and intensity as felt experience. But, in addition, formal legal processes have provided important conditions for the existence of such facts.

4. Law puts its stamp on a vast variety of concrete, particularized policy judgments. But the formality of legal processes meant that these processes were highly abstract, in the sense that procedures of legislating or litigating could be used to serve a great variety of ends or provide a great variety of means. This abstract character of legal processes meant that they produced formal records of an unusual range of social experience, from lawsuits over dog bites to lawsuits over combinations in restraint of trade, from statutes about abortions to statutes about zoning. This abstract character has helped to promote the pervasive range of law which makes legal records useful to define or identify so many factors in social life. And it has contributed to the continuous availability of legal processes, because it has meant that their standard procedures could accommodate a shifting variety of particular issues. Thus the abstractness of its procedures has enabled law to work toward the emergence of large institutions like the market or large instrumental policies like the insurance principle. Another distinctive role of law derives from the abstract character of its procedures. If the law's continuity contributed to other institutional continuities, the abstract character of its procedures helped to make action through law an important dimension or area of social change. Le-

289

---

38. John R. Commons, *Legal Foundations of Capitalism* (Madison, 1957), chaps, iv, vii; Fleming James, "Accident Liability Reconsidered: The Impact of Liability Insurance," *Yale Law Journal*, 57 (1948), 549.

gal records evidence a good deal of social change, because availability of legal processes has been a significant ground of existence for social change. This is not to claim that public or private use of law was likely to initiate change. The sources and dynamics of social change almost always originated in experience outside the law. Indeed, this was the condition most consistent with our constitutional tradition, which demanded that law serve values not finally determined by the state. But the capacity of legislative or litigious processes to entertain a great variety of complaints and proposals for organized action meant that ideas about new life goals or life content or about new means of pursuing familiar goals were likely at some point to find expression in legislative bills or in lawsuits or in petitions to administrative or executive agencies. This is the solid reality behind the often aimless popular cry that "There ought to be a law." Because of the nature of the processes from which they come, formal legal records thus offer riches for studying social change in areas other than the law—riches for historians of ideas (for evidence of new life styles or new concepts of individuality, for example), for historians of economic growth (for evidence of responses to scientific or technical change, or of shifts in the structure of private decision making), or for historians of social structure (for evidence of shifting attitudes toward class or caste, or realignments of roles or power within the relations of husband and wife, parent and child, teacher and student, church and state).[39]

290

5. Let us note, also, that formal legal records may be useful evidence of different social relations according to the immediate function performed by a type of formal legal action. Consider some implications of comparing legislative and adjudicative action. If the immediate function of law is to make a generalization, whether by setting regulatory standards or rules for behavior (as by a statute forbidding sale of adulterated foods) or by providing a service (as by a statute providing unemployment compensation), the legal activity helps us to identify shared interests of some sort or the presence of some fairly broad type of tension or want. On the other

39. Roscoe Pound, *Jurisprudence* (St. Paul, 1959), III, chap. xiv.

hand, the immediate function of law may be to determine a proper particular application of the state's power, whether by making a public service available to a given applicant (a welfare claimant) or by providing a punitive or compensatory response for a particular invasion of general interest (as by fine or jail sentence in a specific instance of law violation, or by judgment for damages arising out of breach of contract). Here the legal activity suggests and helps to identify focused impacts of the social context on individual life, including evidence of breakdowns or departures from desired norms. In other words, the formal qualities of legal action are likely to express different functions of legal action—the court's judgment or decree has a different function from that of the court's opinion —and the researcher should note that the aspects of social experience reflected in legal records will vary with the function of the legal action.[40]

These comments have pointed to positive qualities that formal legal evidence offers the historian. However, this kind of evidence is not without defects or limitations in reflecting the course of social experience.

a. The pervasiveness of legal operations means that legal records help to identify a wide range of social interactions. It also entails a daunting volume of potentially relevant records, posing practical problems of physical access, costs of processing, and reliability of findings. Access and cost problems mount fast as research moves down the hierarchy of authority in government (greater difficulties appear in studying what local governments did about public health than what the state legislature did) or as research moves from larger to smaller private entities (the researcher's problems in studying the law's relation to the life history of a billion-dollar corporation will be primarily political ones, of breaking through barriers of institutional secrecy; his problems in studying law's relation to the life history of a one-million dollar corporation are likely to be primarily created by lost, scattered, unindexed records). The volume of legal records presses the researcher toward

40. Edgar Bodenheimer, *Jurisprudence* (Cambridge, 1962), pp. 272–276; Lon Fuller, *The Law in Quest of Itself* (Chicago, 1940), pp. 131–135.

sampling. If records reflect transactions of simple, standard character, this may be workable. But many legal operations are not interchangeable; actions against public or private nuisances, suits over business torts, contests over water rights will take too much color from particular facts to allow ready sampling, and the sharper the definitions the scholar must draw as to what is in issue in particular cases, the more he is driven to look at all the raw data he can find.[41]

b. The costs of moving matters over the law's thresholds (costs of assembling data and defining issues, costs of the risk of failure, costs of opposing or conciliating other interests, for example) reduce the areas of experience brought to formal legal action. These costs help to maintain or enlarge areas of informal action lacking formal records, such as informal settlements of contract disputes or tort claims, spillover costs suffered in silence, uncontested illegal actions of public officers. In other words, the processes which generate formal legal records—the need or requirement to have formal legal records for some purposes—help create costs which materially limit the extent to which such records evidence the interactions of law and other patterns of social action.[42]

c. The continuing availability of formal legal processes may help to destroy or change the practical meaning of action apparently brought about by those processes. So in days before the Securities and Exchange Commission legislation, state statutory requirements that corporations report periodically to public officers or to shareholders bred a fiction of accountability, either because the reporting requirements were thin or wholly lacking in sanctions. Stereotypes in pleading lawsuits not only made much pleading empty evidence of what was in fact going on among the parties, but sometimes worked contrary to good public policy. Thus for some years the Supreme Court failed to see the propriety of extending federal admiralty jurisdiction to cover inland navigable

41. Richard Eells, *The Government of Corporations* (Giencoe, Ill., 1962), chap. i; Spencer L. Kimball, *Insurance and Public Policy* (Madison, 1960), pp. vi, vii; Laurent, *The Business of a Trial Court*, pp. viii–ix, 32, 38, 44–45.

42. Stewart Macaulay, "Non-Contractual Relations in Business: A Preliminary Study," *American Sociological Review*, 28 (1963), 55.

292

waters, because it drew its concept of admiralty from English pleaders who always alleged that the cause of action arose on tide-water because England knew no other major watercourses for transport. Again, professionals tend to develop vested interests in their specialized knowledge or familiar habits of characterizing situations. The continuity of legal processes may, on this basis of vested professional interest, perpetuate formal requirements which become sufficiently dysfunctional to breed significant informal counter action which the formal records do not reflect. So, early distrust of corporations fostered limited statutory charters out of which judges erected an elaborate body of doctrine declaring the invalidity or ineffectiveness of *ultra vires* activity. Judges continued to voice this learning after statute law had turned to granting incorporators such scope in drawing charters as to render hollow most claims that corporate action was *ultra vires*. Indeed, there was a reciprocal effect here. Some of the pressure for greater liberality in general incorporation acts came from lawyers' desire to escape the worries raised by the judges' dire talk of the consequences that might flow, or fail to flow, if a corporation exceeded its chartered authority.[43]

293

SOME PARTICULAR USES OF FORMAL LEGAL RECORDS

There are special skills to learn in order to squeeze as much juice as possible out of formal legal records. As a minimum the researcher should know some things about legal bibliography. He should appreciate the full range of official records. Thus he ought to know that potentially useful legislative records include not only statute books, legislative journals, and published legislative hearings, committee reports, and debates, but also the text of floor amendments, preserved in bill jackets kept by records custodians, and unpublished committee files. He should know that there are specialized

43. Katz, "The Philosophy of Midcentury Corporation Statutes," 177, 179–181 ("enabling" corporation acts, compared with *ultra vires*); Robert L. Knauss, "A Reappraisal of the Role of Disclosure," *Michigan Law Review*, 62 (1964), 607, 625 (corporate reports); *The Propeller Genesee Chief v. Fitzhugh*, 12 How. 443 (U.S. 1851) (pleading practice and admiralty jurisdiction).

utilities even in the published records; that, for example, hearings of appropriations subcommittees sometimes preserve evidence of particular executive or administrative action brought under fire when an agency seeks fresh money. In dealing with the courts, he should know that, though trial court records are usually hard to get at, commonly there will be libraries which preserve records and briefs of cases appealed. These auxiliary appellate records may flesh out what appears in court opinions, and may also offer considerable evidence not elsewhere so readily available, as to facts of life—business structure and practice, for example—put in evidence incident to pressing a claim or making a defense. In exploring executive or administrative action, the researcher should be aware that in addition to published rules or orders, he may find in the files internal policy memoranda or handbooks of operating policy to guide agents in the field.[44] The possibilities of evidence are varied and diverse, but the tools for locating the evidence are of uneven quality. Indexing of official volumes is typically poor, as is the selection of classifications for digests of court opinions; the scholar needs to learn sophistication against allowing the hack work of an index-maker or digester to define his subject for him. One tool of high reliability which he will learn to use wherever he can in tracing the course of both statute and case law is *Shepard's Citations*, whose tables will tell him almost always when a statute has been amended or repealed, or a judicial opinion followed, distinguished, or overruled.

The more subtle and productive skill needed is that of reading formal legal materials so as to find all that they say, including what they say between the lines or what they indicate by significant silence, omission, or question begging. There is not much that is mysterious or highly technical here. But without some disciplined study of how to read legal sources, the researcher is likely to take them too much at their formal face value.[45] There are two respects

294

44. Wright v. Vinton Branch of the Mountain Trust Bank, 300 U.S. 440, 463, note 8 (1937); Allen v. Grand Central Aircraft Co., 347 U.S. 535, 544 (1954); Richard R. Robinson, "Liability Without Fault in the Fish and Game Statutes," *Wisconsin Law Review*, (1956), 656, 663–666.

45. Note 22, above.

in which reading skill is particularly needed to extract all that formal legal records can offer. First, though purposes (ends, and means to achieve them) may be clearly stated or indicated, can we establish that lawmakers really meant them to have impact? One needs to learn to look for the points where statutes or decisions pay off in terms of particular gains or costs provided. For example, legislation franchising power developments on navigable streams may say that transportation is to be preferred over waterpower, but the legislature more convincingly shows that it means this when the statutes impose on grantees the costs of providing locks or other devices to allow transport to pass.[46] Second, the bulk of the law's formal product, in statutes and decisions and administrative rules and orders, shows legal action sharply focused on particular social relations or tensions, with larger objectives left implicit. To define the more general social ends sought through law, the ranking of such values, and the functional (or, sometimes, dysfunctional) relations of law to other social institutions often requires that we look for trends or patterns that are not openly declared. Important dimensions of social existence become visible and to some extent measurable only when we look at the sequence and the context of events—when we look at events in time, that is, historically. Thus the preeminent value which public policy from the late-eighteenth century into the mid-twentieth century attached to enlarging economic productivity emerges most powerfully from the law's presumptions favoring market expansion (in favor of free contract, the fee simple title, and limited tort liability of economic actors), widely dispersed association (in the shift from special to general incorporation acts, and then to general incorporation acts increasing the options open to private draftsmen of corporate articles), and public subsidy of applications of technical innovation (as in hard-surfaced roads to underwrite the automobile industry and mass use of the automobile).[47] To identify

46. James Willard Hurst, *Law and Economic Growth* (Cambridge, 1964), p. 221.

47. Sidney Fine, *Laissez Faire and the General Welfare State* (Ann Arbor, 1956), chap. v; James Willard Hurst, *Law and the Conditions of Freedom in the Nineteenth-Century United States* (Madison, 1956), chap. i; Malcolm M. Willey and Stuart A. Rice, "The Agencies of Communication," in President's Research Committee on Social Trends, *Recent Social Trends in the United States* (New York, 1934), p. 167.

public policy in this way calls for patient, competent handling of large amounts of specific and often technical legal material, with skills that can elicit generalizations from details.

There are three aspects of formal legal materials which may be particularly productive of insights into the broader reaches of public policy.

1. The legal historian should look closely at the facts, events, or actions which the law says must be established in order to obtain a given action of law.

a. Policy may take on one dimension or another according to whether the law states a standard or a rule—or, more broadly, according to how much discretion central lawmakers delegate at points of immediate use or application of law. (1) Policy may be established by roles allotted between levels of sovereignty or authority. Thus the Federal Constitution assigned specific priority to national markets over state revenue when it stipulated that no state should, without the consent of Congress, lay any duty on imports or exports, except as absolutely necessary to execute its inspection laws; in contrast, the broad terms of the grant to Congress of power to regulate commerce among the states left to the haul and pull of federal and state legislative and judicial processes the adjustment among other national and local policies affecting the economy.[48] (2) The generality or specificity of legal regulation apportions the exercise of will as between public and private decision makers. Thus statutes forbidding loss leaders put one technique of price competition under strict ban, reflecting a particular point of tension between chain and independent retailers; on the other hand, the sweeping generality of the Sherman Act's prohibition of combinations in restraint of trade among the states left the initiative to private organizers, subject to government challenge after the fact.[49] The contrast suggests how narrowly pragmatic the legislative process has usually been, with its focus fixed by the kind of pressure brought to bear on it. (3) The choice in law between standard and

48. United States Constitution, 1, 8, 10; Gibbons v. Ogden, 9 Wheat. 1 (U.S. 1824); Pensacola Telegraph Co. v. Western Union Telegraph Co., 96 U.S. 1 (1877).

49. 29 Stat. 209 (1890); Wis. Stat., 100.30 (1969); cf. James M. Landis, "Statutes and the Sources of Law," in Harvard Legal Essays (Cambridge, 1934), p. 213.

rule also allocated decision-making power, or substantially affected the apportionment of risks or of costs and gains among private parties. Thus the common law acknowledged a social interest in individual life and in the community's effective manpower by requiring an employer to furnish his employee a safe place in which to work. This standard, however, put claimants under the burden of suing to spell out its application in particular circumstances. Twentieth-century factory safety laws typically delegated to an administrative agency authority to define and enforce specifications as to clean air, guards on moving machinery, or safety brakes on elevators. The shift to this style of law meant shifting burdens of action for safety more on to the state and on to employers, reducing the risks and costs of claims which common law had laid on employees.[50]

297

b. Law deals much in classifications or categories of behavior or situations: "persons," "property," "navigable waters." The legal historian must cultivate sophistication in sizing up the functions of such generalizations. That lawmakers feel moved to generalize fits the constitutional tradition; generalization helps lawmaking meet the constitutional criterion of utility, by promoting better awareness of relationships, and serves the constitutional criterion of justice by inclining men to appraise more closely the likenesses or differences which should guide law toward equality and rational adaptation of means to ends. But classifications may be used to avoid closer definition of policy in action, whether because this is the easier way or because some interest which might be questioned if it were more openly declared can be more readily pursued under disguise of a conventional concept. Thus, for the law to allow unchecked discretion to the "owner" of standing timber to clear-cut his land, because it was his "property," served in fact to by-pass the social interest in a continuing, productive forest. In a mid-nineteenth-century context, lawmakers probably followed the "property" idea here primarily from inertia and from a lack of countervailing pressures for conserving productive resources for the general economy. Toward the end of the century the "private property" shibboleth became more suspect, as an instrument of

50. John R. Commons, *Myself* (New York, 1934), pp. 141–143, 153–160.

particular interests. By the mid-twentieth century calculations of social gain and cost found sufficient statutory expression so that to say that a man had a private property in a given relationship of man and things which might yield him profit was treated as stating a conclusion rather than explaining it, and in various ways conservation law now made "property" only a qualified license.[51]

c. Law also establishes and ranks values when it stipulates that a certain state of mind must be shown as a condition of putting the law into application, or in contrast stipulates that proof of simple cause will suffice. Thus, to make out some criminal offenses the state must prove that a defendant had either a general intent to bring about the result the law does not want (as where murder is shown when a defendant acted to take life, not in self defense) or a specific intent to produce a specifically forbidden outcome (as where law punishes with greater severity than for mere assault, an assault with intent to do grievous bodily harm). But from the late-nineteenth century more and more we used the criminal law to penalize conduct or the production of specified states of fact where the state need prove only that a defendant acted and that his action brought about the objective condition against which the law was directed. For example, by statute the seller of foodstuffs might be guilty of an offense of selling dirty or diseased food with no requirement that the state prove that he intended to do so or was even guilty of negligence in doing so. To require that the state prove a guilty mind in the defendant was a way of holding down the reach of public regulation; to omit wrongful intent as an element in an offense was to enlarge the scope of public action. To require proof of a guilty mind was to emphasize the social dangers in certain calculated purposes or in careless behavior; to omit wrongful intent in defining an offense was to recognize in law that certain cause-and-effect relationships could not be accepted in closely interlocking society, regardless of the actors' states of mind. Whatever the indicated judgment, the presence or absence of a

298

---

51. Richard F. Babcock, *The Zoning Game* (Madison, 1966), chap. vii; Hurst, *Law and Economic Growth*, pp. 368, 428, 459.

mental element in the law's definition of crimes was an indicator of trends in the growth of public policy.[52]

d. Law may declare detailed terms or conditions on which it makes available its privileges, protections, subsidies, and services. To be eligible for publicly provided unemployment compensation a claimant must show that within statutory definitions he was a benefited employee, of a covered employer, and that he was unemployed in conditions that met the statutory policy. To obtain a statute-granted credit against income tax liability on account of new investment, a taxpayer must fit the terms of investment prescribed, while the income against which the credit would be given must fit standards set out by statute, administrative rules, and court decisions. Explicit or implicit in such terms for the law's application were dispositions favorable toward some behavior or outcomes and unfavorable toward others, as well as indications of the relative ranking of favor and disfavor. Most of the evidence of public policy lay in such specifications; broad expositions of public policy objectives were the exception rather than the rule. The historian, therefore, must learn to extract the larger generalizations from the more particular statements.[53] Unemployment compensation laws stated their large objectives more openly than most legislation. Still, indicated in the specifications of claims was a host of important, if subsidiary, policy patterns concerning the social interest in the continuity of economic relationships, judgments on diligence and the will to work, provisions for equality between men and women as workers, and many others. An investment credit provision in the tax law might rather openly show its general promotional policy, but implicit in its detail were other significant judgments, as on social priorities in allocating capital among competing uses.

e. To identify the law's specific commitments to stability or change in particular relationships of individuals and society, or

299

52. Edgar Bodenheimer, *Treatise on Justice* (New York, 1967), pp. 202–210, 216–218; Livingston Hall, "Strict or Liberal Construction of Penal Statutes," *Harvard Law Review*, 48 (1935), 548.

53. Roscoe Pound, "Common Law and Legislation," *Harvard Law Review*, 21 (1908), 383, 385.

of individuals and government, or among individuals and groups, is another inquiry which brings the uses of law into clearer view. One kind of commitment to stability was made through the choice between writing arrangements into constitutional form, or leaving them to legislation. Thus we get a measure of the importance attached to the potentials of a national economy, when the makers of the Federal Constitution commit to the United States a monopoly over direct creation of money by government. In contrast, we get some measure of nineteenth-century favor toward broadly dispersed private power when, in the face of the rapid emergence of the corporate form of business enterprise, the shape of corporation law is left to state legislation and judge-made law without any serious question of amending the Federal Constitution to impose uniform regulatory standards for the national economy. The contrast is the sharper when we observe that state-chartered, note-issuing banks fast grew to supply a major part of the money supply, outside the central government's monopoly of direct government issue of coins or paper money.[54] Treatment of corporations provided another early example of values reflected in the law's commitments to stability or change. The *Dartmouth College Case* cast the protection of the contract clause over corporate charters. Thus a state legislature might not by later statute upset organizational expectations created by an earlier charter. But considerable public distrust accompanied growing use of the corporate form. State policy expressed this distrust by putting into state constitutions or into legislation reservations of power to legislatures to alter, amend, or repeal corporate charters. The Supreme Court stamped such reserved powers as legitimate, so far at least as they were not used to destroy vested assets. However, state legislatures proved conservative in exercising the reserved powers. Such powers were rarely used against the desires of corporate stockholders or management, and then typically only on some cause shown in

54. United States Constitution, 1, 8, 10; Craig v. Missouri, 4 Pet. 410 (U.S. 1830); Briscoe v. The Bank of the Commonwealth of Kentucky, 11 Pet. 257 (U.S. 1837); Veazie Bank v. Fenno, 8 Wall. 533 (U.S. 1869); Robert L. Stern, "The Commerce Clause and the National Economy, 1933–1946," *Harvard Law Review*, 59 (1946), 645, 883.

public interest. Legislative practice thus substantially restored the commitment to charter security earlier made by the *Dartmouth College Case*, though within the framework of broad regulatory authority in the legislature.[55] In these shifts in the extent to which the law was committed to various courses of action, we can trace shifts in prevailing attitudes toward private power organized through incorporation.

    f. Another way in which law expresses and ranks values is by distinctions between loss or cost for which law will enforce reparation (wrongs or injuries), and those burdens or detriments which it does not treat as bases for invoking law's help. Thus the law expressed its favor for regular market operations by holding that loss suffered by a business enterprise through ordinary competition did not create a cause of action, though if a businessman took customers away from another by force, or fraud, or for no purpose save to inflict loss, he would be liable. Of analogous character as evidence of social values was the development in the law of eminent domain (defining situations in which government must compensate for taking private property for a public use) compared with the growth of economic regulatory law (for the impact of which law did not require compensation). The law banning child labor might have the effect of putting some manufacturers out of business, but they were allowed no money claim against the state. In contrast, if government took a man's land for a highway right of way, it must pay him for the land; government generally need not pay for value lost to private assets from the law's action, unless government employed or destroyed the economic utility of the private assets to produce the specific result it sought.[56] Implicit in distinctions between takings of private property for which government must pay and losses to private property from the impact

301

55. The Trustees of Dartmouth College v. Woodward, 4 Wheat. 518 (U.S. 1819); Greenwood v. Freight Co., 105 U.S. 13 (1882); John W. Cadman, Jr., *The Corporation in New Jersey* (Cambridge, 1949), pp. 94–96, 379, 380–382; Louis Hartz, *Economic Policy and Democratic Thought: Pennsylvania, 1776–1860* (Cambridge, 1948), pp. 240–242.

56. Robert L. Hale, *Freedom Through Law* (New York, 1952), p. 427; Max Radin, *Manners and Morals of Business* (Indianapolis, 1939), chaps. vii, viii; Henry Rottschaefer, *Handbook of American Constitutional Law* (St. Paul, 1939), pp. 694, 695.

of social regulations for which government need not pay were propositions of social income and cost accounting. Compensation requirements ordinarily followed from focused burdens of social action; freedom from compensation ordinarily went with diffused burdens of social action. Compensation requirements reflected concern for individuality and for guarding areas of some private autonomy against state incursion; freedom from compensation implied value put on productive social relations.

2. Emphasis on creating and maintaining regular procedures for bringing issues to definition and to some kind of decision has been a prime characteristic of the constitutional legal order. The historian should learn to look at the structure of legal procedures, and at their operations, for significant evidence of law's social roles. For this purpose, consider five aspects of legal procedures.

302

a. To put legal processes in motion the law has required that persons have some particular standing—be in some particular condition of fact or of law—relative to the action they seek from law. The requirement of standing has its most varied and substantial effect upon the work of the courts, where it marks constitutional bounds of judicial authority. By Article III of the Federal Constitution federal courts may decide only "cases" or "controversies," which exist only where suitors have standing in court, and (except for special provision for advisory opinions) a like limitation inheres in state constitutions' grants of "judicial power." There is considerable ambiguity in the idea of standing in court. But at least its core meaning—if, perhaps, not its whole meaning —is that a court will only decide a point of law at the request of a suitor who shows that decision on the point is likely to have some focused, factual effect on him for good or ill, different from the shared interest that everybody has in legal order. So the Supreme Court held that a federal taxpayer, as such, lacked standing to challenge the constitutionality of Congressional appropriations on the grounds that the object of expenditure (to promote the health of mothers and infants) exceeded Congress's authority in violation of the Tenth Amendment; any federal taxpayer's contribution to the total federal budget was deemed too small to make any particular expenditure of specially focused concern in fact to his affairs. Contrary to the restrictive indications of this classic decision, the mid-twentieth-century trend seemed to be increasingly to recognize standing in litigants who, though they might not be within a class immediately subject to the law's impact, could yet show that they were or would be materially affected in some particularized way. Analogous to the standing question was the doctrine which barred collusive suits, where ostensibly opposed interests contrived a combat which was in fact fictitious because both sought the same outcome. A test case was, however, distinguished, where interests were in genuine conflict, but the parties, or at least one party, arranged behavior to give rise to an issue in order to obtain a ruling on the validity or meaning of a statute. In the courts' treatment of questions of standing or collusion the historian could find some measure of the state of men's perception of interests at a given time, and of the readiness or disinclination of the courts to intervene in the haul and pull of interests in arenas of action outside courtrooms. So, too, insofar as a trend appeared to relax requirements to show standing in court, one might sense shifts in value judgments on the increasingly pervasive roles of law, and especially of law effected through administrative agencies.[57]

It was the courts which developed the most broadly effective doctrines of standing. This was natural to our institutional inheritance, in which courts were identified with handling specific claims of specially affected suitors. In contrast, the institutional inheritance was much less confining in ideas of legislative or executive authority. The legislative tradition and the trend of legislative growth pointed to broad, open-ended functions of the legislature as the grand inquest of the polity—the instrument through which any question of felt public concern might be ventilated—and as the principal agent on the frontier of formal policy-making, charged to adopt or reject additions to the body of law-supported policy.

57. Kenneth Culp Davis, *Administrative Law Treatise* (St. Paul, 1958), III, 208–294; *cf.* Frothingham v. Mellon, 262 U.S. 447 (1923); Flast v. Cohen, 392 U.S. 83 (1968); Brennan, J., concurring and dissenting in Association of Data Processing Service Organizations, Inc. v. Camp, 90 S. Ct. 838 (1970).

Symbols of the open doors to legislative consideration were the great reluctance of courts to put judicially enforceable limits on legislative investigation, and the absence in either constitutions or legislative rules of any limits on the subject matter of introduced bills. An enacted statute of a given character might be ruled unconstitutional in later litigation, but this hazard did not make it out of order to introduce a bill to create such a statute and press it through the regular stages to enactment.[58] Restriction or flexibility as to standing to seek or oppose action of executive or administrative agencies almost always depended, in the first instance, on what the legislature had done. Apart from quite limited areas our law recognized no executive prerogatives of law-making, but made all depend on what the legislature delegated. However, the courts played a substantial role here, too, insofar as it fell to them to interpret the scope of delegations made to the executive by the legislature.[59] The one major exception to the absence of restrictive standing requirements in approaching the legislature was the common late-nineteenth-century adoption of state constitutional bans on special and local laws. This development emphasized the main line of functional growth, which was that generalization of public policy was the normal role of the legislature.[60] Comparison of treatment of standing in the legislative and executive processes on the one hand and in the judicial process on the other serves mainly to highlight differences in legal-institutional roles; only with regard to the courts did standing doctrine take on enough detail to reflect differentiated judgments on the law's relations to life outside the law.

b. Law used various devices—allocations of the burden of proof, creation of presumptions, allowance or disallowance of parties' options to contract themselves out of otherwise binding legal obligations—which implicitly defined or ranked values by assign-

58. Norwegian Nitrogen Products Co. v. United States, 288 U.S. 294 (1933); Townsend v. Yeomans, 301 U.S. 441 (1937); Watkins v. United States, 354 U.S. 178 (1957); Goodland v. Zimmerman, 243 Wis. 459, 10 N.W. 2d 180 (1943); Rose Manor Realty Co. v. City of Milwaukee, 272 Wis. 339, 75 N.W. 2d 274 (1956).

59. Note 57, above.

60. Wisconsin Constitution, IV, 31; Harvey Walker, *Law Making in the United States* (New York, 1934), p. 258.

ing among concerned parties the burden of taking initiatives to use the law. Consider the value implications of allocating the burden of proof. By the late-nineteenth century prevailing opinion favored the corporate form of business for its utility in mustering and disciplining capital. One reflection of this judgment was in the doctrine which said that complaining stockholders must show gross abuse of trust or gross negligence, to obtain legal redress for errors of their board of directors.[61] Presumptions might likewise reflect social value judgments. A market-oriented society favored energy of will vented through contract; law indicated this bias by presuming the legality of private agreements, placing on the party who sought to avoid his bargain the burden of coming forward with evidence or argument to show that the contract should for some reason be deemed unenforceable as against public policy.[62] Presumptions were adaptable to varied directions of policy. Sometimes the law recognized gross inequality of position between parties to a transaction, and redressed the balance with a presumption against the stronger; so a contract of insurance would be construed against the insurer, unless the insurer made a contrary intent plain; so where a passenger suffered injury from an accident to a train, because the train was wholly in the railroad's control the fact of the mishap was itself normally taken to show negligence in the railroad (*res ipsa loquitur*). Changing appraisals of social costs and gains showed up, also, when courts interpreted regulatory legislation to decide whether it would permit a regulated party to contract himself out of his statutory liability. Early decisions favored allowing a common carrier to stipulate against liability for negligent handling of passengers or goods. Partly by statute, partly by judge-made law, the later current of policy rejected this presumption in favor of contracting out, and made the law the full arbiter of the carrier's liabilities; dropping the old presumption which favored the carrier's freedom of contract amounted to recognizing realities

305

61. Robert S. Stevens, *Handbook on the Law of Private Corporations* (2nd ed. St. Paul, 1949), pp. 650–651, 705.

62. Diamond Match Co. v. Roeber, 106 N.Y. 473, 13 N.E. 419 (1887); *cf.* Sir George Jessel, M.R., in Printing and Numerical Registering Co. v. Sampson (1875) L. R. 19 Eq. 462, 465.

of dependence bred of modern technology and organization.[63]

c. Another dimension of legal history is created by judge-made law and statutory and administrative rules defining what is evidence legally competent for admission before legal officers to decide a controversy or obtain some other legal result. The historian will find here reflections of ideas about man's nature as an observer—as a truth-teller or as a liar or creature of bias; as one who uses reason and knowledge or as one moved by emotion and habit. The other side of these considerations is what they reflect of stable or changing estimates of the practical capacity of legal processes themselves to function within certain ideas of the qualities and defects of men.[64] So, for example, shifts in the law of evidence indicate changed estimates of the working norms of marriage and of legal procedures as well. Older policy tended to bar a wife's testimony in matters affecting her husband, out of concern for marital harmony or for the likelihood that she would be an unreliable witness from fear of the husband's coercion or from unreasoning bias of sympathy. In the mid-twentieth century the law grew more relaxed, was willing to trust triers of fact to make a hardheaded appraisal of the wife's credibility, and no longer found such plausibility in fears of coercion or bias as would warrant ruling the wife out altogether as a witness. The law of evidence reflects other factual and value judgments on society besides those turning on theories of human nature. The historian might trace in the law on the qualification of expert witnesses how we moved from a narrowly pragmatic community which exalted the jack-of-all-trades to one which accepted experts—and perhaps unduly trusted them. Here is one facet among many of the law's responses to the enlarged roles of science and technology. In its willingness to accept evidence of trade or occupational customs in measuring standards of care or fidelity toward customers or members of the public dependent on the quality of service, the law of evidence responded to facts of

306

63. Morris R. Cohen, *Law and the Social Order* (New York, 1933), pp. 69, 103–108; Spencer L. Kimball, *Insurance and Public Policy* (Madison, 1960), pp. 210, 211.

64. Edward W. Cleary, "Evidence as a Problem in Communication," *Vanderbilt Law Review*, 5 (1952), 277; John Henry Wigmore, *A Treatise on the Anglo-American System of Evidence* (Boston, 1940), I, 239, 242–246, 260–263.

interlocking relations and the growth of more and more institu-tionalized patterns of associated action in the economy.[65]

d. Closely related in function to the law of evidence is the law of official notice—the doctrine that official agencies may, with-out requiring formal submission of testimony or documents, find the factual bases for their actions in knowledge commonly ac-cepted by those qualified to appraise the realities of the matter in hand. The law of this kind most familiar to lawyers is the doctrine of judicial notice. Employed in place of direct production of wit-ness-stand or documentary evidence, official notice entered agency actions in two styles. Sometimes an overt issue might be made, or at least overt attention given, as to the proper applicability of offi-cial notice. More often perhaps, no question was raised and the court or other legal agency grounded its policy determinations on the assumption that it knew certain facts to be true, though no supporting evidence was put into the record. The legal historian should sharpen his eye to identify the use of official notice—and especially to detect unacknowledged use of official notice—in pro-viding the grounds of judicial opinions, legislative reports and stat-utory preambles, or other formal declarations and explanations of agency reaction. The most compelling drives behind men's actions are often their taken-for-granted assumptions as to what is real and true in affairs; this is no less so of the law than of other institutions, but especially important there because law holds special means of bringing things about. The official-notice dimension of formal le-gal documents can provide unusually broad evidence of many going assumptions of the society or of particular institutions in it. The evidence is the weightier because it is produced as an incident of structured processes for defining and resolving public policy choices and private transactions and tensions—often under the sober-ing check of adversary proceedings.[66] Official notice may be taken

307

65. Funk v. United States, 290 U.S. 371 (1933); United States v. Dege, 364 U.S. 51 (1960); Boyce v. Wilbur Lumber Co., 119 Wis. 642, 97 N.W. 563 (1903); Wigmore, *Anglo-American System of Evidence*, II, chap. xxiii.

66. Edmund M. Morgan, *Some Problems of Proof under the Anglo-American System of Litigation* (New York, 1956), pp. 36–69; Wigmore, *Anglo-American System of Evidence*, IX, 535, 539–546, 571–577.

of matters which are value-neutral—as that insurance agents' commissions are large enough in fact to account for a substantial part of the cost of insurance. Or official notice may be taken of values commonly held in the community—as that insurance is a useful and almost necessary device to break the impact of unforeseen and otherwise shattering loss. From such premises a legislature might reasonably conclude that there is a public interest in regulating fairness of insurance rates, and hence an auxiliary public interest in regulating insurance agents' commissions. To spell out even so simple a chain of propositions as this is to emphasize that assumptions of fact and judgments of value are woven inextricably together in making public policy, and to suggest that the question posed by the law's criterion for legitimizing official notice is of high practical pertinence: Should a given matter of fact be taken to be so far beyond reasonable dispute by men knowledgeable in the field as to warrant accepting it without taking evidence? The historian will not examine legal operations long before he learns how much that is questionable in fact is treated as unquestionable, and how much light is cast on the working realities of the law if one measures them against the law's formal test for valid official notice.[67] The legitimate and the (usually unacknowledged) bastard uses of official notice can offer revealing insights for the historian of ideas, of common culture, of interest perception and conflict, and of the habit, custom, and inertia which form great parts of the web of social existence.

308

     e. The law developed a considerable armory of weapons by which to make itself felt, including judgments for damages, penal sentences carrying fines or terms in jail, decrees enjoining specified conduct or compelling specified conduct, orders creating a lien or attachment on particular assets, findings or orders subjecting individuals to undesired publicity, licenses conditioning access to desired activity. From the ways in which particular sanctions hurt or

67. Compare the majority and dissenting opinions in O'Gorman and Young, Inc. v. Hartford Fire Insurance Co., 282 U.S. 251 (1931); see Henry Wolf Bikle, "Judicial Determination of Questions of Fact Affecting the Constitutional Validity of Legislative Action," *Harvard Law Review*, 38 (1924), 1, 6–9, 11–16, 18–19, 21–22.

reward, from the different interests to which particular sanctions are adapted, the historian can draw evidence of cause-effect relations between law and life outside law, or at least such cause-effect relations as men perceive or believe in, as well as helping himself to define specific values pursued through law. Thus, mechanics liens provide a relatively early nineteenth-century legislative development encouraging the supply of labor. Decrees commanding specific performance of contracts for the sale or purchase of land tell something of the central place of land as a trade commodity in the eighteenth and nineteenth centuries. The growth and abuse of court injunctions against the activities of labor unions, and the legislation which followed to limit injunctions in labor disputes, tell of the critical significance of delay when men of little means contest with men of greater financial staying power. Multiplication of liens and of occupational licensing requirements helps to measure the realities and fictions of competitive markets, and the rise of organized pressure groups confronting legislatures. The turn in consumer-protection efforts, from nineteenth-century reliance on private damages actions or criminal prosecutions before judge and jury to twentieth-century reliance on administrative rules and cease and desist orders, responds to an increased disparity of bargaining power in modern markets; the felt need of more expertness in regulation, and the loss of faith that private interest would provide a sufficient dynamic for action to protect diffuse social interests. Altogether, the remedies or sanctions aspect of the law offers historians a wide range of insights into the law's relations with society. For choice of remedies required both policy-makers and those with interests to press upon the policy-makers to translate general wants and desires and general notions of how to proceed into particular allocations of benefits and burdens and particular procedures. What was done about remedies thus might supply useful supplements or correctives to often vaguer evidence of substantive goals.[68]

309

68. Henry W. Farnam, *Chapters in the History of Social Legislation in the United States to 1860* (Washington, 1938), chaps. xi, xvii, xx; Ernest Freund, *Administrative Powers over Persons and Property* (Chicago, 1928), chap. vii, and Part II, and *Legislative Regulation* (New York, 1932), Parts IV and V.

3. Legal agencies developed distinctive working characteristics, even though their outputs overlapped. There were legislative, executive or administrative, and judicial aspects to the work of legislatures, executive and administrative offices and courts. But, whatever their output, legislatures did their work in ways characteristically different from those of courts or administrators, and judges and executive or administrative officers showed different working styles from legislators, and from each other. Agencies differed in working personality partly because they differed in equipment and partly because they differed in the expectations which prevailing opinion developed toward them. For example, the legislature was treated as properly open to the direct approaches of interest groups in ways considered improper for approaching courts. Our tradition linked lobbies and legislators and separated lobbies and judges. The difference was partly traceable to the fact that the legislature held the power of the purse, which invited a broad range of interest approaches. Judges held the power to determine how the law should be applied to particular persons, which invited caution against approach by outside interests. Entwined with these differences was the fact that groups found the legislature their natural place of resort, because of its representative character; only individuals or small groups usually sought out courts, because technical specialization tended to insulate judges from group pressures and concerns. Given the fact that agencies developed different functional personalities, historians should be alert to exploit these differences for such evidence as they give of the law's roles in society.[69] Let us consider three aspects of the functional characteristics of agency processes which may be useful to historical inquiry.

a. There are often material differences between what men ask and strive to get out of law and what they get; the law's product may be more or less than the claims pressed upon it, and the results of legal operations may prove different from what was foreseen by anyone who set legal processes in motion.

The distinctive procedures of legal agencies tend to create particular types of evidence for comparing input and output in legal

69. Hurst, *The Growth of American Law*, chaps. iii, ix, xi, xiii, xiv.

operations. A statute was once a bill; comparison of the introduced bill—and possibly also of amendments introduced in course of consideration—with the measure finally enacted or voted down may help to identify interests active in seeking legislation and to assess the extent to which the legislative process mediates them or channels their energies. Among all agencies, the legislature holds the broadest powers of investigation, and legislative hearings provide a spotlighted arena for the play of interest groups as well as arming legislators with the sanctions of publicity. Both the promise and threat of legislative action generate widespread response witnessed in unofficial documents—in news accounts, trade journals, investment advisers' publications, trade association records, institutional advertising, and fugitive pamphlets. Matching what appears in the statute books against what shows up in legislative hearings and committee reports and in unofficial documents may suggest quite different readings of events from those based upon the formal record alone. For example, twentieth-century state statutes multiplied occupational licensing requirements in the name of protecting public safety or assuring honest and capable service. The historian could read in these developments evidence of increased division of labor, specialization, and interdependence in the country's way of life. Another picture emerged from records of lobbyists' appearances, legislative reports, an occasional governor's veto, and from trade group journals or publications—a picture of fence-me-in pressures to limit competition within the favored groups. In this context, the growth of occupational licensing laws must be reckoned with in appraising the vitality of markets as instruments of social control.[70]

Effective tradition kept policy issues before courts more within the bounds of official records than was true with matters pressed on

---

70. Church of the Holy Trinity v. United States, 143 U.S. 457 (1892); Jewell-LaSalle Realty Co. v. Buck, 283 U.S. 202, 206 (1931); Bedno v. Fast, 6 Wis. 2d 471, 476–477, 95 N.W. 2d 396, 399 (1959); Note: "Non-Legislative Intent as an Aid to Statutory Interpretation," *Columbia Law Review*, 49 (1949), 676; Julius Cohen, "Hearings on a Bill: Legislative Folklore," *Minnesota Law Review*, 37 (1952), 34; Julius Cohen and Reginald A. H. Robson, "The Lawyer and the Legislative Hearing Process," *Nebraska Law Review*, 33 (1954), 523.

legislatures. Thus, to compare input and output in the judicial process the historian must usually work by matching litigants' pleadings against what courts decree, or by noting devices by which judicial opinions extend or restrict the impetus they give to public policy. Most readily available is the evidence offered by judges' techniques in writing opinions. Judges and legal commentators familiarly distinguish between holding and dictum. The distinction is between what an opinion says that is necessary to sustain the decision rendered, and what it says that is broader than, or perhaps even irrelevant to what the judges must say to dispose of the case. Dicta can give law a push in one direction rather than another. Yet, being by definition unnecessary to the decision in hand, dicta can be treated as exploratory and readily disavowed. On the other hand, the holding-dictum distinction is a reminder that there is a sobering responsibility about making real decisions which may not attach to announcing hypothetical doctrine. Thus, legal historians need skill in separating out holding from dictum, both to detect all that court opinions reveal about policy-making and also to make realistic assessment of judicial roles by checking what judges say against what they do. Analogous problems and opportunities exist where courts declare alternative grounds of decision.[71]

Another revealing device in judicial opinions is the use of presumptions of policy (to be distinguished from presumptions of fact incident to applying law) governing the courts' treatment of legislative action. These presumptions of policy are of two principal types. One type is the presumption of the constitutionality of statutes. The other embraces rules for interpreting statutes. When courts presume that an economic regulatory statute is constitutional, they cast on the attacker of the statute a heavy burden of proof; the attacker must establish either that the legislators could not reasonably find facts to exist creating the problem with which the statute purports to deal, or that they could not reasonably determine that the statute represents a socially acceptable value or a means rationally calculated to achieve that value. Insofar as this presumption actually works to limit judges' interventions in leg-

312

71. Karl N. Llewellyn, *The Bramble Bush* (New York, 1951), pp. 45-49, 66-69.

islative policy-making, it both limits the bearing of judicial decisions upon the merits of public issues and enlarges the scope for
conflict of interests in the legislative arena. Thus when a court holds
constitutional a statute allowing makers or distributors of goods to
fix and enforce resale prices for the goods, the court is not itself
deciding the social desirability of resale price maintenance, but in
practical effect leaving more room for lobbies of small retailers to
seek legal protection from the legislature against chain competition.[72] Judge-made rules of statutory interpretation, on the other
hand, probably have operated for the most part to limit the effective scope of legislative policy-making in behalf of values preferred
by the judges. It would be hard to make out a case for this generalization from the avowed terms of the courts' canons of construction, which invariably claimed legitimacy as fulfilling the most   313
likely legislative intention. If, however, one compared the kinds of
situations in which courts applied the rule of strict construction of
penal statutes and those in which they did not, their behavior suggested that judicial evaluations were being imposed on the policy
decisions that the legislature had made in the first instance. In the
field of penal statutes regulating economic activity, courts often
applied restrictive interpretation where the likelihood was that the
statute responded to pressures from some lobby focused on the
pocketbook gains of its members (as under statutes regulating access to occupations). In contrast, the strict construction rule was
generally not applied, or not mentioned, and a sympathetically expansive interpretation given to legislation which protected moral
interests (as with regulations against obscene entertainment) or interests shared by broad, diffuse groups, such as consumers.[73] There
were crosscurrents, therefore, in the courts' response to the prac-

72. Paul Freund, *On Understanding the Supreme Court* (Boston, 1949), pp. 50–51, 58–
65, 88–107; *cf.* Note: "The Presumption of Constitutionality Reconsidered," *Columbia
Law Review*, 36 (1936), 283; Note: "The Presentation of Facts Underlying the Constitutionality of Statutes," *Harvard Law Review*, 49 (1936), 631.

73. James M. Landis, "A Note on Statutory Interpretation," *Harvard Law Review*, 43
(1930), 886; Hall, "Strict or Liberal Construction of Penal Statutes," 548; Harry W.
Jones, "Statutory Doubts and Legislative Intention," *Columbia Law Review*, 40 (1940),
957; Felix Frankfurter, "Some Reflections on the Reading of Statutes," *Columbia Law
Review*, 47 (1947), 527.

tical pressures behind legislation. The practical effect of the presumption of constitutionality was to allow much scope for the legislative process to strike balances between competing selfish interests; the practical effect of some rules of statutory construction was to allow courts to take back some of this legislative freedom without acknowledging what they were doing.

Comparison of input and output is no less important for the historian as to law made by executive or administrative offices than as to statute or judge-made law. But there are usually greater difficulties in getting access to the source materials which will allow the comparison. Difficulties lie partly in the specialization and sometimes the highly technical character of executive or administrative law-making. These elements have meant that less unofficial publication has come out of executive or administrative than out of legislative policy-making, and that the researcher needs to acquire more specialized skill to deal with the subject matter. Moreover, executive and administrative offices—staffed by political appointees surrounded by civil service cadres—did not operate as much in public view as popularly elected assemblies. On the other hand, even well into the twentieth century they had not typically developed traditions of confining their business within formal procedural bounds comparable to those observed by courts. These factors promoted both considerable privacy and considerable informality in executive and administrative policy-making. The researcher in these fields must depend to an uncommon degree on interviews and on access to letter files, and in either case was likely to encounter less than enthusiastic response from the agencies. In addition, the further back in time he pushed his study, the less likely that either key persons or key files still existed. Published legislative hearings and investigative reports could make good some, but not many, of these deficiencies. Though asking questions about how the executive was spending public money was a classic prerogative of the legislative branch, legislators (and especially state legislators) failed consistently to pursue this function or to plow sufficient resources into it. Executive and administrative law-making procedures did not highlight the background pressures upon agencies as distinguished from legislatures, and generally did not include analogies to the holding–dictum distinction or the presumptions of policy which helped in comparing the determinants and end-products of judicial findings. In sum, the relatively withdrawn character of executive-administrative law-making and the diversity and relative informality of procedures in these areas meant that study must be tailored to the particular activity of particular agencies.[74]

b. Historical study is an especially realistic mode of studying legal processes at work, because typically they work through time. The costs of putting them in operation (costs not only of interest conflict, but also of inertia, and costs imposed on mind, energy, and pocketbooks by the law's insistence that facts and choices be brought to definition, deliberation, and some degree of formal resolution) plus the institutional toughness (the continued availability) of legal processes mean that the law's workings usually build up chains of events before formal legal action commences. The construction of these chains of events not only constitutes a prime reality of legal-social order, but also provides the historian with good opportunities to see what is going on.

315

The legislative process normally moves through an accumulation of pressures and effort. Legislation which marks any considerable change or new direction in policy will not usually have grown out of the immediate circumstances of its passage. Probably in the background is a record of memorials or petitions, bills introduced without success over some years, legislative hearings, committee reports, perhaps some limited or faltering enactments. Such a background exists, for example, for the Wagner Act which cast the protection of federal law around union organization and collective bargaining. It would be a shallow judgment to assign that legislation simply to the pressures playing on public policy in 1933–1935 without allowances for a prior generation of struggle over labor's legal status.[75] Care is needed to read a legislative record lying be-

74. Frank E. Cooper, *State Administrative Law* (Indianapolis, 1965), I, chap. iii; Davis, *Discretionary Justice*, pp. 9–26.

75. Stephen K. Bailey, *Congress Makes a Law* (New York, 1905), chap. i; Lawrence W. Chamberlain, *The President, Congress and Legislation* (New York, 1946), chaps. i, xii.

hind the statute book, for much tactical maneuvering is likely to have gone into making it. A good deal of the requisite practical caution is embodied in the rules and practices of courts in using legislative history in the interpretation of statutes. Thus a court will give much weight to what it finds in reports of committees which considered the bill that became the statute, and to remarks on the floor by legislators who were in charge of debate or were members of the committee from which the bill came, or sponsors of floor amendments. The court will use such material to help interpret not only the general purpose but also detailed provisions of the act. In contrast, courts will use statements made in legislative hearings or remarks on the floor by legislators not on the committee or in charge of debate only to show the general purposes of legislation or the general circumstances of the times out of which it came. The distinction is between generalists and specialists on the bill, and between those who have official responsibility for the bill and those who speak for private partisan interest; to serve both credibility and integrity in statutory interpretation, the judges will ordinarily draw for detailed guidance only on the official specialists. Even within these bounds there may be cause for skepticism in assessing the record of the legislature's consideration of a bill. Legislator-specialists may manufacture legislative history (by planted questions and planned answers) to try to establish points which they did not deem it prudent to write openly into the bill. Where the legislative record is not marked by such contrivances, it is nevertheless likely to show the ambiguity natural to a bustling, rough-and-tumble, often opportunistic process. Legislative silences or failures to act are particularly ambiguous. Thus the legislature may give short shrift to bills introduced over the years to change a controversial interpretation of a statute by the courts. Such a record offers some circumstantial evidence that the legislature approved the court's reading of its handiwork. But, without more evidence, that record may indicate only that amending bills lost out in the constant competition for time on crowded calendars, or that the particular facet of the statute presented by the court's interpretation was not one which concerned a broad enough spectrum of inter-

316

ested parties to muster the group pressure required to overcome the normal inertia of the legislative process.[76] There is no formula for resolving such doubts about the legislative record. But the doubts do not remove the reality, that legislation (or, often, the want of legislation) typically has behind it a record of policy-making activity which demands attention. The researcher needs to cultivate sophistication in doubting the record and also in reading it in light of his doubts.

Sequential growth of public policy appears also through law made by the accumulation of judicial decisions. From about 1810 to 1890 the courts' contributions were largely in the form of common law—public policy hammered out in lawsuits by the action simply of judges. From the late nineteenth century on legislatures and their executive or administrative delegates took over the principal business of declaring public policy, but courts continued to make substantial contributions in interpreting statutes and administrative regulations.[77] Judge-made law showed chains of development partly because we valued reasonably assured precedent; *stare decisis* had force both at common law and in decisions interpreting statutes. Also, proceeding as it did only on the initiative of suitors, law-making by litigation had no existence except by the accretion of particular contests. Certain working characteristics appeared in the processes of making public policy through the accumulation of court decisions. With different degrees of learning, judges and lawyers shared the task and tradition of inducing generalizations of policy from particular rulings. Their preoccupation with this job produced a greater concern with articulation and symmetry of general ideas than marked the legislative process. This bias in judicial law-making bred more specialized, professional expression of policy than showed itself in much legislation; it bred, too, a greater

317

76. United States v. St. Paul, Minnesota & Manitoba Railway Co., 247 U.S. 310 (1918); Girouard v. United States, 328 U.S. 61 (1946); Learned Hand, circ., j., dissenting in United States v. Ryan, 225 F. 2d 417, 426 (2d Cir. Ct. App. 1955); *cf.* Robert H. Jackson, "The Meaning of Statutes," *American Bar Association Journal*, 34 (1948), 535, and Jackson, J., concurring, in United States v. Public Utilities Commission of California, 345 U.S. 295, 219 (1953).

77. Hurst, *Law and Social Process*, pp. 139–140; Roscoe Pound, *The Formative Era in American Law* (Boston, 1938), *passim*.

tendency than in statute law for concepts to take on a life of their own, affecting decisions; and it bred a use of fictions and artful distinctions of fact or doctrine designed to keep the appearance of symmetry and stability, beyond any counterparts in legislation. Judge-made law was also subject to accidents of litigation and to limitations built into procedure by the adversary presentation of issues through advocates paid by the suitors; human affairs did not always cast up the right litigants with the most appropriate issue for a rounded growth of doctrine, and the advantage in pushing policy one way rather than another might lie with the litigant who had the longer purse.[78] The course of the common law concerning private property rights shows various of these peculiar attributes of litigious law-making. Courts built on the concept of fee simple title as a legally protected relation to the profit-making potentialities of land, to protect an expanding range of other profitable relationships in an economy marked by increasing division of labor —giving protection against private interference with contract, against unfair methods of competition, against pirating of trade-names and trademarks. The formal appeal of concepts sometimes prevailed over the dictates of factual reality; thus, courts borrowed the law which protected possession in the captor of a wild animal, to protect the landowner who first drilled a well and drew oil and gas from beneath his neighbor's land as well as his own. It was in the context of a simple agricultural economy that some courts first decided that an effective mortgage could not be given on assets (growing crops) which the mortgagor did not yet have in possession when he executed the mortgage. The timing of the question plagued with uncertainty later efforts to create after-acquired property clauses to serve more sophisticated systems of credit for building and operating railroads. The sequences in which public policy emerged from judicial decisions thus offered mixtures of patterned ideas, doctrinal confusion or fictions, and accidents of timing or of

318

78. Patterson, *Jurisprudence*, pp. 292–294, 416–417, 560, 579–594. *Cf.* Thurman Arnold, "Trial by Combat and the New Deal," *Harvard Law Review*, 47 (1934), 913; Felix Frankfurter and Henry M. Hart, Jr., "The Business of the Supreme Court at October Term, 1934," *Harvard Law Review*, 49 (1935), 68.

litigants' resources, which peculiarly taxed the historian's capacity —as they taxed the judge's capacity—to extract valid generalizations from what were often opposed or at least ambiguous particulars.[79]

The specialization of much executive and administrative activity brings focused attention to the job, both among public officers and among immediately affected private interests, which may produce distinctive kinds of evidence of sequences of policy-making. Such agencies do a lot of rule-making, from the course of which significant continuities and shifts in values and in means chosen to effect values may appear. They issue handbooks to their field agents, and publish advice or instructions to those whom they regulate. The governing statutes may equip them with advisory committees drawn from the particular publics they affect; further leads to the course of policy-making may turn up in records of the interactions between the agency and such statutory advisers. The legislature is likely to pay only sporadic attention to the content of the policy built up by its delegates over the years, but at least it must regularly review the appropriations it gives them, and appropriations hearings may help to define the lines which the law is taking. Two characteristics are likely to be specially marked in the recorded evidence of administrative or executive law-making—tenacious institutional precedents or traditions (agency policy), and close and growing involvement in the goals and operating problems of the immediately affected interest, at least if that interest is itself organized into disciplined and technically focused units or groups.[80]

319

c. The course of public policy exists not only in sequence, but also in context; sequence and context together make up the time dimension of law. We need to look for evidence of the course

79. Lon L. Fuller, "American Legal Realism," *University of Pennsylvania Law Review*, 82 (1934), 429; Roscoe Pound, "The Economic Interpretation and the Law of Torts," *Harvard Law Review*, 53 (1940), 365; Francis Lynde Stetson, "Preparation of Corporate Bonds, Mortgages, Collateral Trusts and Debenture Indentures," in *Some Legal Phases of Corporate Financing, Reorganization and Regulation* (New York, 1930), pp. 2-13.

80. Marver H. Bernstein, *Regulating Business by Independent Commission* (Princeton, 1955), chaps. vi, viii; Louis M. Kohlmeier, Jr., *The Regulators* (New York, 1969), *passim*; James M. Landis, *The Administrative Process* (New Haven, 1938), chaps. ii, iii; Scheiber, *Ohio Canal Era*, chaps. ii, iii, vii.

of policy horizontally as well as vertically—that is, in functionally analogous or related areas of legal action, as well as in direct lines to particular agencies, programs, or centers of interest. There are both cultural and structural reasons which make it sensible to trace public policy in the horizontal plane. The separation of powers means that related policy activity may be going on at the same time in legislative, executive, or judicial agencies of the same sovereignty. Federalism means that related policy action may be going on at the same time in the central and the state governments and among the states. Within states, the division of labor between state and local governments adds another sector to the context of law-making. In addition to these structural considerations two working characteristics of our legal system require attention to the horizontal plane of policy. The threshold costs of putting legal processes in motion tend to make men approach law with particular problems and along lines of particular pressures; the costs do not encourage broad-scale codification. This economic aspect of legal operations has been powerfully reinforced by a bastard pragmatism, putting a premium on narrow "practicality," bred deep into our approaches to the law out of eighteenth- and nineteenth-century experience of a rush of change, scarce resources, and needs to improvise. This often astigmatically "practical" approach meant that experience taught us to deal with public policy at the points of most immediate pressure only. We often made policy piecemeal and in disconnected efforts and areas, where a more rational practicality would have told us to link our efforts, fill in gaps, and move on a broad front.[81]

Horizontal or parallel growth of public policy was more obvious in common law than in legislation. The courts' tradition included the idea that doctrine adopted in any common law jurisdiction was presumptively applicable in any other; the reported decisions of a state's own courts of course prevailed over those from courts of another state, but otherwise out-of-state cases were treated as also entitled to the respect enjoined by the principle *stare decisis*. The

81. Oliver Wendell Holmes, Jr., *Collected Legal Papers* (New York, 1921), pp. 27, 186, 187.

reach of particular decisions was further extended because common law courts were accustomed to reasoning from precedents by analogy—as, for example, equity courts enlarged the idea of the real estate mortgage to build forms of security for railroad financing, or borrowed ideas from the law of trusts to create some fiduciary obligations of corporate management to shareholders. Indeed, courts carried their analogical style over to link judge-made with statute-made policy, when they ruled that proof of violation of a penal statute might suffice to make the actor civilly liable for negligence according to the common law standard of care.[82]

Compared with the courts' overt borrowings of policy made in one area of social relations to apply in another, the statutory record was more veiled; traditions of legislative operations included no counterpart in volume or continuity to the practice of judicial opinion writing. Yet from the first years of the nation the states borrowed much legislation from each other. Preoccupied with the economy more than with the law, men were impatient of the time costs of policy-making, and grasped at readymade formulas. Moreover, this was a mobile population. Those who settled a new state looked back to the older ones from which they came, when they wanted new laws on corporations, or insurance, or the property rights of married women. Federalism played its part in the states' imitation of each other's statutes. For one thing, the successful creation of a continental federalism meant that over much of our history we saw new sanctions go through phases of growth analogous to those which had already left their marks on older regions. These differences in timing allowed policy-makers to adapt earlier experience to later pressures for legislation. Such a movement showed itself through the country in successive adoptions of the administrative process to meet problems connected with the rise of industry and cities. An occasional impetus to imitation in state law-making was competition. Thus a number of other states copied New Jer-

---

82. E. Merrick Dodd, Jr., "For Whom Are Corporate Managers Trustees," *Harvard Law Review*, 45 (1932), 1145; Albert Kocourek and Harold Koven, "Renovation of the Common Law Through Stare Decisis," *Illinois Law Review*, 29 (1945), 971; Clarence Morris, "The Relation of Criminal Statutes to Tort Liability," *Harvard Law Review*, 46 (1933), 453.

sey's end-of-nineteenth-century liberal incorporation acts in bids for charter business and the fees it would bring. Finally, in the twentieth century the breadth of commercial markets developed under protection of the commerce clause of the Federal Constitution made it functional to introduce calculated uniformity—as by the Uniform Commercial Code—in state statute law affecting titles to personal property and creation of instruments of credit.[83]

Within a given state the legislature normally responded only to particular pressures or problems. Thus statutory treatment of functionally similar or related matters was more likely to turn up at different times and under different headings, than to be provided in a single comprehensive effort. A rudimentary statutory law of public utilities was hammered out in this fashion in the days of special corporate charters, one company at a time. Protection of consumers against fraud or against dangerous goods or incompetent service grew by accumulation of disjointed items in the nineteenth century. Social values and social tensions involved in management-labor relations were dealt with piecemeal, in separate legislation about factory safety, labor liens, wage collection, injunctions in labor disputes, collective bargaining, and unemployment compensation.[84] Courts in effect recognized this fragmented style of legislative policy-making in various rules for handling statutes which came into litigation. For example, statutes *in pari materia* (separate statutes dealing with related subject matter) should be construed together or in harmony, so far as possible; judicial reading might thus supply the generalizations of principle which statutory texts did not.[85] Again: an economic regulatory statute was sometimes challenged as violating the equal protection of the

322

83. E. Merrick Dodd, Jr., "Statutory Developments in Business Corporation Law, 1886–1936," *Harvard Law Review*, 50 (1936), 27, 34, 43, 44; Frank E. Horack, Jr., "The Common Law of Legislation," *Iowa Law Review*, 23 (1937), 41; Hurst, *Law and the Conditions of Freedom*, p. 10; Frederic J. Stimson, *American Statute Law* (Boston, 1886, 1892), *passim; cf.* Draper v. Emerson, 22 Wis. 147 (1859); Febock v. Jefferson County, 219 Wis. 154, 262 N.W. 588 (1935).

84. Freund, *Standards of American Legislation*, chap. iii; Hurst, *Law and Social Process*, pp. 93–102, and Hurst, *Law and Economic Growth*, pp. 173, 548–559, 561–565.

85. J. G. Sutherland, *Statutes and Statutory Construction*, ed. Frank E. Horack, Jr. (Chicago, 1943), II, 529.

laws, because its regulations treated only part of the potential problem area. The courts here normally applied the presumption of constitutionality and ruled that the legislature need not grapple with all dimensions of a social problem at once; until the contrary was shown, the court would presume that the legislature had some rational ground for singling out that part of the whole with which it had dealt. This doctrine sensibly recognized that policy-makers needed room to deliberate and test and learn by experience. Measured in the context of many cases, the doctrine also conveyed wry realism about the incurable tendency of legislators to handle only what they had to at the moment.[86] In handling questions both of constitutionality and interpretation courts thus caution the legal historian that he should expect to find broad trends of statutory policy ordinarily evidenced only in separate, formally unconnected patches of legislation.

323

When we turn to executive or administrative law-making, specialization of experience if not of knowledge in these agencies again determines what their processes yield for legal history. Specialization limits borrowing or functional parallels among offices dealing with different areas of social relations, whether within one sovereignty or among different sovereigns. On the other hand, specialization within any given area of service or regulation tends to promote borrowing or parallel responses within the specialized area. Thus United States legal history includes the development of relatively coherent and sustained bodies of standards, rules, and regulatory procedures among at least some of the states in particular fields such as the law dealing with insurance, the issue and sale of corporate securities, or public utilities.[87] There have been great variations in quality and integrity of performance among offices charged with like responsibilities in different states, and between federal and state offices; these variations are part of the history, too,

---

86. Williamson v. Lee Optical of Oklahoma, 348 U.S. 483, 487–488 (1955); State v. Whitcom, 122 Wis. 110, 114, 99 N.W. 468, 469 (1904).

87. Martin G. Glaeser, *Public Utilities in American Capitalism* (New York, 1957), pp. 113, 115–116, 118–119; Richard W. Jennings, "The Role of the States in Corporate Regulation and Investor Protection," *Law and Contemporary Problems*, 23 (1958), 193, 208–229; Spencer L. Kimball, *Insurance and Public Policy* (Madison, 1960), p. 174.

and awareness of them adds a realistic dimension in appraising the more successful agencies. In sum, though there is little relation in policy growth among executive or administrative offices operating in different sectors of social relations, there is a good deal of policy history to be studied by comparing agencies of like subject matter jurisdiction working within the variety provided by our federal system.

324   II. The Desirable and the Practicable Subject Matter of Legal History

HAVING looked at types of available evidence for the roles of the law, we can return, better equipped, to ask what should be the principal subject matter of legal history. The clearest answers point to two sectors. There is a third sector which cannot be ignored, but in which problems of proof severely limit what we can hope to establish. Legal history should tell of (1) the structure and functions of legal agencies and (2) the uses of law in defining values concerning ends and means in social institutions other than law, in social transactions which law affects, and in the content of individual life affected by law. In addition legal history should describe, if it can, (3) the effects of law on the rest of life, and of the rest of life on law. This third category would include assessing not only the working realities of law-declared values and procedures, but also the impact on legal processes of values and procedures derived from outside the law. From the legal system's own formal records the legal historian can get enough material to develop the first two themes with some confidence. But the third area takes this inquiry beyond the law's own records and into mazes of informal data and multiplied cause-effect relations which should caution us to modest estimates of what we can expect to tell.

ROLES OF LEGAL AGENCIES

The core responsibility of legal historians is to tell the history of the principal legal agencies. For the existence and operations of these agencies have primarily determined the form, and largely the content, of the legal components of life in this society. In some societies the legal elements in social order have little separate expression; rather they appear as but one product or concern of institutions—family, kin group, priesthood, war band, or elders—which serve other functions as well. But even in its simpler stages society in the United States included sharply differentiated structures and processes of formal law-making, and this separate institutional identity of legal processes bulked large in our social experience. The law here put its own impress on affairs by its own means. This institutional division of labor is what gives distinctive reality to the social history of law in the United States.[88]

Legal history should take account of all principal types of federal and state legal agencies, legislative, executive, administrative, and judicial. It should also include the work of those agents in whom the legal system vests particular duties, privileges, or capacities for operating legal processes, though they exercise their functions only occasionally (as with constitution-making apparatus) or do not hold public office (as with most of the bar). Legal history should deal with the organization and functions of a wide range of legal agencies, simply because there has been a substantial division of labor among them—in large part they have done different jobs—and they have developed different ways of doing even similar jobs, with different consequences. To ask attention to a wide range of legal agents might seem to worry an obvious point, were it not that scholarship has exaggerated the judicial process at the expense

325

88. George Lee Haskins, *Law and Authority in Early Massachusetts* (New York, 1960), pp. 25, 43, 62, 77, 79, 136; Mark DeWolfe Howe, "The Sources and Nature of Law in Colonial Massachusetts," in George A. Billias, ed., *Law and Authority in Colonial America* (Barre, Mass., 1965), pp. 1, 15; Hurst, *The Growth of American Law*, passim, and Hurst, *Law and Social Process*, pp. 3–6; *cf.* E. Adamson Hoebel, *The Law of Primitive Man* (Cambridge, 1954), chaps. ii, xi.

of other principal forms of law-making. Apart from neglecting key areas of legal process because courts figure little in them, as in the spending power of legislatures, this bias has distorted estimates of the role of the courts themselves. The distortion is most likely to consist in exaggerating the relative importance of judges' contributions; the scholar does not locate the bulk of the law of legislative investigations, for example, if he looks only at the decisions, and not at legislative practice. But the distortion may also deny the judges full credit for the special impact they do have. Thus, unless we take account of the loose way in which state legislation sanctioned wider discretion in corporate management *vis-à-vis* shareholders after 1890, we shall not fairly estimate the contributions of judge-made law in imposing some fiduciary standards on management. Legal historians need, first, to direct their studies more outside the courts, and, second, when they focus on courts to measure what courts do more closely against related work of other agencies.[89]

Division of labor among legal agencies is embodied in formal differences in organization and authority; state constitutions vest what they designate as "legislative" power in an agency structurally different from that of the courts in which they vest "judicial" power. It is familiar wisdom that, despite these formal divisions, there is considerable sharing of types of legal output among all major agencies; legislative-type action (policy generalization), for example, is taken by legislatures (in statutes), courts (in common law), and executive or administrative offices (by rules made under statutory delegation, or through patterns of decision analogous to the courts' common law). However, these familiar features do not exhaust all aspects of the division of labor among agencies. Agencies have tended to perform different substantive services for the social order beyond the distinctions made by formal organization. The legislature became the prime point of intake for broadly felt

89. Jacob L. Bernheim and Clara Penniman, "A Functional Analysis of Wisconsin Public Expenditures," *Wisconsin Law Review* (1948) 528; Fenno, *The Power of the Purse*, chaps. vii, viii; George David Hornstein, *Corporation Law and Practice* (St. Paul, 1959), I, 472–481, 528, 541, 647; Hurst, *The Growth of American Law*, pp. 24–26, 71–74, 85–86; Yellin v. United States, 374 U.S. 109 (1963).

wants or needs pressed upon the law, the prime ratifier of policy generalizations, the prime agency to legitimize public and private organized effort (whether by chartering municipal or business corporations or sanctioning other kinds of associations), the prime official agency to allocate scarce economic resources (through its powers to tax and spend, borrow on public credit, and control the money supply). The offices of our chief executives emerged as pre-eminent sources of program-making, of quick response to public security emergencies, and of mobilization of public opinion against civic apathy or despair. The general executive and administrative establishment provided the most important official channels for moving scientific and technical knowledge into community application, and for more or less adequate representation of diffuse interests (as of consumers) challenged or exploited by aggressive special interests. As public and private organization of power has become increasingly concentrated, the courts mounted in importance as the best forums open to the claims of individuals and small groups. Functional differences sharpened among levels of government. Care of the vitality and integrity of national markets fell more and more to the central government, responding to a greater scale of private operations, to shifts in the balance of power between public and private centers with which states could not cope, and to demands on the public purse beyond the reach of state taxing ability. Within the states like pressures produced analogous tendencies to shift the definition and enforcement of public policy standards from local governments to the capital city. It was broadly characteristic in the nation's experience that factors of scale thus affected the allocation of tasks among legal agencies.[90]

327

Apart from the emergence of different functional roles, differences in the timing with which roles were played significantly affected the shares which the various legal agencies had in events. Expansion of corporate chartering went on with more cost and under more public suspicion than was necessary, because legisla-

90. Hurst, *Law and Social Process*, pp. 24–25, 36–41, 47, 51, 72, 95–96, 136, 207, 315, 320, 324; Edward W. Weidner, "Decision-Making in a Federal System," in Arthur W. MacMahon ed., *Federalism, Mature and Emergent* (New York, 1955), p. 363.

tures lagged in assuming their proper generalizing job and proceeded still by special charters long after the business community's
acceptance of the corporate device as a matter-of-fact instrument.[91]
Inertia, slow perception of fast-moving business change, and ignorance of what to do about it figured in Congress's failure to
generalize policy fast and effectively concerning the concentration
of private industrial and financial power; within the context of
lagging and vague legislation the United States Supreme Court
thus became the principal maker of antitrust policy.[92] Inexperienced early-nineteenth-century state legislatures were unready to
declare policy on a broad scale, yet the expansion of population and
of private dealings demanded considerable legal adjustment, especially in market; hence we get a larger amount of judge-made
(common) law through the middle decades of the century than
thereafter, owing to the readier availability and greater professionalism of the courts.[93] An inheritance from disagreements with the
mother country was a deepseated distrust of executive power, an
attitude all the more readily continued within the relative simplicity of an agrarian country. The rise of the administrative process
thus had to wait upon pressures created by the growth of cities and
industry, so that it is not until well into the twentieth century that
executive-administrative action becomes an important part of legal
history in the states.[94] The unusual prominence of written constitutions in this legal system had diverse effects on the roles of agencies
and on the timing of their emergence, depending mainly on the
extent to which constitution-makers unwisely froze specific policies into constitutional form. Where constitutions declared general standards, whether in grant or limitation of official power,
legislatures and courts showed considerable ability to use their freedom to adapt their roles to changing facts of community life.

328

91. James Willard Hurst, *The Legitimacy of the Business Corporation* (Charlottesville,
1970), pp. 119, 131–138, 157.
92. Thurman W. Arnold, *The Folklore of Capitalism* (Garden City, N.Y., 1941), pp.
210–218; Edward S. Mason, *Economic Concentration and the Monopoly Problem* (Cambridge, 1957), pp. 23–32, 37–43; Standard Oil Co. v. United States, 221 U.S. 1, 69 (1911).
93. Hurst, *Law and the Conditions of Freedom*, pp. 13, 97.
94. *Ibid.*, pp. 8, 9.

Within the sweep of the commerce clause Congress found it possible steadily to enlarge the fostering and protective functions of federal legislation concerning interstate markets. Within the breadth of the 14th Amendment's due process clause the Supreme Court could enlarge its scrutiny of state legislation to an extent which opened the Justices to criticisms of tending to make themselves more of a superior legislative chamber than a court. On the other hand, highly specific constitutional language could materially delay or rechannel agency response to changing community needs. A conspicuous example was what happened to the purse power of state legislatures under stringent limits on state debt written into many state constitutions in the wake of mid-nineteenth-century fiscal extravagance. As legislatures tried to cope with rising demands for public services in the twentieth century, the unwise rigidity of such fiscal limits hindered response to community needs or else drove legislatures and courts into questionable fictions— such as borrowing through dummy corporations which did not in form produce debts of the state.[95] The influence of the timing of events is of course an aspect of affairs lying specially in the province of the historian. Timing is perhaps of special importance in affecting the impact of the law, which usually operates only with limited resources and on the margin of broader social currents.

329

Finally we should note that for a full-dimensioned treatment of the functional history of official agencies and processes, legal history must pay attention to the organization and operations of other institutions of social order. The wants and needs brought to bear on the law reflected a good deal of what men experienced as the strengths and limitations of other-than-legal ways of ordering their relationships. In their relevant realms, therefore, law and the market shared social functions, as did law and the family, law and the schools, law and the church, law and the organized processes of science and technology.[96] Such comparison of institutional roles

95. Felix Frankfurter, *The Commerce Clause under Marshall, Taney, and Waite* (Chapel Hill, 1937), *passim*; McCloskey, *The American Supreme Court*, pp. 127–135, 185–187; Loomis v. Callahan, 196 Wis. 518, 220 N.W. 816 (1928); State ex rel. Thomson v. Giessel, 267 Wis. 331, 65 N.W. 2d 529 (1954).

96. Robin M. Williams, Jr., *American Society* (New York, 1951), chaps. iv, vi, ix, xii, xiii.

leads naturally to defining the subject matter of legal history to include the full range of social values brought to some definition and resolution through law.

SOCIAL VALUES DEFINED IN LAW

What the law's formal records tell us about law in society is most obviously the structure and processes of legal agencies themselves. The next most conspicuous yield from these records is evidence of formally defined value judgments about ends and means in men's social relations and in the relations of individuals to groups, as well as a good deal of implicit or explicit evidence of how men perceived facts on which they erected these value judgments. Probably no social institution other than law produced such a range and volume of formally declared propositions about men's felt wants and needs and about ways to satisfy those wants and needs.

What legal records show on these counts is important, but also limited. We should carefully note the limitation. With considerable reliability legal records evidence a great body of value judgments and of judgments of facts seen as giving foundations and meaning to those value judgments. It is quite a different matter to ask whether these values were put into practice or how far the fact judgments involved were realistic. The values the law declares do not operate just because the law declares them. Concentrations or combinations in restraint of trade did not disappear because the Sherman Act condemned them and said that they should be visited with penalties.[97] What lawmakers perceive as facts do not exist simply because lawmakers believe they do. A public lands disposal policy designed to encourage grain farming did not mean that men could grow grain in soil suitable for growing trees, and applying the policy to unsuitable land only wasted timber or muddled decisions on what was truly at stake.[98] All that we take note of at this

97. *Staff Report of the Federal Trade Commission, Economic Report on Corporate Mergers* (Washington, 1969), pp. 29–37.
98. Hurst, *Law and Economic Growth*, pp. 66, 94–96, 98, 111, 125, 127, 435, 448, 599, 601, 602.

point is the evidence which legal records give of value judgments and the factual perceptions involved in them. The validity of these perceptions and the effects of these value judgments present a different order of problems of which the second section of this essay took note.

The variety of goals and contrivances men sought to effect with the law's help baffles reduction to any one neat pattern. This variety allows legal historians to pursue many particular themes. But its richness also challenges them to seek large organizing ideas, lest they miss realities which do not lie within narrow bounds. Without claiming exclusive merit for the pattern, let us consider two types of value problems and a third kind of valuation which affected how we handled the first two. Let us look at uses of law in United States society as these (1) dealt with creating and maintaining order (=meaning) in individual and group experience, (2) allocated scarce resources to obtain economic and non-economic satisfactions, (3) subjected particular actions under the foregoing headings to the constitutional ideal that all public and private power be employed responsibly, that is, legitimated by providing utility and justice.

331

1. Men made increasing use of the law to seek values of order. This effort was not just to obtain peace and safety against physical violence, though a basic element in our legal tradition was the idea that law should hold the legitimate monopoly of violence. Beyond this important but elementary proposition ranged much more diverse uses of law to affect the ways in which groups, and individuals in relation to groups or the society at large, structured experience and organized action. So regarded, the use of law to promote order becomes no less than part of man's constant effort to make meaning out of what otherwise would be formless and chaotic experience.[99]

Four major components of social experience weave together and overlap in the legal history of this search for order.

a. The legal historian has a particular concern with roles

99. Edmond N. Cahn, *The Sense of Injustice* (New York, 1949), pp. 51–123; Holmes, *Collected Legal Papers*, p. 248; Hurst, *Law and Social Process*, pp. 62–75, 137–152.

special to the state, compared with those of other social institutions, in pursuing values of individual and group existence. By definition this is not a query to be answered separately, but only relative to what the record shows of factors operating in addition to law. But the questions of the state's particular roles is not meaningless simply because it cannot be answered in isolation. For the record is clear that the country used law substantially to affect individuals, associations, and social transactions, and to affect them in some ways which had no counterparts in other institutions. Thus we used law for legitimating certain kinds of physical force, taxing and spending, creating corporations and franchises for action not open to the generality, setting and enforcing particular rules of procedure for official (and in some matters private) decision of disputes, and defining standards and rules of official and private behavior to be enforced through the state's agencies. Some of these activities had functional analogies in other institutions; in imperfectly competitive markets, for example, large business corporations could in effect tax their customers by pricing goods to yield funds for corporate investment. But only the government might use the tax collector. And only government might ultimately decide whether any given practical power in private hands should be sanctioned or protected by law.[100]

b. In different ways and degrees law entered into the organization and processes of other institutions of social order, including the market, the family, the church, and organized education and scientific and technical research. Law made only limited contributions to these institutions. Markets were mainly the product of businessmen's purposes, their invention of techniques of trade, distribution, finance, and association, and their customs and habits of dealing. In organized religion, doctrine, priestly status and hierarchy, allocation of resources between spiritual and secular concerns, and continuity in association were the products of churchmen and communicants and not of lawmen.

332

100. Jerome Hall, "Authority and the Law," in Carl J. Friedrich, ed., *Nomos I: Authority* (Cambridge, 1958), p. 58, and Talcott Parsons, "Authority, Legitimation, and Political Action," *ibid.*, 197; Hurst, *Law and Social Process*, pp. 5–17.

The other-than-legal sources of most of the content of other-than-legal institutions was primarily a matter of fact. The fact reflected the reality, that social experience was too diverse, the product of too great a variety of chances, calculations, customs and cumulated impacts, to derive from any one source.[101] But in some measure the limited impress of law on other institutions was the result of law-embodied policy. Through the nineteenth and twentieth centuries law fostered a large measure of autonomy in the market, in belief that both individuality and economic productivity gained if private will and energy had large scope. This policy was expressed in the common law presumption that all private agreements were socially acceptable and hence should be enforceable at law, until a challenger sustained the burden of proving good reason to the contrary. It was expressed, also, in legal limitations on public or private power which interfered with free flows of contract activity; thus the antitrust laws spoke against private combinations destructive of vital markets, while under the commerce clause the Supreme Court curbed barriers erected by states against interstate transactions.[102] So, too, the fact that churchmen and the faithful created most of the structure and activity of organized religion was partly the result of law-declared policy favoring separation of church and state, symbolized in Jefferson's Virginia Statute of Religious Liberty and in the First Amendment. The separation doctrine set a standard rather than a rule, leaving room for controversy and for change in its application. But at its core it sharply limited the state's impact on religious institutions; plainly, for example, the state might not pay the salaries of priests or ministers of private congregations, nor impose any oath of religious faith as a condition of voting or holding public office or gaining access to private occupations.[103]

333

101. Benjamin N. Cardozo, *The Nature of the Judicial Process* (New Haven, 1921), pp. 98–141; Holmes, *The Common Law*, p. 1, and Holmes, *Collected Legal Papers*, pp. 27, 186, 187.

102. Welton v. Missouri, 91 U.S. 275 (1875); United States v. Trenton Potteries Co., 273 U.S. 392 (1927); W. M. Bell Co. v. Emerson, 182 Wis. 433, 446–447, 196 N.W. 861, 866 (1924).

103. Mark DeWolfe Howe, *The Garden and the Wilderness* (Chicago, 1965), chaps. i, vi; Waltz v. Tax Commission of the City of New York, 90 S. Ct. 1409 (1970).

Altogether, legally declared limits on the law's intervention in other social institutions stand for one of the basic, pervasive policy themes in United States legal history—the persistent effort to distinguish between what is legitimately "public" and what is legitimately "private" interest, to allow and foster legal support of broad, shared concerns on the one hand, and on the other to guard the dignity and creativity involved in the individual's general claim to be let alone by his fellows.[104] History showed continuing and often severe tension between public and private values, partly because men were greedy for power, partly because reasonable distinctions between public and private concerns could not be divorced from their social context. The pressures of social context meant that lines would quite properly be redrawn from time to time with changing social relations. Thus, somewhat belatedly, in the mid-twentieth century the Supreme Court began to apply the presumption of constitutionality vigorously in favor of state economic regulatory legislation. In effect the Justices recognized that greater interlocking of cause and effect in the economy called for conceding broad discretion to legislators to enlarge definitions of what was of public concern and hence no longer within protected private autonomy.[105]

One area of the law's involvement with other social institutions warrants particular note, because it displayed the law's most distinctive concern with the general frame of social order. Our tradition assigned no more special role to law than that it should successfully assert the legitimate monopoly of violence.[106] Corollary to this assignment was the title to determine what forms of organized public and private power might exist, lest force be usurped or become spread abroad to an extent dangerous to good order. This concern brought law into the structure of social institutions which otherwise mostly derived from non-legal sources.

334

104. Boyd v. United States, 116 U.S. 616 (1886); Brandeis, J., dissenting, in Olmstead v. United States, 277 U.S. 438, 474–479 (1928).

105. Nebbia v. New York, 291 U.S. 502 (1934); Williamson v. Lee Optical of Oklahoma, 348 U.S. 483 (1955); note 72, above.

106. New York ex rel. Bryant v. Zimmerman, 278 U.S. 63 (1928); Hague v. C.I.O., 307 U.S. 496 (1939).

This concern found particular expression in the law's treatment of the corporation. The corporate device was not essential to bring men and assets together under a central decision-making power. But it proved so useful that between about 1850 and the 1920's it became the dominant form of institutional organization, most prominently for business, but also for religious congregations, philanthropic enterprises, research and educational foundations, trade associations and groups organized to advance almost any shared interest. Only the law could confer legally secure corporate status. The terms on which law offered that status, and the extent to which it wrote regulatory provisions into corporate charters, provide one useful measure over the years of prevailing social attitudes toward institutionalized private power. However, corporation law proved too limited a frame of reference within which to deal with all the problems which private organized power created as twentieth-century society moved into conditions of increasing interdependence of relations and increasing prominence of large-scale business corporations. The main emphasis of our constitutional tradition in the eighteenth and nineteenth centuries demanded responsibility in the use of official power. As private organized power grew, in the twentieth century public policy began to enlarge early precedents to insist that private power, too, must be constitutional—that it, like official power, must be responsible according to criteria not wholly in the control of the powerholders. This was a large theme in United States legal history, and one which after some seventy years of growth still lacked formulae adequate to the variety of relational problems with which it dealt. However, the theme could be seen emerging, for example, in antitrust law, in the expansion of the idea of public utilities and their regulation, in the protection and regulation of collective bargaining, in legislation limiting the discipline which automobile makers wielded over their franchised distributors, in statutory and administrative controls on organized stock exchanges, and in judge-made standards for the discipline of students by educational institutions. In proportion as decision-making power concentrated within other-than-legal institutions, so it seemed likely that measures would be taken in law to affect the

335

structure of those institutions, and especially their procedures for bringing their power to bear on individuals and small groups.[107]

Law became involved in some measure in the organization, procedures, and substantive activities of all the other major institutions of social order. But the extent of its intervention varied a great deal among institutions. In particular, law affected the market and related institutions of property more than it did other patterns of social relations.[108] Why this should be so posed questions for legal history, the answers to which might better define the positive capacities of legal processes, as well as their limitations.

c. Law entered into the order of individual lives, as well as that of institutions. It did so when the development of public health regulations and public investment in water supply and waste disposal protected the biological basis of life, when domestic relations law entered into the content and continuity of family relations, when compulsory school laws and government spending on optional education and on mental health related to personality development, when unemployment compensation and workmen's compensation legislation as well as public subsidies to medical care and public provision for old age insurance contributed to the economic framework within which individual and family life went on. The law's most sustained roles regarding the structure of individual life involved subsidy and service, rather than regulation.[109] Here legal history raises questions analogous to those suggested by the different degrees to which law was involved in the character of

107. Abram Chayes, "The Modern Corporation and the Rule of Law," in Edward S. Mason, ed., *The Corporation in Modern Society* (Cambridge, 1960), p. 25, and Earl Latham, "The Body Politic of the Corporation," in Mason, *The Corporation*, p. 218; Hurst, *The Legitimacy of the Business Corporation*, pp. 58–61, 90–105; Arthur S. Miller, "The Constitution and the Voluntary Association: Some Notes Toward a Theory," in J. Roland Pennock and John W. Chapman, eds., *Nomos XI: Voluntary Associations* (New York, 1969), p. 233.

108. Zechariah Chafee, Jr., "The Internal Affairs of Associations Not for Profit," *Harvard Law Review*, 43 (1930), 993; Pound, *Jurisprudence*, III, 353–373.

109. Arthur J. Altmeyer, *The Formative Years of Social Security* (Madison, 1966), chap. i; Howard W. Odum, "Public Welfare Activities," in President's Research Committee, *Recent Social Trends*, chap. xxiv; Charles E. Rosenberg, *The Cholera Years* (Chicago, 1962), chaps. xii, xiii. *Cf.* Stefan A. Riesenfeld, "The Formative Era of American Public Assistance Laws," *California Law Review*, 43 (1955), 175.

other social institutions. Probably the record will show a mixture of fact and of policy. In fact individual life experience included probably more intangible values arising out of relations which no external force could regulate than was true with institutions; law could not create or enforce affection, trust, gratitude, or unselfish sharing within a family.[110] But policy entered too. Our social tradition put high values on individuality, and incident to this, on privacy. The legal history of the United States shows continuing attention to drawing lines between what is properly of public concern and what is properly only of private concern. As social relations grew more intricate and interwoven, public policy found more matters to be of public concern than it once had. Perhaps individual privacy was less valued, or at least accepted as real, as the country moved into a highly urbanized, technically organized style of living. Yet the record did not run all one way. Separation of church and state continued to be a vital principle protective of privacy. On the whole the Court continued to watch jealously any invasions of the Fourth Amendment protection against unreasonable search and seizure. At the mid-twentieth century there were gathering signs of a tendency to narrow legal regulation of morals in situations (notably affecting sexual relations) where there were not clear effects on third persons. Law touched the sequence of individual experience at critical phases and in important respects. But it operated in this domain under specially durable constitutional principles against the state's intrusion into matters felt properly for governance by individuals as private beings.[111]

337

    d. When we examine uses of the law to help bring order into experience—and whether we focus on defining roles peculiar to the state, or on law's relations to other social institutions or to the structure of individual life—we have a special need to keep in mind the massive influence of inertia and drift. Talking about law as an instrument of order, in the broad sense in which this discus-

---

110. Sholberg v. Itynre, 264 Wis. 211, 58 N.W. 2d 698 (1953); cf. J. H. Beuscher, *Farm Law in Wisconsin* (Appleton, Wis., 1951), pp. 142–146.

111. Griswold v. Connecticut, 381 U.S. 479 (1965); Stanley v. Georgia, 394 U.S. 557 (1969).

sion speaks of order, invites exaggerating the amount of awareness and conscious will that enters into determining events. Creating order, in the sense of creating meaning, is man's constant quest, for his existence as man depends on how far the quest succeeds. The effort continues, because men live surrounded by phenomena which in their impersonality, their contingency, their bewildering variety, density, and volume always threaten to deny human meaning in existence. The legal historian needs to guard against the vanity of overestimating how much men bring things about and of underestimating how much things move men. Wherever he studies law's roles in creating order, reality enjoins that he measure the order he finds against the order which was not made, and measure the fragility of order achieved against the threat of undirected flows of events.[112]

2. Institutions and individual life patterns do not exist simply as ends in themselves, though we sometimes treat them so. Generally, they endure because they help people to make decisions which must be made because everyone cannot have everything he wants, and no one can have most of what he gets without cost to himself or to someone else; creating form and content in individual lives and in institutions requires choosing among scarce satisfactions and scarce resources. People in the United States used legal processes as one way of making these inescapable choices. They declared and implemented many of those choices directly through law. They also used law to legitimate or disallow, and to support or oppose choices made through other institutions or by individuals. Legal and economic institutions thus had much in common, for both dealt with adjusting to facts of scarcity.[113] However, law was involved with a wider range of scarcity problems than could be defined just in economic terms. For we used law to deal also with the limits which reality enforced on men's desires for power, for emo-

112. Hurst, *Law and Social Process*, pp. 62–75.

113. John Maurice Clark, *Economic Institutions and Human Welfare* (New York, 1957), chap. x; Jerome Hall, *Living Law of Democratic Society* (Indianapolis, 1949), p. 94; Charles E. Merriam, *Systematic Politics* (Chicago, 1945), pp. 70, 209–210; Joseph J. Spengler, "From Theory to Public Policy," in A. Smithies, *et al., Economics and Public Policy* (Washington, D.C., 1955), pp. 23–44.

tional security or fulfillment, for deference to individual worth and dignity, and for shared faith and shared creativity. Again we must note that law was more involved with some social institutions and some sectors of individual life than with others; it was more involved with the market than with the church, and with the individual as a producer or consumer of goods than as a holder of any particular faith. So law figured with different degrees of involvement in different types of value choices. Most of the particular value choices in which we implicated law concerned the economy, though not only those economic choices immediately relevant to market dealings. We drew law in less measure into non–economic moral choices (as in relations of trust and respect between sexual partners or between parent and child), but where we used law in regulating morals we did not limit its involvement simply to bounds defined by such other institutions as the church or the family; for example, law had its own criteria for regulating marriage and divorce, which differed materially from the values defined in some religious faiths or in various individual ways of life. Part of the legal historian's job should be to mark out the relative uses of law in dealing with different value sectors, and to appraise the positive and limiting qualities of legal processes which may explain why law became more involved with some kinds of value choices than with others.[114]

339

Values written into law in the United States dealt with too wide a range of interests to fit any neat catalog. However, there were certain kinds of value decisions to which legal processes made a special contribution and which were particularly defined in law. These were decisions concerning (a) exercise of particular forms of practical power by some men over others, (b) recognition of social income and social costs incident to individual and group activity, (c) assignment of priorities among competing objectives of socially involved action. There is no sharp dividing line which separates particular value determinations of these kinds from the law's

114. Harold D. Lasswell and Myres J. McDougal, "Legal Education and Public Policy: Professional Training in the Public Interest," *Yale Law Journal*, 52 (1943), 203, 217–232; Pound, *Jurisprudence*, V, 268–325.

concern with the general structure of institutions. But, despite some overlap there were different foci of legal attention involved here. For example, corporation law contributed to the structure of the business corporation and statutes fostering collective bargaining contributed to the structure of trade unions. But, in addition, when statutes and administrative and court decisions spelled out what should be deemed unfair practices by either management or union the law in doing so adjusted the balance of power with consequences for values other than those of the immediate parties—affecting, for example, general social interests in freedom of speech, or in markets, or in the prevention of violence.[115]

340

a. A persistent theme in American legal history has been attention to the location, extent, and related utility and danger in relationships which enable some men to compel other men's wills. Concern has run both to official power and to private power, thus defined—and to power not only in politics or in the economy, but also among groups marked by felt differences in religion, race, or culture.

The legal record embodied many judgments on particular relationships in which some men enjoyed practical ability to compel other men's wills—judgments, that is, on power. The law validated power though its use caused detriment to some, where it was thought to promote economic productivity, as with ordinary competition. Law condemned power where its use was such as to bring private violence or to substitute duress for a rational or fair calculus of gains over costs, as where employers hired spies or thugs to break up legitimate trade unions. Law legitimated power in many situations because of a felt need for effectively concentrated capacity for initiative and decision, but it qualified power by recognizing conditions of dependence which power created and hence attaching fiduciary obligations to it, for example, as between trustee and beneficiary, or as between insiders to corporate management and investors lacking skill or knowledge in a firm's affairs. Law in our

115. Milk Wagon Drivers Union of Chicago v. Meadowmoor Dairies, 312 U.S. 287 (1941); Republic Aviation Corporation v. National Labor Relations Board, 324 U.S. 793 (1945).

tradition held the legitimate monopoly of violence, and held out established and regular procedures (legislative as well as judicial) to help bring contesting private forces under some external definition and appraisal. Our cultural inheritance valued individuality and a broad scope for innovative will and venturing energy. In this legal and social context it was natural that we should make law a principal instrument and deposit of judgments on all sorts of power relationships.[116]

b. Out of communications, transactions, shared nurture and education, and simply out of common occupancy of limited living space men enjoy the gains and suffer the costs of a social existence. Some of this social income and social cost is the purposed product of those who experience it; much of it is uncalculated by-product. Some of the social gain is earned by those who enjoy it, but a great deal is unearned increment derived from those who went before; some of the social costs are incurred by the living, but a good deal of the social cost which the living must bear derives from circumstances to which their predecessors committed them. Because social gains and social costs derive from past or present relationships of a diffuse character, it is difficult for men to find ready means to perceive them and to make reasoned and humane responses to them. Yet, since men realize their humanity only in a social context, they neglect that context at peril to their humanity. Out of these conditions of life various pressures came to bear at different phases of the country's history, to use law to establish some acceptable means of social income and social cost accounting.[117]

Efforts at social accounting found two main kinds of expression in law. First, law helped muster the assets and organization to provide social overhead capital, for services or facilities which were foundations for private activity. Social overhead capital included investment of money and sustained effort for schools, for highways and means of bulk transport (navigation aids, canals, railroads, airports), for basic and applied knowledge (scientific and technolog-

341

116. Hegeman Farms Corporation v. Baldwin, 293 U.S. 163 (1934); Tuttle v. Buck, 107 Minn. 145, 119 N.W. 946 (1909).
117. Hurst, *Justice Holmes*, pp. 66–78.

ical research), for public safety (army and navy and air force, police and fire departments), for public health (safe water and food supplies, and prevention or control of epidemic disease), and for care of dependent persons (public welfare). Through most of the nineteenth century, in a cash-scarce economy which found it difficult to raise taxes, law fostered social capital investment largely by indirection, by incorporating public utilities and philanthropic enterprises and by conferring franchises which enabled and encouraged private actors to supply facilities and enjoy certain privileges (such as the power of eminent domain) not open to everyone. Such delegation of general-interest functions to private management continued into the twentieth century, notably through welfare and research foundations and religious corporations. In the 1960's sharp controversy over the tax-exempt status of such bodies attested both the felt public importance of what they did and the law's involvement in their mobilization and direction of capital. But as the country developed a more flexible money supply and increased the turnover of capital in commerce and industry, the twentieth century witnessed a great increase in the government's practical capacity and hence in its direct action to supply social capital through taxing and spending public moneys. Provision of social capital found conspicuous reflection in nineteenth-century legislation creating corporations and special franchises; in the twentieth century more and more of the values put on social capital investment were declared or implied in the terms of public budgets, and in legislative hearings and executive or administrative reports on how public money was used. In earlier times fiscal policy might properly be treated as relevant mainly to the internal housekeeping of government. Twentieth-century legal history had to recognize public finance as an area of law-declared values of at least as broad reach as the law of franchises or regulations.[118]

The other main legal expression of concern with social account-

118. Francis M. Bator, *The Question of Government Spending: Public Needs and Private Wants* (New York, 1960), pp. 9–39; Solomon Fabricant, *The Trends of Government Activity in the United States Since 1900* (New York, 1952), pp. 140–155; Carter Goodrich, *Government Promotion of American Canals and Railroads, 1800–1890* (New York, 1960), chap. viii; Hurst, *Law and Economic Growth*, pp. 143, 231–232, 235–236.

ing was the growth of public policy addressed to the secondary and more remote results of public and private activity in an increasingly interdependent society. Public policy here came to bear in part on unearned increment. Thus, progressive taxation expressed or implied judgments that substantial parts of individual and corporate income should not fairly be attributed to the recipient's own deserts, but to the social environment which supported and fostered his ability to act productively, and that hence some of that income should be appropriated to needs of that environment. Public policy in this domain came to bear, also, on costs of a given activity which, without the law's intervention, would not fairly be borne by the activity itself—spill-over costs (for example, water pollution as an incident to municipal waste disposal or to private industrial operations), and hidden subsidies and hidden redistribution of wealth or income created by failure to deal openly with such costs. There was some overlap between fiscal policy and policy concerning unearned increment and unacknowledged costs; tax policy took some account of unearned increment, and spending policy (as by public subsidy of sewage treatment plants, or appropriations to support administrative checks on industrial pollution of water) was partly directed toward meeting secondary costs to which the immediately responsible actors were not responsive. But legal action on these fronts included more than social capital investments, and took the form also of a growing body of regulation, especially of regulation expressing dissatisfaction with market processes as a means of allocating the gains and costs of economic activity. Examples were the growth of law dealing with public health and sanitation, with unfair competition, with employment of women and children, and with industrial waste disposal. Involved in legal action on such issues was the exercise of what since the early nineteenth century the courts called "the police power," which was in effect the authority of government to act to promote the good order of social relations.[119]

343

119. Walter J. Blum and Harry Kalven, Jr., *The Uneasy Case for Progressive Taxation* (Chicago, 1953), pp. 36, 66; Harold M. Groves, *Financing Government* (New York, 1939), pp. 32–42; K. William Kapp, *The Social Costs of Private Enterprise* (Cambridge, 1950), chaps. i, ii; Proprietors of the Charles River Bridge v. Proprietors of the Warren Bridge, 11 Pet. 420, 547–548, 552–553 (U.S. 1837).

c. Another way of looking at the law's responses to problems of scarce satisfactions is to note that in these uses of law, we were formally establishing priorities among competing values. So viewed, the law offered a large body of evidence of relations among felt wants and needs in the society. Moreover, in view of the costs of putting legal machinery in motion, it was evidence which could fairly be taken to reflect serious effort and commitment by those who sought or opposed legal action. Before social scientists devised techniques of attitude research, the value judgments embodied in legal records thus offered a special means not only of identifying but of weighting what some people wanted and strove for in adjusting their relations. Public budgets implied priorities, if they did not always declare them; for example, appropriations told of the country's increasing demand for the convenience and commercial utility of the automobile, a demand which matched demands for schools, and overmatched provisions for conserving natural resources. Regulatory laws sometimes openly assigned priorities, as when a legislature explicitly subordinated freedom of contract to the nutritional needs of urban populations and imposed price regulations deemed necessary to keep a regular supply of milk flowing to the city. More often priorities were implicit in regulatory law, as when by abolishing imprisonment for debt and exempting debtors' tools of trade from creditors' execution, the law subordinated the general interest in reliable performance of contracts to the general interest in keeping workers active and available in the stock of productive manpower.[120] It is one thing to find evidence of relationships to which men in the past have assigned value; it is a subtler point to rank their values, and because it is difficult to share the comparative judgments which people made in the past, there is the more reason to draw from the law the evidence it offers on this score.

3. Among values declared in law none was prior to the constitutional ideal—the continuing, if often challenged and defeated de-

120. John Maurice Clark, *Social Control of Business* (Chicago, 1926), chap. iii; John Kenneth Galbraith, *The Affluent Society* (Boston, 1958), chaps. xxii, xxiii, xxv; Frederick C. Mosher and Orville F. Poland, *The Costs of American Governments* (New York, 1964), chap. vii; Nebbia v. New York, 291 U.S. 502 (1934); Spangler v. Corless, 61 Utah 88, 211 Pac. 692 (1922).

mand that all public and private power be legitimate. Legitimacy included substantive dimensions: that power be warranted by being useful and by being just, by standards of humane and rational service to life. Legitimacy also included procedural dimensions: that law should provide or encourage reasonably workable means to assure that all forms of public or private power be accountable to others than the immediate holders of power.[121]

All particular legal action included under the two large heads of values that this essay has just considered—creation of order and accommodation to scarcity of satisfactions—might be measured against demands for legitimacy. Legitimacy, that is, is not a separate subject in legal history, apart from specific uses of law. Rather, legitimacy consists in good working relations of specific uses of law to the broadest and deepest values men seek in society. Yet, it is meaningful to make legitimacy a distinct theme of legal history, because it can be studied only by relating specific uses of law to each other within wider frames of reference than are suitable in examining more focused lines of public policy.

In view of the demand for legitimacy, the uses of law to help create order and to choose among scarce satisfactions can be measured, respectively, by the law's contributions in achieving (a) community and (b) acceptable balances of power in social relations. (a) Law reflected our conviction that individuals could realize their humanity only within constructive, shared values; they needed to belong together, and they needed to feel that they belonged together. Community rested in part on utility; law should help secure the functional requisites of a humane and reasonable society. Community rested in part on justice; law should help men perceive and accept shared values that favored life, fairly and equally. (b) Law also reflected convictions—hard bought from experience both of politics and of the market—that substantial dispersion of public and private decision-making power was necessary to achieve either utility or justice. Dispersion we thought useful because it fostered creatively different responses to experience, and in doing so it also made society sturdier against blows of chance or

345

121. Yick Wo v. Hopkins, 118 U.S. 356, 369 (1886).

miscalculation. Further, dispersion of power guarded justice. The extent and diversity of a continental federal system, the expansion of markets, along with the varieties of organization fostered in the surge of industrial and financial growth, the religious, ethnic, and national-origins differences among our people, and increased pressures for the government's services and protections, all fostered many different sorts and centers of public and private power. The situation thus required that we deal with many sources and drives of power. Our tradition added an individualistic concept of human nature, which at once prized the individual's dignity and creative potential and distrusted his selfishness, fears, and aggressions, especially when he acted with others. Power was real, diverse, functional, yet dangerous. We concluded that we should use law to keep centers of power dispersed and open to critical judgment from outside the circle of immediate powerholders.[122]

The themes of community and balance of power were interrelated. If values were widely shared, and especially in proportion as the people saw them as widely shared, the resulting sense of community reduced tensions that otherwise accented balance-of-power issues. Such was a desired function, for example, of public schools, of public provision for dependent persons, of the 14th Amendment's guaranty of equal protection of the laws—and none the less in any of these respects merely because performance fell far short of the goal. When the law scored some success in holding power in balance among interests likely to conflict, or likely to seek oppressive advantage, its balance of power contributed to community by teaching faith in shared social structures and processes amid a great diversity of wants and ambitions. Farm subsidy programs, thus, were a balance-of-power use of law which also reassured a politically potent sector that, along with commerce and industry and labor, it, too, could get some response from government. Legal protection of trade union organization and of collective bargaining aimed to redress the imbalance of power in the

122. United States Constitution, *Preamble; The Federalist,* ed. Henry Cabot Lodge (New York, 1888), No. 10, p. 51 (Madison); *cf.* John Locke, *The Second Treatise of Civil Government,* ed. J. W. Gough (Oxford, 1948), pp. 5, 62–64, 66–72.

structure of big industry, but it also reassured a new interest group that it was recognized as sharing legitimacy with other economic interests to which public policy had already given favor. Such balance-of-power accomplishments were not without ambiguities which challenge historical appraisal. By conciliating particular pressures law might score narrow gains for the sense of community at the expense of neglecting broader interests and so eventually breeding more serious questions about the legitimacy of the legal order. Thus by the last half of the twentieth century there was gathering unease about the legitimacy of the large-scale business corporation, which had grown to great social power by the accumulation of particular accommodations of the past.[123]

Whether we appraise particular law-declared values by their relevance to larger values of community or of balance of power, or find other concepts useful to the purpose, we cannot ignore the overarching theme of legitimacy in this legal and social order. In many areas of public policy, over much of the time, public policy-making dealt with matter-of-fact functional problems (what kinds of title and security best served market operations, for example) or specifically focused clashes of interest (for example, between retailers and chain stores). But law could handle such functional problems or limited-interest clashes only because prevailing opinion accepted the legal system as on the whole useful and just to larger life goals.[124] There were always challenges severe enough to show that the legal order must obtain some working minimum of acceptance of its legitimacy, if it were to exist. Legitimacy was at stake in contests over the Federal Constitution, the Alien and Sedition Acts, and the Second Bank of the United States, in the jousting of sections and the Civil War, in agrarian and small-business revolt against railroads and trusts, and in issues concerning the Vietnam war and links between a gigantic military establishment and large-scale economic interests. The constitutional ideal was a tough,

347

123. Morris R. Cohen, *American Thought* (Glencoe, Ill., 1954), pp. 118–128; Merle Curti, *The Roots of American Loyalty* (New York, 1946), chap. iv; Theodore J. Lowi, *The End of Liberalism* (New York, 1969), chap. x.

124. *Cf.* Luther v. Borden 7 How. 1 (U.S. 1849); Reynolds v. Sims, 377 U.S. 533 (1964).

persistent reality of American legal history which put the legal order under judgments which conditioned even when they did not
control law's operations. Constitutionalism thus is a dimension of
all more particular values represented in the law, and therefore
must be reckoned with in a realistically comprehensive legal history.

*   *   *

The sum of this inventory might be set down thus: The history
of law in the United States offers many challenges to research, relatively few of which have so far been taken up. That work to date
has moved within much narrower limits than the field allows may
be due somewhat to the failure to define the potential subject matter of legal history in terms adequate to the law's involvement in
the life of the society. Without claiming that the ideas it advances
are definitive, this essay outlines some themes which point up the
range and variety of the social history of law in this country. However, it is realistic to lay out themes with an appreciation of what
the available materials for study are likely to allow us to do. Since
the law has not worked as a self-contained system but has been
concerned in many other aspects of individual and social life, ideally legal history should tell not only what went on in the law's
formal processes, but what were the full actual effects that law and
the life environing the law had on each other. To examine social
legal history in this full sweep would be desirable, and the more
we can learn of the working effects of law and society upon each
other the better for realism. However, this essay does indicate difficulties which should induce modest estimates of how much we
can expect to prove about the interplay of law and society once
we venture outside the formal records yielded by legal processes.
What we can establish with more confidence is the development
of social value judgments—both as to ends and as to means—reflected or embodied in the law's own formal actions. A particular
object of this essay is to argue that such law-declared values carry
significant insights into important sectors of life outside legal institutions, and that by examining them legal history can make special
and weighty contributions to general history. Together with the

348

functional history of legal agencies themselves, delineation of the social value judgments reflected in formal legal processes constitutes the special responsibility of legal historians which they are most likely to be able to meet. No one need be concerned that these estimates lead to narrow and only technically oriented approaches to the subject. In the United States the functions of legal agencies and the social values embodied in law developed within the context of demanding ideals of constitutionalism which pressed legal agencies and their formal processes into rich involvement with institutions and patterns of individual and group experience environing the law. Proper study of legal history will draw it into like involvement.

349

THE LAW IN UNITED STATES HISTORY

WILLARD HURST

Professor of Law, University of Wisconsin

(*Read April 21, 1960*)

1.

NOT only the man in the street but also professional students of society hold very limited images of what "law" means. Most often they take
it to mean simply the drama of criminal trials:
Perry Mason on Saturday night television, the
lurid promise of the murder yarns on drugstore
racks. If they think of law in a little broader
reference, probably it will be in terms of a remembered picture in a high school history text, of
portly gentlemen in frock coats, striking attitudes:
Webster replies to Hayne. If one presses them,
the social scientists at least may concede there is
more to law than this. Law, they will grant, states
a great many doctrines which provide much of
the vocabulary of public policy discussion. But
this is, after all, largely formal stuff; sophisticated
students know that reality lies in the substance,
in operations, in getting behind the law's formalism
to the hard facts of interest and practical maneuver.
So much for law—and little wonder, then, if
neither the man in the street nor the student of
society shows much curiosity to learn what aspects
of social events or social processes might be better
illumined by knowing more about the law's
contribution.

Criminal trials and constitutional debates are
important. Important, too, in ways which to a
distressing degree are not understood even by
well-educated men, is the formality of legal process.
But these aspects of legal order, however important, fall far short altogether of representing
the significance of legal process in this society.
A more adequate definition of the attributes of
our legal order suggests that study of law in these
terms—and in particular study of legal history in
these terms—should contribute more to the understanding of the society than the lay stereotypes
would indicate.

For studying social process, the most useful
definitions of law are made in terms of social
functions of law. What are the most distinctive
and most important jobs we have asked the law
to do in this society? This asks for a modest

definition: not what is "law," anywhere, anytime,
but what has law been in the development of this
particular society. This modesty is appropriate
to the limits of what we know about the social
functions of legal order. It is appropriate also
to a definition of law looked at historically, because
history regards events, that is, looks at processes
always in particular context. Moreover, this
relativist definition of law is peculiarly appropriate
to our situation. For we have taken as a central
value the idea that legal order should find its
warrant in serving men as they strive to realize
the larger potential of being—which means that
law must find its warrant in relation to particular
experience.

Four functions have been specially important
to defining law's roles in the growth of this society. (1) To law we assigned the legitimate
monopoly of violence; normally only the policeman goes armed. As a corollary, to law we assigned ultimate scrutiny of the legitimacy of all
forms of secular power developed within the society—that is, of all means by which some men
may exercise compulsion over the wills of other
men. Modes of competition and forms of private
association thus exist subject to legal regulation
to protect the public interest. (2) We used law
to define and to implement an idea of constitutionalism as the norm of all secular power. This is
an idea which with us had reference to all forms
of secular power, not merely to official power.
It meant, first, that we believed there should be
no center of secular power which was not in some
way subject to review by another center of such
power. If there seems something paradoxical in
this notion, the historic record nonetheless shows
that we lived by it; for example, we used law to
foster and protect the growth of private (that is,
non-official) associations like the business corporation or religious, political and social associations, to build centers of energy and opinion which
might provide counter weights to official power.
Thus we sought to make all secular power responsible to power outside itself, for ends which it

350

alone did not define. But responsibility means nothing until we know, responsibility for what? The second and most distinctive aspect of our insistence that all secular power be responsible (constitutional) power, was that we held the final measure of responsibility to be in serving individual life. (3) We used law to promote formal definition of values and of appropriate means to implement values. In other words, this legal order was characterized by strong insistence on procedural regularity. (4) Finally, we assigned to legal process important roles in allocating scarce resources—of manpower and human talent, as well as of non-human sources of energy—for shaping the general course of economic development. This was an especially important use of law, in a society which believed that in economic creativity it held the means to fashion new standards of human dignity. At the outset government here held the unique asset of the public domain, which we spent to help build turnpikes, canals, and railroads and to create in the Mississippi Valley a republic of family farms. Likewise, we made bold use of taxing and spending powers of national, state, and local governments to help create the framework of economic growth. Resource allocation by law was the more striking in our history because we placed great reliance on broad dispersion of economic decision making into private hands through the market, implemented through the law of property and contract. We supplemented private energies in market by important delegations to non-official persons of powers of public concern. We gave railroads the right of eminent domain; we granted franchises to enterprisers to conduct public utilities and to charge toll for their services; by grant of limited liability to corporation stockholders and by contract, property and tort doctrines which in effect favored venture, we encouraged men to take the risks of action, letting losses lie where they fell unless someone who had been hurt showed compelling reason why the law should help shift the burden.

These uses of law mean that law wove itself into the organization and processes of this society in ways which should make the study of legal process—and in particular of legal history—important to social science. (1) Because it held the legitimate monopoly of force, and incident thereto the authority to call to account all other forms of secular power, law bore some relation to all types of association and all means for mustering

collective will and feeling. The obverse of free religious association here, for example, was the legally embodied policy of separation of church and state. (2) Because North American legal order sought to give content to the idea that all power must be constitutional (responsible) power, law entered into the practical meaning that individuality had in this society. The constitutional character of this legal order likewise meant that law was actually or potentially part of the social structure and social process; there was no pattern of social organization, no procedure of social interaction whose significance could be appraised without taking into account the demands which an ideal of constitutional order either did in fact make on it, or should make on it. Thus, for example, we cannot tell the story of the status and roles of women in the United States without including the meaning which the movements for married women's property legislation and equal suffrage had for defining the condition of woman as an effective member of the society. Again, we cannot understand the social history of the business corporation without including the search for acceptable definitions in law of the grounds on which, first, the practical power of corporate owners, and, more recently, of corporate management may establish legitimacy. (3) Because this legal order emphasized procedural regularity—providing diverse organized means for bringing choices to definition and mustering evidence and reasoned argument for their resolution—law entered significantly into the process by which men created social goals and mobilized energies of mind and feeling to move toward their goals. Of course we must not exaggerate the rationality of the law, any more than of other institutions. Regard for procedures tends to create inertia or complacency with familiar ways; passion and prejudice color legal operations as they color any human operations whe..e men feel deep concern about the stakes. Moreover, how men feel is at least as valid a part of their experience as what they achieve by reason; indeed, reason probably finds justification ultimately only as an instrument by which men achieve more subtle, more varied, and more shared emotion. So qualified, however, and always within the framework of a constitutional ordering of power, the increase in men's rational competence and the extension of more rationalized processes of human relations ranked high among the organizing values of this society. Legal process ranked with industrial technology and with organized science as a major means to enlarge the scope of rationalized behavior. In the second half of the twentieth century the trend of events seemed likely to give larger importance to the law's rationalizing role, in the interests of maintaining a vital constitutional tradition. The pressure of scientific and technical rationalization of social processes increased the scale and intricacy of social organization, the demands made in the name of organizational integrity and efficiency, and the inertia created by organization mass. Legal procedures in part had served and would continue to serve to provide a framework of reasonably assured expectations, backed by the force of the state, within which a complex social division of labor could work. More important, however, in our tradition legal procedure had the ultimate function of implementing the constitutional idea—that choices and the costs as well as gains of choices be brought to definition, that power holders be made to account for their use of power, and all this in last analysis that power be used to serve individual life. That growth proceeded along these lines was witnessed by the painful efforts to hammer out a law of labor relations within which management and labor might create a kind of due process and equal protection of law to govern the discipline of the modern factory. (4) Because we used law boldly as a means of resource allocation—with at least as great effect as we used the market—the history of legal process was woven closely into the general growth of the economy and of key relations of social and economic power in the United States. The terms on which we disposed of the public domain in the Mississippi Valley, for example, materially affected the development of a tradition of agrarian political revolt on the one hand, and on the other the growth of the political as well as business and social power of big corporations, of which the first models were the land-grant railroads. The public domain no longer offers government the unique leverage it afforded for nineteenth-century social planning—though current controversy over franchises for use of the air waves reminds us that social growth may bring new areas of public domain into policy significance. However, through its fiscal powers twentieth-century government plays as large a role in affecting the directions and content of the commonwealth as did nineteenth-century government through the public lands. Demands upon the resources-allocation functions of law continue to involve law in the main processes of social change and stability.

Finally, let me note that these social functions of law mean that legal processes produce uncommonly valuable raw materials for studying institutions, transactions, and events whose main focus lies outside law. Law's procedural emphasis —its provision of varied methods of bringing to definition and decision value choices of all degrees of importance—is at the bottom of the fact that law tends to build a storehouse of data for general social science. But it is the fact that law's procedures work for purposes set by the other three functions of legal order that produces the activity that fills the storehouse. Law scrutinizes the over-all dispositions of power in the society; it embodies and insists upon the constitutional idea that the uses of power show justification; it is used to reach decisions on resource allocation outside the market calculus. These functions mean that a great range of men's economic and social as well as their political objectives, tensions, and strivings are made more visible and are caused to leave more tangible evidences of their presence, through legal records. In constitutions, statutes, judgments, and executive and administrative orders, and in the enormous volume of statement and rationalization which surround these in recorded proceedings, in committee reports, in judicial and administrative opinions, as well as in petitions and bills and such routine forms as the income tax return—in all these we have one of the largest and perhaps on the whole the most ordered body of evidence that any of our institutions produces, to reflect many of our values and the troubles we have in bringing values to awareness and doing something about them. It is a sign of the too narrow ideas that the student as well as the man in the street has of law's functions, that both historical and current cross-sectional study of human relations have made limited use of the data afforded by legal process.

2.

However, if laymen draw less understanding than they might from legal materials, they may properly say that they have had little guidance from law men to do better. Aside from providing concepts and ordering judicial precedents for the immediate operating needs of bench and bar, legal research has a thin record of accomplishment over the past ninety years in which university law schools have grown to some stature. The defects are not primarily defects of method, though when we press more ambitious study of legal order we as

352

soon encounter the hard limits of our present techniques as do students of other aspects of men's behavior. But at this stage the trouble lies much deeper than method. The fundamental defect is a want of philosophy. Legal research has moved within very limited borders, relative to its proper field, because it has not been grounded in ideas adequate to the intellectual challenge which the phenomena of legal order present.

This essay seeks to appraise United States legal history as a field of scholarship, in its promise and in its development to date. I need not, nor could I within this span, take stock of the whole reach of research in law. However, what can be said of the discipline of legal history applies in large measure to other types of legal research.

Research and writing in North American legal history show four major limitations. Implicit are limitations of conception which characterize most of the published work. Here criticism should move carefully. Where men have defined meaningful problems for study it is irrelevant as well as unfair to criticize the particular product because it does not deal with some different subject. Fair criticism may be made of the over-all allocation of energy, where work concentrates on a narrow range of problems to the neglect of others of equal or greater meaning. Fair criticism may be made where the over-all allocation of effort rests on express or implied rejection of other themes for whose development a good case can be made. Fair criticism may be made where particular work is done from a parochial point of view which omits effort to trace relations either to the larger issues of legal order or to the relations of legal to social order. There is much work that needs doing in the study of our legal history, and thus far there are too few able recruits for the work. Hence the most pertinent criticism may be not of particular jobs done, but of the failure of practicing legal historians to show the excitement inherent in the field with enough conviction to enlist more talent for the whole enterprise. Ordered learning is made from the building blocks fashioned by devoted study of particulars. There need be no parochialism in work on a limited subject, if the worker sees the subject in relation to a large context. But significant ordered learning does not consist in rubble, nor does it grow without the skill of master craftsmen who know how to fit building blocks together.

Four limitations of the general product attest the want of philosophy in the study of North American legal history. (1) Historians have exaggerated the work of courts and legal activity immediately related to litigation. (2) They have paid too little attention to the social functions of law. (3) They have not distributed their effort with adequate response to the facts of timing and the reality of major discontinuities in the country's growth in relation to the uses of law. (4) They have exaggerated areas of conscious conflict and deliberated action, at the expense of realistic account of the weight of social inertia and the momentum of social drift.

Anglo-American law men are by tradition and training biased toward equating law with what judges do, to the neglect not only of legislative, executive, and administrative activity, but also to the neglect even of the out-of-court impact of the work of lawyers, let alone the additions or subtractions made in legal order by lay attitudes and practices affecting legal norms. We early trained lawyers by apprenticeship which taught them court pleadings and client-caretaking. When the principal revolution in legal education arrived in the 1870's, it was organized about the case method of instruction, which again emphasized the work of courts. Most of the business of the bar through the nineteenth century had to do with the property and contract affairs of clients, and most of the law of these fields was common (that is, judge-made) law, so that through the formative period of our main legal tradition the focus remained on the judicial process. Thus, first our treatise writing and later the writing done for legal journals dealt mainly with public policy as declared by courts. This bias of professional thinking was not affected by the fact that through the nineteenth century Congress and the state legislatures churned out large quantities of important legislation, or by the fact that in great areas of policy which did not lend themselves easily to common law development the framework of the law was erected mainly in statutes (as in the law of the public lands, public education, public utilities, highways, health and sanitation, or the organization of local government). From limited beginnings in the late nineteenth century, executive and administrative law-making grew to great proportions alongside the statute law. Judicial law-making was never as exclusively important as the concentration of legal writing might seem to show. From the 1870's on, legislative, executive, and administrative processes definitely became the principal sources of formed policy. The course offerings of even the better

353

law schools were slow to reflect this reality. But legal research was even slower, with legal historians badly lagging the field. Of course the work of the courts continues of great importance. In our time legal and non-legal institutions take on increasing size and there is growing readiness to accept demands made on individuals in the name of the security and operating efficiency of large social aggregates. In this context more than ever before the availability of independent courts and an independent class of professional advocates supported not by grace of the state but by private fees, represent basic elements of civil liberty. In the second half of the twentieth century the courts have distinctive importance because they are the forum in which individuals and small groups, of their own resources, can best call organized power to account. To recognize this, however, in no measure justifies the extent to which legal history writing, along with legal philosophy and other legal research, has treated the judicial process as if it were the whole of legal order. Symbolic is the fact, for example, that while twentieth-century scholarship has given us at least four large-scale treatises, a dozen substantial monographs and scores of essays in the law journals on the history of constitutional doctrine as it has been made by the Supreme Court of the United States, we lack a single first-rate modern work on the history of constitutional doctrine as it has been formed in the Congress.

The bulk of legal history writing has been about topics defined by legal categories. We have much writing about commerce clause doctrine, but little about the meaning of commerce clause doctrine for the development or operation of sectional or nationwide marketing organization, or about the impress which such business history may have made on constitutional principles. There is some rather formal history of property law, but little history of the significance of fee simple title for types of land use, for the private and social accounting of income and costs of alternative land uses, or for the political and social balance of power. There are some essays on the history of contract law, but little or no effort to define or appraise the meaning that contract law had for the functioning of the market, the provision of credit, or the allocation of gains and costs of business venture. There are scattered writings about the history of the mortgage, the corporate indenture, the receivership and tax law, but we lack the good studies we should have of the historic relations of law to the growth and channeling of investment capital. There is a good deal in print about various aspects of the Bill of Rights, but no connected story of the implications of civil rights doctrines for the shifting balance of power among various kinds of groups and between the individual and official and private group power at different stages of the country's growth. Though better than a generation has gone by since we heard the call for a sociological jurisprudence, legal history writing has made little response, but continues content on the whole to let the formal headings of the law fix its subject matter. It is an ironic course of affairs, in a society whose tradition is so strongly constitutional, insisting that legal order is not an end in itself but gains legitimate meaning only in terms of its service to ends of life outside law.

In the total distribution of effort, there has been a disproportionate attention in legal history writing to beginnings—and to beginnings in their most obvious sense—at the expense of proper development of hypotheses concerning the main lines of growth through to our own time. Much attention has focused on colonial origins, on the period of constitutional experiment from 1776 to 1790, and on the successive frontier phases of national expansion. I do not quarrel with the worth of attending to such formative periods taken in themselves, but only with the tendency to fasten onto origins without equal curiosity to follow through, and with failure to see that in terms of law's relation to gathering issues of power and social function there were other less obvious periods of beginnings which should also be studied. First, as an example of the want of follow through, it is odd that for so many states we have writing which with care sometimes verging on antiquarian enthusiasm traces the beginnings of territorial and state courts (once again, the excessive preoccupation with judicial process), but little good writing on such basic themes as law's relation to the creation of transportation networks, the law's response to the business cycle, or the relation of tax policy to the fortunes of agriculture and other extractive industries. These omissions are, of course, part of the neglect of the social-function history of law which I have already noted. But they also represent a neglect of a familiar and important time sequence characteristic of the growth of these states, whose people normally established their basic legal institutions in the nineteenth century with some obvious impatience to get on to

354

their central care, which was the expansion of their economy.

Second, on the neglect of the less obvious beginnings, the most notable examples are the relative inattention to the sharp changes in direction and pace of social movement which came about in the 1830's, the 1870's, and the 1930's. The 1830's saw rapid development of markets and marketing emphasis in the public policy-making of one state after another, with reflection especially in the statute books, as we passed from relatively simple agrarian to more commercial and credit-centered economies. The 1870's saw the rapid cumulation of forces channeled or given new impetus by the new scale of organization of men and capital and the new techniques of public and private finance generated out of the North's war effort. Change here was far more drastic than in the 1830's and amounted to a major break in continuity. Due mainly to the shifts in the size of private industrial and financial organization and in the reach of markets which gathered force in the '70s, by the late '90s the United States was a qualitatively different society from what it had been before the Civil War. The strains and conflicts, the gains and losses attendant upon this rapid and major alteration of the country's power structure and modes of operation provide main themes for legal history which we have hardly begun to explore. The 1930's saw the cumulated impact of trends in social and economic interdependence which had been gathering force since World War I. The challenge of these themes is so large, indeed, that one may wonder whether more essays on territorial beginnings represent so much contributions to knowledge as refuges from more exacting studies.

Legal history research may be especially subject to a bias toward themes of conflict, or at least toward themes which emphasize conscious and debated decisions. Such a bias is favored by the emphasis of our legal order on formal procedures. So far as they are efficient, regular procedures for framing, deliberating, and adopting constitutions, statutes, executive orders and administrative rules work toward bringing choices to definition, aligning interested parties, promoting expression and energizing will. Lawsuits and court decisions work even more dramatically to these ends. Hence, so far as legal history research has tended toward exaggerated emphasis upon the judicial process, it has particularly strengthened a bias toward equating men's history with the record of their more or less conscious strivings. Yet, the broader

the reach of our hypotheses and the deeper our concern to study the social functions of legal order, the more we will learn to respect the relative influence of inertia and drift in affairs. The most realistic view of all aspects of man's history leads to the conclusion that most of what has happened to men has happened without their wanting it or striving for it or opposing it or—more important—without their being aware of the meaning of trends until patterns of structure and force have developed past points of revoking. This general judgment seems no less true of legal history in this country. There is peculiar irony in the fact, since it is the business of constitutional legal order to promote responsible control of events. No example is more instructive than the history of antitrust law, whose development both reflected and persistently lagged the imperious course of revolutions in industrial and financial organization. Aside from some efforts either to expound or refute Marxian styles of hypothesis,—and even here the institutional cast of language only thinly disguises villains or heroes felt to be working in the background—the writing of North American legal history has paid little attention to putting legal phenomena in due perspective relative to the massive weight of inertia or to the implacable movement of decisions taken by drift and default.

3.

If legal history research and writing in this country have moved within too narrow limits, the criticisms point to some positive prescriptions. (1) We need allocate more effort to studying legislative, executive, and administrative processes as well as the bar's contributions to these formal processes and to the informal social regulation that goes on through the market and through private association. Likewise we need more attention to ways in which lay attitudes toward law (including laymen's disregard of law or their mistaken images of it) have affected the creation of institutions of social order other than formal legal institutions. (2) Legal history should begin to contribute more to develop fact-based, fact-tested theories of social structure and social process. For example, we should have more legal history written in terms of law's operational significance for the institution of the market, studied in as wide a range of interplay of law and market as the wit and devotion of legal scholarship can compass. (3) Legal history writing should come to bear with greater em-

355

phasis upon the past one hundred years in the United States. Especially should there be substantial scholarly investment in study of the profound shifts in structure, process, and attitudes that occurred in the generations beginning about 1820 and 1861, and in the depression 1930's. Legal history has not been made only by quill pen and candlelight. (4) Not with despair but with realistic estimate of the odds against man's conscious contrivance and out of conviction that his distinctive quality lies in rebellion against the odds, legal history should treat as critical themes the impact of social inertia and social drift. Nor can we afford to take this direction with any moral complacency, weighing our own shrewdness against the blunders of our ancestors. If the more significant decisions regarding natural resources use were made by default in the nineteenth century, no less by default have been the twentieth-century decisions on metropolitan growth; if the nineteenth century allowed market demands for rail transport unduly to determine the course of public policy, no less has the twentieth century allowed the immediate conveniences, comforts, and social status markings of the automobile to determine a fantastic range of matters of public concern, from the safety of life to the location of commerce and industry. The physical size of this country, the invitations to large-scale economic effort posed by its natural resources and population growth, as well as deep-rooted, but little-calculated faith in the self-evident values of growth and movement and change (in intangible senses of status and accomplishment as well as by tangible measures of product and location)—such factors contributed to make provision of transport an element of uncommon influence on our public policy, and a good example in both nineteenth- and twentieth-century settings of the type of unplanned and largely undirected cumulation of events which had basic shaping effect upon what law was asked to do and how it did it.

There are many profitable directions in which a broader conception of legal history might take us. I have drawn specific prescriptions from four criticisms of limitations implicit in the bulk of work so far done. In addition let me note some more general developments that would be useful. Two concern the more effective study of legal institutions themselves. Two concern particularly critical kinds of meaning which the study

of legal history might have for better understanding the general course of this society.

First, as to legal institutions: (1) In times when social change moves fast, wide, and deep amid peril to the prized values of a constitutionally ordered community, we need more sophisticated knowledge of the potentials and the limits of the major agencies of law-making. If no other currents of events enforced this need, it would gain enough urgency because of the extent to which we depend upon public finance to sustain the momentum of the economy and upon foreign policy to maintain the national security. On the whole the organization, procedures, and working traditions of the legislative and executive branches represent responses to conditions which the fast pace of events has put far behind us. If there need be less concern for the adequacy of judicial organization, this is not because it lacks serious defects. However, the most important job for the courts in this highly organized modern society is not that of general policy-making but of insuring some minimum of decent procedural protection for individuals and small groups confronting large organized power. On the whole this is a task simpler enough than general policy-making so that it can be handled with what we have, if bench and bar apply their traditions with intelligence and courage. The situation is quite different as to the sufficiency of the legislature and executive before the daunting challenges of the times; the difference is reflected, for example, in contemporary controversies over the proper roles of legislative investigation, and over functions of the National Security Council or the Joint Chiefs of Staff, or in hearings and debates of the Congressional Joint Committee on the Economic Report of the President's Council of Economic Advisors. Types of public problems vary in distinctive character and challenge; types of public agency vary in distinctive capacities, whether born of formal structure and process or of tradition. Legal history should lend us more insight into the working character, promise, and limitations of formal agencies for making public decisions. (2) There is no more badly neglected area of legal research than that of sanctions, the comparative study of methods of implementing policy. Given life's infinite variety and the hard limits of social science research techniques so far available, the study of sanctions is an area in which we now stand to gain most from history. Nor should we view it as the study of factors of secondary importance. The more difficult the basic policy choices, the more surely must judgments of the promise and costs of implementation enter into the basic decisions. Moreover, we grow into some basic decisions out of experience of what we can expect to do. Sophisticated study of experience in enforcing public policy will require overleaping the limitations which have marked the bulk of legal historical writing—appraising the interplay of legislative and executive with judicial processes, relating law to the functional character of other social institutions on which it impinges, putting legal decisions and procedures into the proper perspective of the times in which they are made, weighing the positive investment of resources which the law must provide or direct to obtain desired results. It is a commentary on the failure of scholarship thus far to tackle many major problems, that, for example, in the 1960's when we confront the difficulties of building equal protection of the laws for Negroes in voting and schooling we have no studied body of experience for guidance in handling problems of large-scale hostility to public policy. If legal historians will set themselves to significant problems in legal sanctions, they will lack no longer for a more searching philosophy of their discipline; their problems will push them into philosophy.

Second, consider two respects in which a broader approach to legal history might yield insights of two types specially important to understanding the general life of the society.

(1) Because of the four key functions we have assigned to law—its scrutiny of all types of secular power, its constitutionalism, its emphasis on procedural regularity and its role in resource allocation—but especially because of law's formality (its attention to regular procedures for examining and taking decisions), law offers peculiarly important evidence of the values which give this society coherence and vitality. Of course this is not true in equal measure of all we find recorded in law; inertia and drift play their roles here, too, so that a prime job for legal history is to distinguish what has living force from what is dead or dying, deceptive or hypocritical. Granted this need of taking distinctions, legal history, just because of its relative formality, offers unusual evidence of the development of the values our people have held. Thus, study of legal history can make special contribution to the general history of ideas. The study of a people's

values has basic importance to understanding a society, for it is the sharing of values that provides the bond of lasting human relations, even where (as with the value we put on the competitive processes of the market) the shared values may express themselves in secondary conflict. Study of the growth of shared values has special importance not only for understanding this particular society, but for contributing to its strength. We have grown fast amid a great bustle of events and subject to major discontinuities in the emergence of new relations of power and process. We need to know ourselves in our strengths and failings much better than we do. There is evidence of this need in the uncertain allegiance which common opinion has shown under stress even to such traditional values as those of the Bill of Rights. A broader concern with legal history as an avenue to study of ideas will bring this discipline into relation to the most fundamental kinds of social analysis as well as into relation with the most critical living problems of our own generation.

(2) Because legal processes and legal records bulk large among ways in which we bring values to definition, a broadly conceived legal history could help us come to terms with the good and the bad features of the pragmatic attitudes that are so central in this culture. Our actions show that we have believed that within a framework of generalized values men must make meaning for themselves, in a universe whose baffling detail and sweep favor drift and inertia as the norm of men's experience. In this light the main theme of man's history is the cultivation of his awareness and of his capacities of mind and will to act upon his greater awareness of his situation. We need to strive to see, and to learn what our creative possibilities are by striving to act upon what we see. The experimental and activist bias of our culture rest upon these valid insights. On the other hand, our preoccupation with directed effort and what it teaches has led us also into a bias toward exalting the immediately practical—in the sense of knowledge which can be translated into immediate operations—at the expense of understanding larger causes and more remote chains of effects. Thus a valid pragmatism is constantly at war with an illegitimate pragmatism in our way of life. Because it brings so much focused effort to bear upon making choices and counting gains and costs, legal process offers rich tangible evidence of these

357

warring brands of pragmatism in our common life. For example, the history of our worship of the fee simple title to land—in its fruitful relation to the development of civil liberty on the one hand, and its unfortunate relation to the waste of natural resources on the other—could be told in ways to show how legal history might illuminate the sound growth and also the distortion of pragmatic values in this society. If the cultivation of awareness is the basic theme which expounds man's most distinctive life role, the most characteristic functions of our legal order—its scrutiny of the arrangements of power, its insistence on the responsibility (constitutional status) of legitimate power, and on procedural regularity, and its uses for resource allocation—point to the intimate relation which the imaginative study of legal history should have to the study of general history.

Implicit in what I have said in appraising some approaches to legal history is the notion that we should study history to learn more about realizing life's possibilities. History itself will teach us not to hold a naive faith that men readily learn from history. Moreover, the view I take of man means that there is no need to apologize for studying history partly because there is pleasure in the effort; the enjoyment lies precisely in man's nature, for his life consists most distinctively in his consciousness. But writing and reading history are more than aesthetic experiences. They are themselves kinds of activity which constitute man's distinctive being, which consists in his response to and rebellion against the challenges of an impersonal universe. It is in this sense that legal history research and writing stand under the functional command to serve the growth of our philosophy.

Old and New Dimensions
of Research in United States
Legal History

by JAMES WILLARD HURST*

The last 30 years have seen a marked increase in the number of law-trained scholars and scholars primarily trained in other disciplines who are investigating United States legal history or legal dimensions of other sectors of the country's experience. Probably several factors have contributed to this development. Concern with grave public policy issues in our own time has stimulated interest in studying the leverage law has given in handling older problems and the uses of law to affect balance or imbalance of power among interests. More immediately, the daunting pace, range and depth of social change has prompted critics to re-examine values embodied in law, and incident to this re-examination students have been stirred to develop more productive ideas to guide research in legal history. This fresh curiosity has tended to put legal history into broader frames of reference to other aspects of social experience, and hence to recruit to the field students who found little interest in older, narrower notions of what legal history was all about.

There is a lot of work to be done; the extent of unexplored territory far exceeds that for which we have charts, most of those obviously imperfect. Thus lawyer historians should welcome recruits from outside the bar. But at the threshold of considering the future of the field, the need for recruiting raises an important tactical matter. One does not have to be a lawyer to do useful research in legal history; a good deal of distinguished publication by non-lawyers already demonstrates that. But the formal materials of the law—constitutions, statutes, executive and administrative rules and orders, court judgments and opinions—present technical barriers to the uninitiated. Getting over these barriers calls for some special skills in dissecting legal source material. Three years of law study are not necessary to develop the level of skills non-

*Vilas Professor of Law, University of Wisconsin

lawyer historians need in order to handle legal sources capably for a good many kinds of legal historical studies. But the non-lawyer would benefit from exposure to a selection of law school courses adding up to about a year of law school study—a couple of courses reflecting processes of common law development, one emphasizing statutory construction, one dealing with judicial review of administrative action and one dealing with a policy area in which administrators shape a large part of the substantive content, and a course in jurisprudence. I raise this point as a plea to law faculties, and law school administrators, and not just to lawyer historians, that schools be flexible enough generously to open selected courses to non-lawyer advanced students who want the courses in order to command the tools for effective contributions to research in legal history. So much for academic mechanics.

The Limited Scope of Work in Legal History

360

Of more basic importance, of course, is the state of ideas which determine how far research matches the inherent challenges of the subject. Unfortunately, what is most prominent over the last 30 years of work in United States legal history are omissions or restrictions which with little change over that time have meant that research has stayed within disappointingly narrow bounds.

Concentration on courts: Above all else work in legal history— by which hereafter I mean, unless I specify otherwise, work in United States legal history—has put disproportionate, indeed nearly exclusive, emphasis on judicial process and courts. Courts are important. But there are reasons to be wary of misallocating research resources by giving them more attention than the whole extent of legal-social order warrants. Court opinions typically offer more explicit and available identification and rationalizations of public policy choices than do legislative and administrative materials. Court cases present relatively sharply drawn dramas of confrontation, which by their demarcation of roles at least give more appearance of explaining what are the relevant interests and issues than do the often more confused or opaque products of other legal processes. Responsive to their different functions, legislative and executive or administrative law making agencies are likely to deal with diffuse or varied interests not as well defined as in the alignment of plaintiffs and defendants in litigation.

There is more justification for emphasizing courts' contributions to the content of public policy before the 1890's than thereafter; the span from about 1810 to 1890 was the great and unique flowering of judge-made law. But in increasing measure since 1890 the bulk of law-embodied public policy has been contained in statute books and in rules and regulations or accretions of precedent created by executive and administrative action. (Hereafter, for convenience, I shall refer simply to administrative action as a shorthand term for law made both by offices in the executive branch and by administrative agencies which enjoy some independence of the executive under powers delegated by the legislature). Judges continue to make contributions to the content of law after 1890. But their creativity now works almost always within limits set by their roles as interpreters of statutes, save as they review the constitutionality of legislative or administrative action. Indeed, before the 1890's, and even in the late 18th century and the first half of the 19th, the statutory component looms large in legal order, in allocating economic resources (by public lands policy), in creating and legitimating public and private organizations for collective action (fixing the structure of national, state and local government offices, chartering philanthropic and business corporations), and in granting to private individuals and groups special franchise privileges (for damming and improving navigable waters, for laying out transportation rights of way and exercising delegated powers of eminent domain to acquire them, and for charging tolls and otherwise setting terms for use of waterpower and transport facilities so created). Through most of the 19th century administrative agencies were scantly developed in the national and state governments, but even in this respect the statute books made significant early beginnings.

361

Two persistent trends in ideas about legal history research partly reveal and partly conceal disproportionate attention to the courts. Both trends seem to lack sound basis.

Commentators sometimes distinguish "law" from "government," with the more or less clearly indicated conclusion that "law" consists only of what courts do. Two things seem wrong here. First, there may be an imputation that once we step outside the area of judicial action we confront only arbitrary exercises of will—that statutes and administrative rules and precedents do not provide principled or predictable lines of public policy. But, viewed in some time perspective, sustained ordering of values and predictable regularities of choice show in the products of legislative and administrative processes. For example, there has been no whimsical or ever changing flux of arbitrary will in the course of statute and administrative law dealing with frames of market dealing, or with public health and sanitation, or with safe working conditions or allocations of costs of accidents on the job, or taxation of persons and property. Of course such bodies of law reflect much pulling and hauling among contending interests. But such maneuvering has been no less present, if a bit more below the surface, of much common law development. Likewise one can identify and predict continuities in development of legislative and administrative as well as of judicial procedures—in such matters as setting terms of notice or hearing to affected interests, fixing relations of legislative committees to their parent bodies, and arranging process for making administrative rules or orders.

Two related aspects of our legal order might seem to warrant distinguishing "law" from "government," so as to give "law" its distinctive realm. Our system has always included the idea that aggrieved individuals or groups should have remedies available in court against actions which exceed legislative or administrative authority as set by constitutions or by statutes. In this sense law created and operated by judges has had an existence apart from the activities of other legal agencies. But noting this does not go far to justify legal historians in fastening most of their attention on the judicial process. In practice relatively little legislative or administrative action comes under judicial review. In most instances legislative and administrative agencies set and enforce their own limits on themselves, defined by their own doctrine and precedents in interpreting relevant constitutional and statutory provisions; in addition, imperfectly, but yet not in trivial degree, administrative law-making stands under surveillance in legislative hearings and in appropriations acts. Another aspect of legal order which may suggest distinguishing "law" from "government" is the great array of statute, judge-made and administrative law which deals with structuring and regulating relations which are in the first instance private— notably relations set within the law of private contract and property and the law of business corporations. Even here, however, as a proper statement of the point shows, the law which thus stretches outside the operations of formal legal agencies is not simply, or even in larger part, judge-made law.

Insofar as a distinction taken between "law" and "government" works in effect to identify law with courts, it implicitly identifies "law" solely with commands—with Thou Shalts and Thou Shall Nots—and conceives of commands simply as judgments or decrees of courts. This is too narrow a view even in terms of commands. At least for the past 100 years the bulk of legal commands have been embodied in statute books, in volumes of administrative rules or regulations, or in bodies of administrative precedent; the trend has increased in this direction until in the 1970's lawyers turn most of the time to legislation or delegated legislation or to administrative case law to find what the law commands their clients to do or not to do. Granted, from the 1790's to the 1870's administrative law making played a relatively small part compared to the surge of common law development. But even in that span legislators put a substantial volume of standards and rules into statute books.

Probably more important than these assessments, however, is the fact that identifying law with commands tends to pass over two great

362

areas of public policy in which statutory and administrative outputs have always dominated. Our constitutional and political tradition puts the power of the public purse firmly in legislative hands; judges have never had authority to impose taxes and only by indirection and marginally have their judgments determined for what public money shall be spent. Resource allocation through public taxing and spending has long been a major source of impact of law on the society. Unmistakably so in the 20th century, this was no less true in substance to the end of the 19th century. Congress—and state legislatures under delegation from Congress—set terms for disposing of a vast public domain —an immensely important style of legal allocation of resources in decades when a cash-scarce economy found it hard to raise tax money. These earlier decades also saw important beginnings of what we now call tax expenditures—using tax exemptions or selectivity in taxable subjects as instruments to promote favored lines of economic activity. In the 20th century the growth of over-all productivity created unprecedented liquidity in the economy. Direct money subsidies from government then assumed the dominant role which land grants had in the cash-scarce 19th century. Through conditions set on government grants in aid, and by elaborating exemptions, credits, and deductions under individual and corporate income taxes, 20th century appropriations and tax law became major factors regulating and channeling economic activity, and affecting the distribution or allocation of purchasing power. Public policy has also been deeply implicated in resource allocation through legislation and administrative action controlling, or at least materially affecting, the supply of money (including the supply of credit), and influencing for better or worse the course of deflationary or inflationary trends in the economy. Courts have had only marginal involvement with these matters, which legal historians have neglected in proportion as they have exaggerated their attention to the judicial process. That special interests succeeded often in turning all of these types of resource allocations to their own rather than public benefit did not lessen the social impacts. Moreover, such resource allocating uses of law, good, bad, or questionable, showed marked continuities, if not always neat coherence, in legislation and administrative outputs.

    Another way in which narrow identification of law with commands ignores major sectors of legal impact is its tendency to scant government licensing or other permissions which have legitimated and fostered and incidentally regulated forms of private collective action. From the late 19th century on the character of the society was shaped to a great extent by activities of business corporations and, especially in the 20th century, by the influence of lobbies organized to pursue profit and nonprofit goals; the structure and governance of business corporations and of pressure groups derived primarily from private initiatives, but also could not be divorced from statutory and administrative law which profoundly affected the scope given to private will.

Finally, overlapping the resource-allocating, licensing, and regulatory roles of law, yet bearing distinctive character, were uses of law to promote or channel the advance of science and technology. Again we confront a major area of public policy, built more from legislative and administrative than from judicial contributions, which tends to be ignored insofar as we identify "law" with courts and with commands issuing from courts.

Another conceptual problem may press researchers to cling to a definition of legal history almost identified with activities of judges. That emphasis can carry the comforting sense that it legitimates limiting inquiry to the output of a single branch of government, one which has more sharply defined character than do legislatures and administrative offices, and which proceeds through techniques of building and applying doctrine more familiar to law-trained students than the less formal ways by which statute and administrative law seem to grow. In contrast, disquietingly broad horizons open up as one views the range, diversity, and often informality of contacts of legislative and administrative activities with the life of the society. It is not just that search now reaches out to more legal agencies. Long established, quite firm traditions of professional ethics as well as common law and constitutional doctrine about the separation of powers together with constitutional standards of procedural due process of law hedge about approaches to courts. In contrast, in our tradition, legislatures and administrative law makers are open to a much wider range of approaches by affected interests. True, here, too, longstanding traditions set fiduciary ideals for these law makers, further supported, however imperfectly, by positive law dealing with questionable or corrupt practices of private-interest representatives. Nonetheless, policy making is a more open and fluid business in the legislative and administrative than it is in judicial arenas, and properly so in a legal order that seeks to be both relatively open and representative. But the student may worry that if he recognizes such contrasts in institutional roles, he may assume responsibility for making himself a master at firsthand of knowledge of politics and political parties, lobbies, and the whole range of processes that go into forming public opinion and nerving will to action. Understandably he may stand dismayed before so ambitious a mission, and look for definitions that will narrow his obligations. But the proper answer seems to be to recognize the propriety of a sensible division of labor, rather than to adopt a truncated idea of the subject matter of legal history which denies the realities of the range and variety of ways in which legal processes pervade social structure and operations. In an efficient division of labor some researchers will concentrate on the immediate operations of official agencies—but on legislative and administrative as well as judicial agencies—and these investigators should be those who have acquired special technical qualifications for dealing perceptively with the formal output of the agencies. Others will specialize in studying elements other than formal legal operations that provide important contexts for formal law making. Each division of specialists must draw on the product of the others; the dense and diverse reality of legal-social order precludes everyone being an expert in everything. But I see no gains and only losses in denying how far a realistic conception of "legal" history should reach into the life of the society.

So much for comment on the costs of allocating research resources disproportionately to the judicial process and its immediate products. There are three other respects, which I note more briefly, in which work in legal history over the past 30 years has proceeded within bounds too narrow to meet the inherent challenge of the subject.

365

Factors of size and scale: Scholarship has so far not matched the importance of geographical and organizational size and scale as elements in the country's legal history. Federalism is of course the prime legal expression of these factors, and has had much scrutiny. But most regard has gone to constitutional doctrine and to related aspects of politics. However, the federal theme should also include the reality of economic and cultural sectionalism, mingled with emergence of a national economy and components of a national culture. Thus far legal historians have not done much to develop the likenesses and differences with which legal doctrine and uses of law have shaped or responded to sectional experiences, different from or in tension with interests perceived on a national scale. It is especially clear that research resources have gone so far disproportionately to law as it has figured in the New England and Middle Atlantic states. The country is too big and diverse to warrant assuming that all that has held for those areas has held for the South, the Mississippi Valley, the Plains, the Southwest or the Pacific Coast.

Moreover, in fashions somewhat analogous to development of public policy aligned to national or regional settings, so public policy has affected or has been affected by changes in the scale of private organization for collective action. Private collective action for both profit and nonprofit ends has provided important elements of social structure and process from the beginnings of the nation. But the impacts of growth of large private organizations took on critical importance in and after the tumultuous decades of change from the 1880's into the 1920's. Legal historians need to assign a higher priority than they yet have given to studying relations of law to the shifting currents of centralized and decentralized private associational power that ran in that decisive period.

Salient periods of change: We need more attention to identifying and examining salient periods of change in relations of law and social structure. Until the last 30 years work badly scanted the 19th century, which in many ways seems more to have determined the character of 20th century society than did courses of public policy in the colonial years or the late 18th century. We have begun to make good this lack. But research output still largely focuses on decades before 1860. Yet the War and the headlong pace, depth and diversity of change from the 1880's into the 1920's so far remade the country as to call imperatively for prime attention to those decades of growth and default in public policy. Moreover, insofar as past allocation of research resources may imply that history resides only in the distant past, the notion does not stand analysis. Obviously, special cautions attach to investigation as it nears the confusions, feelings and interests peculiar to our immediate experience. But this is a caution about technique, not about defining subject matter. In essence, the subject is the time dimension of social experience, and this dimension reaches into today as well as into yesterday. Indeed, the generation since the end of World War II is probably a period of creative and destructive disjunction in the course of roles of law at least as important as any in the prior record.

Law's relations to other institutions: Finally, research in legal history needs to allocate more resources to match the range of the law's relations to the other-than-legal institutions which have been principal components of the society. So far most attention has gone to interplay of law and the changing character of the market. That allocation is appropriate to the centrality of the market in ideas and styles of action which mustered prevailing political power over the last 150 years. Even the record on this head is still spotty, and is notably deficient in studies of concrete particulars of where and how law has helped or hindered in providing functional requisites of market operations. But, beyond studying law and the market, we need more attention to the interplay of law and the family and sex roles, the bearing of law on the church, on the tensions between conventional morality and individual goals, on education, and on the course of change in scientific and technological knowledge. To elaborate such an institutional catalog is not to imply that law has been a dominant factor in the shifting patterns of other institutions. To the contrary, more work in legal history is likely to lead us to modest estimates of the comparative impact of law and other-than-legal institutional factors. What the search may yield is better answers to Roscoe Pound's key question of learning the limits of effective legal action. But no less a range in approach is calculated to lead study of legal history to the contributions it should make to a rich sociology of law.

New Interest in the Theory of the Field

What I have suggested as deficiencies in the scope of work in legal history to date indicates basic deficiencies in developing adequate theory to guide the growth of the field. However, to leave the matter so would be to disregard some significant, encouraging changes in approaches to the subject over the past 30 years, and particularly in the last decade. Increasing attention has gone to critical examination of ideas for defining subjectmatter and analyzing relative impacts of law in the society. This is a marked change from a time when legal historians wrote as if the subject defined itself within narrow limits which came near to identifying law as a wholly self-contained element in society. Three inter-related concerns figure most prominently in this new attention to theory—examination of ideas about consensus, about pluralism, and about dominance and oppression.

Consensus: Critics have attacked much work published over the last 30 years on the history of public policy as being "consensus" history. The term has slipped into almost conventional use as an epithet. The critics find want of realism or sophistication in studies which they read as portraying the United States as a society of one happy family, based on almost universally shared values, marked by little or no use of law to put and keep power in the hands of narrow sectors of wealth to the disadvantage of everyone else, but especially to the disadvantage of workers and the poor. Much of the criticized work is not so simpleminded as the criticism would suggest. The critics are not the first to discover that law has often involved serious conflicts over power and profit, or that the realities of conflict have not always showed on the surface of events. Early texts on these themes include Federalist No. 10, attacks leveled by Jefferson and Madison on Hamilton's programs, and Calhoun's Disquisition on Government. Moreover—a frequent peril for originally useful insights—the critique of "consensus" history shows signs of becoming a dogma or badge of intellectual *chic* which saves its user the hard work and responsibility of making his points out of his own digging in the raw materials of history. The better critics, I believe, concede that our legal-social history in fact reflects the presence of some broadly shared values which have shaped or legitimated uses of law. Indeed, wholesale denial of that proposition could hardly stand against stubborn facts which show this to have been in many respects a functioning society; an operational society spells some substantial sharing of values. The real issue is not Consensus or No Consensus, but how much consensus, on what, among whom, when,

367

and at what gains and costs to various affected interests. Certainly at different times on various matters law-embodied policy has reflected or pursued values shared among broad, yet diverse sectors of interests. Salient examples are the long, broadly held faith in the general benefi- cence of increasing over-all productivity measured in market-transac- tion terms, in many operations of the market as a major institution for allocating scarce economic resources, and in advances in scientific knowledge and in technological capacity to manipulate the physical and biological environments to human advantage. Challenges mounted to these shibboleths in the last generation themselves evidence the felt past reality of these propositions. The spread of those challenges into newly developing public policies itself attests early-stage emergence of some new areas of value consensus. In recent criticism there sometimes seems to lurk confusion between recognizing matters of fact and evalu- ating the social impact of those facts. The critics plainly share moral disapproval of certain values which broad coalitions of opinion have in fact shared in our past. But disapproval now of a shared value of the past is no proof that people then did not in fact share it.

368

Summary rejection of "consensus" history is a poor way of mak- ing some valid points which are potentially constructive contributions of the critique.

(1) Skepticism toward claims that the continued existence and operations of a given legal order has reflected general agreement among all those affected on the values represented in law can be useful in not letting us forget how much the possession of superior physical force has determined who has benefited and who has suffered from patterns of social relations. To the extent that it has been effective, this legal order has rested on successful assertion of a monopoly of physical force in legal agencies, including their ability to govern terms on which force may properly be wielded by private delegates. The declared ideal of our tradition has been that the law's monopoly of force should be legitimated by being held always within and subject to constitutional limitations designed to secure uses of law for public interest, including public interest in respect for the ultimate worth of individuals. No charge is more important on legal historians than to continue to probe the extent of fiction and reality in constitutional limits on the state's command of violence. The record shows uses of law to put its force at the disposal of private greed for power and profit. It shows, too, impositions of unlawful private force against workers, poor people, or racial or ethnic or religious minorities, which legal agencies—corrup- tion apart—have been too weak or incompetent to contain. There is a penetrating admonition for legal historians in criticism of assumptions of consensus which ignore realities of physical force in affairs, brought to bear by law officers who break the law, by private interests which

buy or over-awe law officers, and by collective private action which supplants law unable to over-match it.

(2) Consensus may be the product of indoctrinating people against their best interests, under guidance and for the particular benefit of special interests. Given the prominence in our political and social tradition of the constitutional ideal and the legitimacy it confers on legal order, law may be a useful instrument for such manipulation. The effectiveness in past politics of such rallying cries as "freedom of contract," "law and order," and "due process and equal protection of the laws" bears witness to this fact, as it also attests that quite a range of particular interests have mustered political influence under such symbols. It is useful to sharpen historians' appreciation that, while law may rest on consensus, law may be used to build consensus.

(3) Apparent consensus may reflect a deceptive range of will. It may reflect not so much positive consent or desire as resigned or despairing acceptance of superior force, directly or indirectly applied: "You can't fight city hall." It may reflect, as perhaps it often did in immigrants' acceptance of "Americanization," a sense of insecurity and lost roots. In this aspect of our experience a leading issue for legal, as for general historians, is to grapple with the difficulties of applying the idea of "class war" in our context, where so much interest conflict stayed within bounds of market, political, and legal processes. Contradictions among shared values have also been a significant part of public policy history, weakening or defeating the potential impress of common will. The course of antitrust policy is a notable example. Positive legal protection of the competitive vitality of the market has had broad acceptance since the Sherman Act. On the other hand, general opinion has learned to prize a rising material standard of living, and to associate this satisfaction with fruits of large-scale production and distribution. These attitudes have developed in continuing tension, reflected in the firm institutionalization of antitrust programs, but also in failures of broad public policy—not only in antitrust, but also in tariff, patent, tax, and public spending policies—to withhold government subsidies from or mount effective challenges to growth and entrenchment of concentration of private control in the market. Criticism of "consensus" history could in these respects indicate important directions for research into the origins and quality of will behind value sharing. But so far published work does not show much spadework put in on the raw materials.

(4) The uncertain realities of consensus involve one dimension which the critique, so far as I am aware, does not sufficiently identify. In a society marked by increasing diversity and numbers of functions and roles, economic and cultural, most people most of the time have in fact probably been indifferent to particular uses made of law to fix

369

gains and costs among specialized interests. Most people, that is, have tacitly if not explicitly shared a value distinctive to the legal order— that is, they have accepted certain legitimated, regular peaceful processes for determining particular allocations of gains and costs in particularly focused respects, and have accepted the particular substantive products of operation of those legal processes, whatever they be. True, such indifference may be another case of indoctrinated ignorance. But, also, it may rest on valid, rational perceptions of self-interest; as a creature of limited time, energy and capacity for satisfactions, the individual does not need for his own good to busy himself in helping decide how every competition of focused interests in his society should be worked out. Thus a valid indifference toward many substantive specifics in uses made of law has probably been a continuing element in a real consensus accepting legal processes, and all the more so as the society has grown more diversified in the kinds of life experience its members encounter.

370

Pluralism: Let me state from another perspective the significance of the fact of politically effective consensus which I last noted—that over most of our national history substantial opinion accepted uses of law to channel and legitimate bargains struck among competing interests. An inventory of state session laws and of the federal Statutes at Large through the 19th century, and of both statute law and administrative rules and regulations of the 20th century, will quickly attest the fact. The fact is less overt, and—as I noted earlier—held within close bounds of propriety, but nonetheless present in the growth of common law. Interwoven with these roles of formal legal agencies in providing frameworks for interest bargaining has been varying but continuing resort to political parties and party politics to give a generally centrist character to pursuit of major interest adjustments. A practical division of labor has assigned study of political processes to its own cadre of specialists. But products of formal legal processes have been closely intertwined with political operations; historians who specialize in studying output of formal legal agencies need to borrow appropriately from investigators of political processes, to put their subject in proper context.

This continuing general acceptance of legal processes to structure interest bargaining is a fact of our legal history. How to weigh the social results and to evaluate the social legitimacy of these bargaining uses of law present different questions, more open to dispute. Some may have read this record too complacently, taking this legal role to be a self-evident public good; some of this tone sounds even in the sophistication of Federalist No. 10, and Calhoun pointedly questioned the legitimacy of such interest bargaining in his Disquisition on Government as early as 1831. Modern criticisms of faith in the general benefits of a pluralist social-legal order suggest several useful cautions to legal historians. (1) Over sizeable periods of time and ranges of concerns the distribution of practical as well as of formal legal power has barred or severely limited access to the bargaining arena for Indians, blacks, other disadvantaged ethnic groups, women, and poor people in general. (2) Among those gaining some entry to the arena for competition of interests immediately concerned with roles in producing or marketing goods and services, bargaining power has often been in gross imbalance, as for example between big business and small business, urban creditors and rural debtors, employers and workers. (3) Interests not among the excluded or generally disadvantaged groups have in important matters been so diffuse and unorganized as to have little effective to say about what went on. Such was the situation, for example, in late 19th century relations of farmers and small businessmen to the railroads and in 20th century dealings of consumers with big firms supplying mass markets. This type of deficiency in bargaining patterns worked to the detriment of white middle class people who in other respects shared profits of dominance over less advantaged sectors. In this regard, as in relation to production and marketing relationships, a central theme for legal historians must be the rise of the big business corporation and the substantial but so far inadequate efforts in public policy to resolve the problems these great entities pose for achieving a healthy structure of social power. (4) The most subtle, but probably the most broadly harmful limitation of the bargaining process derived from the prime human factor that energized the process. Bargaining got impetus from what individuals or groups perceived as their interests. Perceptions of self-interest typically brought will to a focus for initiating and sustaining uses of law to serve interest. What did not enter perception did not stir will. In an increasingly diverse and shifting society, even among relatively sophisticated and powerful individuals and groups perceptions of interest tended to concentrate on rather short-term adjustments, specialized and intricate in detail. Such factors fostered narrowly pragmatic uses of law which excluded or subordinated attention to gains and losses calculated in terms of broad reaches of cause and effect and of long-term impacts. Tardy realization of this limitation of interest bargaining contributed pressure for late 20th century moves to invoke law to regulate the course of technological change and even of scientific inquiry as well as to reassess the social gains and costs of market allocation of resources.

371

Thus, there are sensible reasons for critically examining the record of using law to strike bargains among a plurality of interests. Even so, there are positive aspects to this history. For one thing, despite troubling trends toward increasing concentration of private control of economic assets and political influence, the society continued to be marked by a considerable dispersion of different types of practical power; it should be the business of legal historians to learn more about the qualities and defects of legal processes in affecting both concentration and dispersion. Second, interest bargaining through law seems to have contributed to creating socially productive elaboration of the division of labor within and outside of market processes. This is another aspect of a feature I noted in appraising consensus on legal order—that is the generally accepted value of procedures for adjusting specific relationships toward the substance of which most people were indifferent so long as they felt secure with recognized legal means of resolving the particular situations. Third, experience with oppressive uses of various kinds of legal organization of power has suggested no convincing alternative to improve on interest bargaining within constitutional legal processes as a major component of a legal and social order at once efficient and humane. The principal alternatives of which we have comparative historical experience have involved narrowly based, centralized authority which has typically fallen into abuse without serving either efficiency or humanity. It is a plausible thesis from our own experience that an efficient and just society needs more guidance for policy than bargaining among a plurality of interests alone will yield, but that the society cannot afford to do without a substantial bargaining component in its legal order.

372

Ruling class domination: There is a more sharply defined interpretation of United States legal history than what may be suggested by critiques of pluralism. This interpretation reads that history as the record of successes of a narrow sector of society in using law to help them get and hold decisive command of the prinicpal means of production, to the end of dominating all other social sectors for the satisfactions which concentrated wealth and power afford. In this view all else in the law which does not appear to fit this reading—such as constitutional structures, Bill of Rights guarantees, or generalized legal rights of property and contract and association—is but a facade for the real, tight monopoly held by private power. This kind of interpretation sometimes seems cast in tones of conspiracies to cloak coercion or to dupe credulous masses into according unwarranted legitimacy to the system. But the interpretation may be put on broader bases which attribute the outcome largely to trends functionally facilitated by law legitimizing private ownership of means of production. Since I do not qualify as an expert in Marxist doctrine, I hesitate to designate this as "the" or even "a" Marxist interpretation of United States legal history. If my statement does not accurately characterize Marxist interpretation, at least it points in the same direction. It has some similarities to critiques of pluralist analysis, but critics of pluralism are not necessarily proponents of a ruling-class thesis.

Like some analyses of pluralism, interpretation of legal history as a record of successes of a small sector of private controllers of wealth over the dominated generality carries useful insights for legal historians who do not accept the thesis. Wealthy individuals and groups and controllers of organized assets have used law to help create or sustain distinctions between dominated and dominant. This fact stands out most sharply in the situations of such disadvantaged interests as I noted excluded from the circle of effective interest bargainers. Gross imbalances in distribution of control over economic assets caution us to take account of the extent to which possession of organized physical force lies back even of constitutional legal order, and of the standing inducement that possession of such force has given to using law to serve private greed and ambition. Short of resort to overt force, continued gross, relative inequalities in private command of wealth and income under law have fostered and supported unjust uses of law to serve special interests. In the 20th century the might concentrated in a few hundred business corporations of unprecedented size has made control of massed economic assets, rather than personal enjoyment of great wealth and income, a source of social tensions distinctive to the time. That concentration of private control has profoundly challenged traditional reliance on the private market as an institution for healthy dispersion of power. So, too, it has put in question realization of the ideal of constitutional (that is, responsible) power as a standard to measure the legitimacy of both public and private powerholders.

373

However, our legal history seems too rich and diverse to be understood mainly as recording the success of a small class of controllers of major means of production in dominating the generality of the society. Three considerations stand out particularly, to make this interpretation unpersuasive as a sufficient explanation of the whole of this legal-social order, taken with reference both to its virtues and its vices. These defects include (1) underestimation of the realities of value consensus and bargaining among a plurality of interests, (2) neglect of public policy responses to felt functional needs of living in society, and (3) failure to measure qualities and defects in uses of law to confront some stubborn facts of the human predicament.

(1) Some broadly shared values which figured significantly in legal history had important roots other than in the distribution of control of means of production. First the adoption of the First Amendment separation of church and state fast became a substantially unchallenged premise of public policy. Sectarian diversity within a growing population, memories of religious wars and persecutions across the Atlantic, and an individualistic outlook on life born of mixed parentage in religious, economic and cultural influences of some hundreds of years, all went into this consensus on church-state re-

lations. Another salient example is the profound impact on public policy of broadly shared values growing out of experience of developments in science and technology — interlocked, it is true, with workings of the market, but involving reckonings not limited to those simply of a market calculus. Technological advances in ability to manipulate physical and biological elements of the environment nurtured belief in the self-evident social as well as individual benefits of growth in over-all, economic productivity. Teachings of a market-oriented way of life undoubtedly did much to promote this faith. But it seems as evident that technical-and-science-based confidence that material advance would boundlessly improve the quality of life did as much to sustain faith in the social merits of the market as the other way round. In addition to this belief in virtues of increased productivity, continuing exposure to what people saw as evident benefits from additions to technological command of nature built receptivity to change brought by the course of technology; the idea that such change might properly call for legal regulations was therefore the slower to emerge. Of course business exploitation of technological change for profit powerfully determined when, where, and by what calculations of gain and cost such change would be translated into marketable goods and services. Nonetheless, common attitudes derived from outside market experience slowed people's perception of needs to curb market exploitation of new technologies, and especially of new science-based technologies.

374

Likewise a ruling-class interpretation of legal history seems not to weight realistically the extent to which interest bargaining through law curbed private controllers of means of production. Public policy showed serious deficiencies in content and implementation. Nonetheless out of interest group bargaining within legal processes emerged substantial regulations protecting workers, consumers, and small and moderate sized business firms in matters of health, safety, collective bargaining, honest dealing, and maintenance of some extent of competition in market. By the 1970's one could not realistically define the structure and governance of even the largest business corporations without adding to provisions of corporation law proper multiplying elements of legal controls external to corporation law — in matters of finance, credit, marketing practices, taxation and accounting, labor relations, stockholder relations, and impacts on the environment. Apart from expansion of legal controls, another aspect of affairs puts in question a diagnosis which finds a narrow sector of capitalists or capitalist bureaucrats dominating everyone else. Through the 19th century and up to the 1970's a large proportion of interest conflicts fought within the frame of legal processes seem to have been intra-class rather than inter-class collisions, among segments of entrepreneurial property owners who, though of varying means, played capitalist roles. This appraisal seems to fit much of the development of law dealing with creditors and debtors, with the money supply, with regulation of insurance and banking, with relations between corporate promoters and managers and investors, and with antitrust protections of the market. It does not help analysis to label such phenomena as internal contradictions of capitalism, reflecting mere factional clashes within a well demarcated ruling class. What law often reflected in these aspects was an extent of fractionization substantial enough to put in question the dimensions of the high capitalist sector. Moreover, to all of this we must add account of the more or less distinct impact of political processes. Of course these estimates turn on questions of fact, well open to disputes and to differences of judgment. But there seems enough of bargaining impact visible in our legal history to preclude dogmatic acceptance of a theory cast wholly in terms of a small ruling class of wealthy individuals and big business bureaucrats.

375

(2) Important uses of law appear to have responded in substantial measure to what quite broad sectors of opinion perceived to be functional requisites of a going society, including some adjustments among competing demands of individuality and of group norms. In the background always, of course, were more or less explicit values about what kind of a society it should be. But, given some such basic premises, workable patterns for living together inescapably demanded a great detailed attention to more narrowly conceived ends and means. Growth of total population, increased concentrations of population in urban centers, broader and more complex marketing operations, and imperatives derived from advances in rule-of-thumb and science-based technology multiplied pressures of functional considerations from the late 19th century on. In pre-empting people's time, energies and attention, such immediate functional concerns readily generated out of their own momentum substantial proportions of the general content of public policy. This type of pressure seems material, for example, in development of law dealing with predictable regularities in market transactions, with public health and sanitation, and with organizing and administering supply of basic facilities for transport, water supply, and generation of electrical power. Of course the capitalist context often put its distinctive stamp on these developments. But comparisons with operations of non-capitalist societies suggests the presence of elements derived from problems likely to attend large-scale, bureaucratized, technically intricate social arrangements as such. And so far as functional requirements of workable social relations took on a character specially adapted to capitalism, legal historians need to learn more about the concrete particulars of uses of law to serve those functional needs. For whether one's ultimate concern is with likely con-

tinuance or displacement of capitalist elements of the social system, it is relevant to learn the qualities and defects of its organization. Despite the helpful insights it may prompt, a ruling-class interpretation carries the peril that its stripped-down diagnosis may tempt exponents to substitute its recitation for inevitably grubby work with particular raw materials.

(3) Some aspects of social experience are probably grounded in the fact that under all kinds of social organization, capitalist, socialist, or whatever, humans are finite beings. Scarcity of life satisfactions seems to be a constant of life for most people who are not saints. Individuals are born without their consent, live through successive phases and varying degrees of biological, emotional, and intellectual development or decline, and die. We should have learned to be cautious of fixed definitions of "human nature" knowing how often exploitation has justified itself by appeals to that "nature." Granted that caution, the stubborn fact remains that we are creatures of limited physical, intellectual and emotional capacity, with limited capacity to transcend sense of self or of in-group, with limited courage and energy of will. Within such limitations we confront social experience which is overwhelming in detail and density, sometimes moved by changes which in pace, range, depth and intricacy of cause and effect outstrip our understanding. To such limitations on individuals we know that we must add limits set sometimes below awareness by cultural inheritance and by unreasoning mass emotion. Out of this melange which makes up our human predicament as individuals and as members of social groups, general history tells how much has happened from unchosen, unplanned, often unperceived accumulations of events and their consequences.

376

Legal historians need reckon with the extent to which uses of law have partaken of these daunting forces of individual and social drift and inertia. Probably these elements account for more legal history than all of the deliberate strivings which our human vanity likes to dwell on. Here perhaps we confront the most profound limits of effective legal action.

However, along with science and technology, and our acquired experience in contrived collective action outside formal legal means in producing and distributing various kinds of satisfactions, law has been a major instrument for combating mindlessness and chaos in experience. There can hardly be an aspect of legal history more poignantly bearing on our human situation than this, but it is an aspect so far almost unexplored. By definition an interpretation cast in terms of dominant and dominated sectors of society deals with more or less conscious and deliberate striving. Thus, along with all other interpretations that turn on estimates of will, it omits the great darkness that surrounds all striving. Moreover, this consideration brings us back —

again with due caution — to questions of the extent to which problems brought to law derive not just from pursuit of particular roles of people as capitalists or workers, oppressors or oppressed under particular forms of social organization, but from sources rooted in existential fears and insecurities. Whatever the specific organization of social power, general history suggests that under any system we shall see impacts of greed, lust for power over other people's wills, fear of the stranger, and yearning for individual and group security against primitive fears of what lies in the surrounding murk and muddle. Though imperfectly perceived or realized, some responses to such threats and challenges appear in our legal history. They are deep in constitutional structures and in Bill of Rights provisions, in uses of law to allocate resources to advancing knowledge and providing education, and in creating legal standards and rules which may work to enlarge empathy among individuals who stand to each other in no close ties of blood, kin, clan, religion, race, or nationality. So far as uses of law have responded to these profound issues, probably the responses have been conditioned by many features of social context of special weight in our experience—in the setting in North America, growth timed in the surge of the commercial and industrial revolutions and the rise of the middle class, values stamped as predominantly white, middle class and capitalist, Christian, individualist, and pragmatic. But there is a substratum of meaning here which study of such contextual particulars does not reach. No more will it be reached by a ruling-class interpretation. Law has nothing to do with creating these ineluctable terms of existence. But the presence or absence of response to them through law, and the qualities or deficiencies of response, provide inescapable dimensions of legal history, whether or not legal historians have enough sensitivity to see this.

377

Individual experience of legal order: Approaches to more perceptive theory about legal history, through critiques of consensus, pluralism, and ruling class explanations have in common a tendency to lose sight of individuals by concentrating on groups or masses. The omission carries some irony, given the persistence with which the economy, the culture and the constitutional tradition of this society have professed to assign high value to individual will and the dignity of individual life. Moreover, the omission offends against reality, for no one can escape history as an individual; the content of history necessarily includes the individual's own experience of the social context, including the context provided by uses of law. Of course biographers of lawyers, judges, legislators, and other public officers, as well as of politicians have been filling in some of this part of the story—though usually subject to the kinds of limitations which have marked the examination of legal history in the large. But biographers deal almost always with individuals who in some measure have stepped out of the general ranks, have held some degree of leadership, and have hammered out some form of exceptional career. General historians have scarcely begun to work with the ordinary experience of ordinary people, or even with the typical experience of typical members of higher social status or practical power. Legal historians have made even less beginnings in exploring at this level the meaning or lack of meaning that public policy has had for individual life courses. There are obvious difficulties in finding reliable sources. For great sectors of the people of the past, probably evidence is simply not there for even the most ingenious and tireless searcher to find. The general lack of evidence increases the embarrassments of judging what we may find in terms of its comparative meaning or its representative character. A proper sense of these obstacles should induce humility in critics of those who muster the courage and persistence to tackle the job. Meanwhile, we must consider that the catalog of work done shows a serious gap for its want of studies on how legal order has entered or failed to enter into individual life experience.

378

I have disagreements with much recent criticism of the theoretical frame for studying legal history. Overall, however, the extent of fresh concern with theory is constructive. Thirty years ago legal historians seemed generally indifferent to the need of a theoretical structure for making sense of the raw materials. Otherwise, they showed what now seems parochial or naive complacency that everyone knew what the proper subject matter of legal history was, and that for all purposes that counted, it began and ended with the output of judges. By and large, I do not quarrel with the intrinsic worth of the subjects in which scholars invested effort; there has been and probably always will be hack work and sheer antiquarianism, but past scholarship has given us a great deal on which to build. My concern is rather that so far research resources have not been allocated in due proportion to the full range of significant subject matter. More penetrating and wider ranging theory is prerequisite to allocations more realistically aligned to the full realities of legal-social order.

However, the quality of this new direction of interest carries a potential defect that is serious. We don't know much across the board about how law has really worked in social experience. Trying to find out is costly in time, money, energy, thought, courage, and persistence. In contrast, spinning theory can be more fun, less work, and more quickly satisfying to the ego, which is happiest to see itself reflected promptly in print. Turning out solid monographs does not yield such quick and easy returns. If a new generation of legal historians is not wary of its capacity for original sin, it might wind up full of talk and short of matter. Theory must go to work on recalcitrant raw materials, if it is to deserve full respect.

BOOK REVIEWS

Looking Backward: The Early History of American Law

The Rise of the Legal Profession in America (2 volumes). ANTON-HER-
MANN CHROUST. Norman: University of Oklahoma Press, 1965. Vol.
I, Pp. xxiii, 334; Vol. II, Pp. 318. $15.00.

Professional Lives in America. DANIEL H. CALHOUN. Cambridge: Harvard University Press, 1965. Pp. xiv, 231. $5.95.

The Golden Age of American Law. CHARLES M. HAAR, ED. New York: 379
George Braziller, Inc., 1965. Pp. xiv, 533. $8.50.

The Life of the Mind in America. PERRY MILLER. New York: Harcourt,
Brace & World, Inc., 1965. Pp. xi, 338. $7.50.

There has occurred in the last year what may be viewed as a modest
revival of interest in the early history of American law. The bulkiest
manifestation of this renaissance is a two-volume study of the rise of
the legal profession from the seventeenth century to 1860, but at the
same time several other books have appeared which in whole or in
part bear on the same subject. The historian is tantalized but at the
same time troubled by the traditional character of much of the new
work.

Legal historians have tended to define the substance of the law quite
narrowly. We have a great many legal and judicial biographies, treatises on the formal categories of law and procedure, accounts of constitutional development, and histories of particular courts. Legal history has been slow, however, in responding to the newer concerns and
techniques of contemporary historians, particularly in the realm of
social and economic history. The possibility of examining the law in
its actual relation to social and economic process through the systematic exploitation of a fuller range of documents, such as legislative and
administrative records, economic and social data, and the records of
lower courts and ordinary lawyers is now emerging. To keep pace
with the times, legal historians must move from the study of appellate
opinions to the broader context of law in society, from what law was
to how law worked, from substance to process.

Likewise, the chronological horizons of American legal history must be broadened. Legal historians, operating on the unspoken assumption that American law derives from the requirements of industrial society, traditionally have concentrated on a period beginning in the mid-nineteenth century. The colonial period has been neglected almost totally, while even the revolutionary and early national periods have been veiwed merely as a "formative" stage. The periodization which rejects everything before 1776, bows perfunctorily to the antebellum era, and sets to work in earnest after 1861, no longer seems satisfactory. It derives from the formalism which has afflicted legal history quite generally, and seems unlikely to survive the current reexamination of the field. For as the focus of study becomes the law in action and as the socio-economic aspects of legal development are probed, the long-term continuities of legal history are bound to emerge. After all, to demonstrate that our present law would not be the same had the industrial revolution never occurred is not necessarily to show that one aspect of the economy determined the nature of legal development. To the historian it seems more reasonable to suppose that a wide range of phenomena—political, economic, social, and ideological—helped to shape the character of American law. And at least to the colonial historian, it seems likely that the century and three-quarters preceding the Revolution, as well as the first decades of the national period, made a basic contribution to the growth of American law. If we are to turn our attention to the operation of the law in a broad social context, we shall also have to accept a more sweeping definition of the chronological bounds of the problem.

The books under review illustrate some of the possibilities now available to legal historians in terms of sources, techniques, and periodization. None of them is entirely successful, but as a group they hint at what might be done. One day, with a bit of luck and hard work, we shall have an American legal history which looks to the entire range of society for its context and which begins in the beginning.

Professor Anton-Hermann Chroust of the University of Notre Dame prefaces his two volumes on *The Rise of the Legal Profession in America* with the disclaimer that they are intended "primarily, though not exclusively, for the instruction of law students, and, perhaps, for the entertainment of practicing lawyers rather than for the enlightenment of the critical historian." He acknowledges that his book makes "little pretense to original scholarship" and expresses his fear that students of American colonial and legal history will disagree with him

380

"on many points of information."[1] Writing for an audience of lawyers, the historian is compelled to confess that his reservations not only fulfill the author's fears, but also extend to Professor Chroust's underlying suppositions.

The Rise of the Legal Profession in America carries the profession from its origins in the seventeenth century to the decades immediately preceding the Civil War. Chroust sees the seventeenth century (until 1690) as an era of "justice without lawyers and, in consequence, frequently without a stable and reliable body of laws as well as without proper courts of law."[2] The primitive condition of the law obviated the need for trained lawyers, contributed to the widespread distrust of the profession, and allowed "incompetent and irresponsible opportunists" to preempt the transaction of legal business. After 1690, however, the situation improved rapidly. A "regular and independent" system of courts was developed, and a group of trained lawyers appeared, "doing business according to law and in keeping with the strict rules of procedure."[3] Standards for the admission of lawyers to practice were rationalized, and the bar began its first, feeble attempts to organize itself for the achievement of definable standards of professional conduct. By the mid-eighteenth century, the stature of the legal profession had "drastically improved in most colonies," aversion to lawyers had been transformed into admiration, and law-trained men had become the leaders of the revolutionary new nation in response to the popular recognition that the lawyers had sprung "to the defense of the people's rights and liberties."[4]

381

In the years between the American Revolution and the Civil War, Chroust finds a confusion of seemingly contradictory trends. For one thing, there was a serious tendency toward "deprofessionalization" of the bench and bar immediately following the Revolution and again after 1830, caused by an influx of unqualified practitioners and an intrusion of state legislators into the judicial process. By the eve of the Civil War, the egalitarian spirit of Jacksonian democracy had corroded the institutional safeguards of the profession to the extent that men "unfit by character, culture, or training to become members of a learned profession" had brought its public reputation to a new low point.[5] Nevertheless, in several significant ways the profession was "rising" during this period. Public and professional revulsion with

---

1 Vol. I, pp. vii-viii.
2 *Id.* at 331.
3 *Id.* at 332.
4 *Id.* at 334.
5 Vol. II, p. 286.

English common law in the post-revolutionary years resulted in the production of the first American law reports and legal treatises. Legal education was removed from the practitioners' offices and placed in the leading universities. A "golden age" of "creative legal accomplishments" ("mostly concerned with the applicability of traditional legal materials to the specific American circumstances") emerged as American judges and lawyers created a system of law "applicable to the new and unique American social scene."[6] Lawyers attained higher standards of professional skill and, imbued with the national spirit of "rugged individualism," rose to unprecedented heights of "public leadership."[7] Aside from their contributions to public life, "the cumulative though unofficial services which the legal profession rendered the country in the promotion of vital causes are beyond estimate."[8]

The working historian finds that he disagrees with this bold and romantic summary in three major respects. The first has to do with Chroust's treatment of lawyers and their profession. He exaggerates the significance of the lack of a trained bench and bar in the seventeenth century, and poses a misleading dichotomy between "lawyers" and "charlatans."[9] Recent work in colonial legal history indicates that in the seventeenth century both laymen and lawmen (the distinction is not by any means clear before the middle of the eighteenth century) dealt with legal problems in a sophisticated and conscientious manner, acting as lawyers and as judges.[10] That they should have been able to cope with the law is not surprising, for in the seventeenth century English local law was for the most part in the hands of laymen.[11] The emergence of an educated and professionalized bar in the eighteenth century thus did not cause as radical a reorientation in the conduct of legal business as Chroust suggests. At the same time, Chroust underestimates colonial lawyers and overvalues English legal education. Examination of the working materials of American lawyers for the first third of the eighteenth century reveals a surprising familiarity with contemporary English law and a high degree of technical com-

382

---

6 *Id.* at 283.

7 *Id.* at 285.

8 *Id.* at 286.

9 See vol. I, p. 277.

10 See, *e.g.*, Chafee, *Records of the Suffolk County Court, 1671-1680*, 29 COLONIAL SOC'Y OF MASS. PUBLICATIONS xxviii-xciv (1933); COLONIAL JUSTICE IN WESTERN MASSACHUSETTS (1639-1702): THE PYNCHON COURT RECORD 65-68 (Smith ed. 1961); COURT RECORDS OF PRINCE GEORGES COUNTY, MARYLAND 1696-1699, xliii-cxiv (Smith & Crowl eds. 1964); HASKINS, LAW AND AUTHORITY IN EARLY MASSACHUSETTS 113-62 (1960).

11 DAWSON, A HISTORY OF LAY JUDGES 178-264 (1960); HASKINS, *op. cit. supra* note 10, at 163-88; Goebel, *King's Law and Local Custom in Seventeenth Century New England*, 31 COLUM. L. REV. 416 (1931).

petence,[12] and the proposition that men trained in the Inns of Court emerged with "sound legal learning" and "acquired a vast intellectual culture" is highly dubious.[13]

Chroust's treatment of lawyers in the revolutionary period is altogether unsatisfactory, since he is content simply to list the leading Whig lawyers of each colony seriatim, without analyzing their professional stature or revolutionary leadership. He notices the large number of Loyalist lawyers who left the country in the 1770's, but never comes to terms with the really interesting question of whether there was anything in their professional training or outlook which predisposed them to side with Great Britain.[14] Since lawyers are credited with a leading role in the revolutionary and constitution-making eras, Chroust's failure to examine their group attitudes and social functions in the last third of the eighteenth century is especially disappointing.

As far as the nineteenth century is concerned, suffice it to say that Chroust never manages to disentangle the welter of conflicting lines of development which he suggests. Was there no connection between the "deprofessionalization" of bench and bar and the emergence of lawyers as the leading public figures in the United States? Why should bar associations have fallen into disuse at the very time that legal thought and legal education were attaining true distinction? In any case, what is the relevance of the popular reputation of lawyers to their professional development?

383

Second, one must question Professor Chroust's account of the substantive history of law in the one hundred and fifty years following the settlement at Jamestown. One difficulty here is that he rejects the currently accepted interpretation of law in the seventeenth century in favor of the view that:

> English law and English precedents often were neither followed nor used as a guide by the courts. . . . The law itself often was extremely flexible and amateurish. In some instances, it was the highly questionable product of personal caprice, prejudice, or just plain ignorance.[15]

Chroust cites the outdated works of Hilkey[16] and Reinsch[17] in support

---

12 ALEXANDER, A BRIEF NARRATIVE OF THE CASE AND TRIAL OF JOHN PETER ZENGER, 41-105, 139-45, 148-51 (Katz ed. 1963).

13 Vol. I, p. 230.

14 See vol. II, pp. 5-11.

15 Vol. I, p. 26.

16 Hilkey, *Legal Development in Colonial Massachusetts*, 37 COLUMBIA STUDIES IN HISTORY, ECONOMICS, AND PUBLIC LAW (1910).

17 Reinsch, *The English Common Law in the Early American Colonies*, 1 SELECT ESSAYS IN ANGLO-AMERICAN LEGAL HISTORY 367 (1907).

of the view that English common law did not make an appearance in the colonies until the beginning of the eighteenth century, tempering this blunt assessment with the suggestion that colonial law was a "half-remembered and half-understood technical language of English courts and English lawyers" which was "roughly applied" to frontier American conditions.[18] If one examines the actual substance of colonial law, however, it seems difficult not to conclude that early American law was a quite sophisticated combination of English and indigenous ideas which evolved in response to the changed conditions of life in the New World. To notice that the common law was not transported *in toto* to Massachusetts does not demonstrate that English law had no influence there. It was out of the familiar English local law that the Puritans framed their own system.

384

Furthermore, regardless of the precise "sources" of the law, the printed records of seventeenth century courts alone seem sufficient to indicate the complexity and surprising maturity of American law at that time. Professor Chroust's concern with the lack of a legal profession in the early period leads him to the indefensible position that so long as laymen were permitted to manage lawsuits "there was little need and little use for a refined and stable law."[19] Is it not anachronistic to argue that "the administration of justice without a stable and detailed body of laws is at best a constant source of difficulties and uncertainties"?[20] Blackstone would have been appalled by the state of the law in early Massachusetts, but would Michael Dalton have been?[21]

Moreover, Chroust's dark view of the first century of settlement leads him to take the position that the "reception of the common law" was a sudden and widespread phenomenon of the early eighteenth century, a response to the increase in numbers and influence of trained lawyers.[22] This approach minimizes the extent to which common law ideas were known and used in the seventeenth century and ties the growth of substantive law to the formal education of lawyers. In fact, as Chroust himself notes, each colony developed its own primitive common law,[23] and it was into this existing tradition that the common

---

[18] Vol. I, pp. 7, 71.

[19] *Id.* at 17.

[20] *Id.* at 194.

[21] Dalton, a Cambridgeshire justice of the peace in the first half of the seventeenth century, was the author of the best-known handbook on English local justice of the period: THE COUNTREY JUSTICE (1618). The volume was widely used in colonial America; it was one of the small group of legal works imported by the Massachusetts General Court and was still to be found in the libraries of revolutionary American lawyers.

[22] See vol. I, pp. 17-18.

[23] *Id.* at 17.

law of England was gradually fed for reasons of political convenience, intellectual sophistication, and practical necessity. The process was continuous throughout the eighteenth century, and the behavior of American courts in the last quarter of the century makes it appear that the rejection of English common law which Chroust attributes to nationalistic feelings spawned by the Revolution was more rhetorical than practical. Indeed, Professor Levy has made a strong case for the idea that the framers of the state and federal constitutions and the writers of the first amendment accepted the notion of an American common law.[24]

Third, the historian's concern for periodization leads him to feel that Professor Chroust's rigid temporal divisions distort his perception of legal development. We have already noted his arbitrary distinction between the seventeenth and eighteenth centuries according to their supposed receptiveness to English common law, and the division of the eighteenth century itself at the Revolution for the same reason. A similar artificiality characterizes his discussion of the years 1776-1860 as a new and unitary period, the achievements of which "may favorably be compared with the legal achievements of any epoch in Western history."[25] This periodization (and thus the general plan of *The Rise of the Legal Profession in America*) derives from Roscoe Pound's notion of the "formative era" of American law. Pound argued that colonial law bore little relation to the distinctively American law inspired by the independent United States. He emphasized the formal, medieval, and pre-commercial character of colonial law. "[T]he common law as the colonists knew it was the law of the age of Coke, not the law of the age of Mansfield";[26] the entire heritage amounted to no more than "Coke's Second Institute and Blackstone."[27] The task of the formative era was thus to work out a body of law suitable to a modern society "from our inherited legal materials."[28] Admittedly, nineteenth century law responded to economic pressures which had been maturing since the middle of the eighteenth century, but, as we shall see, it seems unlikely that the post-revolutionary generation of lawyers, judges, and legislators was creating an American law *de novo*.

The character of the legal profession from the mid-eighteenth to

---

24 LEVY, LEGACY OF SUPPRESSION: FREEDOM OF SPEECH AND PRESS IN EARLY AMERICAN HISTORY 176-248 (1963); Levy, *Liberty and the First Amendment: 1790-1800*, 68 AMERICAN HISTORICAL REV. 24-27 (1962).

25 Vol. II, p. 283.

26 POUND, THE FORMATIVE ERA OF AMERICAN LAW 6 (1938).

27 *Id.* at 9.

28 *Id.* at 8.

the mid-nineteenth century is one of the subjects of Daniel H. Calhoun's *Professional Lives in America*, which also includes essays on medicine and religion. Calhoun applies some of the techniques of quantitative analysis, as well as a well-trained intuition, to the problem of the interaction of social structure and professional thought. He has singled out the history of a county in the Cumberland River country of middle Tennessee, from roughly 1790 to the Civil War, as a case study of the relationship between American society and the law. During this period, Sumner County evolved from a frontier community to one increasingly characterized by urban and commercial concerns. The lawyers of Sumner County, like the law they practiced, underwent a measurable change as their society changed its character. In the earliest days, lawyers on horseback followed judges on horseback around the judicial circuits of Sumner and its neighboring counties. The peripatetic county bar was small in numbers and quite inflexible in character, but it monopolized the legal business of the communities into which it travelled. The first signs of change occurred in reaction to the economic hard times preceding the War of 1812, when the rapid accumulation of suits for the recovery of debt crowded other types of lawsuits off the calendars of the county courts. In response, Tennessee lawyers remolded the law to suit the new conditions —for example, a statute of limitations set a term on real property disputes. The profession itself was also changing. Lawyers, no longer content merely to assist in the collection of debts, began to reorient themselves toward individual clients rather than local communities, and as Tennessee towns and commerce expanded, the circuit-riding lawyer gave way to the urban commercial lawyer. In the end, "it was not merely the expansion of business, but expansion against the communal rigidities of an earlier system, that forced the emergence of a new kind of legal profession."[29]

Taken by itself, the legal history of Sumner County, Tennessee, is unlikely to quicken many pulses, but Professor Calhoun has used it as an example of the socialization of the American legal profession from 1750 to 1850. He takes the transition from the colonial to the national period, or from the eighteenth century to the nineteenth, quite seriously. He sees a gradual change from a communally-oriented era to an era characterized by liberal, market-oriented values. To a great extent, this shift can be seen in the "continuing, growing spill of town standards over into the countryside."[30] Within this larger so-

---

[29] P. 85.
[30] P. 13. See also pp. 18-19.

cial context, the legal profession was dramatically transformed. The level of the profession had been quite low before 1750, but at about that time a general effort to raise "its intellectual level and practical performance" began. The result was that the status of lawyers was institutionalized, both superficially—gowns and wigs were introduced —and profoundly—legal commentary achieved new heights. This pursuit of professional excellence extended through the revolutionary period, carrying with it aristocratic, hierarchical implications.[31]

Focusing on the middle of the nineteenth century, Calhoun finds a radically changed professional outlook. The egalitarian spirit of Jacksonian democracy forced the legal profession toward mediocrity and individualistic chaos. A bifurcation appeared within professional life as the leveling tendencies of the democratic trend toward conformity forced lawyers to accommodate themselves to popular ideas as well as to pursue "their highest professional concerns in spheres removed from the public."[32] Furthermore, as market relationships rather than the notion of an elite came to determine the social structure of the profession, leadership was transferred from men endowed with intellectual authority to the bureaucrats who administered bar associations and other professional institutions. Lawyers, like physicians and ministers, retained their "sense of being a special in-group, yet seemed to move toward uniformity, away from any individual distinction other than what emerged from impersonal competition in the labor market that the profession itself became."[33] In this situation, the leadership of the legal profession repressed the extraordinary individual lest his efforts endanger the structure of the profession.

Professional Lives in America is a brief book, only tangentially concerned with the history of the legal profession, and the experience of a county in Tennessee is, of course, far removed from the mainstream of the urban profession in the northeastern states. Yet the scope and quality of Calhoun's analysis provide us with a glimpse of some promising avenues open to legal historians. The particular virtue of the book is that it combines the study of lawyers as social beings, caught up in the currents of social change, with the study of legal thought, which takes its meaning from the social context in which it is conceived. Calhoun views lawyers from a sophisticated sociological point of view; he asks how the changing nature of legal business (from debt collection to commercial litigation) affected the structure of the legal profession, how basic economic and social change forced a reorga-

387

---

31 Pp. 178-80.
32 P. 184.
33 P. 187.

nization of that profession, and how professional problems caused lawyers to seek changes in the law. It is clear that legal historians of the early period have much to learn from the techniques of sociological history.

Charles M. Haar's *The Golden Age of American Law*, which anthologizes the legal literature of the forty years before the Civil War, deals with "the interaction of law with the ideals, technology, and physical conditions of these formative years . . . ."[34] The "golden age" of the title, although required by the publisher's series of which this is only one volume, betokens Haar's fundamental agreement with the Pound notion that the pre-Civil War years laid the foundation for the modern American legal system:

388

> Dissolution of the vestiges of feudal society in the New World [during the Revolution] created the need for a fresh analysis of goals, as well as for a legal framework to establish the conditions necessary for community life and order consistent with the approved goals.[35]

The anthology includes extracts from legal treatises, periodicals, judicial opinions, courtroom addresses, and a wide range of nonlegal sources. It is subdivided into five topics: the legal profession, public law, law and reform, law and economic development, and "the search for legal identity."

Haar's introductions to the several sections of the volume are concise, intelligent, and frequently original. With respect to the problems of public law, for example, he addresses himself to the incisive question of why "there was never to be a *McCulloch v. Maryland* for slavery," concluding that for slavery there could never have been, as there was for national banks, "the degree of consensus which permits recourse to law."[36] Haar also contributes to our understanding of nineteenth century social reform by his discussion of the manner in which Americans agreed to use the law "as a tool for evolutionary growth"—permitting judges to act as arbiters of social change while at the same time developing legal agencies through which the reform movements could respond to the needs of the age.[37] The essay on law and the economy succinctly states the major legal problem of the antebellum years: "the need for new legal instrumentalities and fresh

---

[34] P. v.
[35] P. vi.
[36] P. 120.
[37] P. 210.

concepts to give the entrepreneur the organization and discipline he required" in the face of Jacksonian prejudices against the intervention of the state into the economy.[38]

Although *The Golden Age of American Law* is an anthology, Haar's introductions raise an interesting question about the sources of legal history, for it is evident that the editor's most interesting speculations are based, not on the sorts of literary evidence which the anthology preserves, but on the social, economic, and political imperatives of the period. Reviewing contemporary speculation on the nature of law, Haar concludes that two contradictory forces were at work in the law of the "formative era": "the old and the given" (accepted law, English traditions, settled business relations, social and economic privilege) and "the new" (universal suffrage, anti-monopoly, anti-professionalism, a Bill of Rights, hostility to corporations). The task of the law was "to mediate between these two forces and to maintain the status quo until a general consensus could be reached and conflicts resolved. This function made the law of the period unique."[39] Such a "mediatory" function, is however, precisely the sort of aspect of the law which the writings Haar reprints do not in themselves illuminate. In so far as the law is merely a general statement of rules necessary to social order, it can be dealt with in terms of legal "literature." To the extent that law is itself a factor in socio-economic change, however, such literary evidence gives a very limited notion of the process of legal development. It relates to the dead letter of the law in the statute book rather than to the life of the law in legislatures, courts, and counting houses. At bottom, the implication of the "literary" approach to legal history is that the law is essentially a self-conscious creation of men's minds, a branch of the history of thought.

It is from precisely this point of view that the foremost student of American intellectual life, the late Perry Miller of Harvard, deals with the law in his "The Legal Mentality," published in his posthumous volume *The Life of the Mind in America.*[40] Of a projected nine long essays on various aspects of the American intellect in the period from the Revolution to the Civil War, "The Legal Mentality" is one of two completed by Professor Miller before his death. Miller's sources are of the formal literary type collected in Professor Haar's anthology. He is aware that "the life of the mind" has no existence apart from society, but he believes that historical change can best be gauged by

389

---

38 P. 333.

39 P. 423.

40 See also the anthology which preceded Miller's study of the law, THE LEGAL MIND IN AMERICA: FROM INDEPENDENCE TO THE CIVIL WAR (Miller ed. 1962).

the expressions of the human intelligence. Thus, institutional and social developments are inferred from their literary manifestations (using the term broadly), and legal history becomes the study of what lawyers and judges have committed to print.

"The Legal Mentality" surveys the legal profession, the character of legal theory, the relation of law to morality, and the negative character of public law in the period between 1776 and 1860. The argument is too complex to be summarized briefly, but Miller's long chapter on the movement for codification of the law indicates the nature of his approach. He begins by noticing the attempts of James Wilson in Pennsylvania and Thomas Jefferson and others in Virginia to prepare digests of the post-revolutionary laws of their states. These early digests were of the eighteenth century, rational sort and encountered serious opposition even from a populace that passionately feared the mysterious common law which the digests promised to make coherent. Miller notices that this was a phenomenon that persisted throughout the period: an ambivalence "between hostility to the intricacy of the Common Law and . . . reluctance to abandon it as constituting the bulwark of rights and liberties."[41] The layman's fear of codification was, however, dissipated by the gradual realization that the unsystematic character of the common law might lead to rule by the judges empowered to interpret the law, and eventually "believers in democracy found a special appeal in the idea of a digest speaking in a language familiar to everybody."[42] The idea was strengthened by Edward Livingston's success in codifying the procedure and criminal law of Louisiana along the lines of the Code Napoleon, and by the influence of the first legal textbooks, which became "in effect drafts of codes" by reason of their "effort to impose a logical structure upon their material."[43]

The struggle for codification ultimately left the refined atmosphere of the law school and lawyer's club and became the political issue of codification versus common law, driving the common man even more surely into the party of codification.[44] The problem that intrigues Miller is why the profession should have been so bitterly divided over such a question. He remarks that opponents of codification ranged all the way from those who merely desired "to monopolize a profitable mystery" to those who saw in the common law "an intellectual vision

---

[41] P. 241.
[42] P. 243.
[43] P. 245.
[44] P. 246.

of infinite extensibility."[45] He examines the thought of the leading codifier, David Dudley Field, in search of clues, and they are forthcoming. Field was angered by the chaotic state of the law, by the complexities of special pleading, and by the artificial distinction between law and equity. He sought instead a "simple and natural scheme of legal procedure," claiming that his "radical" method of going back to first principles would not introduce substantive novelties into the law.[46] At this point, Miller introduces a characteristic interjection: "Had the crux of the argument, up to the Civil War, been only a matter of the simplicity of codes versus the malleability of precedents, the entire contentious episode would be only a sad footnote to a period of intellectual exertion."[47]

After this remark, we are not startled to find that "something more was involved": "[T]he crevasse which opened within the fraternity represented a division between two opposing ideals of America. At bottom, the dispute over codes was a dispute over the identity of the nation."[48] The point, as Miller sees it, is that Field and his supporters were legal nationalists, seeking an American law derived pragmatically from the American experience. In Field's words:

391

> Not being provided with a literature of his own, the American is subjected to two opposite systems of training; one from books, the other from the life he sees around him.[49]

Field preferred the empirical method—constructing law out of native materials rather than "applying here the customs and maxims which belong to Europe."[50] At the same time, he associated the common law with the corrupt and aristocratic societies of Europe and fervently wished to develop a domestic law which would fulfill the republican promise of the Revolution. Of course the proponents of the common law felt fully as American as Field, but they were inclined to seek the fulfillment of their own civilization "by remaining within the context of an international culture . . . ."[51] Thus, the debate over codification was a conflict about the content of American democracy—the one publicly debatable issue in the law. Miller concludes that in the end, Field was doomed to failure by the onrush of industrial society:

---

45 P. 253.
46 Pp. 260-61.
47 P. 261.
48 P. 254.
49 P. 262.
50 *Ibid.*
51 P. 264.

> Compared with the palatial steamboats, the roaring railroads,
> the Atlantic cable (which David Field's brother laid in 1858),
> wherein was the majesty of a code, or even of the Common
> Law?[52]

Codification, like Puritanism, was too remote and intense a vision to control the forces at work in America.

The legal historian will find that despite its undoubted merits, "The Legal Mentality" is unsatisfactory in several respects. The principal objection arises out of the author's view of the law as only one instance of a general intellectual manifestation, a view which frequently leads him to wrench contours of the history of legal thought in order to fit them into a larger scheme. Miller's language is a case in point, since it reflects the duality he perceives throughout American history: the conflict between the natural and the artificial. He discusses the conflict over the state of the law in post-revolutionary America in terms of a series of parallel antinomies: nature vs. society, nature vs. law, equity vs. sophistication, genius vs. system, romantic vs. Newtonian, heart vs. head.[53] For Miller, the history of law is a revealing test case of the American experience. Man could not live absolutely naturally even in America, though that is the ideal for which he strove, and the types of legal systems he established reflect the degree to which he sacrificed his democratic genius to the demands of social order. This, to be sure, overstates Miller's case, but it points up the fact that most students of the law have been less nostalgic than Miller about the subjugation of nature to legal order.

A more pedestrian objection concerns the periodization employed in "The Legal Mentality." Miller accepts the general idea of the "formative era," even though he selects his terminal dates for more profound, non-legal, reasons. Following Joseph Willard[54] and Henry St. George Tucker,[55] Miller argues that American law had to start

392

---

52 P. 265.

53 See pp. 104-06, 112-13, 121. Professor Calhoun uses similar terminology in noting the conflict between "intensity" and "training" within the legal profession, but the sense of his dichotomy is more obviously related to the social situation of the law. CALHOUN, PROFESSIONAL LIVES IN AMERICA 16, 195-97 (1965).

54 In accordance with the practice in Miller's earlier volumes, *The Life of the Mind in America* is unannotated, so that no specific reference to Willard's views is given. Willard (1798-1865) was a graduate of Harvard College and the Harvard Law School (1820) who established his reputation for legal knowledge during a long career as a master in chancery and Clerk of the Court of Suffolk County, Massachusetts.

55 Miller's reference to Tucker is as unspecific as his citation of Willard. Tucker (1780-1848) was a graduate of William and Mary (1799) and the most distinguished Virginia lawyer of the ante-bellum period. He was successively a judge in chancery, President of the Supreme Court of Appeals of Virginia, and Professor of Law at the University of

afresh after the Revolution: "[C]olonial precedents were of little worth, and . . . therefore we had no such venerable body of antique wisdom as gave the Common Law in England its sacerdotal power."[56] Thus, the legal theorists of the early nineteenth century provide evidence of a rejection of the colonial period through a process which Miller describes as the "shifting from a philosophy of law which was primarily contractual in character to one that was conscious of history" or the "getting out of the eighteenth century and into the nineteenth."[57] Miller also finds support for his analysis in the economic developments taking place in America around 1800: the transformation from landed to corporate property and the socio-economic explosion following the War of 1812: "the new importance of admiralty law, the beginnings of manufactures, and the sudden need of policies for patents, for the development of canals and turnpikes, and soon thereafter for railroads."[58]

393

No one would deny the impact of early nineteenth century economic change upon the law, but it is disappointing that Miller is not more concerned with the colonial roots of nineteenth century law. It is surprising that the leading intellectual historian of the colonial period does not trace a connection between the movement for codification in the nineteenth century and the persistent demands for codification in virtually all of the American colonies in the seventeenth century. Plymouth, Massachusetts Bay, Connecticut, and New Haven all produced one or more legal codes, and there was even a primitive code in the first decade of Virginia's settlement. The demand for certainty in the law and an unsophisticated quest for legal rationality were widespread popular feelings in the first half of the seventeenth century, somewhat as they were in the Jacksonian era. Colonial ideas of law were obviously quite different from those of the 1830's in most respects, but the similarities are at least as important as the differences. Again, the stultifying preconception of the "formative era" is an unfortunate hindrance to what seems a more promising topic—the organic growth of law and legal thought in America from the colonial settlements to the Civil War and after.

The Life of the Mind in America and, by implication, *The Golden Age of American Law* also raise a problem even more disturbing than the one of periodization. They lead one to the belief that the study

---

Virginia. Tucker was the author of learned treatises, including LECTURES ON CONSTITUTIONAL LAW (1843) and COMMENTARIES ON THE LAWS OF VIRGINIA (1836-1837).

56 P. 118.

57 P. 127.

58 *Ibid.* See also p. 232.

of legal literature alone, removing as it does the law from the legislature, the courtroom, and the marketplace, is too restricted an approach. Consider the question of codification once more. Miller examines the debate on codification at the New York Constitutional Convention of 1846 in order to investigate the conflict between Field and the proponents of the common law. He finds that the "opponents of codification planted themselves upon the rational patriotism of an irrational but native development, and so challenged codifiers to wage war with them on the issue of legal allegiance. This the codifiers were more than ready to do."[59] Calhoun chooses the same incident to sample the character of the bar in the mid-nineteenth century and finds that the convention was divided between nativists and anti-nativists, lawyers and farmers.[60] The two points are not necessarily contradictory, and Miller's is obviously profound, but the comparison suggests that the use of purely literary evidence (debates, in this instance) runs the risk of abstracting law from its social significance.

394

A review of the foregoing books suggests two ways in which the study of the early history of American law might profitably be reoriented: a reassessment of the traditional periodization and a broadening of the range of our source materials.

The periodization imposed by the concept of the "formative era" has led to a neglect of colonial legal history and, as a result, a denial of the continuity between the pre-revolutionary years and the period of independence. Colonial history was mere antiquarianism from Pound's point of view. He relegated the seventeenth century to the oblivion of "law without lawyers" and dismissed the earlier eighteenth century as an irrelevant age of outmoded English common law. Chroust, Haar, and Miller all follow Pound in proclaiming the innovative character of the period from 1776 to 1860. Calhoun's choice of 1750 and 1850 as the end points for his study of professional life seems more original and promising, assuming as it does only the profound general transition from eighteenth to nineteenth century social organization. Moreover, it would seem reasonable to argue that 1750-1800 is the critical period for legal historians if continuity between colonial and national law is to be demonstrated. If the judges, lawyers, and legislators of Massachusetts and New York, for example, were not starting from scratch in 1776, there ought to be evidence of the forms and ideas from which they proceeded in the last half of the

---

[59] P. 259.
[60] Pp. 180-82.

eighteenth century. Happily, the recent appearance of the first volume of *The Law Practice of Alexander Hamilton*[61] and the three volumes of *The Legal Papers of John Adams*[62] dramatizes the wealth of material and maturity of analysis which can now be brought to bear on the period. Our concern with the public law and constitution-making of the last part of the century has perhaps blinded us to the persistent characteristics of private law. In any case, the argument for testing the hypothesis of continuity in early American law seems strong.

Similarly, it seems that only an extension of our inquiry to sources such as the working papers of lawyers, manuscript court and legislative records, statutes, and various socio-economic documents will reveal the role of the law in American life. We must not limit ourselves to the study of what men have said about the law, thus treating legal history solely as a branch of the history of ideas. This is the approach taken by both Haar and Miller, and although both the lawyer and the historian broaden their treatment of the law through their unspoken assumptions about social and economic organization, the better view would seem to be that these assumptions are in themselves proper subjects for legal historians. One of the virtues of Calhoun's brief treatment of the legal profession is that it inquires directly into the social origins of the thought and behavior of American lawyers. He analyzes only one limited sample,[63] but he suggests some general lines along which future investigation might proceed. The sources for a broader legal history of the early period are hard to come by, since legal reports and judicial opinions, not to mention printed statutes, were extremely rare in pre-revolutionary days. The gathering of material will be slow, but it is necessary.[64]

Such work as has already been done along these fresh lines[65] suggests that American law in the seventeenth century was far more sophisti-

395

---

[61] 1 THE LAW PRACTICE OF ALEXANDER HAMILTON (Goebel ed. 1964). For Goebel's comment on the persistence of the common law tradition, see *id.* at 9-25.

[62] THE LEGAL PAPERS OF JOHN ADAMS (Wroth & Zobel eds. 1965).

[63] See also Nash, *The Philadelphia Bench and Bar, 1800-1861*, 7 COMPARATIVE STUDIES IN SOCIETY AND HISTORY 204 (1965). Nash provides another sample, but his analysis falls into the more traditional type of social mobility study.

[64] See Kammen, *Colonial Court Records and the Study of Early American History: A Bibliographical Review*, 70 AMERICAN HISTORICAL REV. 732 (1965). A bibliography of American law and trial reports and related materials first printed before 1801 is in an advanced stage of preparation by Professor Wilfred J. Ritz of Washington and Lee University.

[65] In addition to the work of Goebel, Haskins, and Smith which has already been cited, see, *e.g.*, the learned introductions to the several volumes of the American Legal Records series and the superb volume of introduction, 1 SUPREME COURT OF JUDICATURE OF THE PROVINCE OF NEW YORK, 1691-1704 (Hamlin & Baker eds. 1959).

cated than one would have expected and that the "reception" of the common law was a gradual process which bridged the first two centuries. The entire pre-revolutionary period is beginning to emerge as one in which the interaction of several varieties of English law with the requirements of the American situation provides a strong theme of continuity. Work on the law during the revolutionary period is still in a primitive state, but it is beginning to look as though the last part of the eighteenth century was a transitional stage rather than a fresh start. It is clear that in the early nineteenth century sweeping economic change and a new sense of the positive powers of government affected American law. We have ignored, however, the possibilities that the activity of the period did not occur *in vacuo* and that the "formative era" might perhaps better be called the "transformative era." If we expand our methods and extend our view, we may discover that the lawyers and judges of the "golden age" were the children of their fathers.

STANLEY N. KATZ*

* Assistant Professor of History, The University of Wisconsin.

* * * * *Notes and Suggestions* * * * *

Time to Reclaim: The Current Challenge of American Constitutional History

Paul L. Murphy[*]

ONE aspect of the public furor over the Supreme Court's decision striking down the New York Regent's prescribed public school prayer[1] should both bother the consciences and arouse the energies of historians. This was the frequent complaint that Justice Hugo Black in his majority opinion placed his reliance almost solely upon history and not upon solid legal precedents.

Such complaints illustrate a common public misunderstanding of the permissible resources upon which the Court can draw in its work. They also call attention to the history profession's neglect of a vital area for which it is responsible, and about which it has done shamefully little in the last quarter century: American constitutional history and areas related to constitutional problems.

For the distressing aspect of Black's opinion is not that he used history. The Court has always used history;[2] the founding fathers expected it to do so.[3]

[*] Mr. Murphy, associate professor of American constitutional history at the University of Minnesota, is currently engaged in a study of "The Meaning of Freedom of Speech, 1918–1933," a project of the Center for the Study of the History of Liberty in America, Harvard University.

[1] *Engle* v. *Vitale*, 370 US Reports, 421 (1962). On the general question of public attacks on the Court, see Arthur S. Miller, "A Note on the Criticisms of Supreme Court Decisions," *Journal of Public Law*, X (Spring 1961), 139–51.

[2] Edward S. Corwin, "The Constitution as Instrument and Symbol," *American Political Science Review*, XXX (Dec. 1936), 1072, indicates the long and heavy reliance of conservatives upon history, as "a useful device for the consecration of an already established order of things." This suggests that conservatives are not so concerned about the use of history as the purposes for which it is used.

[3] James Madison, writing late in his life of the Confederation and its faults, stated: "Such were the defects, the deformities, the diseases and the ominous prospects for which the convention were to provide a remedy, and which ought never to be overlooked in expounding and appreciating the Constitutional Charter, the remedy that was provided." (Cited in Robert L. Schuyler, *The Constitution of the United States: An Historical Survey of Its Formation* [New York, 1923], 92, and to which Professor Schuyler adds: "These words of the 'Father of the Constitution' sound like a protest against judicial interpretation of the Constitution by judges ignorant of its historical setting and, therefore, unable to fathom the original intent of its provisions. Unfortunately, a knowledge of American history has not yet been made a prerequisite for admission to the Supreme Court.")

What should bother the historian is the type of history Black used in evolving a basis for an important constitutional ruling. For in tracing the historical development of church-state relations, the most recent work he cited was Thomas J. Wertenbaker's 1947 volume, *The Puritan Oligarchy*, and for the most part he relied upon works which may be "historical" given the length of time in the past they were written, but which modern scholars would hesitate to suggest an undergraduate rely upon as anything but a once important, although now outdated view.[4]

This is not so much an unfortunate reflection upon Black, however, as it is upon the historical profession because it points up the urgent need of its members to reclaim and revitalize this area. If we were doing a large body of outstanding research in constitutional development and it were being passed over for archaic sources, then we could legitimately criticize. Unfortunately, this is not and has not been the case for some years.

Why have we neglected constitutional history for so long? The reasons are complex, partially justifiable, and reflective of the tendency of our profession to respond to current needs and sometimes even current fads in the name of scholarly activity. One of the ironies of American historiography is that in the nineteenth century, when the American citizen was hardly touched in his everyday existence by his national government and very little by his state government, constitutional history tended to crowd out almost every other aspect of history. In the twentieth century, social, cultural, and intellectual history has risen in professional status to the rapid exclusion of constitutional, yet Americans have never been more regulated by government. Their social and economic life has increasingly taken on political and constitutional connotations until it has become difficult to point out any area of that life that is not restricted by law. Constitutional history's inability to attract adherents in such a favorable situation, then, must be a reflection, not on the subject matter, but on the nature of its approach, its style, and the

---

[4] E.g., on the English background of the question of church-state relations, Black relies solely upon Leighton Pullan, *The History of the Book of Common Prayer* (London and New York, 1900), and the 1957 edition of the *Encyclopedia Britannica;* on early American practice he uses Vernon Parrington's *Main Currents in American Thought* (3 vols., New York, 1927–30); Leon Whipple's *Our Ancient Liberties: The Story of the Origin and Meaning of Civil and Religious Liberty in the United States* (New York, 1927); and Thomas J. Wertenbaker, *The Puritan Oligarchy: The Founding of American Civilization* (New York, 1947). On the nature of the revolutionary established church controversy, he cites Sanford Cobb, *The Rise of Religious Liberty in America: A History* (New York, 1902); Charles F. James, *Documentary History of the Struggle for Religious Liberty in Virginia* (Lynchburg, Va., 1900); and John Fiske's *The Critical Period in American History* (Boston, 1888); and for Roger Williams he again uses Parrington, citing only his characterization of Williams as "the truest Christian amongst many who sincerely desired to be Christians." (*Engle v. Vitale,* 370 US Reports, 421 at 434 [1962].)

materials that its practitioners have considered usable in its delineation. A look at its history makes this clear.

From its crude beginnings with George Bancroft to its traditional exposition by men such as Homer Hockett and Andrew C. McLaughlin, constitutional history was constrained and confined by a set of rigid assumptions. Because of the peculiar nature of the origin and development of the American constitutional system, there was a strong tendency for its students to be conservative and generally worshipful in their attitudes. This led them to adopt an approach toward the discovery of historical reality that might generously be called one of philosophic-metaphysical analysis geared to establish the validity of political orthodoxy, or more crudely might merely be referred to as "revealed" history to underwrite the virtue of established institutions. The subtlety and sophistication of the approach increased greatly as the cry arose for making history more scientific, yet the essential forms did not change. One started with a series of presumptions about the nature of God, the nature of God's universe, the nature of God's kingdom on earth, and man's proper role within this framework, and having established the correctness of these assumptions, then used them as a yardstick to measure man's behavior. Certainly with such knowledge, it was not difficult to evaluate what was moral, righteous, ethical, and decent behavior, who the right people were, or, by the same token, what was not to be considered proper. This, in turn, made historical inquiry a very simple process. It further made historical judgments relatively easy, if, at times, somewhat rigid.

Bancroft, for all his avid interest in pursuing source materials, found it easy and natural to take the position in his writings that our democracy and constitutional government were God-given—manifestations of the will of Divine Providence. If not responsible for originating the long-accepted myth of the semidivine character of the founding fathers, he did nothing to discourage its full acceptance and created for later scholars the danger of seeming mildly heretical if they openly rejected it.

Then, with the cessation of hostilities in 1865, an attempt was quickly made by both northern and southern historians to wrap a shield of historical orthodoxy and justification around both sections' constitutional position and political leadership in the late secessionist crisis. Principal gospelgiver for the South was former Vice-President of the Confederacy, Alexander H. Stephens, whose two-volume work, *The Constitutional View of the Late War between the States* (Philadelphia, 1868–70), contained a complete constitutional justification for secession argued in terms of enlightened southern leadership correctly supporting state sovereignty and the true preservation of Grecian civilization. He was subsequently joined by Jefferson Davis, whose *The Rise and Fall of the Confederate Government* (New York, 1881), although later, gave no ground on constitutional questions. The northern inspired 128-volume, *Official Records of the Union and Confederate Armies* (Washington, D. C., 1880–1901), conspicuously subtitled *The War of the Rebellion*, by that very term suggested that secession was not legal under our form of government and that southerners had violated constitutional forms and agreements, and by implication the natural and moral order of things, by defying federal authority. Less dispassionate were various popular writers of the day, principally Horace Greeley[5] and Henry Wilson.[6] Wilson, especially, drew northern popular acclaim, but he also aroused some northern scholarly distress, in arguing that the dissolution of the Union was solely the result of a thirty-year conspiracy on the part of southerners led by the detestable rebel John C. Calhoun, who from the 1830's had hidden behind the metaphysical shield of devious constitutional theories as he plotted the destruction of the nation.

Herman Eduard von Holst, probably the first outstanding academic constitutional historian, lent scholarly veneer to the Greeleys and the Wilsons in his seven-volume *Constitutional and Political History of the United States* (Chicago, 1874–92). Utilizing the tedious and ponderous techniques innate in his German training, von Holst argued that at the beginning of our nation under the Constitution the framers had intended no such thing as state sovereignty, the states having relinquished any sovereignty they had earlier when they signed the Articles of Confederation. This, plus his almost irrational hatred of slavery, led him to suggest that immoral southerners had evolved the state sovereignty argument as an illegal defense of an institution in itself illegal. The only happy side of the American past was the victory of the northern forces of light over this heinous conspiracy. Less violent but equally firm in his antislavery convictions was the legally oriented James Schouler, whose seven-volume *History of the United States of America under the Constitution* (Washington, D. C., and New York) reached the public irregularly between 1880 and 1913.

But the methodology of nineteenth-century history generally is also relevant. Historians of the time were committed to an institutional-legal approach to the study of the past, an approach that beautifully complemented the study of the Constitution, but that, as early as the 1880's, was already inducing

[5] Horace Greeley, *The American Conflict: A History of the Great Rebellion in the United States of America, 1860–64* (2 vols., Chicago, 1865–66).
[6] Henry Wilson, *History of the Rise and Fall of the Slave Power in America* (3 vols., Boston, 1876–78).

certain expansive minds to call for emancipation. This approach, defining institutions as forms of social behavior primarily definable by law, confined legitimate areas of inquiry to the origins and continuity of such institutions. This sent would-be historical scholars probing into the past, highly restricted both as to the type of questions they could ask and the type of evidence they could use to construct pertinent answers. The suggestion, for example, that one might study an individual judge in an attempt to learn whether his personal predilections might have affected constitutional development would have been considered both unbecoming and unhistorical. Those who would study the Constitution should especially heed Edmund Burke's suggestion regarding the English constitution: "We ought to understand it according to our measure; and to venerate where we are not able to understand."

By the 1890's the movement to break out of such strictures was gaining apace. Frederick Jackson Turner's suggestion that institutions did not simply evolve within their own set patterns and that external forces could decisively influence their course, while not immediately destroying a legal-institutional approach to historical development, at least suggested that broader areas of inquiry were permissible in seeking to reconstruct the past. Yet Turner and his historical successors were merely part of a scholarly revolution that was taking place generally within the social sciences beginning around the turn of the century. The pragmatic revolt in scholarship, involving a new sophistication and healthy skepticism toward rigid ancient truths and an empirical-rational approach toward the determination of reality, opened the door to the restless and hyperinquisitive historical scholar to begin asking questions previously felt unanswerable. And with the increasing impact of the ideas of Marx, Darwin, Dewey, and Freud, permissible areas of inquiry were extended even further. Yet the response of students of the Constitution was, in all but a few instances, disappointing. Charles A. Beard, certainly not unimpressed with the fact that the law itself was beginning to reflect the new emphasis pressed upon it by advocates of sociological jurisprudence, did try his hand at constitutional reassessment. In re-evaluating the actions of the founding fathers, Beard utilized the analysis of ideas, social forms, and economic needs. But while not as doctrinaire as his Marxist contemporaries, A. M. Simons and Gustavus Myers, he operated on the assumption that to determine primary economic motivations would prove the most revealing avenue for ultimate reality.

Yet contemporary scholars of the Constitution did not follow Beard's lead. The reasons are clear if not totally warranted. Beard had departed sharply and frankly (and unjustifiably) from the traditional set of assumptions about constitutional development. It was inconceivable, that given the virtue

401

of the Constitution and our constitutional system and the type of men the founding fathers were known to have been, that petty human motives, especially those of personal aggrandizement, could have been present in its origin. The type of inquiry Beard was making and even the facts that the inquiry produced were not, they thought, relevant types of information for studying the past. But equally present was the fact that Beard as well as Myers, Simons, and John R. Commons, who wrote *Legal Foundations of Capitalism* (New York, 1924), were not constitutional historians; nor were they interested in writing constitutional history per se. They were interested in analyzing the Constitution and the Supreme Court as a way of finding answers about nonconstitutional areas of American life. As such, the type of information that they put forth was not highly useful to either students of the history of explicit aspects of the law or the development of legal precedents, or to lawyers or judges seeking information on the historical antecedents of explicit modern institutions and practices.

Thus despite the revolution in knowledge and the approach to it fostered by the pragmatic revolt, traditional constitutionalists felt themselves justified in adhering to fixed and ancient patterns. Such a tradition was preserved in the two most well-known works in "pure" constitutional history in the first quarter of the twentieth century, Albert J. Beveridge's four-volume *Life of John Marshall* (New York, 1916-19) and Charles Warren's three-volume *The Supreme Court in United States History* (Boston, 1923). While both Beveridge and Warren were nonacademicians, the academic constitutionalists still plying their trade were apparently inspired more by their success than by the example of Beard's heresy and the condemnation it brought. This does not suggest that the steadily decreasing number of such scholars did not feel compelled to adopt more sophisticated techniques in their scholarship. Certainly the few remaining active constitutional historians, McLaughlin, Hockett, J. G. Randall, conducted their research within a self-conscious frame of scientific historical analysis. Yet the result was seldom more than a far more sophisticated version of nineteenth-century legal-institutional "revealed" history, in a modern package. By the 1930's the literature of American constitutional history revealed both that its old practitioners were largely talking only to each other and that, with exceptions, the profession generally had rejected the discipline for other historical approaches and fields. One immediate result was to create a temporary vacuum. The vacuum, however, was quickly filled by a number of lawyers, political scientists, and journalists who assumed the responsibility for doing what research and writing were still being produced in the area.[7]

[7] Typical of such works are Walton H. Hamilton and Douglass Adair, *The Power to Govern: The Constitution Then and Now* (New York, 1937); Robert H. Jackson, *The Struggle for*

Fortunately, in light of this rejection of responsibility by historians, those constitutional lawyers in political science departments and lawyer-historians who attempted to keep the field alive were not generally bound by the constraints that historians had seemed unable to break. The years between the late 1930's and the 1950's saw much of merit coming from them.

Benjamin F. Wright, who had earlier explored the role of natural law in American constitutional development,[8] made valuable contributions with a work on the contract clause in 1938[9] and a pithy and perceptive summary of *The Growth of American Constitutional Law* in 1942.[10] Carl B. Swisher, with revealing studies of Field and Taney, showed the valuable potentials of judicial biography.[11] This area was one in which much other useful work was done. Historians, peculiarly and inexcusably, left it almost entirely alone.[12]

Judicial Supremacy: A Study of a Crisis in American Power Politics (New York, 1941); Fred Rodell, *Fifty Five Men* (New York, 1936); Felix Frankfurter, *The Commerce Clause under Marshall, Taney and Waite* (Chapel Hill, N.C., 1937); Beryl H. Levy, *Our Constitution: Tool or Testament?* (New York, 1941); Robert K. Carr, *The Supreme Court and Judicial Review* (New York, 1942); Edward S. Corwin, *Twilight of the Supreme Court* (Princeton, N. J., 1934), *The Commerce Power versus States Rights* (Princeton, N. J., 1936), *Court over Constitution: A Study of Judicial Review as an Instrument of Popular Government* (Princeton, N. J., 1938), *The President: Office and Powers* (New York, 1940), and *Constitutional Revolution, Ltd.* (Claremont, Calif., 1941); Carl B. Swisher, *American Constitutional Development* (Boston, 1943); Joseph Alsop and Turner Catledge, *The 168 Days* (Garden City, N. Y., 1938); Irving Brant, *Storm over the Constitution* (Indianapolis, 1936); Drew Pearson and Robert Allen, *The Nine Old Men* (New York, 1937); and Merlo J. Pusey, *The Supreme Court Crisis* (New York, 1937). This is not to infer that no constitutional history was being written by historians. The 1930's saw the publication of two textbooks in the field: Homer Hockett, *The Constitutional History of the United States, 1776–1876* (2 vols., New York, 1939), and Andrew C. McLaughlin, *A Constitutional History of the United States* (New York, 1935). Each was highly traditional, and McLaughlin, like Hockett, paid relatively little attention to developments following 1885. The decade also brought important studies such as Lawrence A. Harper, *The English Navigation Acts: A Seventeenth Century Experiment in Social Engineering* (New York, 1939); Richard B. Morris, *Studies in the History of American Law* (New York, 1930); and Lewis G. Van der Velde, *The Presbyterian Churches and the Federal Union, 1861–1869* (Cambridge, Mass., 1932). It is nonetheless significant that in the 1938 collection of essays commemorating the 150th anniversary of the Constitution, *The Constitution Reconsidered*, ed. Conyers Read (New York, 1938), only two of the twenty-eight contributors were active practitioners of American constitutional history.

[8] Benjamin F. Wright, *American Interpretations of Natural Law* (Cambridge, Mass., 1931).

[9] *Id.*, *The Contract Clause of the Constitution* (Cambridge, Mass., 1938).

[10] *Id.*, *The Growth of American Constitutional Law* (New York, 1942).

[11] Carl B. Swisher, *Stephen J. Field, Craftsman of the Law* (Washington, D. C., 1930), and *Roger B. Taney* (New York, 1935).

[12] Worth noting in the area of judicial biography are: Francis P. Weisenburger, *The Life of John McLean: A Politician on the United States Supreme Court* (Columbus, Ohio, 1937); Bruce R. Trimble, *Chief Justice Waite—Defender of the Public Interest* (Princeton, N. J., 1938); Beryl Levy, *Cardozo and Frontiers of Legal Thinking* (New York, 1938); George S. Hellman, *Benjamin N. Cardozo: American Judge* (New York, 1940); Marie Carolyn Klinkhamer, *Edward Douglas White: Chief Justice of the United States* (Washington, D. C., 1943); Alexander A. Lawrence, *James Moore Wayne: Southern Unionist* (Chapel Hill, N. C., 1943); Joseph E. McLean, *William Rufus Day* (Baltimore, 1947); Willard King, *Melville Weston Fuller: Chief Justice of the United States* (New York, 1950), and *Lincoln's Manager, David Davis* (Cambridge, Mass., 1960); Charlotte Williams, *Hugo L. Black: A Study in the Judicial Process* (Baltimore, 1950); Samuel Hendel, *Charles Evans Hughes and the Supreme Court* (New York, 1951); Joel F. Paschal, *Mr. Justice Sutherland: A Man against the State* (Princeton, N. J., 1951); George Shiras, *Justice George Shiras, Jr., of Pittsburgh, Associate Justice of the Supreme Court, 1892–*

Charles G. Haines, avoiding both the incensement and tendency to produce a lawyer's brief, which had marked the work of Louis Boudin,[13] brought out a useful corrective to the position of Charles Warren in his *Role of the Supreme Court in American Government and Politics* (Berkeley, Calif., 1944). Wallace Mendelson raised a series of important questions about the Dred Scott case and added to historians' knowledge of the evolution of due process.[14] Alpheus T. Mason shamed historians who had apparently feared the legal involvements of twentieth-century constitutional subjects by a long series of historically oriented works, as also did Samuel Konefsky.[15] Edward S. Corwin continued both to make valuable contributions and to inspire his political science graduates to do likewise.[16] Robert McCloskey and C. Herman Pritchett produced generally well-received works on, respectively, nineteenth-century political-judicial thought,[17] and the Roosevelt, Vinson, and Warren Courts.[18] Law professors such as Charles Fairman,[19] Mark DeWolfe

404

1903 (Pittsburgh, 1953); Henry Steele Commager, "Joseph Story," in *Bacon Lectures on the Constitution of the United States, 1940–1950* (Boston, 1953), 33–94; Donald Morgan, *Justice William Johnson: The First Dissenter* (Columbia, S. C., 1954); Charles Page Smith, *James Wilson, Founding Father, 1742–1798* (Chapel Hill, N. C., 1956); for Howe's work on Holmes, see note 20, below; Leonard W. Levy, *The Law of the Commonwealth and Chief Justice Shaw* (Cambridge, Mass., 1957); Eugene C. Gerhart, *Robert H. Jackson, America's Advocate* (Indianapolis, 1958); H. Landon Warner, *The Life of Mr. Justice Clarke* (Cleveland, 1959); Helen S. Thomas, *Felix Frankfurter, Scholar on the Bench* (Baltimore, 1960); Wallace Mendelson, *Justices Black and Frankfurter: Conflict in the Court* (Chicago, 1961); Robert K. Newmeyer, "Justice Joseph Story—A Political and Constitutional Study," unpublished doctoral dissertation, University of Nebraska, 1957; Lewis Maddocks, "Justice John M. Harlan," unpublished doctoral dissertation, Ohio State University, 1959; and Stephen R. Mitchell, "Mr. Justice Horace Gray," unpublished doctoral dissertation, University of Wisconsin, 1960. Worth noting also is that of this group only three, Commager, Klinkhamer, and L. Levy, are primarily constitutional historians.

[13] Louis B. Boudin, *Government by Judiciary* (2 vols., New York, 1932).

[14] Wallace Mendelson, "Dred Scott's Case—Reconsidered," *Minnesota Law Review,* XXXVIII (Dec. 1953), 16–28, and "A Missing Link in the Evolution of Due Process," *Vanderbilt Law Review,* X (Dec. 1956), 125–37.

[15] Alpheus T. Mason, *Organized Labor and the Law* (Durham, N. C., 1925), *Brandeis: Lawyer and Judge in the Modern State* (Princeton, N. J., 1933), *Brandeis: A Free Man's Life* (New York, 1947), *Harlan Fiske Stone: Pillar of the Law* (New York, 1956), *The Supreme Court from Taft to Warren* (Baton Rouge, La., 1958); Samuel J. Konefsky, *Chief Justice Stone and the Supreme Court* (New York, 1945), *The Constitutional World of Mr. Justice Frankfurter* (New York, 1949), *The Legacy of Holmes and Brandeis: A Study in the Influence of Ideas* (New York, 1956).

[16] Edward S. Corwin, *Total War and the Constitution* (New York, 1947), *Liberty against Government* (Baton Rouge, La., 1948), and *A Constitution of Powers in a Secular State* (Charlottesville, Va., 1951); Clinton Rossiter, *Constitutional Dictatorship: Crisis Government in the Modern Democracies* (Princeton, N. J., 1948), *The Supreme Court and the Commander in Chief* (Ithaca, N. Y., 1951), and *Seedtime of the Republic: The Origin of the American Tradition of Political Liberty* (New York, 1953); and Benjamin R. Twiss, *Lawyers and the Constitution: How Laissez Faire Came to the Supreme Court* (Princeton, N. J., 1942).

[17] Robert McCloskey, *Conservatism in an Age of Enterprise: A Study of William Graham Sumner, Stephen J. Field and Andrew Carnegie* (Cambridge, Mass., 1951).

[18] C. Herman Pritchett, *The Roosevelt Court: A Study in Judicial Politics and Values* (New York, 1948), *Civil Liberties and the Vinson Court* (Chicago, 1954), *The Political Offender and the Warren Court* (Boston, 1958); and *Congress versus the Supreme Court* (Minneapolis, 1961).

[19] Charles Fairman, *Mr. Justice Miller and the Supreme Court, 1862–1890* (Cambridge, Mass., 1939), "The So-Called Granger Cases, Lord Hale and Justice Bradley," *Stanford Law Review,* V (July 1953), 587–679, and "What Makes a Great Justice? Mr. Justice Bradley and the

Howe,[20] Zechariah Chafee,[21] Julius Goebel,[22] Jacobus Ten Broek,[23] Bernard Schwartz,[24] and Howard J. Graham[25] also shouldered historical burdens. And, as a demonstration that the subject matter of constitutional development did not lack popular appeal, Merlo Pusey's biography of Charles Evans Hughes won the Pulitzer Prize for biography in 1952, while Catherine Drinker Bowen's jejune biography of Justice Oliver Wendell Holmes, a choice of the Book-of-the-Month Club, made best seller lists and eventually the theaters in an even less satisfying grade *B* movie.[26]

Historians were frequently aroused to strong and just criticism of the efforts of nonhistorians to produce such historical works. Much of the writing of Corwin and his students was present-minded and done as a response to current crises. Clinton Rossiter's *Seedtime of the Republic,* although it won the Bancroft Prize for history, distressed many historians as little more than a compilation of well-known material valuable largely in that it brought together in one place much useful information. A. T. Mason, while highly knowledgeable in law and judicial procedure, drew fire for his distressing lack of internal consistency and his questionable use of material, especially in his biography of Stone,[27] and also for his failure to set his figures in anything but a judicial world, despite their frequent ventures into other environments. Konefsky sinned similarly, while one reviewer candidly branded the second volume of Charles G. Haines's work (completed by Foster H. Sherwood) a "stale rehash"[28] and another pointed out McCloskey's naïveté in failing to understand that Andrew Carnegie relied heavily upon the ghost writer James H. Bridge and that it is dangerous to use the writings

405

Supreme Court, 1870–1892," in *Bacon Lectures on the Constitution of the United States, 1940–1950* (Boston, 1953), 423–85.

[20] Mark DeWolfe Howe, *Readings in American Legal History* (Cambridge, Mass., 1949), and *Justice Oliver Wendell Holmes: The Shaping Years* (Cambridge, Mass., 1957).

[21] Zechariah Chafee, *Free Speech in the United States* (Cambridge, Mass., 1941), *How Human Rights Got into the Constitution* (Boston, 1952), *Three Human Rights in the Constitution of 1787* (Lawrence, Kan., 1956), and *The Blessings of Liberty* (Philadelphia, 1956).

[22] Julius Goebel and T. Raymond Naughton, *Law Enforcement in Colonial New York, 1614–1776* (New York, 1944).

[23] Jacobus Ten Broek, *The Anti-Slavery Origins of the Fourteenth Amendment* (Berkeley, Calif., 1951).

[24] Bernard Schwartz, *The Supreme Court: Constitutional Revolution in Retrospect* (New York, 1957).

[25] Howard J. Graham, "The Conspiracy Theory of the Fourteenth Amendment," *Yale Law Journal,* XLVII, XLVIII (Jan., Dec. 1938), 371–403, 171–94, "Our 'Declaratory' Fourteenth Amendment," *Stanford Law Review,* VII (Dec. 1954), 3–39, "Builded Better Than They Knew—The Framers, the Railroads and the Fourteenth Amendment," *University of Pittsburgh Law Review,* XVII (Summer 1956), 537–84.

[26] Merlo J. Pusey, *Charles Evans Hughes* (2 vols., New York, 1951); Catherine Drinker Bowen, *Yankee from Olympus: Justice Holmes and His Family* (Boston, 1944).

[27] Among others, see my review in *Western Political Quarterly,* XI (June 1958), 413–15.

[28] Review by Leonard W. Levy in *American Historical Review,* LXIII (Apr. 1958), 696.

of any business leader for analysis either of his mind or his times.[29] Pusey's *Charles Evans Hughes*, which voted against Franklin D. Roosevelt on virtually every page and ignored large segments of that leader's public career, and Mrs. Bowen's *Yankee from Olympus* were frequently either ignored or taken lightly for what they were, undisciplined and subjective narratives. Historians, however, were in a poor position to be too hostile since they were doing so little themselves in the constitutional area.

The luxury of having someone do one's job and then caviling at his efforts, however, began to be undercut in the 1950's as political scientists' interest waned and shifted. With the rise especially of what Dwight Waldo in 1954 was to call "the behavioral vogue," and the tendency, as Waldo further pointed out "of the larger foundations to support empirical study in the social sciences, as against more traditional studies,"[30] political scientists turned rapidly away from the constitutional area. The transition, while not without its valuable sides, especially in pointing out new ways to look at and assess judicial behavior, initially aroused concern among more traditional political scientists. V. O. Key and Frank J. Munger in 1954 questioned the inroads that the behaviorists were making because of their tendency to sublimate totally the historical content of political and constitutional behavior.[31] By 1961 William Beaney began a review of James Willard Hurst's *Law and Social Process in United States History* with the statement: "Because of the profession's diminished interest in law and its indifference toward history, it is unlikely that many political scientists will read this book."[32] Thus, if historians criticized their brethren for the use of Guttman scalogram analyses,[33] or Shapley-Shubik empirical power indexes,[34] or for creating psychometric models of the Supreme Court,[35] it was more apt to be on the grounds of skeptical bewilderment than improper use of history.

[29] Review by Fritz Redlich, *ibid.*, LVII (Apr. 1952), 707.

[30] Dwight Waldo, *Political Science in the United States of America* (Paris, 1956), 29. Waldo also includes a careful study, prepared by Gerald D. Nash, of articles in general political science journals for the periods 1925–1929, 1939–1941, and 1952–1954, showing, for example, that by the last period, public law and jurisprudence had declined to 7 per cent of the total of articles published by the profession; he concluded simply that "public law has been declining in attention, relatively speaking" (p. 46). See also Robert A. Dahl, "The Behavioral Approach in Political Science: Epitaph for a Monument to a Successful Protest," *American Political Science Review*, LV (Dec. 1961), 763–72.

[31] Cited in *Handbook of Social Psychology*, ed. Gardner Lindzey (2 vols., Cambridge, Mass., 1954), II, 1125.

[32] Review by William Beaney in *American Political Science Review*, LX (Sept. 1961), 643.

[33] S. Sidney Ulmer, "Supreme Court Behavior and Civil Rights," *Western Political Quarterly*, XIII (June 1960), 288–311.

[34] Glendon A. Schubert, Jr., "The Study of Judicial Decision-Making as an Aspect of Political Behavior," *American Political Science Review*, LII (Dec. 1958), 1007–25.

[35] *Id.*, "A Psychometric Model of the Supreme Court," *American Behavioral Scientist*, V (Nov. 1961), 14–18.

Yet, again, popular trends tended to move at crosscurrents with scholarly fads, for while public law specialists in political science departments were convincing themselves they were no longer historians and were really empirical behaviorists (and by so doing, as some critics have suggested, losing their professional identity) the use of history, as a key reliance in the shaping of public policy, rose to a new level of importance. This development was the product of the Supreme Court's new willingness to accept the role of public policy maker in a variety of congressionally stalemated areas of domestic development, combined with its traditional and well-accepted duty of construing the language used in the Constitution. This periodic supercession of Congress meant the utilization of different tools as the basis for public policy.

For Congress, while not unconcerned with history, sees its role largely in the present, with emphasis upon legislating for current needs and in the context of current problems. The Courts have traditionally fulfilled the function of construing established statutes and legal language. This is done in the context of both initial meaning and intent and later recasting, which has occurred when precedents have been inadequate to cope with the needs produced by changing situations. The judicial tradition, in other words, directs itself much more naturally than does the legislative to historical study—not merely to discover the precise locus of the productive language of, say, the Bill of Rights, but also to ascertain its thrust, its deep and enduring implications, and its over-all philosophical justification in a democratic society.

This development has occurred during the same time as the revolutionary constitutional changes that the last three decades have necessitated, a period in which the Court's role, while in many ways still traditional, took on an importance greater than at any previous time in American history. The rapid shift toward positive government and the leviathan state necessitated a complete reassessment of all the clauses of the Constitution with politico-economic implications from commerce and taxing power to delegation of executive authority and the Tenth Amendment. The complete reassessment of the relationship between government and the individual as related to personal liberties, which has also dominated our times, has not only brought constitutional change but the assurance of the current Chief Justice that over the next few years virtually every clause in the Bill of Rights will have to be reinterpreted. To reinterpret for the Court means to reassess the logical extension of first principles. In such a process not only will history play a vital role, but a new role as an auxiliary tool for the jurist, not for "the consecration of an already established order of things," but for a new order seeking a new level of equal rights and social justice through law.

When in 1925 the Court took its first faltering but significant steps toward assuming an activist role (in this instance by laying the groundwork for the subsequent "nationalization" of the Bill of Rights by suggesting that certain of those guarantees might be enforceable against the states through a return to the original meaning of the Fourteenth Amendment),[36] a turn to history was essential. This trend was brought to fruition in 1931 in cases involving freedom of speech,[37] and freedom of the press,[38] and later extended by application to freedom of assembly in 1937,[39] and the "free exercise" section of the religious provisions of the First Amendment with a long series of Jehovah's Witnesses' rulings between 1938 and 1946. These cases necessitated a clear reassessment both of the actual intent of the framers of that amendment and the development and rationale of fifty years of erosion of the amendment as a device for the protection of individual rights. Conversely, the Court, starting with the O'Gorman case of 1931,[40] and going on through Nebbia in 1934,[41] and Stone's famous 1938 Carolene footnote (stating the "preferred freedoms" concept of the supercession of individual rights over property rights in cases involving state police power),[42] wiped much of the antiregulatory sheen off the due process clause. And while not agreeing that it should confess its historic sins of ever having taken this interpretive turn in the first place (as new Justice Hugo Black urged in 1938),[43] the Court nonetheless made clear that it was willing to return, as well as it could in conformity with good judgment and *stare decisis,* to an earlier day. Similarly, starting in 1931 the Court took the activist position in reassessing certain of the procedural guarantees of the Bill of Rights. This trend was less clear cut and frequently involved backtracking. Cardozo, for example, in 1937 seriously questioned the advisability

408

---

[36] *Gitlow* v. *New York,* 268 US Reports 652 (1925).

[37] *Stromberg* v. *California,* 283 US Reports 359 (1931).

[38] *Near* v. *Minnesota,* 283 US Reports 697 (1931). On the historical background of the Near case, see John E. Hartmann, "The Minnesota Gag Law and the Fourteenth Amendment," *Minnesota History,* XXXVII (Dec. 1960), 161–73.

[39] *DeJonge* v. *Oregon,* 299 US Reports 353 (1937).

[40] *O'Gorman & Young, Inc.,* v. *Hartford Ins. Co.,* 282 US Reports 251 (1931). On the importance of the O'Gorman case, see Harry Shulman, "The Supreme Court's Attitude toward Liberty of Contract and Freedom of Speech," in *Selected Essays on Constitutional Law* (4 vols., Chicago, 1938), II, 1098–1106.

[41] *Nebbia* v. *New York,* 291 US Reports 502 (1934). In his majority opinion Justice Owen J. Roberts ruled that there was no class of business which was not "clothed with a public interest," thereby removing a historic hurdle from the path of broad-scale state regulation of economic activities.

[42] *United States* v. *Carolene Products Co.,* 304 US Reports 114 (1938). The footnote, although not having the force of law, nonetheless marked the first frank acknowledgment from the bench that in the future the justices would take a much longer and more critical look at state restrictions upon individual liberties than upon economic activities.

[43] *Connecticut General Life Ins. Co.* v. *Johnson,* 303 US Reports 77 (1938). For a discussion of the implications of Black's suggestions and their historical setting, see Andrew C. McLaughlin, "The Court, the Constitution and Conkling," *American Historical Review,* XLVI (Oct. 1940), 45–63.

of an absolutist position with regard to the guarantees of the Second through Eighth Amendment. He also suggested at the same time, however, that the Court might make it its business to activate the Bill of Rights in new areas "implicit in the concept of ordered liberty."[44] This suggestion found picketing redefined as free speech in 1940[45] and similar "sacredness" placed around labor union organization in 1944.[46]

In other areas, history became a vital reliance for sweeping changes of public policy. Justice George Sutherland in 1936, relying upon a shockingly inaccurate use of historical data concerning the original transferal of power from the Continental Congress to the new government under the Constitution, laid the constitutional basis for virtual plenary executive authority in the area of foreign relations.[47] Having previously avowed his belief while Attorney General that utilization of the commerce clause as the essential device for the regulation of virtually every aspect of the economy was actually carrying out the initial intentions of John Marshall,[48] Justice Robert H. Jackson wrote that position into judicial precedent in 1943, with a long historical discussion documenting more fully its evolution.[49]

409

More recent times have found the Court returning to the "true meaning" of the Fifteenth Amendment in eliminating a great variety of state restrictions upon voting rights, from grandfather clauses,[50] and white primaries,[51] to unequal and unmodernized districting procedures.[52] More familiarly it has erased the 1896 "separate but equal" gloss on the Fourteenth Amendment's equal protection clause, thereby eliminating over fifty years of obstacles to the equality before the law that the framers of the amendment had sought to guarantee.[53]

[44] *Palko* v. *Connecticut*, 302 US Reports 319 (1937).
[45] *Thornhill* v. *Alabama*, 310 US Reports 88 (1940).
[46] *Thomas* v. *Collins*, 323 US Reports 516 (1945). Despite its heavy reliance on history in reassessing the Fourteenth Amendment, as late as 1949, three of the justices confessed they were reading H. E. Flack, *Adoption of the Fourteenth Amendment* (Baltimore, 1908), as the historical authority on the amendment. (Walter P. Armstrong, "What Do the Justices Read? Books of Interest to Supreme Court Members," *American Bar Association Journal*, XXXV (Apr. 1949), 295–300.
[47] *United States* v. *Curtiss-Wright Export Corp.*, 299 US Reports 304 (1936).
[48] Robert H. Jackson, *The Struggle for Judicial Supremacy* (New York, 1941); see also Robert L. Stern, "The Commerce Clause and the National Economy, 1933–1946," *Harvard Law Review*, LIX (May, June 1946), 645–93, 883–947; and Paul L. Murphy, "The New Deal and the Commerce Clause," unpublished doctoral dissertation, University of California, 1953.
[49] *Wickard* v. *Filburn*, 317 US Reports 111 (1942).
[50] *Lane* v. *Wilson*, 307 US Reports 268 (1939).
[51] *United States* v. *Classic*, 313 US Reports 299 (1941); *Smith* v. *Allwright*, 321 US Reports 649 (1944); *Terry* v. *Adams*, 345 US Reports 461 (1953).
[52] *Baker* v. *Carr*, 369 US Reports 186 (1962).
[53] Although it can only be speculation, an interesting question is raised as to whether the subsequent public castigation of the Court for relying upon the "modern authority" of six sociological and psychological texts in rendering the famed 1954 integration ruling, *Brown* v. *Board of Education*, 347 US Reports 483 (1954), may not have had the effect of pushing it

In virtually all of these rulings, the Court, when it cited history, either relied upon archaic historical works of the earlier devotees of "revealed" history, turned to history written by nonhistorians, or trusted its own ability to reconstruct historical evidence from the sources themselves.[54] The fact should disturb sensitive historians. Yet it should also force them to reassess the way the Court uses history and should challenge them to examine carefully what steps they can take to improve the situation.

History, to the legal profession—"law office history," as Howard J. Graham has frequently called it—has a peculiarly functional quality as an aspect of legal advocacy. The law clerk assigned to provide historical materials for the bolstering of a brief or an opinion knows that his job is to find those materials which will best serve to persuade the judges to rule favorably in the immediate case. That he may choose his evidence from only one side, or in such a way as partially to distort the record, will neither cause him qualms nor greatly distress the judge. The ultimate object, that of gaining a certain legal determination, is the focus. "Law office history," then, is not only deliberately calculated to win cases, but its inadequacy as academic history is never questioned by the bench and bar. As Saul Touster has so well pointed out, "The questions asked, the values expressed, and the factors considered in a law-making context are not the same as those present in a research context."[55]

Granted, then, there is little that the history profession can do to change the methodology of legal decision making. And with the Court using history, even if in nonacademic fashion, to attack many of the legal myths of a static society and thereby reach new and significant plateaus of social and economic justice, there is even less incentive to try. Yet, the historian can take positive steps that can be of relevance. If the Court is intent upon building new and dramatic legal structures to meet the requirements of a dynamic

back toward the use of history and precedent in subsequent rulings, especially those calculated to arouse strong public emotions. (See Mason, *Supreme Court from Taft to Warren*, Chap. VI.) The Court certainly had adequate historical information at hand, since historian Alfred H. Kelly had compiled thorough background information which was embodied in the appellants' brief on reargument. (See Alfred H. Kelly, "The Fourteenth Amendment Reconsidered—The Segregation Question," *Michigan Law Review*, LIV [June 1956], 1049–86.)

[54] Justice Harold H. Burton told an interviewer in 1953: "The Justices of the Supreme Court do take judicial notice of historical facts. We usually go back to original sources for our information rather than looking into secondary historical writings." He, himself, he stated, "went way back into colonial times" to investigate certain historical facts that illuminate issues of a case under study. (John J. Daly, *The Use of History in the Decisions of the Supreme Court: 1900–1930* [Washington, D. C., 1954], ix.) For a current reminder of the danger inherent in writing history from pure source material, see the wise comments of C. Vann Woodward, "The Anti-Slavery Myth," *American Scholar*, XXXI (Spring 1962), 318 ff.

[55] Saul Touster, "Law and Psychology: How the Twain Might Meet," *American Behavioral Scientist*, V (May 1962), 3–4.

society, the historian can at least furnish it with complementary modern architectural materials, so that it does not have to rely upon scrap lumber, salvage bricks, and raw stones for its buildings.

What the profession can profitably and easily do is to accept the responsibility that the new judicial emphasis, and the declining interest of political scientists, forces upon it. Despite the labors of a few brave pilgrims in recent years,[56] vast areas of constitutional and constitutionally related subject matter, some of which have scarcely been touched for decades, lie crying for attention. Further, if these areas were subjected to the rigorous and modern research techniques that historians and social scientists generally have perfected in the last decade, their results might well be startling.

Further, the opportunity is a unique and exciting one. With the Courts more and more shaping public policy, the opportunity to play a coordinate

[56] In 1948 Alfred H. Kelly and Winfred A. Harbison published the first textbook in the field to treat thoroughly constitutional development from English\ antecedents to the present, *The American Constitution: Its Origins and Development* (New York, 1948); see also note 7, above. The year 1958 saw the publication of James M. Smith and Paul L. Murphy, *Liberty and Justice: A Historical Record of American Constitutional Development* (New York), the first reading collection devoted solely to constitutional history since the companion set of Allen Johnson, *Readings in American Constitutional History, 1776–1876* (Boston, 1912); and *id.* and William A. Robinson, *Readings in Recent American Constitutional History, 1876–1926* (New York, 1927). Special studies of note coming from historians included: Edmund S. Morgan and Helen M. Morgan, *The Stamp Act Crisis: Prologue to Revolution* (Chapel Hill, N. C., 1953), and Edmund S. Morgan, *Prologue to Revolution: Sources and Documents on the Stamp Act Crisis, 1764–1766* (Chapel Hill, N. C., 1959); Harold M. Hyman, *Era of the Oath: Northern Loyalty Oaths during the Civil War and Reconstruction* (Philadelphia, 1954) and *To Try Men's Souls: Loyalty Tests in American History* (Berkeley, Calif., 1959); James M. Smith, *Freedom's Fetters: The Alien and Sedition Laws and American Civil Liberties* (Ithaca, N. Y., 1956); Robert E. Brown, *Charles A. Beard and the Constitution* (Princeton, N. J., 1956); David M. Silver, *Lincoln's Supreme Court* (Urbana, Ill., 1957); Robert S. Hunt, *Law and Locomotives: The Impact of the Railroad on Wisconsin Law in the 19th Century* (Madison, Wis., 1958); Winton U. Solberg, *The Federal Convention and the Formation of the Union* (New York, 1958); Forrest McDonald, *We the People: The Economic Origins of the Constitution* (Chicago, 1958); Leonard W. Levy, *Legacy of Suppression: Freedom of Speech and Press in Early American History* (Cambridge, Mass., 1960); Arnold Paul, *Conservative Crisis and the Rule of Law* (Ithaca, N. Y., 1960); Jackson T. Main, *The Antifederalists: Critics of the Constitution* (Chapel Hill, N. C., 1961); William R. Leslie, "The *Gaspée* Affair: A Study of Its Constitutional Significance," *Mississippi Valley Historical Review*, XXXIX (Sept. 1952), 233–56, and "Similarities in Lord Mansfield's and Joseph Story's View of Fundamental Law," *American Journal of Legal History*, I (July 1957), 278–307; Kelly, "Fourteenth Amendment Reconsidered"; Arthur Bestor, "State Sovereignty and Slavery," *Journal of the Illinois State Historical Society*, LIII (Summer 1961), 117–80; Stanley I. Kutler, "Labor, the Clayton Act, and the Supreme Court," *Labor History*, III (Winter 1962), 19–38, and "Chief Justice Taft, Judicial Unanimity and Labor," *Historian*, XXIV (Nov. 1961), 68–83; Everett Swinney, "Enforcing the Fifteenth Amendment, 1870–1877," *Journal of Southern History*, XXVIII (May 1962), 202–18; Leonard W. Levy, "Liberty and the First Amendment: 1790–1800," *American Historical Review*, LXVIII (Oct. 1962), 22–37, and *id.* and Lawrence H. Leder, "'Exotic Fruit': The Right against Compulsory Self-Incrimination in Colonial New York," *William and Mary Quarterly*, 3d Ser., XX (Jan. 1963), 3–32. In their article, Levy and Leder respond vigorously to the barbs of Law Professor Julius Goebel concerning the inability of nonlawyers to write legal history (p. 5). The 1950's also saw the creation of the American Society for Legal History, with an organ, *The American Journal of Legal History*, and eventually even a Lawyer's Literary Club to furnish monthly selections of legal history to its members. Unfortunately the orientation of the movement was more one that sought to stimulate members of the bench and bar to try their hand in the historical area than to encourage academic participation in legal research.

role through the furnishing of new historical materials, a role so often coveted and seldom realized by our profession, affords itself. Yet it does so without necessitating the compromise of professional standards by making our work present-minded. On the contrary, what is needed from historians is the most accurate, thoroughly documented, and impeccable history we are capable of producing. This certainly does not guarantee that the present Court will cease to be criticized when its decisions rely upon historical evidence for points of law, but should at least exempt us from the charge that we are not providing the Court with modern research findings, a charge that we cannot afford to ignore.

412

IN RE RADICAL INTERPRETATIONS OF AMERICAN LAW: THE RELATION OF LAW AND HISTORY

A.E. Keir Nash *

TABLE OF CONTENTS

413

INTRODUCTION

The past decade has seen the emergence of at least four types of analysis of American law that variously challenge conventional legal research undertaken within the intellectual boundaries of American empirical and normative pragmatism. Two of these types — post-

---

* Professor of Political Science, University of California, Santa Barbara. A.B. 1958, Harvard University; M.A. 1961, University of North Carolina; Ph.D. 1968, Harvard University, 1968. — Ed.
I wish to thank Martin Shapiro for critiquing an earlier draft of this article and making valuable suggestions—some of which I followed.

positivist legal philosophy[1] and Posnerian neo-positivist economic-legal analysis[2] — have been much debated elsewhere[3] and are only peripherally touched upon in this Article. Neither is primarily concerned with assessing the historical relationships among American law, polity, and economy for any reason, whether to understand a historical problem in itself, to develop a historically grounded theory of the American legal experience, or to ascertain the limits, if any, that history places upon the law's role in the solution of contemporary American problems.

This Article centers instead upon assessing two types of legal analysis — non-Marxist radical interpretation and "non-reductionist" Marxist theory — which, despite conspicuous differences, share the belief that understanding the American historical experience is a prerequisite to understanding American law. Both approaches also share two other important convictions. One is that a "consensual" or "liberal pluralist"[4] version of American history has little explanatory

414

---

1. *See, e.g.,* B. ACKERMAN, SOCIAL JUSTICE IN THE LIBERAL STATE (1980); R. DWORKIN, TAKING RIGHTS SERIOUSLY (1978); R. NOZICK, ANARCHY, STATE, AND UTOPIA (1974); J. RAWLS, A THEORY OF JUSTICE (1971). For a useful overview and critique of Rawls, Nozick, and utilitarian philosophy, see P. PETTIT, JUDGING JUSTICE: AN INTRODUCTION TO CONTEMPORARY POLITICAL PHILOSOPHY (1980).

2. *See* R. POSNER, ECONOMIC ANALYSIS OF LAW (2d ed. 1977); Posner, *Some Uses and Abuses of Economics in Law,* 46 U. CHI. L. REV. 281 (1979); Posner, *Utilitarianism, Economics, and Legal Theory,* 8 J. LEGAL STUD. 103 (1979).

3. *See, e.g.,* READING RAWLS: CRITICAL STUDIES ON RAWLS' *A Theory of Justice* (N. Daniels ed. 1975); Coleman, *Efficiency, Exchange, and Auction: Philosophic Aspects of the Economic Approach to Law,* 68 CALIF. L. REV. 221 (1980); *A Spectrum of Responses to John Rawls's Theory,* 69 AM. POL. SCI. REV. 588 (1975) (articles by Chapman, Harsanyi, Van Dyke, Fishkin, Rae, Bloom and Barber); *Jurisprudence Symposium,* 11 GA. L. REV. 969 (1972) (discussing Dworkin); *Symposium on Efficiency as a Legal Concern,* 8 HOFSTRA L. REV. 485 (1980) (on economics and law); *Change in the Common Law: Legal and Economic Perspectives,* 9 J. LEGAL STUD. 189 (1980).

4. "Consensual" is the term many American historians favor, while "liberal pluralist" is the one that political scientists typically use. Each term amounts to much the same view of American history and contemporary politics, emphasizing the broad measure of agreement on Lockean liberal political philosophy and the consequent generally low level of conflict perceived to characterize the course of United States history. In 1955, Professor Louis Hartz wrote a brilliant book, *The Liberal Tradition in America,* arguing that America

> was the prisoner of a bourgeois frame of political reference that had forestalled the development of either a strong radical or a strong conservative political tradition . . . . The only political theorist for Americans, Hartz insisted, was the quintessential bourgeois Englishman, John Locke. . . . Hartz's book captured the imagination of a generation of students of American culture.

Howe, *European Sources of Political Ideas in Jeffersonian America,* 10 REVIEWS IN AM. HIST. 28, 28 (1982). For some examinations of new American historiographical trends that question Hartz's consensual interpretation, see Bartley, *In Search of the New South: Southern Politics After Reconstruction,* 10 REVIEWS IN AM. HIST. 150 (1982); Chudacoff, *Success and Security: The Meaning of Social Mobility in America,* 10 REVIEWS IN AM. HIST. 101 (1982); Foner, *Reconstruction Revisited,* 10 REVIEWS IN AM. HIST. 82 (1982); Hollinger, *American Intellectual History: Issues for the 1980s,* 10 REVIEWS IN AM. HIST. 306 (1982); Rodgers, *In Search of Progressivism,* 10 REVIEWS IN AM. HIST. 113 (1982); Wilentz, *On Class and Politics in Jacksonian America,* 10 REVIEWS IN AM. HIST. 45 (1982).

validity, at least in regard to such major problems as the political and legal breakdown represented by the Civil War, and the law's role in American economic development. They also agree that historical explanations which downplay discussion of economic forces in the law's evolution are explanations which downplay truth. These common convictions cause me to group these two approaches, despite their deep-seated differences, as "radical interpretations of American law."

One of these radical interpretations is explicitly Marxist. The other is not. This observation suggests perhaps the most important of three major differences. That difference has to do with the extent to which American law has merely reflected the economic and political interests of dominant groups or classes versus the extent to which American law has had a separate life of its own, evolving autonomously from the larger polity or economy. Surprisingly, at least for those whose understanding of Marxism was formed before the 1970s, the current sophisticated Marxist view is the less determinist of the two radical interpretations. Indeed, this type of Marxist view strongly criticizes non-Marxist radical interpretations for engaging in "instrumental reductionism" — for adopting a view of American legal history that reduces American law to a mere instrument of dominant classes.

415

The second difference flows from the first. It is that contemporary American Marxist analysis displays fairly intense concern for working out knotty aspects of the problem of the law's autonomy, while contemporary non-Marxist radical analysis does not. In this sense, non-Marxist radical analysis is simultaneously closer to, and further from, more conventional liberal-individualist and American conservative interpretations of law in society. On the one hand, its almost "populist" simplicity as to who gets what and who doesn't, and its tendencies to quasi-melodrama about who controls the law and who doesn't, make it seem very much in the American tradition. On the other hand, the result of that quasi-melodramatic approach —yielding less autonomy to the law — places it analytically further away from formalist legal approaches than is current American Marxist analysis.

The third major difference pertains to scope. Non-Marxist analysis, uninterested in — or, if you prefer, unencumbered by — the task of working out a general theory of American law, tends to be much more compartmentalized in its analysis on two chief counts. First, it compartmentalizes quite unself-consciously within history, both as to time and geography as well as to legal subject. Thus, it is not fazed by the compartmentalization entailed in writing about the transformation of American law using nineteenth century industrialization as the explanation and Northeastern United States private law as the dominant data base — while largely ignoring relationships among Northeastern and Southern or Middle Western economies and relationships between constitutional and private law.[5] Similarly, in analyzing the law's role in the quarrel over slavery, non-Marxist radical analysis separates problems of comity-and-slavery from relationships with the criminal administration of justice in a slave society or from relationships with issues of economic growth and competing economic forms.[6] In marked contrast, Marxist analysis, which aims at a general theory of American law in its more ambitious moments, is both considerably more holistic and considerably more troubled by the way in which different "parts of history" fit together. The second major count on which Marxist theory is less compartmentalized pertains to time past and time present. Marxist analysis has much more to say about contemporary problems in American law and polity and their linkages to the past.

These differences and similarities account for the structure of this Article. Part I undertakes, after briefly comparing Marxist and non-Marxist radical approaches to analyzing the law of American slavery, to assess Paul Finkelman's *An Imperfect Union*,[7] the most recent substantial non-Marxist radical essay on the subject. This task is undertaken first because it is, from a nonradical perspective, more straightforward.

Part II lays the ground for understanding and evaluating Marxist analysis of American law. It focuses primarily on the work of Mark

---

5. *See* M. HORWITZ, THE TRANSFORMATION OF AMERICAN LAW, 1780-1860 (1977); *see also* L. FRIEDMAN, A HISTORY OF AMERICAN LAW (1973). For a good defense of this approach, see L. Friedman, The Law Between the States: Some Remarks on Southern Legal History (unpublished paper delivered at the Second Conference on Southern Legal History, Gulfport, Mississippi, Feb. 1983). In regard to the tendency of books on 19th American law to downplay or omit Southern legal history, Friedman observes:

> Why are these Southern instances ignored? Simply because, from the standpoint of the North, including Northern courts, they were regional . . . not mainstream . . . . [I]n the nineteenth-century, there was a commonly accepted *core* of the legal system; and it was certainly not in the South . . . . [T]oday . . . the core has been redefined. California is the most frequently cited state court today . . . . This has to be recognized. Keir Nash, in a rather nasty passage in . . . "Reason of Slavery" which appeared in . . . the Vanderbilt Law Review, in 1979 . . . accused me of appalling sloppiness and ignorance on this subject . . . .

Id. at 6-7. It *was* a nasty passage. The devil made me do it.

For a favorable commentary on Horwitz's book, see Nash, Book Review, 73 AM. POL. SCI. REV. 244 (1979).

6. *See* P. FINKELMAN, AN IMPERFECT UNION: SLAVERY, FEDERALISM, AND COMITY (1981).

7. *Id.*

Tushnet, the Marxist scholar whose work to date most amply covers issues in both contemporary American law and American legal history even as it exemplifies and enunciates some of the problems inherent in working out an adequate Marxist theory of American law. Part II lays this ground in three steps. First, it briefly examines the reactions of non-Marxist legal historians to Tushnet's principal historical work, *The American Law of Slavery, 1810-1860*.[8] Second, it examines in parallel fashion non-Marxist reactions in the area of Tushnet's other major concentration, current issues in constitutional law. Both sets of reactions indicate a "threshold problem" that Marxist legal scholars face: getting their arguments read accurately and taken seriously. Thus, the third step consists of removing some of the barriers to understanding by "defanging" Marxist language that appears particularly troublesome to non-Marxists, and by describing what contemporary Marxist scholars such as Tushnet take to be appropriate goals for Marxist analysis of American law.

417

An additional aspect of this analysis, to be explored in a later article, will undertake to evaluate Marxist work in the areas of current constitutional law and the legal history of slavery, focusing again primarily but not exclusively on "Tushnetian Marxism." That analysis will develop two main themes. The first is whether and to what extent Tushnetian criticism of contemporary legal scholarship flows from an internally coherent Marxist theory, or from a less coherent series of Marxist insights, or from something much less "foreign" — to wit, "Neo-Legal-Realism" run rampant. The second main theme is the adequacy and promise of such criticism, regardless of its intellectual origin, as it pertains to four areas of intense current controversy: slavery's legal history, the defensibility of constitutional structural review, the question of interpretivist versus noninterpretivist constitutional construction, and the viability of "democratic-process-protecting" judicial review versus "substantive-due-process review revived."

I. Non-Marxist Radical Interpretation: Conflict of Laws and the Legal History of Slavery

A. *Comparing Marxist and Non-Marxist Approaches to Analyzing the Law of Slavery*

Finkelman's *An Imperfect Union* and Tushnet's *The American Law of Slavery, 1810-1860*, together with Eugene Genovese's lengthy review essay, *Slavery in the Legal History of the South and the Na-*

---

8. M. Tushnet, The American Law of Slavery, 1810-1860 (1981).

tion,[9] suggest the rough contours of a radical interpretation of the relations between law and society in the era of American slavery.[10] These analyses also suggest some major obstacles to a comprehensive radical interpretation of the development of American law. Although I shall at times criticize the manner in which Tushnet and Finkelman marshal and assess evidence, even where I disagree on the specifics I am fairly sympathetic to their main purposes, more so, I expect, than a number of other commentators.[11] To the extent that Finkelman attempts to relate the judiciary and slave law to the coming of the Civil War and to the extent that Tushnet tries to provide both a "Restatement" of the law of slavery[12] and an account of rela-

---

9. Genovese, *Slavery in the Legal History of the South and the Nation* (Book Review), 59 TEX. L. REV. 969 (1981). A version of Genovese's essay that has been expanded to include analysis of Morton Horwitz's writings has just appeared in L. FOX-GENOVESE & E. GENOVESE, FRUITS OF MERCHANT CAPITAL: SLAVERY AND BOURGEOIS PROPERTY IN THE RISE AND EXPANSION OF CAPITALISM 337 (1983).

10. Although I say here "*a* radical interpretation," Finkelman's approach, *see* Part I-A *infra*, differs significantly from those of Tushnet and Genovese, which are much more explicitly Marxist. Finkelman's radicalism is almost as chaste of leftist "deep structure" as the McGovernite 1972 Democratic Party National Platform. Tushnet, by contrast, is striving for systematic critical analysis, even if his results often appear no more threatening to American capitalism and its legal-historical superstructures than the Faculty Club luncheon menu at the University of Belgrad.

11. Finkelman's book has come off quite well, though it has taken occasional knocks. *See* Ely, Book Review, 69 CALIF. L. REV. 1755 (1981); Jackson, Book Review, 66 J. NEGRO HIST. 329 (1981) (a much less analytical review); *see also* Reid, *Lessons of Lumpkin: A Review of Recent Literature on Law, Comity, and the Impending Crisis*, 23 WM. & MARY L. REV. 571 (1982). Reid is good reading but not, on this subject, well-read. *Lessons of Lumpkin* proceeds on the basis of two mistakes. Mistake One is assuming that the most vocal case is also indicative of Southern judicial attitudes in general. "Of these [Deep South] states, none should be more revealing than Georgia." *Id.* at 578. Why should it be? Prior research suggests the contrary. That indicates Mistake Two — giving us as if novel and probably representative what is at least a thrice-told tale of uniquely ardent pro-slavery rhetoric in the antebellum Georgia Supreme Court under Chief Justice Joseph Lumpkin. *See* Nash, *The Texas Supreme Court and Trial Rights of Blacks 1845-1860*, 58 J. AM. HIST. 622, 624 n.11 (1971) [hereinafter cited as Nash, *Trial Rights of Blacks*] ("The Georgia supreme court, from its creation in 1845, had the solitary distinction of being the only continuously pro-slavery, 'fire-eating' state supreme court."); *see also* Nash, *Reason of Slavery: Understanding the Judicial Role in the Peculiar Institution*, 32 VAND. L. REV. 7, 104-23 (1979) [hereinafter cited as Nash, *Reason of Slavery*]; Stephenson & Stephenson, *"To Protect and Defend:" Joseph Henry Lumpkin, The Supreme Court of Georgia, and Slavery*, 25 EMORY L.J. 579 (1976). Generally, Reid's essay takes analysis of the law of slavery backward rather than forward. For forward progress, see Morris, *"As if the Injury was Effected by the Natural Elements of Air, or Fire": Slave Wrongs and the Liability of Masters*, 16 LAW & SOCY. REV. 569 (1981-1982).

Tushnet's book has taken harder knocks. Except for Genovese's extended paean, *see* Genovese, *supra* note 9, at 998, the more substantial reviews have ranged from somewhat to very critical. *See, e.g.,* Finkelman, *The Peculiar Laws of the Peculiar Institution* (Book Review), 10 REVIEWS IN AM. HIST. 358 (1982); Watson, *Slave Law: History and Ideology* (Book Review), 91 YALE L.J. 1034 (1982). *But see* Wiecek, Book Review, 1982 AM. B. FOUND. RESEARCH J. 274 (mixed review). For generally favorable shorter reviews, see Hall, Book Review, 87 AM. HIST. REV. 855 (1982); Hyman, Book Review, 69 J. AM. HIST. 158 (1982).

12. *See* M. TUSHNET, *supra* note 8, at 9.

tionships among the law, ideology and economy of slavery, each is pursuing worthwhile objectives.

It is important to understand at the outset the major differences in the purposes and methods of Finkelman and Tushnet. Unlike Tushnet's book, which explicitly doubts the utility of legal decisions in illuminating attitudinal currents in political history,[13] Finkelman's *An Imperfect Union* is legal history solidly anchored in political and social history. Where Tushnet's core aim is "to pry apart the cases to disclose the ordering implicit in slave law,"[14] Finkelman is as interested in using the materials of legal history to explain the impending Civil War as he is in using political events to clarify the development of the law of slavery. Where Tushnet's version of Marxist analysis[15] rejects "[c]riteria of justice and fairness . . . [as] far too simple . . . ordering principles,"[16] Finkelman frequently evaluates developments in those terms. Thus, for example, he evaluates state supreme courts in terms of their "fidelity to law" and "impartiality of decision making."[17] In marked contrast, Tushnet's primary search is for a structure of rules evolving toward autonomy from Northern and British nineteenth century law and toward semi-autonomy from the economic substructure of slavery.[18] It is almost as if Tushnet's perfect analytic product would be an a-chronological distillate from his-

419

---

13. *See id.* at 11-27. Note, however, that Tushnet does not reject judicial opinions as "a useful source of insight into the ideological structures from which slavery drew support." *Id.* at 11.

14. *Id.* at 25.

15. I say "Tushnet's version" advisedly because scholars differ as to whether Marx himself thought, and whether modern Marxists should think, it analytically meaningful to assess capitalist and other pre-revolutionary legal structures in terms of moral categories, such as justice, injustice, fairness, unfairness, and the like, that transcend the then-prevailing mode of production. *Compare* Wood, *The Marxian Critique of Justice*, in MARX, JUSTICE, AND HISTORY 3 (M. Cohen, T. Nagel & T. Scanlon eds. 1980) (Marx does not condemn capitalism as unjust), *with* Husami, *Marx on Distributive Justice*, in MARX, JUSTICE, AND HISTORY, *supra*, at 42 (Marx does condemn capitalism as unjust).

16. M. TUSHNET, *supra* note 8, at 25.

17. P. FINKELMAN, *supra* note 6, at 182.

18. Exactly what Tushnet means by autonomy of the law of slavery has given non-Marxist analysts trouble. *See, e.g.,* Wiecek, *supra* note 11, at 277:

Tushnet posits that the law, as a social artifact, exercises a "relative autonomy" in any society, a position that I find odd from one operating within a Marxian framework. Tushnet maintains this position as a more acceptable alternative to a view that he ascribes to Elkins and others who saw law as nothing more than a reflex of economic or social relationships in society. But where, in Marxian terms, the superstructure of a society is determined by the relations of production, it is difficult to see law as being anything but a reflection of the interests of the hegemonic classes.

The source of some of the difficulties *may* be indicated by Finkelman's remark that "to be blunt, this is one of the most poorly written books I have ever reviewed." Finkelman, *supra* note 11, at 358. That seems a bit harsh. At least some of the complexity *is* in the eye of the non-Marxist beholder *ex necessitate*. For discussion of a similar misreading of Tushnet by Nash, see L. FOX-GENOVESE & E. GENOVESE, *supra* note 9, at 372.

tory — as if he wished to map a timeless, perfected form of slave law upon the historiographical equivalent of Keats' Grecian urn, to transfix it there, forever changeless and beyond all human passion.[19] In marked contrast, Finkelman takes us through an analysis whose temporal progressions are far more familiar to the pragmatic American historical sensibility.

This, however, does not mean that Finkelman is right and Tushnet wrong. At a minimum, we should consider the potential relevance of Fredric Jameson's comment that the empiricism of the Anglo-American analytic tradition, though intimately tied to philosophic liberalism, is profoundly conservative in its political consequences. Thus:

> [T]he bankruptcy of the liberal tradition . . . does not mean that it has lost its prestige or ideological potency. On the contrary: the anti-speculative bias of that tradition, its emphasis on the individual fact or item at the expense of the network of relationships in which that item may be embedded, continue to encourage submission to what is by preventing its followers from making connections, and in particular from drawing the otherwise unavoidable conclusions on the political level. It is therefore time for those of us in the sphere of influence of the Anglo-American tradition to learn to think dialectically, to acquire the rudiments of a dialectical culture and the essential critical weapons which it provides.[20]

Although this Article is hardly the place to venture a complete dialectic education, we should note the difficulties that the dialectic writer's basic formal problem imposes for understanding legal history:

> He who has so intense a feeling for the massive continuity of history itself is somehow paralyzed by that very awareness. . . . Where all the dimensions of history cohere in synchronic fashion, the simple linear stories of . . . historians are no longer possible: now it is diachrony and continuity which become problematical . . . .[21]

That problem is substantial. Equally troubling is the second-order problem produced by the critical reflexes of Anglo-American traditional minds reacting to essays venturing a dialectic interpretation of legal history. These problems are not restricted to the dialectical historian alone — at least if those of us who are not Marxists (or Hegelians) wish to avoid ruling out *ab initio* a possible truth or two. We

420

---

19. *See* J. KEATS, *Ode on a Grecian Urn*, in THE POETICAL WORKS OF JOHN KEATS 295-97 (H. Forman ed. 1908). My point in making this reference is to single out this characteristic in Tushnet's intellectual modeling because it has vexed others as if it arose regardless of, rather than in substantial measure due to, the Marxist analysis.

20. F. JAMESON, MARXISM AND FORM: TWENTIETH CENTURY DIALECTICAL THEORIES OF LITERATURE at x-xi (1971).

21. *Id*. at 50-51.

make, after all, two assumptions about the relationships among form, knowledge, and truth that the dialectian does not. One is that truth of a historical sort is best captured in a narrative essay. In contrast, the dialectician's "larger form will . . . be a construct rather than a narrative."[22] Our other assumption is that, though truth is captured in the narrative form, the capturing is best done via facts that are both separable from the language used to narrate them and selected and arranged in objectified, if not objective, structures by a narrating subject (an author) whose subjectivity and subjective relations with the objectified facts are (on behalf of both good form and maximized knowledge) kept well suppressed. For us, good taste, factual thickness, and subjective detachment go hand in hand. They yield sufficient insight if not systematic explanation. But is that necessarily so?

421

B. *Finkelman's Instrumentalist "Breakdown of Comity" Thesis*

Finkelman's central argument is that decision making in the antebellum state court systems, both North and South, roughly paralleled the development of broader political opinion about slavery and the Federal Union. Specifically, he contends that the willingness of Northern judiciaries to honor, out of comity, laws and decisions of Southern states — and vice versa — moved through three phases. In the first phase, extending from the ratification of the Constitution to roughly 1830, slave states and free states "tried to accommodate each other in a spirit of comity and national unity" despite their "competing interests and ideologies."[23] During this phase, Southern courts generally "recognized and accepted the acts and judicial decisions of free states that emancipated visiting slaves."[24] Although most Northern states by the 1820s had moved gradually from slavery toward freedom (though hardly equality) for all blacks,[25] and although some Northern states limited the time that Southern slaveholders could spend visiting in the North with their slaves,[26] "the free states tried to accommodate their slaveholding neighbors who traveled or

---

22. *Id.* at 51.

23. P. FINKELMAN, *supra* note 6, at 46.

24. *Id.* at 11.

25. In retrospect, one sometimes underestimates how early the Northern states freed their slaves. Vermont's 1777 constitution abolished slavery. *See* VT. CONST. ch. 1, art. 1. New Jersey, under its gradual emancipation statutes, still had a few slaves in 1860. *See* State v. Post, 21 N.J.L. 699 (1848); N.J. REV. STAT. tit. xi, ch. 6, § 1 (1846).

26. For example, in the 1780s Pennsylvania established a six-month limitation, while New York provided for a nine-month limitation in 1817. *See* 1780 Pa. Laws ch. 68, § 10; P. FINKELMAN, *supra* note 6, at 46 n.1.

sojourned in the North."[27]

During the second phase, which stretched from the 1830s into the 1850s,[28] accommodation gave way to confrontation. This second phase displayed at least three characteristics. The first pertained to the types of comity issues that produced litigation in Northern courts. In general, four broad situations, other than unlawful flight[29] or manumittory intent on the part of the master,[30] could explain a slave's presence in a Northern jurisdiction and provide grounds for arguing that the master should be divested of his human property. These were, in diminishing order of duration in a free state or territory: (1) in-migrant residency or domicile; (2) sojourn (nonpermanent presence longer than a visit); (3) visit; and (4) transit. Pre-1830 court cases almost always involved longer-duration issues — for example, when it was reasonable for a court to conclude that an in-migrating master had forfeited his human property by falling short of Pennsylanvia's statutory registration-of-blacks requirements.[31] A signal feature of litigation in Northern courts of the 1830s, 1840s and 1850s was the shift towards litigating claims of freedom based on

422

---

27. P. FINKELMAN, *supra* note 6, at 11.

28. Finkleman's thesis is ambiguous as to the precise dates of the beginning and ending of the breakdown of comity and as to whether the dates are those of the general political breakdown between the sections or those of judicial decisions. He sometimes seems to perceive the second phase as beginning and/or ending earlier than he does at other times. At one point, for example, he observes that "[o]ne critical but long-overlooked aspect of the federal Union was the system of interstate comity that began to break down as early as the 1820s and was well on the road to self-destruction by the 1840s." *Id.* at 11-12. Finkelman later states:

   By 1832 slavery had become a major political issue in the nation. The Missouri crisis of 1820 . . . [and] Nat Turner's rebellion . . . focused national attention on slavery. Yet throughout all of this the state courts of the North maintained their desire for interstate comity and harmony. Only in Pennsylvania was any real attempt made to interfere with the movement of slaves. . . . But in the decade of the 1830s this pattern began to change. Starting in Massachusetts . . . [t]he legal harmony of the nation's first five decades was about to end.

Id. at 99-100. For a useful discussion of Northern judicial and legislative attitudes and slavery rulings, see T. MORRIS, FREE MEN ALL: THE PERSONAL LIBERTY LAWS OF THE NORTH, 1780-1861 (1974) (focusing not on comity and interstate "voluntary" travel but on attempts to protect blacks from being kidnapped and returned to the South as fugitive slaves). Morris' work accords more closely with the earlier dating than with the later.

   In part the ambiguity in dating is inherent in Finkelman's subject matter. But it is greater than it need be because of his text's blurred quality on a critical point — the extent to which judicial decisions merely reflected general political events versus the extent to which the decisions constituted or contributed to those events. His "legal-historical instrumentalism" is, on this point, "soft."

29. Unlawful flight triggered the provisions of the Constitution's fugitive slave clause and the pursuant Fugitive Slave Acts of 1793 and 1850. These are not matters of novel exploration in Finkelman's essay. For such, see S. CAMPBELL, THE SLAVE CATCHERS: ENFORCEMENT OF THE FUGITIVE SLAVE LAW, 1850-1860 (1970); T. MORRIS, *supra* note 28.

30. There is as yet no published, analytically-satisfactory, exhaustive account of manumission cases "at" the South or "at" the North. *But see* A. Nash, Negro Rights and Judicial Behavior in the Old South 1-376 (1968) (unpublished dissertation, Harvard University).

31. *See* 1780 Pa. Laws ch. 68, § 5; P. FINKELMAN, *supra* note 6, at 101-80.

much shorter periods of presence in the North — for example, those arising from master-with-accompanying-slave visits or transits.

The second characteristic was a parallel shift in the options that courts exercised in resolving conflict of laws issues.[32] The first option was to "grant comity to all visitors, based on a desire to maintain interstate harmony and friendship, even at the expense of local laws and institutions."[33] The second was to "balance free-state interests against slave-state interests."[34] Option three "was the enforcement of the *lex loci* (law of the state of residence) of the slaves involved."[35] The final option was to "ignore all issues of local policy or conflict of laws theory, by deferring to the United States Constitution."[36] The second phase saw the disappearance of any impulses toward exercising the first option, a diminution of even-handed balancing, and acceptance of the third option in most states.

423

A third characteristic of the second phase pertained to shifts in substantive doctrines. The first phase had seen occasional confusion as to applicable law and, the rest of the time, judicial rejection of the *Somerset* doctrine, which held that a slave could not be returned to slavery against his will if a master voluntarily brought him to England.[37] The second phase saw, first in Massachusetts[38] and later in most other Northern states, the acceptance of *Somerset*-like doctrine and rejection of the master's right even to mere speedy transit with his slave across a free state. That same phase also saw, according to Finkelman, a converse Southern judicial movement away from ear-

---

32. *See* P. FINKELMAN, *supra* note 6, at 14-15. Note that the four options are Finkelman's array. His is not the only way to read the choices available or the propriety of various selections. *See generally* R. CRAMTON, D. CURRIE & H. KAY, CONFLICT OF LAWS 1-145 (3d ed. 1981).

33. P. FINKELMAN, *supra* note 6, at 14.

34. *Id.* at 15.

35. *Id.*

36. *Id.* at 15. This is hardly a parallel to the second and third options. Constitutional deference describes a necessary juridical effort, not an insulatable option. Few judges thought they could put local interests above the Constitution. Rather, their differences involved what the Constitution required on this score.

37. *See* Somerset v. Stewart, 98 Eng. Rep. 499 (1772). Antebellum America generally thought Lord Mansfield to have held that a master's voluntary bringing of a slave from the West Indies to England freed the slave. Although the actual scope of Mansfield's opinion has been questioned in recent years, that dispute pertains more to the actual English holding than to the way Americans interpreted it. *See generally* W. WIECEK, SOURCES OF ANTISLAVERY CONSTITUTIONALISM IN AMERICA, 1760-1848 (1977); Nadelhaft, *The Somersett Case and Slavery: Myth, Reality, and Repercussions,* 51 J. NEGRO HIST. 193 (1966); Wiecek, Somerset: *Lord Mansfield and the Legitimacy of Slavery in the Anglo-American World,* 42 U. CHI. L. REV. 86 (1974).

38. *See* Commonwealth v. Aves, 35 Mass. (18 Pick.) 193 (1836) (a slave girl brought voluntarily from New Orleans to Massachusetts by her mistress could not be removed to the South again unless she were willing to go).

lier tendencies that had led to a "surprising number of slaves [being] . . . freed by courts in slave states, especially in the period before 1840."[39]

The third phase, which arrived on the eve of the Civil War, was marked generally by a collapse of comity. According to Finkelman:

> In the South freedom suits based on previous free-state residence were, with a few exceptions, virtually impossible to win. Only in Kentucky were blacks still able to vindicate such claims with any degree of consistency. Free blacks were barred from most states in the South, and emancipation was unlawful in many. The rights of free blacks from the North were totally ignored by a number of Southern States.[40]

Finkelman concludes that "[w]e must reject the contention that most of the South continued to recognize the freedom of slaves who were domiciled in the North."[41] Rather, "[w]ell before the secession crisis of 1860-61, the comity provisions of the Constitution were usually ignored when state courts decided cases involving slavery and the rights of free blacks."[42] Indeed,

> [t]he decisions and statutes of northern and southern states indicate that, in some ways, a division of the Union took place before the secession winter of 1860-61. The legal institutions of the free states reflected an antislavery attitude as strong as, and sometimes stronger than, that attitude among the general populace. . . . In the South extreme pro-slavery advocates were leaders of the bar and bench. Southern courts were willing to give total protection . . . at the expense of free-state laws, the rights of free-state citizens, and interstate comity.[43]

Thus, even before Lincoln's election a "judicial secession had taken place"[44] and "the firing on Fort Sumter was only a military manifestation of a judicial and legislative war that had been going on for some time between the States."[45] The import of Finkelman's argument is that contemporaries perceived the Civil War and Northern victory as rendering impossible a counterfactual future, a phase four in which the Taney Court, dominated by a pro-slave majority, could have extended some of the implications of the *Dred Scott* decision to "nationalizing slavery."[46]

Professor Finkelman tells us a good story with considerable art-

424

---

39. P. FINKELMAN, *supra* note 6, at 181.

40. P. FINKELMAN, *supra* note 6, at 285. The reader could correctly observe that "a number" could be anything from one to fifteen in the instant case.

41. *Id*. at 184.

42. *Id*. at 11.

43. *Id*. at 285.

44. *Id*. at 183.

45. *Id*. at 11.

46. *Id*. at 325.

fulness.[47] At times I found myself close to believing that *An Imperfect Union* is not only good narrative but also entirely true, at least until Finkelman begins his hypothetical account of what the Taney Court might have done during the 1860s in the absence of the Civil War.[48] But the suspicious reader may detect in the previous passages a reason for second thoughts. Finkelman tells us that the firing on Fort Sumter was "only a military manifestation" of a judicial and legislative war. I should have thought that whatever one might say about the rude shots that arched across Charleston Harbor on April 12 and 13, 1861, one would not say that they were *only* that. I single out these words because they point up an important characteristic of Finkelman's analytic style: overstating or not quite accurately stating something.[49]

425

C. *Assessing Finkelman's Thesis*

I shall offer an alternate reading of Finkelman's data and urge

---

47. Finkelman's analysis often displays sensitivity to points that have escaped other scholars. Four such instances occur to me. One is that he notes important cases omitted from H. CATTERALL, JUDICIAL CASES CONCERNING AMERICAN SLAVERY AND THE NEGRO (1937), for example, State v. Laselle, 1 Blackf. 60 (Ind. 1820) (slavery prohibited in Indiana). *See* P. FINKELMAN, *supra* note 6, at 93. Second, Finkelman carefully disentangles inaccurate federal reports of Oliver v. Kauffman, 18 F. Cas. 657 (C.C.E.D. Pa. 1850) (No. 10,497), *reargued sub nom.* Oliver v. Weakley, 18 F. Cas. 678 (C.C.E.D. Pa. 1853) (No. 10,502) (involving enforcement of the federal Fugitive Slave Laws). *See* P. FINKELMAN, *supra* note 6, at 252 n.42. In a third instance, he highlights a little known but significant fact about the Articles of Confederation debates. Article IV of the Articles of Confederation guaranteed the "free inhabitants" of each state "all privileges and immunities of free citizens in the several States." THE ARTICLES OF CONFEDERATION AND PERPETUAL UNION art. IV. During the debates over adoption of the Articles, South Carolina had moved to insert the word "white" between "free" and "inhabitants." P. FINKELMAN, *supra* note 6, at 31 n.36 (citing D. ROBINSON, SLAVERY IN THE STRUCTURE OF AMERICAN POLITICS, 1765-1820, at 153-54 (1971)). Finkelman suggests that if haste was indeed the reason that the word "white" was omitted, "then South Carolina and other Deep South states may have felt no obligation, under the Articles or the Constitution, to grant comity to free blacks from other states." *Id.* Whether sound or not, the suggestion is interesting. Fourth, Finkelman points to the ambiguous wording of the privileges and immunities clause of article IV of the 1787 Constitution, and to the unsettled questions the ambiguity provoked. For example, could a Massachusetts black, venturing into a slave state, demand the right to testify that he would have enjoyed in his home state? Or could a slaveowner, visiting the North and finding himself embroiled in a legal controversy, demand that the testimony of his own slave be excluded? *Id.* at 33-34. That suggestion is, of course, more striking than historically sound.

48. Although I agree with much of James Ely's critique of Finkelman on this score, *see* Ely, *supra* note 11, at 1759-63, I think Finkelman is to be commended for squarely facing a circumstance that, though suppressed from historical narrative at least since the era of Rankean scientific history, is nonetheless present. Any judgment as to historical responsibility implies a counterfactual possibility. Finkelman's effort at being explicit about the matter is laudable.

49. To use the currently popular "deconstructionist" jargon, *An Imperfect Union* is a "strong reading" of the slavery cases it reads. (See H. BLOOM, THE BREAKING OF THE VESSELS (1982), for an example of the deconstructionist jargon.) The question is whether *An Imperfect Union* is also a "headstrong misreading."

that such a reading is at least as plausible as his. Before addressing the question of Southern comity that lies at the heart of Finkelman's narrative, I will suggest that his reading contains certain characteristics that undermine major components of his interpretation and that intimate the wisdom of a less catastrophic reading of the course of antebellum judicial relations between North and South.

The first of these characteristics is Finkelman's tendency to overlook, in certain cases, critical details that would undercut the interpretation that Finkelman offers. This is perhaps a manifestation of Finkelman's general inclination to use a case to support some generalization that he wishes to establish, even when the best reading of the case does not offer such support. Combined with his geographical selectivity in sampling cases,[50] these failings cast doubt on some of the major generalizations that Finkelman defends. More broadly, Finkelman gives insufficient consideration to the question of law as a dependent variable versus law as an internally evolving entity. He sometimes classifies decisions dichotomously on the basis of insufficiently documented assertions about judicial aims — for example, and somewhat simplistically, as responding to the conflict of laws issues raised by slavery *either* with "automatic comity" *or* with judicial "war-making." In evaluating decisions, Finkelman tends to erect antinomies, that is, "good law" versus "bad law", or even, "non-law." In the next subsection I will attempt to detail some of these tendencies.[51] Although these failings by no means eliminate my respect for Finkelman's intellectual effort, their presence affects the convincingness of some of its chief generalizations.

1. *Interpretation of Vermont and New Jersey Cases*

Finkelman must first establish that harmony prevailed in phase one. I do not totally disagree with him on this score. But I confess to being disconcerted at his treatment of some of the case evidence on the way to establishing his contention. Let us consider his treatment, first, of *Selectmen of Windsor v. Jacob*,[52] the single early nineteenth century Vermont case that he finds relevant to comity, and, second,

426

---

50. *See* Part I-D *infra*.

51. Full discussion of all of these characteristics is not feasible within the confines of this essay. Particularly note that I do not here challenge in any detail an arguable assumption at the base of Finkelman's comity argument: the notion that the only "correct" solutions to the conflict of laws problems involved had to weigh heavily the policy interests expressed in the *lex loci*. Modern conflict of laws analysis might well cavil at the assumption. *See generally* R. CRAMTON, D. CURRIE & H. KAY, *supra* note 32, at 201-309 (1981).

52. 2 Tyl. 192 (Vt. 1802).

of *State v. Quick*,[53] an 1807 New Jersey case that Finkelman thinks "indicates a certain bias"[54] in the New Jersey court for not granting comity when it could well have been granted. Finkelman has this to say about the Vermont case:

> The . . . case . . . indicates the attitude of the Vermont Supreme Court toward slavery and comity. In 1802 the Board of Selectmen of the Town of Windsor sued Stephen Jacob for the maintenance of an "infirm, sick, and blind" black woman, whom Jacob allegedly purchased as a slave in 1793 and later abandoned. All parties in the case agreed slavery could not legally exist in Vermont. But counsel for Windsor claimed that a de facto slavery existed before Jacob abandoned the woman and thus he was responsible for her care. The state supreme court had to decide if the bill of sale from the 1793 purchase was admissible as evidence against Jacob. Without the bill . . . the case . . . would dissolve.
>
> Judge Royal [*sic*] Tyler ruled that the bill of sale was not valid in Vermont, because the state's constitution was 'express' and 'no inhabitant' could 'hold a slave' in the state. Thus Jacob was not liable for the upkeep of the old woman. [Slaves entering Vermont became free unless they were fugitives.] Tyler asserted that the "good people of Vermont" would submit "with cheerfulness" to the enforcement of the Fugitive Slave Law, even though they might wish that the federal requirements were "more congenial to our modes of thinking." In the spirit of comity and nationalism that pervaded this period, Judge Tyler declared that Vermonters were "sensible . . . of numerous right blessings to us as individuals, and to the State as an integral of the Union."[55]

427]

I have quoted at some length because I want the reader first to form in her or his mind a clear image of what (going by Finkelman's description) she or he thinks the case is about, and then to ask whether the generalization about "the spirit of comity" follows from that image. Doesn't the description conjure up something like: (1) a miscreant Vermonter, one Jacob, who purchases a slave in 1793, (ab)uses her for a while, then turns her out to starve when she is old and feeble; and (2) some high-minded Town Selectmen who want to require the miscreant Jacob to do the "decent slaveowner's thing" — support her in old age and infirmity? However, Jacob escapes his rightful burden because the 1793 bill of sale was never valid under Vermont law. Then, ignoring the resulting pitiful welfare situation, Finkelman winds up on a "congenial" note of interpretation regarding the attitudes of the Vermont Supreme Court.

There are two problems here. One has to do with getting the

---

53. 2 N.J.L. 393 (1807).

54. P. FINKELMAN, *supra* note 6, at 76-77.

55. *Id.* at 78-79.

facts of the case straight. The other has to do with their appropriate interpretation.

As to facts, my going to the Vermont Reports and reading the case was triggered by a mere typographic suspicion, a dim recollection that Chief Judge Tyler spelled his first name differently than Finkelman spelled it in his text — a suspicion that turned out to be well-founded.[56]   A reading of the case also revealed that the bill of sale was dated 1783, not 1793 — three years before rather than seven years after the passage of a 1786 state law prohibiting the export of slaves from the state.[57]

Reading further disclosed that the miscreant Jacob's account of what had happened and what the Selectmen were up to was rather different from Finkelman's. According to Jacob's counsel, certain inhabitants of Windsor had "inveigled . . . [the black woman] from her master's family [Jacob's family] and service by the syren [*sic*] songs of *liberty and equality* . . . ."[58] She went off and worked for them, while he, miscreant Jacob, "did not attempt . . . to reclaim her. As an inhabitant of the state, in obedience to the constitution, he considered that he could not hold her as a slave."[59]

There is one final, interesting aspect of the case that Finkelman doesn't bother to tell us. It is that Jacob was himself a colleague of Royall Tyler on the Vermont Supreme Court. *Judge* Jacob excused himself from participating in the case for obvious reasons.[60]   Why doesn't Finkelman tell us this? Surely Judge Jacob's involvement has some bearing on interpreting the case's outcome as an indicator of the attitudes of the Vermont Supreme Court.

As to the interpretation of Judge Jacob's case, what does the substantive situation and the case holding really indicate about comity? Does it say anything at all about the issues that later were so to arouse Southerners — whether they could sojourn, visit, or even transit without losing their slaves? Given that Jacob was off the case and apparently had not attempted to prevent the black woman's departure (surely he was not seeking to inveigle her west and south to some new promised land of slavery across the wide Missouri), what real test of comity was there? And this, after all, is the only Vermont example given.

---

56. Judge Tyler's first name was "Royall," not "Royal."

57. *See* Selectmen of Windsor v. Jacob, 2 Tyl. at 192, 193.

58. 2 Tyl. at 196-97.

59. 2 Tyl. at 197.

60. 2 Tyl. at 198.

Now let us consider the New Jersey case, *State v. Quick*.[61] Finkelman seems to be considerably less admiring of New Jersey's record of protecting an "unlimited right of transit and sojourn for non-resident slaveowners and their human 'property' . . . until 1865"[62] than he is of Vermont's. At any rate, he says of *Quick*:

> Because New Jersey protected the rights of slaveowners only one case dealing with the problem of comity and slavery was recorded. *State v. Quick* (1807) involved a slave purchased in New York and brought to New Jersey. The case was a classic problem in the choice of laws. New York prohibited the selling of a slave for export. New Jersey, on the other hand, had no objection to the introduction of new slaves, provided they were purchased outside the state and not resold within the state. There was no New Jersey law that could free the slave. In reaching his decision, Justice William Pennington noted that if the slave was free under New York law, "it must be that he was free before he was brought into this State; for . . . New York cannot extend into this State and attach itself to any act done here, in order to give him freedom."[63]

429

So much for what Pennington ruled. As to what Finkelman thinks Pennington might have done, "Pennington could have determined that under New York law the slave was free before he came to New Jersey, because the *intent* to export a slave purchased in the state was an offense, as well as the actual exportation"[64] and that "since the exportation began with preparations in New York, the crime against New York law was committed *before* the slave ever reached New Jersey."[65] But Pennington rendered no such interpretation.

> Instead he ruled that the slave would be free under New York law only if the original purchase of the slave was made with the intent of illegally exporting the slave from New York. Since the purchase took place two years prior to the removal, Pennington held that the purchase had not been an attempt to evade the New York law; thus the slave was not freed.[66]

Finkelman's moral is that the decision "indicates a certain bias. . . . Unlike other northern states that leaned toward liberty while at the same time granting rights to nonresidents, New Jersey gave rights to all slaveowners and refused to enforce a New York law for the benefit of a slave owned by a New Jersey resident."[67] Thus, according to Finkelman, "State v. Quick and the protection offered slaves in

---

61. 2 N.J.L. 393 (1807).
62. P. FINKELMAN, *supra* note 6, at 76.
63. *Id.* at 76-77 (footnote omitted).
64. *Id.* at 77 (emphasis in original).
65. *Id.* (emphasis in original).
66. *Id.*
67. *Id.*

transit . . . indicate that New Jersey was one of the least pro-freedom states in the North."[68]

Now, let us picture to ourselves, drawing from Finkelman's narrative, what has been going on. Does it seem that the New Jersey judges didn't do what they really ought to have done — free the slave by applying New York law in the spirit of comity against the New Jersey resident who exported the slave from New York? Particularly, don't you get the impression that this is a New Jersey Supreme Court case? The book itself clearly gives that impression — given that the case is embedded between discussions of New York and New England appellate cases, and given that Finkelman treats the result as indicative of the stand on comity of the whole state of New Jersey. Yet *Quick* was not a state supreme court case at all. Rather, it was a case in the Bergen, New Jersey circuit decided by one judge.

Further, doesn't one get the impression that "Quick" must be either the slave seeking freedom or his owner, and that the owner is the exporter from New York and importer into New Jersey? Doesn't one get the sense that since the owner has been so naughty in avoiding the intent of the New York statute it would serve him right to lose the slave? Lastly, is it not obvious from Finkelman's exposition that the core of his objection to Judge Pennington's opinion is that the judge ignored the "appropriate" comity implications of the second of the New York law's described offenses — one offense being *exporting* a slave purchased in New York and the other offense being *intending to export* a slave purchased in New York?

In fact, Dick was the slave and Quick, his owner, was several sales removed from the erring exporter/importer. The exporting/importing had not been a recent occurrence. The supposedly offensive New York purchase of the slave Dick had taken place not two years, but rather some twelve or thirteen years before the trial in New Jersey. The New York purchaser was one Sir James Jay who, from a time prior to the purchase, had been accustomed to splitting his time between residing in New York and residing on his Bergen County, New Jersey plantation. At some point after purchasing the slave Dick, Sir James had sent him from Sir James' New York house to his New Jersey farm. The alert reader will note that this circumstance is not first cousin, let alone identical twin, to the kind of New-York-law-evading action that Finkelman's narrative contemplates. At some time after sending the slave from his New York to his New

430

---

68. *Id.* at n.27.

Jersey property, seemingly about two years, Sir James committed Dick to jail for what the defense lawyer described as "bad behavior."[69] Sir James later "sold him out of it" to get rid of him as troublesome.[70] The slave "passed through the hands of several masters, when at length the defendant bought him."[71]

If that account of the events, which is the best I can piece together, is correct, it does not provide evidence of any wicked exporter/importer behavior contravening New York law — even the version of the New York law that Finkelman has given us. The case simply does not establish any intent to export from New York at the time of Sir James' (not Quick's) purchase of Dick.

Moreover, Finkelman reads the New York law as penalizing a person who purchases a New York slave with the intent to export. I put the best gloss possible on Finkelman's prose which, read literally, states that the New York statute sought to punish intent to export *without* any act. What *did* the New York law say? According to the New Jersey Court Report, it penalized anyone who "shall, at any time, purchase or buy, or . . . take or receive any slave, *with intent* to remove, export, or carry such slave . . . to any other place without the State and there to be sold."[72] The slave, as I (and Judge Pennington) read the New York statute, was to go free if "Sir James, immediately on purchasing him, had brought him into [New Jersey], and sold him."[73] But, if anything at all is plain about the case, it is that neither Sir James nor the not-so-fast Mr. Quick had such an intent.

To reach this conclusion is to observe a possible cause of Finkelman's analytic slip and to suggest a problem of authorial attitude that bedevils much of *An Imperfect Union*. Pushing the case facts around, Finkelman seeks to open up a hole toward freedom. Then he blames the court in question for not leading the slave through the illusory hole he creates. On any objective analysis, the circumstances of Quick's case and the New York law as stated in the New Jersey Reports require the result that Judge Pennington reached. Finkelman's interpretations of *Jacob* and *Quick* are not the only "strong readings" — or, as I would put it, "headstrong misreadings" — that occur in *An Imperfect Union*.[74]

431

---

69. 2 N.J.L. at 394.

70. 2 N.J.L. at 394.

71. 2 N.J.L. at 393.

72. 2 N.J.L. at 394.

73. 2 N.J.L. at 395.

74. Space does not permit instancing all the cases where I think it at least arguable that

2. *Judicial Motivation and Attitudes*

Finkelman's moral sensibilities, joined with his radical "instrumentalist" tendency to treat lines of case outcomes as dependent variables of political inputs, lead him to explain variations among the states of a single section in ways that I find less than compelling. I shall take just a few examples by way of illustration.

a. *Variation from Aves.* One variation in outcomes among Northern jurisdictions is that the State Supreme Courts of Illinois, Indiana, and New Jersey did not decide to follow *Commonwealth v. Aves*[75] when similar cases came before them.[76] Finkelman "explains" these decisions by observing that all three states had weak antislavery movements, major borders with slave states, and were Negrophobic Democratic strongholds.[77] Putative statewide political and geographic characteristics turn themselves into direct determinants of case decisions. Finkelman's explanation is not made more satisfactory by relegating to a footnote[78] the State of California — a jurisdiction that also rejected *Aves*[79] but did not share similar geopolitical characteristics.

b. Judicial motivations or reasoning. Finkelman sometimes has difficulty with judicial motivations or reasoning, occasionally reach-

432

Finkelman's reading is either wrong or leaves out something. Instances include the following, however. With respect to Lewis v. Fullerton, 22 Va. (1 Rand.) 15 (1821), a case that Finkelman describes as an unfortunate inveigling of slaves to return from Ohio to Virginia, *see* P. FINKELMAN, *supra* note 6, at 89, two alternate readings of the case are already in circulation. At least one is more plausible than Finkelman's. He ignores both. *Compare* R. COVER, JUSTICE ACCUSED 95-98 (1975), *with* Nash, *Reason of Slavery*, *supra* note 11, at 134. With respect to *Ex parte* Bushnell, 9 Ohio St. 77 (1851), Finkelman uses the case to show that the Ohio court remained "antislavery until the Civil War" but omits telling us that the court split closely, 3-2, on the case. Perhaps the most egregious "strong misreading" is his version of John Marshall's opinion in Cohens v. Virginia, 19 U.S. (6 Wheat.) 82 (1821). The case now is best remembered for Marshall's lengthy defense of the United States Supreme Court's jurisdiction in the case notwithstanding the eleventh amendment and the attacks of the Virginia Court of Appeals. But there is a second part to it — namely, whether the defendants could be punished by the State of Virginia for selling in Virginia, contrary to state law, federal lottery tickets putatively authorized by a District of Columbia lottery commission. Considering the case as one of many relating to the possibility of Northern and Southern courts denying right of passage to slaves notwithstanding the commerce clause, Finkelman states, "in Cohens . . . the court had upheld a Virginia prohibition on the sale of lottery tickets, even though the lottery had been authorized by Congress." P. FINKELMAN, *supra* note 6, at 260 n.60. He makes it seem as if *Cohens* endorsed a state's right to regulate interstate commerce against congressional will. But Marshall's opinion held no such thing. Rather, it allowed Virginia to prosecute a Norfolk sale explicitly on the ground that Congress intended to authorize the sale of lottery tickets *only* within the District of Columbia. 19 U.S. (6 Wheat.) at 119.

75. 35 Mass. (18 Pick.) 193 (1836).

76. *See* P. FINKELMAN, *supra* note 6, at 127.

77. *See id.*

78. *Id.* at 127 n.4.

79. *See Ex parte* Archy, 9 Cal. 147 (1858).

ing conclusions without any buttressing evidence. Thus, at a crucial
juncture in the book's argument, he asserts of Southern judicial
motivations: "[F]idelity to the law itself may go a long way in explaining why the courts in a number of Southern states were willing
to liberate slaves who had lived in free states. It was not sympathy
for blacks nor a desire to end slavery that led to these decisions."[80]
Given the number of occasions on which Southern judges did express something much like sympathy for blacks,[81] this sweeping conclusion is not well supported. At other times Finkelman has
difficulty believing evidence when, arguably, the difficulty lies in his
own mind-set. Thus, of a Kentucky case, *Carney v. Hampton*,[82]
which involved the same New York anti-exportation-to-sell statute
as *State v. Quick*,[83] he observes:

> [T]he Kentucky Supreme Court refused to enforce New York's prohi-
> bition against selling slaves and removing them from the State. The
> Kentucky court would not "believe" that New York "intended wholly
> to prevent the exportation of slaves" and thus ruled that a man who
> had purchased a slave without any intention to export him and then
> later left that state had not in fact violated New York's law. Ken-
> tucky's inability to "believe" that New York could truly mean to end
> *all* exportation of slaves indicates how difficult it was for states to grant
> comity to each other's laws. In this case New York's interests were so
> alien to those of Kentucky that the latter state simply found it impossi-
> ble to understand New York's law.[84]

433

Here is palpable confusion. First, the New York law prohibited
purchasing-and-exporting, *not* selling-and-exporting. Once you sell,
the sold "object" is difficult to remove from the state — it's no longer
yours. Second, the Kentucky court's discussion of the various exceptions to the law[85] makes plain the fact that New York did not intend
to forbid *all* exportation. Third, because a neutral reading of the
New York statute indicates that it is a prohibition against *purchase-
with-intent*-to-sell-out-of-state,[86] it is hard to resist the conclusion

---

80. P. FINKELMAN, *supra* note 6, at 182.

81. *See generally* Nash, *Fairness and Formalism in the Trials of Blacks in the State Supreme
Courts of the Old South*, 56 VA. L. REV. 64 (1970); Nash, *Negro Rights, Unionism, and Great-
ness on the South Carolina Court of Appeals: The Extraordinary Chief Justice John Belton
O'Neall*, 21 S.C. L. REV. 141 (1969).

82. 19 Ky. (3 T.B. Mon.) 228 (1826).

83. 2 N.J.L. 393 (1807); *see* notes 61-63 *supra* and accompanying text.

84. P. FINKELMAN, *supra* note 6, at 71.

85. Exceptions included, for example, taking one's own slaves from New York to settle in
another jurisdiction and inheritance of slaves by a non-New Yorker who removed them without intent to sell. Carney v. Hampton, 19 Ky. (3 T.B. Mon.) 228, 230 (1826).

86. *See* note 72 *supra* and accompanying text.

that Finkelman, not Kentucky, "simply found it impossible to understand New York's law" because *his* perspectives are so "alien."

Finally, a neutral reading of *Carney v. Hampton* indicates that the Kentucky court did a passable job of observing comity. Finkelman fails to tell the reader that the lower court's finding for the defendant slave owner was "reversed . . . and the cause . . . remanded for new proceedings"[87] because the lower court erred by instructing the jury to find for the slaveowner and against the claimant slave if it believed that the purchaser-and-exporter of the plaintiff's mother "did not sell her, but gave her to his daughter."[88] The Kentucky Supreme Court said that the instruction was improper because it overlooked the fact that a change of heart after exportation and a pursuant decision not to sell (but rather to keep or give) would not bar the slave's right to claim freedom. That right accrued once there had been purchase-with-intent-to-export and could not be abridged by later change of intent.[89] Thus, the Kentucky Court surely did not in this case show a complete inability to understand or to observe comity.

Arguably, Finkelman's understanding goes astray on a number of other occasions for like reasons — for example, when he finds it difficult to credit that not only in the North but also in the South there might be a difference between a state's legislature and its appeals court on some slavery issue, that there might be something less than complete and intense pro-slavery unity. Another instance is when he discounts as an example of anti-abolition sentiment an Illinois Senator's observation in the United States Senate that, until the late 1840s, " 'the courts of the slave States had been much more liberal in their adjudications upon the question of slavery than the free States.' "[90] So too, he seems to wear analytic blinders when he conclusively characterizes as anti-abolitionist a New York judge who, following his understanding of New York law, first freed slaves in transit with their master and mistress from Virginia through New York City to Texas, and then gave money to the cause of the suddenly impecunious master and mistress.

---

87. 19 Ky. (3 T.B. Mon.) at 233.

88. 19 Ky. (3 T.B. Mon.) at 229.

89. 19 Ky. (3 T.B. Mon.) at 229.

90. P. FINKELMAN, *supra* note 6, at 99. *Compare id.* at 99 & n.101 (where Finkelman feels compelled to qualify and explain the statement quoted in text), *with id.* at 150-55 (where Finkelman has no difficulty perceiving an attitudinal split between the Illinois legislature and the Illinois Supreme Court). Finkelman's book also omits discussion of almost all of the instances of similar legislative/judicial splits in attitudes and manumission policy in the Southern states.

There is no point in belaboring these sorts of arguable interpretations, but they do illustrate how Finkelman's argument can push beyond the evidence he offers to support it. This in mind, I turn to the
issue most vital to the overall success of Finkelman's argument —
the collapse of comity during the phase immediately preceding the
Civil War.

D. *Sampling and the Question of a Collapse of Southern Comity — Finkelman's Problematic Generalizations and the Evidence*

At the heart of *An Imperfect Union* is the contention that during
the 1840s and 1850s judicial matters went seriously awry in the
North and South. I will put aside whether Finkelman is right or
wrong about Northern judicial decisions and concentrate on ten of
his core generalizations about the Southern judiciaries. I shall argue
that only one of these ten is unexceptionable, and that the others are
variously false, simplistic or otherwise problematic, as follows:

435

(1) "The development of . . . doctrine in the American South is best
illustrated by an examination of the case law in four slave states: Kentucky, Louisiana, Missouri, and Mississippi."[91] (False)

(2) "[S]outhern courts, gradually at first and then almost in unison,
began to deny comity to blacks who had lived in the North, where they
had gained their liberty."[92] (False)

(3) "By 1860 . . . most Southern states refused to recognize or uphold
freedom based on free state residence or sojourn, or even direct emancipation in a free state."[93] (False)

(4) "[F]idelity to law — this impartiality of decisionmaking — began
to fade in the 1830s and disappeared throughout most of the South
before 1860. By then fidelity to the institution of slavery was more important than fidelity to abstract concepts of law."[94] (Simplistic)

(5) "Slave-state courts reflected the attitudes of the people they
served. . . ."[95] (Simplistic)

(6) "Kentucky and a few other slave states continued to recognize freedom claims based on the laws of other states throughout the antebellum period. But even in these liberal states the trend was moving away
from decisions in favor of liberty."[96] (Unexceptionable, in respect to
Kentucky)

(7) "By the 1850s most of the South had, to one degree or another,
decided that interstate comity could not extend to cases involving

---

91. *Id.* at 187.
92. *Id.* at 179.
93. *Id.* at 11.
94. *Id.* at 182.
95. *Id.* at 234.
96. *Id.* at 189.

slaves who claimed to be free."[97] (Muddy — either trivially true or wrong)

(8) "It would be convenient . . . to argue that southern courts ceased granting comity . . . in response to northern decisions denying comity to slaveowners in transit. . . . [I]t is not at all clear that the change came about in this way."[98] (Problematic)

(9) "[S]outhern courts freed slaves who had spent time in the North well *before* northern courts freed slaves in transit. It surely would be absurd to argue that southern jurists reversed their own precedents because northern jurists had endorsed them."[99] (Confused)

(10) "Within the realm of state action *Lemmon* [a New York case] represents the final development in the law of freedom, while *Mitchell* [a Mississippi case] symbolized the ultimate logic of the law of bondage." Finkelman concludes that what the dissenting judge in *Lemmon*, and the judge in *Mitchell* "sensed, but could not admit, was that the legal systems of the North and South could no longer coexist."[100] (Problematic)

436

1. *Finkelman's False Generalizations*

Perhaps the most curious generalization in *An Imperfect Union* is the assertion that the development of legal doctrine concerning slavery in the American South is best illustrated by examining case law in Kentucky, Louisiana, Missouri, and Mississippi.[101] A moment's thought suggests that the best way of illustrating the development of Southern slavery case law is to examine it in all fifteen slave states, or at least in all eleven of the secession states. Complete enumeration simply is better than sampling, especially when the "universe" is so small and its component members, the states, are so likely to diverge in ways that no sampling technique can control.

Moreover, given a decision to sample rather than to consider all the slave state jurisdictions, the combination of states chosen — surely not a random selection on Finkelman's part — contains two characteristics which suggest that they might make a singularly unrepresentative "quad." One characteristic is that Finkelman's sample contains a greater percentage of nonseceding than seceding slave states.[102] A second characteristic is that all of the sample states border the Mississippi River. None is east of the Appalachians; thus,

---

97. *Id.* at 189-90.

98. *Id.* at 182-83.

99. *Id.* at 183.

100. *Id.* at 310.

101. P. FINKELMAN, *supra* note 6, at 187.

102. Of the four that did not withdraw from the Union (four states, incidentally, that contained a very small minority of the Union's slaves), Finkelman selects two, or 50%. Of the 11 states that did withdraw, Professor Finkelman also picks two, or 18%.

none is one of the original thirteen colonies. None is one of the older slave-holding jurisdictions. To the extent that jurisprudential characteristics vary accordingly, Finkelman's sample will not detect the variance. His selection is roughly equivalent to a Northern sample consisting of Iowa, Illinois, Wisconsin, and the Minnesota Territory. These states might fairly represent the Northern Mississippi Valley but, absent any New England or North Atlantic states, would be manifestly unreliable as an "all-Northern" sample.

Finkelman's sampling apparently leads him to believe two of his other crucial, but incorrect, assertions: that Southern courts began to deny comity to blacks who had gained liberty in the North "gradually at first and then almost in unison"[103] and the closely related assertion that by 1860 "most" Southern states rejected claims of freedom based on "free-state residence or sojourn, or even direct emancipation in a free state."[104] Although indeed related, the two assertions are not entirely four-square with each other as to the number of Southern states denying comity and as to subjects covered in the comity denials. The second generalization tells us only that "most" states did so — which presumably means *either* six or more of the seceding states *or* eight or more of the slave-holding states. The first generalization claims more — that the denial was almost unanimous by the eve of the Civil War. It also seems to make a stronger claim as to the subjects covered — and a counter-intuitive one at that. Where the second generalization has *most* Southern states rejecting claims in *several* circumstances — free state emancipation, free state residence and free state sojourn — the first describes an almost unanimous denial of claims based on the strongest "pro-freedom" situations, where (ex-)slaves had actually gained liberty by judicial action in the North. This is a bit odd, unless we try an unusual and very awkward reading of Finkelman's first generalization by taking it to mean that although Southern courts nearly unanimously *did begin* to deny comity, they *did not finish* so doing.

A glance at relevant cases in the jurisdictions that Finkelman omits entirely or handles insufficiently in stray footnotes will show that, in any event, both generalizations are false. The only way that one can come close to counting a majority of Southern state jurisdictions as denying comity during the period from 1855-1860 is if one includes as "failing to grant comity" courts to whom no such cases were appealed during those years.

---

103. P. FINKELMAN, *supra* note 6, at 179.
104. *Id.* at 11.

If part of Finkelman's counting trouble is caused by his peculiar sampling, much of the rest results because he isolates what one might call the explicit conflict-of-laws/comity cases, with which he does deal, from the implicit conflict-of-laws/comity cases,[105] with which he deals little or not at all. Yet implicit comity cases involved judges in allied issues whose disposition should (especially in the absence of more explicit conflict-of-laws cases on the relevant dockets) be indicative if not dispositive of whether or not the court in question was bent on an "anti-comity" warlike judicial course.

Whatever the merits of this objection to Finkelman's thesis,[106] let us for the moment examine the disposition of the last few important antebellum cases raising comity issues in each slave state's appellate court. To give every advantage to Finkelman's thesis, we shall say that it succeeds if *either* a bare majority (six) of the seceding states *or* a bare majority (eight) of all of the slave states can be shown to have denied comity as a general late antebellum practice. We shall also give Finkelman's thesis a leg up by counting the box-score of his four sample states as he does: one remaining on the whole disinclined to wage judicial war on comity (Kentucky), and three moving to an anti-comity position (Mississippi, Missouri, and Louisiana).[107] Finkelman's thesis thus produces: (1) a score of zero for and two against comity among the seceding jurisdictions; and (2) a score of one for to three against among all the slaveholding jurisdictions. What happens if we now add in the states Finkelman doesn't sample?

Let us take the two omitted border states, Maryland and Delaware, first. The fruits of my research do not help Finkelman's "off to war" thesis. With respect to the Delaware Supreme Court, I cannot find any cases that explicitly or implicitly deny the efficacy of other states' laws in conferring the benefits of freedom. Indeed, the laws of Delaware aimed at the opposite result. An act of 1787 freed slaves imported into Delaware "for sale, or otherwise."[108] A 1793 act outlawed both kidnapping free blacks into slavery and exporting slaves for sale without a license.[109] Early judicial decisions favored the

438

---

105. For example, those involving wills that directed out-of-state manumission of slaves in instances where the estate was saddled with in-state debts, or wills that permitted slaves to choose between Northern freedom and Southern slavery.

106. I have on an earlier occasion dealt with the dispositions of some thirteen manumission and comity-related issues in five Southern jurisdictions, and shall not repeat the entire demonstration here. *See* Nash, *Reason of Slavery, supra* note 11, at 200-02.

107. There is room for argument about the import of the Louisiana court's holdings, but I shall not develop the point here for reasons of space.

108. Act of Feb. 3, 1787, ch. 145 b, § 7, 2 Del. Laws 884, 886-87.

109. Act of June 14, 1793, ch. 22 c, 2 Del. Laws 1093.

slave. In *Negro Guy v. Hutchins*,[110] a master who had merely brought his slave into Delaware with a cartload of wheat seed to sow on his Delaware farm lost his black to liberty. In *Negro Abram v. Burrows*,[111] a Maryland master sent a slave, Negro Abram, to work one week for the master's brother, who was a tenant on the master's Delaware farm, some three miles distant from the master's Maryland residence. So doing, the master lost his property in Abram forever. Later Delaware decisions ran in the same direction.[112] Maryland had much more slavery than Delaware although Maryland's slavery docket was by no means comparable to those of states such as North Carolina, Tennessee, or Louisiana. Although space limitations render impractical a complete analysis of the Maryland decisions, brief examination of the five Maryland Court of Appeals cases that arose during the 1850s and have some bearing upon matters of comity do not buttress Finkelman's generalizations. Of these five cases, only one — *Northern Central Railway v. Scholl*[113] — goes off in an "anti-freedom direction." But one must push the analysis very hard to argue that the holding in *Northern Central Railway* indicates a reprehensible flouting of comity. The question was whether a railroad was liable in Maryland courts for the carelessness of one of its ticket agents in selling in Pennsylvania a ticket to a runaway Maryland slave notwithstanding a warning to the ticket agent by a third party that the black had unlawfully absconded from his Maryland master.[114] In the view of Maryland Chief Justice Le Grand, Pennsylvania might "forbid its courts to grant redress for the wrong, but it cannot oust the jurisdiction of the courts of the State of the injured party . . . [w]henever the wrong-doer comes within [that State's] limits."[115] Thus, the Court of Appeals of Maryland applied the law of the forum and the law of the locus of residence though not of the locus of the ticket sale. Any doubts that the Maryland court's han-

439

---

110. Unreported case, *cited in* Thoroughgood v. Anderson, 5 Del. (5 Harr.) 97, 103-04 n.a, *affd.*, 5 Del. (5 Harr.) 199 (1848). *Thoroughgood* draws on a judge's notebook of earlier cases. Although the notebook is reprinted in DELAWARE CASES, neither *Negro Guy* nor *Negro Abram*, *see* text at note 111 *infra*, appears there.

111. Unreported case, *cited in* Thoroughgood v. Anderson, 5 Del. (5 Harr.) 97, 102-03 n.a, *affd.*, 5 Del. (5 Harr.) 199 (1848).

112. For example, in State v. Dillahunt, 3 Del. (3 Harr.) 551 (1840), and State v. Jeans, 4 Del. (4 Harr.) 570 (1845), the Delaware Court found a presumption that, at least for the purpose of being a witness, Negroes were not slaves, but free.

113. 16 Md. 331 (1860). On the question of whether Southern slavery decisions could be meaningfully pro- or anti-slavery, see Nash, *Reason of Slavery*, *supra* note 11, at 156-72.

114. There was contradictory testimony as to whether the warning immediately preceded or immediately followed the sale. 16 Md. at 347. The Maryland court treats the case as if the priority of the warning had been demonstrated. 16 Md. at 349.

115. 16 Md. at 351.

dling of the case might cause are not borne out by the resolutions of the other four Maryland cases. In *Brown v. Brown*,[116] the 1858 Maryland court took an approach to a bequest of freedom that surely would have failed before a judiciary hostile to such grants. *Brown v. Brown* upheld a will with several provisions each of which would probably have been voided by the Georgia or post-1859 Mississippi benches. One provision granted freedom after varying terms of years during which the slaves were to be hired out. During that time they would have been *statu liberi* with a quasi-free status — precisely the status that Southern extremist judges feared would provide bad, envy-inducing examples to other less favored slaves. Another provision of the will required that the testator's plantation be rented out with the annual proceeds to be spent on the welfare of his blacks. That is not the sort of practice that would have commended itself to Judge Harris of Mississippi and *Mitchell v. Wells*[117] fame.

440

An 1853 case, *Ringgold v. Barley*,[118] found the Maryland court holding — in contrast to an earlier case[119] — that a master who had taken his Maryland slaves with him to Missouri to establish a farm and who farmed there for approximately a year before becoming ill and returning to Maryland, lost his slaves on bringing them back with him. That is not the sort of ruling that would have commended itself to a pro-slavery judge seeking loopholes in the law of domicile to benefit the master. Furthermore, in *Alexander v. Worthington*,[120] Judge Le Grand observed:

> To permit the heirs at law who have availed themselves of their proximity in blood to obtain administration on the personal estate of the testator, to sell the negroes into ceaseless bondage in foreign climes, for the purpose of providing for payment of debts which are justly chargeable on the lands descended to the heirs at law, . . . would seem to be an act of injustice of which a court composed of slaveholders . . . could not possibly be guilty.[121]

---

116. 12 Md. 87 (1858).

117. 37 Miss. 235 (1859); *see* notes 126-30 *infra* and accompanying text.

118. 5 Md. 186 (1853).

119. The earlier case was Cross v. Black, 9 G. & J. 198 (Md. 1837), which held that time spent in Ohio during an abortive trip to Missouri did not, in conjunction with a relevant Maryland statute of 1831, operate to divest the master of his property in slaves on return to Maryland. The court reached this result despite the fact that the master had signed deeds of manumission while in Ohio. Although I can imagine Finkelman arguing that this case showed the 1837 Maryland court's disregard for comity with Ohio, the evidence showed fairly clearly that a large Ohio anti-slavery crowd had intimidated the master into executing the manumittory devices. *See* 9 G. & J. at 206.

120. 5 Md. 471 (1854).

121. 5 Md. at 494.

In *Smith v. Smith*,[122] decided in the same year, the sale of a *statu liberi* out of Maryland in frustration of a bequest of freedom caused the Chief Justice to express in dictum "our condemnation of the contrivance, by whoever made, to deprive a helpless negress of the freedom to which she was entitled by her master's will. Such conduct . . . ought to be visited with the severest penalties of the criminal law."[123]

Whether mere words or tell-tales of judicial attitudes, these passages in *Alexander* and *Smith*, in conjunction with the other cases discussed, indicate that Maryland should not be included in the "warlike" comity-denying "camp" of Mississippi and Missouri. Thus, we find that the relevant decisions of three of the four non-seceding slaveholding states — two of which Finkelman dealt with and two of which he ignored — do not support Finkelman's hypothesis. Considering the South as a whole, we now have a tie of three in favor of comity (Kentucky, Delaware, and Maryland) to three against (Mississippi, Louisiana, and Missouri).

441

What happens if we examine the records of the slave states that did secede? Will we find in the comparison that the Maryland and Delaware results are atypical, border-state phenomena? The answer is a reasonably clear "No." Indeed, if there is any real puzzle it is that Finkelman could have thought his sample representative. That is because abundant evidence contrary to his hypothesis already exists in other historical analyses for at least four of these nonborder states: Texas, Tennessee, and the two Carolinas.

Texas can be dealt with by quoting a relevant paragraph from my 1971 article:

> Between 1845 and 1860, the Texas judges were asked to rule on six issues which afforded them ample room to determine either for or against liberty: whether a will seeking to free blacks and remove them from the state was valid, when Texas law forbade domestic liberation; whether slaves could make a legally cognizable choice between freedom and slavery; *whether interstate comity required Texas to apply another jurisdiction's "pro-freedom" laws*; whether a slave could obtain not only freedom but also monetary damages for unlawful detention; whether a free black had the right to rescind an agreement selling himself into slavery; and whether oral, as distinct from written, gifts of freedom were valid. On all six issues the Texas judges aligned themselves with the "libertarians."[124]

Texas ought to have been reckoned with in a manner more adequate

---

122. 6 Md. 496 (1854).

123. 6 Md. at 500.

124. Nash, *Trial Rights of Blacks*, *supra* note 11, at 630-31 (emphasis added).

than the single misleading footnote that Finkelman offers.[125] I will take the liberty of quoting from my earlier article again. That article not only ought to have put Finkelman on notice about Texas specifics, but should have put him on guard with respect to his tendency to wave the fire-eating Mississippi decision, *Mitchell v. Wells*,[126] as if it were an amazingly-red red-flag that Finkelman himself had first discovered. To continue:

> In two other cases, the Texas judges followed Tennessee in refusing to allow a claim of "interstate comity" to interfere with an owner's attempt to manumit his slaves. In *Jones v. Laney*, they refused to accept the argument that a Chickasaw Indian's right to free a slave was invalid in Texas because it was contrary to the laws of the state within which the "Chickasaw nation" dwelt. . . . Neither the state where the will had been made nor the State where the suit for freedom was being heard, however hostile to manumission their policies might be, could abrogate the Indian's right to bestow freedom on his slave.[127]

442

At this point a footnote intervenes:

> Contrast the Mississippi court which, after veering between neutrality and libertarianism until the late 1850s refused to recognize the claims of comity even to the extent of allowing a former Mississippi slave duly freed in Ohio to collect a bequest of money left by her former master in Mississippi. Judge William L. Harris insisted that . . . Ohio was denying comity in freeing blacks at all. He went on . . . "[should] Ohio, further afflicted with her peculiar philanthropy, . . . claim to confer citizenship on the chimpanzee . . . are we to be told that 'comity' will require . . . the States not thus demented, to . . . meet the necessities of the mongrel race thus attempted to be introduced into . . . this confederacy?" In fairness it should be noted that Judge Alex Handy, though also an ardent secessionist, delivered a passionate twenty-four page dissent, arguing that Harris was adopting "barbarian rules which prevailed in the dark ages."[128]

Finkelman, though frequently making much of *Mitchell v. Wells* from near the outset of *An Imperfect Union*,[129] does not mention Judge Handy's dissent until we get to page 293 and, while featuring the "secessionist impulse" in the opinion, nowhere mentions the "anti-barbarian objection." Finkelman's *Mitchell v. Wells* is rather like a mini-Southern mirror-image of a Lincoln-Douglas debate

---

125. The only Texas case cited in *An Imperfect Union*'s list of cases, *see* P. FINKELMAN, *supra* note 6, at 364, is Moore's Admr. v. Minerva, 17 Tex. 20 (1856). The list of cases indicates that the sole discussion of *Minerva* appears at page 189 n.17. Note 17 cites *Minerva* as authority for the proposition that "even in these liberal states the trend was moving away from decisions in favor of liberty." *Minerva* was hardly authority for that. *See* text accompanying note 130 *infra*.

126. 37 Miss. 235 (1859).

127. Nash, *Trial Rights of Blacks*, *supra* note 11, at 634-35 (footnote omitted).

128. *Id.* at 635 n.72 (quoting Mitchell v. Wells, 37 Miss. 235, 282 (1859)).

129. *See, e.g.*, P. FINKELMAN, *supra* note 6, at 5-6.

without a "mini-Douglas." To conclude with a final passage from my 1971 essay:

> In 1856 *Moore v. Minerva* brought up once again the issue of interstate comity, and . . . raised a further question: that of damages due to an allegedly freed slave for unlawful detention. . . . Mary Minerva's appeal sought both freedom for herself and her children and damages from the administrator of the master's will. In defense, the administrator argued that Minerva's right to freedom under a deed . . . in Ohio was forfeited by her illegal entry into Texas and that the laws of Alabama—where her master had . . . owned most of his property—barred freedom because he had died leaving large debts. . . . Declaring Minerva and her children free, Lipscomb argued that the claims of Ohio law were superior to those of Alabama and Texas. . . . Finally, in regard to damages, Virginia and Kentucky might . . . deny payment for illegal detention. . . . Lipscomb did not agree . . . .[130]

Texas, in other words, moves the totals of our pro-comity/anti-comity jurisdictions to one-to-two in the secession states and four-to-three in the slave states as a whole.

443

An examination of Tennessee's cases produces the same results — if anything even more clearly. Finkelman disposes of the Tennessee position in a footnote that is, frankly, off-the-wall. He says: "Especially see Virginia and Tennessee cases, which indicate that those states remained almost as consistent as Kentucky. . . . Yet, these moderate states showed some change away from comity. Tennessee's cases do not provide a large enough sample to draw any clear conclusions . . . ."[131]

Quite apart from the fact that the next-to-last sentence quoted seems to contradict its predecessor, the last sentence is simply untrue. The Tennessee Supreme Court's slavery docket was among the most substantial. Its holdings were surely the most consistently libertarian of any of the longer-settled secession states.[132] Nowhere in the annals of antebellum Tennessee Reports is there a denial of comity claimed on the basis of a reasonable Northern state holding.[133] Only Tennessee confronted all thirteen of the following issues, answering each in the "pro-liberty" affirmative. Thus Tennessee: (1) assured fair hearings of manumission claims;[134] (2) allowed damages for wrongful detention in slavery;[135] (3) restricted the presumption

---

130. Nash, *Trial Rights of Blacks, supra* note 11, at 635-36.

131. P. FINKELMAN, *supra* note 6, at 205 n.66.

132. *See* Nash, *Reason of Slavery, supra* note 11, at 123-84, 201 (summary table).

133. Or, for that matter, as far as I can recall, on the basis of an *unreasonable* Northern state comity-related holding.

134. *See, e.g.,* Sylvia v. Covey, 12 Tenn. (4 Yer.) 247 (1833) (removal of slaves from owner to prevent their sale prior to judicial hearing of their claim to freedom).

135. *See* Woodfolk v. Sweeper, 21 Tenn. (2 Hum.) 64 (1840); Matilda v. Crenshaw, 12

against freedom of dark skin color;[136] (4) relaxed the rules of evidence to permit hearsay testimony in a claim of freedom;[137] (5) presumed freedom when confronted with defective court records;[138] (6) ruled that slaves should be sent to freedom in a place where it was permitted even when the will seemed to condition the grant of freedom on its being exercised in a particular place;[139] (7) awarded liberty to the children of *statu liberi*;[140] (8) ruled in favor of freedom for slaves notwithstanding allegations of testator insanity;[141] (9) winked at "quasi-emancipations";[142] (10) permitted masters to restrict the force of anti-manumission statutes by taking slaves out of state to free them, then upholding the out-of-state bequest;[143] (11) permitted slaves to choose between freedom or slavery when the will gave them that choice;[144] (12) permitted manumission societies to receive bequests of slaves and take them to free states, territories, or countries;[145] and (13) observed comity in giving effect to other states' laws concerning freeing slaves and bequeathing property to blacks.[146]

444

There is no record on these issues that even begins to approach Tennessee's in scope, number, and consistency. One can get a rough

---

Tenn. (4 Yer.) 249 (1833) (permitting a second suit, after a successful first suit for freedom, to recover from the ex-master court costs and wages for the time of the first suit's pendency).

136. Vaughan v. Phebe, 7-8 Tenn. (Mart. & Yer.) 389, 400 (1827).

137. *See* Isaac v. Farnsworth, 40 Tenn. (3 Head.) 189, 191 (1859) (freeing a slave sold absolutely in a written conveyance by permitting introduction of oral evidence that the slave had had an oral understanding that he would be freed after eight years; "Perhaps in no case was the proof ever more irreconcilably conflicting. . . . [But] it is revolting to see to what an extent some men will go against the rights of the weak, in the eager pursuit of gain."); Miller v. Denman, 16 Tenn. (8 Yer.) 156, 158 (1835) (court statement that it had extended "the right to introduce hearsay evidence to the utmost limit and further than other courts of high authority have gone . . .").

138. *See* Elias v. Smith, 25 Tenn. (6 Hum.) 14 (1845).

139. *See* Lewis v. Daniel, 29 Tenn. (10 Hum.) 177 (1849).

140. *See* Harris v. Clarissa, 14 Tenn. (6 Yer.) 153 (1834). The court dismissed a contrary Kentucky holding with the words, "With the reasons for this decision we are not satisfied," 14 Tenn. (6 Yer.) at 163, and criticized the Virginia holding in Maria v. Surbaugh, 23 Va. (2 Rand.) 228 (1824), as "a most strict construction, not to say a strained one, in prejudice of human liberty . . . ." 14 Tenn. (6 Yer.) at 163. The *Harris* decision was reaffirmed unanimously (including the vote of Judge Nathan Green, who had dissented in *Harris*) in Hartsell v. George, 22 Tenn. (3 Hum.) 189 (1842).

141. *See* Gass' Heirs v. Gass' Executor, 22 Tenn. (3 Hum.) 207 (1842).

142. *See* Elias v. Smith, 25 Tenn. (6 Hum.) 14 (1845).

143. *See* Blackmore v. Negro Phill, 15 Tenn. (7 Yer.) 297, 307-09 (1835) (statement to the effect that emancipation in the North would be recognized as valid in Tennessee even if the master had intended to evade Tennessee laws restricting grants of freedom).

144. *See* Stephenson v. Harrison, 40 Tenn. (3 Head.) 500, 505 (1859) (also reaffirming that slaves had standing to sue in court and rejecting the contrary view of some then-recent Southern decisions with the words, "It would be entirely inconsistent with *our* liberal slave and emancipation Code, let *others* be as they may.") (emphasis added).

145. *See* Fisher's Negroes v. Dabbs, 14 Tenn. (6 Yer.) 78, 84-86 (1834).

146. *See* Blackmore v. Negro Phill, 15 Tenn. (7 Yer.) 297 (1835).

sense of the differences by comparing results in five jurisdictions on these thirteen issues. North Carolina's court (the runner-up) gave eight yeses, two noes, and did not hear three of these issues. South Carolina gave three clear yeses, did not hear three issues, and split among its judges and chancellors on the remaining seven. Virginia had three consistent yeses, one clear no, and split on the remaining nine issues. The Georgia court (the single Southern court whose jurisprudence closely resembles that of the *post-Mitchell* Mississippi court) delivered one yes and seven noes on the eight issues that it heard.[147]

For Finkelman to tell us that there is not enough Tennessee data to draw any clear conclusions is astonishing. For our purposes, at least two conclusions are quite clear. First, counting Tennessee, the box scores in favor of comity are now: within the secession states only, two-to-two; among all the slave jurisdictions, five-to-three. Second, had Finkelman chosen to "sample" Tennessee rather than Mississippi or Louisiana, his conclusions might have been quite different. With a better "spread," his extrapolations to the South as a whole might have been more accurate.

To continue, I would argue that neither Carolina judiciary had clearly swung over to "war-like anti-comity" by the time of the firing on Fort Sumter. That North Carolina did not is plain from any number of cases but especially from two in the 1850s. In December 1853, Judge Richmond Pearson upheld, in *Alvany v. Powell*,[148] a bequest of over $9000 to slaves freed and taken out of state by the master's executor. The circumstances are similar, though not identical, to those in *Mitchell v. Wells*.[149] But the judicial reactions are dissimilar in the extreme. Where Harris of Mississippi fulminated about chimpanzees and comity, Pearson of North Carolina stated that "the humanity of our laws strikes off his fetters at once, and says, go 'enjoy life, liberty and the pursuit of happiness.' "[150] Another case, *Redding v. Findley*,[151] decided at the late date of December 1858, expressly permitted slaves given a choice by their owner's will to choose between slavery and freedom, thus upholding the very sort of "choice in the will" provision that madly pro-slavery judges thundered should be voided for allowing an object to exercise free will.

445

---

147. *See* Nash, *Reason of Slavery, supra* note 11, at 201.
148. 54 N.C. (1 Jones Eq.) 39 (1853).
149. 37 Miss. 235 (1859).
150. 54 N.C. (1 Jones Eq.) at 43.
151. 57 N.C. (4 Jones Eq.) 210 (1858).

There is, in sum, no reason to consider North Carolina slavery jurisprudence less typical of the Southern legal movement relating to the comity issues than that of *either* (and fairly similar) Tennessee *or* (and quite different) that of Mississippi or Georgia. Thus, we score, so far: the seceding states alone, three-to-two for comity; the slave states, six-to-three for comity.

It is not practical at this juncture to explore the comity-related jurisprudence of the other six slave jurisdictions in quite the detail that we have so far. But it is not altogether necessary to our present purpose, in part because to resolve the point at issue we have only to "count" as far as is needed to determine whether a majority can be found "against comity," and in part because the evidence regarding some of the remaining six is so plain as to require little debate.

The latter is the case with respect to three jurisdictions — Georgia, Florida, and Arkansas. Georgia belongs on the anti-comity side of the ledger[152] — though admittedly the court majority was occasionally restrained by contrary precedent. The evidence from Florida is sparse because slavery litigation in that state was rare. However, what there is does not support Finkelman's thesis. In the only case directly raising a comity issue, *Sibley v. Maria*,[153] the Florida court in 1849 interpreted an 1820 South Carolina anti-manumission statute in a way that freed a South Carolina slave removed to Florida, notwithstanding the fact that eight years earlier the South Carolina legislature had rebuffed the South Carolina Court of Appeals for choosing that same interpretation. Indeed, as Sibley's counsel expressly noted before the Florida Court, the South Carolina Equity Court had in the intervening years altered its interpretation to follow that legislative judgment.[154] There was a second comity aspect to *Sibley v. Maria*. Since both interpretations agreed that manumission in South Carolina would have been illegal, in order to free Maria it was necessary to presume that she had been removed to Ohio (designated in the testator's alternate instruction) and that she had there posted the required $500 good behavior bond. Neither presumption was very likely to be accurate. Yet the court so presumed despite the absence of any Ohio record of manumission.[155] Consequently, I disagree with Finkelman and would score Florida pro-comity.

The same may be said for Arkansas. As I have argued else-

446

152. *See* Reid, *supra* note 11, at 578-81; Stephenson & Stephenson, *supra* note 11, at 602.
153. 2 Fla. 553 (1849). For a detailed discussion, see A. Nash, *supra* note 30, at 337-43.
154. 2 Fla. at 557.
155. 2 Fla. at 555-56.

where,[156] what evidence we have of the not-very-well-known judges of that state's antebellum appellate court goes generally and strongly to the view that its members, though themselves sympathetic to the peculiar institution and much aware of external pressures upon it, nonetheless strove for neutrality of judicial decision making. A statement of Judge Hubert Fairchild on the very eve of Civil War, in July 1860, well exemplifies this:[157]

> The question of freedom should be determined . . . solely upon its legal aspects, without partiality to an applicant for freedom, because he may be defenseless, and a member of an inferior race, and certainly without prejudice to his kind and color, and without regard to the sincere convictions that all candid, observing men must entertain, that a change from the condition of servitude and protection, to that of being free negroes, is injurious to the community, and more unfortunate to the emancipated negro than to anyone else.[158]

447

Though speaking with a forked racist tongue, Judge Fairchild in 1860 freed slaves slated to receive liberty, notwithstanding an 1859 Arkansas statute forbidding all post-mortem manumission. Georgia and Mississippi judges of the Lumpkin and Harris "anti-comity" sort surely would not have so held.

Our final count of the slave states we discussed is expressed in Table I:

TABLE I

For Comity	Against Comity
Seceding states	
Arkansas	Georgia
Florida	Louisiana
North Carolina	Mississippi (after 1859)
Tennessee	
Texas	
Other slave states	
Delaware	Missouri
Kentucky	
Maryland	

Comity was favored five-to-three among the seceding states alone, and eight-to-four among all the slaveholding jurisdictions. On *my* reading of the cases in the various jurisdictions that we have so far

---

156. *See* A. Nash, *supra* note 30, at 333-36.

157. Finkelman cites only one Arkansas case, Rheubottom v. Sadler, 19 Ark. 491 (1858), apparently as evidence of an anti-comity inclination. *See* P. FINKELMAN, *supra* note 6, at 190 n.18. The case does not bear out any such imputation.

158. Phebe v. Quillin, 21 Ark. 490, 500 (1860).

considered, *and* ignoring any doubting queries as to Finkelman's readings of his "own four States," *and* without giving the best "strong reading" of Virginia, South Carolina, and Alabama cases, then the notion that denial of comity was almost unanimous on the eve of the Civil War is plainly false whichever way one counts. Moreover, Finkelman's related generalization — that *most* Southern states began to reject comity-based claims of freedom — is false at least for slaveholding states as a whole. After all, as a majority of those states did not reject comity, "most" cannot be "against." And if anything is obvious at all, it is that the Southern states *did not* deny comity "almost in unison."

Thus, Finkelman's "strong reading" *is* a misreading. His "weaker reading" is also a misreading for the slaveholding states as a whole. To prove his point for the seceding states alone, he would have to demonstrate that the judicial behavior in the three states we have not looked at support his hypothesis. While I do not propose to conduct a jurisdiction-by-jurisdiction examination of the remaining states in order to show the impossibility of such a demonstration, I shall make two quick points going in that direction. First, an examination of the South Carolina Court of Appeals under the leadership of Judge John Belton O'Neall suggests that comity's foes in that state lost out at the highest judicial level.[159] Second, even Finkelman seems to think that an "anti-comity case" against the Virginia Court of Appeals is not very strong.[160]

These observations made, it is possible to show quite swiftly the problems with Professor Finkelman's other generalizations.

2. *Two Simplistic Generalizations*

Finkelman asserts that "fidelity to law — this impartiality of decision making — began to fade in the 1830s and disappeared throughout most of the South before 1860" and also that "fidelity to . . . slavery was more important than fidelity to abstract concepts of law."[161] There are two difficulties here.

First, assuming that "fidelity to law" and "impartiality of decision-making" are fungible and obvious entities, the evidence that either one or (fungibly) both disappeared throughout most of the South simply is not there — assuming also, of course, that here as elsewhere in *An Imperfect Union* Finkelman is talking about states'

---

159. *See* Nash, *Negro Rights, Unionism, and Greatness on the South Carolina Court of Appeals: The Extraordinary Chief Justice John Belton O'Neall*, 21 S.C. L. REV. 141, 175 (1969).

160. *See* P. FINKELMAN, *supra* note 6, at 189 n.17.

161. *Id.* at 182.

appellate courts and not about plantation (in)justice or lynch-mobs. The difficulty is similar to that which we have found in our enumeration of comity-related holdings. Professor Finkelman's generalizations about Southern appellate judiciaries have, exposed to mundane facts, a Cheshire cat aspect about them: they tend to disappear.

The second difficulty relates to the assumption just made *arguendo* — namely, that there is something clear and certain called "fidelity to law," that, moreover, can be measured against something else called "fidelity to slavery."

Two oversimplifications are intertwined here. The first lies in Finkelman's unstated major premise that by 1860 Southern appellate judges were, willy-nilly and by the force of greater historical events, placed in the awkward position of having to choose between "abstract concepts of law" and "slavery." Again, our examination so far suggests that for many Southern judges this was simply not so.

449

The second oversimplification is what Marxist historians might call a "bourgeois oversimplification." That is to say, there is a hidden identification of "law" with certain identifiable values that "reasonable men" would agree about. On this view of the matter, law that does not display these values in the "right" hierarchy is implicitly "not law." The latter half of the generalization, in other words, is arguably simplistic because of its legal ontology. It conflates "good law" and "true law" and sets up a polar opposite, also conflated, which is sometimes thought of just as "bad law" but which often is thought of as "un-law" or "not law." It is, if you will, a simplifying bourgeois variant of "natural lawism" that is bothersomely afoot.

The problem with another of Finkelman's generalizations can be put in a single sentence. It is not very helpful to assert that "slave state courts reflected the attitudes of the people they served"[162] without specifying further: (a) how they "reflected"; (b) whom they "served"; and (c) whether the "reflecting" was in some fashion unique to the slave South or whether such "reflecting" as occurred was merely an instance of a general American attitude.

3. *Muddy, Confused, or Otherwise Problematic Generalizations*

Finkelman generalizes that by the 1850s "most of the South had, to one degree or another, decided that interstate comity could not extend to cases involving slaves who claimed to be free."[163] This is

---

162. *Id.* at 234.
163. *Id.* at 189-90.

muddy. If "most of the South" means a majority of all adult Southerners, then there is no practical way of verifying the contention. If "most of the South" means "most Southern appellate court judges," then the statement is *either* false *or* meaninglessly true. It is false if "to one degree or another" means roughly to cover the span from "somewhat disinclined to extend comity" to "very disinclined to extend comity." It is meaninglessly true if "to one degree or another" includes roughly the range from "not so deciding" to "definitely deciding." That includes almost every viewpoint. The resulting "truth" is meaningless because the sentence's opposite — "most . . . had, to one degree or another, decided that interstate comity *could be* extended" — is equally true.

450   Two generalizations deserve treatment together because both aim at explaining the shift in Southern slavery jurisprudence that Finkelman (rightly or wrongly) perceives. The first of these asserts that although "it would be convenient . . . to argue" that the decline in Southern tendencies to grant comity was a "response to northern decisions denying comity to slaveowners in transit. . . . it is not at all clear that the change came about in this way."[164] The other generalization notes that Southern courts liberated slaves "who had spent time in the North well *before* northern courts freed slaves in transit" and then concludes that "[i]t surely would be absurd to argue that southern jurists reversed their own precedents because northern jurists had endorsed them."[165]

These sentences are both important and artless. They are important in two ways. First, they are part of a central passage in which Finkelman seeks to explain the course of Southern comity-related adjudications in a fashion that exculpates Northern courts from causing any Southern reversal, and that lays responsibility more generally on the changing climate of opinion North and South.

Second, the sentences are important because of what their very artlessness gives away. Their artlessness consists primarily in two parts. Part one lies in the tell-tale phrase, "it would be convenient." Convenient to what? It might be convenient because it would sustain, according to Finkelman, "some legal historians"[166] who have argued that Southern courts "ceased granting comity . . . in response to northern decisions denying comity to slaveowners in transit."[167] I suspect that, in fact, this would prove *in*convenient to

---

164. *Id*. at 182-83.

165. *Id*. (emphasis in original). For similar statements, see *id*. at 234-35.

166. Finkelman cites only one, Don Fehrenbacher. *See id*. at 183.

167. *Id*. at 183.

Finkelman just because it would be convenient for Fehrenbacher, whom Finkelman is seeking to discredit on the issue. And it would be convenient (read "*in*convenient to Finkelman") for the purpose of "exculpating" Southern judicial behavior. That it would be *in*convenient to Finkelman is strongly suggested by the wording of the other generalization's conclusion — which amounts to the second artlessness of the analysis.

A close look at what Finkelman says reveals that he does not say what I imagine most readers would, after a quick reading, tell you he had said. How so? The second generalization contains two sentences that, on hurried inspection, appear to be four-square both with each other and with the notion that the decline in Southern grants of comity was a "response to northern decisions denying comity to slaveowners in transit." Quickly read, the second generalization appears to tell us: (1) that Southern courts freed slaves on the basis of certain conditions or events obtaining in the North before Northern courts did the same sort of thing; (2) that it would be silly to think that Southern courts got annoyed because Northern courts started to follow Southern precedents; and (3) that therefore, the Southern reaction must have originated in some other reason — a reason not traceable to Northern judicial behavior.

But Finkelman doesn't really establish this at all. Of course it is true that it would be absurd to argue that "Southern jurists reversed their own precedents because northern jurists had endorsed them." But *in fact*, Southern jurists never did what too quick a reading of Finkelman's generalizations would suggest they did — free slaves whose masters had "transitted" them across the North.

The vagueness of the phrase "freed slaves who had spent time," is critical to the consequent misreading. All that earlier Southern courts actually did in this connection was to free in some instances *either* slaves who had worked for a considerable period of time with their masters' permission in free states *or* slaves who had been brought into Northern states for periods exceeding some statutory period not perceived by Southern courts as intolerably short. In addition, these courts sometimes permitted Southern masters to evade the restrictive terms of Southern anti-manumission laws by taking favored slaves to the North, there executing manumissions in accordance with Northern law, and then returning south.

But these Southern courts had *never* freed slaves from the grasp of masters in transit through free territories. Of course, it *would* be absurd to suppose that Southern courts reacted adversely to the Northern courts that followed Southern precedents. But that was

451

not at all what Northern courts of the later antebellum era began to do.

Finkelman's generalizations on this matter reveal a crucial flaw in his mode of analysis. He fails to work out what is needed for a satisfactory analysis of the problem of comity and antebellum slavery: a "neutral model" of what comity might be said to require, under what circumstances, and under what readings of "comity."

The consequences of this analytic flaw are several. One is that it makes possible uncritical assertions such as the last of the two generalizations over which we have just paused. It also facilitates Finkelman's assertion that the late antebellum years witnessed a trend "away from decisions in favor of liberty."[168] That is true but rather indefinite. A third unfortunate consequence is the aid lent Finkelman's attempt to specify further trends away from comity by stating that the dissenting judges of *Mitchell v. Wells*[169] and of *Lemmon v. People*[170] "sensed, but could not admit . . . that the legal systems of the North and South could no longer coexist. . . . Within the realm of state action *Lemmon* represented the final development in the law of freedom, while *Mitchell* symbolized the ultimate logic of the law of bondage."[171]

Part of this generalization is mere assertion. Finkelman offers no convincing evidence that *none* of the judges in the two cases were able to admit that the legal systems of the North and South could not coexist. Indeed, Harris of Mississippi seemed boldly to assert the point. One other part of this generalization is also, as yet, mere assertion. Finkelman declares that *Lemmon* is a "final development" and that *Mitchell* "symbolized the ultimate logic of the law of bondage." Perhaps. Perhaps not. The way that Finkelman states the contention prevents the reader from determining whether it is intended as an empirical generalization as to where the laws of the two sections were going, or whether it is intended as some kind of deductive assertion about the necessary evolution of nineteenth century American law.

As we have seen, such an empirical generalization lacks adequate supporting evidence. Such a deductive assertion is not susceptible to testing within Finkelman's explicit framework, in part because of his failure to specify a clear model of what a neutral comity would have looked like. It is also so in part because the relations among law-

452

---

168. *Id.* at 189 (footnote omitted).
169. 37 Miss. 235 (1859).
170. 20 N.Y. 562 (1860).
171. P. FINKELMAN, *supra* note 6, at 310.

made-by-judges, law-made-by-legislators, climates of opinion, and the underlying forces of economy, society, and polity remain ill-worked out in *An Imperfect Union*.

Finkelman's work does not contain, in other words, an adequate key to some of its mystifying and important assertions. For that reason, it is now appropriate to consider Mark Tushnet's approach to radical interpretation of American law. Whatever its other virtues and vices, it *does* proceed from an explicit (Marxist) set of assumptions about the relations of law, individual, and economy.

II. The Possibility of a "Non-Reductionist" Marxist General Theory of American Law

A. *Non-Marxist Criticisms of Tushnet on the Law of Slavery*   453

Mark Tushnet's much-critiqued *The American Law of Slavery, 1810-1860* has baffled in whole or in part a fair number of lawyers and legal historians. Only two of the four main causes of this bafflement have been much pointed out. One is that his writing is less clear than it might be. The other is that he proceeds in an ahistorical fashion — both "externally" and "internally." By "externally" I mean, pursuant to the usual jargon of legal history,[172] that he does not relate the legal history with which he is grappling to the society, polity, and economy "external to" the law. Thus, for example, Wiecek asks:

> What then accounts for the relative "liberalism" . . . of the early Mississippi Court . . . and the harsh posture of the later Mississippi court . . . ? If Tushnet had explored outside the case reports, he would have discovered that the minds of white southerners were traumatized by a series of incidents . . . that led them universally to repudiate it [relative "liberalism"] with a . . . garrison mentality that, as one of its necessary consequences, suppressed the humanity of the slaves.[173]

Wiecek then lists a set of well-known events beginning with the 1819-1820 congressional debates surrounding Missouri's admission to statehood and ending with Nat Turner's Virginia rebellion in 1831. He continues: "Judicial attitudes changed promptly and reflexively. . . . I . . . suggest that . . . obvious events outside the legal arena more readily explain southern judicial behavior."[174] Putting aside the problematic historical question whether and how

---

172. *See* Gordon, *Introduction: J. Willard Hurst and the Common Law Tradition in American Legal Historiography*, 10 Law & Socy. Rev. 9 (1975).

173. Wiecek, *supra* note 11, at 281.

174. *Id.* at 282.

directly judicial attitudes in fact "promptly changed,"[175] we can at least see the main criticism directed against the writing of legal history: the contention that a better (read "simpler") explanation can be found in the law's "external" reflexive response to the larger political world.

By "internally" I mean, again pursuant to legal-historical jargon, the criticism that Tushnet does not get the order of events straight within the law — within its relevant cases and statutes, or between and among its cases and statutes. Thus, Finkelman observes that "Tushnet . . . has little regard for chronology . . . . For example, in a 'largely chronological' discussion of Georgia manumission cases, Tushnet discusses, in the following order, cases from 1858, 1860, 1857, 1858, and 1860."[176] He also commits, according to Finkelman, a spatial error related to this temporal heresy. Tushnet makes "no distinctions between the upper South and the lower South. He writes about 'the slave states' or 'the South' as if all fifteen states were part of a jurisdictional monolith. He quotes from three or more state courts without ever mentioning that his materials come from different jurisdictions."[177]   Perhaps worse, from Finkelman's viewpoint, Tushnet plays fast and loose with the "internal" data when it comes to explaining slavery law's development: "He seriously misstates the facts in State v. Jarrott (p. 112), and alters them in his discussion of State v. Tackett (p. 100)."[178]

The third of four sources of bafflement is itself composed of two factors. One factor is, seemingly, unease that Marxists are around in the late twentieth century United States, not, as at mid-century, restricting themselves to stealing A-bomb secrets and attacking the X in Xmas, but actually now (re)writing (sacred) American history. The other is an American reflex-assumption that Marxist historiography will necessarily be intellectually simplistic in its accounting of the relationships between economic infra-structure and the super-structure of "the law." After all, and especially in America, "no one is ever neutral about Marx."[179] That, however, does not mean that everyone is knowledgeable about Old Karl. Even those of us who, educated to think of *Das Kapital* as belonging to an "outside the first

454

---

175. The balance of the historiography on the subject suggests that the change was both slower than "prompt" and more complicated than merely "reflexive."

176. Finkelman, *supra* note 11, at 359.

177. *Id.*

178. *Id.* Finkelman does not, however, specify how the facts are altered.

179. E. KURZWEIL, THE AGE OF STRUCTURALISM: LEVY-STRAUSS TO FOUCAULT 53 (1980).

amendment" category of unprotected quasi-obscene literary essays, consider ourselves unlikely to be subverted, may be mistaken in how we approach Marxist legal analysis.

To say that is to indicate the fourth, and perhaps the most important, source of bafflement that some may experience when reading Tushnet on the law of American slavery. It comes from not realizing that *The American Law of Slavery* is as much connected to Tushnet's intellectual explorations in twentieth century American constitutional law as it is to the debate over nineteenth century slavery law. To understand Tushnet on slavery, one must understand Tushnet's work as a whole, those "innumerable" articles which Milner S. Ball has characterized as "the fallout of a Mt. St. Helen's eruption of scholarship."[180] That is so in part because of the clues these works provide as to the main features of Tushnet's Marxist intellectual topography and in turn as to why Tushnet may make slip-ups that from his own angle seem relatively unimportant whereas to a non-Marxist they seem devastating.[181]

455

But there is a more important reason for looking at Tushnet-on-slavery in light of Tushnet-on-the-American-Constitution-today. Tushnet is, among the current generation of American law scholars, the only individual who has essayed sustained, serious endeavors both in legal history and in constitutional law while being reasonably *au courant* in a third approach to the law — political science's judicial-process-and-behavior approach. In addition, Tushnet says he is a Marxist. Is there a potentially important moral for the study

---

180. Ball, *Don't Die Don Quixote: A Response and Alternative to Tushnet, Bobbitt, and the Revised Texas Version of Constitutional Law*, 59 TEX. L. REV. 787, 793 n.42 (1981).

181. *See* Watson, *Slave Law: History and Ideology* (Book Review), 91 YALE L.J. 1034 (1982). Briefly, Watson makes the following points about four of Tushnet's chief "case-studies":

(a) that Tushnet's argument about the omission of a tort rationale from the leading antebellum Southern "fellow servant rule" case, Ponton v. Wilmington & Weldon R.R., 51 N.C. 246, 6 Jones 245 (1858), is not convincing. Watson, *supra*, at 1038;

(b) that Tushnet errs in arguing that rules of liability adopted in a particular Georgia case, Gorman v. Campbell, 14 Ga. 137 (1853), could only have been justified by claims of humanity (rather than, as Watson argues, on grounds of appropriate rules of contract). Watson, *supra*, at 1040–42;

(c) that Tushnet misreads Thomas Ruffin's opinion in the much-debated North Carolina case, State v. Mann, 13 N.C. 229, 2 Dev. 263 (1829). Watson, *supra*, at 1042–44; and

(d) that Tushnet's explanation for the fourth case in question, Jourdan v. Patton, 5 Mart. 615 (La. 1818) also is erroneous:

[T]his is nonsense on various levels. First, Tushnet has no right, without evidence or argument, to posit the theory on which the trial court based liability. In fact, Tushnet in this case is demonstrably wrong — the rule was simply taken from Spanish and French law, which in turn had taken it from Roman law.

Watson, *supra*, at 1045. In all, for Watson, "Tushnet's Marxist analysis reveals itself as fundamentally sterile." *Id.* at 1044. "Tushnet's failure in his analysis of the cases . . . should mean that the book will convince only those predisposed to believe the theory." *Id.* at 1047.

of American law in general at a time of crisis in the American polity? This part lays the ground for examining this question by considering other non-Marxist reactions to Tushnet's writing on constitutional issues and linking them with more general reactions to radical interpretations in legal history and political science. It then further develops the basis for inquiry by exploring Tushnet's broader, if shifting, program for a Marxist analysis of American Law.

B. *Non-Marxist Criticism of Tushnet on "Liberal" Constitutional Interpretation, or: Coming At Constitutional Debating Issues From the Extra-Paradigmatic North*

456

Writing three years ago in this *Review*, Tushnet (easily the most prolific of younger constitutional law scholars) expressed the wish that his critique of Professor Laurence Tribe (easily the most cited of almost-as-young constitutional law scholars) be taken, not as coming from a particular point on the conventional left-right political spectrum, but rather from some unrelated direction, "say, the north."[182] To a certain extent, Professor Tushnet got his wish. Judge Richard A. Posner took Tushnet's critique to be coming from off-the-street and aiming several inches below the belt. Indeed, then-Professor Posner thought Tushnet's imputation of Tribe's motives in writing *American Constitutional Law*[183] illustrative of a broader problem in recent legal scholarship coming from the "Critical Legal Studies" movement.[184] Said Posner in a recent Yale Law School Symposium on the state of legal education and scholarship:

Some Marxists play by different rules from those of the other norma-

---

182. Tushnet, *Dia-Tribe*, 78 MICH. L. REV. 694, 694 (1980) (reviewing L. TRIBE, AMERICAN CONSTITUTIONAL LAW (1978)).

183. L. TRIBE, AMERICAN CONSTITUTIONAL LAW (1978). Presumably, it was Tushnet's concluding paragraphs that most distressed Judge Posner:

I hope that what has gone before raises a serious puzzle: how could so morally obtuse a work be taken so seriously? The answer can be found in Professor Tribe's ambition, which, like that of constitutional scholars generally, lies outside the world of scholarship and in the world of contemporary public affairs. Not that there is anything intrinsically wrong with ambition. . . . Most of us have imagined ourselves as Justices of the Supreme Court, and Professor Tribe . . . would surely be a better Justice than many.

The question, though, is to what activities the rewards of ambition accrue. In . . . public affairs, they accrue not necessarily to intellectual substance. One who addresses the real questions of justice is by that fact alone disqualified . . . . I take some pleasure, not however unmixed with regret, in noting that the Framers would have understood the phenomenon that Professor Tribe's work represents: they called it corruption.

Tushnet, *supra* note 182, at 710 (footnote omitted).

184. For a recent discussion of the "Conference on Critical Legal Studies," which "attempts to bring together scholars involved in radical legal studies and includes such notables as Duncan Kennedy, Morton Horwitz, Karl Klare, Mark Tushnet, and Roberto Unger," see Note, *'Round and 'Round the Bramble Bush: From Legal Realism to Critical Legal Scholarship*, 95 HARV. L. REV. 1669, 1669 n.3 (1982); *see also* Unger, *The Critical Legal Studies Movement*, 96 HARV. L. REV. 563 (1983).

tive scholars, and rather ugly ones. I am thinking, for example, of Tushnet's recent unpardonable personal abuse of Laurence Tribe. The Marxist scholars question the objectivity and integrity of the non-Marxists, whom they accuse of prostituting their intellectual abilities to personal or class interests. By this reasoning, the Marxists' motives should be equally suspect. Their emphasis on scholars' motives is, however, a distraction. Scholarship should be evaluated on its merits; it should not be disparaged by reference to the presumed motives of its practitioners.[185]

Posner's reaction may not be exactly what Tushnet hoped for. The Siberian North was probably not the direction Tushnet intended to come from — although it is conceivable that he sought to exacerbate the internal contradictions of capitalist legal scholarship by raising its blood-pressure. Given my own diffidence about readily getting inside other people's minds, I cannot say. Yet two observations do seem fairly inferrable. The lesser is that Tushnet should deem discretion the better part of valor and stay out of Judge Posner's jurisdiction lest some of Tushnet's goods and baggage be seized and transferred to other persons valuing them more highly.[186]

457

The more important, and more serious, observation is that Posner's reaction itself exemplifies a recurrent problem in American legal scholarship, indeed in American intellectual life generally. The problem is the difficulty that Marxists face in getting themselves taken seriously, or even read accurately. In the instant case, Posner seems to skip over both the substance of Tushnet's argument and the qualifying sentence preceding Tushnet's comments about Tribe's motivations. Although Tushnet's argument can be questioned, it is nonetheless seriously intended and novel. It is grounded in the general contention that *American Constitutional Law*, like much else in contemporary constitutional scholarship, mistakes at its base the "central issue in political philosophy today."[187]

Specifically, Tushnet contends that *American Constitutional Law*, having mistaken the central issue, (mis)organizes itself around four

---

185. Posner, *The Present Situation in Legal Scholarship*, 90 YALE L.J. 1113, 1127 (1981) (footnote omitted).

186. See the discussion of the forcible taking from Derek of a book he values at $2 and the giving of it to Amartya, who values it at $3, so as to increase the total societal wealth, in Dworkin, *Is Wealth a Value?*, 9 J. LEGAL STUD. 191, 197-99 (1980), and Posner's reply in Posner, *The Value of Wealth: A Comment on Dworkin and Kronman*, 9 J. LEGAL STUD. 243, 244-50 (1980).

187. Tushnet, *supra* note 182, at 696. The central issue is, according to Tushnet, not what one would think "from reading law reviews, . . . whether abortion is morally permissible, . . . [or] whether remedial action that takes race explicitly into account is justified." *Id.* Rather, "the real one that has animated philosophical discussion . . . is which social-economic system, capitalism or socialism, justice demands. That is what John Rawls and Robert Nozick are concerned with . . . ." *Id.*

premises: (1) that the Constitution aims at securing justice; (2) that the Constitution "can fairly be interpreted to . . . approximate the accomplishment of justice";[188] (3) that the Supreme Court should engage in constitutional interpretation that promotes justice, the "premise . . . around which the standard controversies in constitutional theory rage";[189] and (4) (whence "the fundamental contradictions withiñ the treatise emanate"[190]) that the Supreme Court's recent decisions, be they those of the late Warren Court or of the Burger Court, "are reasonable approximations of justice."[191] I do not agree with much of this.[192] Nonetheless, the driving moral intent behind Tushnet's critique seems clear.

Tushnet's criticism proceeds, after all, regardless of its merits or lack thereof, from the moral judgment that there is something deeply wrong both with what gets onto the agenda of public law discussion and what is left off. His concern addresses what professors of law, that part of the nation's intellectual elite most influential in determining the perception of the law's role in shaping public needs, do and don't do. The mode of conducting the debates, the determination of what the "de rigeur" debate topics are (for example, whether "interpretivism" is, or is not, an intellectually viable approach to the constitutionality of statutes,[193] and whether a particular notorious

458

---

188. *Id*. at 694.

189. *Id*.

190. *Id*. at 695.

191. *Id*.

192. Let me just note here two points of divergence — at the risk of being taken as an immoderate "originalist" and hence a constitutional fundamentalist of either the Protestant or Catholic legal persuasion. For discussions of "originalism" and "the civil religion of the constitution," see Brest, *The Misconceived Quest for the Original Understanding*, 60 B.U. L. REV. 204 (1980); Levinson, *"The Constitution" in American Civil Religion*, 1979 SUP. CT. REV. 123. I find it problematic that Tushnet's description of Tribe's first premise does not separate out two of its possible meanings. One is whether *the single* (or even *the main*) aim of the Framers was "to secure justice" — which seems to me doubtful — or whether it was more centrally to improve the ex-Colonies' commercial conditions and capacity for external defense. The other matter of meaning is whether now, after nearly two centuries of amendment and interpretation, it is better to speak of a "glossed Constitution" as itself "aiming at justice" or whether it is more helpful to think in a less reifying fashion *either* of it as containing specific propositions that so "aim" *or* of it or its particular propositions as something(s) that individuals (or groups, or classes) "aim" at justice in particular (sets of) circumstances.

Putting aside the question of whether these four premises all in fact best describe the underpinnings of Professor Tribe's organizational modes and analytic objectives, I should have thought that more of the current "standard controversies in constitutional theory rage," if they rage at all, around the content of the fourth premise (whether recent Supreme Court decisions approximate justice), than around the content of the third (whether the Court should aim at accomplishing justice). Even Justice Rehnquist rarely argues for a contrary aim.

193. *See* C. BLACK, STRUCTURE AND RELATIONSHIP IN CONSTITUTIONAL LAW (1969); J. ELY, DEMOCRACY AND DISTRUST (1980); Brest, *supra* note 192; Fiss, *Objectivity and Interpretation*, 34 STAN. L. REV. 739 (1982); Grey, *Origins of the Unwritten Constitution: Fundamental Law in American Revolutionary Thought*, 30 STAN. L. REV. 843 (1978); Grey, *Do We Have an*

case — be it *Kras*,[194] *Bellotti*,[195] *National League of Cities*,[196] or *Roe v. Wade*[197] — can be squared with justice), and, ultimately, how much justice and how much injustice will be done are all to an important extent prima facie "responsibilities" of that elite. If one starts from that position, as does Tushnet, it is much less gratuitously insulting than ethically and analytically necessary to ask why a scholar building so enormous an intellectual edifice as Tribe's treatise (mis)constructs it as he does. In turn, an inquiry into motivations and, if the inquiry calls for it, an adverse judgment concerning those motivations flow quite naturally from Tushnet's normative starting point. He is simply instancing a particular "trahison des clercs"[198] — in this case the "treason" of a once-clerk and, Tushnet

---

Unwritten Constitution?, 27 STAN. L. REV. 703 (1975); Kurland, *Curia Regis, Some Comments on the Divine Right of Kings and Courts "To Say What the Law Is"*, 23 ARIZ. L. REV. 581 (1981); Linde, *Judges, Critics, and the Realist Tradition*, 82 YALE L.J. 227 (1972); Monaghan, *Taking Supreme Court Opinions Seriously*, 39 MD. L. REV. 1 (1979); Parker, *The Past of Constitutional Theory — and its Future*, 42 OHIO ST. L.J. 223 (1981); Perry, *Interpretivism, Freedom of Expression, and Equal Protection*, 42 OHIO ST. L.J. 261 (1981); Laycock, *Taking Constitutions Seriously: A Theory of Judicial Review* (Book Review), 59 TEX. L. REV. 343 (1981); Levinson, *Judicial Review and the Problem of the Comprehensible Constitution* (Book Review), 59 TEX. L. REV. 395 (1981).

194. United States v. Kras, 409 U.S. 434 (1973) (sustaining the constitutionality of a law requiring payment of a $50 filing fee, spreadable over a maximum of nine months, as a condition precedent to obtaining bankruptcy discharge). This case is notorious as far as Tushnet and the four dissenters, Douglas, Brennan, Stewart, and Marshall, are concerned. *See* Tushnet, *". . . And Only Wealth Will Buy You Justice" — Some Notes on the Supreme Court, 1972 Term*, 1974 WIS. L. REV. 177, 184-85 (discussing the Term during which Tushnet was one of Justice Marshall's clerks and *Kras* was handed down). For other critical commentary on *Kras*, see L. TRIBE, *supra* note 183, at 1009, 1120-22; Binion, *The Disadvantaged Before the Burger Court: The Newest Unequal Protection*, 4 LAW & POL. Q. 37, 44-47 (1982); Clune, *The Supreme Court's Treatment of Wealth Discriminations Under the Fourteenth Amendment*, 1975 SUP. CT. REV. 289, 314-15.

195. First Natl. Bank v. Bellotti, 435 U.S. 765 (1978) (striking down, as violative of first and fourteenth amendment free speech rights, a Massachusetts statute limiting corporations' expenditures for expressing company views concerning upcoming referenda proposals that did not materially affect its business interests).

196. National League of Cities v. Usery, 426 U.S. 833 (1976) (invalidating the 1974 amendments to the Fair Labor Standards Act extending maximum hours and minimum wage provisions to state, county, and municipal employees). Tushnet characterizes Tribe's sympathetic treatment of the majority position, *see* L. TRIBE, *supra* note 183, at 308-18, as "tendentious," and the majority position itself as one "that reeks of the American Enterprise Institute." Tushnet, *supra* note 182, at 698.

197. 410 U.S. 113 (1973). Tushnet, at least as to outcome, would not consider that case "notorious." *But see* Ely, *The Wages of Crying Wolf: A Comment on Roe v. Wade*, 82 YALE L.J. 920 (1973); J. ELY, *supra* note 193, at 248 n.52 (updating of Ely's view on the issue); *see also* Epstein, *Substantive Due Process By Any Other Name: The Abortion Cases*, 1973 SUP. CT. REV. 159.

198. *See* J. BENDA, LA TRAHISON DES CLERCS (1927). Benda's objection to many intellectuals of his generation was to be sure a bit different as to what they betrayed:

> About 1890, the men of letters, especially in France and Italy, realized with astonishing astuteness that the doctrines of arbitrary authority . . . contempt for the spirit of liberty, assertion of the morality of war . . . were . . . poses infinitely more likely to strike the imagination of simple souls than . . . Liberalism and Humanitarianism.

thinks, would-be future king (or at least judicial employer) of clerks.

On this view of the matter, Posner's reprimand for "un-bour-geois" intellectual manners misses the point. There are two points really. One is that it does not accomplish much for us bourgeois, who are thereby made uncomfortable, simply to enjoin those who are deliberately rejecting "bourgeois niceties." The other is that we may be better off being less dismissive and more enquiring into the sources of the objectionable behavior. We might learn something unpleasant but useful.

Before leaving Posner's reprimand, we need to note two further costs of such a peremptory dismissal. First, note how casually it leaps from ruling beyond the pale *"some* Marxists" who play by ugly rules (and note how "some" at first equals one, Tushnet) to all Marx-ists: *"The* Marxist scholars question the objectivity and integrity of the non-Marxists . . . . By this reasoning, *the* Marxists' motives should be equally suspect."[199] This *non sequitur* is as sloppy as any-thing I have seen Tushnet pen in a rush.

Second, but more important, the phrase "by this reasoning" mis-understands the Marxist position on three counts. One, it is no sur-prise that Marxist scholars question (whether politely or rudely) the objectivity of non-Marxist scholars. Marxism "expects" non-Marxist scholars to wear ideological blinders, and in this case they are argua-bly right. But, two, it does not follow from "this reasoning" that the Marxists' motives should be equally suspect because, of course (and this is the very devil of it from our non-Marxist viewpoint), Marxism argues that "its" scholars transcend ideologically induced mispercep-tion and achieve objectivity. Three, in arguing that "emphasis on scholars' motives is a distraction" and that scholarship should "not be disparaged by reference to . . . presumed motives" but rather "evaluated on its merits,"[200] Posner adopts by fiat precisely the bourgeois interpretive canons that Marxist analysis rejects. Interest-ingly, given recent articles in law reviews and political science jour-nals urging the applicability to constitutional interpretation of hermeneutics and post-structuralist methods of literary interpreta-tion,[201] these canons have lately been much questioned in ancillary

J. Benda, Betrayal of the Intellectuals 135 (R. Aldington trans. 1955).

199. Posner, *supra* note 185, at 1127 (emphasis added).

200. Posner's position respecting legal scholarship curiously approximates that of the New Critical School of the 1940s in American literary criticism.

201. *See* Abraham, *Statutory Interpretation and Literary Theory*, 32 Rutgers L. Rev. 676 (1979) (discussing statutory interpretation, but also applicable to constitutional interpretation); Brest, *Interpretation and Interest*, 34 Stan. L. Rev. 765 (1982); Deutsch, *Law As Metaphor: A Structural Analysis of the Legal Process*, 66 Geo. L.J. 1339 (1978); Harris, *Bonding Word and*

interpretive disciplines by non-Marxists.[202] Posner's fiat, in short, makes us — if we accept it — adopt blinders that prevent us from learning much beyond good etiquette. They exemplify a cross-epistemological and cross-ontological problem of divergent analytic approaches more than they solve it.

I have belabored Posner's comments a bit both because I think they may resemble the reactions of many constitutional scholars when confronted with Marxist legal analysis and because they have symptomatic counterparts in reactions to "radical analysis" arising in two domains of inquiry relatively proximate to constitutional scholarship — legal history and political science. I shall give just one example pertaining to each.

The first comes from American legal history. I have in mind *Boundaries of Realism*,[203] Professor Peter Teachout's lengthy review of G. Edward White's *Tort Law in America*.[204] *Boundaries* is almost as much an attack upon what he calls " 'the new orthodoxy' in American legal historical thought"[205] as it is a panegyric on White's book. Interesting as much of *Boundaries*' analysis is, it displays a strong reactive pattern. Thus:

461

In recent years, the world of American legal historiography has be-

---

Polity: The Logic of American Constitutionalism, 76 AM. POL. SCI. REV. 34 (1982). For criticisms of this attempt to apply "deconstruction," see Kurland, *supra* note 193; Fiss, *supra* note 193.

202. Useful discussions of the structuralist and post-structuralist trends in literary interpretation and related interpretation in the humanities and anthropology include: T. HAWKES, STRUCTURALISM AND SEMIOTICS (1977); F. JAMESON, THE PRISON-HOUSE OF LANGUAGE: A CRITICAL ACCOUNT OF STRUCTURALISM AND RUSSIAN FORMALISM (1972); E. KURZWEIL, THE AGE OF STRUCTURALISM: LEVI-STRAUSS TO FOUCAULT (1980) (especially the essays therein entitled *Hermeneutics and Structuralism* and *Literary Structuralism and Erotics*); P. PETTIT, THE CONCEPT OF STRUCTURALISM: A CRITICAL ANALYSIS (1975); *see also* H. GADAMER, PHILOSOPHICAL HERMENEUTICS (D. Linge ed. 1976).

I find it hard to resist concluding that most of the legal scholars' and political scientists' "importing" of structuralist, post-structuralist, and particularly deconstructionist analytic modes into constitutional interpretation look more like capitalizations on those imports' capacity to bedazzle in aid of constitutional noninterpretivism than like genuine analytic advances. Conspicuously absent so far is any serious reckoning with discussions of the shortcomings of such analytic modes in the disciplines where they originated. Among the critiques of deconstruction in literary analysis, see DONAGHUE, *Deconstructing Deconstruction: Review of Harold Bloom, Paul de Man, Jacques Derrida, and J. Hillis Miller*, Deconstruction and Criticism, N.Y. REV. BOOKS, June 12, 1980, at 37 (de Man comes in for particularly strong criticism); Graff, *Fear and Trembling at Yale*, 46 AM. SCHOLAR 467 (1977) (attacking Yale English faculty, leaders of American post-structuralist movement, for advancing a "no-fault" theory of interpretation); Kenner, *Decoding Roland Barthes*, 261 HARPER'S 68 (Aug., 1980). The reader who shares the concern of Fiss, *see* Fiss, *supra* note 193, with where deconstruction might lead in constitutional interpretation might profitably examine H. BLOOM, THE BREAKING OF THE VESSELS (1982).

203. Teachout, *Boundaries of Realism*, 67 VA. L. REV. 815 (1981).

204. G. WHITE, TORT LAW IN AMERICA: AN INTELLECTUAL HISTORY (1980).

205. Teachout, *supra* note 203, at 819.

come deeply divided over the question of how the basic patterns of American legal historical experience ought to be viewed. During the seventies there emerged a "new school" of American legal historians who reject what they call "the conservative tradition" in American legal historiography and advance in its place an alternative historiography centered in and structured by ideological theory. Because of its doctrinaire character, this new historiography has come to be regarded as "the new orthodoxy" in American legal historical thought.

The central thrust of the new historiography is its attack upon . . . classic liberalism. According to the new orthodoxy, a culture based on liberal premises is destructively competitive, individualistic, and legalistic. The primary task of the new historian, accordingly, is to write revisionist history that "demonstrates" the corrupting and disintegrating tendencies of liberalism. Professor Horwitz's recent *Transformation of American Law*, for example, can be read as an attempt to demonstrate how . . . a world of simple communal justice was transformed into one dominated by legalism, manipulation, and greed. Against this unhappy picture of liberalism and its consequences, the new orthodoxy holds out an alternative vision of society based on "communitarian" principles.[206]

462

In my judgment, this description of the state of affairs in current American legal history contains three major flaws.

First, unless I utterly misapprehend the distribution of political philosophy and analytic proclivity among the more research-active members of that learned field (going, for example, by the tenor of papers, commentaries, and questions at the annual meetings of the American Society for Legal History), at most a tiny minority of those members write or speak as though they think their central objective is attacking classical liberalism *or* demonstrating its corrupting and disintegrating tendencies. Nor do many appear to me to be ideologues believing in a bygone world of simple communal justice or even thinking about alternative visions of future society based on "communitarian" principles. Far more than being deeply "anti-law," a charge Teachout elsewhere amplifies,[207] the great majority of

---

206. *Id.* at 819-20 (footnotes omitted).

207. *See* Teachout, *Light in Ashes: The Problem of "Respect for the Rule of Law" in American Legal History,* 53 N.Y.U. L. REV. 241, 244-47, 272-78 (1978). Presser, *Legal History or History of the Law,* 35 VAND. L. REV. 849, 857-68 (1982), offers another way of dividing up recent American legal historical scholarship, into four discernible schools: (1) conservative, adopting "the notion that law has followed an orderly evolution according to fixed intellectual principles," *id.* at 857; (2) "the Wisconsin School," viewing "economic needs as the primary determinants of law," *id.* at 858; (3) the "radical transformation school," also economically focused but "reject[ing] some of the relatively benign implications of the Wisconsin school's historiography," *id.* at 859; and (4) a "heroic school" which "can be likened to Elizabethan tragedy or Greek mythology because it focuses on great men of the law," *id.* at 863. Presser's divisions have the advantage of being less "alarmist" than Teachout's perceptions. But I think they are too simple, leaving out a considerable amount of legal historical scholarship that doesn't pigeonhole so readily, finding substantial schools where at most there may be enough scholars to form a transitory one-room schoolhouse, and putting certain scholars where they

legal historians strikes me as eminently enamored of law — especially its most antiquarian obscurities. Indeed, Professor Teachout's list of radicals is barely enough for a "teach-in": "The leading representative of the new school is Professor Morton Horwitz of Harvard Law School."[208] Teachout finds that Horwitz's themes are also expressed by Nelson, Unger, Levinson, and Tushnet.[209] That's five. Given my lack of conviction that Sanford Levinson and Roberto Mangabeira Unger are primarily legal historians, I am constrained to think that the "new orthodoxy" has come to be regarded as such mainly in Professor Teachout's head. I suspect that the Church of England has at least as good a chance of being reestablished in Virginia as Teachout's neo-orthodoxy has of coming to be so regarded generally among American legal historians.

A second major defect in Teachout's description of the state of affairs in American legal history is that the members of this none-too-numerous band of "neo's" disagree among themselves. The third and most important defect in Teachout's position is that it reaches, albeit via a different route, an intellectual station-stop uncomfortably like that of Judge Posner. It wants to get those "coming from the North" off the train in one lumpy group, and to send the "neo-orthodox" packing back up North. Quite apart from the circumstance that so doing reminds me uncomfortably of the antebellum Southern solution for dealing with visiting abolitionist dignitaries, I would like to hear more precisely what each of these "neo-orthodox" scholars has to say, and why.

463

Having said this much, I shall relegate most of the political science example to the footnotes and to another occasion, pausing only to declare that roughly a decade and a half ago there erupted in political science a normative cry against the dominant pluralist description of the distribution of American political power. I have in mind the "non-decisionmaking" critique of American pluralism.[210] Succinctly put, that critique argued that a prime characteris-

---

don't really fit. Robert Cover's *Justice Accused* (1975) and Grant Gilmore's *The Ages of American Law* (1977) don't really measure up to Elizabethan tragedy or Greek mythology; nor do I think Cover is so simplistic as to view Lemuel Shaw and his legal decisions as wholly independent "of the economics of his time or . . . a particular legal tradition . . . ." Presser, *supra* at 863. Presser's approval of Teachout's judgment that "the writers in this school are not really generating historical scholarship . . . [but] producing literature," *id.* at 864, is a bit unkind both to these legal historians and to writers of literature.

208. Teachout, *supra* note 203, at 819 n.17.

209. *Id.*

210. *See* Bachrach & Baratz, *Two Faces of Power*, 56 AM. POL. SCI. REV. 947 (1962); Bachrach & Baratz, *Power and its Two Faces Revisited: A Reply to Geoffrey Debnam*, 69 AM. POL. SCI. REV. 900 (1975); *see also* Bachrach & Baratz, *Decisions and Nondecisions: An Analytical Framework*, 57 AM. POL. SCI. REV. 632 (1963).

tic of American politics was a pattern of elites keeping really pressing problems inherent in post-industrial American democracy off the political agenda by controlling what was, and what was not, "legitimate" to raise in government fora.

Without declaring my position on the "non-decisionmaking debate," I think it pertinent to stress one similarity and one difference in the treatment that political science accorded its "visitation from the North" and the treatment that the law's method of analysis has accorded similar visitations. The similarity is that both approaches were rejected by the dominant school of analysis.[211] The difference is that in political science, the "dissident tendency" got its "day in court," including a detailed assessment and rebuttal. Succinctly put, the "non-decisionmaking" critique was "sent packing up North" by the intellectually respectable technique of arguing its methodological deficiencies.[212] But in constitutional law and, to a lesser extent, in legal history, the "dissident tendency" has so far been more often met with "open pages for expression" than with painstaking assessment.

The remainder of this Article is devoted to such an assessment. Such an undertaking is required not only by the "civil obligation" of giving a response, but also by the very uncertainties about the purposes and effectiveness of legal research and teaching recently expressed by such "establishment" representatives as Harvard University President Derek Bok, as well as others who, along with Posner, were heard at the Yale Law School Symposium.[213] The

464

---

211. If we go by the content of articles in major political science journals, the nondecisionmaking critique had been quashed by the mid-70s.

212. *See, e.g.,* Wolfinger, *Nondecisions and the Study of Local Politics*, 65 AM. POL. SCI. REV. 1063 (1971); Frey, *Comment: On Issues and Nonissues in the Study of Power*, 65 AM. POL. SCI. REV. 1081 (1971); Wolfinger, *Rejoinder to Frey's "Comment"*, 65 AM. POL. SCI. REV. 1102 (1971); *see also* Debnam. *Nondecisions and Power: The Two Faces of Bachrach and Baratz*, 69 AM. POL. SCI. REV. 889 (1975); Debnam, *Rejoinder to "Comment" by Peter Bachrach and Morton S. Baratz*, 69 AM. POL. SCI. REV. 905 (1975).

213. Bok's 1981-1982 Report to the Harvard Overseers dealt with problems of legal education at Harvard in the 1980s. *See* Bok, *A Flawed System*, 85 HARV. MAG. 38 (1983). For further discussion of these problems, see Stone, *From a Language Perspective*, 90 YALE L.J. 1149, 1149 (1981) ("My thesis is that law scholarship . . . is fragmented and drifting." Stone argues that research into law as language would give law a clearer sense of purpose.); *see also* Fiss, *The Varieties of Positivism*, 90 YALE L.J. 1007, 1007, 1016 (1981) ("Positivism is an idea that has generated a great deal of confusion . . . . Stumped, especially by these papers, Professor Robert Gordon announced that he had 'come to the conclusion that a positivist is someone who sounds very positive.' ") ("The law, as opposed to history, is lacking a literature on its scholarship. . . . The hour is late . . . ."); Fletcher, *Two Modes of Legal Thought*, 90 YALE L.J. 970, 970 (1981) ("We have no jurisprudence of legal scholarship. . . . Yet we reflect little about what we are doing when we write about the law."); Michelman, *Politics As Medicine: On Misdiagnosing Legal Scholarship*, 90 YALE L.J. 1224, 1124 (1981) ("Here it is, Sunday morning. Something . . . makes me think it must be my role to counter Mark Tushnet's message of despair with the message of hope—and to wrestle with Alan Freeman for the soul of Paul

need is also suggested by the differences in the contemporary states of two "law-and" areas of inquiry — "law-and-history" (robust and expansive) and "law-and-political science" (much less robust, even in the doldrums between normative analysis and the search for that in the law which is both distinctively political and readily quantifiable).[214] More broadly, this assessment is called for by the conditions of the larger American polity — especially the stasis or retrogression of social and economic goods distribution characterizing the past few years, the Democratic opposition's extraordinary inability to mount a coherent critique of this stasis or retrogression, and the Administration's seeming inability to do more in foreign relations than to separate the country further from Western Europe

---

Brest. The problem posed to us by Professor Tushnet is the failure of contemporary legal scholarship, as he sees it, to participate significantly in what he takes to be the one true intellectual calling of our times . . . ."); Shapiro, *On The Regrettable Decline of Law French: Or Shapiro Jettet Le Brickbat*, 90 YALE L.J. 1198, 1198 (1981) ("Professor Stone's call . . . may well be the first trumpet call of an essentially reactionary movement . . . .").

214. Defending fully the proposition that law-and-political-science is in the doldrums would require an essay in itself. That is not possible here. Certain phenomena evident at the 1982 American Political Science Association and the 1983 Western Political Science Association annual meetings, however, might be considered at least indicative. Each meeting featured panel discussions that revolved around questions such as "Where are we going now?" and "Are we really scientists of the law's processes?" Those discussions also betrayed unease as to how political scientists specializing in law could become more central to the "discipline" of political science — that is, less peripheral compared to, for example, students of voting or of legislative processes. Arguably, the public law speciality in political science continues to suffer to a peculiar degree from identity-anxiety and a perceived failure to attain the "science status" sought by some. Be that as it may, it is interesting that only one of the panelists at the W.P.S.A. meeting continued to speak in the optimistic behavioral terms common in the 1960s. It is also indicative that, after a generation of seeking independence, the references to discussion-relevant articles in the five W.P.S.A. papers came by a ratio of about three-to-one from law reviews rather than political science journals. *See Whither Political Jurisprudence?*, W. POL. Q. (forthcoming, Dec. 1983) (collecting the W.P.S.A. papers as a symposium).

The A.P.S.A. convention papers showed sufficient diversity on the subject of public law's methodological paradigm to establish one "negative pregnant" — that if such a paradigm is one necessary condition of a scientific speciality, public law just is not in the ballpark. *Compare* L. Carter, Models of Public Law Scholarship and Their Payoffs (Sept. 2-5, 1982) (unpublished paper delivered at A.P.S.A. annual meeting), *with* C. Tate, The Development of the Methodology of Judicial Behavior Research: A Historical Review and Critique of the Use and Teaching of Methods (Sept. 2-5, 1982) (unpublished paper delivered at A.P.S.A. annual meeting). Carter maintains that "[o]f the several current political science uses of the label 'public law,' the most inclusive (and the one most frequently used) refers to no coherent theory or body of knowledge about either law or the public." L. Carter, *supra* at 3. Generally, his essay takes a line somewhat analogous to that of Stone, arguing for a "new public law" concerned with "how language shapes and limits the perception of normative issues . ..." *Id*. at 11. Tate, on the other hand, is still very positive about positivist science's possibilities. Methodological deficiencies, rather than something amiss in the scientific undertaking itself, explain for Tate the sub-optimal progress of political-science-in-law. *See also*, B.C. Canon, Studying the Impact of Judicial Decisions: A Period of Stagnation and Prospects for the Future; D.M. Provine, Research on the Judicial Process, 1970-82: What Have We Learned?; A. Villmoare, What Is the Conceptual Future of the Analysis of Public Law? One Perspective on the Questions (all presented at the A.P.S.A. meeting; Canon the most critical as to disciplinary progress, Villmoare "fishing" for useful approaches from other disciplines' methodologies and conceptualizations, Provine less pessimistic but well short of positive positivism).

and to re-stage the Vietnamese peasant-shooting enterprise in Central America. All of these factors argue for a "critical liberal" examination of the insights, if any, that the "Critical Legal Studies Movement" offers in examining the role of law in shaping, or misshaping, the American polity's destiny and the life-situations of its members.

So, deférring for now whether we would be better advised "to call on God to speak"[215] or to "find the mind's opportunity in the heart's revenge," rather than standing "in tedious embarrassment before cold altars,"[216] let us play with fire a bit.

C. *Marxist Language as a Barrier to Understanding, and Tushnet's Maximum and Minimum Goals for a Marxist Theory of American Law*

466

Of course, Tushnet is not really coming at us from the (non-Siberian) North. That was a red herring. But neither is he quite coming at us from the People's Cossack-dancing revels in the birch forests around Moscow or from the Central European tradition of Dracula-like pointy-headed Marxist intellectuals out to sap the vitality of the monopoly-capitalist Western European and North American bodies politic.[217]

Any American intellectual who is seriously committed to socio-economic reform and who organizes his critique of American folk- and corporate-ways around a Marxist framework of analysis runs great risks. I do not mean, however, to doubt that one can critique American trends with impunity or even reward. One can. There are indeed at least eight safe ways within the domain of American legal scholarship to critique American ways. Starting with the most spacious, one may pen a philosophical treatise at a level of abstraction that avoids having clearly to resolve whether its distributive judgments are compatible with socialism or capitalism.[218] Second, one may pen constitutional treatises that make straight (or at least show

---

215. After showing conclusively, at least in the eyes of Tushnet, the pitfalls of liberalism, Roberto Mangabeira Unger concludes *Knowledge and Politics* with the words (he likes quasi-literary, post-analytic flourishes): "Desirous of faith, touched by hope, and moved by love, men look unceasingly for God. . . . But our days pass, and still we do not know you fully. Why then do you remain silent? Speak, God." R. UNGER, KNOWLEDGE AND POLITICS 295 (1975).

216. Unger, *The Critical Studies Movement*, 96 HARV L. REV. 561, 675 (1983) (where Unger gets meta-analytic again).

217. Note that I do not say "bodies economic." Clearly he would like to change substantially at least the distribution of economic goods.

218. *See* B. ACKERMAN, SOCIAL JUSTICE IN THE LIBERAL STATE (1980); J. RAWLS, A THEORY OF JUSTICE (1971).

the way to making more straight) the Supreme Court's way through the political wilderness.[219] This approach usually avoids altogether the question of whether its distributive prescriptions are compatible with socialism or capitalism.

The third safe method is to compose historical treatises that plainly disapprove of some past American evil and that contain vaguely well-intentioned implications for current American justice and justices;[220] this approach also avoids questions of compatibility. Alternatively, there is a fourth approach: writing casebooks that seek to rectify judicially wrought (or aided) wrongs by, variously, locating the source of primal error in some unfortunate formalist law professor who, long deceased, cannot defend his failure to bring about legal coherence or social justice;[221] anticipating improvement in solving a core problem of scarce resources by increasing judicial limitation of state power in favor of national power;[222] or imbuing the student simultaneously with the complexity of constitutional questions and the desirability of measured legal-doctrinal change as the way to bring about social, economic, and political progress.[223]

467

Fifth, one can "critique" by documenting alarming changes in the "who owns what" of the American economy, or "who damages what" of American nature, and suggesting "cures" that no political majority is likely to take seriously. A sixth option is to write articles demonstrating that, while not everything is improving, at least the Court's handling of a particular invidious distinction may be. Seventh, the critic can write articles that support affirmative action, or eighth, produce articles showing that the Burger Court has reached a sensible middle-of-the-road disposition of one or more problems of late-industrial capitalism, such as the terms under which middle-class public employees work or are fired.[224]

---

219. *See* J. CHOPER, JUDICIAL REVIEW AND THE NATIONAL POLITICAL PROCESS (1980); J. ELY, DEMOCRACY AND DISTRUST (1981); L. TRIBE, *supra* note 183; *see also* Easterbrook, *Ways of Criticizing the Court*, 95 HARV. L. REV. 802 (1982) (useful analysis of ways in which, given that the Supreme Court consists of nine persons who often disagree with each other in their value priorities, it is and is not sensible to criticize the Court).

220. *See, e.g.*, R. COVER, JUSTICE ACCUSED (1975). *Justice Accused* has become a bit the "darling" of law professors skimming the law of slavery topic (somewhat less so of legal historians burrowing into it). For a rare adverse judgment by a lawyer, see Tushnet, Book Review, 20 AM. J. LEGAL HIST. 168 (1976).

221. *See* R. CRAMTON, D. CURRIE & H. KAY, *supra* note 32, at 6 (Joseph Beale takes it on the chin for having tried to solve conflict-of-laws problems by "territorializing" them).

222. *See, e.g.*, G. COGGINS & C. WILKINSON, FEDERAL PUBLIC LAND AND RESOURCES LAW (1981).

223. *See generally* G. GUNTHER, CONSTITUTIONAL LAW: CASES AND MATERIALS (10th ed. 1980).

224. *See* Simon, *Liberty and Property in the Supreme Court: A Defense of Roth and Perry*, 71 CALIF. L. REV. 146, 192 (1983).

Why should Professor Tushnet find the breadth of all this critical room insufficient? Why should a Marxist critique be necessary for him? After all, if none of these methods is sufficient, he could busy himself with what at least one legal scholar takes to be the central problem of contemporary constitutional scholarship — the adequacies and inadequacies of "interpretivist" versus "non-interpretivist" approaches to constitutional decision making.[225] Why won't this do? The answers to these questions are important — if (though not) only because of Tushnet's analytic uniqueness among Marxist Anglo-American legal scholars.

A common characteristic divides these scholars from Tushnet. The characteristic is that they take Marxist analysis very seriously in an "interpretivist sense." Either they do so in a fundamentalist fashion, and quite illiterately,[226] or they do so in a less fundamentalist — and more literate — manner. In this the members of the more literate sub-group have much in common with the best Marxist historians, such as Eugene Genovese, who, whatever else they may be, are neither fundamentalist nor lacking in linguistic felicity, but who think that the "source" is interpretively crucial to an adequate analysis. For Tushnet, the role of Marx/Engels "scripture" is much less clear, as is the appropriate maximum goal of a Marxist analysis of American law. Tushnet, in other words, waffles on whether a powerful Marxist analysis of law is really possible. In an odd sense, that is why his analysis ought to be taken seriously and ought to be carefully scrutinized. What makes the examination of Tushnet's work interesting is, in large measure, his oscillation among three positions — whether Marxism is capable of a "strong" analysis of American law (one covering both the specific and the general characteristics of that law), or whether it can only hope to attain a "weak" analysis (one embracing general trends but having little or nothing to say about particular cases or doctrinal devolutions), or whether, yet more weakly, Marxism is merely useful as an existential "anti-" position (one more valuable for affirming differences from "establishment" analyses than for describing general or specific propositions about the path of American law).

In addition, Tushnet exhibits at least three Marxist faces whose alternating appearances in various essays make Tushnet's overall po-

468

---

225. *See* Brest, *supra* note 192; Brest, *supra* note 201; *see also* Brest, *The Fundamental Rights Controversy: The Essential Contradictions of Normative Constitutional Scholarship*, 90 YALE L.J. 1063 (1981) (arguing that both interpretivism and non-interpretivism are ultimately failures).

226. *See, e.g.,* Hunt, *Dichotomy and Contradiction in the Sociology of Law*, 8 BRIT. J. LAW & SOCY. 47 (1981).

sition difficult to grasp.[227] The first "face" is concerned chiefly with assessing, at a fairly high level of abstraction, the value and limitations of Marxist analysis of American law.[228] The second "face" is concerned primarily with using Marxist analysis to critique both conventional liberal American legal scholarship in general and particular issues that such conventional scholarship prominently discusses, such as "Structural Constitutional Review" and "Interpretivism versus Non-Interpretivism."[229] The third "face" is the "legal historical" one. It is concerned both with applying Marxist analysis to nineteenth century American law and with criticizing the shortcomings of conventional liberal and non-Marxist radical essays on that subject.

Beyond the confused situation in which the scattering of Tushnet's analyses across so many essays leaves his readers, there are at least four main barriers to speedy overall assessment. One is contained in what, from the American liberal standpoint, appear as the linguistic peculiarities of Marxist writing — especially the use of certain recurrent "evidence-summing" metaphors with pejorative connotations.

469

The second barrier springs from the fact that Tushnet's views as to how much specificity and explanatory power can be displayed by Marxist analysis of American law have shifted over time. The third barrier, which is most apparent in his "second face" analyses of post-Realist legal scholarship, is that those analyses merge critical axioms flowing from Legal Realism and from Marxism variously in a sometimes opaque fashion.

---

227. That is to say nothing of those of his articles that are entirely or almost entirely conventional case or doctrinal discussions. *See, e.g.,* Tushnet, *The Sociology of Article III: A Response to Professor Brilmayer*, 93 HARV. L. REV. 1698 (1980); Tushnet, *Rethinking the Dormant Commerce Clause*, 1979 WIS. L. REV. 125; Tushnet, *Constitutional and Statutory Analyses in the Law of Federal Jurisdiction*, 25 UCLA L. REV. 1301 (1978); Tushnet, *Constitutional Limitation of Substantive Criminal Law: An Examination of the Meaning of* Mullaney v. Wilbur, 55 B.U. L. REV. 775 (1975).

228. This face is manifested chiefly in five essays published or written since 1978. *See* Tushnet, *A Marxist Analysis of American Law*, in MARXIST PERSPECTIVES 96 (1978) [hereinafter cited as Tushnet, 1978 MARXIST PERSPECTIVES]; Tushnet, Book Review, 7 BRIT. J. L. & SOCY. 122 (1980) (reviewing M. CAIN & A. HUNT, MARX AND ENGELS ON LAW (1979), P. HIRST, ON LAW AND IDEOLOGY (1979), and C. SUMNER, READING IDEOLOGIES (1979)) [hereinafter cited as Tushnet, BRITISH REVIEW]; M. Tushnet, Marxism as Metaphor (unpublished paper, forthcoming in 1983) [hereinafter cited as Tushnet, 1983 Marxism as Metaphor]; M. Tushnet, Marxism and Law (unpublished paper, forthcoming in 1983) [hereinafter cited as Tushnet, 1983 Marxism and Law]; M. Tushnet, Is There A Marxist Theory of Law? (Sept. 2-6, 1981) (paper presented at Annual Meeting of the American Society for Political and Legal Philosophy) [hereinafter cited as Tushnet, 1981 Marxist Theory].

229. *See* Tushnet, *Truth, Justice, and the American Way: An Interpretation of Public Law Scholarship in the Seventies*, 57 TEX. L. REV. 1307 (1979). This article also contains a discussion of what a Marxist theory of law ought to be about. *See id.* at 1346-58.

The fourth barrier is something of an "evidentiary analogue" to the third, but it arises in the area of nineteenth century American legal history. Part of the problem is suggested by recalling Alan Watson's argument that some of the peculiarities of Southern slave law could be explained in terms of the natural legal evolution of any slave society and thus were understandable without recourse to what he took to be Marxism's not very insightful insights into the antebellum South. More broadly, the problem relates to an observation by Frederic Jameson quoted near the outset of this Article. Does, to state it somewhat differently, Marxist dialectic's focus upon the historiographic equivalent of twentieth century physics' "wave theory" explanations of "light" merely amount to a vaguer and more cumbrous mode of explanation of history than Anglo-American empirical history's focus upon (to continue the analogy) a "particle theory" of historical individuals' activities? Or are Marxism's different insights somehow "worthwhile"? Lastly, in this connection, are the "canons of sufficient evidence" properly thought to be the same when judging between the two historiographical approaches: does Ockham's razor properly apply to both?[230] In the remainder of this Part we shall consider the first two of these four barriers.[231]

470

I wish to deal with the first of these difficulties — Marxism's linguistic peculiarities — in a two-step fashion. First, we must bring to the surface our (bourgeois) sense of objection to some common Marxist terms by simply lining them up. The second step is to see whether we can profitably "de-fang" them with whimsy yet leave them with some explanatory value by turning them into non-Marxist or "less Marxist" phrases with sense-meanings apprehendable from a liberal perspective.

I choose selectively from a long list of potentially "annoying" Marxist words and phrases by limiting the examples to a small sample drawn mainly from Tushnet's writings and from three other recent Marxist essays on law.[232] Here is a short list, with "de-fanged" substitutes:

---

230. Another radical legal historian puts the point well:
One cannot repeat too often that Marx's dialectical approach involves the rejection of a familiar bourgeois way of looking at the world in favor of the development of a more comprehensive, qualitative, substantive approach which, among other things, disavows the liberal fact/value distinction and the liberal mode of definition-by-isolation.
Holt, *Morton Horwitz and the Transformation of American Legal History*, 23 WM. & MARY L. REV. 663, 701 n.133 (1982).

231. The other two require a separate essay in themselves.

232. Abel, *A Critique of American Tort Law*, 8 BRIT. J. LAW & SOCY. 199 (1981); Balbus, *Commodity Form and Legal Form: An Essay on the "Relative Autonomy" of the Law*, 11 LAW & SOCY. REV. 571 (1977); Hunt, *supra* note 226.

"Socialist camp," "imperialist camp," "death agony of capitalism." The first two are annoying to some of us who associate "camp" fondly with childhood summers but who don't want to be thought of as having nothing better than army cots to sleep in the rest of the year. "Death agony" seems a bit overdrawn; possibly capitalism is better than Italian opera stars at lengthy death scenes. Let's say "Marxist-Leninist countries," "democratic-pluralist countries," and "bad day on Wall Street."

"Ruthless imperialist beast," "jackal legal henchmen," and "paper tiger." Let's say "that nice David Rockefeller," "the distinguished law-and-economics professors," and *"papier mâché* pussycat."

So much for the general nouns and noun-phrases of Marxist name-calling. What about verbs?

"Emanate," "mystify," "generate," "be implicated in," "exploit, "oppress." The first three only suggest confusion, while the last three imply guilt. It is, oddly perhaps, easier to defang the latter trio — respectively, "be functionally related to," "give foreign aid to assist in the economic development of," and "anti-inflationary wage-restraining." The first three verbs are typical analytic conjunctures linking fairly reified abstract nouns and noun phrases — for example, "Capitalism generates liberal ideology." We will have to defang them as they come along individually. What of Marxist legal analysis terms-of-art?

471

"Legal fetishism," "fetishism of commodities." These are particularly irritating, but more for Freudian than Marxian reasons. After all, Karl preceded Sigmund. "Characterized by greater concern with the rule of law than with socioeconomic inequalities," and "being more concerned with 'keeping up with the Joneses' than with the human costs of work-conditions," will have to do as restatements.

"Internal contradictions of liberal law," "economic infrastructure versus legal superstructure," "hegemony of liberal legal ideology," "dilemmas of liberal-capitalist legal theory," and *"formal legal reflections of ruling class interests."* These are all particularly irritating to lawyers and legal scholars. Metaphoric animal names may not break bones. Indeed, they're a bit funny — though Marxist-Leninists intellectuals, who almost uniformly seem to be below the tenth percentile in capacity for humor, often do not realize this. But these phrases all go straight to our sense of intellectual independence. They put us in a kind of Platonic cave of legal analysis, implying that we labor long and hard with mere legal shadows of what really matters intellectually. The implication that we do not know that dilemmas and contradictions suffuse even our most hard-headed thinking is also

disconcerting. Moreover, they defy general defanging. Again we shall have to take them up as we come to them.

If it is important in understanding contemporary American Marxist analysis of law not to be put off at the start by some of the general phraseology I have just lampooned, it is *very* important to realize that as that analysis emerged during the late 1970s and early 1980s, its more sophisticated practitioners, including Tushnet, put considerable distance between their view of the relationships of law and economy, on the one hand, and a simple determinist view of those relationships, on the other. Thus, to offer an illustration "outside of" Tushnet, Balbus has outlined the essentials of his own theory of law. He states that:

472

> This theory . . . entails a simultaneous rejection of both an *instrumentalist* or reductionist approach, which denies that the legal order possesses any autonomy from the demand imposed on it by actors of the capitalist society in which it is embedded, and a *formalist* approach, which asserts an absolute . . . autonomy of the legal order from this society.[233]

Balbus goes on to argue that formalist analysis and reductionist, instrumentalist analysis are equally unsatisfactory. Formalism's focus on the specifics of the forms of American law produces elegant descriptions of a closed, wholly autonomous legal system but avoids the knotty problem of conceptualizing and locating the relationships between those forms and the "capitalist whole of which [such forms are] a part."[234] Both "pluralist . . . [and] crude-Marxist"[235] instrumental approaches misconstrue the law "as a mere instrument or tool of the will of dominant social actors."[236] Consequently, such instrumental approaches neither explain why the forms of law in a particular society are as they are, nor ascertain, with respect to a capitalist economy, how those forms link to "the overall requirements of the . . . system."[237]

Now that is something that any halfway critical liberal or conservative could have said.[238] It explains, incidentally, why I earlier

---

233. Balbus, *supra* note 232, at 571 (emphasis in original). Note the implicit separation of "actors" from the status of mere unthinking "robots" of the economy's dictates.

234. *Id.* at 572.

235. *Id.* at 571.

236. *Id.*

237. *Id.*

238. *Cf.* Gordon, Gordon, *Historicism in Legal Scholarship*, 90 YALE L.J. 1017 (1981); *Introduction: J. Willard Hurst and the Common Law Tradition in American Legal Historiography*, 10 LAW & SOCY. REV. 9, 10-11 (1975) (comparing American legal history concerned with the "inside the black box" of the law's forms with American legal history concerned with the "external relations" of the law).

said that Teachout's lumping of persons such as Tushnet and Horwitz into a "neo-orthodox" school won't do,[239] and why "not-so-crude" Marxists like Tushnet have attacked both Horwitz's and Friedman's "radicalism."[240] An interesting footnote in Balbus's argument is worth pausing on for its equation of pluralist and "crude-Marxist" legal analysis.

> Despite their obvious opposition, there is no *theoretical* difference between a Pluralist and an Instrumentalist-Marxist approach to law. Both bypass entirely the problem of the form or structure of the legal order in order to conceive it as a direct reflection of consciously articulated and organized pressures. Thus the difference between them is merely empirical: Pluralists deny that there is a systematic bias to the interplay of pressures; Instrumentalist Marxists argue that this interplay is dominated by specifically capitalist interests.[241]

Very similar judgments as to the insufficiency of crude instrumentalist Marxism are prominent in the writings of other Marxists. Closely related are two other characteristics of such writing. One characteristic is the rejection of an approach that tries to bring order into all of Marx's and Engel's various legal writings, followed *either* by an attempt to make sense of the literal and implied meanings of certain restricted "chunks" of text[242] *or* by giving up the exegetical task entirely as not worthwhile. The latter, as we have already noted, is Tushnet's mode.[243]

473

The other characteristic is an attempt to construct something like

---

239. *See* text accompanying notes 203-09 *supra*.

240. *See* Tushnet, 1978 MARXIST PERSPECTIVES, *supra* note 228, at 106; Tushnet, *Perspectives on the Development of American Law: A Critical Review of Friedman's "A History of American Law"*, 1977 WIS. L. REV. 81; *see also* Tushnet, *The Dialectics of Legal History*, 57 TEX. L. REV. 1295 (1975) (critical of Teachout's "hero" — G. Edward White). *But see* Holt, *supra* note 230 (Marxist defense of Morton Horwitz).

241. Balbus, *supra* note 232, at 571 n.1; *cf.* Freeman, *Truth and Mystification in Legal Scholarship*, 90 YALE L.J. 1229, 1232 (1981) (seeing law as grounded in its social setting "can lead to explanatory models as divergent as conspiratorial Marxist instrumentalism and liberal pluralist instumentalism. That approach seems to underestimate the importance of law and legal ideology, to reduce it to a reflexive fact of social life, to demean the human activity associated with legal consciousness . . . ."). The latter clause, incidentally, may explain partially the unpopularity among lawyers of behavioral political science's legal analysis.

242. As, for example, Gary Young's exegesis of "only Marx's mature writings." Young, *Marx on Bourgeois Law*, in 2 RESEARCH IN LAW AND SOCIOLOGY 133, 134 (1979).

243. *See* Tushnet, BRITISH REVIEW, *supra* note 228, at 123. In discussing M. CAIN & A. HUNT, MARX AND ENGELS ON LAW (1979), Tushnet notes:

> [The authors] have expended enormous effort in discovering and collecting the fugitive writings of Marx and Engels that deal with law. . . .
>
> This method of presentation . . . establishes that exegesis cannot give us a Marxist theory of law. The texts will support any position from reductionism to something just short of liberalism. Nor is it the case that we can distinguish between an early Hegelian Marx and a mature *post-coupure* Marx, or between Marx as analyst of general structures and Marx as analyst of particular conjunctures. The various inconsistent approaches simply coexist.

Tushnet, BRITISH REVIEW, *supra* note 228, at 123; *see also* Tushnet, 1981 Marxist Theory,

a "legitimizing pedigree" for contemporary noninstrumentalist Marxist analysis by reexamining the work, not of Marx and Engels themselves, but rather of, typically, early twentieth century Marxists — especially the Austrians Karl Renner and Rudolf Hilferding and the Russian E.B. Pashukanis.[244] Pashukanis's rejection of both formalism and "the vulgar materialism which was becoming dominant in the USSR in his day"[245] differs, it is said, from Renner's neo-Kantian conception of the scientific method and concurrence with Hans Kelsen's formalist view of law as an autonomous sphere. Yet both views legitimize "non-vulgar" late twentieth century Marxist analyses of law.

However, such legitimation of current nonfundamentalist approaches as genuinely Marxist does not lead to quick concurrence as to "Shto Sdyelat?"[246] The uncertainty is evident not only among scholars seeking to apply Marxist analysis to American law but even *within* the work of the scholar with whom we are here most concerned. Furthermore, the shift in Tushnet's views developed over a very short span of time. Consider the variation between late-1970s and early-1980s "Tushnetian Marxist" legal analysis.

Tushnet's 1978 essay, *A Marxist Analysis of American Law*,[247] lays out quite clearly a not unambitious program as to what an adequate Marxist theory of American law would entail. Basically, such a theory would have to undertake three tasks. First, it "must show the material basis for both the existence of a legal form in capitalist society and for the specific ideological content of that form . . . ."[248] In other words, without falling into "the reductionist trap of viewing the form and content of the law as direct expressions of the interests, narrowly defined, of the bourgeoisie,"[249] it must explain: (a) why there is a rule of law in capitalist polities at all; and, (b) why the legal rules in such polities prioritize certain values but not others. For example, it should be able to explain why nineteenth century American law enforced harsh contracts rationally entered into rather than, as at an earlier phase, adjusting the contracts' terms to reach more

474

---

supra note 228, at 2 ("I will avoid exegetical exercises . . . partly because the texts make exegesis futile . . . .").

244. *See* P. HIRST, ON LAW AND IDEOLOGY 106-22, 122-26 (1979) (discussing Pashukanis and Renner).

245. *Id.* at 107.

246. This is a transliteration of the title of Lenin's famous essay — in English, *What is To Be Done? See* V. LENIN, *What is to Be Done*, in COLLECTED WORKS 347 (V. Jerome ed. 1961).

247. Tushnet, 1978 MARXIST PERSPECTIVES, *supra* note 228.

248. *Id.* at 96.

249. *Id.*

equitable results,[250] and why twentieth century American constitutional law arguably carries equality of access to travel and entertainment accommodations well beyond the Framers' original intent, but makes no such advances with respect to equality in school resources or in effective rights to settle in choice neighborhoods.[251]

Moreover, the explanation of why the law thus favors formal rights and liberty over substantive concern for lessening disparities in "real" capacity to exercise such rights cannot be adequate for the Marxist, if it is limited to exercises in "mere" liberal intellectual history, "mere" pluralist political science, or to "mere" philosophic analysis of the content of talismanic review-triggering clauses such as "equal protection of the laws." Accordingly, the preference for "negative liberty"[252] over "positive equality" could not be adequately "explained" in terms, for example, of the Framers' concepts of a nonarbitrary form of government or in terms of successive generations' evolving conceptions[253] of liberty, contractual fairness, and the like. It is equally insufficient, from the Marxist vantage point, *either* to "explain" judicial rejection of constitutional arguments that would equalize school resources or reduce exclusionary zoning of suburbs by referring only to pluralist accounts of the liberal or conservative mind-sets of the judges, *or* to "explain away" the substance of constitutional "trigger-clauses" by arguing that they are formally empty.[254] Rather, an adequate Marxist explanation would need to relate these judicial doctrines and the ideas and politics underlying them to structural economic facts of American life.

475

---

250. If, in fact, the earlier era was properly so characterized. For argument that Horwitz and others err on this, see Schwartz, *Tort Law and the Economy in Nineteenth-Century America: A Reinterpretation*, 90 YALE L.J. 1717 (1981); Schwartz, *The Vitality of Negligence and the Ethics of Strict Liability*, 15 GA. L. REV. 963 (1981). For a defense of Horwitz, see Holt, *supra* note 230, at 667-70.

251. See the conflicting majority and minority opinions in San Antonio Indep. School Dist. v. Rodriguez, 411 U.S. 1 (1972).

252. *See* I. BERLIN, TWO CONCEPTS OF LIBERTY (1958). I have changed "positive liberty" to "positive equality" deliberately.

253. For a useful, but problematic, distinction between "concepts" (generalized ideas about X and Y — *e.g.*, free speech and right to counsel — that were "put once and for all" in the Constitution by the various Framers and that remain constant) and "conceptions" (more specific ideas of same that may evolve from generation to generation), see R. DWORKIN, TAKING RIGHTS SERIOUSLY 134-36 (1978).

254. It is also insufficient to explain that the use of terms like "liberty" or "equality" is intellectually or politically confusing. *See* Westen, *The Empty Idea of Equality*, 95 HARV. L. REV. 537 (1982) (elegant argument to that effect); Westen, *On "Confusing Ideas": Reply*, 91 YALE L.J. 1153 (1982); Westen, *The Meaning of Equality in Law, Science, Math, and Morals: A Reply*, 81 MICH. L. REV. 604 (1983). *But see* Burton, *Comment on "Empty Ideas": Logical Positivist Analyses of Equality and Rules*, 91 YALE L.J. 1136 (1982); Chemerinsky, *In Defense of Equality: A Reply to Professor Westen*, 81 MICH. L. REV. 575 (1983); D'Amato, *Is Equality A Totally Empty Idea?*, 81 MICH. L. REV. 600 (1983).

Tushnet's second necessary task for a Marxist theory of American law is to "show how the structure of the legal system supports its autonomy from the political and economic structures of capitalism,"[255] without regarding that autonomy as absolute. His third necessary task is closely related, giving "content to the idea of the relative autonomy of the law."[256]

In other words, a Marxist theory needs to explain: (a) what it means to say that the legal system appears to function, in at least some aspects, independently of "economic and political dictates" but less so in other aspects; (b) which are the more, and which the less, apparently independent aspects both of structure and of process; (c) why some aspects push toward functional independence yet others do not; and (d) how and why factors external to the law brake or limit that independence, by making the law's autonomy only "relative," or better (since the word "relative" in non-Marxist language seems to demand a "with respect to what" clause about which Marxist analysis remains vague), "incomplete" or "partial."[257]

Following a comment concerning the "pernicious reductionism" of Lawrence-Friedman-style legal history,[258] Tushnet states quite optimistically that recent Marxist discussions have both "shifted attention to the significance of the legal form itself and provided a solid foundation for a return to . . . analysis of the specific content of the law."[259] This view envisages Marxist theory as potentially capable of explaining not merely the *form* of capitalist law — for example, why state-provided welfare "to the dominated classes . . . proceed[s] according to general rules applied by lower-level officials not thought to have substantial discretion."[260] It also conceives of Marxist theory as capable of explaining the *content* of that law — for example, why "regulation of collective workers' activity [became] collective bargaining in an essentially contractual framework."[261]

After discussing three possible responses to the Neo-Realist contention that large sectors of the law "which might seem to express the

476

---

255. Tushnet, 1978 MARXIST PERSPECTIVES, *supra* note 228, at 96.

256. *Id.*

257. "Partial," of course, has its ambiguities too.

258. The non-Marxist reader should be alerted that the phrase "pernicious reductionism" is used in Marxist prose less to distinguish it from "non-pernicious" or "deft" reductionism (for example, reducing 111111/555555ths to 1/5th) than to differentiate the merely "pernicious" (no evidence of mens rea) from the "heinous" (evidence of mens rea) form of reductionism.

259. Tushnet, 1978 MARXIST PERSPECTIVES, *supra* note 228, at 96.

260. *Id.* at 97.

261. *Id.*

fundamental presuppositions of capitalist society [are in fact] essentially irrelevant to the transactions of capitalists"[262] — an attack which, if successful, might undermine any Marxist theory of law — Tushnet goes on to argue that an adequate Marxist theory needs to focus on three issues: (1) how ideologies are generated; (2) whether capitalist material conditions give rise to distinctively capitalist legal forms of ideology; and (3) what the consequences are of "the contradictions inherent in the capitalist mode of production."[263] The essay concludes with brief discussions of, in Tushnet's view, significant but flawed examinations of these issues.[264] The details of Tushnet's characterizations of these examinations need not detain us here; the important point involves the scope of the Marxist analytic enterprise contemplated. Tushnet seeks a *general* theory of American law that explains both the form and content of that law as well as how each rests upon a "material basis" that pins down the extent of autonomy in the law, and that, having determined the genesis and operation of capitalist ideology, works out the consequences.

477

Now let us contrast that fairly tall order with Tushnet's more recent formulations, half a decade later. A fair characterization of Tushnet's more recent position(s) — as laid out particularly in *Is There A Marxist Theory of Law?*, *Marxism as Metaphor*, and *Marxism and Law*[265] — is that it recedes substantially from his 1978 position on at least the following scores: (1) the feasibility of a general Marxist theory of American law which explains adequately and systematically both the law's content(s) and its form(s); and (2) in turn, the likely potential scope of Marxist explanation and the satisfactory minimum content of a Marxist theory of law.

At times, indeed, he turns almost puckishly cynical, as when he says: "It may be . . . that to the degree that a theory is distinctively Marxist, it is not a good theory, and conversely."[266] Tushnet's non-

---

262. *Id.* Tushnet is particularly concerned with Stewart Macaulay's studies. *See* Macaulay, *Non-Contractual Relations in Business: A Preliminary Study*, 28 AM. SOC. REV. 55 (1963); *see also* Epstein, *The Social Consequences of Common Law Rules*, 95 HARV. L. REV. 1717 (1982) (challenging the view that common law doctrines may determine significantly the allocation of resources in society).

263. Tushnet, 1978 MARXIST PERSPECTIVES, *supra* note 228, at 101.

264. *See* Gabel, *Intention and Structure in Contractual Conditions: Outline of a Method for Critical Legal Theory*, 61 MINN. L. REV. 601 (1977) (perceived by Tushnet as demonstrating the potential for using phenomenological approaches in tandem with Marxist analysis); Kennedy, *Form and Substance in Private Law Adjudication*, 89 HARV. L. REV. 1685 (1976) (perceived by Tushnet as fruitful but incomplete analysis of internal contradictions in legal thought); Unger, *supra* note 184 (same).

265. *See* Tushnet, 198 Marxism as Metaphor, *supra* note 228; Tushnet, 1983 Marxism and Law, *supra* note 228; Tushnet, 1981 Marxist Theory, *supra* note 228.

266. Tushnet, 1981 Marxist Theory, *supra* note 228, at 15.

Marxist reader could, I think, be pardoned for drawing from this sort
of statement the conclusion that the pursuit of a Marxist theory of
American law is hardly worth the candle. But the conclusion would
be premature. A more cautious, middle-of-the-journey assessment
would come in two parts. The first consists in determining the main
features of what Tushnet describes in his less throw-in-the-towel moments as a weak or minimum-satisfactory Marxist approach, and to
try to account for this particular more-moderate recession from the
"1978 high." The second (which we shall defer) is to see to what
extent, if at all, it is Marxist theory ("strong" or "weak") that lies at
the base of Tushnet's critiques of "main-line" positions in the current debates over constitutional issues, in the scholarship of legal history, and more generally in conventional law school research.

478

Let us, therefore, conclude this Article by sketching, and accounting for, Tushnet's more modest, but still ostensibly Marxist position on the law's analysis. I begin with the "accounting for"
because, if I am right, it makes the substance of Tushnet's position
more easily understandable.

First, let us try to explain his retreat from the 1978 idea of a
grand theory explaining both form and content in American law. I
detect three prime causes.

One lies in the extent to which he is consistently impressed by
what he takes to be the "true truths" of early twentieth century
American Legal Realism as well as of its more recent manifestations.
Over and over again, in his critiques of conventional "liberal pluralist" and conventional "formalist" legal scholarship, he uses a "legal
realist truth" to (he thinks) show conclusively that a particular contention (from either "school") is wrong. The "truth" is that there is
no principled order in the law because any clever[267] judge can manipulate precedent to reach any result he wishes. Therefore, asserts
Tushnet, any argument for a principled formalist order in the set of
cases under consideration is erroneous.

Yet, and this is the second cause, the most obvious analytic
stance to derive from this "truth" — legal nihilism — appalls him
morally more than it appeals to him intellectually. Although he
seems at times fascinated by the "cold steel" side of, for example,
Holmes' legal realism (with small letters), he does not share the
Holmesian delight in perceiving the mailed fist beneath the velvet

---

267. *See* Tushnet, 1978 MARXIST PERSPECTIVES, *supra* note 228, at 99. The "relative clev-
erness" of judges is also a theme in Tushnet's legal historical writing. It relates, though he
never quite says so, to "relative autonomy."

glove,[268] or for that matter, Posner's delight in taking from X to give to Y for reasons of economic efficiency. It may be sensible judicial behavior for judges to recognize, as Holmes would have had them do,[269] imminent shifts in the balance of power among more and less fortunate societal groupings, and "a-morally" rubber-stamp such shifts rather than blocking the redistributive way. But, for Tushnet, that is not enough. For, even if judges do not block the shift for long,[270] people suffer in the meantime. Moreover, nothing in legal nihilism explains why some politicians, including judges, block the shift while others stand aside and still others abet the shift. Nor do the intellectual puerilities of political science's "behavioralism derivative" explanations of judicial behavior begin genuinely to explain why judges behave as they do,[271] why they participate in the judicially wrought wrongs this day, or any other day, done let alone atone for them.[272] Hence, Tushnet is driven to search out an explanatory model of law and humanity, and inhumanity, that might explain, even as it might partially exculpate, that which contemporary judges, legal scholars, and mere persons do and do not do in hurting each other. Having described as his most important concern the hurts inflicted on mere persons in this vale of post-industrial existence, Tushnet goes straight, not to a single, but to one primary, and two secondary goals. The primary recourse is to a, if not *the*, major

479

---

268. *See* Tushnet, *The Logic of Experience: Oliver Wendell Holmes on the Supreme Judicial Court*, 63 VA. L. REV. 975 (1977).

269. *See id.* at 1030.

270. As did, according to the conventional liberal pluralist view of the matter, the Supreme Court majority from the *Lochner* era until 1937. For a more benign view of the Court during much of that time, see J. SEMONCHE, CHARTING THE FUTURE: THE SUPREME COURT RESPONDS TO A CHANGING SOCIETY, 1890-1920 (1978).

271. Tushnet is generally among the more sympathetic of law school scholars toward political-science-in-law. But he can be severe about certain aspects of its behavioral branch. Thus:

The next move was to look for the origins of . . . policy preferences in the social origins and political experiences of the judges. [Citing G. SCHUBERT, THE JUDICIAL MIND: THE ATTITUDES AND IDEOLOGIES OF SUPREME COURT JUSTICES, 1946-1963 (1965).]

There is of course something to this kind of argument, but it suffers from an unbearable simple-mindedness. Many law professors . . . have spent one or two years as a law clerk to a judge. They know from experience that the vote-counters do not describe what really happens when a judge makes a decision and, with the assistance of people like themselves, writes an opinion. Further, the reductionist account may have had a core of truth in it, but it eliminated much of the richness of the system of legal rules and institutions. Even if it was all a silly game, that game was elaborately choreographed in ways that the vote-counters could not understand.

Tushnet, *Post-Realist Legal Scholarship*, 1980 WIS. L. REV. 1383, 1397 (1980). He concludes with beautiful aptness: "It is as if a scene in a ballet were described by saying that the male character moved from left to right while the female character moved upstage. It is true enough—but somehow lacking in flavor." *Id.*

272. *See* Plessy v. Ferguson, 163 U.S. 537, 562 (1896) (Harlan, J., dissenting): "The thin disguise of 'equal' accommodations for passengers in railroad coaches will not mislead anyone, nor atone for the wrong this day done."

mode of post-1800 Western analysis that purports to explain the material sources of the human condition in industrial society — to Marxism.[273]

The two secondary goals flow from this primary recourse. One secondary goal, really an embrace, is phenomenology. It is pursued, I surmise, on the assumption that it may explain part of the gap left by "crude Marxism" — namely, why the normal run of persons, and judges, (mis)perceive as they do. The other secondary goal, also involving an embrace out of faith, is semiology. Thus:

> The most promising line of investigation . . . is . . . opened up by . . . the unholy trinity of semiology, phenomenology, and Marxism. . . . [W]hy do people think the way they do? The essential contribution of semiology has been to show how complex ways of thinking are—how ways of thinking indeed make totalistic claims on all who share them. The essential contribution of phenomenology has been to show how forms of life work themselves into complex ways of thinking. And the essential contribution of Marxism has been to show that the fundamental forms of life are those implicated in material social relations of production—and that those relations, because they contain contradictions, allow contradictory ways of thinking to develop.[274]

Thus, Tushnet opts for "Marxism-plus."

To say this is to point to the instability of Tushnet's 1978 grand theory solution, and to the third cause of his recession from predicting the success of grand theory. The combination of "Marxism-plus-semiology-plus-phenomenology" leads toward scrutiny of the "meaning-content" of Marxist language, in part because of analytic queries about language common to both semiology and phenomenology and in part because both have developed at least in "Continental" part against the "Viennese-Anglo-American" backdrop of linguistic positivism and its progeny. Therein, arguably, at least from the perspective of its Anglo-American reception, has lain Marxism's Achilles' heel. It has been, in its pre-revisionist forms at least, notoriously un-self-analytic as to how its language, in summing human experience, reconstructs, elides, and foreshortens that experience. That lack of self-critical awareness has made it easy — for better or worse — for the Anglo-American empiricist mode of

480

---

273. Let me emphasize that I mean Marxism, not Leninism or Maoism. The recourse is tempting for any thinking and feeling academic who is neither endowed at a deep level with the whimsical pessimism about human destiny that makes for cavalier conservatism, nor possessed of the possessions that make for self-interested conservatism, nor imbued with the capacity to truncate intellectual from psychic terms of existence that lead to adopting conventional law or social science pluralist research norms while "voting for (a little) change" as persons, nor yet endowed with the sheer unoriginality, the moral indifference, of most essentially derivative academic intellects.

274. Tushnet, *supra* note 271, at 1399.

thinking to reject Marxism as verbally careless, hence not to be taken seriously.

This, very likely, accounts for the first of four main characteristics that differentiate Tushnet's "weaker Marxist approach" from his 1978 grand version. Those four characteristics are (1) a sense that Marxist language is often awkwardly metaphorical; (2) a concomitant uncertainty about whether such language can adequately cope with four recurrent criticisms of Marxist theory in general; (3) doubt not only as to the capacity of a Marxist explanation of law to explain its "content" but also about its capacity to explain much of the law's form; and (4) substantial inspecificity concerning that which remains distinctively Marxist about what is left in the approach.

With respect to the first characteristic — the metaphoric deficiencies of Marxist explanatory language — the "current Tushnet" almost gives up on any concerted defense, saying, for example: "A Marxist analysis of law claims that there is a reasonably systematic relation between the law and the relations of production, with the latter *more or less sort of determining* the former. (The fuzziness is . . . inevitable.)"[275] Elsewhere, he contrasts reductionism and liberalism, which appear to have adequate metaphors as to what law is and how it functions, with Marxism, which does "not have the metaphors at hand for 'relative autonomy.' "[276]

481

As to the second characteristic, Tushnet recognizes four recurrent criticisms of Marxism: (a) a problem of mechanism, which most non-Marxists attack;[277] (b) the problem of law as constitutive, which "arises pretty much within the Marxist camp";[278] (c) the problem of reification, which he argues is "the peculiar American contribution to the discussion";[279] and (d) the problem of the extent to which

---

275. Tushnet, 1983 Marxism as Metaphor, *supra* note 228, at 1 (emphasis added).

276. Tushnet, British Review, *supra* note 228, at 123.

277. The problem is to explain the mechanism by which capitalist law subserves ruling class interests — given judges' formal independence from class pressures as well as the scantiness of evidence indicating that judges believe that they are not independent or that they act as "instruments of the ruling class." Tushnet, 1983 Marxism as Metaphor, *supra* note 228, at 1.

278. *Id.* The problem of law as constitutive is:

[i]n its simplest version . . . : class relations are defined in terms of whether or not members of a class own the means of production. Yet ownership is a legal category which takes on its meaning only because of its relation to all the other available legal categories. Law thus seems to define or constitute class relations, in which case it is circular to say that the relations of production sort of determine the law. How then is a Marxist analysis of law possible?

Id. at 1-2.

279. *Id.* at 2. One could argue with Tushnet's view that there is something particularly distinctive about American legal realism as a source of objections that Marxist language is unduly prone to reification. But here is his statement of the problem:

Most Marxists seem to want to say that a rule of law — the fellow servant rule is a classic

Marxist analysis is "scientific" or "normative."[280] Tushnet's discussion of these problems is disarmingly frank. But some of his conclusions — for example, that the most satisfactory answers to the problems of mechanism and of law as constitutive "weaken the claim that Marxists have a special way of analyzing the law"[281] — run the risk of disarming the analysis entirely. So too, his declarations "that one cannot readily distinguish within the Marxist tradition between Marxism as a sociological/historical theory and Marxism as a normative critique of capitalism,"[282] and that "it is more fruitful"[283] to assume that a Marxist theory must be sociological with "the normative critique . . . immanent in the theory,"[284] do not really get us very far.

With respect to the third characteristic, Tushnet, after deciding that Marxism is not likely to explain effectively the content of capitalist law, even waffles as to Marxism's ability to explain that law's form. Having agreed with Hugh Collins that the only explanatory candidate is "one that deals with the form and not the content of the law," and that the "commodity exchange theory is the leading, perhaps the only, contender of that [form-only-explaining] sort,"[285] Tushnet goes on to argue that a "Marxist theory of the legal form may be impossible."[286]

What, then, are we left with if not substantial uncertainty as to what is distinctively Marxist? We have a concern for setting about the hard work of developing a position between liberalism and reductionism,[287] a concern for explaining the law's "relative autonomy," and a set of unsolved analytic problems about the law's relationship to the economic infrastructure. We have also an inher-

482

---

example—serves class interests. Yet the legal realists taught us that there never was a "fellow servant rule" that could be a dependent variable to be explained in terms of its links to the economic base. There were and always are rules and counterrules, rules with exceptions of such scope as to threaten the rule itself, rules whose force can be eliminated by creatively drawing on analogies to apparently unrelated areas of law, and so on. Statutes too have to be interpreted . . . and cannot be understood as . . . words whose meaning is fixed at the time of enactment. What then can Marxist analysis try to analyze? *Id.* at 2. I am not convinced that all these problems are exactly mind-stumpers.

280. Tushnet, 1981 Marxist Theory, *supra* note 228, at 3.

281. Tushnet, 1983 Marxism as Metaphor, *supra* note 228, at 2 (discussing Hugh Collins' answer to these problems in H. COLLINS, MARXISM AND LAW (1982)).

282. Tushnet, 1981 Marxist Theory, *supra* note 228, at 3.

283. *Id.*

284. *Id.*

285. Tushnet, 1983 Marxism as Metaphor, *supra* note 228, at 15 (discussing H. COLLINS, *supra* note 281).

286. Tushnet, 1983 Marxism as Metaphor, *supra* note 228, at 15.

287. *See* Tushnet, BRITISH REVIEW, *supra* note 228, at 122.

Michigan Law Review

ent normative critique of capitalism and of legal scholars who do their scholarship, whether as liberals or as conservatives, without regard to the norms embraced in that critique. What does that amount to? Tushnet concedes the resultant analytic anemia, though he declares that he is "comfortable with such an anemic reconstruction of a Marxist theory of law"[288] — even if the reconstruction looks more like destruction and even if the end point seems very "close to liberal sociology."[289]

THE ROAD AHEAD

If that were all that could be said about Tushnet's Marxist theory of American law, non-Marxists might reasonably close the book on it without more. Nor would Tushnet's three reasons for referring to his position as Marxist, given just after the above-quoted declaration of satisfaction with analytic anemia, convince us otherwise: (1) that "the effort to produce a sociological theory that is both good and distinctively Marxist may be thought to have failed, but negative results . . . are nonetheless important";[290] (2) that "calling the theory Marxist is a statement of affiliation with an international tradition of struggle for liberation [including] the upheavals in Poland";[291] and (3) that it is important to "emphasiz[e] . . . political distance from liberalism."[292] This runs the danger of seeming closer to moral posturing than to something worth examining at length.

483

There are, however, the other "two faces" of Tushnet — those that appear when he turns from attempts to develop systematic theory to legal history and to critiques of contemporary constitutional scholarship. These represent, after all, the bulk of his analytic contributions to legal scholarship. Their examination may be worthwhile.

To anticipate the sequel to this Article, it may be argued that such examination *is* fruitful for three reasons. First, analysis of those contributions reveals that many of their strengths and weaknesses come from a curiously disjointed shoving together of "strong" Neo-Legal-Realist and "weak" Marxist approaches. Second and more specifically, this shoving together produces not analytic chaos or anemia in applied analysis, but rather a recurrent and unintentionally patterned series of insights and blindnesses about the state of con-

---

288. Tushnet, 1981 Marxist Theory, *supra* note 228, at 29.
289. *Id.*
290. *Id.*
291. *Id.* at 30.
292. *Id.*

temporary legal scholarship and late twentieth century American law. Third, construed together with other recent radical analyses — for example, those of Karl Klare and Roberto Unger — the upshot is a correct diagnosis of severe strain in the law's capacity to deal with American social and economic problems but an incorrect diagnosis as to the primary culprit — liberalism. American problems, I would argúe, are more complex than that. So too, both their solutions and the roles of laws, judges, and legal scholars in venturing toward such solutions are more complicated than the problem-solving analytic recourse explicit in much "radical analysis" of American law — abjuring liberal law and liberal legalism in favor of Karl Marx.

484

"Legal History" or the History of Law: A Primer on Bringing the Law's Past into the Present*

*Stephen B. Presser***

I. INTRODUCTION

Ten years ago, legal history was not taken particularly seriously, and there was still much truth in Daniel Boorstin's 1965 lament that "while lawyers, judges, and law professors repeat platitudes about their glorious professional past, they find no respectable place for legal history in their extensive curricula."[1] With the publication in 1973 of Lawrence Friedman's *A History of American Law*,[2] however, American law professors could quickly gain an overview of their own disciplines and bring law school legal history courses out of thirteenth century England.[3] Five years later, Morton J. Horwitz' book on American legal history[4] won the Bancroft Prize, whicʰ is Columbia University's award for outstand-

* This Article is based on remarks that the author gave on June 1, 1981, as an address at the American Association of Law Schools' Conference on Teaching Contracts, which was held at the University of Wisconsin Law School in Madison, Wisconsin.

** Professor of Law, Northwestern University School of Law. A.B. 1968, J.D. 1971, Harvard University. My colleagues Timothy Breen and Brook Manville made helpful criticisms of an early draft, for which I thank them.

1. D. BOORSTIN, THE AMERICANS: THE NATIONAL EXPERIENCE 444 (1965).

2. L. FRIEDMAN, A HISTORY OF AMERICAN LAW (1973).

3. The materials always had been available for the few people who had the substantial fortitude to assemble them. The pioneers were Mark De Wolfe Howe, J. Willard Hurst, George Haskins, and Julius Goebel, Jr. *See, e.g.*, C. AUERBACH, L. GARRISON, J. W. HURST & S. MERMIN, THE LEGAL PROCESS: AN INTRODUCTION TO DECISION-MAKING BY JUDICIAL, LEGISLATIVE, EXECUTIVE, AND ADMINISTRATIVE AGENCIES (1961); J. GOEBEL, CASES AND MATERIALS ON THE DEVELOPMENT OF LEGAL INSTITUTIONS (1931); G. HASKINS, LAW AND AUTHORITY IN EARLY MASSACHUSETTS: A STUDY IN TRADITION AND DESIGN (1960); M. HOWE, READINGS IN AMERICAN LEGAL HISTORY (1949).

Friedman synthesized and built upon the work of Hurst and his school. The availability of Friedman's work made it more likely that American law schools would be able to offer legal history courses that met Calvin Woodard's prescription for "relevance" by concentrating on nineteenth-century America—a period that law students might find more pertinent than the traditional focus of late medieval England. *See* Woodard, *History, Legal History, and Legal Education*, 53 VA. L. REV. 89, 113-21 (1967).

4. M. HORWITZ, THE TRANSFORMATION OF AMERICAN LAW 1780-1860 (1977).

ing historical scholarship and probably the history discipline's highest professional honor. This selection marked the first time that a work in American legal history had won the award, and it conferred a new mantle of legitimacy on legal historians in general. These two books, plus a few significant others,[5] generated dozens of reviews in legal publications,[6] and those periodicals began to publish pieces concerning the history of American law on a far more regular basis.[7] By 1979 two major lawbook publishers apparently had become convinced that a new potential market existed for American legal history textbooks,[8] and almost all law schools now offer either a course or a seminar in American legal history.

486

Two other factors besides the recent effusion of scholarship have contributed to the growing respectability of American legal history in the legal curricula. One is the newly perceived, post-Watergate need for ethics in the law. Legal history, as it is practiced currently, concerns the discovery, articulation, and evaluation of the norms that have guided American courts, legislatures, and lawyers in the past; this information supposedly sharpens one's judgment about the appropriate values to implement in the future. Second, many undergraduates contemplating law school now are pursuing increasingly specialized curricula. Until recently, many schools simply did not encourage a generalized course of study, and educational specialization seemed to offer a surer and safer chance to achieve the high grade point averages now needed for admission to law school. As a result, some students believe that law school offers the last chance to obtain a dose of humanistic learning. These students often conclude that although philosophical insights might not readily be gained in most law school courses, the perspective acquired in courses such as American legal history can contribute both a missing sense of community of endeavor and an antidote to the cynical instrumentalism that so often prevails in law schools.[9]

---

5. *See, e.g.,* M. BLOOMFIELD, AMERICAN LAWYERS IN A CHANGING SOCIETY 1776-1876 (1976); W. NELSON, AMERICANIZATION OF THE COMMON LAW (1975); G. WHITE, THE AMERICAN JUDICIAL TRADITION (1976).

6. For a collection of many of some reviews, see LAW IN THE AMERICAN REVOLUTION AND THE REVOLUTION IN THE LAW: A COLLECTION OF REVIEW ESSAYS ON AMERICAN LEGAL HISTORY (H. Hartog ed. 1981) [hereinafter cited as LAW IN THE AMERICAN REVOLUTION].

7. *See, e.g.,* ESSAYS IN NINETEENTH CENTURY AMERICAN LEGAL HISTORY (W. Holt ed. 1976) (collecting many law review articles on legal history).

8. *See, e.g.,* S. PRESSER & J. ZAINALDIN, LAW AND AMERICAN HISTORY: CASES AND MATERIALS (1980); READINGS ON THE AMERICAN LEGAL PROFESSION (D. Nolan ed. 1980).

9. *Cf.* Kronman, *Foreword: Legal Scholarship and Moral Education,* 90 YALE L.J. 955

The increasing opportunities to teach legal history in law schools and the lamentable decline of positions available to historians in undergraduate institutions have resulted in more historians either teaching in law schools or combining graduate training in history with graduate training in law. As a result, several methodologies or approaches to legal history have emerged. Although legal history has generated a great deal of comment,[10] few have written about how this spate of scholarship and criticism might affect law school teaching. This Article attempts to categorize and to review, therefore, the kinds of insights that American legal history currently offers both to law students and to law professors. Parts II and III of the Article sketch the parameters of the legal history discipline and describe the variant historiographical approaches that scholars recently have adopted. Part IV then offers some suggestions for integrating legal history into selected law school courses.

487

II. The Core Values of American Legal History

As a "perspective course," legal history seeks to raise law students to a new level of insight; to permit them, in Holmes' memorable phrase, to hear some of "the echoes of the infinite";[11] and to make them appreciate that the nature of what has gone before facilitates and circumscribes what happens in the law today. Because legal history necessarily deals with longer time periods than do other law school courses, legal history professors more easily can discern and elaborate on the nature of the past and the process of change in the law. Like other law professors, those who teach legal history seek ultimately to prepare lawyers to condition their legal actions not only to the immediate needs of their clients, but also to the continuing needs of the constitutional order. The advantage of an extra degree of removal from the more immediate doctrinal and procedural requirements of practice, however, puts legal historians in a unique position to underscore these duties and obligations of prospective lawyers.

This broader aspect of American legal history teaching potentially offers the greatest reward for both teacher and student. Since one can assume that many law students could have pursued alter-

---

(1981) (discussing law professors' obligations to use their scholarship and teaching to promote a reverence for truth and to fight cynicism in their students).

10. *See, e.g.,* Law in the American Revolution, *supra* note 6.

11. Holmes, *The Path of the Law,* 10 Harv. L. Rev. 457, 478 (1897).

native graduate business courses that could have provided quicker and more substantial financial reward than could the practice of law, one can also assume that law students are after more than money. At some level, then, although one must probe very deeply in some stubborn cases, a law professor may draw on a shared commitment to altruistic enterprise, a shared desire to implement ideals of justice, and a shared realization that the law—whatever its current or past limitations—has been a principal instrument in the physical betterment of mankind's condition. Actually showing law students that they are engaged in a worthy struggle of this sort provides an experience that confirms the value of instruction for both teacher and student and can lead to some of the solutions modern society so desperately needs in its search for meaning in human existence.

488

One can also describe this value of legal history teaching in Edmund Burke's metaphorical terms by characterizing the job of law professors in general, and legal historians in particular, as an attempt to convince students that they must view the law as Burke viewed the social contract. Burke argued that this contract does not constitute an agreement which is easily dissolvable by one of its parties, but is instead an ongoing partnership among members of society in all science, art, and virtue.[12] Since the ends of such a partnership cannot be obtained without the effort of many generations, Burke suggested, "it becomes a partnership not only between those who are living, but between those who are living, those who are dead, and those who are to be born."[13] Similarly, the law professor's task is to suggest to students the dangers of pursuing legal quests for instantaneous transformations, utopian solutions, or even short-term manipulations that eventually might undermine the long-term goals of American law. To make all these glittering generalities meaningful, as well as to set some manageable and intelligible limits on the multi-generational partnership, one necessarily must specify what the goals of American law have been. Fortunately, this task has preoccupied the teaching and scholarship of most recent legal historians.[14]

---

12. E. Burke, Reflections on the Revolution in France 194-95 (O'Brien ed. 1969).
13. *Id.*
14. Another way to state these ultimate goals of law teaching is to suggest that professors should communicate to students that they are involved in an important international human dialogue which seeks to determine the appropriate modern jurisprudential principles for the promotion of justice. This dialogue—or search—attempts to uncover American equivalents for the civil-law concepts of "Recht" or "Droit," which are used to formulate

As suggested below,[15] however, no general agreement exists among legal historians about the prominence of any single, over-arching theme in American legal history. Consequently, perhaps the best approach to the study of legal history is to stress the variety and the richness of the goals of the various legal doctrines as they have evolved and to emphasize that much of American law has concerned the reconciliation of conflicting aims and values in our legal culture.[16] Since at least the early nineteenth century, several prominent ideals, which properly can be characterized as "core values," have been evident in American law. Although lawyers and laymen generally agree that these several ideals are desirable, the problem of their order of priority has been a source of great conflict, since the ideals, when pushed to their limits, exclude or diminish one another. This part of the Article describes these core values and then uses them as a means of thematic discrimination to explain some of the current variant approaches to American legal history.

489

The most basic core value of American law[17]—and, indeed, of virtually any human society—is the ideal enshrined in the concept of the "rule of law" itself: any compulsion in the society must not take place arbitrarily, but must be subject to some restraints. These restraints might develop from a variety of diverse sources, including the law of nature, God, the social contract, or clearly announced and procedurally valid acts of the temporal sovereign.

---

standards for evaluating the specific positive rules of law. *See* Fletcher, *Two Modes of Legal Thought*, 90 YALE L. J. 970, 980-84 (1981).

15. *See infra* notes 34-96 and accompanying text.

16. The effort to stress competing values is emerging as a useful corrective for both "legal nominalism"—the notion that no legal rules are inherently better than any others—and the "efficiency" or "wealth maximization" school of economic analysis of law, which holds out greater material prosperity as the aim of the law. Fletcher, *supra* note 14, at 995-96. Fletcher emphasizes two recent efforts to study the variated nature of legal values. *See* B. ACKERMAN, PRIVATE PROPERTY AND THE CONSTITUTION (1977) (differing approaches to compensation for governmental appropriation of private property); Kennedy, *Form and Substance in Private Law Adjudication*, 89 HARV. L. REV. 1685 (1976) (relative influences of altruism and idealism in the history of contract law).

17. The four core values that are described below might well be criticized as "cartesianism, the construction of drastically simplified models of social reality," and thus as an unacceptable reduction of the real complexities of the historical context. *See* Gordon, *Historicism in Legal Scholarship*, 90 YALE L.J. 1017, 1025-28 (1981). Nevertheless, the approach *has* proved heuristic, and—at least as far as beginning legal history students are concerned—the process of illuminating the richness of the historical context must start somewhere. Some cartesianism, therefore, may be necessary to perform a current "criticial academic task, . . . to clarify the competing ideals currently struggling for ascendency . . . by placing them in historical . . . context." Ackerman, *The Marketplace of Ideas*, 90 YALE L.J. 1131, 1140 (1981).

This most basic principle represents the idea that the legal system must provide *restraints on arbitrary power*.[18] Because of the primacy of this core value, it can be discerned earliest in what might be characterized as the beginning of the American legal culture—the time during our colonial period in which we mirrored the struggles of the English in their civil wars and their Glorious Revolution through American events such as the Zenger Trial,[19] the Writs of Assistance Case,[20] and the writing of the Declaration of Independence.

The second core value of the American legal culture is the ideal of *popular sovereignty*. Following its rebirth in Europe,[21] this notion emerged in America as people began to accept the idea that the best way to prevent the exercise of arbitrary power is to disperse political power as widely as possible and to lodge ultimate sovereignty in the citizenry. The second core value was born soon after the first[22] and was certainly of paramount importance in the theoretical framework both of the Declaration of Independence and of the federal constitution of 1787. This legal ideal, however, is perhaps the most problematic—if not the most hypocritical—of all the four values: women and racial and ethnic minorities effectively have been excluded from the definition of "people" throughout much of American history, and the people themselves can never effectively exercise sovereignty because some representative must exercise it on their behalf. For these reasons, the founding fathers proclaimed the United States to be a republic and not a democracy. Nevertheless, as American history has unfolded, many people often have equated the principle of popular sovereignty with the

490

---

18. Many of the assertions that are made in this part of the Article are developed in their historical context in the Teacher's Manual to S. PRESSER & J. ZAINALDIN, *supra* note 8. For one of the most influential statements of freedom as the absence of subjection to arbitrary power, see J. LOCKE, THE SECOND TREATISE OF GOVERNMENT ch. IV, ¶ 22 (1690).

19. *See* J. ALEXANDER, A BRIEF NARRATIVE OF THE CASE AND TRIAL OF JOHN PETER ZENGER 1 (1972). Peter Zenger was tried in New York in 1735 for seditious libel, and a jury acquitted him after an historic argument by his lawyer, Andrew Hamilton. The case marked an early statement in colonial America that the sovereign was not immune from criticism. *Id.* at 34-35.

20. For the primary sources on this case—also known as "Paxton's Case"—in which American Whigs argued that unlimited search warrants were unconstitutional instruments of tyranny, see S. PRESSER & J. ZAINALDIN, *supra* note 8, at 61-89.

21. *See, e.g.,* J. LOCKE, *supra* note 18.

22. An example of its operation in colonial America is Andrew Hamilton's rhetoric in the Zenger trial. *See* J. ALEXANDER, *supra* note 19. The controversy over proprietary quitrents in New Jersey in the 1740's provides another example of this second core value. *See* Presser, *An Introduction to the Legal History of Colonial New Jersey*, 7 RUT.-CAM. L.J. 262 (1976).

idea of democracy, and they have never made it universally clear whether our legal system exists to implement the wishes of the people, or whether it exists merely to effect what the representa-tives think best benefits the people.

The tensions brought about by the impossibility of the complete implementation of popular sovereignty and, in particular, the risk of divergent interests among the people and their rulers, fairly quickly generated a third core value of American law, which can be characterized as the *maintenance of maximum economic opportunity and social mobility.* Pursuant to this ideal, Americans rejected the institution of privileged orders and social deference—because it led to the exercise of arbitrary powers—and fairly early focused on the idea that oppression would be minimized and something akin to democracy would be best assured by allowing capable individuals to accumulate wealth and rise in social standing and commercial power. This principle of American law was in full operation by the time of the Jacksonian entrepreneurs[23] and may have reached its fullest expression in Chief Justice Taney's opinion in *Charles River Bridge v. Warren Bridge.*[24] This third core value, however, was influential from the beginning of American history and manifested itself in a hatred both of the English aristocratic feudal order and of any remnants of that order in the English common law. One of the clearest early displays of this antipathy occurred in the late 1780's, when the Boston Merchant Honestus questioned the need for lawyers, a group which he believed to be an unnecessary and odiously privileged class in a republic.[25] Nevertheless, the principle did not receive what was probably its most coherent form until well into the nineteenth century, when its most profound legal impact was to end the hegemony of the *rentier* interest in American law and to substitute the ascendence of fluid, entrepreneurial, commercial, and manufacturing

491

---

23. For studies of how the egalitarian philosophy of the Jacksonian years included a component that stressed the duty of each man enterpreneurially to accumulate as much wealth as possible, see S. BRUCHEY, THE ROOTS OF AMERICAN ECONOMIC GROWTH 1607-1861, at 193-207 (1968); S. PRESSER & J. ZAINALDIN, *supra* note 8, at 260-63; P. TEMIN, THE JACKSONIAN ECONOMY (1965).

24. 36 U.S. (11 Pet.) 420 (1837). *See also* K. NEWMYER, THE SUPREME COURT UNDER MARSHALL AND TANEY 95-98 (1968). In the *Charles River Bridge* case Chief Justice Taney held that a new bridge company's charter was constitutional, even though it arguably contravened a conferral of an implied monopoly in an old bridge company's charter. *See infra* notes 154-61 and accompanying text.

25. B. Austin, *Observations on the Pernicious Practice of the Law, As Published Occasionally in the Independent Chronicle in the Year 1786,* at 7-10 (1819), *reprinted in part in* S. PRESSER & J. ZAINALDIN, *supra* note 8, at 264-66.

wealth.[26]

A final core value of American law began to evolve at the turn of the nineteenth century, when it became increasingly evident that democracy, social mobility, and the ideal of restraints on arbitrary power might best be realized if the legal system allowed the primary economic and industrial development decisions to be directed by Adam Smith's "invisible hand."[27] By according primacy to doctrines such as freedom of contract,[28] American law increasingly recognized that the national interest would best be served by carving out a large sphere of private initiatives and interests—immune from governmental intervention or regulation—where the free market, rather than the state, might maximize development.[29] In the late nineteenth and early twentieth centuries, this free enterprise ideal of the *maximum protection and promotion of private interests and initiatives* became perhaps the dominant value of American public and private law,[30] although it has lost considerable ground since the New Deal years. The ideal of protected spheres of private interests was evident in crude form in the early years following the American revolution—both in the state declarations of rights[31] and in the Federal Bill of Rights of 1791[32]—although in those early years the primary protected private interests probably were more spiritual and political than economic in nature. Nevertheless, explicit reference in American law to Smith's market-oriented views can be found as early as the Philadelphia Cordwainers trial in 1806.[33]

492

---

26. The manner in which the *rentier* interest—that is, the power, wealth, and influence of great landowners—lost out to entrepreneurial sectors in the battle over who ought to benefit most from legal doctrines is the subject of M. HORWITZ, *supra* note 4.

27. The "invisible hand" notion suggests that the accumulation and conflict of individual private interests will lead to the most efficient allocation of resources and production. For an accessible introductory treatment of Smith's "invisible hand" idea, see R. HEILBRONER, THE WORLDLY PHILOSOPHERS 38-44 (rev. ed. 1967).

28. For descriptions of how freedom of contract became a dominant concept in antebellum law, see M. HORWITZ, *supra* note 4; W. NELSON, *supra* note 5.

29. *Cf.* C. MACPHERSON, THE POLITICAL THEORY OF POSSESSIVE INDIVIDUALISM: HOBBES TO LOCKE 272-73 (1962) (discussing how Hobbes' and Locke's work has been interpreted in modern democracies to support capitalist enterprise and individual effort).

30. *See, e.g.,* S. PRESSER & J. ZAINALDIN, *supra* note 8, at 674-705 and sources cited therein.

31. *See, e.g.,* PA. CONST. of 1776, ch. I, art. I ("inherent and unalienable rights" include "acquiring possessing and protecting property"), *reprinted in* S. PRESSER & J. ZAINALDIN, *supra* note 8, at 114.

32. *See, e.g.,* U.S. CONST. amends. I, IV, and V (protection for religion, speech, privacy in dwellings, and property).

33. Commonwealth v. Pullis, Mayor's Ct. of Philadelphia (1806).

With these four core values of American legal history delineated, we now can articulate and evaluate the divergent approaches that scholars have taken to the study of American legal history. In elaborating upon these current schools of legal history, the next part of the Article also suggests some of the outstanding writings in the area that profitably might be consulted by beginners.

III. CURRENT "SCHOOLS" OF AMERICAN LEGAL HISTORY

Four schools of legal history are discernible from the current literature in the area. This literature includes major works that are representative of each school, as well as critical book reviews that often are as important as the works themselves, in part because they provide a format for the intellectual sniping that recently has enlivened legal historical scholarship. As should be evident from the discussion below, legal history, along with the subject of law and economics,[34] is today generating some of the most sharply divided scholarship in legal literature.

493

The first school of legal history that seems to be discernible adopts the notion that law has followed an orderly evolution according to fixed intellectual principles and, thus, may be labelled the "conservative school." These legal historians come closest to replicating the thinking of the great English and American Whig historians like Lord Macaulay or George Bancroft.[35] To begin with the first of several sweeping generalizations, the practitioners of this school believe that the enterprise of legal decisionmaking predominantly has proceeded according to certain neutral principles. They posit that although the substantive law might have varied over time and might have been created to meet particular social or economic needs, the basic principles of the law have not changed. By focusing on the maintenance of particular principles, the practitioners of this first school emphasize the first core value of American law that was discussed above[36]—namely, the restraint of arbitrary power, the "rule of law" itself, or, simply, the notion of adherence to precedent.

---

34. For the latest examinations of law and economics, see *Symposium on Efficiency as a Legal Concern*, 8 HOFSTRA L. REV. 485 (1980); *A Response to the Efficiency Symposium*, 8 HOFSTRA L. REV. 811 (1980).

35. *See, e.g.*, G. BANCROFT, HISTORY OF THE UNITED STATES OF AMERICA, FROM THE DISCOVERY OF THE CONTINENT (1883); H. BUTTERFIELD, THE WHIG INTERPRETATION OF HISTORY (1931); T. MACAULAY, THE HISTORY OF ENGLAND, FROM THE ACCESSION OF JAMES THE SECOND (1866).

36. *See supra* notes 17-20 and accompanying text.

Oliver Wendell Holmes, Jr., for example, explained much of American tort law by pointing to the courts' efforts to maintain the principle of no liability without fault, and he explained much of American and English contract law using the principle of consideration.[37] Similarly, Roscoe Pound characterized legal developments as the orderly evolution of legal doctrines brought about by judges' searching for principles in previous cases and applying them to new situations, a process which he described as a "taught legal tradition."[38] G. Edward White, the latest proponent of this school, pushes the analysis to a slightly different level,[39] but he nevertheless contends that certain legal principles—mostly procedural ones—circumscribe the role of judges and ensure that they adhere to a coherent "American judicial tradition."[40] The common thread that ties together the work of all these scholars, then, is a primary emphasis on intellectual judging paradigms and a relegation of economic, political, and social influences to a secondary level.

494

The practitioners of the second group of legal historians, the "Wisconsin school,"[41] view economic needs as the primary determinants of law. Although any generalization slights the subtlety of the school's best analysis, its adherents widely perceive law as a tool to be used by the most productive sectors of American society in "releasing their energy."[42] This group as a rule focuses primarily on the third core value discussed above of maintaining maximum economic progress and social mobility.[43] Adherents of the Wisconsin school apparently are more prepared than their conservative school counterparts to conclude that judges, legislators, lawyers, and other actors in the legal system often have been willing to abolish even the most fundamental principles or tenets of legal doctrines in the promotion of economic progress, and that the law can be almost totally malleable in the hands of those bent on

---

37. *See* O.W. HOLMES, THE COMMON LAW (1881).

38. *See* R. POUND, THE FORMATIVE ERA OF AMERICAN LAW (1938).

39. Although White appears to recognize to a greater degree than Pound or Holmes that judges self-consciously may be molding doctrines that are influenced by current political issues, he still finds dominant elements that continue from John Marshall to Earl Warren. G. WHITE, *supra* note 5.

40. *Id.*

41. This group is so named because its most distinguished practitioners taught or studied at the University of Wisconsin Law School. *See* White, Book Review, 59 VA. L. REV. 1130, 1132 (1973).

42. *See* J. HURST, LAW AND THE CONDITIONS OF FREEDOM IN THE NINETEENTH CENTURY UNITED STATES 3-32 (1956).

43. *See supra* notes 23-26 and accompanying text.

achieving their economic or political ends.[44] Practitioners of the
two schools seem to agree, however, that legal change reflects a
fundamental societal consensus on the appropriate values and
principles of the legal system. The Wisconsin school thus explains
much of nineteenth-century legal development as the result
of many—if not all—Americans concluding after the rise of the
Jacksonian entrepreneurs[45] that democracy could best be achieved
by promoting economic progress and social mobility.[46] If de
Tocqueville's findings are still considered valid, the evidence supporting this conclusion certainly seems strong.[47]

The work of the third school of legal history, of which Morton
J. Horwitz is perhaps the chief proponent,[48] shares with the Wisconsin school a focus on both the economic implications of legal
doctrines and the economic influences that create those doctrines.[49]
The practitioners of this "radical transformation school," however,
reject some of the relatively benign implications of the Wisconsin
school's historiography.[50] Instead of accepting that changes in
American law have transpired because of a consensus on appropriate legal values, for example, Horwitz suggests that a minority
comprised of merchants, industrial entrepreneurs, and lawyers—foisted a new legal order on an unwilling—or at least a hood-
winked—general populace.[51] According to this view, late eighteenth-century contract law focused primarily on principles of
substantive equity, including such formidable doctrines as the
sound price rule,[52] and the law in general was administered principally through the equitable discretion of juries. Horwitz, however,

495

---

44. *See, e.g.*, L. FRIEDMAN, *supra* note 2, at 14 ("The basic premise of this book is that
despite a strong dash of history and idiosyncrasy, the strongest ingredient in American law,
at any given time, is the present: current emotions, real economic interests, concrete political groups.").

45. *See supra* note 23.

46. *See, e.g.*, J. HURST, *supra* note 42 (nineteenth-century law promoted a "release of
energy" to secure the widest benefits of the American Revolution's political gains).

47. *See* I & II A. DE TOQUEVILLE, DEMOCRACY IN AMERICA (P. Bradley ed. 1945).

48. *See* M. HORWITZ, *supra* note 4.

49. *Id.* at xvi ("American legal system after the Revolution was transformed successfully to promote developmental goals.").

50. *See* Tushnet, *Perspectives on the Development of American Law: A Critical Review of Friedman's "A History of American Law,"* 1977 WIS. L. REV. 81.

51. For an explanation and critique of his analysis, see Presser, *Revising the Conservative Tradition: Towards a New American Legal History*, 52 N.Y.U. L. REV. 700 (1977),
reprinted in LAW IN THE AMERICAN REVOLUTION, *supra* note 6, at 113.

52. The payment of a "sound price" creates an enforceable, implied obligation that
the goods purchased be "sound"—that is, fit for the purpose for which they were purchased.
See M. HORWITZ, *supra* note 4, at 161-73, 180.

argues that in the nineteenth century the rule of *caveat emptor* replaced the sound price rule, the rules of contract generally were rigidified, and juries were forced more often to accept and act on the law as the judges delivered it to them.[53] According to Horwitz, certainty replaced equity as the central value of contract law, and the market mentality of industrial capitalism replaced the communitarian mentality of preindustrial America.[54] Putting the work of this school into the scheme of values that this Article has delineated then, Horwitz and others of his school are most interested in pursuing the conflict between the value of popular sovereignty[55]—to the extent that this value might be interpreted to dictate adherence to widely shared community standards of fairness and equity—and the value of maintaining maximum economic opportunity and social mobility.[56]

496

At least one commentator has called Horwitz' work marxist,[57] and, indeed, some of his views on the evolution of contract law do sound similar to Marx' notorious assertion in *The Poverty of Philosophy* that "[t]he Handmill gives you society with the feudal lord; the steam mill, society with the industrial capitalist."[58] According to Horwitz, the merchant and entrepreneurial class, once it gained ascendence in American society, proceeded to refashion the law to prevent further fundamental change and to ensure its continued dominance.[59] Horwitz argues that this development led to a period of "formalism" in the law which began in the middle of the nineteenth century[60] and to an era of outrageous and inequitable

---

53. *Id.* at 180, 197-201.

54. *See id.*; Presser, *supra* note 51.

55. *See supra* notes 21-22 and accompanying text.

56. *See supra* notes 23-26 and accompanying text. In his recent excellent work on the law of slavery, Mark Tushnet, the most prolific writer of the radical transformation school, described a similar conflict in Southern slavery law as "the competing pressures of humanity and interest." M. TUSHNET, THE AMERICAN LAW OF SLAVERY 1810-1860: CONSIDERATIONS OF HUMANITY AND INTEREST 5-6 (1981).

57. *See, e.g.*, Nelson, *Legal and Constitutional History*, 1978 ANN. SURV. AM. LAW 395, 397. Some of the other scholars in this school—for example, Tushnet and Feinman—use the theories of Marxism much more explicitly than Horwitz. *See, e.g.*, Feinman, *The Role of Ideas in Legal History*, 78 MICH. L. REV. 722 (1980); Tushnet, *A Marxist Analysis of American Law*, 1 MARXIST PERSPS. 96 (1979).

58. K. MARX, THE POVERTY OF PHILOSOPHY 202 (n.d.), *quoted in* P. SINGER, MARX 36 (1980).

59. M. HORWITZ, *supra* note 4, at 266.

60. *Id.* at 253-66. The idea of formalism as an exclusive, dominant, and deceptive strategy of jurisprudence apparently is no longer tenable. *See, e.g.*, Presser, *Judicial Ajax: John Thompson Nixon and the Federal Courts of New Jersey in the Late Nineteenth Century*, 76 Nw. U.L. REV. 423, 426 (1981), and sources cited therein. A distinctive, bom-

maldistribution of American society's material assets.[61] Unlike
Marx, however, Horwitz does not necessarily view the development
of the means of production as the primary force in history, nor
does he appear to share the classic Marxist idea that the inevitability of certain dialectical transformations in society ultimately will
lead to a proletarian revolution and a withering away of the state.
Nevertheless, one can find a strain of utopian socialism in Horwitz'
work, which manifests itself in his belief that if America can free
itself from the constraints of nineteenth-century legal concepts, it
might be able to fashion a truly equitable legal system.[62] Horwitz
presumably believes society then could return to some of the organizing principles of an earlier, uncorrupted America.

When Horwitz won Columbia's Bancroft Price in 1977, he naturally became a prominent target for criticism. Some commentators have suggested that these critical attacks have devastated his
scholarship,[63] but this proposition goes too far. The criticisms usually have focused on Horwitz' use of relatively few cases to support
his assertions, on other cases or legal sources that contradict his
readings of doctrinal development, or on his reliance upon authority from only a particular area of the country.[64] These criticisms

497

---

bastic judicial style clearly existed in the late nineteenth century, but it may have reflected
the resurgence of individualistic religious and moral fervor following the chaos of the American Civil War as much as it did a particular class attempt to impose its hegemony through
the law. *Id.* at 427-28. Horwitz, of course, does not argue in *The Transformation of American Law* that late nineteenth-century formalism represented some sort of self-conscious
conspiracy on the part of judges and other legal figures. *See* Presser, *Book Review*, 22 Am. J.
Leg. Hist. 359 (1978). Nevertheless, considering the prevalence and inevitability of "bourgeois individualism" in nineteenth-century American political life, one must question Horwitz' frequent use of the "deception" or "concealment" metaphor for what transpired in
American legal history. *Cf.* C. MacPherson, *supra* note 29, at 262-77 (underlying unit of
English political thought from the seventeenth to the nineteenth centuries was based on the
concept of "possessive individualism" from sixteenth-century political courts).

61. M. Horwitz, *supra* note 4, at 253-66.

62. *See, e.g.*, Horwitz, *The Legacy of 1776 in Legal and Economic Thought*, 19 J. L. &
Econ. 621 (1976) [hereinafter cited as *Legacy*]; Horwitz, *The Rule of Law: An Unqualified
Human Good?* (Book Review), 86 Yale L.J. 561 (1977) [hereinafter cited as Book Review].
Horwitz' concentration on the limiting effects of dominant legal paradigms reflects the influ-
ence of Thomas Kuhn's book, The Structure of Scientific Revolution (2d ed. 1971). *See*
Horwitz, *The Conservative Tradition in the Writing of American Legal History*, 17 Am. J.
Leg. Hist. 275, 282-83 (1973) [hereinafter cited as *The Conservative Tradition*]. Horwitz'
work thus appears to bear a strong resemblance to the work of the European "structuralist
Marxists," who explored the limiting characteristics of intellectual paradigms—*i.e.*, the
"structures" of human thought and action. *See* D. McClellan, Marxism after Marx, 298-
306 (1979) and sources cited therein.

63. *See, e.g.*, Scheiber, *Public Economic Policy and the American Legal System: Historical Perspectives*, 1980 Wis. L. Rev. 1159, 1168 n.45, and sources cited therein.

64. *Id.; see generally*, Bridwell, *Theme v. Reality in American Legal History*, 53 Ind.

for the most part are well reasoned, but their total impact may be less than the sum of their parts. Horwitz, as well as other members of the radical transformation school, still have much to contribute to our understanding both of the nature of change in the legal order and of how the work of particular actors influences others. Critics of this school often appear not to realize that one essential premise in the radical transformation theorists' work is that while the way society thinks about the law may change dramatically, at any given point in time only certain elements of the changes are perceptible.⁶⁵ Furthermore, Horwitz and his colleagues appear to assert that some doctrines of the law, or some legal actors, may at any given time be much more influential than others.⁶⁶ Thus, even if only five out of fifty cases decided at a particular time support their view, they might argue that those five decisions signal a dominant attitudinal change and thus should be entitled to the most weight in any analysis. Horwitz, therefore, generates criticism simply because he must deal with any historian's most perplexing problem—namely, assigning weight and order to a virtually infinite and contradictory body of fact. Since Horwitz' strong polemical statements often obscure this methodological problem, however, his critics have had an easy time pointing out evidence that contradicts his thesis.

On a final—and paradoxical⁶⁷—note before considering the last group of legal historians, the work of the radical transformation and conservative schools of legal history share a common problem: both schools—and, to a more limited extent, the Wisconsin school—base their historical interpretations on elusive premises concerning both the subjective nature of the nineteenth-century legal mind and how various patterns of thought influenced the law and each other. Since patterns of thought do not lend themselves to exact empirical verification, their theses are impossible ultimately to prove or disprove. To the extent that the radical transformation school explores the availability of *competing* intellectual paradigms—indeed, this type of inquiry lies at the heart of

498

L.J. 449 (1978).

65. *See, e.g.*, M. Horwitz, *supra* note 4, at 1-30 (discussing the emergence of an "instrumental conception" of law).

66. For instance, Horwitz' analysis suggests that Joseph Story is perhaps the best example of a jurist who was much more influential than others. *Id.* at 38-39, 55-56, 112, 118, 196-97, 205, 248-52, 258.

67. The radical transformationists level their most rigorous criticisms at the work of the conservatives. *See, e.g.*, Feinman, *supra* note 57; *The Conservative Tradition, supra* note 62.

the radical transformation thesis[68]—its analysis is inherently more satisfying than that of either the conservative school or the Wisconsin school, since the availability of competing intellectual paradigms appears to be an inevitable result of the competing values that are inherent in our legal culture.[69]

Viewed in this light, the radical transformation approach to legal history resembles the final discernible school of thought, which can be likened to Elizabethan tragedy or Greek mythology because it focuses on great men of the law. Like Horwitz, the proponents of the "heroic school" of legal history believe that exploring all the empirical minutiae of the law may prove misleading or counter-productive. Unlike the radical transformation theorists, however, heroic school historians believe that psychological and philosophical problems of the human condition determine their subjects' legal behavior more than do the means of production or economic development. In particular, heroic school historians study the ways in which their subjects constructed legal systems that initially were intended to resolve personal internal conflicts, but which were later applied in an effort to heal general societal conflicts. Heroic school scholars, therefore, are most comfortable in the mode of biography, and Leonard Levy's and Robert Cover's works on Chief Justice Shaw[70] are indicative of this preference. Levy and Cover do not view Shaw and his legal decisions either as the products of the economics of his time or as the results of a particular legal tradition, but rather as the results of the sheer force of his own personality. These authors believe that Shaw used his dynamic personality to implement a passionate commitment to particular and conflicting social, ethical, and political values that were not necessarily accepted in the legal system which existed at the time. Levy and Cover, for example, identify a central problem in Shaw's deep commitments both to abolish slavery and to preserve the federal union—namely, that the commitments place in conflict the legal values of democracy, private ordering, and adherence to the existing legal order.[71] Thus, the authors present Shaw's slavery decisions as an effort to resolve his inner conflict through the law. In following Shaw's attempts to determine the

499

---

68. *See supra* notes 55-56 and accompanying text.

69. *See supra* notes 11-33 and accompanying text.

70. *See* R. COVER, JUSTICE ACCUSED: ANTI-SLAVERY AND THE JUDICIAL PROCESS (1975); L. LEVY, THE LAW OF THE COMMONWEALTH AND CHIEF JUSTICE SHAW (1957).

71. *See* R. COVER, *supra* note 70, at 227-58, 249-56; L. LEVY, *supra* note 70, at 315-21, 323-30, 332-36.

proper obeisance to be accorded particular personal values or their legal analogues—in other words, in studying the allocative process of the heroic judge—the writer and the reader leave the realm of law and enter the realm of justice.

The heroic writers' perspective, therefore, is neither provincial nor particularly legal; on the contrary, it is universal. These writers transcend the four legal values delineated above because their work usually goes beyond the doctrines to study personalities. Nevertheless, one might characterize their work as the study of human attempts to reconcile the irreconcilable aspects of various legal and personal values. As Peter Teachout recently declared, the writers in this school are not really generating historical scholarship; they are producing literature.[72] These writers—among whom the author immodestly includes himself[73]—do not prove assertions by exhaustively marshalling and analyzing vast amounts of data. They probably perceive that an empirical analysis of law cannot be performed comfortably in a human lifetime and inevitably would lead to contradictory interpretations.[74]   Instead, therefore, they have written relatively short essays that are essentially more literary than historical.[75]

500

As Teachout has suggested, Gilmore remains the most visible practitioner of this methodology,[76] and his writing indeed may be works of allegory rather than history.[77] He rejects the conceptualists such as Holmes, Langdell, and Williston who would impose a rigid authoritarian order of "classical contract doctrines," perhaps because of weaknesses within themselves.[78] Gilmore's heroes are the Corbins, the Llewellyns, and, indeed, the Gilmores—great-spirited men who would infuse the law with pluralism, humanity,

---

72. Teachout, *Gilmore's New Book: Turning and Turning in the Widening Gyre* (Book Review), 2 Vt. L. Rev. 229 (1977).

73. *See, e.g.,* Presser, *supra* note 60; Presser, *A Tale of Two Judges: Richard Peters, Samuel Chase, and the Broken Promise of Federalist Jurisprudence,* 73 Nw. U.L. Rev. 26 (1978).

74. *See* Gordon, *Book Review,* 1974 Wis. L. Rev. 1216, 1238-39.

75. Some radical transformation work also lends itself to this "literary" characterization. Horwitz' book, for example, might be described as "Dark and Dostoyevskyan." *See* Presser, *supra* note 51, at 700.

76. *See generally* Teachout, *supra* note 72.

77. *See, e.g.,* G. Gilmore, The Ages of American Law (1977); G. Gilmore, The Death of Contract (1974).

78. For Gilmore's explanation of the influence of Langdell, Holmes, and Williston on the rise of the "classical" theory of contract, see G. Gilmore, The Death of Contract, *supra* note 77.

and flexibility.[79] Gilmore uses his allegory of these legal figures to show us both how bad the law might be or might become and how one might seek good and avoid evil.[80] He fears the new conceptualists like Posner—and, perhaps Horwitz—and warns of the injustices of magnificient Langdellian Gothic legal cathedrals.[81] Although Richard Speidel has argued that Gilmore's description of these legal giants' work is based more on myth or fantasy than reality,[82] his criticism may be off the mark. Gilmore, like the Greeks,[83] perceives that myth is often greater than reality.[84]

While each legal history school culls reality to organize their interpretations and create myths about the law, the heroic school—more than the others—constructs myths that underscore the uncertainty and paradoxes of life. In this way the heroic school's myths more closely resemble those of the great Greek writers of tragedy and epic poetry. Another distinctive characteristic of the heroic school is a nuance that Teachout appears to devine from Gilmore[85]—the recognition of the Elizabethan[86] character of legal man in general and of Oliver Wendell Holmes, Jr., in particular. According to Teachout, Gilmore, by reminding us both of Holmes' colossal creativity and of his massive insensitivity, "pulls into sharp focus the powerful contradictions in his character and thought, and explores searchingly the paradoxical connections be-

501

---

79. Gilmore's general tendency is to lavish praise on Corbin and censure on Langdell, Holmes, and Williston. *Id.* Corbin best captures what Gilmore lauds in the one-volume student edition of his famous treatise, *Contracts.* A CORBIN, CONTRACTS (1952). Llewellyn also demonstrates the humanistic sympathies that Gilmore seems to praise. *See* K. LLEWELLYN, THE COMMON LAW TRADITION: DECIDING APPEALS (1954).

80. *See* Teachout, *supra* note 72.

81. *Id.* at 235-37, 268.

82. *See* Speidel, *An Essay on the Reported Death and Continued Vitality of Contract,* 27 STAN. L. REV. 1161 (1975).

83. The suggestion that myth is greater than reality, for example, may be interpreted as a central theme of Plato's *Republic.* One can discern this theme both in his theory of the ideal forms (Books V and VII) and in his comments that his guardians must not be taught the works of some of the great Greek poets lest the poets' critical views of the gods corrupt them (Books II and III).

84. This cryptic statement simply means that since myth need not be circumscribed by what actually occurs, its range is great: since it need not take account of the complexities of reality, its power of expression is more perfect. Because myth, if believed, is as influential as reality, its power to influence may thus be greater.

85. Teachout, *supra* note 72 at 254-55 n.90.

86. Teachout's source for the description of Elizabethan character is D. BUSH, PREFACES TO RENAISSANCE LITERATURE 89 (1966), *cited in* Teachout, *supra* note 72, at 255 n. 90. Perhaps one of Shakespeare's best demonstrations of the duality of man's nature is the tragedy of Leontes, which is found in the first half of *The Winter's Tale.*

tween Holmes's darker and nobler natures."[87] This paradox might
be referred to as Elizabethan because late Renaissance thought in
England was characterized by its recognition of the "troubled, even
despairing, sense of man's inescapable duality, of his being pulled
at once toward the bestial and the angelic."[88] This view enables
Gilmore and the other proponents of the heroic school to embrace
at once, as did the Greeks and the Elizabethans, "lower depths and
loftier heights and richer tensions"[89] than are included in the views
that practitioners of the other schools espouse. This quasi-literary
view of man as inherently complex and contradictory better enables heroic school historians to describe legal development; it at
least enables them to communicate their insights more immediately to the reader. The practitioners of the fourth school thus are
better equipped to account simultaneously for all the inconsistent
core values in American law than are the writers who adhere to the
other schools.

502

Like the conservative school scholars, then, the heroic school
legal historians are interested primarily in the intellectual paradigms that their subjects utilized. The writings of the heroic
school, however, posit the existence of conflicting and competing
elements within the thought and philosophy of their subjects to a
greater extent than does the work of the conservatives. Like the
writers of other forms of literature, the writers of the fourth school
assume that man is after more than mere economic survival, and
they study legal man as he searches for spiritual as well as temporal salvation. Many of these characteristic elements of heroic
school writings appear in the work of other schools. In particular,
adherents of the radical transformation school[90]—particularly Horwitz—exhibit messianic or millenarian elements in their work and
are preoccupied with questions of justice and of human salvation.[91]
Nevertheless, while the radical transformationists ultimately seem
to believe that justice will best be secured—and a high quality of
life best assured—through a fundamental redistribution of material wealth and a new communitarian attitude in the law, the work
of the fourth school suggests no such prescription for utopia. He-

---

87. Teachout, *supra* note 72, at 255.

88. *Id.; see supra* note 86.

89. D. Bush, *supra* note 86, at 89, *quoted in* Teachout, *supra* note 72, at 255 n.90.

90. *See supra* notes 48-69 and accompanying text.

91. For statements of Horwitz' belief that society might be improved if we could shed
the odious aspects of our "rule of law" see *Legacy, supra* note 62; *Book Review, supra* note
62.

roic school scholars simply imply that to the extent salvation and a high quality of life are attainable, they will come only through individual striving and concentration on the unique characteristics and potential of particular individuals, rather than through concerted action based on the needs of the entire community. The fourth school's "heroic" concern, therefore, is more often with how the law enables heroic individuals to flourish, than with how some group might have misused the law to oppress the masses, or with how the law might be reformed to terminate the inherent alienation among the people and their rulers in an atomistic market society.

In sum, the four schools of legal history outlined above probably can be classified and distinguished according to their preoccupations with particular aspects of American law's four leading values. Thus, conservative school writers emphasize the first or paramount core value of the restraint of arbitrary power and the adherence to the rule of law concept.[92] Wisconsin school scholars, on the other hand, draw insights from the third value of American law—the maintenance of maximum economic opportunity and social mobility.[93] Members of the radical transformation school are preoccupied with questions of how the notion of popular sovereignty or democracy can be preserved and shielded from the arbitrary power that the law's promotion of economic progress creates.[94] Finally, heroic school writers concentrate on the contributions to the American legal culture of strong individuals, and, in so doing, they often consider the fourth value of American law—the maintenance of maximum freedom for private initiative.[95] This fourth value, more than any other, recognizes the need for competing conceptions of what is good for society and suggests that conflicts between and among the other legal values create a need for individuals to reach creative, unique, and different resolutions of the ordering of priorities in implementing the values of American law.

With the four values and the four schools of American legal history thus examined, this Article next suggests several ways in which the insights gained from current studies in legal history—particularly from the characterization of American legal history as a series of conflicts over competing values—might be inte-

503

---

92. *See supra* notes 17-20 & 35-40 and accompanying text.
93. *See supra* notes 23-26 & 41-47 and accompanying text.
94. *See supra* notes 21-26 & 48-69 and accompanying text.
95. *See supra* notes 27-33 & 70-91 and accompanying text.

grated into classroom teaching. Under the rubric of each school of
legal history, the Article examines several approaches that law
professors might adopt to use the history of law to illuminate current issues in their courses. Many of these approaches will be familiar to most professors; several are traditional "old chestnuts" of
law teaching. The aim, however, is to suggest how the "old
chestnuts," together with some new developments in legal historiography, might be employed to provide law students with a deeper
understanding of American law. Ultimately, the digestion of these
insights with the other classroom materials might lead to the satisfaction of law students' hunger for spiritual as well as instrumental
instruction. This possibility is particularly likely in first-year
courses, both because the first year is the most shattering, penetrating, and powerful experience for law students and because the
need for unifying philosophical explanations is strongest during
that time.[96]

504

IV. Selected Approaches to Integrating American Legal History into Legal Education

A. The Conservative School and the Containment of Arbitrary Power by the Rule of Law

1. Contracts

The dispute between Sir Edward Coke and James I over the
extent of the royal prerogative and its possible circumscription by
the English common law[97] provides perhaps the greatest vehicle for
the use of historical episodes in contracts courses to explain the
emergence of the rule of law as a restraint on arbitrary power. Although almost all contracts teachers probably make at least some
reference to the conflict between the common-law and equity
courts in the early seventeenth century, focusing on the several
face-to-face confrontations between Coke—as the common law's
representative—and assorted royal officials is perhaps the best way
to illuminate this historical controversy. Professors should comment on Coke's disputes over the question whether the King
should be subject to the constraints of the common law with Chancellors Ellesmere and Bacon, as the representatives of the preroga-

---

96. Most of the approaches suggested below are drawn from materials in first-year
courses—particularly contracts—because these are the courses with which most legal historians teaching in law schools are familiar.

97. For an excellent treatment of this conflict, see C. BOWEN, THE LION AND THE
THRONE 291-306 (1956).

tive courts of equity, with Archbishop Bancroft, as the representative of the Ecclesiastical Court of High Commission, and, finally, with James I himself. Although the conflict began as a personal struggle between Coke and the King and his ministers, it concluded with the assertion of parliamentary sovereignty and the execution of James' successor, Charles I, during the English Civil Wars. This struggle, therefore, is fascinating both for what it reveals about the emergence of the rule of law as a restraint on arbitrary power and for what it eventually signified in the American and English revolutions—namely, the idea that the English common law and the "fundamental rights of Englishmen" embody the essence of popular sovereignty.[98]

While this episode provides the traditional historical tool for underscoring the difficulties of concentrating discretion in equity judges, a great many other developments in early American history are instructive when addressing the core value of restraining arbitrary power. Perhaps the most helpful of these historical developments is the hostility with which Americans came to view the colonial Vice-Admiralty courts, which operated without juries. Examining that hostility naturally leads to the question of how the arbitrary power of jury discretion might itself frustrate contracts, and one ultimately might suggest that colonial reliance on juries —because of the colonists' belief in popular sovereignty —resulted in a conflict between the American legal values of popular sovereignty and the restraint of arbitrary power. Horwitz,[99] William Nelson,[100] and John Reid[101] have shown that colonial juries often used their equitable discretion to enforce popular prejudices, and this practice occasionally extended to voiding contracts that the English common law might have enforced.[102] In short, reference to English and American colonial history enables a contracts professor to explore one dimension of a traditional conflict in contracts courses—the conflict between certainty and equity.

When exploring the arbitrary operation of equity, one should always consider the methodological comments of perhaps our most famous Chancellor, James Kent, who said,

505

---

98. *See, e.g.,* B. BAILYN, THE IDEOLOGICAL ORIGINS OF THE AMERICAN REVOLUTION (1967); G. WOOD, THE CREATION OF THE AMERICAN REPUBLIC 1776-1787 (1969).

99. M. HORWITZ, *supra* note 4.

100. W. NELSON, *supra* note 5.

101. J. REID, IN A DEFIANT STANCE: THE CONDITIONS OF LAW IN MASSACHUSETTS BAY, THE IRISH COMPARISON, AND THE COMING OF THE AMERICAN REVOLUTION 27-28 (1977).

102. *Id.*

In 1814 I was appointed Chancellor. The office I took with considerable reluctance. . . . The person who left it was stupid, and it is a curious fact that for the nine years I was in that office there was not a single decision, opinion, or dictum of either of my two predecessors . . . , from 1777 to 1814, cited to me or even suggested. I took the court as if it has been a new institution, and never before known in the United States. I had nothing to guide me, and was left at liberty to assume all such English Chancery powers and _jurisdiction as I thought applicable under our Constitution. This gave me grand scope . . . .

. . . .

My practice was, first, to make myself perfectly and accurately . . . master of the facts. . . . I saw where justice lay, and the moral sense decided the [cause] half the time; and I then sat down to search the authorities until I had [exhausted] my books. I might once in a while be embarrassed by a technical rule, but I most always found principles suited to my views of the case . . . .[103]

2. Constitutional Law

506

One advantage of an historical approach to American law that emphasizes the overarching values of American legal culture is that it illuminates the correspondence between American public and private law.[104] Accordingly, the same difficulties with arbitrary power that are evident in contracts doctrines can be observed in the principles of American constitutional law. One prominent example illustrates the underpinnings of the fourth amendment's prohibition against unreasonable searches and seizures.[105] In the "Writs of Assistance"[106] case of 1761 the court considered whether colonial customs officials forcibly could search homes for contraband without first obtaining a special search warrant from a responsible magistrate that clearly identified the premises to be searched and the goods sought. English statutes authorized warrantless searches pursuant to "Writs of Assistance," which the Court of Exchequer routinely issued to customs officials when they assumed office.[107] The practice appears to have been followed in

---

103. W. KENT, MEMOIRS AND LETTERS OF JAMES KENT, LL.D. 157-59 (1898).

104. *Cf.* Hall, Book Review 77 Nw. U.L. REV. 112 (1982) (reflecting on the need to integrate the fields of constitutional and legal history).

105. U.S. CONST. amend. IV. The fourth amendment states that

[T]he right of the people to be secure in their persons, houses, papers, and effects, against unreasonable searches and seizures, shall not be violated, and no Warrants shall issue, but upon probable cause, supported by Oath or affirmation, and particularly describing the place to be searched, and the persons or things to be seized.

Id.

106. Paxton's Case of the Writ of Assistance, Quincy's Mass. Reports 51 (Sup. Ct. of the Province of Mass. 1761); *see* S. PRESSER & J. ZAINALDIN, *supra* note 8, at 61-89; M. SMITH, THE WRITS OF ASSISTANCE CASE (1978).

107. *See* 2 LEGAL PAPERS OF JOHN ADAMS 106-23 (L. Wroth & H. Zobel eds. 1965).

Massachusetts from 1755 until 1761, when, for various personal and political reasons, James Otis, Jr., a brilliant and fiery lawyer who was soon to emerge as a leader of the Whig opposition to England, appeared in Massachusetts court to challenge the legality of the writs.[108] Although Otis might have used several sophisticated and technical arguments to suggest that the English statutes authorizing the issuance of the general writs of assistance were inapplicable in America,[109] he instead grounded his argument on the assertion that employment of the writs constituted an absolutist exercise reminiscent of King John's and the Stuarts' abuses of the prerogative and, therefore, was "constitutionally" impermissible. Otis accused the writs of being "the worst instrument of arbitrary power, the most destructive of English liberty, and the fundamental principles of the constitution, that ever was found in an English law-book."[110] Otis reminded his listeners that such exercises of arbitrary power had "cost one King of England his head [Charles I] and another [James II] his Throne."[111] Pointing to the "fundamental principle" of the English Constitution that would justify invalidating the writs, Otis announced that "one of the most essential branches of English liberty . . . is the freedom of one's house. A man's house is his castle; . . . and while he is quiet, he is as well guarded as a prince in his castle. This writ . . . would totally annihilate this privilege."[112]

507

Attempting to bolster his arguments with a dubious misreading of Coke's opinion in *Dr. Bonham's Case*,[113] Otis demanded that the Massachusetts court throw out the writs because "AN ACT AGAINST THE CONSTITUTION IS VOID."[114] Although Otis eventually lost this particular battle, his ardent rhetoric had two

---

108. M. SMITH, *supra* note 106, at 216-17.

109. Otis, for example, could have argued that English statutes ought to be construed as not condoning "general" warrants. He also could have argued that the practices of the Exchequer court could not be duplicated in America. *See* 2 LEGAL PAPERS OF JOHN ADAMS, *supra* note 107, at 106-23.

110. S. PRESSER & J. ZAINALDIN, *supra* note 8, at 69 (quoting Massachusetts Spy, April 29, 1773, at 3, cols. 1-3).

111. *Id.*

112. *Id.* at 70.

113. Dr. Bonham's Case, 77 Eng. Rep. 638 (K. B. 1610) (according to the principles of the English common law, a statute could not be construed to make the Royal College of Physicians both a party and a judge in the same case). For the most lucid discussions of this "misreading" of Coke to find a general principle of the common law that permitted courts to invalidate parliamentary legislation as "unconstitutional," see 1 PAMPHLETS OF THE AMERICAN REVOLUTION 1750-1776, at 411-13 (B. Bailyn ed. 1965), and sources cited therein.

114. S. PRESSER & J. ZAINALDIN, *supra* note 8, at 71 (quoting Massachusetts Spy, *supra* note 110).

profound effects on American law. First, constitutional protection from unreasonable searches and seizures became enshrined in the Bill of Rights,[115] and, second, the notion of judicial review of legislation based on the principles and provisions of a constitution became the most original and enduring institution of American government.[116] The federal constitution's permanent establishment of judicial review resulted from myriad causes, but the principal one appears to have been the commercial uncertainty that the excessively democratic and prodebtor state legislation created during the period in which the Articles of Confederation were in force.[117] Although the arguments for the institution of judicial review may have been couched in terms of popular sovereignty,[118] the fear of arbitrary power permeates the philosophy of judicial review, which in its early American manifestations was shaped by the historical abuses of the English royal prerogative.

508

3. Antitrust Law

By the late nineteenth century, the legal and cultural value of restraining arbitrary power in America had become divorced from its foundations in resistance to Stuart absolutism. Fears that society once had directed against human beings began to be focused on supposedly impersonal, artificial creations—the American corporations. Instructors can pursue this aspect of the historical theme in many contexts, but it is perhaps best considered in the framework of the evolution of federal antitrust law in America. The passage of the Sherman Antitrust Act of 1890[119] may have constituted no more than a cosmetic gesture by a business-dominated Congress that was intent on quieting a massive public uproar by producing "some bill headed: 'A Bill to Punish Trusts' with which to go to the country."[120] Whatever the intention of the Act's drafters, however, the judicial perception that corporations were odious instruments of arbitrary power led the courts to attempt to restrain that

---

115. U.S. CONST. amend. IV.

116. For the classic theoretical statement of this notion, see THE FEDERALIST No. 78 (A. Hamilton). *See* Marbury v. Madison, 5 U.S. (1 Cranch) 137 (1803). A bolder articulation of the doctrine by a Federalist judge can be found in Chase's opinion in United States v. Callender, 25 F. Cas. 239, 254-58 (C.C.D. Va. 1800) (No. 14,709).

117. *See* G. WOOD, *supra* note 98, at 403-25.

118. *Id.* at 453-63, *see* THE FEDERALIST No. 78, *supra* note 116.

119. Ch. 647, § 1, 26 Stat. 209 (1890) (current version at 15 U.S.C. § 1 (1976)).

120. Letwin, *Congress and the Sherman Antitrust Law: 1887-1890*, 23 U. CHI. L. REV. 221, 221 n.4 (1956) (quoting L. COOLIDGE, AN OLD-FASHIONED SENATOR: ORVILLE H. PLATT 444 (1919)).

perceived arbitrary power through the antitrust laws. This development illustrates the importance of American cultural values both as social forces acting on—but ultimately independent of—legislators and as ideas capable of turning a legal placebo into a potent instrument of regulation or reform.

Prior to the Sherman Act state courts first articulated a "devil theory" of corporations. Some members of Congress had alluded to this notion in their rhetoric during the debates over the 1890 Act,[121] and the courts that subsequently interpreted the statute seemed to adopt the view rather consistently. In *Central Ohio Salt Co. v. Guthrie*,[122] for example, the state court declared that the "inevitable tendency" of manufacturers to allocate territories between themselves was "injurious to the public," and that even if such agreements were deemed not to have resulted either in the destruction of competition or in an unreasonable increase in price, courts would not enforce them because agreements among competitors eventually would damage the public.[123] Similarly, the Michigan Supreme Court remarked in *Richardson v. Buhl*[124] that this damage naturally resulted because "[t]he sole object of [such a] corporation is to make money, by having it in its power to raise the price of the article, or diminish the quantity to be made and used, at its pleasure."[125] The *Richardson* court stated that these corporations were nefarious, "artificial person[s], governed by a single motive or purpose, which is to accumulate money regardless of the wants or necessities of over 60,000,000 people."[126] Reflecting the deep-seated American fear of arbitrary power, the court concluded that the tendency of any monopoly was "destructive of free institutions, and repugnant to the instincts of a free people, and contrary to the whole scope and spirit of the federal constitution . . . . "[127] In sum, these courts were engaging in an elaborate exercise of reifying corporations[128]—imagining these "artificial beings" as blood-

509

---

121. *See, e.g.*, 21 CONG. REC. 2457 (1890) (Senator Sherman's statement that combinations in restraint of trade smacked of "kingly prerogative"); S. PRESSER & J. ZAINALDIN, *supra* note 8, at 584 (quoting 21 CONG. REC. 2726 (1890) (Senator Edmunds stated that "all human experience and all human philosophy have proved that [monopolies] are destructive of the public welfare and come to be tyrannies, grinding tyrannies.")). *See generally infra* notes 129-32 and accompanying text.

122. 35 Ohio St. 666 (1880).

123. *Id.* at 672.

124. 77 Mich. 632, 43 N.W. 1102 (1889).

125. *Id.* at 657, 43 N.W. at 1110.

126. *Id.* .

127. *Id.* at 658, 43 N.W. at 1110.

128. For a discussion of the "reification" of the corporation, see R. WINTER, GOVERN-

less monsters that were unmoved by any human feelings and bent simply on monetary gain at public expense.

Senate proponents of the Sherman Antitrust Act also focused on this theme. John Sherman himself declared that trusts were governed only by "[t]he law of selfishness, uncontrolled by competition, [which] compels [them] to disregard the interest of the consumer."[129] Sherman expressly linked the bill to the fear of Stuart absolutism by concluding that a trust controlled by a single man "is a kingly prerogative, inconsistent with our form of government . . . ."[130] Senator Edmunds joined Sherman and declared that the bill was necessary to "repress and break up and destroy forever" monopolies such as the sugar and oil trusts "because in the long run, however seductive they may appear in lowering prices to the consumer, for the time being, all human experience and all human philosophy has proved that they are destructive of the public welfare and come to be tyrannies, grinding tyrannies."[131] Unfortunately, the Senator never explained what he meant by the phrase "all human experience and all human philosophy." Indeed, the drafters of the Sherman Act clearly did not intend to proscribe *all* monopolies, but only those that the common law would have deemed impermissible.[132]

510

Even though the common law may have supported the condemnation of only those monopolies that operated "unreasonably" to restrain trade, some of the earliest constructions of the Sherman Act suggested that the statutory language prohibited *all* agreements in restraint of trade.[133] In the first Supreme Court opinion to adopt this position, Justice Peckham apparently rejected a "rule of reason" analysis because of his personal ideology, which emphasized the legal restraint of big business' arbitrary power. Peckham, for example, repeated the state court litany that trusts or

---

MENT AND THE CORPORATION (1978).

129. S. PRESSER & J. ZAINALDIN, *supra* note 8, at 581 (quoting 21 CONG. REC. 2457 (1890)). For the entire debate, see 21 CONG. REC. 2456-68 (1890).

130. S. PRESSER & J. ZAINALDIN, *supra* note 8, at 581 (quoting 21 CONG. REC. 2457 (1890)).

131. *Id.* at 584.

132. *See, e.g.*, 21 CONG. REC. 2457-68 (1890). *See generally*, Letwin, *supra* note 120, 221-43 (1956). For the English common law authorities, see Letwin, *The English Common Law Concerning Monopolies*, 21 U. CHI. L. REV. 355 (1954) (although English common law condemned prerogative grants of monopoly, engrossing and charging extortionate prices for necessities, unreasonable agreements not to compete between employers and employees, and certain conspiracies to raise or lower wages, its proscriptions were not as broad as the provisions of the Sherman Act).

133. *See, e.g.*, United States v. Trans-Missouri Freight Ass'n, 166 U.S. 290 (1897).

combinations

all have an essential similarity, and have been induced by motives of individual or corporate aggrandizement as against the public interest. In business or trading combinations they may even temporarily, or perhaps permanently, reduce the price of the article traded in or manufactured, by reducing the expense inseparable from the running of many different companies for the same purpose.[134]

Peckham also observed that although these combinations might provide some cost savings for consumers, their ultimate result would be to drive "out of business the small dealers and worthy men whose lives have been spent therein, and who might be unable to readjust themselves to their altered surroundings. Mere reduction in the price of the commodity . . . might be dearly paid for by the ruin of such a class . . . ."[135] While acknowledging that this dislocation inevitably might result from the normal course of changes in business methods, Peckham suggested that no such inevitability ought to attach in law to business ruinations that result from "combinations of capital."[136] Even though the combinations initially might lower an article's price, "[i]t is in the power of the combination to raise it, and the result in any event is unfortunate for the country by depriving it of the services of a large number of small but independent dealers . . . ."[137]

511

Thus, Peckham's concern for the small businessman in America, coupled with his conclusion that "combinations of capital" inevitably harmed the public interest, led him to construe the antitrust laws in a way that would avoid the ruination of the class of "small but independent dealers."[138] Peckham's romantic, antebellum notions[139] of what sparked "real prosperity" caused him to

---

134. *Id.* at 322-23.
135. *Id.* at 323.
136. *Id.*
137. *Id.* at 324.
138. According to Peckham,

Whether [such independent businessmen] be able to find other avenues to earn their livelihood is not so material, because it is not for the real prosperity of any country that such changes should occur which result in transferring an independent businessman, the head of his establishment, small though it might be, into a mere servant or agent of a corporation for selling the commodities which he once manufactured or dealt in, having no voice in shaping the business policy of the company and bound to obey orders issued by others.

Id. at 324.

139. *See supra* note 138. For a discussion of Peckham's romantic wish to return to simpler antebellum times and its influence on his jurisprudence, see Skolnik, *Rufus Peckham,* in 3 THE JUSTICES OF THE UNITED STATES SUPREME COURT, 1789-1969, at 1685 (L. Friedman & F. Israel eds. 1969).

utilize the Sherman Act as a vehicle for preserving a "big is bad, small is beautiful," ideology of independent business. Remarkably, Peckham failed to make the distinction that the instant case concerned railroads, which were characterized by their attendant public regulation and their demonstrated need for economies of scale. He argued that at the time of the Sherman Act's passage,

> [t]here were many and loud complaints from some portions of the public regarding the railroads and the prices they were charging . . . and it was alleged that the prices . . . were unduly and improperly enhanced by combinations among the different roads. . . . [T]he evil to be remedied is similar in both [manufacturing and railroad] corporations, . . . we see no reason why similar rules should not be promulgated in regard to both, and both be covered in the same statute by general language sufficiently broad to include them both.[140]

512

By reading the general language of the Sherman Antitrust Act to cover railroads, Peckham undermined the new regulatory efforts of the Interstate Commerce Commission[141] and appeared to take a firm stand in favor of a transcontinental transportation system that was dominated by individually operated, small business enterprises. Of course, the Supreme Court eventually accepted the rule of reason analysis that Peckham rejected and recognized the intent of the Act's framers to implement only the rule of the common law at the federal level.[142] Nevertheless, one who considers Peckham's ideology as it related to the influence on the Act of the desire to restrain arbitrary power—in the form of large business enterprises—is better equipped to explain current debates on that issue. The idea of "per se" antitrust law rules, for example, owes much to ideologies like Peckham's.[143] Furthermore, the resistance to argu-

---

140. United States v. Trans-Missouri Freight Ass'n, 166 U.S. 290, 319-20, 324-25 (1897).

141. Peckham strongly suggested that the Interstate Commerce Commission (ICC) condoned the railroad's practices of entering into "rate agreements" to ensure the continuation of railroad service at reasonable rates and free from ruinous competition. *Id.* at 314-15, 321. Although the ICC apparently had been directed to enforce the law against "pooling agreements"—agreements to parcel out freight and territories between competitors that were forbidden by the Interstate Commerce Act, ch. 104, § 1, 24 Stat. 379 (1887) (current version at 49 U.S.C. § 10101 (Supp. III 1979)) — it did not interpret "pooling agreements" to include rate agreements. J. GARRATY, THE NEW COMMONWEALTH 1877-1890, at 112-19 (1968).

142. Standard Oil Co. of N.J. v. United States, 221 U.S. 1 (1910); *see supra* note 132 and accompanying text.

143. Several practices in restraint of trade have been regarded as so obviously odious that no "rule of reason" is applied, and a violation of the antitrust laws is made out once evidence of the particular practice is established. Some examples of these practices are price fixing, collective boycotts, and market sharing. *See* A. NEALE, THE ANTITRUST LAWS OF THE U.S.A. 27-28 (2d students' ed. 1970).

ments that these and other "inefficient" antitrust law rules should be abandoned in the interest of wealth maximization[144] perhaps is attributable to the continued viability of Peckham's free enterprise notions about the nature of real prosperity. This continued viability in turn supports the conservative school's contention that the law progresses according to fixed intellectual principles that judges apply to new situations.[145]

Advocates of a market-oriented, wealth-maximizing system appear to have the upper hand in the current federal administration. In a statement that directly contravened Peckham's perspective, Attorney General William French Smith recently announced that the Justice Department's Antitrust Division was reexamining "inefficient" prior official positions on antitrust law interpretation pursuant to the insight that "bigness is not necessarily bad."[146] This new policy illustrates how perceived popular demand for economic progress—in this case, for an end to perceived unnecessary restraints on productive capital and economies of scale—may result in the change or abandonment of statutory or common-law legal rules. The next section considers other opportunities for exploring this phenomenon by suggesting insights of the Wisconsin school of legal historians, who concentrate on legal change resulting from the pressures of a societal consensus on the desirability of economic progress.

513

B. *The Wisconsin School and the Alteration of Rules of Law in Service of Economic Progress and Social Wealth*

1. *Groves v. John Wunder Co.*

One can conjure up many historical examples to support the Wisconsin school's contention that American law has changed to accommodate the needs of industrial capitalists in a market economy. Perhaps the best starting point for this analysis, however, is the traditional contracts case of *Groves v. John Wunder Co.*[147] Defendant in *Groves* had agreed to leave plaintiff's property at a uniform grade after removing sand and gravel from the land. Since the cost of levelling the land would be $60,000 and the resulting

---

144. For arguments regarding the supposed inefficiencies that are inherent in much of current antitrust law, see R. POSNER, ECONOMIC ANALYSIS OF LAW, 210-552 (2d ed. 1977) and sources cited therein.

145. *See supra* notes 35-40 and accompanying text.

146. Wall St. J., June 25, 1981, at 6, col. 2.

147. 205 Minn. 163, 286 N.W. 235 (1939).

value of the property would be only about $12,000, defendant deliberately breached the contract and refused to level the land. Defendant argued that damages to plaintiff should be the difference in the value of the property before and after it was graded. Plaintiff, on the other hand, contended that damages should be calculated as the cost of performance.

- The *Groves* majority held for plaintiff and awarded damages based on the cost of levelling plaintiff's land. The court in essence reasoned that land is unique, stating that "[t]he owner's right to improve his property is not trammelled by its small value."[148] A strong dissent, however, argued that damages should be calculated based on the diminished value rule—as long as no evidence existed to support the contention that plaintiff wanted the land levelled to satisfy his personal tastes—and rejected the proposition that the measure of damages should be increased because the breach was willful.[149]

514

To put the *Groves* majority's decision into context, one must understand the special treatment that the English and American common law has accorded land. Although the availability of specific performance in disputes over land illustrates this treatment most clearly, the same considerations apparently influenced the majority's decision to award Groves the cost of contract completion rather than the decrease in the land's value caused by the breach. The majority's thesis in effect was that one simply cannot put an objective market value on land; the *Groves* dissent, on the other hand, would reject this thesis when the purpose of a specific transaction is clearly and measurably economic. To gain more than a mere intuitive grasp of the majority's uniqueness-of-land concept, one must consider centuries of English and American colonial cultural and legal history, in which all life centered around land, and people's status, social duties, and responsibilities arose from their relationships to that land.[150]

One fairly can speculate that the *Groves* majority missed the essential economic purpose of the transaction in question because it accepted the Jeffersonian vision that Americans should continue to attach primacy to land. In his *Notes on Virginia*, Jefferson posited that Americans should make their livelihood on small plots of

---

148. *Id.* at 168, 286 N.W. at 237.
149. *Id.* at 171-85, 268 N.W. at 239-45; *see* Peevyhouse v. Garland Coal & Mining Co., 382 P.2d 109 (Okla. 1963).
150. *See, e.g.*, F. Ganshof, Feudalism (3d ed. 1964); P. Laslett, The World We Have Lost (1965); L. Wright, The Cultural Life of the American Colonies 1607-1763 (1957).

land by continuing as brave yeomen farmers who would shun commerce, industrial expansion, and luxury.[151] What Groves did with his land and money is not what Jefferson suggested, of course, but that is not the point—the point is that the law of contracts sometimes allows judges to ignore the economic valuation of the market and to impose remedies based on the supposedly unique value of a particular piece of land. The *Groves* case thus demonstrates the law's accounting for personal idiosyncrasy, a characteristic that also supports the position of those who stress the legal value of the operation of private wishes in public regulation.[152]

The relevance of the *Groves* case in this context is that it presents the tension between a traditional rule—supporting individuality by recognizing the uniqueness of land when measuring value—and a more modern approach—calculating damages based solely on economic loss. According to the Wisconsin school's thesis, both these rules arose because of the economic needs of society. As these needs have changed over time, the holding in *Groves* has become almost an exception to a general rule; the *Groves* dissent appears more in keeping with the trend of American law to weigh market considerations most heavily in reaching economic results that diminish the importance of individual idiosyncrasy, reduce uncertainty, and presumably minimize inefficiency while maximizing production.[153] Thus, by approaching the *Groves* case from the Wisconsin school's perspective, one can better examine the role of market forces in judicial decisionmaking.

515

2. *Charles River Bridge v. Warren Bridge*

The first great constitutional law case that most fully embraces the core value of American law of maximizing economic progress at the expense of other property interests is the Supreme Court's decision in *Charles River Bridge v. Warren Bridge*.[154]

---

151. The most famous section in which this point is made in the *Notes* is Jefferson's response to query XIX. T. JEFFERSON, *Notes on the State of Virginia* (1781-82), in THE LIFE AND SELECTED WRITINGS OF THOMAS JEFFERSON 279-81 (A. Koch & W. Peden eds. 1944); *see* Letters from Thomas Jefferson to Charles Van Ogendorp (Oct. 13, 1785), J. Bannister, Jr. (Oct. 15, 1785), and A. Stuart (January 25, 1786), *reprinted in* THE LIFE AND SELECTED WRITINGS OF THOMAS JEFFERSON, *supra* at 384-85, 385-88, 390-91.

152. *See supra* notes 27-33 and accompanying text; J. DAWSON & W. B. HARVEY, CASES AND COMMENT ON CONTRACTS 12-13 (3d ed. 1977) (quoting RESTATEMENT OF CONTRACTS § 346, illustration 4).

153. *See, e.g.*, M. HORWITZ, *supra* note 4, at 196-201 (the "objective" theory of contract helps ensure certainty and predictability in mature markets).

154. 36 U.S. (11 Pet.) 419 (1837). *See supra* notes 23-29 and accompanying text. For

Eighteen years before the *Charles River Bridge* case, the Court in *Dartmouth College v. Woodward*[155] held that the grant of a corporate charter to Dartmouth College was a contract that the contract clause of the Constitution[156] protected from state interference in the absence of a reserved power of amendment. The *Charles River Bridge* case presented the question of how narrowly the state contractual obligations incurred in the granting of charters should be construed. In 1785 the State of Massachusetts chartered the Charles River Bridge Company to build a toll bridge across the Charles River and granted the company a franchise to collect tolls for an extended number of years. In 1828, when the Charles River Bridge franchise still had a substantial time to run, the State chartered a competing bridge company to operate a toll-free bridge. The effect of the second charter, of course, was to render the Charles River Bridge Company's franchise worthless. The Charles River Bridge charter contained no language dealing with the state's authority to grant competing charters; the new bridge company, therefore, argued that the strictly construed language of the document and the State's obligation to act in the public interest justified new bridge charters whenever the interests of commerce or public transportation made them necessary. The Charles River Bridge Company, on the other hand, argued that since an undertaking not to breach can be implied in every contract, the original charter should be construed to contain an implicit assurance that the State would do nothing to render the charter worthless. Both the new and the old bridge proprietors based their arguments on the country's need for economic development: the Charles River Bridge Company argued that this development would be stymied if initial investments were not assured full contractual protection, and the Warren Bridge Company argued that the same development would be frustrated if newer forms of transportation were not allowed easily and freely to compete with old ones.[157] As Justice Taney explained in his majority opinion holding for the Warren Bridge Company, the real issue in the case might have been whether the newly burgeoning railroad industry would be checked by lawsuits from the moribund turnpike companies,

516

---

an excellent Wisconsin school analysis of this case, see S. KUTLER, PRIVILEGE AND CREATIVE DESTRUCTION: THE CHARLES RIVER BRIDGE CASE (1971).

155. Dartmouth College v. Woodward, 17 U.S. (4 Wheat.) 518 (1819).

156. U.S. CONST. art. I, § 10 ("No state shall . . . pass any . . . law impairing the obligation of contracts . . . .").

157. S. KUTLER, *supra* note 154, at 43-44.

whose business the railroads were then seizing.

The *Charles River Bridge* case dramatically illustrates how public pressures for economic progress can change either the applications of constitutional rules or the conceptions of property or contract. Indeed, the depth of the chagrin that Justice Story and Chancellor Kent felt after the rendering of the decision is indicative of the extreme nature of legal change during the mid-nineteenth century. Thus, Kent "thought Taney's opinion . . . was miserable and [Story's] gigantic," and reportedly could read Taney's opinion only with "shuddering disgust" and "increased repugnance."[158] Story himself, who dissented in the case, wrote in 1837 that "I am sick at heart, . . . and now go to the discharge of my judicial duties . . . with a firm belief that the future cannot be as the past."[159]

Although Wisconsin school historians would attribute the legal change signaled by the *Charles River Bridge* case to a difference over the best method of achieving the concensus goal of economic development, members of the radical transformation school[160] examining the same case would probably be more struck by the perceptions of extreme change on the part of Story and Kent revealed both by the application to constitutional law of the "instrumental conception"[161] of law and the malleability of legal doctrines, which jurists such as Story and Kent themselves had poineered in the private law area. This Article, therefore, next considers some radical transformation school concepts that can be used to develop understanding of American private law.

517

C. *Conflict Between Core Values and Radical Transformation in Private Law*

One of the primary premises of the radical transformation school is that the power centers of American society in the nineteenth century used the law as a vehicle for promoting fluid, entrepreneurial uses of capital at the expense of *rentier* interests.[162] The seminal work of this school, Horwitz' *The Transformation of*

---

158.   G. Dunne, Justice Joseph Story and the Rise of the Supreme Court 365-66 (1970).

159.   Letter from Joseph Story to James Kent (June 26, 1837), *quoted in* 5 C. Swisher, History of the Supreme Court of the United States: The Taney Period 1836-64, at 93 (1974).

160.   *See supra* notes 48-69 and accompanying text.

161.   *Id.; see* M. Horwitz, *supra* note 4, at 1-30.

162.   *See supra* notes 48-69 and accompanying text.

American Law,[163] provides many examples in tort, property, and contract law to support this proposition. Horwitz' book, for example, discusses Justice Story's intent in cases such as *Van Ness v. Pacard*[164] and argues that Story altered American property rules to enable American tenants to invest in productive capital without risking their landlords' appropriating their investments by applying the English "waste" doctrine.[165] Horwitz' work also facilitates a study of Chancellor Kent's efforts to mold American common law in a manner consistent with his ideals of economic progress.[166] Furthermore, Horwitz' analysis is particularly useful when studying how the nineteenth century case of *Seymour v. Delancey*[167] altered the rules regarding adequacy of consideration; Horwitz claims that the court in *Delancey* effected this change because it deemed objective market principles to be more important than popular equitable considerations.[168]

518

Another leading work of this school, Richard Danzig's brilliant article[169] on *Hadley v. Baxendale*[170] provides a further radical transformation study of the competition between popular equitable notions and particularized demands of industrial organizations. Danzig thoroughly examined the facts of the case and offered the thesis that the needs of an increasingly organized English national market prompted the court to adopt the *Hadley* forseeability rule as a means of minimizing the unpredictable exercise of jury discretion in the local courts. Extending Danzig's analysis, one might also conclude that the quick acceptance of the forseeability principle in America followed from similar needs.

Studies like Horwitz' and Danzig's suggest that in the process of transforming legal doctrines to accommodate emerging national markets, older equitable concepts, and their democratic manifestations—for example, jury discretion in setting breach of contract damage awards—impersonally were dismissed from the law. These scholars' perspectives can provide valuable insights into the cur-

---

163. *See supra* notes 4 & 48-69 and accompanying text.

164. 27 U.S. (2 Pet.) 137 (1829).

165. M. Horwitz, *supra* note 4, at 55-56. According to the English "waste" doctrine, any fixtures removed by the tenant—unless they were "trade fixtures" used in some nonagricultural trade would create tenant liability for the value of the fixtures removed. *Id.*

166. *Id.* at 117-18, 124-26, 138-39, 165, 190.

167. 6 Johns. Ch. 222 (N.Y. Ch. Ct. 1822), *rev'd*, 3 Cow. 445 (N.Y. Sup. Ct. 1824).

168. M. Horwitz, *supra* note 4, at 179-80.

169. Danzig, Hadley v. Baxendale: *A Study in the Industrialization of the Law,* 4 J. Legal Stud. 249 (1975).

170. 156 Eng. Rep. 145 (1854).

rent state of the law and how it progressed to this point. Nevertheless, as the discussion above of Peckham's opinion and the *Groves* decision suggests, American legal history seems never really to bury old equitable or social concepts completely. Our legal system, therefore, is perhaps best described as a system for reconciling new and old values, mores, and perspectives. The next section of this Article thus examines the conflict between, and the occasional reconciliation of, these conflicting legal pressures.

D. *Reconciling Diverse Demands: The Heroic Mode in Legal History*

The works of the radical transformation theorists provide a fruitful source for examining the simultaneous existence of competing perspectives, since the methodological care of those theorists usually leads them to present enough data that one can derive interpretations which are quite different from their own occasionally polemic conclusions.[171] The pressures of competing ideological imperatives, however, usually emerge with more clarity in the work of the heroic school writers. As discussed above,[172] the heroic mode of doing legal history takes as its foundation the premise that changes in the law are the result of individual strivings and personalities. Consequently, the historiography of this school often focuses on the internal forces at work on a particular jurist's decisionmaking. These forces are perhaps best examined by reference to literary parables that illuminate the character of the decisionmaker in question. What follows, therefore, are two examples of how the legal careers of great lawyers or jurists might be examined allegorically to divine a humanistic understanding of legal development.

519

1.   Lemuel Shaw

Lemuel Shaw, who was the Chief Justice of the Supreme Judicial Court of Massachusetts, is perhaps best known for his labor law work[173] and, in particular, for his opinions in *Farwell v. Boston & Worcester Rail Road*[174] and *Commonwealth v. Hunt*.[175] This body of Shaw's work provides an excellent example for applying

---

171. *See* Presser, *supra* note 51, at 716-24.
172. *See supra* notes 70-91 and accompanying text.
173. *See* L. LEVY, *supra* note 70.
174. 45 Mass. (4 Met.) 49 (1842).
175. 45 Mass. (4 Met.) 111 (1842).

the historiographic technique outlined above, which in essence results in a confluence of law, history, and literature. In *Farwell*
Shaw held that the English "fellow-servant" doctrine applied in
America and, therefore, that a railroad laborer could not recover
from his employer for an injury that the negligence of a fellow
worker caused. In *Hunt*, however, Shaw determined that labor un-
-ions did not constitute conspiracies, a conclusion that contravened
the English and American law which existed at the time.[176] The
surface inconsistencies between the two opinions generated a fascinating historical debate,[177] which no one has resolved definitively.
In keeping with the "literary" emphasis of heroic school analysis,
one might wish to resolve this inconsistency by considering the
work of Herman Melville.

520

Melville dedicated his first book, *Typee*, to Shaw, who was his
father-in-law. Shaw, in turn, was in love with Melville's aunt and
always carried two love letters from her in his wallet. Since their
families appear to have been exceptionally intimate,[178] considering
Melville's Captain Vere in *Billy Budd* as a character based at least
in part on Shaw is certainly a fair assumption. In allegorical
terms, then, the character of Billy Budd could represent the American workingman—a simple laborer such as *Farwell*—and Vere's
judgment that Billy Budd must hang could represent Shaw's treatment of workers in the *Farwell* case. In the novel, Vere incorrectly
asserts that Billy acted of his own free will when he killed Claggart, and in *Farwell*, Shaw asserts the social fiction that workers
are free to contract as they wish. Vere, like Shaw, professes to be a
just, if stern, man, but just as the readers of *Billy Budd* are not
persuaded initially by this attitude, so the contemporary reader of
Farwell is not persuaded that Shaw rendered "justice" to those
who suffered from the ravages of the "fellow-servant" rule.

On the other hand, one can probe deeper into the themes of
the novelist and the judge and reach a different conclusion. For
example, one might present Billy as negligent, even evil, and
thereby raise the possibility that Vere is in fact good and just. In
the novel, Billy Budd fails to report plans of a mutiny because his

---

176. For the contemporary English law, see Rex v. Journeymen Taylors, 8 Mod. Rep.
10 (K.B. 1721). For the American law, see People v. Fisher, 14 Wend. 10 (N.Y. Sup. Ct.
1835).

177. *Compare* Nelles, Commonwealth v. Hunt, 32 COLUM. L. REV. 1128 (1932) *with* R.
POUND, *supra* note 38, at 86-88 (1938).

178. For the link between Shaw and Melville, see R. COVER, *supra* note 70, at 4-6
(1975).

personal honor prevents him from informing on his peers. He then proceeds to kill Claggart because of his frustration at Claggart's false accusations. Billy's behavior threatens shipboard discipline, and, since a state of war then existed, any breach in discipline threatened the survival of the entire crew. Vere's treatment of Billy, therefore, becomes necessary and inevitable. Similarly, the labor unrest in New York City at the time of *Farwell*[179] perhaps suggested to Shaw the necessity for some demonstration to secure discipline among workers.

In any event, both Vere and Shaw clearly transcended personal morality when they attempted to act according to a "higher morality," a reaction which they believed the needs of the commonwealth required. Sailors engaged in a war cannot be permitted to behave like savages, and workers must be treated as free agents who contract for their own independence and are paid higher wages for any higher risks that they assume. The interests of the nineteenth-century economy in *Farwell*, like the interests of the war effort in *Billy Budd*, are better protected under such a scheme; private interests must be subordinated, at least in part, to the collective interest. Melville's ambiguous *Billy Budd*, however, offers no simple answer to the question whether Vere's behavior was correct or praiseworthy. Shaw's treatment of laborers in *Hunt*, on the other hand, does display a higher regard for the common good, since he condones the organization of labor to preserve the contractual bargaining power of workers. *Hunt* thus is consistent with the free market model that Shaw employed in *Farwell*, and this model in turn becomes a higher morality with which to reconcile the surface inconsistency between the *Hunt* and *Farwell* opinions. The diverse themes in Melville's *Billy Budd*, therefore, help magnify the diverse themes in Shaw's jurisprudence.[180]

521

2.   Benjamin Cardozo

One other example, which is drawn from comparing Justice Cardozo to Greek literature, helps underscore the flexibility, diversity, and reach of the heroic school approach. Thus, perhaps the best way to explain the multiple considerations at issue in Cardozo's opinion in *Allegheny College v. National Chautauqua*

179. The unrest referred to in the text concerned a mass meeting of 27,000 people, which was described as "the greatest meeting of working men ever held in the United States" until that time. L. LEVY, *supra* note 70, at 193.

180. *See* S. PRESSER & J. ZAINALDIN, TEACHER'S MANUAL FOR LAW AND AMERICAN HISTORY: CASES AND MATERIALS 63-64 (1980).

Bank[181] is to approach the case after examining the problem in Aeschylus' *Oresteia.* In *Oresteia*, Agamemnon, the Greek leader in the battle against Troy, is brutally murdered by his wife, Clytemnestra, and her lover. Orestes, Agamemnon's son, then punishes his mother for this foul deed by slaying her. In her last moments, Clytemnestra summons the Furies to hound and torment Orestes for murdering her. The play, then, concerns the resolution of the conflict between an old morality—requiring one always to respect blood ties—and a new morality, which suggests that, under certain circumstances, matricide is justifiable. The play represents the movement from the primitive, authoritarian, and aristocratic morality and social order to the more subtle and conditional democratic society and morality that was then emerging in fifth-century Athens.[182]

522   In *Allegheny College* Cardozo recognized the doctrine of promissory estoppel and enforced a promise of a decedent to have her executor grant a sum of money to a college. Judge Kellogg in dissent, however, focused on the lack of contractual formalities in the transaction and appeared to emphasize the need for bright-line rules in contract law. Drawing upon the *Oresteia* analogy, one can suggest that Kellogg's dissent represents an old morality and that Cardozo's opinion casts him as a proponent of a new morality represented by the doctrine of promissory estoppel.[183]

This new morality, like that in the Golden Age of Athens, is far more subtle than the old. Cardozo did not care what the parties called their arrangement, or what they thought they were doing; he was prepared to "weav[e] gossamer spider webs of consideration"[184] to advance the greater good of higher education over personal greed. Cardozo's new morality, therefore, subordinated the wishes of the individual to the interests of the collectivity, which is precisely what *Oresteia* and much of Greek tragedy took as its

---

181.   246 N.Y. 369, 159 N.E. 173 (1927).

182.   *See* Lattimore, *Introduction* to AESCHYLUS, ORESTEIA 5-31 (R. Lattimore trans. 1953). *See generally*, AESCHYLUS, EUMENIDES (H. Lloyd-Jones trans. 1970); E. DODDS, THE ANCIENT CONCEPT OF PROGRESS AND OTHER ESSAYS ON GREEK LITERATURE AND BELIEF (1973); K. DOVER, THE GREEKS (1981). Aeschylus was working through the use of several dichotomies, which now might simply be thought of as the distinction between the public and the private interests—the fourth significant core value of American legal history discussed above. *See supra* notes 27-33 and accompanying text.

I am indebted to my colleague in the department of classics at Northwestern, Brook Manville, both for his suggestion of these sources and for his willingness to share his deep understanding of Aeschylus with me.

183.   *See* U.C.C. § 2-302; RESTATEMENT (SECOND) OF CONTRACTS § 90 (1979).

184.   G. GILMORE, *supra* note 77, at 62 (1974).

foundation.[185] Thus, comparing Cardozo's jurisprudence to the thematic strains in Greek literature can provide expanded insights into the process of legal change that Cardozo so significantly affected.

V. CONCLUSION

That historians in law schools practice something called "legal" history seems to require some sort of explanation. "Legal" history seems to imply the existence of its opposite, and it is difficult to imagine an "illegal" history without envisioning a group of masked and surreptitious scholars bent on some nefarious purpose. Perhaps this is why so many books that might have been entitled "legal history" have been labelled histories "of," "and" or "in" law.[186] In another sense, however, the endeavor might be labelled "legal history," rather than "the history of law." In teaching the law's past, previous events illuminate the present and mark out desirable choices for future conduct. In this sense, then, the teaching of history serves the same societal pattern-maintenance function as legal rules.

523

This pedagogical technique increases our understanding not only of the nature of the American legal culture, but also, pursuant to the particular possibilities that heroic school scholars have created, of the nature of mankind.[187] These scholars teach us that a great danger exists in preoccupation—at the individual or cultural level—with a single value to the exclusion of others. As a result, these scholars stress the need to remain simultaneously committed to a variety of values. The implementation of this lesson requires an openness of spirit and a maturity that is not always forthcoming in either societies or individuals; it also requires a willingness to attempt the impossible and to run the risk of being labelled a hypocrite.

In those eras of history when some Americans and their laws were overly preoccupied with one of the four values described

---

185. As discussed above, *see supra* notes 173-80 and accompanying text, this theme also concerned Shaw.

186. *See, e.g.,* L. FRIEDMAN, *supra* note 2; LAW IN AMERICAN HISTORY (B. Bailyn & D. Fleming eds. 1971); S. PRESSER & J. ZAINALDIN, *supra* note 8.

187. The mythological insights that this school offers may be a sign that legal thinkers have begun to explore the same territory as European structuralists such as Claude Lévi-Strauss. *See, e.g.,* C. LÉVI-STRAUSS, MYTHOLOGIQUES (1967-1971); C. LÉVI-STRAUSS, 2 STRUCTURAL ANTHROPOLOGY (1967); *cf.* Tushnet, *Post-Realist Legal Scholarship,* 1980 WIS. L. REV. 1383, 1400 (suggesting the need for American legal scholars to focus on the implications of the work of Lévi-Strauss, Habermas, Lacan, Barthes, and Althusser).

above,[188] tensions resulted that severely strained the fabric of American society. In the early years of the Republic, rampant popular sovereignty resulted in arbitrary mob actions that made government all but impossible.[189] In the mid-nineteenth century, Southern orators' and lawyers' excessive emphasis on the private sphere of protected property rights in slaves led to a gag rule in Congress, to exaggerated fears of a Southern conspiracy among the abolitionists, and ultimately to an orgy of Northern democratic sentiment that resulted in the Civil War.[190] In the years preceding the New Deal, preoccupation with private property rights to contract led to a constitutional revolution that fundamentally reordered the nature of American government and led to an unhealthy emphasis on restraining arbitrary private power through governmental intervention.[191] If the recent efforts of federal and state courts represent a trend,[192] American society now is apparently attempting to regain some sense of balance and to retreat from the

524

---

188. *See supra* notes 11-33 and accompanying text.

189. Maier, *Popular Uprisings and Civil Authority in Eighteenth-Century America*, 27 Wm. & Mary Q. 3, 34-35 (3d Ser. 1970) (describing how post revolutionary Whig leaders believed that continued mob activity after the American revolution, although arguably based on notions of popular sovereignty, constituted "insults to government that were likely to discredit American republicanism in the eyes of European observers").

190. For an excellent treatment of all these historical developments, see D. Potter, The Impending Crisis 1848-1861 (1976).

191. *See, e.g.,* A. Bickel, The Supreme Court and the Idea of Progress (1970).

192. Such a "trend" may be observed in a number of different substantive legal categories. In contracts, for example, certain signs suggest that state courts may be seeking to reinforce private bargaining behavior rather than constantly reanalyzing the fairness of individual transactions. *See, e.g.,* Patterson v. Walker-Thomas Furniture Co., 277 A.2d 111 (D.C. 1971); Weisz v. Parke-Bernet Galleries, Inc., 77 Misc. 2d 80, 351 N.Y.S.2d 911 (App. Term 1974).

One theorist remarked in 1976 that it is inappropriate both to use judicial activism to advance social objectives through private tort cases and to fashion negligence rules on a case by case basis. Henderson, *Expanding the Negligence Concept: Retreat from the Rule of Law*, 51 Ind. L.J. 467, 468 (1976). At least some recent negligence and products liability decisions seem to share this concern that there must be some limits on the expansive construction of the doctrines. *See In re* Kinsman Transit Co., 388 F.2d 821 (1968); Tibbetts v. Ford Motor Co., 358 N.E.2d 460 (Mass. App. Ct. 1976). Finally, strong signs are appearing that the United States Supreme Court wants to diminish the reach of the federal securities laws. Federal authorities probably went far beyond the congressional intent when, in the late 1960's and early 1970's, they used these laws to punish almost any conceivable fraudulent behavior in connection with the issuance of securities. *See* The Securities Exchange Act of 1934, 15 U.S.C. §§ 78a-78kk (1976 & Supp. IV 1980). *Compare* Superintendent of Ins. of New York v. Bankers Life & Cas. Co., 404 U.S. 6 (1971) *and* S.E.C. v. Texas Gulf Sulphur Co., 401 F.2d 833 (2d Cir. 1968), *cert. denied*, 394 U.S. 976 (1969) (apogee of liability for fraud under securities laws) *with* Aaron v. S.E.C., 446 U.S. 680 (1980) *and* Chiarella v. United States, 445 U.S. 222 (1980) (apparently constricting the reach of the federal securities laws).

rampant judicial activism of the past. The maintenance of this balance, however, never will be easy because no single core value ever can be realized fully without endangering the others. Indeed, our institutions always can be condemned for failing to honor the promises that they were designed to fulfill.

Because we can never have true democracy, the efforts of our legislatures often appear hypocritical. We can never have a totally free market, or a maximum of economic progress and social mobility, without running the risk that monopolies will exercise intolerable arbitrary power. The most desirable course for society eventually may be to arrive at a communitarian existence, in which these and other antinomies of the liberal perspective would be dissolved, and society somehow would become free to discard the contradictory imperatives of the old individualistic values. The most brilliant recent attempt to lay the groundwork for such an existence, however, apparently confesses frankly that reaching this utopian state would be impossible without clearly articulated divine direction, which generally has not been available for two millenia.[193]

525

Perhaps the best available alternative to such a goal is to consider why relative peace and prosperity have existed during much of our legal past, and whether this tranquility has affected American law's commitment continually to reconcile the irreconcilable in diverse values. As suggested earlier, then, because of the manner in which selected parts of the history of law can suggest the proper course to follow in the future, labelling this activity "legal history" is perhaps correct. In teaching lawyers, at least, it seems appropriate to adopt this shamelessly presentist mode of history.[194] "Legal history," then, is really *applied* history, and it is probably theoretically distinguishable from "pure history"—the search for the objective truth of the past—in the same sense that applied mathematics differs from pure mathematics. Nevertheless, since the totality of past experience can never be recovered in full detail, even the most scrupulous scholars must employ some principles of selection, and each historian of the law, therefore, must make methodological assumptions that are consistent with the values which he or she holds.

At some point, then, all history of law may be "legal" history,

---

193. *See* R. UNGER, KNOWLEDGE AND POLITICS 295 (1975).

194. In this sense, Hendrik Hartog's characterization of several legal historians appears accurate. Hartog, *Distancing Oneself from the Eighteenth Century: A Commentary on Changing Pictures of American Legal History*, in LAW IN THE AMERICAN REVOLUTION, *supra* note 6, at 230.

even though some forms may be more "pure" than others. Indeed, a complex dialectical interplay probably exists between the values one expects to discover during the study of "pure" history of law and the values one seeks to transmit when teaching. For now, however, law teachers should be concerned with "legal history" and not, alas, the history of law. Some legal scholars, impatient with Laskian or Bickelian pluralism,[195] once again are searching for the single key to achieving a perfectly functioning legal system.[196] Some of them profess to find the solution in the "new conceptualism" of the Posnerian wealth maximization or efficiency analysis of law and economics,[197] while others seek it in the "unholy trinity" of Marxism, semiology, and phenomenology.[198] Nevertheless, formulating the law along the lines of the first philosophy would generate the same arbitrary power problem encountered in the late-nineteenth century, and subscribing to the second ultimately would lead to a socialism that—if much of recent world history is a guide—inevitably would result in the suppression of valuable private diversity and initiative. One could do much worse than to settle for an enlightened Burkianism[199] that is content to revel in inconsistency, to eschew simple or complex, one-track modes of analysis, and to accept Holmes' view that repose is not the destiny of man.[200]   Short of divine revelation, then, we are not likely to find a means to unlock the ultimate mysteries of our destiny, but legal history still can be used to understand how best to fumble for the keys.

---

195. *Cf.* S. PRESSER & J. ZAINALDIN, *supra* note 8, at 734-65 (noting that unhappiness with Harold Laski's and Alexander Bickel's ethical position that society ought to maximize competition between different values simply by maintaining access to the political process led both Circuit Judge J. Skelly Wright and the Warren Court to seek to implement their own vision of a jurisprudence of "goodness").

196. For evidence of this trend, see Tushnet, *supra* note 187; *Legal Scholarship: Its Nature and Purposes*, 90 Yale L.J. 955-1296 (1981).

197. For these professions, see *Symposium on Efficiency as a Legal Concern, supra* note 34.

198. Tushnet, *supra* note 187, at 1399.

199. "Enlightened Burkianism" denotes adherence to Edmund Burke's "chief articles" of a "universal constitution for civilized peoples." R. KIRK, THE CONSERVATIVE MIND FROM BURKE TO SANTAYANA 15 (1953). Kirk derived these articles from Burke's speeches and writings as "reverence for the divine origin of social disposition; reliance upon tradition . . . for public and private guidance; conviction that men are equal in the sight of God, but equal only so; devotion to personal freedom and private property; opposition to doctrinaire alteration." *Id.* Since Burke limned an implicit philosophy that culled superior from inferior principles of the past, limiting an interpretation of Burke to the notion that what has gone before ought to be repeated would be incomplete. *See* Tushnet, *Darkness on the Edge of Town: The Contributions of John Hart Ely to Constitutional Theory*, 89 YALE L.J. 1037, 1039 (1980).

200. Holmes, *supra* note 11, at 466.

BOOK REVIEW

REVISING THE CONSERVATIVE TRADITION: TOWARDS A NEW AMERICAN LEGAL HISTORY

THE TRANSFORMATION OF AMERICAN LAW 1780-1860. By Morton J. Horwitz. Cambridge, Massachusetts: Harvard University Press. 1977. Pp. xvii, 356. $16.50.

INTRODUCTION

Dark and Doestoyevskyan is the world of Morton Horwitz. In *The Transformation of American Law,* Professor Horwitz portrays nineteenth-century private law as a battleground where God and the Devil fight over the soul of man. Legal principles are subverted (p. 99), "class bias" prevails (p. 188), and "gross disparities of bargaining power" are brushed behind a facade of "neutral and formal rules" (p. 201). In sum, legal power is ruthlessly exercised to bring about economic redistributions, by powerful groups who carefully "disguise" their activities from the majority of Americans (p. 266). When all of this is over, the forces of goodness and morality in private law have been completely thrashed by emergent entrepreneurial and commercial groups, who manage "to win a disproportionate share of wealth and power in American society" (p. xvi).

Horwitz's primary purpose in writing this book was to correct an error made by "consensus" American historians, who ignored the redistributive effects of private law doctrines. These historians, who Horwitz believes were writing to provide an historical pedigree for the New Deal (p. xiii), "discovered" the long American tradition of governmental and legal activity to regulate and promote the economy.[1] They failed, however, to ask: "in whose interests were regulations forged?" This question Horwitz now attempts to answer. Primarily addressed to general American historians, the book employs a minimum of complex legal terminology.[2]

527

---

[1] Horwitz refers expressly to "the Handlins and Hartz" (p. xiii). The reference is to O. HANDLIN & M. HANDLIN, COMMONWEALTH: A STUDY OF THE ROLE OF GOVERNMENT IN THE AMERICAN ECONOMY: MASSACHUSETTS, 1744-1861 (rev. ed. 1969), and L. HARTZ, ECONOMIC POLICY AND DEMOCRATIC THOUGHT, PENNSYLVANIA, 1776-1860 (1948).

[2] For example, Horwitz manages to discuss the "holder in due course" doctrine without once calling it by name (pp. 213, 224).

From other writings of Horwitz[3] and from hints thrown out here (pp. xiii, 266), a second aim can be discerned. Horwitz seeks to correct what he believes to be a misconception held by most lawyers and some legal historians — the notion that American law has a valid claim to political and moral neutrality. Most of this book is an analysis of the private law doctrines with which every lawyer and law student is familiar. Horwitz draws the legally trained reader in, and then forces him to reexamine the foundation of "scientific" reason on which the case-method system of instruction is founded. This is a disturbing enterprise, and if Horwitz's views on the law and legal change gain acceptance, we may soon see a major modification in the way legal history is taught in the law schools. This, in turn, may lead to some basic changes in the way lawyers think and act about law.

528

While it contains some problems on the polemical level, Horwitz's view of legal history is brilliantly conceived and should affect the teaching and writing of legal history for some years to come. In the remainder of this review, I will summarize Horwitz's argument as I understand it, explain why I think its impact will be substantial, and finally explore some of the limits of Horwitz's analysis.

I

LAW AS A CAPITALIST TOOL: AMERICAN LEGAL DEVELOPMENT 1780-1860

A. A New Kind of Judging

Chapter I is derived from Professor Horwitz's seminal article, *The Emergence of an Instrumental Conception of Law, 1780-1820.*[4]

---

[3] E.g., Horwitz, *The Conservative Tradition in The Writing of American Legal History*, 17 AM. J. LEGAL HIST. 275, 277-78 (1973) [hereinafter Horwitz, *The Conservative Tradition*].

[4] 5 PERSPECTIVES AM. HIST. 287 (1971), *reprinted in* D. FLEMING & B. BAILYN, LAW IN AMERICAN HISTORY 287 (1971). Chapter II first appeared as Horwitz, *The Transformation in the Conception of Property in American Law, 1780-1860*, 40 U. CHI. L. REV. 248 (1973). Chapters III, IV and V are published for the first time here. Portions of Chapter VI appeared as Horwitz, *The Historical Foundations of Modern Contract Law*, 87 HARV. L. REV. 917 (1974). Chapter VII is new and Chapter VIII originally appeared as Horwitz, *The Rise of Legal Formalism*, 19 AM. J. LEGAL HIST. 251 (1975). The articles have undergone some editing for inclusion in this volume and seem to be more accessible than when they first appeared. The increase in readability is nearly offset, however, by the damnable and execrable practice (common to the volumes in Harvard's *Studies in Legal History* series) of placing all the footnotes at the end of the book.

Unlike the rest of the book, which is principally concerned with the use of nineteenth-century law to promote economic development, Chapter I focuses on political theory.

Horwitz believes that a fundamental change in attitudes toward substantive legal doctrines came about as a result of the American Revolution. In the eighteenth century, he argues, the law (or at least the English common law) was thought to be a fixed set of divinely inspired principles, which judges accepted on faith and applied in a consistent and unvarying manner. The war with England, however, forced Americans to rethink their institutions to bring the workings of government into line with the theories of popular sovereignty and social contract that were used to explain and justify the Revolution and the state and federal constitutions.[5] It became impossible to view the English common law in the same manner as before Independence. Some English doctrines, such as the common law crimes of seditious libel and malicious shooting, were clearly inconsistent with new conceptions of American liberty, reflecting values more appropriate to a monarchical or feudal society.[6]

529

Moreover, if the substantive common law was a product of a hierarchical and probably corrupt[7] Old World, then perhaps the English common law judges were not simply applying unvarying rules of divine reason. This realization, Horwitz maintains, emancipated American judges from the slavish bonds of common law precedent and freed them to function as quasi-legislators, fashioning a new American common law consonant with the social and economic needs of the young Republic (pp. 18-19, 22-23).

Chapter I suggests the promise of a flowering of American law sprouting from the fertile soil of Enlightenment rationalism. In American courts, freed from nonsensical trappings of English justice like wigs and feudal doctrines, a new law based on equity and liberty could take shape. In his following chapters, Horwitz argues that this promise went unfulfilled.

---

[5] For a general discussion of this trend, see W. NELSON, THE AMERICANIZATION OF THE COMMON LAW: THE IMPACT OF LEGAL CHANGE ON MASSACHUSETTS SOCIETY, 1760-1830 (1975), and G. WOOD, THE CREATION OF THE AMERICAN REPUBLIC, 1776-1787 (1969).

[6] For a discussion of libel, see *Hitherto Unpublished Correspondence Between Chief Justice Cushing and John Adams,* 27 MASS. L. QUAR. 11 (1942), and on malicious shooting, see State v. Campbell, Charlt. T.U.P. 166 (Ga. 1808).

[7] *See* B. BAILYN. THE IDEOLOGICAL ORIGINS OF THE AMERICAN REVOLUTION 144-59 (1967); M. BLOOMFIELD, AMERICAN LAWYERS IN A CHANGING SOCIETY, 1776-1876, at 18-20 (1976).

B. Property Law

Horwitz begins by describing the transformation in the conception of property, using the doctrines of riparian rights as his paradigm. First, he shows how American courts in the colonial and early national periods enforced the doctrine of "natural flow," which barred riparian owners from interrupting the flow of water to others. This preserved the stable, quiet situation of the past, permitting only agricultural or domestic uses while occasionally allowing the operation of grist mills. Other uses could be enjoined as nuisances (pp. 35-36).

When judges sensed, however, that economic progress demanded the encouragement of new forms of manufacturing based on water power, the natural flow rule was replaced by the doctrines of "prior appropriation" and "prescription." These new doctrines encouraged the initial investments necessary to put up new mills by permitting the first mill owner to continue using the flow, even if this interrupted the natural flow to his fellow riparians, and even if his use of the water prevented a similar use by them (pp. 34, 36, 42-43).

Finally, in a manner that Horwitz characterizes as Machiavellian (p. 34), the prescription and prior appropriation theories were in turn abandoned, when judges sensed that economic progress required a new rule. They were succeeded by "reasonable use" doctrines, which required courts to balance conflicting uses, ultimately permitting new owners to come onstream and jeopardizing the initial investments encouraged by the abandoned doctrines. By this time, "quiet enjoyment" and "absolute dominion," the basic principles of eighteenth-century property law, had been all but forgotten in the push for efficiency and material progress.[8] Property, once valued for its own ascriptive nature, became merely a tool of economic growth.

C. Tort Law

A similar transformation occurred in tort law. Eighteenth-century doctrines, such as "strict liability" in nuisance, had imposed a high cost for interfering with the tranquility or livelihood of another. In the nineteenth century, these doctrines were replaced with new legal concepts, like negligence. When the negligence doctrine was fully developed, by the mid-nineteenth century, it permitted substantial

530

---

[8] The adjustment of common law doctrines to favor economic progress is also illustrated by Horwitz's discussion of the mill acts and the waste and dower doctrines (pp. 47-58).

interference with the property of another, so long as the interfering actor adhered to an accepted standard of care. The move from nuisance to negligence was accomplished in fits and starts. For instance, Horwitz describes the modification and eventual destruction of nuisance law by the public-nuisance exception,[9] statutory justification,[10] and the exceptions for consequential or remote injury (pp. 71-74, 83). In their efforts to protect "infant" industry, ostensibly for the benefit of the public at large, the courts eventually extended the limited liability afforded by the statutory-justification doctrine to both franchised and unfranchised entrepreneurs, resulting in the "triumph" of modern negligence. The new American transportation and manufacturing establishment found its liability in nuisance virtually eliminated, so long as its activities were undertaken with "due care" (pp. 97-99).

Examining the consequences of these new tort doctrines, Horwitz stresses that the encouragement of industry was achieved at great cost. First, removing the damage remedies provided by the old doctrines placed what Horwitz believes is a disproportionate share of the cost of manufacturing and transportation development on landowners and artisans who were no longer assured recovery for injury. Had development been encouraged by direct subsidies through taxation, the cost of development would have been spread over a greater segment of the population, and the process would have been much more open to public discussion and scrutiny (pp. 99-101). Second, judges used the new legal rules of public nuisance, consequential damages, and negligence to restrict the traditional power of juries to award damages according to their sense of fairness and equity. Judges' notions about how best to promote industrialization became more important than jurors' sense of justice (pp. 80-84).

531

D. The Law of Competition

The development of laws regulating competition provides still another variation on the theme of nineteenth-century common law's transforming itself to meet judicially perceived commercial needs. At the beginning of the nineteenth century, the spirit of Jeffersonian

---

[9] This doctrine denied any private right of recovery where the general public was injured (pp. 76-78).

[10] This doctrine permitted the holders of state franchises, such as turnpikes or canals, to cause damage when acting pursuant to a statutory plan (pp. 78-80).

egalitarianism had seeped into the courts, and judges tended to reject the Blackstonian rule that certain "public" enterprises, like transportation, could secure injunctive relief to prevent competition. Soon, however, judges became convinced that the inducement of exclusive franchises and injunctive protection would increase investment in new transportation technologies. Thus, in *Livingston v. Van Ingen*,[11] the New York Court for the Correction of Errors held that Livingston's monopoly on steamboat transportation was entitled to injunctive relief against competitors.[12] The use of the injunctive remedy, of course, insulated the question of protection of monopolies from jury intervention.

As still newer technological developments became available, some legal theorists began to see that the recently entrenched monopolies might themselves have to be destroyed to make way for progress. And so the third stage of the nineteenth-century common law of competition came about. Horwitz uses as the paradigm for this stage the great *Charles River Bridge* case,[13] which, he argues, "represented the last great contest in America between two different models of economic development" (p. 134). The first model, which was rejected in *Charles River Bridge*, was the notion that "certainty of expectations and predictability of legal consequences" were of paramount importance (p. 134). Therefore, once the state granted a transportation franchise, as Massachusetts had to the Charles River Bridge Company, that investment had to be protected from competition. The competing model, which prevailed in the case, held that "fair and equal competition" was the best means to promote economic progress.[14]

The real winners in the *Charles River Bridge* case, those who stood to benefit the most from this second transformation of competition doctrine, were the railroads. Because the Supreme Court had affirmed the states' power to license competing public works, the railroads no longer had to fear that some state-franchised canal or bridge company could enjoin their operation. The stage was set for the explosion in railroad development that followed (pp. 137-39).

---

[11] 9 Johns. 507 (N.Y. 1812).

[12] *Id.* at 589-90.

[13] Charles River Bridge v. Warren Bridge, 24 Mass. (7 Pick.) 344 (1829), *aff'd*, 36 U.S. (11 Pet.) 341 (1837).

[14] *Id.* at 462.

E. The Lawyer-Merchant Alliance

Obvious questions are raised by this description of the American common law's fashioning and dismantling of legal rights in the service of economic growth. How was it that judges could be so obviously inconsistent in their adherence to legal doctrines? How could rational men so cavalierly condone the creation and destruction of important legal rights? Horwitz answers these questions with his theory of the lawyer-merchant alliance.

In colonial times, Horwitz explains, lawyers chiefly served the interests of landed wealth. The common law rules enforced in the courts were suited to this service, and were not particularly hospitable to other areas of economic exchange, such as trade, finance, and manufacturing (pp. 140-41). As a consequence, merchants employed their own mechanisms for dispute settlement, like arbitration and penal bonds. The common law even encouraged this self-regulation by permitting the practice of "struck" juries—juries composed solely of members of the merchant class.

533

After about 1790, however, the merchant and entrepreneurial classes began to seek advice from lawyers in such matters as marine insurance and speculation in state securities (pp. 140-41, 174). This shift in their clientele encouraged lawyers (and thus courts) to focus more closely on commercial interests. Toward the end of the nineteenth century, two developments occurred that accelerated the shift in the nature of the lawyers' practices and subsequently changed the substantive nature of the common law. First, a split developed in the merchant community as different types of commercial enterprise began competing for wealth and influence. In marine insurance, for example, distinct groups of underwriters and insured formed even as early as 1790. Prior to that time, shipowners had combined haphazardly to insure each other as a means of mutual risk-pooling. After 1790, however, separate insurance companies, devoted solely to underwriting, began to emerge. The effect of specialization in the commercial community was to diminish the role of self-regulation, since the increasing fragmentation of interest made consensus difficult to achieve. This drove merchants to litigation, and thus gave lawyers and courts a more prominent role in the settlement of commercial disputes.

The second late nineteenth-century development pinpointed by Horwitz as affecting the relation between the bar and commercial interests was the growing tendency of courts to consolidate their law-declaring function. Jury discretion became strictly limited to matters of fact; all questions of law were reserved for the court. Cutting back the role of the jury, Horwitz argues, enhanced the prospects for certainty and predictability of judicial decisions, thus promoting merchant resort to the courts. At the same time, the courts' consolidation of their law-declaring function explains the increasing hostility to extra-judicial dispute settlement, manifested by refusals to enforce arbitration awards or to permit struck juries.

The increasing judicial hostility to merchants' settling their own disputes did not, however, reflect a more general hostility to merchants. In his most provocative stroke, Horwitz argues that the exact opposite inference should be made. Perhaps seeing where the future of lucrative legal practice lay, the courts embarked on a program of writing a procommercial common law. According to this view, the transformations of tort, property, and competition doctrines explored above occurred because the lawyers and judges shifted from protecting the landed gentry of the eighteenth century to promoting the emerging entrepreneurial, transportation, and manufacturing interests of the nineteenth century. This procommercial transformation of the common law was most striking in the area with the most immediate impact on trade—the law of contracts. Horwitz forcefully maintains that, despite ostensible justification in the needs of the whole society, the procommercial transformation in contracts disproportionately benefitted the newly blessed merchant and entrepreneurial interests.

F. Contract Law

Eighteenth-century rules of exchange required that bargains be "fair" and generally permitted courts to set aside transactions that resulted in harshness to one of the parties. These doctrines well suited an economy in which complicated long-distance executory exchanges were rare, prices and trade patterns were stable, and the community had a good sense of "fair" prices for virtually all items.[15] With the advent of speculation in state securities after the Revolution, and with the beginnings of national commodities markets after about 1815, however, the American economy underwent fundamental change. In this more complex market society, it was important that merchants be able to rely on getting the exchanges for which they bargained.

---

[15] *See* W. NELSON, *supra* note 5, at 54-63.

For this reason, Horwitz argues, the rules of contract damages were rewritten to shift from the equitable eighteenth-century theory of fair exchange to the nineteenth-century model of expectation or "benefit of the bargain." A new central organizing principle, the "will theory" of contract, was articulated by nineteenth-century judges to bring about this change. The relevant inquiry shifted from the community's sense of what a fair bargain in a similar contractual situation would be to the parties' "intent" as set forth in their particular arrangement. Old ideas about the existence of "objective" values of goods were discarded by judges and legal theorists and new ideas and techniques took their place (pp. 173-85). These new concepts, still the basis of modern contract law, included the supremacy of express over implied contracts, the refusal to set aside contracts in law or equity for inadequacy of consideration, and the widespread acceptance of the rule of *caveat emptor.*

535

By mid-nineteenth century, Horwitz argues, a further transformation in contract law had begun. The will theory, which relied on the intention of the parties, was becoming less useful as an instrument for meeting the increased needs for certainty and predictability in the expanding American market. So the will theory gave way to a new "objective" theory of contract, which focused on the practices and desires of the commercial group itself. Somehow, states Horwitz, judges managed to disguise this "class legislation" (p. 192), and a new law of commercial contracts was written to favor sophisticated insiders at the expense of consumers and laborers (p. 200).

According to Horwitz, the greatest victory of the lawyer-merchant alliance was this objective theory, specifically its acceptance of the fiction that equal bargaining power existed in virtually all business arrangements. Judges like Lemuel Shaw were prepared to assume that their contract model existed in the real world, and that when a laborer took a job with a railroad he held out for wages that truly reflected the risks of fellow-servant negligence (p. 210). Horwitz believes that the pressure to transform contract law to incorporate the rules of the marketplace led judges to redefine all economic relationships in terms of contract, and to assume that the rules of the marketplace governed in many situations in which they actually did not.

Seduced by the intellectual (and business) appeal of these new contract notions, judges began to undermine the body of eighteenth- and nineteenth-century tort law, which had imposed reciprocal duties and obligations wholly apart from contract. Eventually, it became possible to ignore the law of torts when the parties had arrived at some arrangement that could be characterized as a "contract." Judges were fully prepared to allow parties to "contract" away their tort law rights and, in ambiguous cases, equally prepared to erect presumptions to that effect. This triumph of contract over tort law in the mid-nineteenth century meant that the law would henceforth ratify any form of inequality that the market system produced (p. 210).

G. Legal Formalism

For these commercial doctrines to triumph, Horwitz believes, their political implications had to be disguised to an extent that has completely escaped contemporary historians. The chief instrument of deception was the fiction that in implementing commercial doctrines, judges were merely applying "scientific" general principles of law. This attitude, Horwitz argues (pp. 245-50), occurs as early as 1842 in Chief Justice Story's opinion in *Swift v. Tyson*.[16] In *Swift*, Story overruled New York decisions on the basis of a "general" commercial law that, Story said, the federal courts were qualified to expound authoritatively.[17] In Horwitz's view, *Swift* was designed to impose procommercial doctrines on reluctant state courts (p. 250), but in light of the prevailing anticommercial attitudes in the states, it was premature.

Horwitz's final chapter details the eventual victory of the attitudes reflected in *Swift v. Tyson*. In the first half of the nineteenth century, the ease with which early nineteenth-century private law decisions dispensed with contrary precedent had bothered some of the more conservative and "scientifically minded" treatise writers. These commentators felt that, for law to call itself a science, it was at least necessary for rules and doctrines to be consistently applied (p. 258).

In the beginning of the nineteenth century, this conservative attitude was reflected in the law as well as the treatises, although its ambit was restricted to a strain of constitutional law doctrines that protected vested rights from public appropriation (p. 255). The *Dartmouth College*[18] case is a fine example of this trend. Private law, however, had played fast and loose with vested rights, and seemed to

536

---

[16] 41 U.S. (16 Pet.) 1 (1842).

[17] *Id.* at 12-14.

[18] Trustees of Dartmouth College v. Woodward, 17 U.S. (4 Wheat.) 517 (1819).

set them aside with impunity.[19] By about 1850, according to Horwitz, the lawyer-merchant alliance, having secured most of the things it wanted out of private law, made the tactical decision to freeze legal doctrines where they were. The adherence to precedent required by this strategy dovetailed nicely with the treatise writers' "scientific" attitudes, and with the lawyers' aspirations to the mantle of non-political professionals. So it was that the conservative doctrines of public law began to merge with private law. By the middle of the century, the same notion of protection of vested rights prevailed in both private law and constitutional cases, and the inventiveness of early nineteenth-century private law was no more. No longer would judges rewrite the rules of property, torts, and contracts to conform with their notions of social policy. Now, with the advent of "formalism," *stare decisis* would be the rule, the inherent redistributive dangers of an expansive private law would be diminished, and the lawyer-merchant alliance would be able to consolidate its gains. This is where Horwitz leaves the laws of the nineteenth century.

537

II

THE IMPACT OF HORWITZIAN LEGAL HISTORY:
THE LAW STUDENTS' PERPLEXITY DIMINISHED

A. *Law Students and Legal History*

To law students, law professors seem like lighthouses. Lighthouses, as Dean Prosser pointed out, are no good for fog. They whistle, they blow, they ring bells, they flash lights, they raise hell; but the fog comes in just the same.[20] Most law students, especially those in their first year, are bombarded with holdings and dissents; they watch the prestidigitations of their teachers with awe, but to no apparent avail. There are too many conflicting doctrines and policies from too many seemingly discrete bodies of law.

For a few lucky ones, the light begins streaming in the window a few days or hours before the final exam, and these few begin to perceive the outlines of some principles for the resolution of problems in

---

[19] Examples include the cases involving mill acts, water rights, nuisance, and negligence. *See* pp. 703-04 *supra*.

[20] Prosser, *Lighthouse No Good*, 1 J. LEGAL. EDUC. 257, 257 (1948).

particular courses. They get A's on their individual exams, but very few ever find a way of relating their courses to each other. Few are able to see the law as more than different lines of precedent found under different key numbers.

And so, from out of their fog, law students view legal history. They find bits and snatches of it in their casebooks, but it is usually related to doctrinal problems, like the origin of particular writs underlying forms of action in contracts and torts, or the evolution of the courts of equity and common law in legal process or civil procedure. As Professor Calvin Woodard noted ten years ago, this focus on the "origin" and "development" of the institutions of the Anglo-American common law seems narrow and remote to the twentieth-century law student.[21]

538

Hence the recent push for a new synthesis in legal history, a new "field theory" that will bring to the teaching of legal history something of value to modern law students.[22] Something is needed that will make law students and practitioners appreciate that legal history may be an "antidote to the provincialism inherent in the insularity of the twentieth century,"[23] something that will provide an organizing focus for discrete substantive courses on law.

There is an emerging consensus among legal historians that the future of legal history does not lie in tracing the evolution of narrow legal topics.[24] Legal historians have been censured for their past concentration on the internal logic or lack of logic in pleading, procedure, and case law—for their insistence on staying within the "box" of lawyers' legal history.[25] Thus, the new generation of legal historians has been urged to concentrate on societal factors outside the law which have actually been responsible for the course of American legal history. Instead of the development of legal institutions, in short, legal historians should study and teach about the influence of extralegal environmental factors and human or personality factors on the law.[26]

---

[21] Woodard, *History, Legal History, and Legal Education*, 53 VA. L. REV. 89, 105 (1967).

[22] For a discussion of "field theories" in nineteenth-century legal history, see Holt, *Now and Then: The Uncertain State of Nineteenth-Century Legal History*, 7 IND. L. REV. 615 (1974).

[23] Woodard, *supra* note 21, at 113.

[24] *See* Boorstin, *Tradition and Method in Legal History*, 54 HARV. L. REV. 424, 434 (1941); Gordon, *Introduction: J. Willard Hurst and the Common Law Tradition in American Legal Historiography*, 10 LAW & SOC. REV. 9 (1975).

[25] Gordon, *supra* note 24, at 11.

[26] Woodard, *supra* note 21, at 116.

B. A New Perspective on Legal History: Horwitz's Method

In *The Transformation of American Law*, Horwitz offers his alternative to the "conservative tradition" of legal historiography reflected in Dean Roscoe Pound's *The Formative Era of American Law*. Pound suggested that the nineteenth-century common law judges arrived at their decisions simply on the basis of tradition, honesty, and application of "reason," unaffected by the economics of emerging capitalism or the political issues of the day.[27]   One of the central themes that shapes Horwitz's work is that Pound's tenacious "taught legal tradition" is a myth.[28]   Few, if any, legal historians would seriously advance Pound's perspective today, and "Pound-pounding"[29] has been a favorite indoor sport for legal historiographers for almost forty years.[30]   Until Horwitz, however, no one had built the case against Pound with such richness, complexity, and power. As Horwitz leads us from level to level, it becomes increasingly clear that what went on in nineteenth-century law was not the work of "reason" alone.

At the first level, Horwitz describes substantive legal doctrines. Here, by showing how new doctrines were radically grafted onto old,[31] and by demonstrating the variable nature of property and contract rights in the nineteenth century,[32] he makes a powerful case against Pound's theory of the internal consistency of legal doctrine. Horwitz, like Crosskey before him,[33] shows that even simple legal words like "contract"[34] and "negligence"[35] could be given completely dissimilar meanings at different times.

539

---

[27] R. POUND, THE FORMATIVE ERA OF AMERICAN LAW 83-84 (1st ed. 1938).

[28] *See* Horwitz, *The Conservative Tradition, supra* note 3, at 277-78.

[29] The noun "Pound-pounding" is the creation of Carole S. Presser.

[30] Criticism perhaps began with Boorstin, *supra* note 24, and it reached its latest and most elegant expression in Gordon, *supra* note 24.

[31] For example, Horwitz notes that in Livingston v. Van Ingen, 9 Johns. 507, 589-90 (N.Y. 1812), the New York Court for the Correction of Errors treated a franchise as a form of property to be protected by the common law (pp. 123-24).

[32] For example, Horwitz uses the shifts in contract theory from objective to subjective and finally to a new objective theory to illustrate the vagaries of nineteenth-century commercial law (pp. 161-73, 180-85, 188-201).

[33] *See* W. CROSSKEY, POLITICS AND THE CONSTITUTION IN THE HISTORY OF THE UNITED STATES 352-57 (1st ed. 1953).

[34] The word "contract" has defined a mode of transferring title (pp. 162-63) as well as a method of ensuring expectation damges (pp. 173-77).

[35] The word "negligence" has meant nonfeasance (pp. 85-87) as well as misfeasance or carelessness (pp. 94-99).

Working at a second level of analysis, Horwitz explores judges' intellectual processes in order to explain the inconsistencies of their decisions. This bit of judicial intellectual history has two foci: the ideologies of judges, and their choices of theoretical models to implement those ideologies. The individual ideology component is used to explain such diverse matters as James Kent's morally based defense of usury laws (pp. 242-43) and the rejection of the "reasonable use" test for percolating waters by judges conditioned to "laissez-faire" and "rugged individualism" (pp. 105-08). According to Horwitz, a judge's ideology may lead him to select a particular model of legal analysis, which model then tends to circumscribe the result the judge is able to reach. Thus, judges in the middle part of the nineteenth century, who were strongly influenced by the prevailing economic philosophy, chose to interpret ambiguous problems through a contract mode of analysis, rather than a tort model. This choice of analytical framework made it much less likely that judges would impose liability for tortious acts, because they would presume that parties had (at least impliedly) defined their rights and liabilities according to a contract with risks rationally analyzed and appropriately compensated.[36]

540

Carrying the analysis still further, Horwitz shows how different theoretical models within the chosen doctrines profoundly influenced results. In the law of competition, he argues, judges' differing models on how best to promote economic development (as expressed in the *Charles River Bridge* case) led to opposite holdings.[37] In the law of insurance, those judges using the "actuarial risk" model were prepared to enforce liability against insurers when judges adhering to an earlier model of "implied warranties" would not (pp. 226-37). In the law of contract, taking "implied contract" or "express contract" as the model could result in widely disparate damage judgments (pp. 170-72, 180, 185-86).

Moving to a third level, Horwitz seeks to demonstrate how changes in the character of business and legal practice resulted in different judicial modes of analysis. Each new business practice—the organization of national commodities markets (pp. 173-80), the technology of water power (pp. 40-41, 49-52), the strategies of dispute settling among merchants (pp. 145-59, 167-70)—influenced lawmakers and shaped legal doctrine. Lying behind all of these develop-

---

[36] *See* text accompanying note 15 *supra*.
[37] *See* text accompanying notes 13-14 *supra*.

ments is Horwitz's posited lawyer-merchant alliance, which made the law's broadscale push for economic progress possible. Of course, Horwitz is not the first to suggest that economics was the major shaping force in nineteenth-century legal history.[38] In this book, however, he has contributed the fullest analysis to date of the characteristics of the economic environment and their effect on the intellectual concepts of nineteenth-century lawmakers.

Horwitz's intellectual history draws not only on cases and economic history; he gives special weight to the influence of legal treatises.[39] Roscoe Pound noted the influence of the treatise tradition in shaping legal development in the nineteenth century, but Pound saw the process mainly as one of consistent logical refinement.[40] Horwitz's interpretation is quite different. He shows how some treatise writers' solutions to legal problems were influenced by a conservative desire to return to the simpler values of the past, while others sought to move the law forward by combining principles from disparate doctrines in a distinctly activist manner (pp. 181-83). Still other treatise writers, like Gulian C. Verplanck and John Milton Goodenow, are shown to have altered the very nature of the way men thought about law and to have been responsible for the shift to judicial policymaking and the procommercial character of the law (pp. 15-16, 181-83). Instead of a neutral development, then, the treatise tradition becomes for Horwitz a major factor in forging the lawyer-merchant alliance.

541

All these themes coalesce in the discussion of Joseph Story, whom Horwitz seems to regard as the most important nineteenth-century jurist. At this level, Horwitz is writing a sort of judicial biography and is seeking to correct earlier writing on Story.[41] Horwitz has Story participating at every stage of nineteenth-century legal development and shows how the philosophy of Story's opinions mirrored most of the changes in law. In the early years of the century,

---

[38] See, e.g., L. FRIEDMAN, A HISTORY OF AMERICAN LAW (1973); W. HURST, LAW AND THE CONDITIONS OF FREEDOM IN THE NINETEENTH CENTURY UNITED STATES (1956).

[39] For Horwitz's views on the importance of the treatise writers, see Horwitz, *Treatise Literature*, 69 LAW. LIB. J. 460 (1976). For an excellent recent article on nineteenth-century American legal history, also drawing on the treatise literature, see White, *The Intellectual Origins of Torts in America*, 86 YALE L.J. 671 (1977).

[40] R. POUND, *supra* note 27, at 138-67.

[41] E.g., G. DUNNE, JUSTICE JOSEPH STORY AND THE RISE OF THE SUPREME COURT (1971); J. MCCLELLAN, JOSEPH STORY AND THE AMERICAN CONSTITUTION (1971). For Horwitz's criticism of these works, see Horwitz, *The Conservative Tradition*, *supra* note 3, at 283-94.

Story wrote from an eighteenth-century natural law perspective in *United States v. Coolidge,* [42] which announced the inevitable existence of a federal common law of crimes. [43] A few years later, however, Story's treatise on conflict of laws adopted a positivistic position and announced that each independent sovereignty was free to make its own laws. [44]

Horwitz suggests that Story's leading opinion on riparian rights, *Tyler v. Wilkinson,* [45] is a transparent attempt to reconcile a welter of conflicting doctrines, while leaving some freedom for courts to reassess riparian rights as the needs of the times changed (pp. 38-39). Nevertheless, Story in his *Dartmouth College* [46] and *Charles River Bridge* [47] opinions, again reflecting prevailing sentiments, indicates his belief that the state could not cavalierly meddle with private property. When Story ultimately writes *Swift v. Tyson* [48] in 1842, it seems, on the surface at least, as if he has returned to the discredited natural law viewpoint. In *Swift,* he announces the existence of a general law of commerce for which the federal courts are to be the ultimate authority, [49] much like his earlier opinion on federal jurisdiction over common law crimes.

Story's seeming judicial schizophrenia can be explained. For Horwitz, Story's early work on conflict of laws and his opinion in *Coolidge* mark an attempt to promote America's political development, while his later opinion in *Swift* is aimed at encouraging economic progress. Like his brethren generally, Story embraced a flexible jurisprudence when economic initiatives required encouragement, but staunchly defended vested property rights when the security of investment demanded protection. While Story could occasionally be out of step with other judges in his perception of the country's best interests, [50] no one outdid him in attempting to formulate a new American law designed to ensure commercial progress.

---

[42] 25 F. Cas. 619 (D. Mass. 1813) (No. 14,857), *rev'd,* 14 U.S. (1 Wheat.) 191 (1816).

[43] *Id.* at 619.

[44] J. STORY, COMMENTARIES ON CONFLICT OF LAWS § 7 (1st ed. 1834).

[45] 24 F. Cas. 472 (C.C.D.R.I. 1827) (No. 14,312).

[46] 17 U.S. (4 Wheat.) 250, 335-37 (1819).

[47] 36 U.S. (11 Pet.) 341, 504-05 (1837) (dissenting opinion).

[48] 41 U.S. (16 Pet.) 1 (1842).

[49] *Id.* at 17-18.

[50] His opinion in *Coolidge,* 25 F. Cas. 619 (D. Mass. 1813) (No. 14,857), was reversed, 14 U.S. (1 Wheat.) 191 (1816), and he dissented in *Charles River Bridge,* 36 U.S. (4 Wheat.) 250 (1819).

What motivated Story? That he was a bank president, as well as a Supreme Court Justice, and thus a charter card-carrying member of the lawyer-merchant alliance [51] is presumably of some significance for Horwitz.

With this comprehensive examination of doctrinal development, intellectual history, economic reality, and judicial biography, Horwitz has built the strongest case against Pound to date. No one who seeks to write in this area will be able to ignore this book, and Horwitz's hypotheses about the scope and the nature of doctrinal change have been so carefully constructed that it is difficult to imagine their being convincingly refuted in the near future. In short, the book is a tour-de-force and may well be, as its jacket triumphantly proclaims, "[o]ne of the five most significant books ever published in the field of American legal history." [52]

543

C. *The Relevance of Horwitz*

The basic lessons Horwitz offers are first, that diverse forces—moral, political, and economic—go into making the law, and second, that the law does *not* develop along strictly logical lines. Moreover, Horwitz's work teaches that different cultural forces are prominent at different times as the character of society itself changes. Thus, vastly dissimilar areas of substantive law often develop in parallel fashion, and radical shifts occur as new values take prominence in the minds of judges. The course of the law, then, is not a straight-line development but, as is true of societies generally,[53] one of staged growth. Ultimately, legal history in the Horwitz mold can demonstrate that American law is a reflection of different philosophies of American life and that the meaning of law must be understood in this broader cultural context.

To a great extent, Horwitz begins where law schools leave off. The modern contract doctrines of "consent," "bargain," and "consideration" are still preeminent (or at least ambient);[54] property is still

---

[51] *But see* G. DUNNE, *supra* note 41, at 141-44 (1970) (Story's bank presidency viewed as a quasi-public service).

[52] The comment is attributed to Professor William E. Nelson, Yale University. Professor Nelson circumspectly did not list the other four; neither will I.

[53] W. ROSTOW, THE STAGES OF ECONOMIC GROWTH (2d ed. 1971).

[54] *See generally* Henderson, Book Review, 124 U. PA. L. REV. 1466 (1976). The exaggerated report of the demise of these doctrines is to be found in G. GILMORE, THE DEATH OF CONTRACT (1974). For a sample of the controversy Gilmore has prompted, see Speidel, *An Essay on the Reputed Death and Continued Validity of Contract,* 27 STAN. L. REV. 1161 (1975).

viewed as a tool of the individual in the marketplace; "free competition" is the goal of antitrust law; and "negligence" is central to torts. In illuminating the cultural derivations of these various doctrines, an approach like Horwitz's could go far towards burning away the fog that shrouds our law students.

If any consensus on the goal of legal education exists today, it is that law students should be imbued with the sense that law is "much more than a complex of rules for settling disputes between litigants in court." [55] In George Haskin's summation, law "is both an anchor to tradition and a vehicle for change—a pressure upon social organization and a device for accomodating new and emerging forces." [56] Legal history like that wrought by Horwitz can sharpen students' awareness of law's use as a vehicle for social change, and thus complement learning in the substantive law courses that seek to demonstrate uses of the law in society.

544

The unique role that courses or writings in legal history can have is to clearly delineate "social purpose." [57] It is through the study of history that overarching cultural ideals are made more intelligible. The notion that legal history should be primarily concerned with the discovery, articulation, and evaluation of the values that have shaped and guided the legal past is the central insight and organizing principle of Horwitz's book. By comparing and contrasting the legal doctrines which were spun out in response to the change in ideologies from the eighteenth to the nineteenth century, Horwitz dramatizes the spectrum of needs and interests that American law has served in the past. By stressing what he believes to be the "disproportionate" share of American wealth and power that some groups received from nineteenth-century law, and by showing precisely which legal changes achieved this misallocation, Horwitz invites legal reform, or at least debate in the classroom. By suggesting that legal doctrines represent political and moral choices, he makes it difficult for the student of law to approach legal problems as matters of purely logical analysis.

A little more than a decade ago, it seemed to a perceptive observer of American law and life that American legal history was a

---

[55] Haskins, *The Legal Heritage of Plymouth Colony*, 110 U. Pa. L. Rev. 847, 850 (1962).
[56] *Id.* at 851.
[57] The phrase "social purpose" is used by George Haskins in opposition to the other function of law, maintaining "social organization." *Id.*

"Dark Continent."[58]   "Decades pass," he wrote, "and, while lawyers, judges, and law professors repeat platitudes about their glorious professional past, they find no respectable place for legal history in their extensive curricula."[59]   The problem, as this critic saw it, was that the history of American private law—the body of doctrines taught to law students and practiced by most lawyers—remained unexplored,[60] and thus the materials for passing on American legal history to law students were unavailable. Horwitz, Willard Hurst, William Nelson, Lawrence Freidman, G. Edward White, and others are now supplying these materials,[61] and, if Horwitz's success at Harvard is not atypical, the time may be coming when law students will not consider their legal education complete without a course in legal history. But should the interpretations supplied by Horwitz be the ones passed on to this new generation of legal history students?

III

EVALUATING THE REVISION: HORWITZ'S ALTERNATIVE
TO THE CONSERVATIVE TRADITION

A. The Polemical Challenge

The Transformation of American Law persuasively demonstrates that nineteenth-century judges altered legal doctrines in a manner that promoted certain social policies, usually economic development. To this extent, Horwitz succeeds in his effort to show that nineteenth-century lawyers and judges were neither objective nor politically neutral.[62] In a society that purports to be governed by the popular will on most nonconstitutional issues, the place of the judge

---

[58] D. BOORSTIN, THE AMERICANS: THE NATIONAL EXPERIENCE 444 (1965) [hereinafter D. BOORSTIN, THE AMERICANS]. Boorstin, who is now best known as a generalist-historian of American culture, began his work in legal history. *See* D. BOORSTIN, THE MYSTERIOUS SCIENCE OF THE LAW (1941); Boorstin, *supra* note 24.

[59] D. BOORSTIN, THE AMERICANS, *supra* note 58, at 444.

[60] *Id.*

[61] For a discussion of Willard Hurst's contribution, see Gordon, *supra* note 24, and on American legal history generally, see L. FRIEDMAN, *supra* note 38, G. WHITE, THE AMERICAN JUDICIAL TRADITION (1976), and W. NELSON, *supra* note 5. In addition to the authors mentioned in the text, see M. BLOOMFIELD, *supra* note 7, and W. HOLT, ESSAYS IN NINETEENTH CENTURY AMERICAN LEGAL HISTORY (1976).

[62] Unless, of course, one is prepared to assume that the goal of economic growth is an "objective" or "politically neutral" goal.

is a tenuous one. The basic justification for the institution in America seems to have been that judges would decide cases impartially and would act as agents of the entire populace, in whose best interests they were to resolve disputes.[63]   Some states subject judges to election to keep them responsive to the people, but in other states and the federal system, good behavior tenure gives a measure of political independence that needs to be justified in a democratic society. If Horwitz is correct about the ideological struggles that went on in nineteenth-century law, and also correct in asserting that judges tipped the legal scales to give emerging entrepreneurial and manufacturing groups a disproportionate share of wealth and power in American society, then perhaps the judicial institution has proved inconsistent with basic American democratic beliefs. If there is a polemical message in Horwitz, then, it might be that we should redress the imbalances in private law created by nineteenth-century judges and should either restructure the institution of judging, or frankly acknowledge that it is not as objective as it purports to be.

546

Standing alone, however, *The Transformation of American Law* is not enough to support a movement for radical legal reform. Although Horwitz is brilliant and provocative, the case has not yet been made that the weak and relatively powerless segments of American society were legally overwhelmed by nineteenth-century anti-democratic judges.

As I understand it, the argument for judicial betrayal of the masses depends on the fact that the judges fostered commercial doctrines and attitudes in the face of a clearly dominant "precommercial consciousness" particularly among rural and religious Americans. These people, who presumably made up the majority of American society, are pictured by Horwitz as resisting the judicial implementation of the rules of the market economy and as being the economic losers when those rules were enforced (pp. 253-54).

B. "Losers" as Winners

Horwitz himself concedes that the group he regards as losers were still a powerful force (p. 210). Furthermore, he occasionally acknowledges changes in nineteenth-century law that clearly favored their interests. The good-faith possession statutes, widely passed in the first half of the nineteenth century, offered some measure of pro-

---

[63] G. Wood, *supra* note 5, at 453-63.

tection to occupying claimants whether or not they had good legal title. Although one such law was invalidated by the Supreme Court,[64] and Chancellor Kent blasted good-faith possession laws in his *Commentaries*,[65] Horwitz concedes that the laws remained in effect in most states (pp. 61-62). While the statutes did serve to protect speculating sellers, they also must have been a great benefit to small farmers and squatters.

Similarly, Horwitz admits that, at least in Massachusetts, courts eventually cushioned the impact of the infamous mill acts (pp. 52-53). Interpretation of the acts in the early part of the century had favored mill owners over other riparians; the owners were permitted to flood neighboring properties and amortize their damages, resulting in a forced loan from those whose lands were damaged. In 1830, however, the Massachusetts legislature responded to dissatisfaction with the mill acts by permitting the recovery of permanent damages. In the next few years, says Horwitz, the Massachusetts courts read the mill acts more narrowly, resulting in greater damage liability for mill owners who flooded adjoining property (p. 52). The beneficiaries of this trend, of course, were not the entrepreneurial mill owners, but their agricultural neighbors.

547

While most private law doctrines that were litigated in the appellate courts support Horwitz's thesis of merchant and entrepreneurial ascendancy in the law, there must have been many other legal developments in the nineteenth century that had little to do with these groups. For example, *The Transformation of American Law* tells us relatively little about the effects of legislative action, although Horwitz occasionally hints that state legislatures were pressured into passing legislation antithetical to commercial interests (pp. 211, 243). Other action by state legislatures may have had a significant social impact on American life in realms apart from economics.[66] If we were able to add up the impact of the court decisions Horwitz reviews, and somehow compare this with the impact of other forms of law on nineteenth-century society, we might find that the overall result was very different from that which Horwitz's court decisions alone reveal.

---

[64] Green v. Biddle, 21 U.S. (8 Wheat.) 1 (1823).

[65] 2 J. KENT, COMMENTARIES ON AMERICAN LAW *337-38 (4th ed. 1840).

[66] *E.g.*, R. M. COVER, JUSTICE ACCUSED 63-82 (1975) (legislative action to free slaves); L. FRIEDMAN, *supra* note 38, at 182 (liberalization of divorce laws); Presser, *The Historical Background of the American Law of Adoption*, 11 J. FAM. L. 443, 465-89 (1976) (legislation permitting legal adoption of children).

Finally, even if Horwitz is correct in viewing nineteenth-century legal development as a tale of great gains by merchants and entre-preneurs, it does not necessarily follow that these gains came at the expense of other groups such as farmers and consumers. Horwitz does not give us any examination of "free-riders"—the filtering down of economic gains to society generally.[67] For all we know, most of the consumers and farmers, in absolute terms, were better off after the nineteenth-century legal changes than before. In addition, Hor-witz's assertion that definable "classes" in American society could be characterized as "gainers" or "losers" in legal development may be wrong. Perhaps in nineteenth-century America, particularly in the West, people moved so freely from one occupational group to another that attempts to draw sharp distinctions between "farmers" and "mer-chants" distort social reality. Twentieth-century social classifications may be anachronistic in the nineteenth century.[68]

C. Alternative Interpretations

Horwitz's work is most impressive not because it demonstrates the ascendance of any particular group in the law, but because it suggests that the development of American law reflects a continuing struggle between competing economic and social interests. Just as modern American law is composed of different doctrines promoting both certainty or predictability *and* equity, perhaps the American law of the nineteenth century is also a mass of doctrines with contrary purposes. Horwitz makes relatively few references to American pri-vate law development in places other than the eastern seaboard. From preliminary work on western law, however, one gets the im-pression that western private law doctrines and even styles of judicial reasoning may have differed sharply from those in the East.[69] When

---

[67] This is not properly a criticism of Horwitz, since a major macro-economic study would have been beyond the scope of his undertaking.

[68] Horwitz may have a better case for his proposition in the Northeast, from which he draws much of his data, than in the rest of the country. On the notion of fluid society in nineteenth-century America, see D. BOORSTIN, THE AMERICANS, *supra* note 58, at 113-61.

[69] For example, Daniel Boorstin has suggested that the rule of prior appropriation in water rights, which Horwitz believes went out of favor in the early nineteenth century, was still alive in the West in 1866 when it was codified in federal law. *Id.* at 80. Boorstin believes that the principle of priority continued strong in western law until the end of the nineteenth century. *Id.* In addition, it has been argued that "formalism" was not dominant in the West in the late nineteenth century, and that the whole idea of ascendancy and decline of instrumentalist juris-prudence is open to question. Scheiber, *Instrumentalism and Property Rights: A Reconsidera-tion of American "Styles of Judicial Reasoning" in the Nineteenth Century,* 1975 WIS. L. REV. 1, 12-17.

American legal historians are able to synthesize data on *all* American private law in the nineteenth century, their conclusions may be that the course of American legal history is far more diverse than that presented in *The Transformation of American Law*.

Even if developments in other parts of the country are relatively insignificant, and even if Horwitz is correct about the freezing of legal doctrines in a procommercial mode, his conclusions about the triumph of the merchant-lawyer elite and its *disproportionate* gains may not hold. While nineteenth-century legal change promoted economic development and commerce, it may well have done so not to protect any one favored segment of the economy, but to promote economic and social mobility generally. In the limited sense that the law may have provided equal economic opportunity for those willing and able to learn the techniques of commerce and for those able to employ native intelligence, inventiveness, and shrewdness, the law may have been much more democratic than Horwitz suggests. If one can take nineteenth-century legal commentators at face value,[70] one can read some of Horwitz's evidence as supporting this legal fostering of the development of native abilities. Thus, Gulian Verplanck's insistence in his *Essay on the Doctrine of Contracts* that contractors be permitted to capitalize on "peculiar advantages of skill, shrewdness, and experience"[71] may reflect a desire to encourage those with native talent to rise in stature according to their abilities. Similarly, one can read the New York Court for the Correction of Errors' opinion that Livingston and Fulton were entitled to an injunction to protect their steamboat monopoly as a way "to compensate genius for introducing, extending, and perfecting, the invention of others."[72] The whole trend in water rights and negligence cases that promoted the development of industry at the expense of landed wealth may, in fact, be as much a weakening of the *rentier* interest as it was a blow to the small farmers. In short, before we can safely generalize we need to know more about who the real winners and losers were in nineteenth-century legal development.

549

---

[70] Admittedly, a dangerous assumption. *See, e.g.,* Katz, *Looking Backward: The Early History of American Law,* 33 U. Chi. L. Rev. 867, 881-82 (1966).

[71] G. Verplanck, An Essay on the Doctrine of Contracts: Being an Inquiry How Contracts are Affected in Law and Morals 135 (1825).

[72] Livingston v. Van Ingen, 9 Johns. 507, 547 (N.Y. 1812) (argument of counsel); *see id.* at 560 (opinion of Yates, J.).

Part of our difficulties may be solved if Horwitz, or another legal or economic historian, is able to link up the theories discussed here with the actual social composition of the merchant and entrepreneurial class. One immediate problem is that we need to know more about the supposed split in the commercial interest that Horwitz says developed in the early nineteenth century (p. 154). Horwitz discusses this split only in the context of marine insurance (pp. 228-37) and his discussion seems to suggest that there, at least, the law eventually promoted the interests of the insured, not the insurers. Since the insured were arguably smaller enterprises, this instance of the merchant "split" may have resulted in the law's favoring less powerful economic interests. If this result can be generalized to other areas of the merchant community, it may be difficult to read nineteenth-century law as a well organized movement of the most powerful interests to crush the weakest.

Finally, to test whether some groups in American society managed *disproportionate* gains in nineteenth-century law, one ought really to compare the American legal experience with that of other countries. Horwitz provides some hints in his references to English developments. Horwitz's model of an increasingly stratified society seems to fit England much better than America, and contemporary English law does seem to have given certain groups a disproportionate influence to a greater degree than did American law.[73]

Both English and American law appear to show a reworking of commercial law to favor merchant interests.[74] But it appears that the merchant interest, at least in the area of marine insurance, was more homogeneous in England than in America. American law favored tenants, by permitting them to profit from their improvements as early as 1829 (pp. 55-56). In England, tenants had to wait until the 1880's to win comparable rights.[75] Similarly, the English rule for breach of title warranty in a land sale was less favorable to tenant farmers (or the "industrious citizen or mechanic") than the American rule (pp. 58-62).[76] Nineteenth-century English tort law did not encourage the

550

---

[73] *Compare* D. BOORSTIN, THE AMERICANS, *supra* note 58, at 65-90 *with* W. WILLCOX, THE AGE OF ARISTOCRACY 1688 TO 1830, at 256-61 (3d ed. 1976).

[74] On the process in England, see Horwitz's references to the work of Lord Mansfield in the late eighteenth century (pp. 18, 114, 142-44, 148, 155, 168, 170-71, 174, 178-80, 189-94, 214, 219 & 227).

[75] W. ARNSTEIN, BRITAIN YESTERDAY AND TODAY 145 (3d ed. 1976).

[76] The American position was implemented at first through litigation that expressly rejected the English rule, and later, after the English rule was apparently adopted by the courts, through "good faith possession" statutes (pp. 58-62).

instrumental uses of property to the extent American law did. England enforced strict liability in trespass after America had begun to implement the negligence doctrine (p. 94), and English courts apparently tended to give damages in nuisance actions with more consistency than did American courts.[77]   Finally, in the beginning of the nineteenth century the English courts were restraining competition through the granting of injunctions to franchise holders at a time when American courts favored competition (p. 122). In short, while both English and American law promoted commercial developments through commercial law, the English law of property, torts, and competition appeared to favor vested property interests to a greater degree than the American law did. In the nineteenth century at least, it seems plausible that. English law tended to produce greater disproportionate wealth and power (in the landed property class), than American law did (in a merchant and entrepreneurial class).

551

Conclusion

None of the criticisms advanced here disprove the Horwitz thesis, of course, but before legal scholars accept his alternative to the conservative tradition in legal history, more must be learned about the social and economic effects of the doctrines that Horwitz analyzes. There is a chapter in Doestoyevsky's *The Brothers Karamazov*,[78] in which Christ returns to earth, to sixteenth-century Seville, and is lectured by the Grand Inquisitor on the shortcomings of Christian teaching. The Grand Inquisitor points out to Christ that men are perfectly willing, indeed eager to live by bread alone, and that the organized church has done them a tremendous favor by offering them sustenance in return for their freedom. Free choice between good and evil, explains the Grand Inquisitor, is a terrible burden and men are happier if they can be supplied miracle, mystery, and authority by the church. Doestoyevsky leaves the reader wondering whether the Grand Inquisitor and the organized church were simply lusting after power or were really rendering a service to mankind. In *The Transformation of American Law*, Professor Horwitz poses similar questions about the development of nineteenth-century

---

[77] This is suggested by Horwitz's observation that it was only *after* 1865 that English courts "acknowledge[d] that a process of weighing utilities and not the mere existence of injury was necessary for deciding whether a particular use of land constituted a nuisance" (p. 75).

[78] F. Doestoyevsky, The Brothers Karamazov 227-44 (Signet Classics ed. 1957).

American law. Was legal change benign and in the best interests of all, or was it a clandestine grab for power and wealth? Is the law, like the Grand Inquisitor, hiding its lack of objectivity behind a screen of mysterious rules and doctrines? With Doestoyevskyan passion, Horwitz has argued that nineteenth-century law was an instrument of injustice. As with the Russian master, when one finishes Horwitz's book, one isn't quite sure.

STEPHEN B. PRESSER*

* Associate Professor of Law, Northwestern University School of Law. A.B., 1968, J.D., 1971, Harvard University. Part of the research for this review was made possible by a summer stipend from the National Endowment for the Humanities.

552

Volume XXXV]   *October, 1929*   [*Number 1*

The

American Historical Review

THE INTERRELATION OF SOCIAL AND CONSTITUTIONAL HISTORY[1]

THE happily increasing output of social history has produced much comment on the new garb which the historical muse is assuming. Since adopting the habit of the flapper and making her appeal to the tabloid reading public, Clio is no longer preoccupied with presidents, congresses, court decisions, and the like. She is now concerned with mobs, crazes, fads, Jesse James, P. T. Barnum, the fabulous 'forties, the gay 'nineties, and a thousand other such things. To this modern Clio constitutional history may seem " mid-Victorian ", and therefore hopeless. But looking more closely one finds that social history is not a new thing (Macaulay's third chapter, for instance, is one of the finest passages in social history that we have) ; and that it is not Clio alone that has been watching the modes. With increasing emphasis political scientists are now stressing the note of correlation with the findings of sociology, economics, psychiatry, psychology, and kindred fields. Any scholastic treatment of government as a static, inflexible thing resting upon an abstract conception of sovereignty is out of tune with prevailing scholarship among political scientists themselves.[2] The social historian is himself a sign of the times. He is undergoing a tendency which manifests itself also in political science, in literature, in art, in philosophy, and in the human studies generally. Naturally one asks what will be the reaction of these social studies upon civil history. It is the view of the present writer that this reaction, which has already appeared, is favorable, and that political history has much to gain from these social correlations.

Constitutional history, as understood in this paper, is not merely the history of a constitution. It is not constitutional law, which is a specialized and technical subject for lawyers. It does not resolve

553

[1] This paper was read in part at the meeting of the American Historical Association at Indianapolis, Dec. 28, 1928.

[2] An introduction to current political thought is to be found in C. E. Merriam and H. E. Barnes (eds.), *A History of Political Theories: Recent Times.*

itself into a justification of everything that has been done under a constitutional label. One should not read into constitutional history a consistency and harmony that is not there. The constitutional historian should be best able to reveal legal fictions, to expose constitutional follies, and to criticize the anomalies and abuses that come within the field of his inquiry. He examines civil processes as the biologist examines living cells; and his function is to observe critically and study objectively civil and governmental data. He must bring to his task the scientific skepticism and the careful critique of modern historical research. Besides statutes, proclamations, resolutions, decisions, and other " strictly constitutional documents ", he will need to explore a wide variety of sources which illustrate the drift of social philosophy and the direction of social influence. Constitutional history is no subject for a legalist. It is no subject for one whose interest in the forms of law blinds him to the essential forces that work through law.

Political and constitutional history can not be adequately treated apart from their social and economic bearings. " Politics ", as Woodrow Wilson has said, " can only be studied as life." [3] It is no longer sufficient to follow Austin in defining law as the command of a sovereign. One might better define law as order in society, and think of legal development in terms of an evolutionary process by which rules of human conduct are developed and obeyed not because a sovereign requires it, even though that sovereign be the people, but because such obedience is engendered by the practical necessities of social relations, so that disaster attends communities in which such obedience does not exist.

Even in treating such a topic as the interpretation of the Constitution by the Supreme Court, the legalistic method breaks down. The Supreme Court does not merely apply logical rules of construction to the instrument of 1787. The court has its rules of construction, to be sure; but they involve many contradictions. There are cases which hold that the Constitution, so far as not affected by amendment, is changeless; [4] but there have been enough instances of opposite interpretations being given to the same clause to weaken

[3] Ray Stannard Baker, *Woodrow Wilson: Princeton*, p. 98. See also Woodrow Wilson, *Constitutional Government in the United States*, p. 192.

[4] " The Constitution is a written document, and, as such, its meaning does not alter." South Carolina *v.* U. S., 199 U. S. 437, 448. " It [the Constitution] speaks . . . with the same meaning and intent with which it spoke when it came from the hands of its framers." Ch. J. Taney in Dred Scott *v.* Sandford, 19 How. 393, 426.

the practical import of this doctrine of changelessness.[5] There is the rule that the intention of the framers must be followed;[6] but even if you could know what the intention of the framers was, which is often doubtful,[7] you would be confronted by another " rule of construction " which says that if a certain interpretation is within the letter of the Constitution, it is not to be excluded because the framers

[5] In Lochner *v.* New York, 198 U. S. 45 (1905), the Supreme Court held that a New York law limiting hours of labor in bakeries was void under the federal Constitution as an interference with liberty of contract. In later cases the authority of this decision was worn away. (Muller *v.* Oregon, 208 U. S., 412; Bunting *v.* Oregon, 243 U. S., 426; Adkins *v.* Children's Hospital, 216 U. S. 525.) In the Adkins case Chief Justice Taft, in dissenting from the opinion of the Court, remarked: " It is impossible for me to reconcile the *Bunting Case* and the *Lochner Case,* and I have always supposed that the *Lochner Case* was thus overruled *sub silentio.*" 261 U. S. 564. The income tax law of June 30, 1864, was interpreted as not being a " direct tax " and its constitutionality was upheld in Pacific Ins. Co. *v.* Soulé, 7 Wall. 433 (1868). This position was reversed in Pollock *v.* Farmers' Loan and Trust Co., 158 U. S. 601 (1895). The doctrine that state laws restricting rates to be charged by public utility corporations were not violative of the Fourteenth Amendment was announced in Munn *v.* Illinois, 94 U. S. 113 (1877); but this opinion was reversed in C. M. and St. P. Ry. Co. *v.* Minn., 134 U. S. 418 (1890). In Hepburn *v.* Griswold, 8 Wall. 603, the Legal Tender Act of 1862 was held to be unconstitutional. The opposite opinion was announced in the Legal Tender Cases, 12 Wall. 457. The court held in *Ex parte* Vallandigham, 1 Wall. 243, that a judgment by a military commission is not reviewable by the Supreme Court; but in *Ex parte* Milligan, 71 U. S. 2, the decree of such a commission was reviewed and set aside. Rogers *v.* Burlington, 3 Wall. 654, was reversed in Brenhan *v.* German American Bank, 144 U. S. 173; Doyle *v.* Central Ins. Co., 94 U. S. 535, was reversed in Terral *v.* Burke Construction Co., 257 U. S. 529. For other instances of the " victory of dissent ", see Charles E. Hughes, *The Supreme Court of the United States: its Formation, Methods and Achievements,* pp. 69–70.

[6] " The object of construction, applied to a constitution, is to give effect to the intent of its framers, and of the people in adopting it." Lake County *v.* Rollins, 130 U. S. 662, 670. See also Gibbons *v.* Ogden, 9 Wheaton 1, 188.

[7] In seeking to determine the " intention of the framers " of the Constitution one finds that the members of the convention, even the majority, did not intend the same thing; that in the process of ratification votes were cast by no more than one-sixth of the adult males; that voters for delegates in the state ratifying conventions had only superficially read the Constitution if they had read it at all; that their layman's understanding might differ from the interpretation which lawyer-judges later placed upon the document; that the delegates in the state conventions were influenced by log-rolling as well as by the exercise of pure reason, and that their votes were, in the last analysis, limited to *Yes* or *No* on the whole instrument. Under these circumstances it would be very difficult to determine as to particular clauses, especially the more debatable ones, just what was the intention of those responsible for putting the Constitution into effect. C. A. Beard, *Economic Interpretation of the Constitution*; C. E. Miner, *The Ratification of the Federal Constitution by the State of New York*; A. C. McLaughlin, *The Confederation and the Constitution*; A. J. Beveridge, *Life of John Marshall,* vol. I., chs. VIII., IX. (For further bibliography on ratification, see Charles Warren, *The Making of the Constitution,* p. 744 *n.*)

did not foresee or intend it.[8]　Construing the words of the Constitution according to their contemporary meaning[9] is another rule which the court does not uniformly follow.　For instance, in deciding the income tax of the second Cleveland administration to be unconstitutional, the court applied the words " direct taxes" in the sense of the economist, which was not the sense intended by the framers, who seem to have had in mind land and capitation taxes raised by the states according to quotas fixed by Congress.[10]　The maxim *stare decisis* is a powerful force in conserving legal doctrine; yet at any time the court may depart from precedent.　Construing according to context is another " rule";[11] yet the context of a particular clause may be a mere accident traceable to the committee on style in the convention,[12] and various occasions arise in which the rule is properly disregarded.　The court will at times derive an affirmative from a negative (*e.g.*, Congress is held to have power over navigation because, among other reasons, it is prohibited from giving preference to one port over another),[13] and there are also instances of deriving a negative from an affirmative;[14] but neither of these processes of judicial construction is uniformly applied.

556

[8] " It is not enough to say, that this particular case was not in the mind of the Convention, when the article was framed, nor of the American people when it was adopted. . . . The case being within the words of the rule, must be within its operation likewise." Dartmouth College *v.* Woodward, 4 Wheaton 518, 644–645.

[9] " The convention must have used the word [*commerce*] in that sense [*i.e.*, *navigation*]; because all have understood it in that sense; and the attempt to restrict it comes too late." Gibbons *v.* Ogden, 9 Wheaton 190. See also The Propeller *Genessee Chief et al. v.* Fitzhugh *et al.*, 12 How. 443, 458; Locke *v.* New Orleans, 4 Wall. 172.

[10] Pollock *v.* Farmers' Loan and Trust Co., 158 U. S. 601 (see esp. dissenting opinion, pp. 638 ff.). See also Chase's opinion in Veazie Bank *v.* Fenno, 8 Wall. 533, 542.

[11] " *Noscitur a sociis* is a rule of construction applicable to all written instruments." Va. *v.* Tenn., 148 U. S. 519.

[12] Since the *habeas corpus* clause appears among the limitations placed upon Congress (Art. I., sec. 9), it has been argued that the power to suspend the writ in an emergency belongs to Congress instead of the President (Ch. J. Taney in *Ex parte* Merryman, 17 Fed. Cas. 144). Turning back to the history of the clause in the convention, however, one finds that the subject was discussed in connection with provisions concerning the judiciary, and that it was the committee on style which, as a final touch, placed the clause with the paragraphs concerning Congress. G. Hunt and J. B. Scott (eds.), *Debates in the Federal Convention . . . Reported by James Madison*, pp. 427, 477.

[13] Gibbons *v.* Ogden, 9 Wheaton 191.

[14] This was done in Marbury *v.* Madison, 1 Cranch 137, as to the original jurisdiction of the Supreme Court. The affirmative statement that the court shall have original jurisdiction in specified cases was held to imply that it shall not have original jurisdiction in any other cases. But in Cohens *v.* Virginia, 6 Wheaton 264, the court refused to derive a negative from an affirmative as urged by the counsel

What, then, has happened to the court's "rules of construction"? When one reads the hundreds of pertinent cases involved in pursuing this inquiry he finds that the adjustment of certain. practical interests—it may be those of a bank or a steamship company or a grain elevator corporation or a railroad—and the safeguarding of public interest in connection with these adjustments, have induced a modification here and a restatement there until the court's rules have been flattened into broad doctrines which permit an expansive and flexible interpretation. The court says, in sweeping phrase, that the Constitution must be so construed as to promote its broad purposes. It deals in general language and must not be given·the literal interpretation suitable to a legal code. While enumerating the powers of Congress, it does not attempt to define them. To state the meaning of any of the enumerated powers is a judicial function, a function to be performed in the light of reason. Thus the court, struggling with its task of applying this and that part of the Constitution, is led by the continual modification of its rules of construction to a situation in which almost no line of interpretation is absolutely fixed; for at all points the court reserves to itself a large freedom of judgment in attuning its decisions to changing conditions of society. The very process of finding solutions for "legal questions" in a practical world leads to their social and economic relationships. We have Story's *Commentaries* and Kent's *Commentaries,* but the commentary on the Constitution which appears in American social history is still to be developed; and it may not be venturing too far to suppose that it is the most important of all.

It is an interesting exercise to ponder what we mean by "legal questions". The question of a man's good name and the location of his fence-line may both be legal matters; which indicates that when you call something a "legal question" you have not classified it. To say that the Supreme Court deals with legal questions is about as illuminating as to say that a printing press is used in the manufacture of books. The most diverse kinds of subject-matter, from shrimp canning to radio, may come before the Supreme Court. Admitting that the court deals only with legal questions (or, more strictly, with judicial questions, for political issues·are avoided), the fact remains that when the court gives a decision approving or disapproving the activities of an industry, its decision profoundly affects that industry; and in many of its decisions a wide range of indus-

557

for Virginia, and held that the conferring of original jurisdiction where a state is a party did not have the negative force of excluding appellate jurisdiction where a state is a party. Deriving the negative from the affirmative in the Marbury case, said the court, was necessary to give effect to the purpose of the Constitution, while in the Cohens case it would have had the opposite effect.

trial practices throughout the whole country is involved. To the academic legal writer the points of law may make the chief appeal; but in the business world it is the industrial subject-matter that signifies. A lawyer may be interested in a given decision because it concerns a certain use of the injunction; but the social historian finds it notable because it controls the activities of organized labor. Constitutional history is more than a legal study.

A question that is judicial in its manner of adjustment may be financial or economic or social in its essential character. The Supreme Court today is largely an arbiter of economic problems; and stock brokers closely watch its decisions. To decide, for instance, whether certain legislation is " confiscatory ", and whether property is being taken without " due process of law ", the court must determine what a corporation's property is, tangible and intangible, whether the corporation is overcapitalized, what its earnings are, gross and net, how far capitalized earnings may be taken as a basis for valuation, whether earnings are assisted by an artificially controlled market, what present value attaches to future profits, what attention should be given to " cost of reproduction " in evaluating corporate property, and many other complex questions of capitalistic organization.[15]   In reading many of its decisions, one is impelled to ask, Is the court interpreting the Constitution and the laws, or is it making an economic adjustment? It might in a sense be said that the judge is a part of our industrial régime. Judicial reaction to economic environment is a factor that can not be escaped. Every judge has his economic philosophy, his social ethics on questions of property, landholding, appropriation of socially created values, protection of capital by a public guarantee of profits, and the like. A man with the economic views of Henry George would decide certain legal questions differently than a man holding the economic opinions of, let us say, John Adams. When presidents appoint judges, the economic doctrines of available men are considered; and the Senate gives heed to this factor in confirming nominees. Certain of the court's decisions are more memorable for their economic doctrines than for purely legal principles; and some of the notable dissents are traceable to a difference of economic approach between the dissenting justice and his associates.[16]

---

[15] To show the complex factors of capitalistic economics that come before the Supreme Court one needs only to select at random from a multitude of cases, of which the following are typical: Smyth *v.* Ames, 169 U. S. 466; Galveston Electric Co. *v.* Galveston, 258 U. S. 388; Wilcox *v.* Consolidated Gas Co., 212 U. S. 19; United Gas Co. *v.* Railroad Commission of Ky., Oct. term, 1928, no. 1.

[16] In one of his famous dissenting opinions Justice Holmes brought this element of judicial economics, if we may call it that, into focus when he said: " This

Often what we call constitutional processes are social processes with a constitutional manifestation. As Dr. Jameson has shown, the American Revolution involved important changes in landholding, in the " status of persons ", in the educational horizon, and in social conditions generally.[17] Beard's researches as to property interests involved in the adoption of the Constitution and as to capitalistic-agrarian antagonisms manifest in later controversies are indispensable to the constitutional historian.[18] Southern interests as to race adjustment produced the constitutional defense of slavery; while the impulse for social reform produced such Northern arguments as those of Chase to show that the fugitive slave acts were unconstitutional. Nullification was an economic and social issue, though it produced one of our constitutional classics in the Webster-Hayne debate. As to secession, the constitutional phases should not be ignored, for they were a part of our history; and it should be remembered that the South was justifying state withdrawal as a peaceful, legal affair. Yet one can not read the proceedings of the commercial conventions of the ante-bellum South, or turn the pages of T. P. Kettell,[19] or explore *DeBow's Review*, without realizing the pull of

559

case is decided upon an economic theory which a large part of the country does not entertain. . . . But a constitution is not intended to embody a particular economic theory, whether of paternalism and the organic relation of the citizen to the state or of *laissez faire*. It is made for people of fundamentally differing views, and the accident of our finding certain opinions natural and familiar or novel and even shocking ought not to conclude our judgment upon the question whether statutes embodying them conflict with the Constitution of the United States." Lochner *v.* N. Y., 198 U. S. 75–76. Chief Justice Taft expressed a similar sentiment when dissenting in the Adkins case. 261 U. S. 562. It was the pressure of the capitalistic age that turned the attitude of the Supreme Court on the Fourteenth Amendment. Having formerly restricted the amendment to the protection of the negro as intended by the framers, the court later reversed its position and extended federal protection under the amendment to corporations when confronted with adverse state laws. (Compare the Slaughter-house Cases, 16 Wall. 36, with the Minnesota Rate Case, 134 U. S. 418.) By 1911 the Supreme Court issued 604 opinions under the Fourteenth Amendment, which has been productive of more cases than any other phase of constitutional law. Of these 604 cases, only 28 involved the rights of the negro as such. Charles W. Collins, *The Fourteenth Amendment and the States*; R. E. Cushman, *Leading Constitutional Decisions*, p. 34. See also Charles Warren, *Supreme Court in United States History*, II. 741; Rodney L. Mott, *Due Process of Law*, p. iii.

17 J. F. Jameson, *The American Revolution Considered as a Social Movement*.

18 C. A. Beard, *Economic Interpretation of the Constitution*; id., *Economic Origins of Jeffersonian Democracy*.

19 Kettell's fundamental thesis was that the South, while producing the great bulk of the nation's wealth, was sapped of its just profits by the partiality of the federal government to the North, and by Northern control of cotton marketing, international exchange, banking, manufactures, and shipping. T. P. Kettell, *Southern Wealth and Northern Profits* (N. Y., 1860). See also Robert R. Russel, *Economic*

social and economic forces in the secession movement. In the development of minor parties since the Civil War, the element of social motive is fundamental.[20] Third parties, indeed, seem to belong more to social than to political history. Though failing from the political standpoint in the sense of never winning an election, a minor party may nevertheless achieve success by agitation in favor of its programme until that programme is adopted by one of the major parties and put into execution. The whole movement for the development of nationalism following the Civil War is to be explained chiefly in economic terms. The "unwillingness of absentee capital to rely upon State courts for the vindication of constitutional rights"[21] is a factor that entered powerfully into certain developments since 1865 by which federal courts have become the protectors of capital. Among the links in this process were the Removals Act of 1875,[22] permitting any party asserting a right under the federal Constitution, laws, or treaties, to begin suit in a federal tribunal or have his case removed from a state to a federal court; the development of the doctrine of corporate citizenship,[23] and the opening of new avenues of corporation law by the modern application of the "due process" clause of the Fourteenth Amendment.

The question whether our Constitution is effective is largely a social question. What we call constitutional guarantees are conditioned by social forces. The Constitution prohibits Congress from abridging freedom of speech and press; but (leaving aside the fact that, according to competent authorities, this constitutional prohibition has been violated by Congress in 1798 and 1918) the question whether we actually have liberty of spoken and written opinion is a matter that rests with the community. André Siegfried, who may perhaps be ranked with De Tocqueville and Bryce as a foreign interpreter of American institutions, has remarked that the United States is a Protestant country;[24] and if that is true it is a factor of greater

Aspects of Southern Sectionalism (Univ. of Ill. Studies in Soc. Sciences, XI., nos. 1 and 2, 1924).

[20] Fred E. Haynes, *Social Politics in the United States*, ch. VII.

[21] Felix Frankfurter and J. Landis, *The Business of the Supreme Court*, p. 65 n.

[22] "The Act of 1875 opened wide a flood of totally new business for the federal courts. This development in the federal judiciary, which in the retrospect seems revolutionary, received hardly a contemporary comment." Frankfurter and Landis, *op. cit.*, p. 65. For the act see *U. S. Stat. at Large*, XVIII. 470.

[23] For the development after the Civil War of the "fiction" as to the citizenship of a corporation and of the legal principle that a corporation is a "person", see Gerard Carl Henderson, *The Position of Foreign Corporations in American Constitutional Law*.

[24] André Siegfried, *America Comes of Age*, p. 33.

potency than the constitutional guarantee that office-holding shall be free from any religious test. In certain kinds of cases trials are not impartial despite our bills of rights, for social sentiment amounts to a stacking of the cards for or against the accused. The courts allow a change of venue to avoid prejudice; but this becomes useless if a certain prejudice is state-wide or nation-wide. The protection of jury trial becomes a broken reed in times of social strain or intense popular feeling.[25] In view of such factors it would seem that the most vital subject for the political scientist is to be found in the social bearings of politics.

But there is another side to this question of interrelations. The social historian finds a reciprocal profit in the study of legal and political data. With his insight into social factors he will be able to illuminate many a ·subject by exploring legal records for the indirect light they throw upon conditions of society. Early Kentucky decisions reflect the frontier society of that time.[26] The rulings of these pioneer courts concerning slaves, their anxiety to protect the settler in his land titles, their circumspection when dealing with such outlawed but socially respectable practices as duelling and gambling, their respect for horseflesh, their Latin maxims combined with their practical directness in bringing the pioneer conscience to bear upon particular cases, can not fail to impress the student of society. The investigator of slavery will find useful data in the judicial reports of slave states.[27] Many interesting factors in the transition from the Mexican to the American régime in California are revealed in the earliest legal records of that commonwealth. With the unprecedented rush of immigration the necessities of actual settlement outran law. The old Mexican code, the only constituted law, was a sealed book to the Americans. Justice was somehow administered in advance of settled constitutional government and "custom was for all purposes law".[28] The old Mexican law prohibiting usury, for instance, was quickly overruled by California judges.[29] With the help of legal sources interesting dissertations could be prepared on such subjects as the English common law on the American frontier; legal education in pioneer communities; Kentucky's modified inheritance of Virginian institutions; the supplanting of English landlordism in Virginia;[30] conditions affecting the

561

[25] Z. Chafee, *Freedom of Speech*, pp. 76–80.

[26] 1 Littell (Ky. Reps.), *passim*.

[27] Helen T. Catterall (ed.), *Judicial Cases concerning American Slavery and the Negro*.

[28] Fowler *v.* Smith (1882), 2 Cal. 39, 48.

[29] *Ibid.*

[30] W. E. Dodd, "Chief Justice Marshall and Virginia", *Am. Hist. Rev.*, XLI. 776–787.

Southern Unionist in the Civil War,[31] and so forth. Legal records
are so elaborate; they reveal so much of human nature, and they cover
so many phases of life that they can not safely be ignored by the
historian of social conditions. Much law is ineffective and much
of it involves maladjustment; but the great body of effective law
consists of crystallized social experience expressed in terms of working rules. Precisely because of the social experience which it embodies, law becomes important in the social description of any people.

Law is not as wooden as is sometimes supposed. There is such
a thing as social craftsmanship in the application of law. It has
its procedures as well as its substantive provisions. It may be considered an art, or at least a technique, as well as a science. It gives
a certain play to skill in the utilization of its devices and in the discretion reposed in its agents.[32] An imperfect system of law carries
the germs of its own evolution. Representation has often been enlarged and the franchise extended through the imperfect agency of
a narrower franchise or a more limited representation. It was the
unreformed Parliament of 1832 which passed the Reform Bill and
opened the way for succeeding social reforms. Woman suffrage
was obtained not by revolution but by political processes under male
control. In ratifying the Seventeenth Amendment our state legislatures put into force a constitutional provision by which the right of
those very legislatures to elect United States Senators was transferred to the people. When one studies new branches of jurisprudence such as radio law or the law of air travel he finds not so
much new legal elements, as new applications of principles that have
long been recognized. The law of radio derives much from the
previous law of interstate commerce;[33] and in a recent brief Charles
E. Hughes argues that the right to exclusive use of a certain wave-
length bears an analogy to the law of trademarks.[34] Law is evolu-

562

[31] The reports of the United States Court of Claims throw unexpected light
upon conditions surrounding the Southern Unionist during the Civil War. 3 Ct. Cl.
19, 177, 218, 390; 4: 337; 5: 412, 586, 706.

[32] Roscoe Pound, *Interpretations of Legal History*, pp. 156–157.

[33] Stephen Davis, *The Law of Radio Communication*, p. 28.

[34] It is argued in this connection that, while originally there is no property
right in a particular wave-length, yet the same is true as to a particular sign or
combination of words which in the beginning any one may adopt as a trademark;
and it is an established principle that the person who first makes use of a certain
name or sign without initially interfering with anyone else, and who establishes
the use of such a sign in business, acquires a property right therein. The taking
over of this principle from trademark law to radio law is one of the most interesting current examples of legal evolution. Brief of Charles E. Hughes in General Electric Company's Station WGY *v.* the Federal Radio Commission, Court of
Appeals, District of Columbia (N. Y. *Times*, Dec. 16, 1928, sec. X., p. 16).

tionary. It is for this reason that the leader of social reform often finds that his purpose can be served by using or adapting instead of smashing the political or legal structure.[35]

The social importance of political factors is illustrated in connection with those European movements that have been grouped under the expression " the pragmatic revolt in politics ".[36] Under the stress of post-war struggles, traditional constitutional democracy has been under fire from two directions—from the Right as in Italy and from the Left as in Russia. With the introduction of Mussolini's hand-picked " four hundred " and with the constitutionalizing of the Fascist Grand Council, the last vestige of parliamentary government according to the Constitution of 1848 disappears in that country. The establishment of new dictatorships in Europe has now become so familiar that the recent overthrow of constitutionalism in Jugoslavia was accepted as an ordinary occurrence. This ability of a group within a country to jettison the fabric of constitutionalism, or the inability of other groups or of the country at large to salvage the constitutional structure, has had profound social effects. On the other hand it is of social significance that constitutionalism maintained itself against the threat of the general strike in England. Constitutional control is social control. Or, to put it another way, social control must embrace control through constitutional methods or else through some substitute for those methods; and the choice of the substitute, involving as it may violence and some form of " direct action ", may profoundly affect the social changes themselves. The legal mind is, in any community, a part of social history. No picture of the social institutions of a people is complete without bringing into view its constitutional experience, its governmental aptitudes, and its political background.

563

[35] Lest the student of social questions make the mistake of thinking of law as the product of a legislature, it may be well to emphasize the distinction between legislation and that great body of accumulated law which we may call the *corpus juris* of our courts. Legislation may be thought of as manufactured law; but in the common law, in the whole mass of legal principles as applied in the courts, one sees a slow developing plant that has grown through the centuries and has unfolded in the practical adjustment of human relations with gradual modification to meet new conditions. We should have that kind of law if we had never had any legislatures. The difference between *law* and *legislation* may be illustrated in the fact that a legislature may do a certain thing by statute, and yet the courts may hold that it is invalid because it is not done by " due process of law " (R. L. Mott, *Due Process of Law*, pp. 192–207). Our federal Constitution (Art. III., sec. 3, par. 2) recognizes judicial " attainder of treason ", but declares a bill of attainder prohibited. Thus attainder of treason by legislative act is unconstitutional; but attainder of treason by due process of law is approved.

[36] W. Y. Elliott, *The Pragmatic Revolt in Politics: Syndicalism, Fascism,* and *the Constitutional State.*

The present day specialist in civics is confronted with a new orientation. He must struggle as best he can to grasp the magnitude of social forces in their impact upon politics. Mass formation in modern industry, the development by the working classes of new political theories which threaten the dominant position of capitalism, the growth of feminism, the sharpening of nationalistic tendencies that has accompanied the hostile international contacts of imperialism, the strain upon democratic theory as differential psychology and biological research are undermining the doctrine of equality—these are a few of the factors with which the new political science must deal.[37] In the place of old conceptions of representation have come new formulas such as occupational representation, gild socialism and the like; and social parliaments have been proposed by the Webbs to supplement political parliaments.[38] The validity of the central state itself is challenged as the " pluralists " come forward with their formulas for giving expression to some form of group solidarity. Public opinion is being subjected to many new inquiries, as the writings of Graham Wallas and Walter Lippmann suggest. Government has lost prestige, as Merriam points out, " the old prestige . . . [of the] occult, the divine, the sacred "[39] not having been matched by any new prestige born of the proved advantages of modern types of government.

In this new orientation there is great need for a critical scientific attitude in matters of politics. Much of our public opinion consists of political *clichés*—mere stereotyped mental pictures concerning affairs of government. Many of our citizens have stopped their civic thinking at the grammar school age. The specialist in civics, and his allies, the political and social historian, have a challenging task in clarifying the distinction between scientific thinking in politics and that form of theory-making which is a mere rationalization of the claims of certain social groups. There is much to be done in substituting the scientific approach for a political fundamentalism that is content to juggle with such terms as " sovereignty " and " liberty ", taking terms whose interpretation requires the most careful study and degrading them into mere catchwords. Matters of political philosophy are blurred by the propagandist on the one hand and the oversophisticated intellectual on the other. Yet the importance of political philosophy can not be gainsaid. A social philosopher such as Marx or Paine writes in his study or garret, and it may be that, as

[37] An attempt is made here to summarize the illuminating discussion by Merriam in Merriam and Barnes, *Political Theories: Recent Times*, ch. I.

[38] Sidney and Beatrice Webb, *Constitution for the Socialist Commonwealth of Great Britain*. See also G. D. H. Cole, *Guild Socialism Restated*.

[39] Merriam and Barnes, *op. cit.*, p. 42.

a result of ideas thus launched, a nation may be drenched in blood. Fateful consequences are bound up in the question as to what the people of a community believe. Where belief in witchcraft prevails, persecution and violence result. Influences that act upon the social mind are among the powerful forces of history.

A philosophy expressing itself in outworn orthodoxy is no longer sufficient; and the attitude of opportunism, "habit without philosophy" as Plato calls it [40]—a hard practicality that pushes on to "do things" with no broad vision as to purposes—fails to satisfy. But a sophisticated philosophy that expresses itself only in revolt, that discards all values, and issues only in shifting sands, is no better than orthodoxy or opportunism. Even though one may stop short of a completed political philosophy, he will go far if he substitutes tested conclusions for prejudices and cultivates sound-mindedness in matters of government, an attitude that is critical, modern, and evolutionary, but does not cynically abandon all values as fictions. As the civic student reads current works on political theory he will doubtless envy a Jefferson or a Wilson for their confident political creeds. Somewhere between blind fundamentalism and destructive sophistication he may hope to find a middle ground where a balanced and informed philosophy is in some adjustment with life, and where one may have a political confession of faith without ignoring the realities of politics. Whatever the outcome of such a quest may be, it is submitted that the most useful objects to be promoted by the historical gild will come, not by an isolation of economic or social or constitutional history as if any of these were a self-sufficient field, but by each specialist welcoming the contribution of his allies.

565

J. G. RANDALL.

[40] Plato, *Republic X* (*Dialogues of Plato*: Selections from the translation by B. Jowett, ed. by W. C. Greene), p. 428; Graham Wallas, *The Great Society*, p. 83.

American Constitutional History and the New Legal History: Complementary Themes in Two Modes

Harry N. Scheiber

The approaching bicentennial of the Constitution promises to stimulate interest in scholarship on the history of American law. This prospect coincides with what many practitioners of constitutional history consider to be a genuine crisis in their field—a crisis that recently inspired the program committee of a major scholarly organization to feature the theme "Is Constitutional History Dead?" in preparing its annual meeting.[1] The essence of the field's problem, as many contend, is that scholarly interest in the traditional core of constitutional history—the doctrines and behavior of courts—has been overshadowed during the last two decades by a distinctly different mode of investigation, one that is often termed the "new legal history."

My contention is that, while some troubles do beset the field of constitutional history, there is little reason to proclaim or even seriously debate the "death" of that field. The new legal history, taking the whole legal system as its province and stressing the interactions of change in law with socioeconomic developments, offers perspectives on American history in many vital respects different from the perspectives of constitutional history; yet the two approaches are necessarily complementary both in their logical structures and in their evidentiary bases. Only by integrating their concerns can the full context and significance of change in American legal history be understood.

Harry N. Scheiber is professor of law at the University of California, Berkeley. He acknowledges with thanks research support provided by a humanities fellowship of the Rockefeller Foundation.

[1] This pessimistic session title was adopted by the American Society for Legal History program committee in the planning for the fall 1980 annual meeting. When the final program was prepared, however, the more cautious title "The Crisis in American Constitutional History and Public Law" was adopted. No creation of a straw man was intended; the validity of each title was seriously debated. As to rising interest in constitutional history vis-à-vis the bicentennial: Project '87 has pursued a program of research fellowships and public and scholarly conferences; an encyclopedia of the Constitution, funded by National Endowment for the Humanities, has been announced under the editorship of Leonard W. Levy and Kenneth Karst; and the American Historical Association has embarked on a project for publication of pamphlets on constitutional history for teachers and students. These activities are in addition to pending bills in Congress providing for various types of recognition of the bicentennial.

Such troubles as may beset constitutional history—if one defines "troubles" as lack of vitality in scholarship in the field, lack of attention given the field by sister specialties and disciplines, and the like—are not exclusively of recent vintage, nor do they relate alone to the challenge posed by the new legal history. Indeed, a long and distinguished line of friendly critics has faulted constitutional historians for too often writing as if law were divorced from life, giving too much attention to doctrine and to judges.[2] In the 1960s and 1970s, however, what long had been a major source of support for constitutional history, the interest of political scientists in historical studies of constitutional law, began to weaken. Behavioral theory, quantification, and self-proclaimed "value-free" analysis crowded constitutional law from the center stage of political science; serious scholarly engagement with constitutional history and law became less and less common. In the last few years, the pendulum has swung back. Political science has rediscovered the importance of ideology, social class, and, more generally, normative values in political analysis.[3] Yet ironically an important segment of the discipline that has led in the return from behavioralism to these normative concerns remains fundamentally hostile to one of the controlling premises of public law and of constitutional history—the premise that traditional constitutional principles have a content and historical importance that go beyond mere rhetoric. Many of the critics of behavioralism have a radical-critical orientation; they view constitutional and statutory principles as mere "rule formalism and proceduralism" that attempt to mask but cannot really hide an exploitative political system's machinations.[4] Often, then, the core tradition of constitutional law is dismissed out of hand as empty pretension. From political scientists of this persuasion, there is little interest in scholarship in the traditional mode of American constitutional history.[5]

567

Another element of the difficulties being experienced by constitutional history is what can fairly be termed a loss of prestige in the academy. Admittedly, my evidence is only impressionistic, based upon four years' service during the last ten years on major book-prize committees in the profession and upon systematic discussions with fellow scholars engaged in constructing standardized

[2] See, for example, J. G. Randall, "The Interrelation of Social and Constitutional History," *American Historical Review*, XXXV (Oct. 1929), 1–13. Cf. Paul L. Murphy, "Time to Reclaim: The Current Challenge of American Constitutional History," *American Historical Review*, LXIX (Oct. 1963), 64–79; and Lawrence M. Friedman, "Some Problems and Possibilities of American Legal History," in *The State of American History*, ed. Herbert J. Bass (Chicago, 1970), 3–5.

[3] Murphy, "Time to Reclaim," 73; David Easton, "The New Revolution in Political Science," *American Political Science Review*, 63 (Dec. 1969), 1051–61. The latter is a critique and partial repudiation of behavioralism by one of its early architects. For a book that reflects the optimism of the behavioral/quantitative movement, see Walter F. Murphy and Joseph Tanenhaus, *The Study of Public Law* (New York, 1972).

[4] Gordon J. Schochet, "Constitutionalism, Liberalism, and the Study of Politics," *Nomos*, XX (1979), 8–9. See also Herman Belz, "New Left Reverberations in the Academy: The Antipluralist Critique of Constitutionalism," *Review of Politics*, 36 (April 1974), 265–83.

[5] This is not to say, of course, that a radical-critical scholarly posture precludes taking constitutionalism and its values seriously. See, for example, Thomas I. Emerson, *The System of Freedom of Expression* (New York, 1970).

tests, organizing conferences, and conducting searches to fill faculty posts.[6] Nearly all the evidence points to a serious erosion of concern with constitutional law and history in the training of both undergraduate and graduate students. It appears that in many, perhaps most, of the leading centers of learning today it is entirely possible to obtain the Ph.D. in American history without a firm command of the substantive history of American constitutional law (let alone command of the broader concerns that represent the new legal history). Many undergraduate curricula, and even the introductory survey courses or the courses that substitute for the old-line survey, seem to give far less attention to constitutional themes than they did twenty years ago.[7]

Still another dimension of what many practitioners see as the crisis in constitutional history is the general lack of attention to the history of public-sector themes that characterizes much of the current scholarship in history. Symptomatic of this tendency is the recently published volume *The Past before Us*, a book of essays carrying the imprimatur of the American Historical Association.[8] The message of these essays, one critic contends, seems to be that "we are all social historians now." The new social history, presented as the dominant genre of current scholarship, subordinates law, policy, and public affairs generally to what is termed " 'private place': the family, the bedroom and nursery, voluntary associations, and nonpolitical social institutions."[9] The Civil War, another critic has noted, fails even of mention in *The Past before Us*, except as part of the furniture of historical consciousness.[10] It should be self-evident that a style of scholarship that finds no place for the Civil War as a landmark event cannot be expected to generate much respect for, say, the *Passenger* cases or the Contract Clause, let alone the fellow-servant doctrine.

With these considerations in mind as to the broader dimensions of the perceived "crisis" in the study of constitutional history, let us consider next the view, held by many, that the new legal history bears special responsibility for the field's problems.

Traditionally the province of constitutional history embraced the decisions of the Supreme Court, the institutional history of the Court, and biography of the justices. Although a few outstanding scholars such as Edward S. Corwin, Benjamin Wright, and Fletcher M. Green defined the field much more broadly than that, not so with the great majority of researchers in history, law, and political science. The field therefore proved an easy target for critics who deplored limiting study to what they denounced as a rarified universe of data

568

---

[6] Reference here is to service on the Beveridge and Dunning prize committees, organizing activity for two Project '87 conferences, program-committee work for several scholarly organizations, and College Board committee activities.

[7] This statement is based on data from survey-course syllabi provided by several dozen college and university departments to the College Board's Advanced Placement Committee.

[8] Michael Kammen, ed., *The Past before Us: Contemporary Historical Writing in the United States* (Ithaca, 1980).

[9] Gertrude Himmelfarb, "The New History," *New York Times Book Review*, Aug. 17, 1980, p. 3.

[10] Eric Foner, "Yes, Va., There Was a Civil War," *New York Times*, Sept. 14, 1980, sec. iv, p. 21.

and issues out of touch with the realities of social, economic, and cultural change.

Much of such criticism came from the "legal realists," who dominated legal analysis in academic discourse of the 1940s and 1950s.[11] Further inspiration for criticism on these lines came from British historians who were stripping away the facade of formal law and constitutionalism in the quest for the hard realities of administrative history and "government in action."[12] It was but a short step from the position of such realist critics as Karl Llewellyn—author of the most developed position attacking older-style constitutional analysis as arid and formalistic—to the position taken in early methodological statements by Willard Hurst, a scholar who with Richard Morris, George Haskins, Leonard Levy, and Lawrence Friedman has virtually rewritten the conceptual foundations of American legal history.[13] Historians, in Hurst's view, had greatly exaggerated the importance of "the work of courts and legal activity immediately related to litigation."[14] Attention should be directed instead to "the social functions of law." In his own work, Hurst stressed such long-term continuities as the effects of "social inertia and the momentum of social drift." He broke very decisively with the framework-of-analysis subject categories that traditionally had been dictated by the content of constitutional law.[15] The history of the legal system should be considered, Hurst contended, by use of an analytic framework that reflected instead law's real-life functions and impact.[16]

569

The literature of the new legal history well reflects the ascendancy of such views. No longer is "the evolution of the law [treated] as if it had all happened

[11] Robert W. Gordon, "Willard Hurst and the Common Law Tradition in American Legal Historiography," *Law and Society Review*, 10 (Fall 1975), 9–56; Harry N. Scheiber, "Federalism and the American Economic Order, 1789–1910," *ibid.*, 58–67. Stephen Diamond, "Legal Realism and Historical Method: J. Willard Hurst and American Legal History," *Michigan Law Review*, 77 (Jan.–March 1979), 784–94.

[12] This strain in British scholarship dates from Walter Bagehot, *The English Constitution* (London, 1867). The great modern exponent of constitutional analysis in terms of working government institutions is G. R. Elton.

[13] Cf. Harry N. Scheiber, "At the Borderland of Law and Economic History: The Contributions of Willard Hurst," *American Historical Review*, LXXV (Feb. 1970), 744–56; Herbert Alan Johnson, "American Colonial Legal History: A Historiographical Interpretation," in *Perspectives on Early American History*, ed. Alden T. Vaughan and George Athan Billias (New York, 1973), 250–81. Emblematic of a new realism in the study of legislation and its enforcement was the work in the 1930s and 1940s of Paul Wallace Gates on American land policy. See Paul Wallace Gates, "The Homestead Law in an Incongruous Land System," *American Historical Review*, XLI (July 1936), 652–81; Paul Wallace Gates, "Land Policy and Tenancy in the Prairie States," *Journal of Economic History*, I (May 1941), 60–82.

[14] Willard Hurst, "The Law in United States History," *Proceedings of the American Philosophical Society*, 104 (Aug. 15, 1960), 521.

[15] *Ibid.*, 521, 524. Hurst used the term "instrumentalism" to describe typical uses of law in nineteenth-century America; subsequently, the term has been used extensively by others as equivalent to pragmatism in uses of law. Willard Hurst, "Changing Responsibilities of the Law School, 1868–1968," *Wisconsin Law Review* (1968), 336–37.

[16] For others who advocated this conceptual change, see D. J. Boorstin, "Tradition and Method in Legal History," *Harvard Law Review*, 54 (Jan. 1941), 424–36; George L. Haskins, "Law and Colonial Society," *American Quarterly*, IX (Fall 1957), 354–64. See also the classic historiographical essay by Lawrence M. Friedman, "Heart against Head: Perry Miller and the Legal Mind," *Yale Law Journal*, 77 (May 1968), 1244–59.

in outer space rather than in the real world," as Peter Coleman has written; "Langdell [is] out, and Hurst in. . . ."[17] The new legal history has greatly expanded the province of materials and analysis that define the law's past. Studies in this mode have pushed the common law—especially themes such as how judges have shaped contract and tort law and with what consequences for economic institutions and allocations of income and power—to the very center of the analytic focus. Moreover, there is now considerable attention to law-making agencies other than the federal courts, to the making and incidence of state law, and to reappraisal of landmarks in constitutional law in the light of legal, social, and political developments in the states.[18] The new-mode practitioners of legal history acknowledge that the field must not only examine "how developments in American society shaped the law," but must seek also, as David Rothman has written, "to run the lines the other way, to explore the implications of the structure and substance of the American legal system" for social change.[19] Some of the new legal history's exponents proclaim explicitly the importance of maintaining the old intellectual-history tradition of investigating the law as an "autonomous" system of ideas and doctrines; but their emphasis is upon how this system expresses (or challenges) other social values and norms rather than upon how one idea led to another, in follow-the-dots fashion, as an exclusive investigative concern.[20]

570

What are the functional linkages between these methodological developments and the "crisis" in the study of constitutional history? In the first place, some of the new legal history's best-known substantive scholarship has been notable for its lack of attention to the concerns of traditional constitutional history. For example, Lawrence M. Friedman's *History of American Law* is universally recognized as a landmark work in the study of American legal history;[21] yet even while appreciative of its achievements, one prominent commentator complained that the book gave too little attention to the nation's high politics, to the Supreme Court, and withal to the interaction of "law, politics, and ideology . . . defin[ing] the social values of a nation."[22] Another work, by Morton Horwitz,[23] purports (despite a slender geographical

[17] Peter J. Coleman, "The New Realism in American Legal History," *Law and Liberty*, 3 (Autumn 1976), 3.

[18] See Stanley I. Kutler, *Privilege and Creative Destruction: The Charles River Bridge Case* (Philadelphia, 1971). Some of the new literature is discussed in Jamil S. Zainaldin, "The New Legal History: A Review Essay," *Northwestern University Law Review*, 73 (no. 1, 1978), 205–25; and William E. Nelson, "Legal History," *Annual Survey of American Law, 1973–74* (New York, 1974), 625–28. See also Stanley Katz, "Looking Backward: The Early History of American Law," *University of Chicago Law Review*, 33 (Summer 1966), 867–84.

[19] David J. Rothman, "The Promise of American Legal History," *Reviews in American History*, 2 (March 1974), 19.

[20] See Harry N. Scheiber, "Back to the 'Legal Mind'? Doctrinal Analysis and the History of Law," *Reviews in American History*, 5 (Dec. 1977), 458–66; Mark Tushnet, "The American Law of Slavery, 1810–1860: A Study in the Persistence of Legal Autonomy," *Law and Society Review*, 10 (Fall 1975), 119–83; Lawrence M. Friedman, "Legal Culture and Social Development," *ibid.*, 4 (Aug. 1969), 29–44. See also Friedman, "Problems and Possibilities of American Legal History."

[21] Lawrence M. Friedman, *A History of American Law* (New York, 1973).

[22] G. Edward White, review, *Virginia Law Review*, 59 (Sept. 1973), 1130–31, 1140.

[23] Morton J. Horwitz, *The Transformation of American Law, 1780–1860* (Cambridge, Mass., 1977).

data base) to describe "the transformation of [all of] American law," yet it fails to give sustained attention to constitutional issues. The book fails even to consider the doctrines of dual federalism, which underlay validation of the states' authority in the very areas of judicial rule-making that the book stresses.[24]

Some constitutional historians have expressed a legitimate concern that this sort of subordination or neglect threatens to become endemic. They fear that blocking constitutional law out of legal-history studies might easily become a touchstone of new legal history—an entry card, as it were, to the club. This worry is reinforced by the fact that many monographs in the literature of the new legal history deal with family relations, criminal law, private-law doctrines, and other matters that did not play much part in federal constitutional litigation until late in the nineteenth century.[25] In many of these studies, there seems to be little interest in linkages that imaginative analysis might suggest between movements in state law and the contemporary history of constitutionalism (as opposed to constitutional litigation narrowly defined)—linkages that would broaden and enrich the new legal history.

571

In the second place, the new legal history is perceived as threatening to constitutional history because some of the new-mode historians subscribe to a view that constitutionalism is nothing more than hypocrisy. This view goes far beyond the realists' skepticism of democratic or egalitarian constitutional doctrine. It also goes beyond a recognition that law can be exploitative and that it has worked in exploitative ways in the course of American history.[26] It is a view that has serious functional implications for research because it portrays American law as undeviatingly exploitative, anti-egalitarian, and anti-democratic. The classic constitutional values are seen as mere smokescreens that obscure exploitation. Some scholars who adhere to this view reserve a special measure of contempt for movements and beliefs that are associated with what may be termed centrist American liberalism.[27] The most strident and polemical of such attacks are directed against some of the pioneers of the new mode of legal history who are alleged to hold a bland "consensus" view; thus, any notion that the new legal history is a monolith, without its own schisms, is dispelled quickly once one examines the polemical literature.[28]

[24] Cf. Scheiber, "Federalism and the American Economic Order," 72–100; Morton Grodzins, *The American System: A New View of Government in the United States*, ed. Daniel J. Elazar (Chicago, 1966).

[25] See Wythe Holt, ed., *Essays in Nineteenth-Century American Legal History* (Westport, 1976); Lawrence M. Friedman and Harry N. Scheiber, eds., *American Law and the Constitutional Order: Historical Perspectives* (Cambridge, Mass. 1978). The Commission on Undergraduate Education in Law and Humanities is now publishing a series of works offering classroom materials on themes in American legal history, including themes mentioned in this article.

[26] That courts have allocated resources and privileges in a manner that is redistributive, and often exploitative, in its effects has long been a main theme of Hurst's work and of such studies as Richard B. Morris, *Government and Labor in Early America* (New York, 1946).

[27] Morton J. Horwitz asserts, for example, that "the historical writing of the last generation tended to ignore all questions about the effects of governmental activity on the distribution of wealth and power in American society." Horwitz, *Transformation of American Law*, xiv. This assertion seems to me entirely spurious.

[28] For a recent reply to such criticism, see Willard Hurst, "Old and New Dimensions of Research in United States Legal History," *American Journal of Legal History*, 25 (Jan. 1979), 9–18. Cf.

Nor are scholars of the left wholly exempt from similar criticism based on the premise that any judge's assertion of such constitutional values as rule of law, dignity of the individual, or equal rights is to be viewed as sheer hypocrisy.[29]

A third dimension of the threat to constitutional history is the association that some critics regard as prevailing between the new-style social history and current scholarship in the Hurst mode. At least on a semantical level, it may seem plausible that the ideal Hurst and Friedman admire, of a "*social* history of American law,"[30] threatens to merge with a type of social history which, given its methodology and interests, will pay little attention to constitutional law. The threat of such a merger gains further credibility from the fact that many new legal historians lean toward social-scientific model building or at least have strong affinities with social science and economic history.[31]

So much for the forces producing stress, if not to say a crisis, in the field of constitutional history. Are there any tendencies, one may ask, in the new legal history that portend a brighter future—if not for a "revival" of constitutional history, assuming it needs one, then at least for a fruitful reintegration of its concerns and techniques with those of legal history in the new mode?

What follows here is inherently optimistic and ecumenical (though not, I like to think, hopelessly eclectic!). The optimism derives from my belief that the best of the new legal history does, in fact, incorporate the traditional concerns and themes from constitutional history. Above all, the optimism is founded on the contention that the very logic of legal history, new or old, absolutely requires functional integration of constitutional history.

Both as a matter of basic methodology and as a matter of accurate reflection of the issues of law in relation to real-life social change, it makes little sense to banish the traditional subject matter of constitutional history from the research compound now under effective control of the new legal history. The

572

Wythe Holt, "Now and Then: The Uncertain State of Nineteenth-Century American Legal History," *Indiana Law Review*, 7 (no. 4, 1974), 615–43. For useful commentary on this matter, see Charles J. McClain, Jr., "Legal Change and Class Interests: A Review Essay on Morton Horwitz's *The Transformation of American Law*," *California Law Review*, 68 (March 1980), 382–97.

[29] Thus E. P. Thompson is attacked for stating that the ideal of "rule of law" is "an unqualified human good" even though, as Thompson demonstrates by his research, it is an ideal that can be manipulated cynically for exploitative purposes. This view, his critic argues, is in error because rule of law always unleashes the most selfish forces in society and is uniformly used to promote "substantive inequality." Morton J. Horwitz, "The Rule of Law: An Unqualified Good?" *Yale Law Journal*, 86 (Jan. 1977), 566. The quotations from Thompson are from E. P. Thompson, *Whigs and Hunters: The Origin of the Black Act* (London, 1975), 266. This sort of criticism ends all dialogue and creates an impasse from the confines of a closed intellectual system.

[30] Friedman, *History of American Law*, 10.

[31] Two examples from the literature on the nineteenth-century criminal law and on litigation will illustrate the point: Michael Stephen Hundus, *Prison and Plantation: Crime, Justice, and Authority in Massachusetts and South Carolina, 1767–1878* (Chapel Hill, 1980); Lawrence M. Friedman and Robert V. Percival, "A Tale of Two Courts: Litigation in Alameda and San Benito Counties," *Law and Society Review*, 10 (Winter 1976), 267–301. The serious possibility of a merger with new-mode social history that cuts legal history off from the constitutional-history tradition is probably slight. Even when the new legal history manages to push landmarks like federalism or the Civil War into the background, its focus remains squarely in the public sector; moreover, the core of the field's evidentiary materials—judicial decisions, statutes, administrative decisions—tends to hold analysis within a strongly chronological framework.

subject matter of the two fields considered together constitutes a set of complementary themes in two modes.

In support of this view, one ought to consider first of all the perdurable, if all too frequently overlooked, concern with constitutionalism that marks the work of Hurst, Haskins, and Levy. This concern permeates both substantive scholarship and methodological statements on legal history. Hurst repeatedly stresses that "ours is by its deepest tradition a *constitutional* legal order."[32] The central ideal of constitutionalism, in Hurst's formulation, is "the responsibility of organized power to be useful and to be just," in order that a "substantial accountability" can be required of every center of power, public and private.[33]

Hurst's judgment as to how well or badly the American legal system has performed, historically, never rests on a blind faith (which some critics impute to him) that the constitutional ideal has been consistently achieved. On the contrary, he takes pains to indicate that "so far as this society achieved the constitutional ideal" it was "dependent as much on the relative independence of political processes from total constraint wielded by other social institutions or by any one political faction as it [depended] on the relative independence of other social institutions from total restraints of law."[34] Furthermore, Hurst has provided a substantive and normative assessment of the legal system's performance that it is sharply critical in vital respects. His critique of the system's operation is based partly on a well-delineated model of how it would work if it were consummately efficient. The critique is also based on an equally explicit model of how the system must work to be fair and to be responsible. That is to say, Hurst uses the constitutional ideal as a normative model against which historic performance is to be measured.[35] Therefore, insofar as Hurst's studies provide many of the new legal historians with a "field theory" for their research, it is one that ought to give a central place to issues of constitutionalism. This feature of Hurst's methodology in itself provides a powerful linkage between traditional constitutional history and the newer-style studies.

573

Indeed, a robust concern with constitutionalism permeates even studies that may superficially appear to be at the farthest remove from traditional modes of constitutional analysis—studies within the new legal history that deal in a sociological vein with lawyers, judges, and other elements of the legal system's authority structure. Jerold S. Auerbach's *Unequal Justice*, for exam-

[32] Hurst, "Changing Responsibilities of the Law School," 340.

[33] James Willard Hurst, "Legal Elements in United States History," *Perspectives in American History*, V (1971), 14; James Willard Hurst, *Law and Social Process in United States History* (Ann Arbor, 1960), 301. The major synthetic work in the literature integrating these classic constitutional concerns with findings from the new legal history is Harold M. Hyman, *A More Perfect Union: The Impact of the Civil War and Reconstruction on the Constitution* (New York, 1973). Several important studies of colonial law that perform a comparable function are collected in *Essays in the History of Early American Law*, ed. David H. Flaherty (Chapel Hill, 1969).

[34] Hurst, *Law and Social Process*, 301. See also James Willard Hurst, *Law and Social Order in the United States* (Ithaca, N.Y., 1977), 45.

[35] See Scheiber, "At the Borderland of Law and Economic History," 746–52.

ple, is interesting above all, perhaps, for the appraisal it provides in normative terms of lawyers' behavior and roles. His appraisal is founded solidly on the values of constitutionalism; Auerbach places at the core of his analysis "the disparity between democratic ideals and hierarchical realities."[36] Even studies in prosopography and group behavior that deal with collective biography of lawyers, judges, or such officers as justices of the peace, located far down in the hierarchical structure of officialdom—whether or not such studies are explicitly concerned to apply normative standards—still serve to enrich our understanding of the working legal system.[37] Can they possibly be viewed as irrelevant to constitutional history? They cast light in a unique way upon the problem of class bias in the behavior of legal institutions and actors; and they give us a better understanding of what "discretion" can mean in the workaday operations of the system. In addition, they provide a more comprehensive portrait of the persons and structures whose functions are essential to the working constitution. Such empirical studies complement the more traditional constitutional history, just as they beneficially stretch outward the boundaries of the new legal history.

574

A different, but no less important, integration of concerns between the new legal history and constitutional history comes from research in the history of administration and in state-level judicial history. This research has examined, in many instances, the classic issues of constitutional law; it investigates these issues from the bottom up, as it were, instead of approaching them by taking Supreme Court consideration and action as the starting point. Traditional constitutional historians too often regarded Supreme Court decisions as an accurate "map" of how power actually was exercised and limited in the governance of the nation.[38] This is too simplistic an approach, as evidenced by certain policy areas where Congress proved notoriously inclined to abdicate responsibility—or became hopelessly deadlocked because of its own members' constitutional objections to its taking action—and so devolved power effectively on the states. Moreover, a moment's reflection on even the "great cases" of constitutional law must pique some curiosity about the state judges who are often found articulating doctrines directly contrary to prevailing Supreme Court doctrines. Typically, historians have tended to treat such evidence from the states as merely the "stuff" of constitutional adjudication—that is to say, as an essential element in the drama of the great cases, but otherwise as being of little historical importance. Yet the challenges to federal

[36] Jerold S. Auerbach, *Unequal Justice: Lawyers and Social Change in Modern America* (New York, 1976), 307.

[37] Among the best of such recent studies are Kermit L. Hall, *The Politics of Justice: Lower Federal Judicial Selection and the Second Party System, 1829-61* (Lincoln, Neb., 1979); Maxwell Bloomfield, *American Lawyers in a Changing Society, 1776-1876* (Cambridge, Mass., 1976); John R. Wunder, *Inferior Courts, Superior Justice: A History of the Justices of the Peace on the Northwest Frontier, 1853-1889* (Westport, Conn., 1979).

[38] For an illustration of the parallel situation in state law (Wisconsin, 1836-1958), see Lawrence M. Friedman, *Contract Law in America: A Social and Economic Case Study* (Madison, 1965). On national law and governmental behavior, see Harry N. Scheiber, "American Federalism and the Diffusion of Power: Historical and Contemporary Perspectives," *University of Toledo Law Review*, 9 (Summer 1978), 619-80.

judicial rulings that repeatedly issued from the state courts were often the surface expression of a pattern of real-life governmental action quite at variance
with the Supreme Court's official prescriptions.

In other words, the federal system frequently worked differently from what a
reading of decisions in the great cases would suggest. By focusing research initially on the economic and social situations that produced state decisions, the
new legal history provides a richer understanding of what the Supreme Court
was confronting; at the same time, investigation in this mode reveals elements
of the working governmental system that are obscured when we give exclusive
attention to federal constitutional cases.

Two examples will suffice. The first is the Commerce Clause in the nineteenth century. From research in state archives scholars have learned the way
in which state canal officials rigged tolls so as to disadvantage out-of-state
interests. These policies were blatantly in violation of the Marshall Court's
nationalistic commerce doctrines; still, they remained unchallenged until the
railroad era opened. Other recent research—notably by Charles W. McCurdy   575
on big business's objectives and tactics in both state and federal courts,
research complementing Gabriel Kolko's and Albro Martin's studies of the
problem of railroad regulation—similarly has forced scholars to refashion their
understanding of the content of the Commerce Clause in constitutional law
and of the actual exercise of power in the states.[39]

A second example of the possibilities of reintegrating constitutional history
with the new legal history is in property law. Through close analysis of doctrinal areas in which enormous discretion was left to state judges—nuisance
law, trespass, torts generally, eminent domain—we can identify differences
among the states, thereby obtaining a much more accurate sense of working
federalism. We can seek to correlate doctrinal tendencies with differential
patterns of economic structure and of development, and we achieve a basis for
appraising how constitutional values constrained or prompted specific types of
behavior in the private sector, especially by entrepreneurial interests seeking
governmental largess, privileges, or immunities.[40] Repeatedly, those who are
working in this area are drawn back to the reintegration of property law with
constitutional law—not because it makes for nice logic or is aesthetically

[39] Charles W. McCurdy, "American Law and the Marketing Structure of the Large Corporation,
1875-1890," *Journal of Economic History*, XXXVIII (Sept. 1978), 631-49; Charles W. McCurdy,
"The *Knight* Sugar Decision of 1895 and the Modernization of American Corporation Law, 1869-
1903," *Business History Review*, 53 (Autumn 1979), 304-43; Harry N. Scheiber, *Ohio Canal Era:
A Case Study of Government and the Economy, 1820-1861* (Athens, Ohio, 1969), 247-67; Gabriel
Kolko, *Railroads and Regulation, 1877-1916* (Princeton, 1965); Albro Martin, "The Troubled Sub-
ject of Railroad Regulation in the Gilded Age—A Reappraisal," *Journal of American History*, LXI
(Sept. 1974), 339-71.

[40] James Willard Hurst, *Law and Economic Growth: The Legal History of the Lumber Industry
in Wisconsin, 1836-1915* (Cambridge, Mass., 1964), explores these themes in the context of one
industry's development. See also Horwitz, *Transformation of American Law*; Harry N. Scheiber,
"Property Law, Expropriation, and Resource Allocation by Government: The United States, 1789-
1910," *Journal of Economic History*, XXXIII (March 1973), 232-51; Paul M. Kurtz, "Nineteenth
Century Anti-Entrepreneurial Nuisance Injunctions: Avoiding the Chancellor," *William and
Mary Law Review*, 17 (Summer 1976).

acceptable in a scholarly world that is more comfortable with the Contract Clause than with, say, "offsetting doctrines," but rather because litigants, lawyers, and judges in the nineteenth century manifestly functioned with a very high consciousness of constitutional values and mandates.[41]

An important by-product of research in this area is the discovery of legal doctrines that served as validating canons in American jurisprudence—and hence are historically of vital importance—yet cannot be discovered by reading only Supreme Court decisions. The new legal history has shown, for example, how the "release of energy" (Hurst's phrase, referring to entrepreneurial energy and subsuming a concept of open opportunity) became a major doctrine of the legal system in action[42] A particularly rich strategy of research is demonstrated by Levy's brilliant work on the Massachusetts court under Chief Justice Lemuel Shaw; here, Levy traces fascinating doctrinal connections between state decisions and federal constitutional law of both contemporary and subsequent times.[43] Building on Hurst's findings and Levy's study, I have contended that a doctrine termed "rights of the public"—evident in the law of police power, eminent domain, and public trust—became an important force shaping governmental responses to pressures from development in the economy's private sector.[44] This doctrine served as a lodestone at crucial moments when courts had to give rank order and priorities to certain private rights. It operated in a vivid counterpoint with two other themes in American law: the doctrine of "vested rights," which Corwin declared was the "basic doctrine" of American law; and the pragmatic principle giving high priority to "release of energy," stressed in Hurst's work.[45] Ultimately, even the classic constitutional doctrines, especially regarding the Contract Clause, were profoundly influenced by movements in state law that involved this three-way doctrinal counterpoint in adjudication of property rights. What is vital to recognize here

576

[41] A brilliant case study illustrating this contention is Leonard W. Levy, *The Law of the Commonwealth and Chief Justice Shaw: The Evolution of American Law, 1830-1860* (Cambridge, Mass., 1954). On the historic constitutional and natural-law context of eminent domain, see William B. Stoebuck, "A General Theory of Eminent Domain," *Washington Law Review,* 47 (Aug. 1972), 553-603. On the nineteenth-century context, see Harry N. Scheiber, "The Road to *Munn*: Eminent Domain and the Concept of Public Purpose in the State Courts," *Perspectives in American History,* V (1971), 327-402.

[42] See James Willard Hurst, *Law and the Conditions of Freedom in the Nineteenth-Century United States* (Madison, 1956), 3-32. Cf. Scott M. Reznick, "Empiricism and the Principle of Conditions in the Evolution of the Police Power: A Model for Definitional Scrutiny," *Washington University Law Quarterly* (Winter 1978), 1-92.

[43] Levy, *Law of the Commonwealth.* The larger national picture is canvassed in Morton Keller, *Affairs of State: Public Life in Late Nineteenth Century America* (Cambridge, Mass., 1977).

[44] Scheiber, "Road to *Munn*"; Harry N. Scheiber, "Law and the Imperatives of Progress: Private Rights and Public Values in American Legal History," *Nomos,* XXII (1981).

[45] Edward S. Corwin, "The Basic Doctrine of American Constitutional Law," *Michigan Law Review,* XII (Feb. 1914), 247-76; Charles W. McCurdy, "Stephen J. Field and Public Land Law Development in California, 1850-1866," *Law and Society Review,* 10 (1976), 235-66; Molly Selvin, "The Public Trust Doctrine in American Law and Economic Policy, 1789-1820," *Wisconsin Law Review* (1980). For a fresh perspective on the issue of property rights in the public sector, see Hendrik Hartog, "Because All the World Was Not New York City: Governance, Property Rights, and the State in the Changing Definition of a Corporation, 1730-1860," *Buffalo Law Review,* XXVIII (Fall 1979), 91-109.

is that a symbiosis of this sort infuses much of American legal and constitutional history, not only property-law development.

The findings of the new legal history mesh with knowledge drawn from traditional constitutional historiography in another important way: we now understand that the validating canons of American law—the principles and doctrines that influenced "judicial style"[46] and legitimated uses of the law by governmental agencies generally—included some important doctrines that stood outside the traditional constitutional categories. The doctrine of "public rights" has already been mentioned. The Hurstian concept of "release of energy" has had a profound impact on our understanding of law and economic development.[47] "Instrumentalism" and "formalism" have been identified as judicial styles; each constitutes a category of judicial thought and behavior that served to define the relationship of courts to the process of economic development.[48] Whatever the limitations of these descriptive categories, the reconceptualization of American legal history that they express vividly points out that the classic concerns of Commerce Clause history, Contract Clause history, "Marshall Court nationalism," and the like, do not cover the entire range of law's operations.

577

These categories are historian's constructs, which are imposed on the realities of the past. When we say that the *Charles River Bridge* case[49] concerned the Contract Clause or analyze Roger B. Taney's opinion for the Court in terms of Contract Clause development, we are on firm evidentiary ground. It is indisputable that (at the formal level) the Court was wrestling with a Contract Clause issue. When we say, however, that *Charles River Bridge* exemplified "instrumental" or "pragmatic" judicial style, that it was consistent with the principle of "release of energy," or that law underwent in the 1830s a "crisis of legitimacy," we are venturing onto a different sort of evidentiary turf. Concepts such as these can become catchall receptacles for the data. Allowing the historical imagination to tear loose from empirical moorings and go into free flight is an occupational hazard; it is not the monopoly of any one "school" or ideological faction in the discipline.

Whatever the differences of emphasis and methodology among legal historians—or between the new legal history and traditional constitutional history—legal history has recently enjoyed a rising influence on research in some other areas of historical study. This has been true most notably in the study of business and economic history. Little more than a decade ago, it was

[46] "Judicial style" is a phrase often used, in the new legal history, as synonymous with "modes of legal reasoning"—the premises and canons of jurisprudence by which judges provide the justifications of their decisions—or else simply with judicial ideology.

[47] Consider uses of the concept, for example, in Kutler, *Privilege and Creative Destruction*. See also Morton Keller, "Business History and Legal History," *Business History Review*, 53 (Autumn 1979), 295–303.

[48] For analysis and criticism of historians' use of these constructs, see Lynda S. Paine, "Instrumentalism vs. Formalism: Dissolving the Dichotomy," *Wisconsin Law Review* (1978), 997–1013.

[49] *Charles River Bridge* v. *Warren Bridge*, 11 Pet. 420 (1837). Cf. Kutler, *Privilege and Creative Destruction*.

fashionable in economic history to consider the institutional dimensions of the economy as "soft" factors, hardly worthy of serious analytical efforts.[50] Anything that could not be quantified was considered beyond verification; any forces other than "market forces" expressing supply and demand were taken as "givens" in the research called the new economic history or cliometrics.[51] This variant of "mod" social science has had its day—much as has happened with behavioralism in political science. Indeed, in an extraordinary reversal, some of the early leaders of cliometrics have given their efforts in recent years to the study of property rights, of the relationships between constitutional doctrines and shaping of the market by conscious governmental decision making (including common law), and of institutional change. There has also been a rediscovery of constitutional and legal change as a component and regulator of the dynamics by which market economies evolve—by which wealth is allocated, privilege allocated or challenged, power asserted, social dislocations and suffering induced, and happiness sought.[52] Historians of public law have compelled a major reconsideration of basic methodologies and conceptions in a sister discipline—no mean achievement. A similar reorientation of interests, with a movement evident now toward disciplinary cross-fertilization, has occurred in one segment of social history, exemplified by the work of Rothman and Gerald Grob on public policy, public law, and institutional change.[53] Such developments in economic history and in social history will, in turn, reveal new dimensions of legal and constitutional history that need to be explored.

These movements in historical studies today bespeak eloquently the vitality of legal-constitutional study. To be sure, there are some disappointments in the recent literature in sister fields; for example, a legal historian is dismayed at how little historical information or perspective—let alone citation of the best recent historical scholarship—can be found in the most important lawyer's treatise on general constitutional law published in this century.[54] Moreover, despite the natural affinities of the two subjects, legal history and constitutional history still tend to be taught separately, with the particular biases of law, history, and political science faculties often working on a prac-

578

---

[50] See Constance Holden, "Cliometrics: Book on Slavery Stirs up a Scholarly Storm," *Science*, 186 (Dec. 13, 1974), 1004–07.

[51] William N. Parker, "Historiography of American Economic History," in *Encyclopedia of American Economic History*, ed. Glenn Porter (3 vols., New York, 1980), I, 3–16.

[52] On the conceptualization and study of law and economic history, see Harry N. Scheiber, "Regulation, Property Rights, and Definition of 'The Market': Law and the American Economy," *Journal of Economic History*, XLI (March 1981); Harry N. Scheiber, "Law and American Agricultural Development," *Agricultural History*, 52 (Oct. 1978), 439–57. A work that fuses cliometric analysis with study of institutional development is Roger L. Ransom and Richard Sutch, *One Kind of Freedom: The Economic Consequences of Emancipation* (New York, 1977).

[53] David J. Rothman, *The Discovery of the Asylum: Social Order and Disorder in the New Republic* (Boston, 1971); Gerald N. Grob, "Reflections on the History of Social Policy in America," *Reviews in American History*, 7 (Sept. 1979), 293–306. Public policy in the economic arena is considered in Harry N. Scheiber, "Public Economic Policy and the American Legal System: Historical Perspectives," *Wisconsin Law Review* (1980), 1159–89.

[54] Laurence H. Tribe, *American Constitutional Law* (Mineola, N.Y., 1978).

tical level against their integration.[55] Still, the achievements already on the record, together with logical and evidentiary requirements of public-law study, promise a new phase of interest in legal and constitutional history as vitally interrelated fields. In reintegrated form, research in legal and constitutional history can hope to attain something like its former standing and influence in the historical profession.

[55] It is common practice in law schools to teach the historical themes in the classic constitutional law course quite separately from legal history. Similarly, the study of private law or even historical development of law in the state governments seldom finds a way into the standard constitutional history courses, let alone the constitutional law courses in departments of political science. The newest textbook materials in the field generally seek to provide a basis for capturing some of the full range and complexity of legal history—including its reintegration with constitutional history—in the classroom.

At the Borderland of Law and Economic History: The Contributions of Willard Hurst

HARRY N. SCHEIBER

HARRY N. SCHEIBER

580

BOTH historians and students of law have long engaged in analysis of how legal systems are interrelated with the processes of social and economic change. In the literature of American economic history, there is a long tradition of scholarship on the subject of "government and the economy," dating from Guy Callender's writings of fifty years ago. The historians have sought to establish how public policy decisions have affected institutional and economic development and also to assess the decision-making process itself. In the last two decades such scholars as Paul Gates, Oscar and Mary Handlin, Carter Goodrich, and Louis Hartz have given special attention to the study of policy-making processes and effects at the state level in the early nineteenth century.[1] In the field of law, since the revolution in jurisprudence led by Oliver Wendell Holmes and Roscoe Pound early in this century, there has been a conscious effort to uncover the realities of the legal process—to determine how legal systems respond to pressures from the economic market place and from society at large, to assess how formal legal doctrines and rules have been forged in relation to the social milieux and contending real interests, and to discover the varying patterns, in different social contexts and over time, of the interrelationships of law and social change.[2]

▶ *Mr. Scheiber is a professor at Dartmouth College. He worked under Paul Wallace Gates while at Cornell University, where he obtained a Ph.D. in 1962. The author of* Ohio Canal Era: A Case Study of Government and the Economy, 1820–1861 *(Athens, Ohio, 1969), he is interested in American economic history. This article, the revised version of a paper presented at the AHA Annual Meeting in December 1968, is based on studies undertaken while he held joint fellowships from the American Council of Learned Societies and the Center for Advanced Study in the Behavioral Sciences.*

[1] Guy S. Callender, "The Early Transportation and Banking Enterprises of the States in Relation to the Growth of Corporations," *Quarterly Journal of Economics,* XVII (Nov. 1902), 111–62; Paul W. Gates, *The Illinois Central Railroad and Its Colonization Work* (Cambridge, Mass., 1935), and his numerous studies of land and timber policies; Carter Goodrich, *Government Promotion of Canals and Railroads in the United States, 1800–1890* (New York, 1960), a synthesis, citing in full the studies by the Handlins, Milton Heath, and others. James Willard Hurst, *Law and the Conditions of Freedom in the Nineteenth Century United States* (Madison, Wis., 1956), is a pioneering effort to blend the data and analytic concerns of legal history with the more traditional public policy studies. After the publication of this volume Hurst seldom used his first name and wrote as Willard Hurst.

[2] A methodological introduction is provided by Willard Hurst in his essay, "Perspectives upon Research into the Legal Order," *Wisconsin Law Review,* 1961 Vol. (May 1961), 356–67; and his ideas are expounded in a different context in his *Justice Holmes on Legal History* (New York, 1964). Important statements on the need for a broadening of traditional concerns in legal history include Daniel J. Boorstin, "Tradition and Method in Legal History," *Harvard Law Review,* LIV (Jan. 1941), 424–36; and Stanley Katz, "Looking Backward: The Early History of American Law," *University of Chicago Law Review,* XXXIII (Summer 1966), 867–84. Representative examples of the new mode of legal history include Leonard W. Levy, *The Law of the Commonwealth and Chief Justice Shaw* (Cambridge, Mass., 1957); Lawrence M. Friedman, *Contract Law in America: A Social and Economic Case*

The subject defines the interactions between law and other systems or institutions, and, therefore, its study naturally occupies a borderland area between formal scholarly disciplines. To define the legal order as something apart from the other segments of social order and to trace causal interconnections between law and the larger society is a demanding task; its full dimensions and difficulties are perhaps nowhere better revealed than in the complex schema set forth long ago by Max Weber.[3] Little wonder, then, that when Justice Holmes argued the need to study the origins of formal rules and doctrines in their full historical context, he relied upon an especially terrifying metaphor: the legal historian, he warned, must first "get the dragon out of his cave onto the plain and in the daylight, [where] you can count his teeth and claws, and see just what is his strength. But to get him out is only the first step. The next is either to kill him, or to make him a useful animal."[4]

No scholar of our day has responded to Holmes's challenge so successfully as Willard Hurst. A graduate of the Harvard Law School, later clerk to Justice Louis Brandeis, and now professor of law at the University of Wisconsin, Hurst has written extensively on the history of the American legal system. In his *Growth of American Law: The Law Makers,* published in 1950, Hurst provided a brilliant overview of the history of legal institutions in the United States. But in his later studies, he made a sharp break with the traditional premises of formal constitutional-legal history. In two of his major studies, *Law and the Conditions of Freedom in the Nineteenth Century United States* (1956) and *Law and Social Process in United States History* (1960), Hurst explicitly departs from the view that federal Supreme Court cases are an accurate historical index of the principal points of conflict in the legal system. One finds no assumption, either, that all doctrines pronounced by the Supreme Court were necessarily enforced in the states. Hurst seeks, instead, to define the law as a working system. Exhaustive research is devoted to classification of the business of the courts at the trial and appellate levels in the states, especially in Wisconsin. Hurst has sought to distill the "guiding principles" of the law, moreover, from a variety of evidence left by politicians as well as lawyers and judges; he has attempted as well to read the inarticulate premises of men and organizations that made demands on the legal system; and he has been explicitly concerned with how both the law and legal values conditioned the actions of men in the society at large. In short, Hurst has sought to deal with the impact of law on informal behavior, not alone with the focused demands on the legal system. In his massive study of *Law and Economic*

581

Study (Madison, Wis., 1965); Robert S. Hunt, *Law and Locomotives: The Impact of the Railroad on Wisconsin Law in the Nineteenth Century* (Madison, Wis., 1958); Samuel Mermin, *Jurisprudence and Statecraft: The Wisconsin Development Authority and Its Implications* (Madison, Wis., 1963); and the works of Willard Hurst, cited below.

[3] *Max Weber on Law in Economy and Society,* ed. Max Rheinstein (Cambridge, Mass., 1954).

[4] Oliver Wendell Holmes, "The Path of the Law" (1897), reprinted in *Landmarks of Law,* ed. Ray D. Henson (New York, 1960), 50.

Growth (1964), a rich analysis of law and the Wisconsin lumber industry from 1836 to 1915, Hurst has provided a case study that shows how a functional treatment of the law (in this case, the treatment of one industry) can bring to light historical change in legal doctrines and also the diverse effects of the law on society. Hurst has not engaged in what Holmes termed a sterile "striving for a useless quintessence of all systems, instead of an accurate anatomy of one."[5] For in Hurst's works, there is a unique mastery of the concrete particulars of historical "context" and "environment." Yet Hurst has also derived from the data of this nation's experience a set of generalizations about law and social changes, with major ramifications for jurisprudential theory.[6]

In this article I shall seek, first, to abstract the essence of Hurst's historical reconstruction, or model, of how the legal process actually functioned during the nineteenth century. Second, I shall indicate some of the value judgments that underlie Hurst's critique of the legal order of the nineteenth century.[7] Finally, I shall venture a critique of his historical model, suggesting a somewhat different view of legal and policy processes in American history prior to 1900.

Let us consider at the outset Hurst's historical model of how the legal process actually functioned.[8] On the input side, Hurst first defines the major variables that affected policy-making style and function. Of overarching importance is the *Volksgeist* of the nineteenth century—the full range of shared assumptions in the society and, as Holmes put it, of the "instinctive preferences and inarticulate convictions" that underlay what men expected of their lawmakers.[9] A prime place is assigned in Hurst's model to what he terms the widespread popular "faith in the beneficient dynamics of increased productivity." Nineteenth-century America was a society which "expect[ed] substantial change as the norm, which [was] not shocked or afraid of this reality, and which expect[ed] its legal order to take the reality in stride."[10] The "common belief" among Americans, he writes, "the article of faith which made almost all men in this country (save Henry Thoreau)

582

[5] *Ibid.*, 55. Hurst, writes the historian David H. Flaherty, "has created an entirely new school of legal historians by taking a very broad approach. . . . Hurst has made all of us conscious of the need to move beyond the traditional framework in the study of the history of American law." (David H. Flaherty, "An Introduction to Early American Legal History," *Essays in the History of Early American Law*, ed. *id.* [Chapel Hill, N. C., 1969], 20, 38.)

[6] See Earl F. Murphy, "The Jurisprudence of Legal History: Willard Hurst as Legal Historian," *New York University Law Review*, XXXIX (Nov. 1964), 900–43.

[7] Admittedly, separating the purely historical analysis from jurisprudential concerns in Hurst's studies does risk fragmenting a coherent, unitary scheme of analysis. Yet this is necessary in order to deal with Hurst's contributions to jurisprudence.

[8] Hurst's definition of legal process includes nearly the full range of phenomena that political scientists commonly subsume when they refer to the "political system." Though Hurst gives relatively little attention to the roles of political parties, he is concerned with the articulation of interest, communications, leadership roles, and other features of political systems. But the dynamic process on which he mainly concentrates is that of policy making, or decision making.

[9] Oliver Wendell Holmes, *The Common Law*, ed. M. DeW. Howe (Boston, 1963), 32.

[10] Willard Hurst, *Law and Social Process in United States History* (Ann Arbor, Mich., 1960), 236, 26, and *Law and Economic Growth: The Legal History of the Lumber Industry in Wisconsin, 1836–1915* (Cambridge, Mass., 1964), 106–107.

Hamiltonians or Whigs," was "that it was common sense, and it was good, to use law to multiply the productive power of the economy."[11] The pervasive view of legal and policy processes in American history prior to 1900.
to help shape an environment which gave men more liberty by increasing the practical range of choices open to them and minimizing the limiting force of circumstances."[12]

In addition to identifying broadly shared basic values, Hurst seeks to define popular views of various specific policy problems. Hurst asserts, for example, that the people of Wisconsin "were busy with private business, from which public affairs were an annoying distraction," and so they were not inclined to conceptualize taxation as an instrumental policy which might be made part of "a rational . . . program in the interest of the general economy."[13] Nor did they exert any pressure on lawmakers to develop a coherent general policy for timberlands or mineral resources. Men commonly regarded these resources as almost inexhaustible; therefore, they accepted fee simple landownership uncritically, without consideration of its long-term social costs. Similarly, their view of property, contract, and torts was predicated on a faith in short-term productivity, on a belief that law should provide mechanisms for releasing private energies, for mobilizing scarce capital, and for devolving resources on private interests toward the goal of maximizing growth.[14]

583

Also on the input side were the specific pressures from society and the economic market place—the well focused demands articulated by what Stewart Macaulay has called the consumers of law. Hurst portrays both the Wisconsin community and the larger American society as communities of expectant capitalists. On specific policy issues that evoked action by "a powerful and dissatisfied interest group" or by several contending interests (regional, functional, or class-oriented), there was sometimes debate that led to consideration of the larger public interest.[15] But, on the whole, special interest demands were either so narrow as to arouse little controversy (and therefore little extension of men's perception), or so well geared to the prevailing philosophy favoring "productivity" as to win a consensus approval.

The inputs in the policy process as they arose from men's demands of law were not all self-interested or characterized by a "bastard pragmatism" that subordinated a long-run calculus of costs and benefits to a "short-term, limited-factor" definition of policy goals. For as Hurst asserts, "this society [also] sought constitutional order, which meant order continuously responsible." This, too, was in a sense pragmatic: just as men accepted change as a natural (and desirable) condition, they wanted their government to reserve its power to institute "reason-

[11] *Ibid.*, 171–72, 203.
[12] Hurst, *Law and the Conditions of Freedom*, 6.
[13] *Id., Law and Economic Growth*, 518; cf. *ibid.*, 220, 597–601.
[14] Hurst, *Law and Social Process*, 79, and *Law and Economic Growth*, 98–108, 461–65.
[15] *Ibid.*, 518; see also *ibid.*, 270–81.

able adjustment of values and procedures" when change altered material circumstances or new experience altered perceptions. "Manifestly," Hurst writes,
"our society wanted to keep its hands on its destiny."[16]

This faith in a constitutional order required that government itself be accountable, even while it was leaving to the market the exercise of important social
functions. This faith also underlay the vitality of police power, as the nineteenth-
century courts reasserted government's reserved right to regulate for the common
weal.[17] In a word, when "irrevocable" policy choices were manifest, as when the
police power was explicitly tested or implicitly threatened, men wanted to avoid
irrevocable acts. Opting instead for short-range, incremental decisions was entirely
consistent with a pragmatic turn of mind. As Hurst repeatedly underlines, however, many basic policy choices, including such truly irrevocable decisions as
allowing Wisconsin's timberlands to be stripped bare, were in fact made by
default and without significant debate, because bastard pragmatism kept real
long-range costs from the threshold of consciousness.[18]

The remaining policy-process inputs in Hurst's model were physical environment and resources, such as the abundance of natural endowments, the scarcity
of liquid cash and long-term investment capital, and the quick pace of material
change. There was, in addition, the dynamic effect of "drift and cumulation"—
institutions and attitudes surviving because they existed, laws perpetuated because
they were not intelligently reappraised, and popular attitudes frozen in fixed
postures despite changes of circumstances.[19]

Of primary importance, in Hurst's model of the policy process itself, is the
fact that government was "underdeveloped." Fact-finding was not aided by supportive agencies of the legislatures or the executive branch of government, and
expertise was lacking. The failure to develop bureaucracies deprived state government of the advantages and insight that it might have derived from greater
continuity of operations. Despite the sustaining of the police power by the
judiciary, Hurst declares, the courts generally shared the community bias for
productivity. Judicial power was constrained in any case, because the initiatives
in lawmaking resided with the legislature, and judges consistently validated the
legislatures' promotional policies and devolutions of power and function to the
private sector. Lumber industry litigation, Hurst finds, offers no "forerunner of
the Brandeis brief," for lawyers, like judges, failed to transcend the mundane
business of applying policy; they made no effort to examine and redefine funda-

---

[16] *Ibid.*, 204. On "bastard pragmatism" and antipathy toward application of theory, see Hurst, *Law
and Social Process*, 238–39 *et passim*, and "Perspectives upon Research," 349–50.
[17] *Id.*, *Law and Social Process*, 165; see also *ibid.*, 146–67; on the police powers, see Hurst, *Law
and Economic Growth*, 204, 760, n. 258.
[18] *Ibid.*, 262–63; Hurst, *Law and Social Process*, 165–67, and "The Law in United States History,"
Proceedings of the American Philosophical Society, CIV (Oct. 1960), 524.
[19] *Id.*, *Law and Social Process*, 23, 63, and *Law and Economic Growth*, 47–52, 117–25, 467; see
also Thomas Cochran, *The Inner Revolution* (New York, 1964), 143.

mental policy itself.[20] The antitaxation bias of the community reinforced "the poverty and weakness" of government and vitiated its capacity to withstand bastard pragmatism.

The objective limitations of governmental institutions and their basic incapacity to formulate policy on long-range, scientific considerations made legal process responsive, but not genuinely responsible. Lawmakers reacted to the multitude of special interest demands in the spirit of a consensus favoring productivity: "In no public forum, national or state, was there focused, sustained, public examination of the choices to be made, in degree even minimally measuring up to the stakes. . . . Decision making on matters inherently of public concern [consequently] was atomized into many market decisions. This was done so early and so completely that no public agency ever attempted an overview of the whole."[21] "The excessive localism and particularity with which legislative process perceived issues delayed the creation of a sensible administrative process capable of coming to terms with the real problems of flexible application of general standards. . . . The legislative process was simply not geared to generalize perception out of particular issues."[22]

585

Men of large vision who held high office apparently made little difference, given the weight of drift and inertia (including laziness, greed, and indifference). There were a few farseeing political leaders whom Hurst can identify as having perceived the larger cost-accounting problems of economic policy. But even they remained "prisoners of the familiar, and of unspoken assumptions" and proved incapable of producing, even as a matter of theory, "a full-blown twentieth century model of legal control."[23]

Given the inputs, especially the restlessness, impatience, and materialism of society—and given the inadequacies of governmental capacity—it is not surprising that policy outputs tended to be shaped by "drift and default" instead of by considered, rational decision making. The functions that ought properly to have been exercised by a government of "independent energy" were instead largely assigned to the market.[24] The policies adopted were fragmented and were incongruent with the real dimensions of the problems confronting the society. Private energies were mobilized by tort law, the law of contract, and corporation and property law; power was consequently widely dispersed. But in proportion to dispersion of

[20] Hurst, *Law and Economic Growth*, 250, 256; see also *ibid.*, 230–31, 246–48. Prior to the Civil War, Hurst has written, a special burden was carried by the lawyer; for in a society that relied upon common law to order its relationships in vital respects, "the lawyer stood out . . . as the guardian and the possessor of a specialized body of knowledge pertaining to man's highest concerns for justice and good order." (Willard Hurst, "The Legal Profession," *Wisconsin Law Review*, 1966 Vol. [Fall 1966], 1969.)

[21] *Id., Law and Economic Growth*, 123.

[22] *Ibid.*, 253.

[23] *Ibid.*, 207; see also *ibid.*, 164–65, and 711, n. 49, and 712–14, nn., on eminent domain and the courts' "disquiet" with regard to legislative mandates.

[24] *Ibid.*, 262–63.

power there occurred a loss of coherence and reduction of the visibility of "public interest."[25]

The key descriptive words, then, in Hurst's portrayal of policy outcomes are drift, default, dispersion, atomization, opportunism, and fragmentation.[26] Though government was responsive to particularized and parochial demands, it was effective only in so far as it maintained a politically acceptable—not a rational—distributive policy. Government was ineffective in so far as it failed to bring policy choices to the threshold of perception and rational debate, and as it failed to define policy in each functional area on a basis congruent with the scope of the problem.

The foregoing model of legal process and its effectiveness in the nineteenth century is based, in Hurst's studies, on the empirical evidence of the times. Hurst has greatly enriched our knowledge of that period, for he integrates data from litigation in the trial courts with more traditional evidence drawn from appellate decisions and statutes. He is specifically concerned, moreover, with how law and legal values conditioned the behavior of men in the market place, that is, with the impact of law on informal behavior and institutional functions in the private sector.

Underlying Hurst's historical model is a value-laden theoretical model of how law in a democratic polity ought to function. This theoretical model provides the standard by which Hurst forms his normative judgments both of the American legal process and of policy outcomes. Three distinct normative premises are evident. First, legal process should perform an educative function, sensitizing men to large policy choices so that they may govern themselves rationally.[27] Second, legal process ought to be systematic in its fact-finding, scientific in its formulation of general policy from particulars, and thorough in public administration once policies are set. Only so may the constitutional ideal of responsibile government be fulfilled, an ideal, Hurst asserts, that coexisted in American thought along with pragmatism and faith in productivity. "The way men do things determines what kind of men they are."[28] Loose, irrational procedures for ordering the society will not only reflect but will also perpetuate an irrational legal process.

---

[25] *Ibid.*, 107, 123. On men's "sloth, bafflement, and weariness" as obstacles to rational process, cf. *ibid.*, 140.

[26] This is a common characteristic of the studies of Wisconsin's legal history inspired by Hurst. In Friedman, *Contract Law in America*, 147–49, for instance, there is comment on the "waste and futility" of pursuing the public interest through the medium of special charters, on the general lack of "social control," and on social policy as "fragmentary in concept and local in implementation." Similarly, in his analysis of the Wisconsin milldams policy Daniel Dykstra avers that "local economic interests" prevailed and that the legislators lacked "comprehensive understanding . . . of the effect on society of the policies which they were pursuing." (Daniel Dykstra, "Legislation and Change," *Wisconsin Law Review*, 1950 Vol. [Summer 1950], 528, 530.)

[27] Hurst, *Law and Social Process*, 164–67, "Themes in United States Legal History," in *Felix Frankfurter: A Tribute*, ed. Wallace Mendelson (New York, 1964), 202–203, 220, and *Law and Economic Growth*, 561, 572.

[28] *Id.*, "Themes in United States Legal History," 367.

The third premise of Hurst's normative model is that dispersion of both power and property is a source of individual dignity—indeed, it may provide a vital shield for political rights. Dispersion of this sort is thus entirely consistent with the political and social ideals of a democratic order.[29] But ideally legal process must balance dispersion of power against the society's needs over a long-term future. A legal order that performs this balancing function explicitly and rationally will convey its values to the society; it will have an effect on informal behavior and temper bastard pragmatism. One that fails to do so will merely legitimate similar narrowness and default of responsibility in men's private behavior and social relations.[30]

In sum, then, the ideal of responsible government requires standards of due process in lawmaking. Hurst insists that such due process can be achieved only if government displays independent energy. Otherwise, it cannot act as a force that will give vitality to the conception of "the public interest."[31] If the legal process fails to meet this standard, according to Hurst's jurisprudential values, the result is no less "magisterial caprice" than, for example, mindless adherence by judges to formal rules and sterile logic. Just as Pound championed "scientific law"—the antithesis of mechanical jurisprudence—so does Hurst hold up this standard of responsible legal process. Hurst finds shortcomings in the quality of the American system's historic performance not because of any mere failure of internal niceties, but rather because procedure can be the stuff of law and because, by pragmatic standards alone, the results of American lawmaking (such as the depletion of the forests) were wasteful.[32]

It is important for the historian to inquire whether the American legal process failed to fulfill Hurst's normative criteria because it was simply beyond men's imaginations to conceive of deliberated policy making; or whether, plausibly,

587

[29] *Id., Law and Economic Growth*, 10, 23–34, 56, 106. "The law," Hurst asserts, "contributed to the creation of individuality. Law likewise attested the value we put upon this individuality." (*Id., Law and Social Process*, 114.) "We believed that the unique opportunity in North America was to build a more self-respecting life for the individual out of the expanding options created by an ever mounting curve of material productivity." (*Ibid.*, 121.) The degree to which political rights may be affected by the dispersion of property is a theme pursued in a fresh context by Charles Reich in his studies of "welfare" and "the public-interest state." In contrast to the kind of legal process that Hurst describes for the nineteenth century, the modern administrative apparatus of the twentieth century has tended to downgrade "individual liberty and privacy" in favor of "the interests of the community." (See Charles Reich, "The Law of the Planned Society," *Yale Law Journal*, LXXV [July 1966], 1244, and "The New Property," *ibid.*, LXXIII [Apr. 1964], 771.)

[30] Hurst, *Law and Economic Growth*, 26–31, 52–53, 520.

[31] *Ibid.*, 262. There is an abundant literature on the concept of "the public interest," but for purposes of comparison with Hurst's discussion, see especially Samuel P. Huntington, "Political Development and Political Decay," *World Politics*, XVII (Apr. 1965), 411–12; and William H. Riker, *Democracy in the United States* (2d ed., New York, 1965), 98–104.

[32] Roscoe Pound, "Mechanical Jurisprudence," in *Landmarks of Law*, ed. Henson, 101–12. Hurst defines Wisconsin timberlands policy and other nineteenth-century policies for the use of resources as "wasteful" and "irrational" because in the long run they created unnecessary social dislocation. This is a view that embodies the implicit "counterfactual" argument that a different policy—one mandating sustained-yield practices—would have been less costly to the society despite short-run sacrifices of income. (For a discussion of counterfactual argument, see Fritz Redlich, " 'New' and Traditional Approaches to Economic History," *Journal of Economic History*, XXV [Dec. 1965], 480–95; see also Harry N. Scheiber, "On the New Economic History," *Agricultural History*, XLI [Oct. 1967], 383–95.)

men may have had understanding of (possibly even actual experience with) "good" legal process, but did not relate it functionally to their resource-allocation problems. Unless I misread Hurst, he believes that the system's failures were in this sense practically inevitable. He says of land policy, for instance, that "some sense of planning responsibility" was present "in the background," but it was not brought to fruition. He asserts, too, that "the legislature, and the country, got about what they actually wanted or were ready to pay for in the way of public lands administration." He explains perpetuation of drift and default by reference to "the environmental odds against major change of direction." Hurst declares elsewhere that even down to the 1880's men failed to adopt a comprehensive policy because they "did not see the long range values."[33]

Resolution of this problem depends on whether or not it is indeed plausible to hypothesize that legal process might have worked differently than Hurst indicates it did. If his historical model neglects instances when legal process in the nineteenth century *did* conform closely to the prescriptions of his normative model, then the whole inevitability question has to be reopened.

I would query whether it is correct to argue, as Hurst does, that nineteenth-century Americans were mainly concerned with legal process for material reasons (to sustain rising productivity), albeit tempered by considerations of responsible government. It appears to me debatable, at best, that decision making in noneconomic areas became a focal concern of the people only "grudgingly or as a form of diversion and excitement in spurts of bad conscience over neglected problems."[34] This view may underestimate greatly the importance of conflicts over such basic rights as the suffrage—touching the very foundations of law and legal process—which was debated most explicitly in the state constitutional conventions of the 1820's.[35] Hurst avers that the nation had finished with "fashioning the principles of power organization" by about 1800. While acknowledging that the constitutional conventions were important episodes, he treats them mainly as part of the larger quest for release of individual energies and for material growth.[36] Yet the constitutional conventions embodied "the people's sovereignty; they were unsurpassed arenas of ideological encounter," as Merrill Peterson writes; and they were "potent instruments of reform."[37] These debates over "the principles of power organization" reflected cleavages basically different from those Hurst describes in his historical model, for the conventions excited class antagonisms,

---

[33] Hurst, *Law and Economic Growth,* 22, 60–61, 410.

[34] *Id., Law and the Conditions of Freedom,* 29, 43.

[35] This subject receives only a few lines' notice, *ibid.,* 30–31.

[36] *Ibid.,* 43.

[37] *Democracy, Liberty, and Property: The State Constitutional Conventions of the 1820's,* ed. Merrill L. Peterson (Indianapolis, 1966), xv. Popular pressures for reapportionment were often closely linked to economic policy questions; in the South Atlantic States, for example, the underrepresented districts failed to obtain their full share of state expenditures for internal improvements; this impelled them to seek constitutional reform. (Fletcher M. Green, *Constitutional Development in the South Atlantic States, 1776–1860* [Chapel Hill, N. C., 1930; reprinted New York, 1966], 150–52, 161–63.)

basic sectional divisions, and, not least important, conflicting ideologies. It is impossible, I think, to find only a single *Volksgeist* or "consensus" when one examines these conflicts. Decisions on such issues as the suffrage or representational apportionment could not be disaggregated and dispensed piecemeal, as happened with resource-allocative policy (water power, timber resources, minerals, and the like). Demands were well focused, and large policy was in the forefront; political status and rights could not be doled out on an *ad hoc* basis to atomistic, particularized interests.

If this argument is correct, it raises a second basic question of historical interpretation: does Hurst's model accurately (indeed brilliantly) describe one, *but only one,* type of historic American legal process?[38] This question is pertinent, I think, even if one narrows the scope of inquiry to embrace only government and the economy. Consider especially the legal process as it worked in the states that undertook major internal improvements in the early canal era. The main task of the policy process then was governmental construction and operation of bulk transport. Wisconsin's initial state constitution, to be sure, prohibited such activity by the state government, and it barred incurring of debt for internal improvements.[39] As a result, the main focus of economic policy in the Wisconsin case was on the state government's allocation of seemingly abundant resources and on the ordering of the market through contract, tort, and property law. But the central focus of policy rested elsewhere in New York, Ohio, Pennsylvania, Michigan, Indiana, and numerous other states. In fact, their ambitious efforts (and accompanying fiscal disasters) in canal projects and other transport enterprises impelled Wisconsin to eschew such activity.[40]

589

In the early period of canal construction in these states, only public enterprise appeared feasible. To undertake state enterprise, in turn, required mobilizing capital, that is, mobilizing a scarce resource. The success of each enterprise depended on erecting a bureaucratic structure that far exceeded in size and complexity any official agency of the state of Wisconsin in the mid-nineteenth century. The products of policy making, moreover—the canals and other bulk transport

---

[38] The following critique of Hurst's policy process model owes much to the theory of "arenas of policy" presented by Theodore J. Lowi, in "American Business, Public Policy, Case-Studies, and Political Theory," *World Politics*, XVI (July 1964), 677–715. One type of policy in Lowi's scheme conforms precisely to Hurst's portrayal of the Wisconsin lumber policy: it is the arena of "distributive" policy, which embraces resource allocation and the devolution of governmental largesse. (Consistent with Hurst's view, Lowi finds that distribution was "almost the exclusive type of national policy from 1789 until virtually 1890.") Because resources distributed by government can be "disaggregated and dispensed unit by small unit," distributive policies tend to be "not policies at all, but . . . highly individualized decisions. . . ." (*Ibid.,* 689–90.) Lowi distinguishes the distributive arena from the "regulatory" arena, in which policy cannot be disaggregated so thoroughly, so that manifest deprivation and denial must occur. Third is the "redistributive" arena, in which disaggregation is nearly impossible since "the categories of impact are much broader, approaching social classes"; examples of policy in this arena are income taxation and broad welfare-state measures such as Social Security. (*Ibid.,* 691, 703–704.)

[39] See Frank Mallare, "Comment: Wisconsin's Internal Improvements Prohibition," *Wisconsin Law Review,* 1961 Vol. (Mar. 1961), 294.

[40] *Ibid.,* 296–98. The experience of the canal states is examined in Goodrich, *Government Promotion, passim.*

facilities—would at first benefit only a few regions and deprive other localities of equal advantages.[41] Finally, the social costs were to be felt immediately, in the burden of taxation to service and amortize state debts. Though men commonly underestimated the debt to be incurred, or overestimated the canals' revenue potential, there was no escaping the tax question on grounds that it was a busy society, not much interested in taxation as part of larger developmental policy.

The resultant variations from Hurst's historical model of "process" were numerous and dramatic. First, a ranking of priorities among contending interests could not be evaded, as certain regions would be indulged and others deprived. Second, the engineers characteristically became spokesmen for long-range planning and comprehensive principles for development of the transport system. Nineteenth-century engineers dedicated much effort to rational calculation of costs and benefits, even to quantification, much as engineers do today. From the regional and functional interest groups, in turn, came pressure of a more particularized kind, admittedly much like the pressures exerted by atomized interests in the Wisconsin lumber industry. But there was another dimension even to these pressures: men articulated their demands for transport not only by a calculus of productivity, but also in terms of equity. Egalitarian precepts required, ideally, that burdens (taxes) and benefits (transport facilities) be distributed equally among all districts of a state. Though material self-interest was hardly lacking, the egalitarian ideal conditioned policy processes significantly. On the basis of men's actions as well as their rhetoric, one can, I think, make as good a case for the impact of egalitarian ideals as one can make for Hurst's version of the contemporary *Volksgeist,* which stresses the primacy of more materialistic social goals.[42] Rather than a consensus of popular views, there was a tension among three distinct and competing "validating principles": planning, particularism, and ideology qua egalitarianism.[43] Moreover, in the policy debates that surrounded the granting of special charters to railroads, when the private sector finally acquired the fiscal capacity to build bulk transport lines, the public canal officials did operate with independent energy. Although in the end they were overwhelmed, they did bring general policy issues past the threshold of consciousness, and they forced railroad promoters to adduce cost-benefit analyses of their own to justify

[41] Of course, once the fiscal restraints on expansion of state canal systems disappeared in the mid-1830's, the by-passed (deprived) regions of each state successfully pressed for the construction of new ancillary lines and "comprehensive programs." (See Harvey H. Segal on "the role of rivalry," in *Canals and American Economic Development,* ed. Carter Goodrich [New York, 1963], 176–79; Harry N. Scheiber, "Urban Rivalry and Internal Improvements in the Old Northwest, 1820–1860," *Ohio History,* LXXI [Oct. 1962], 232–35; Ronald Shaw, *Erie Water West: A History of the Erie Canal, 1792–1854* [Lexington, Ky., 1966], 305–13.) On the size and tasks of state bureaucracy where canals were built as public enterprises, and the "independent energy" that such public agencies displayed, see Nathan Miller, *The Enterprise of a Free People: Aspects of Economic Development in New York State during the Canal Period, 1792–1838* (Ithaca, N. Y., 1962); and Harry N. Scheiber, *Ohio Canal Era: A Case Study of Government and the Economy, 1820–1861* (Athens, Ohio, 1969), Chaps. I, IV, XIII.

[42] See Hurst, *Law and Economic Growth,* 28, 572, on action as an expression of thought in "this unphilosophical society."

[43] Scheiber, *Ohio Canal Era,* 88–92, 355–58.

charters and other public aid (including state and local subsidies) for their projects.[44]

Further historical inquiry may suggest the need to revise Hurst's model further, to allow for still a third major arena of economic policy which was distinct from either resource allocation or transport building. This third arena was economic regulation, especially as it concerned banks and corporations. Hurst has perhaps given insufficient weight to the impact of ideological and partisan cleavages on such issues. In essence, Hurst takes the victor's view of history: he emphasizes that Democratic legislatures churned out special charters despite Jacksonian strictures against such "monopolies" and that "eventually" legislatures ceased to "deal by mere fiat" with the banking mechanism.[45] But this misses the point that in certain states, for periods of varying duration, the very question of whether capitalism was to be permitted to spawn larger-scale forms of organization became an intensely felt issue in politics, occasionally even delaying the course of capitalist development on new lines.[46] To relegate these controversies and struggle to the category of mere interim is to risk hiding from sight a segment of policy process that is basically distinguishable from the Hurst model.

My final caveat relates to the very concept of *Volksgeist* and consensus, which lies at the heart of Hurst's analyses.[47] In the South was a segment of society where deference politics were perpetuated, where maintenance of a caste system (militating against status mobility) was of high priority, and where the expectant capitalist apparently encountered deeply rooted prejudices favoring continued agrarian dominance of the society.[48] To say that even in the North and West we were all Federalists, all Republicans "in possessing a common instrumental belief which shaped the nineteenth century legal order," may treat too lightly the political conflicts that once loomed so large in historical analysis.[49] The Democrats

591

---

[44] *Ibid.*, Chap. x; Frederick Merk, "Eastern Antecedents of the Grangers," *Agricultural History*, XXIII (Jan. 1949), 1–8. Although the administrators of state and federal land policy did not exhibit the same degree of initiative, there was abundant attention to ideological questions in the formulation of public policy in this area. (See Mary E. Young, "Congress Looks West: Liberal Ideology and Public Land Policy in the Nineteenth Century," in *The Frontier in American Development: Essays in Honor of Paul Wallace Gates* [Ithaca, N. Y., 1969], 74–112.)

[45] Hurst, *Law and the Conditions of Freedom*, 56, 53–54, *et passim*.

[46] A case in point is the banking policies of Ohio, where the pendulum of regulation swung from one limit to the other as Whig and Democratic majorities alternated in successive legislatures in the 1830's and early 1840's. (See Francis P. Weisenburger, *The Passing of the Frontier* [Columbus, Ohio, 1941], 337–62; Scheiber, *Ohio Canal Era*, 145–54; cf. Michael A. Lebowitz, "The Jacksonians: Paradox Lost?" in *Towards a New Past: Dissenting Essays in American History*, ed. Barton Bernstein [New York, 1968], 65–89.)

[47] Hurst, *Law and Social Process*, 254–55, and *Law and the Conditions of Freedom*, 6–10, 33.

[48] Green, *Constitutional Development*, 162, 170, and Chap. xiv; Eugene Genovese, *The Political Economy of Slavery* (New York, 1965), 180–220; Stanley M. Elkins and Eric McKitrick, "A Meaning for Turner's Frontier," *Political Science Quarterly*, LXIX (Sept., Dec. 1954), 321–53, 565–602, in which a restatement is attempted of the fundamentally different political styles of the West and Southwest.

[49] Hurst, *Law and the Conditions of Freedom*, 33. Cf. the discussion in Seymour Martin Lipset, *The First New Nation: The United States in Historical and Comparative Perspective* (New York, 1963; reprint ed., Garden City, N. Y., 1967), 54–68. The concept of a historic American "consensus," popular among political scientists, requires re-evaluation in light of Hurst's evidence respecting dynamic change within the federal system, as the result of independent legal processes in the individual states,

may have been Whigs in disguise, but, if so, they maintained their false identity for a very long period, especially considering the depth and intensity of party differences—in the states, on which Hurst has so brilliantly focused attention—on such issues as the privileges to be granted corporations, or the regulation of banking.

These are difficult questions. The full depth of their perplexities and their importance have become clear only because Hurst's confrontation of legal-economic history has been so productive. He has built on a confidence that the concrete particulars of life are worthy of attention from mature scholars in law and history. He has demonstrated how the legal process defined the market and how it set rules for operation of the price system (mechanisms that often are treated as disembodied abstractions by even eminent economic historians). Moreover, Hurst has portrayed with rare acuity the complex interplay of our legal system with cultural traits and values, thereby providing a conceptual basis for fresh re-evaluation of the core issues in jurisprudence—all this mainly with the stuff of local history, a perilous field (because it can be so workaday) even for scholars with far less ambitious research purposes. It is thus appropriate to close with Hurst's own observation, in another context, that "as men expanded their knowledge, they enlarged their ignorance too—specialization drove creative minds farther apart rather than closer together."[50] In an era of intensive academic specialization, Hurst's studies are valuable, above all, because they remind us that the historian must deal with the whole fabric of life. He has made this great borderland between law and history a far richer and more challenging place than when he first began to explore it.

---

and dynamic change in the content of state policies. (See Samuel P. Huntington, "Political Modernization: America vs. Europe," *World Politics*, XVIII [Apr. 1966], 406–407 *et passim;* cf. Harry N. Scheiber, *The Condition of American Federalism: An Historian's View* [89 Cong., 2 sess., Senate Committee on Government Operations, print, Oct. 15, 1966], 1–12; and Carl J. Friedrich, *Trends of Federalism in Theory and Practice* [New York, 1968], 7–9.)

[50] Hurst, *Law and Social Process,* 70.

HISTORY, LEGAL HISTORY AND LEGAL EDUCATION

Calvin Woodard*

IN MANY ways the question "What is wrong with Legal History?" is neither pertinent nor seasonable. After all, the subject is probably more widely pursued and better taught today than ever before. Most of the better law schools offer, and many require, at least one course describable as "Legal History." Moreover, the Selden Society provides a steady stream of impeccably erudite publications,[1] and in this country the *Journal of Legal History* attracts ever wider interest among both lay readers and lawyers. Bearing in mind all this activity, as well as various experiments of an interdisciplinary nature designed to encourage yet more scholarly interest and productivity, one might reasonably hold that Legal History now flourishes to a degree that it never has before.

593

Such a conclusion, to repeat, would not be unreasonable and might, indeed, be substantially correct. Nevertheless it is not, I think, altogether trivial, and neither captious nor a mere counsel of perfection, to question the value of Legal History as a part of contemporary legal education.

There are two reasons for the foregoing assertion. First, notwithstanding various indicia of robust activity and interest, few would deny that the significance of Legal History to legal education is, to put it bluntly, marginal. According to an elaborate survey of American law schools conducted in 1963 by Professor Edward Re,[2] only 31 of 115 responding institutions included in their curricula a course that could, by any stretch of the imagination, be categorized as "Legal History"; and undoubtedly, the great bulk of the graduates of American law schools proceed to their degrees without ever having had the slightest taste of Legal History. This simple fact cannot, I think, be gainsaid; and it stands as my first reason for questioning the role of that subject today.

---

* Associate Professor of Law, University of Virginia. B.A., 1950, University of North Carolina; LL.B., 1953, Yale University; Ph.D., 1960, Cambridge University.

[1] For a list of Selden Society publications, see SELDEN SOCIETY, GENERAL GUIDE TO THE SOCIETY'S PUBLICATIONS (1960).

[2] Re, *Legal History Courses in American Law Schools*, 13 AM. U.L. REV. 45, 47 (1964).

A second and more disturbing reason concerns not those law schools that pass over, but those that do in fact offer, Legal History. Speaking as a teacher of the subject, I believe most students (including, no doubt, my own) find the subject, at best, a bore. To some, those most strongly oriented towards the work-a-day world, it seems to have nothing to do with the business of learning to be a lawyer. To others, made weary by a seemingly endless trek through a Sahara of academia, it is yet another barren stretch of arid "culture," to be endured as painlessly and as passively as possible. To the wide-eyed, eager, enthusiastic youths searching for what they are pleased to call "meaningful relationships" between "law and society"—to them, Legal History is, though interesting enough, an appallingly uneconomic expenditure of time.

594　　To these last students—those whom no teacher can forgive himself for not reaching—we live in a "critical" age beset by "crucial" and "vital" issues that threaten the very existence of human civilization. Hence, they are wont to say, no academic sin can now be so disastrous, none quite so unforgiveable, as a waste of valuable learning time. In their view, the precious hours of instruction should—must—be spent where they will do the utmost good: not dabbling in dusty folios and forgotten files that have rightfully become (in Hallam's phrase) the "property of moths," but on the frontiers of knowledge, mastering and integrating into the law the exciting new discoveries of the physical and social sciences.

In other words, for a variety of reasons, virtually all students—good and bad, diligent and indolent, alert and indifferent—have essentially the same reaction to Legal History: that reaction is uniformly negative, varying only in its intensity. Perhaps the worst condemnation of all is that few find it worth condemning.

The answer, then, to the question posed at the outset—"What is wrong with Legal History?"—must be something like this: the subject is totally neglected in most law schools, and where it is taught it is, by and large, an ineffective, sterile part of legal education. Except in the hands of a few brilliantly stimulating teachers (such as Mark Howe of Harvard or Willard Hurst of Wisconsin) it is, often rightfully, regarded as a barren estate of useless literary lumber; and except for the occasional antiquarian-minded law students—historians by nature, who, happily or otherwise, find themselves in law school—it probably destroys more genuine interest in the subject than it stimulates. Thus, though more legal historians now write back and forth to each other than ever before, undoubtedly to their own edification, one supposes that students and lawyers generally read such works, if at all, only for amusement and general diversion. Even, therefore, as Legal History flourishes as a branch of learning, it seems to drift further and further from the center of legal studies. Insofar as Legal History has, or can have, a more constructive, a more positive role in training lawyers, this situation is both lamentable and deplorable.

I.

If we ask why Legal History languishes in its present baleful state (and, I might add, Professor Re paints a picture no less grim than that depicted above) our answer might consist of any of at least three archetypical explanations, each of which leads (by altogether diverse routes) to the same conclusion. The three explanations are that the place of Legal History in legal education either (a) cannot, (b) need not, or (c) should not, be substantially altered.

595

In the first instance, bearing in mind the practical (professional) purpose of legal education and the largely impractical (scholarly) aim of history (legal or otherwise) we might adjudge the situation, however lamentable, inevitable. Many years ago Maitland pointed out that though lawyers and historians share a common interest in the legal past they do so for different reasons. In a familiar passage, he noted:

> A lawyer finds on his table a case about rights of common which sends him to the Statute of Merton. But is it really the law of 1236 that he wants to know? No, it is the ultimate result of the interpretations set on the statute by the judges of twenty generations. The more modern the decision the more valuable for his purpose. That process by which old principles and old phrases are charged with a new content, is from the lawyer's point of view an evolution of the true intent and meaning of the old law; from the historian's point of view it is almost of necessity a process of perversion and misunderstanding. Thus we are tempted to mix up two different logics, the *logic of authority*, and the *logic of evidence*. What the lawyer wants is authority and the newer the better; what the historian wants is evidence and the older the better.[3]

Now if what Maitland says is true—and it is very difficult to deny that the "logic" of law and the "logic" of history are intrinsically anti-

---

[3] 1 MAITLAND, COLLECTED PAPERS 490-91 (Fisher ed. 1911). (Emphasis added.)

thetical—the chilly indifference of modern lawyers and law students to Legal History can be no great surprise. Indeed it would seem that nothing can be done to prevent Legal History from playing at most a minor, not to say trivial, role in training lawyers. Like Hardy's Jude, Legal History is doomed from the outset to be obscure—and all our piety and our wit cannot make it otherwise.

A second, slightly less deterministic explanation might take a rather different tack. While conceding the lowly status of Legal History, one could assert that the situation as described is by no means deplorable and certainly not alarming (except, of course, to legal historians). This conclusion is based on the premise that the ultimate justification for Legal History as a part of legal training is its "humanizing" attributes: attributes that help transform legal technicians into wise lawgivers, groveling pettifogs into enlightened philosophers. In a singularly forceful statement of this point of view, T. F. T. Plucknett, the *doyen* of Anglo-American legal historians, wrote:

596

> It is still too often said that English law can only be understood historically. Now English law may be bad, but is it really as bad as that? Is the law of contract unintelligible without the history of *indebitatus assumpsit*? Is tort a closed book to those who do not understand the history of trespass on the case? Surely not. But then another will get up and say 'if that be so, why bother about legal history?'
>
> Why, indeed? . . . The real question is not whether we should teach legal history, but whether we can give to students law, and nothing but law, and still call it a liberal education.[4]

Assuming that Professor Plucknett has stated the question accurately, let us answer it with yet another question: Why should the study of law be tantamount to a "liberal education?" In one sense every educational experience, certainly every university experience, should be "liberal." All teachers, including law professors, should endeavor to impart to their students wisdom as well as learning, in order to help them become "complete men" aware of their duties or responsibilities to society, as well as merely skilled craftsmen and technicians. But surely this does not mean that law schools must forfeit their commitment to legal learning in order to give their students broad, general liberal educations. And we can make two telling retorts to the suggestion that

---

[4] Plucknett, Early English Legal Literature 17 (1958).

more Legal History should be introduced into law studies in order to educate the bar "liberally." In the first place many American law students, as contrasted to Professor Plucknett's English law students, already have a "liberal education," or at least a bachelor's degree, before commencing their legal studies. And, secondly, even if we do need to "humanize" lawyers more thoroughly, we might legitimately doubt that Legal History is the best subject for that purpose. Let us briefly consider each of these rejoinders.

The difference between American and English legal education is well known: most English law students plunge directly into their legal studies after leaving the equivalent of high school, at the early age of eighteen or so. In other words those who go up to a university (and many do not) spend their three undergraduate years reading for the B.A. degree in law. This, together with an optional (and by no means customary) fourth year for the LL.B. degree, constitutes the sum of university education for most English lawyers. Hence Professor Plucknett's very pertinent question: Can we "give to students law, and nothing but law, and still call it a liberal education?" Hence also his suggestion that Legal History is a necessary addition to the law syllabus as a means of broadening the outlook of, as well as humanizing, these youthful students of the law.

Consider, however, the situation in this country. Our legal education is almost exclusively of a post-graduate character. So much so that at the moment there is a strong movement afoot to have lawyers recognized as academic "doctors." [5] Given their undergraduate background, it would seem that our law students can, quite properly, concentrate on law, and nothing but law without stunting their "cultural" development. It would certainly seem that the need for more Legal History as a humanizing agent is much less critical in this country than in England.

Moreover, even if we agree that our law students need to be liberally educated further we might question the value of Legal History for that purpose. Why, one might ask, is Legal History any more humanizing than, say sociology, philosophy, religion, economics, or any of half-a-hundred other extra-legal subjects? The answer, without a powerful showing to the contrary, must be that there is no more intrinsic value in Legal History than in any of several other "cultural" subjects. Cold

---

[5] See Hervey, *Time for a Change From LL.B. to J.D. Degree*, Student Law. J., June 1965. p. 5.

experience, in the form of the widespread negative student reaction to the subject, suggests that other subjects might well be more effective.

If "cultural" value be the ultimate justification for Legal History, its proponents (including myself) must show first, the existence of a genuine and compelling need for more culture and, second, that Legal History can somehow effectively give law students those missing "cultural" attributes. Until there is such a showing, the perceptive critic may with justice conclude that, though Legal History is an undeniably ineffectual facet of legal education, there is no cause for concern, no need to make any radical change to improve its status or standing.

The third explanation for the lowly state of Legal History is that the attitude of lawyers and law teachers toward Legal History is in fact a reflection of their general conception of law. The more they, like Blackstone, are preoccupied with history and historical developments, the more likely they are to glorify the past, and, by so doing, to become its victims. Conversely, the less deference they pay to the past in the form of preoccupation with Legal History, the more likely they are to possess a mature, sophisticated attitude toward the law: to regard precedent, however hoary, as the work of ordinary mortals, no more and no less, and at the same time to see the legal process realistically, as an instrument to be used by living men to build a better present and future—not as a dead-handed tyrant dictating the maintenance and perpetuation of absurd and useless rules and practices. Thus, one might conclude, the lowly state of Legal History today, far from being a lamentable circumstance, is in fact evidence of an eminently enlightened, forward-looking development in American law. Certainly this would be the view of one of our greatest legal philosophers and prophets. Justice Holmes wrote in 1896:

> We must beware of the pitfalls of antiquarianism, and must remember that for our purposes our only interest in the past is for the light it throws on the present. I look forward to a time when the part played by history in the explanation of dogma shall be very small, and instead of ingenious research we shall spend our energy on a study of the ends sought to be attained and the reasons for desiring them.[6]

With this elevating thought in mind, who can possibly lament the

---

[6] HOLMES, *The Path of the Law*, in COLLECTED LEGAL PAPERS 195 (1920).

lack of attention given to, and the trivial role played by, Legal History? Is it not evidence of our deliverance from the strangling tentacles of an oppressive past?

We may now summarize these three hypothetical explanations of the lowly state of Legal History in modern legal education: insofar as lawyers show a properly lawyer-like interest in their business, the logic of the law makes it inevitable that Legal History can be, at most, of indirect value to lawyers—from which it follows that *nothing can be done* about the current plight of Legal History. Again, bearing in mind the maturity, and broad educational background of most of our law students, the cultural attributes of Legal History, such as they are, are by no means essential to the liberal education of the American bar— from which it follows that *nothing need be done* to make the role of Legal History more effective. Finally, considering the obnoxious limitations of the several schools of legal thought that have in the past laid the greatest stress on Legal History—those that hallow precedent and defer most meekly to stare decisis—the lowly status of Legal History is itself a healthy sign of enlightened progress—from which it follows that *nothing should be done* to alter the situation. Anyone who calls for a change in the role of Legal History in legal education must, at the very least, counter these arguments. I shall endeavor to do so below.

599

II.

My first task is to refute the notion that the current lowly status of Legal History is inevitable. We can admit that the logic of history is fundamentally different from the logic of law; moreover, we can agree that lawyers are—indeed must and should be—primarily concerned with the latter. Nevertheless, we can still deny that the chief value and interest of Legal History must or should be narrowly limited to a small group of antiquarian-minded lawyers and scholars. The foregoing assertion (brave as it is) assumes that the present state of Legal History is dictated by neither the "logic of law" nor the "logic of history" but by the characteristics of a particular conception of Legal History. It will bear explanation.

Abstractly conceived, Legal History is neither more nor less than that part of the past that lawyers, judges and legal scholars deem germane to understanding the law. As such, no irresistible "logic" [7]

---

[7] The history of logic itself seems to suggest that even *that* most rational of sub-

mechanically preordains it to a fixed, immutable place in legal education. The true determinant is ideas, persuasive ideas about the nature of both law and history, but especially of law. For such ideas carry with them implicit assumptions about the source of "law," and those assumptions in turn, determine what aspects of that vast wasteland of the past will be reclaimed for the purposes of establishing, explaining and defending those ideas. Hence that which we now call "Legal History" is, in fact, nothing more than the echo (with a full time lag included) of certain ideas about law and history. Those ideas, and not some inexorable logic, determine, and delimit the current usefulness of "Legal History" in legal education.

The seminal ideas about law and history underlying the presently prevailing conception of Legal History were forged, and came to be generally accepted, toward the end of the last century; and with one notable exception (the work of Professor Willard Hurst[8]) the prime efforts of all subsequent legal historians have been to execute, and to document in a scholarly way, the relationship between law and the past, as defined by those seminal ideas. However, since 1900, when Legal History took its present form, the most powerful ideas about the nature of both law and legal education have been dramatically revised.[9] With continued debate about the nature of law, and almost none about the scope or relevance of Legal History, we have witnessed in the past forty or so years the development among lawyers of a strikingly a-historical outlook in dealing with current legal problems: one that acknowledges the existence of, but makes no use of, and has no need for, "Legal History."

---

jects is not altogether above the winds of change. "There is as great diversity among authors in the modes which they have adopted of defining logic, as in their treatment of the details of it."—So wrote J. S. Mill in his 1 SYSTEMS OF LOGIC 1 (8th ed. 1872), a book that supplanted Archbishop Whateley's treatise on the same subject which had, in its turn, ended the century-long reign, at least in Oxford, of Aldrich's *Artis Logicae*—and a book that itself yielded eventually to the various innovations and attacks of such logicians as Boole, deMorgan, Peirce, Bradley, Bosanquet, Lotz, Windelband, Sigwart, Cohen, Wittengstein and Ayer—to mention but a few.

[8] See note 40 *infra*.

[9] We may measure this disparaging intensity of intellectual ferment in Legal History and legal education during the last fifty or so years by comparing the place currently accorded Maitland, the leading legal historian at the turn of the century, with that of Christopher Langdell, the foremost reformer of legal education during the same period: whereas both men are still uniformly regarded as formative thinkers, indeed master-builders, Maitland's ideas about the nature and scope of Legal History remain vital and virtually unchallenged whereas Langdell's "case method" has been under more or less constant fire.

Now one might say that it is as natural, indeed inevitable, for ideas about law to change as it is for ideas about the nature of History to remain unchanged. After all, history is history and nothing can be said or done to alter it. But to hold this view, to make this assumption, is to do a grave injustice to the best historians. Specifically, it vastly underrates and fails to recognize the true genius of the men who cast the mold of Legal History. Furthermore, it conceals from the unwary the modernity—that is the temporal quality—of their work.

Undoubtedly the most formative single idea underlying modern Legal History is that there is such a subject as "Legal History." Certainly it did not exist as such until the last half of the 19th century. Down to that time the past played such a formidable part in the thoughts of men that they could scarcely distinguish it, as such, from their speculations. It was simply too pervasive, too powerful, too subtle to be separated from the present.

601

Consequently, "History" (conscious concern about the past) played a most insignificant academic role, though the past was of paramount intellectual import. Burke is an obvious example of an 18th-century thinker who wove the past inextricably into his political philosophy— yet, as full of history as his works are, they are not what we, today, would call "Political History." Again, Adam Smith buried his theories on political economy in such an amazing array of historical data that Henry Thomas Buckle was pushed to the very limits of his creative genius to "prove" the *Wealth of Nations* to be the product of "deductive" rather than "inductive" reasoning—though, whichever we may call it, it is clearly not what we now know as "Economic History." And, of course, Blackstone's *Commentaries* is the example par excellence of a law book literally full of history and yet totally different in conception from a modern text on "Legal History."

To Burke, Smith, Blackstone, and to their less articulate contemporaries as well, the past was too potent a reality to be identifiable and isolatable as an academic science. In the form of custom, tradition, continuity, and a deep reverence for things established and vested, it not only gave flavor and color to particular ideas: it shaped the mind that formed the ideas. So it was that Auguste Comte lamented in 1850: "la siècle actuel sera principalement caractérisé par l'irrevocable prépondérance de l'histoire, en philosophie, en politique, et même en poésie." [10]

---

[10] "The present century will be principally characterized by the indelible impression

Around 1850, however, a new notion of history became gradually accepted among scholars—the idea of "Scientific History." ("It has not yet become superfluous," declared the Regius Professor of Modern History in the University of Cambridge in 1902, "to insist that History is a science, no less and no more." [11]) That conception of history was a part of the great renaissance of social sciences that has characterized, increasingly, Western thought ever since: a movement reflecting man's growing awareness of the multiplicity of "forces" conscious and unconscious, environmental and hereditary, social and personal, impinging upon him. And the subsequent history of "history," like that of the other social sciences, has been the chronicle of man's efforts to free himself from those forces—which, in the case of history, means cutting the tentacles of the stultifying past.

In undertaking this task, all social scientists, including "scientific historians," have pursued a common method. First they have endeavored to identify, as precisely as possible, the several forces—such as the "social," the "psychological," the "economic," the "political"—impinging upon man. Then they have *isolated* each force from the rest; finally, they have delegated, to trained scholars and experts, the responsibility of scrutinizing, with meticulous detail, every scrutinizable aspect of each of the several forces.

Scientific historians, following the pattern described above, have carefully subdivided the past into areas equivalent to the chief categories used to analyze the present. In this way "Economics" begot "Economic History," "Political Science" begot "Political History," "Sociology" begot "Social History," "Religion" begot "Ecclesiastical History," and so forth. Also, of course "Law" (which modern legal philosophers assure us is a social science) begot "Legal History."

Such was, in brief, the manner in which Legal History came into being. And like scientific history itself, it is still very much a newcomer, an experiment as it were, in educational techniques. The extent to which it is a newcomer is well indicated by the following passage from a book published in 1902, in which Maitland briefly traced the history of history-teaching in English universities.

> The tale need not be long, and indeed could not be long unless it
> became minute. The attempt to teach history, if thereby be meant

602

---

of history on philosophy, on politics, and even on poetry," 3 COMTE, POLITIQUE POSITIVE 1 (1850), quoted in ACTON, LECTURES ON MODERN HISTORY 338 (1921).

[11] PAUL, LIFE OF JAMES ANTHONY FROUDE 72 (1906).

a serious endeavor to make historical study one of the main studies of the Universities, is very new. We can admit that it has attained the manly estate of one-and-twenty years and a little more. But not much more. Some of those who watched its cradle are still among us, are still active and still hopeful.[12]

Now the point of this discourse on the origins of the "science of history" is simply to remind the reader of a well-known and obvious, but often overlooked fact, namely that this form of history is very much the creation of the modern mind. From which I conclude that, whatever form it may currently take, it is by no means the inevitable, or sole form that History, or its adjunct Legal History—must take; and from which I further conclude that the part Legal History now plays in legal education is not the only one it can or must play. It may be that the present form and place is the right and the best one. But we simply do not know without having examined the premise of modern Legal History more closely, and considered the alternatives. Given the present unsatisfactory state of the subject, I for one refuse to concede that nothing can be done to alter the situation.

603

I repeat: my task has been to show simply that the relationship between law and history is by no means inevitably that which we now know as "Legal History." That conception depends upon, and is only as valid as the precepts of "scientific history."

III.

We have seen that Legal History, as an academic discipline, derives largely from ideas about notions of history that became current in the last half of the 19th century. Now we shall consider more particularly how Legal History, once conceived, came to take the particular form we now give it.

The main burden of applying the more general ideas about the "science of history" to the domain of the law fell to two truly architectonic scholars, Sir Henry Maine and F. W. Maitland. As the most influential expounders, and initial executors (though not the sole formulators) of those general ideas, they inevitably played roles of utmost importance in the history of Legal History. Through their efforts the fledgling subject took on a precise and practically undisputed meaning that has provided both the inspiration and the direction for the intellec-

---

[12] Maitland, *Introduction*, in Essays on the Teaching of History at ix (1901).

tual efforts of all succeeding generations of legal historians. Moreover, this achievement was, or so I contend, the supreme evidence of their creative genius as well as their chief contribution to legal scholarship.

Maine and Maitland taught that Legal History means, properly speaking, "the development of legal institutions"—a phrase that is still frequently used, both in books and in law school curricula, interchangeably with "Legal History" itself. To show how the foregoing definition reflects the personal influence and interests of these two great historians (rather than the dictates of some omnipotent logic), we shall examine, first, the term "legal institutions," then the term "development," and finally, how both came to be limited; for all practical purposes, to Medieval England.

Turning, then, to the phrase "legal institutions" we may note that, as a focus of legal scholarship, it must be attributed to Maine. True, Niebuhr, the marvelous German historian, deserves more credit for the idea ("He had grasped," Gooch tells us, "the truth that the early history of every nation must be rather of institutions than of events, of classes than of individuals, and customs than of lawgivers." [13]), but in the English-speaking world Maine was indisputably the author most closely identified with (to quote the title of one of his books) "The Early History of Institutions."

The novelty of Maine's line of inquiry is best measured by the impact of his work on his contemporaries. It contributed decidedly to the development of anthropology and his name justly ranks with Tylor and Morgan, Sir James Frazier and William Graham Sumner as pioneers in that young science. But it was with respect to legal institutions (and hence with lawyers) that his ideas were most influential. In addition to making him putative father to "Comparative Law" (another youthful academic discipline), Maine's ideas, in effect, redetermined the part of the past relevant to explaining and understanding the law. That is, he convincingly asserted that the focus of research in Legal History should be "legal institutions"—but legal institutions instead of what?

Prior to Maine's immensely successful series of publications (his *Ancient Law* appeared in 1861) the only book of any size on what we would call Legal History was John Reeve's *History of the English Law*, a five volume treatise published between 1783 and 1814. Pluck-

---

[13] Gooch, History and Historians in the Nineteenth Century 18 (1913).

nett rightfully describes this work as being "abominably technical" [14] —so much so, he adds, that "it is unthinkable that Reeves should have attracted anyone to the study of legal history." [15] Maine's works, by contrast, were anything but narrow and technical (in a pejorative sense). Deeply versed in (and indeed Regius Professor of) Roman Law, widely read in the most recondite subjects (such as the Hindu "Laws of Manu" and the "Brehon Law" of Ancient Ireland), and personally acquainted with the folkways and customs of India, Maine quite naturally defined the relationship between the Past and the legal present in broader, more catholic terms than Reeves, a rather insular practitioner of the common law. And it was through his knowledge of "institutions," particularly "ancient institutions," that he convinced lawyers and legal scholars of the inadequacy of "history" based exclusively on common-law technicalities. That is, he redefined the part of the past germane to understanding the law.

605

Maine's works are full of references to institutions that are only remotely "legal"; and when he did treat of "legal institutions" he did so in anything but a narrow legalistic manner. The "Geilfine Group" of the ancient Irish family, which ranked the youngest member highest, is an example of a nonlegal, or at best quasi-legal institution discussed by Maine. (He accounted for it by reference to the mystical number Five and concluded, with a characteristically provocative generalization: "If you ask why in a large number of ancient societies Five is the representative number, no answer can be given except that there are five fingers on the human hand." [16]) "Equity," a staple of Legal History, will serve as an illustration of Maine's broad, nonlegalistic treatment of a genuine legal institution. Rather than confine his researches to the rise of the English Court of Chancery, or even to the Edicts of Roman Praetors, he treated the subject as one of three types of "agencies by which law is brought into harmony with society." [17] (He concluded that there are three such instrumentalities: fictions, whereby law is in fact changed while the continuity of the Law is preserved; equity, whereby law is changed by appealing to external principles invested with a higher sacredness than the Law itself; and legislation, whereby law is changed by appeals to an external body subject, theoretically anyway, to no restraints other than "public opinion.") The inherent interest in Maine's

---

14 PLUCKNETT, *op. cit. supra* note 4, at 5.
15 *Id.* at 6; see HOLDSWORTH, THE HISTORIANS OF ANGLO-AMERICAN LAW 60-64 (1928).
16 MAINE, LECTURES ON THE EARLY HISTORY OF INSTITUTIONS 220-21 (1888).
17 MAINE, ANCIENT LAW 25 (10th ed. 1885).

topics, and his intensely interesting way of treating them left an indelible imprint on the legal mind of the 19th century. From that time to this, "Legal History" has reflected Maine's interest in, and has in fact largely consisted of the study of, legal "institutions."

We need only add that, whereas Maine used the term "institution" to broaden the scope of his historical inquiry—to use the past creatively to explain the present—many modern legal historians (more in the tradition of Reeves than of Maine) use the same term to narrow their inquiry. By concentrating on "institutions" they consciously or otherwise exclude a wealth of "human," "environmental" and other "extralegal" factors from the corpus of Legal History; and at the same time they (again more like Reeves than Maine) define "legal institutions" as unimaginatively and legalistically as possible. Today, in nine out of ten Legal History books and courses, the term has the same narrow meaning—the law-making bodies (courts, juries, and other tribunals), and the formal aspects of practice and the administration of justice (pleading, writs, and forms of action). That and nothing else.

My point is not to condemn this conception of Legal History as wrong or false. It is, rather, to suggest that Legal History, so defined, must be largely irrelevant to (and hence no great help in understanding) the modern conception of law. Furthermore, this more or less obvious irrelevance of Legal History has driven many responsible lawyers and legal philosophers to conclude that history—meaning the past in all its variegated forms—also has nothing to offer to contemporary legal problems. This is an error that can, I think, lead to the most unfortunate consequences.

Be that as it may, the present preoccupation of lawyers and legal historians with legal institutions is, I submit, a legacy of Sir Henry Maine—one man's influence—and not some inexorable force in "law" and "history" dictating that "Legal History" must be so limited.

The second characteristic (I almost said "property") of modern Legal History is a commitment to the notion of "development," and particularly (as we have seen) development of legal institutions. Of course this characteristic cannot be attributed exclusively to any one author or even school of thinkers. Like the Nile its sources are too numerous, and its influence too pervasive, to be traced. Nevertheless we can say with some certainty that this idea came to be an intellectual *tour de force* only in the mid-19th century.

Today we find it difficult to fathom, let alone to appreciate, the rapidity with which the idea penetrated the 19th-century mind. True, of course, there were earlier thinkers such as Ibn Khaldûn, Jean Bodin and Giovanni Vico, who discussed society and history in terms of "stages" of development; and church historians and theologians, committed to the doctrine of eschatology,[18] looked for (and found) in history the hand of God moving man ever closer to Judgment. But, generally speaking, as of 1800 the idea of "development" played no significant role in the minds of lawyers or men of letters, and certainly it did not govern their attitudes toward history. That attitude is probably more accurately reflected by Dr. Johnson. "History," he tells us, has three meanings:

(i)   a narrative of events and facts delivered with dignity
(ii) narration, relation
(iii) the knowledge of facts and events.[19]

Nowhere in these meanings does one find the idea, or even the hint, that history entails "development," a word implying a certain motion or movement possibly along a preordained course or pattern.

By 1870, in striking contrast, the idea of development, in one form or another, abounds in virtually every book on virtually every subject. To mention but a few of the more conspicuous sources: Hegel (influenced by Herder) spread the notion that history was really the repetition of a three-staged (thesis-antithesis-synthesis) dialectic process moving man and society ever closer to "freedom"; and, later, Marx, his irreverent student (Marx, believing Hegel's dialectic

---

[18] For a discussion of this doctrine and its historical significance, see BULTMANN, HISTORY AND ESCHATOLOGY—THE PRESENCE OF ETERNITY (1955).

[19] JOHNSON, A DICTIONARY OF THE ENGLISH LANGUAGE (1822 ed.). In 1735, Lord Bolingbroke expressed a commonly shared view of "history": "We ought always to keep in mind, that history is philosophy teaching by examples how to conduct ourselves in all the situations of private and public life . . . ." BOLINGBROKE, LETTERS ON THE STUDY AND USE OF HISTORY 48 (1770). Edward Gibbon, whose celebrated *Decline and Fall of the Roman Empire* seems more in keeping with the modern conception of history than with the eighteenth-century style of story-telling, was criticized by his contemporaries on precisely that ground. "Is anything more tedious," one of his censurers asked, "than a Mr. Gibbon, who, in his never ending history of the Roman Emperors, interrupts every instant his slow and insipid narration to explain to you the causes of events that you are going to read." SHEFFIELD, THE AUTOBIOGRAPHY OF EDWARD GIBBON, ESQ. 199 (1846). By 1839 the conception of history had changed sufficiently to cause one commentator to lament: "Histories used often to be stories. The fashion now is to leave out the story. Our histories are stall-fed: the facts are absorbed by the reflexions, as the meat sometimes is by the fat." TWO BROTHERS, [A. W. & J. C. Hare] GUESSES AT TRUTH 445 (written in the 1830's but not published until 1871).

to be "standing on its head," brashly undertook to put it "right side up again." [20]) found in history a process moving society through three rather different stages—from aristocratic feudalism to bourgeois capitalism to proletarian communism. Auguste Comte, rather like Fichte before him, convinced countless readers that the human intellect progressed from the "mystical" to the "religious" to the "scientific" stages, and Lewis Henry Morgan taught that whole societies move, in stages, from "savagery" to "barbarism" to "civilization." All of these thinkers, and others, found in their researches a "process" or "development" suggesting a causal link between the past and present—and then came Darwin.

"Evolution," as established by Darwin and Wallace, elevated the notion of development to the status of a "natural law." And from then on, of course, men concerned themselves essentially with what Herbert Spencer called "social dynamics." [21] To some, like Alfred Marshall, the economist, it meant the "principle of continuity." [22] To others, like Herman von Holst, it meant the "germ" theory of history, but to almost all it meant, in one way or another, that the inevitable movement in history made for a better world. History was, in short, the documentation of "progress." [23]

Lawyers, and the law, were of course not immune to the intellectual ferment taking place around them. Dean Pound has brilliantly demonstrated how *all* the various and contending schools of legal philosophy shared a commitment to the idea of "progress." [24] And in the Anglo-American world it was through the teachings of Sir Henry Maine that these ideas were introduced into legal studies. Maine, Sir Frederick Pollock tells us, "did nothing less than create the natural history of law."

> He showed [Pollock continued], on the one hand, that legal ideas and institutions have a real course of development as much as the genera and species of living creatures, and in every stage of that development have their normal characters; on the other hand, he made it clear that these processes deserve and require distinct study, and cannot be

---

[20] Marx, Capital 25 (Modern Library ed. 1906).

[21] Spencer, Social Statics 409 (1851).

[22] 1 Marshall, Principles of Economics at vi (9th (variorum) ed. 1961).

[23] For a fully documented history of the idea of "progress," see Bury, The Idea of Progress (Dover ed. 1955).

[24] Pound, Interpretations of Legal History 9-10 (1923).

treated as mere incidents in the general history of the societies where they occur.[25]

The "natural history" analogy, as well as the optimism of "progress," have long since ceased to dominate 20th-century legal philosophy or even ideas about the nature of law. Of course the "historical school" of legal philosophy remains, and is still given nodding recognition in most Jurisprudence courses. But few would say that it is now, as it was at the end of the last century, the dominant school of legal philosophy. Yet Legal History remains as deeply concerned about, and closely identified with, the idea of development as it was in Maine's day.[26]

I trust I have shown that the unsophisticated acceptance of the link between Legal History and the idea of "development" is the result of men's ideas and not of some innate, unalterable characteristic of "history." This has had two deleterious effects on Legal History and legal education. In the first place, it means that the subject must be essentially a "survey." Part one must be a study of "origins" and part two "developments" of those origins to the present date. The value of such courses cannot be denied—but anyone who has ever taught a "survey" course on *any* subject knows the inevitable limitations. They must, in their nature, be dull. "1066 and all that" is expressive of the reaction such a form of history, legal or otherwise, inevitably engenders. If Legal History must be taught as a survey course more thought should go into ways of avoiding the dullness inherent not in Legal History but in survey courses. If (as I think) it can be taught otherwise more effectively—with or without the idea of "development"—I should think it would be preferable to do so.

The second objection to the "development" type of Legal History is that it is too remote from contemporary conceptions of law to be pertinent. The true function of Legal History, I submit, is to help lawyers and legal scholars, who are essentially concerned with current problems, to be meaningfully aware of the past as a healthy check on our often overly-optimistic and unfounded hopes; to provide gentle

609

---

[25] POLLOCK, INTRODUCTION AND NOTES TO SIR HENRY MAINE'S "ANCIENT LAW" at viii (1906).

[26] Cardozo spoke of "the historical method, or the method of evolution," and was quoted with approval in the most recent text on Legal History. See SMITH, DEVELOPMENT OF LEGAL INSTITUTIONS 10 (1965), quoting CARDOZO, THE NATURE OF THE JUDICIAL PROCESS 51 (1921).

redress in our moments of frustration and disappointment; to act as an indispensable aid in drawing the ever-difficult distinction between the "temporal" and the "eternal," the changing and the unchanging; and, above all, to provide awareness and appreciation of the value and meaning of "civilization."

Such, I say, is the particular charge, or responsibility, of Legal History. If it can be done by stressing the "Development of Legal Institutions"—good. If it cannot (as experience seems to suggest) I should think something else ought to be tried. In any event, however, the commitment of Legal History to the idea of "development" is certainly no more inevitable than our own thoughts on the subject.

We have seen how two ideas attributable to (or at least closely identified with) Sir Henry Maine—the idea of "development" and the idea of "legal institutions"—have become so completely accepted that now they not only dominate, but define, "Legal History." With, that is, one additional element: the influence and example of F. W. Maitland.

Whereas Maine has been subjected to a full measure of criticism and even ridicule,[27] Maitland is, and has been since his death, the object of unstinted acclaim and veneration. Indeed, with minor exceptions, his works probably carry more authority, and his name commands more respect, today than they did at the time of his death. And quite understandably: the charm, the wit, the genius of the man are unmistakable. No historian has produced more scholarship of such uniform excellence; no teacher has inspired more genuine enthusiasm in fields of recondite research; no scholar ever wore the mantle of learning more lightly. None of the new sciences coming into academic existence at the end of the 19th century had a more humane, civilized sponsor, and it is quite unnecessary to say that Legal History was singularly fortunate to have had, in its formative stages, such a guiding genius both to learn from and to emulate.

The only unfortunate legacy of Maitland's marvelous career is traceable to his scintillating brilliance. According to legend an infallible distinction between Satan and mortal men is the inability of the former to cast a shadow. Maitland was a man. And he cast an uncommonly long shadow. Maitland was an historian both by proclivity and by preference—but chiefly by love. The object of his researches was neither "functional" nor "utilitarian" in the ordinary senses of the

---

[27] "It is not unusual nowadays to talk in a rather supercilious manner of the lack of erudition and accuracy, of the allusiveness and vagueness of Maine's writings," Vinogradoff, *The Teaching of Sir Henry Maine*, 20 L.Q. Rev. 119, 120 (1904).

610

words. To the contrary, as G. M. Young said, he sought "the origin, content, and articulation of that objective mind which controls the thinking and doing of an age or race, as our mother-tongue controls our speaking." [28]

Given this magnificent quest he was rather like Thoreau who, when asked if he traveled much, responded that he had traveled extensively in Concord. So Maitland. No man ever traveled more extensively, or intensively, into the far reaches of English medieval history. And in the course of his peregrinations he incidentally rewrote the history of the origins of the common law.[29] But for all the expansive and humane qualities of Maitland's mind, his books—by which subsequent generations of lawyers and legal historians have known him—deal essentially with a limited brief: (i) the institutions (ii) of the English common law during (iii) the medieval period. And the brilliance of his work, affirming as it were the correctness of Maine's emphasis on "legal institutions," served in fact to create the general impression that Legal History is and must be essentially a study of medieval English legal institutions.

611

Because of the very brilliance of Maitland's works he inspired followers who carried on his work with great loyalty and ability. Thus, the overwhelming preponderance of first-class scholarship in Legal History—by such worthy successors to Maitland as Plucknett, Thorne and Fifoot—has dealt with various aspects of precisely that subject. Only the occasional scholar—such as D. E. C. Yale, the author who has single-handedly resurrected the eminent works of Lord Nottingham[30]—

---

[28] YOUNG, VICTORIAN ENGLAND—PORTRAIT OF AN AGE 275 (1954).

Upon rereading Young's remark I find that it may have been directed to Samuel Roffey Maitland, grandfather of F. W. Maitland. Even so, the point in the text still stands: F. W. Maitland took his grandfather as his inspiration as he wrote: "One still has to do for legal history something like the work that S.R.M. did for ecclesiastical history . . . ." FIFOOT, THE LETTERS OF FREDERICK WILLIAM MAITLAND 95 (1965). And Young, one of the most discriminating historians of the 19th century, admired the younger Maitland, if anything, more than the grandfather. See, e.g., YOUNG, *Maitland*, in DAYLIGHT AND CHAMPAGNE: ESSAYS 271 (1965).

[29] According to J. N. Figgis:

[He] more than anyone else is responsible for the annihilation of what may be called the lawyer's view of history, which dates everything from the thirteenth century, and regards the reign of Henry II as equally with that of Henry I in legal twilight. . . . Just as it needed Freeman, with all his faults, to induce the ordinary historical reader to believe that anything really happened before 1066, so it needed Maitland, with all his genius, to break down the even more intolerable tyranny of insular jurists, and to limit the empire of Coke.

FIGGIS, CHURCHES IN THE MODERN STATE 244 (2d ed. 1914).

[30] See YALE, LORD NOTTINGHAM'S MANUAL OF CHANCERY PRACTICE AND PROLEGOMENA OF CHANCERY AND EQUITY (1965).

has done work of comparable quality in the post-medieval period; virtually none (with the exception of Holdsworth[31]) have gone beyond the "legal institutions" limitation. Maitland has, in short, become so faithfully emulated that Legal History now suffers from a not uncommon academic disease: the hardening of ideas inherent in total acceptance—a hardening that repels innovation even as it quells the imagination and interest of the uninitiated.

This means, in effect, that Legal History, as we now know and teach it, is essentially a subject built on medieval sources, to which we subjoin a thin survey of "developments" in the succeeding three and a half centuries. Probably something over half of most Legal History courses deal with origins and developments prior to 1500. To lawyers, who are (if I may say) extraordinarily suspicious of ideas alien to current experience and unsympathetic with things remote in time, this approach carries with it the seeds of self-destruction.

A taste, indeed even a sympathy for medieval subjects is normally acquired only after long, loving study. Not all historians, and almost no law students are willing to make the effort. And we may be certain that if history is ever to play an important part in training those many lawyers who do not possess an antecedent interest in things medieval, it must put much more emphasis on subjects less remote in time from current experience. To do this is quite possible. It simply requires getting out from under the shadow of Maitland and examining other ages of the past as intelligently as he did medieval England.

Neither Maine nor Maitland nor any of the other great legal historians would, I think, disagree with what I have said. It only remains for us to redefine Legal History so as to make it more pertinent to modern law. We can do that by making use of other parts of the past and by broadening in a word, the scope of Legal History beyond "The Development of the Legal Institutions of Medieval England."

IV.

Thus far I have endeavored to show that the present form, and hence current sad state, of Legal History is by no means inevitable,

---

[31] See 10 HOLDSWORTH, A HISTORY OF ENGLISH LAW (1938). J. H. Plumb, perhaps the foremost living authority on 18th-century English history, and certainly no tender critic, has called Holdsworth's chapter on "The Historical Background" "by far the best brief survey" of that period, "a masterpiece in miniature, buried in this vast and important work." PLUMB, ENGLAND IN THE EIGHTEENTH CENTURY (1714-1815), at 215 (1950).

Legal History

and that it *can* be changed. My second task is to counter the notions that nothing *need* be done to improve the situation. That argument (to repeat it) ran along these lines: The ultimate justification for Legal History, at least as a part of legal education, is its unique cultural value —whereas, in fact, most American law students already hold first degrees and are as "cultured" as they, *qua* lawyers, need be; and furthermore, even assuming our law students need more "culture" there is no real reason for believing that Legal History is the best, or (in the light of experience) even an effective, agency for imparting it.

My reply, in the first place, is to dismiss altogether the term "culture" from the discussion. It carries with it overtones that obscure rather than enlighten the matter. At the same time, however, I shall assert that American law students are, despite their maturity and advanced academic standing, presently being deprived of an extra-legal element of capital importance to their legal education. Moreover, I shall assert that the missing element can be best provided by, and logically should be a part of, Legal History. The element to which I refer is a broad understanding and appreciation of the past as a factor in present-day law-making practices.

American students more than any others need an acquaintance with the past because they are increasingly being subjected to a form of legal education that is frighteningly a-historical. And by "a-historical" I do not mean simply that Legal History is neglected or coldly received. I mean that legal education, like our whole legal system, is focusing increasingly upon the present, both in defining, and in seeking the remedy for, current legal (and other) problems. And this is no doubt what a former Dean of the Yale Law School meant when he recently issued a solemn warning against "the erosion of the historical outlook." According to Dean Rostow:

> The pressure of events and the piling up of statutes and decisions tend to confine perspective, both in the classroom and in much legal writing, to yesterday or the day before, or even to today and tomorrow. Social institutions have deep roots. And social groups have powerful memories. If law is cut off from its history, the student tends to emerge as a limited technician, who may find himself at sea as the law he has learned in school vanishes before his eyes. By the same token our legal literature could become more and more trivial, and inadequate to its responsibilities.[32]

---

[32] YALE LAW SCHOOL, REPORT OF THE DEAN 15 (1966). I should like to take this

613

Besides the pressure of events and the gargantuan number of statutes and decisions referred to by Dean Rostow, we can attribute the "a-historicalness" of contemporary law to at least three other separate, if interrelated, developments. In the first place, during the past forty or so years precedent, which is the most obvious link between law and the past, has been severely weakened and thoroughly discredited. The campaign waged by the school of Legal Realists,[33] calculated to demonstrate that contemporary judges make, rather than discover some preexisting (historic) law, has been so .thoroughly effective that it is not now too much to say that the doctrine of stare decisis, like Justice, "stinks in the nostrils of lawyers." And an amazing number of legal scholars, lawyers and law students are not satisfied with celebrating the demise of an odious principle of law; they would have us believe that the law now stands totally free of the entanglements of the past—as if stare decisis were the sum and substance of the past. No thought could be more absurdly erroneous or potentially dangerous.

In the second place, while stare decisis was falling into general disrepute (dragging along with it everything tainted with or smacking of "oldness") Legal History was being locked ever tighter into the Maine-Maitland mold. That is, the one group of legal scholars interested in and responsible for making the past intelligible to lawyers closed their eyes to the need to redefine the part to be played by history in legal education. Rather unconcernedly, they continued to research, write about and teach "the origins and development of legal institutions in medieval England," despite the tremendous reaction against the established law-history relationship going on around them. Under such circumstances nothing could have been more remote from current ideas about the nature and function of law (and hence less germane to legal education) than "Legal History." In this way legal historians themselves rendered Legal History less, not more useful to training lawyers; they also helped widen the unnatural rift now dividing "law" from "history."

Third, while stare decisis was being savagely (and successfully) un-

614

opportunity to express my appreciation to Dean Rostow for many courtesies, not the least of which have been conversations upon the subject of this Article. Of course he is in no way responsible for the ideas expressed here; still I may fairly say that but for him I would not have written it.

[33] For discussion of American Legal Realism see Rostow, *American Legal Realism and the Sense of the Profession*, in THE SOVEREIGN PREROGATIVES, THE SUPREME COURT AND THE QUEST FOR THE LAW 3 (1962); Gilmore, *Legal Realism: Its Cause and Cure*, 70 YALE L.J. 1037 (1961).

dermined, and while the young science of "Legal History" maintained
an air of scholarly indifference to the drastic changes taking place in
the established relationship between past and present, a new, strikingly
a-historical conception of law was coming into being. And the extraordinary rapidity with which that notion gained acceptance in this country is largely explained, I think, by the vacuum created in the legal
mind as a result of the apparent debasement of History.

Lawyers and legal scholars, no longer under the illusion that authority reposed in precedent, and somewhat intoxicated by the delusion of
complete freedom from the past, came easily to the idea that law, real
law, is an "instrument" or "tool" to be used for what Dean Pound
first called "social engineering" and others (notably Professor Popper)
have been pleased to call "piece-meal tinkering." [34] And this is the
a-historical conception of law to which I have referred.

615

The "tool" or "instrument" conception of law is a-historical, not
anti-historical. That is, it is not hostile to history. To the contrary its
adherents are often warm enthusiasts, and even close students, of historical scholarship. In fact, some of them are invariably among the first
to deplore that certain aspects of the law (for example the admiralty
courts in colonial Connecticut or Jamaica) have not yet found their
Maitland; and most of them are constantly promising themselves to take
time off from their labors to read Holdsworth's or Holmes' *The Common
Law* or Toynbee or Charles Warren's *The Supreme Court in United
States History* or (like H. M. Pulham, Esq.) *The Education of Henry
Adams*. No, the "tool" conception of law is not anti-historical.

The adherents of this conception of law, or many of them, would
willingly indulge their interest in the past, but they are simply too busy
(with the really decisive aspects of the law) to do so. Which is precisely what I mean when I say that that conception of law is a-historical: its adherents know well enough the source, nature and meaning
of both law and history; and they assume (as a result) that the two
meet only under the most leisurely, not to say effete circumstances. In
the workaday legal world, where the *real* issues are dealt with, there
is no place for history. History is, in short, irrelevant. Totally irrelevant.

And why? Because no one has yet demonstrated, except in the most
general way, how history *can* help either the lawyer to use the "tool"
of law to win more cases or the wielders of authority to mold better

---

[34] POPPER, THE POVERTY OF HISTORICISM 58 (1954).

policy. Nor, I suggest, is one likely to do so. For (to repeat my assertion) that conception of law is intrinsically a-historical. When we say that law is a "tool" we are, in effect, saying that the past has, and *can* have, no more to do with present day law-making than the history of hammers and nails has for builders, architects and carpenters. For lawyers and legal scholars implicitly assume, as do those denizens of the construction trade, that, though tools we need and tools we use, tools we have—and so it is with that most complicated and delicate of all tools, the law. The law is here, not indeed in Lord Coke's green bag, but here in the 20th century, at our disposal. Thus, it follows that the chief problems of legal education today do not involve the origins or sources, but the uses, of law. Hence also the dominant trend in legal education during the last forty or so years: the quest, through law and the social sciences, for "policy" (the underlying rationale for legal action) and "values" (the ideals giving direction to legal change). The "thrust" (to use a revealing expression much in current use) of modern legal education, is, in a word, forward—to the future. The significance of the past, if any, remains undefined.

616

Today, American law students, subjected to this a-historical conception of law, sedulously learn that they, as lawyers, will stand, or have the power to get, beyond the forces, the pulls and tugs of amorphous history. They know that judges (contemporary mortals) make the law in accordance with good or bad "policy," socially desirable or reprehensible "values." And the past neither restrains them from, nor aids them in determining how modern law makers should wield the awesome tool. That determination (they are taught) must be found in the "circumstances" and "available alternatives." And of course these determinants only serve to lock the student even more firmly into the 20th century. For they learn, on the one hand, to marvel at the uniqueness of the "circumstance" in which we live—an epoch characterized by such unprecedented "phenomena" as "industrialism," "automation," "urbanization," "mass-culture," and "affluence." On the other hand, they regard themselves as the heirs to the intellectual and scientific revolution of the past fifty years, possessing, in the form of positive knowledge, exacting skills and delicate techniques of analysis, "alternatives" unknown to the wisest seers and prophets of yore. Why, the young lawyer student must wonder (if he ever has occasion to do so) *should* he look to history? What *can* we possibly learn from the past? Surely answers to our problems cannot be found in the ignorance of pre-scientific, pre-industrial man.

Such is, I think, the tenor, the tendency, and the end result of modern American legal education. And if history shows anything, if it teaches any lesson at all, it is the poverty, the hollowness of such reasoning.

Given the "tool" conception of law with its built-in a-historicalness I am frank to admit that I cannot see how history is, or can be of any relevance to legal education. But for that very reason—and there could be none better—we should make every effort to acquaint our law students with more history. I think, in other words, the fact that we *cannot* show the relevance of the past to legal education is itself the best evidence that there is a genuine need to counterbalance the a-historical tendencies of the modern legal process.

And Legal History properly conceived—not simply "The Development of Medieval English Legal Institutions" but an intelligent, sensitive awareness and appreciation of the past as a part of the legal process —is, I submit, the *only* viable antidote to the provincialism inherent in the insularity of the 20th century. It, and only it, provides an escape from the compelling logic which ever alienates modern man, with all his newly won splendor, from the transcendent wisdom of History.

To repeat my assertion: the a-historical character of modern legal education is itself sufficient reason to establish the need for teaching law students more history. Also it is sufficient cause to lament the feckless role of Legal History in training lawyers and a powerful motive for seeking a change for the better.

V.

The need for more Legal History, I have said, stems ultimately from the widespread, and not altogether critical, acceptance of an a-historical ("tool") conception of law. And this brings me to my third task: granted that a genuine need for more history of some kind exists, I must convincingly demonstrate that we *should* satisfy that need. The argument to be countered, it will be recalled, is that the present lack of Legal History is evidence that man has, for the first time, freed himself from the restraints of the past and progressed quite beyond to a new level of social maturity—a trend to be saluted, not lamented, and certainly not to be reversed.

In the foregoing discussion of the need for more Legal History I have attempted to show why that need should, indeed must be satisfied. Now I only add that the a-historical "tool" conception of law was itself originally a reaction against the widespread, uncritical acceptance of the history-imbued Blackstonian conception of law. And this reform movement—call it "sociological jurisprudence" or "legal pragmatism" or whatever—has so achieved its purposes that its truths have now become a part of what J. K. Galbraith called the "conventional wisdom" of the day.[35] So much so that it is not at all uncommon today for law students to commence their legal career aware of little other than the "heresies" of the late Judge Jerome Frank. They leave law school believing that judges make the law in accordance with something called "policy" and that the "reasoning" of the cases is so much rationalization—a form of "window dressing."

Now these convictions in the mouth of a great scholar and judge like Frank is one thing; in the mouths of fledgling lawyers, garnished with all the glibness of *Time* magazine, it is quite another. What it harbingers for the future I dare not say. I am sure, however, that introducing more of a sense of history, including a healthy respect for what Dean Pound once called the "tenacity of the legal tradition," [36] would be neither degrading nor retrogressive to the Bar or to our society.

Surely, lawyers and judges who believe law to be a "brooding omnipresence in the sky" no longer dominate or even give tone to American law and legal education. Hence, I do not believe there is any real danger of modern law students binding themselves blindly and slavishly to past precedent. The problem today is, as I have indicated, quite the opposite: to show them that law, our system of law, is *more* than the vector of so many mid-20th-century social forces rationalized in accordance with the personal preferences of so many contemporary judges and legislators. The need is real; only some sense of history can fulfill it; hence (I conclude) we *should* make every effort to give history a more positive place in legal education than it currently holds.

VI.

Such, then, are my retorts to those who assert that nothing can, or need, or should be done to alter the place of history (call it "Legal" or whatever) in training lawyers. Yet, granting the validity of my conclusion, the nagging question remains: *What* should be done? To even the most charitable reader my prolonged discussion must appear to be little more than a cacophanous chorus of vapid truism interspersed

---

[35] GALBRAITH, THE AFFLUENT SOCIETY 6 (1958).
[36] POUND, THE FORMATIVE ERA OF AMERICAN LAW 82-84 (1938).

618

with hoary exhortations. (The overall effect is, no doubt, something like that of Henry Sidgwick's long and fruitless search for a rationally tenable religion: "[H]e never did anything," so Maynard Keynes tells us, "but wonder whether Christianity were true and prove that it wasn't and hope that it was." [37]) In order to minimize, or at least to anticipate, this criticism I shall offer a few concrete, though embarrassingly obvious, suggestions that might be of some practical value in improving the situation I have branded deplorable.

At the outset, however, let me remind the reader, that I assume the central problem is *not* lack of historical scholarship or research into legal sources. It is, rather, law students who have no intelligent awareness of the part the past plays in defining (and limiting the efficacy of) our conception of law. Scholars—historians and lawyers—to carry on the work of Maitland and Holdsworth are of course always needed and always (I hope) welcome; but we now suffer more from a dearth of history-conscious lawyers than we do from a lack of law-conscious historians. And it is to *this* problem that I now address myself.

619

The means of inspiring scholarly research by historians may or may not be the same as those of imparting a sense of history among law students. Nevertheless I believe that both causes now suffer from the same malady and that, accordingly, they would both benefit from the remedies here proposed. The malady to which I refer is, at bottom, a lack of speculation about the relationship between the past and the legal process as we now know it; and the remedy is simply (though by no means a simple matter) to stimulate such speculation by breaking the shell, cracking the crust encasing what we call "Legal History." So long as that phrase connotes a known quantity of fixed dimensions, and so long as it is regarded by lawyers and scholars as the sole authoritative link between law and history, speculation must dwindle and scholarship languish. This is true because speculation, about history or anything else, depends essentially upon a multiplicity of juxtapositions affording opportunity for comparisons.[38] And 20th century insularity (and alienation) is a result of the paucity of conscious contact between present-day law and "the past," which discourages animated and fruitful speculation about the relationship between the two. With "Legal History" a fixed quantity; and with modern legal education based on

---

[37] HARROD, THE LIFE OF JOHN MAYNARD KEYNES 116 (1951).
[38] *Cf.* Maitland's remark: "History involves comparison and the English lawyer who knew nothing and cared nothing for any system but his own hardly came in sight of legal history." 1 MAITLAND, *op. cit. supra* note 3, at 488.

the "tool" conception of law, the past, understandably, seems to be dead, dull and irrelevant.

Proceeding, then, on the assumption that speculation of the kind desired will be inspired by increasing the number of points of conscious contact between past and present, we can readily see that two lines of attack can be pursued simultaneously and altogether independently of each other. The first is to broaden the scope of the course of instruction known as "Legal History"; the second is to introduce more historical matter into other law courses. But the paramount unanswered question we have raised is this: What is the meaning and content of this term "history" we have used so often and so loosely? What, in short, should be added to "The Development of Legal Institutions" to inspire more speculation about the relationship between the past and present? We shall first try to answer this question and then consider how it can be more effectively introduced into the law school curriculum.

The "history" now used in legal education is, I have asserted, too narrow in scope. I shall now try to justify the indictment by indicating some of the elements heretofore excluded from Legal History. By stressing "legal institutions" as the focus of Legal History, two other factors of equal significance to law-making have been comparatively neglected. I mean, of course, extra-legal environmental factors and human or personality factors. Both of these factors are familiar to every reader and neither of them is altogether excluded from Legal History. They are not, however, adequately integrated into the subject.

Of course today we are most familiar with the idea that "economic" factors, such as "industrialism," [39] have had a formative impact on the law. Professor Willard Hurst, and the "Wisconsin School," have been extremely diligent in correlating legal and economic change.[40] But

[39] I have attempted to illustrate some of the ways in which "industrialism" has affected law and society in Woodard, *Reality and Social Reform: The Transition from Laissez-Faire to the Welfare State*, 72 YALE L.J. 286 (1962).

[40] The most influential books published by Professor Hurst are THE GROWTH OF AMERICAN LAW: THE LAW MAKERS (1950); LAW AND THE CONDITIONS OF FREEDOM IN THE NINETEENTH-CENTURY UNITED STATES (1956); LAW AND SOCIAL PROCESS IN UNITED STATES HISTORY (1960) and, more recently, LAW AND ECONOMIC GROWTH: THE LEGAL HISTORY OF THE LUMBER INDUSTRY IN WISCONSIN 1836-1915 (1964). These works have been widely recognized as a significant contribution to both jurisprudence and legal history. See, e.g., Brooks, *The Jurisprudence of Willard Hurst*, 18 J. LEGAL ED. 257 (1966); Frank, *American Legal History: The Hurst Approach*, 18 J. LEGAL ED. 395 (1966); Murphy, Book Review, *The Jurisprudence of Legal History: Willard Hurst as a Legal Historian*, 39 N.Y.U.L. REV. 900 (1964). For a slight dissent from some of Profes-

other, scarcely less formative environmental factors, receive scant attention indeed. For example, the religious attitudes of the Evangelical revival of the early 19th century (led by lawyer Charles Finney[41]) gave rise, among other things, to "Teetotalism," and the idea grew up to become "Prohibition," a genuine chapter in Legal History. Again, the "Clapham Sect" of London left an indelible imprint on the mind and character of such lawyers as William Wilberforce (renowned for his work in abolishing slavery) and Sir James Fitzjames Stephen, a leading authority on criminal law who learned, believed and taught that it was "morally right to hate criminals" and "moral cowardice" not to hang murderers.[42] Who can say that that Sect is beyond the purview of "Legal History" when so much law school time is spent trying to refute the very ideas Stephen taught? Still speaking of environmental factors, the growing influence of the colonies, and particularly India, on the 19th-century English legal mind, is almost totally neglected as a part of Legal History. Yet the experience of God-fearing English lawyers living amidst, and having to make laws for, non-Christians led to reforms in the common law as well as to a broader conception of law. Lord Hardwick's dictum that "the Christian religion . . . is a part of the law of the land,"[43] was largely assumed to be true in 1800. Not so by 1900. What happened to the idea? In some ways the closer contact with the colonies was the beginning of what might be called Anglo-American International Law, a topic itself not, I think, beyond the scope of Legal History.

621

Now, I ask, who can say that these topics have no place in Legal History? And who can say that they are less important to Legal History or legal education than the origin of the courts of Chancery or the intricacies of common-law pleading? The test is whether a topic

---

sor Hurst's more general conclusions, as well as his approach to history, see Woodard, Book Review, 19 LA. L. REV. 560 (1959).

[41] For an interesting discussion of Finney, the leading figure in the series of "revivals" of the first forty years of the 19th century, see MILLER, THE LIFE OF THE MIND IN AMERICA 24-35 (1965). "I was bred a lawyer," said Finney. "I came forth from a law office to the pulpit, and talked to the people as I would talk to a jury." *Id.* at 25. Accordingly, he delivered sermons in the form of a lawyer's brief; and, acting as God's attorney, he interrogated penitents, "criminals on their own admission . . . employing the most unsentimental of nineteenth-century techniques for cross-examination." *Id.* at 24.

Miller's book is an excellent example of an attempt to integrate legal change ("the legal mentality") into the intellectual history of the period.

[42] See RADZINOWICZ, SIR JAMES FITZJAMES STEPHEN, 1829-1894 (1957).

[43] De Costa v. De Paz, 2 Swans. 532, 36 Eng. Rep. 715, 716 (Ch. 1743).

can be used to attract the interest of law students, and to help them to understand better that subject we call law. And it is, I suggest, a test to be empirically administered.

So much for "environmental" factors that could properly, and with profit, be added to the scope of Legal History. Now a word about the personality factor. I do not labor the "psychological" aspect, which is perhaps overstressed in some biographies today. Nor do I stress the "great-man" approach which has always been powerful enough to assure us a steady and large number of memoirs, autobiographies and the like. The bar has always tended to venerate if not apotheosize both its more eminent members and the bench. And it would, indeed, be difficult to conceive of a course in Legal History that did not include some allusions to such majestic (as they now appear) figures as Bracton, More, Coke, Hale, Mansfield, Blackstone, Marshall, Story and Holmes.

622

No, the complaint is not that Legal History ignores the personal factor. It is clearly there in the references to these larger-than-life individuals. The complaint is that the personal factor is not adequately integrated into Legal History so as to increase our understanding of the legal system beyond the bald truism that it has always produced some great men. It teaches us absolutely nothing about the way the greatness of one age differs from that of another—or why. For example, we learn nothing of the change that, in this country, catapulted the humble office-type lawyer to the head of the profession in the place of the stately court room barrister. (According to Robert T. Swaine, Paul D. Cravath, the senior partner in the famous Wall Street firm bearing both their names, first grasped the fact that, at least as regards corporate clients, the real need was for lawyers who could stay out of court, counselors who could anticipate and avert litigation rather than advocates capable of delivering sparkling perorations in their defense.[44])

But Legal History, no less than any other history, consists of work done by ordinary men, most of whom were innocent of both intellectual brilliance and philosophical enlightenment. As the historian of Cambridge University observed: "[T]he history of a university, like the history of a nation, is not exclusively a record of the achievements of great men. Mediocrities play their part in binding up the whole . . . ."[45] So, too, it was with the law. And in American legal history

44 1 SWAINE, THE CRAVATH FIRM 1819-1947, at 573-75 (1946).

45 WINSTANLEY, THE UNIVERSITY OF CAMBRIDGE IN THE EIGHTEENTH CENTURY 1 (1958).

especially, another personal element, not so much of mediocrity as ignorance, must be weighed and measured. It was Justice Miller who pointed out that our early judges "did not know enough to do the wrong thing, so they did the right thing." [46]

Greatness, mediocrity, ignorance—all these factors gave color and character to the bar; and that color and character changed from age to age. Why? How? The whole edifice of learning—that which Mannheim called the "sociology of knowledge" [47]—is and could be introduced into Legal History, helping us better to comprehend the relationship between the legal mind of a given time and the so-called *Zeitgeist,* and serving as a means of understanding how we ourselves differ from the past and got to be the way we are. Legal History, so conceived, would surely be more meaningful than that which prevails today.

623

It will be noted that in the foregoing discussion of environmental and personality factors, most of the illustrations were taken from the 19th century. That period is near enough in time for the nonspecialist law student to understand. So also, to a lesser extent, is the 18th century. Prior to that time, however, it is more difficult for them to do so. Yet most Legal History courses start with and concentrate upon the period prior to the 16th century, thereby killing interest before it is ever engendered. This logical, but forbidding approach recently moved a member of the bar to propose that Legal History "be taught backwards." [48] And though professional historians may look askance at the suggestion, it does have the merit of appealing to the interest of ordinary law students more than topics in medieval history.

Of course this "teaching backwards" approach carries with it a danger that may outweigh its virtues. That danger is the temptation to use history to play what Michael Oakeshott has called "Retrospective Politics." [49] Opinion on topics of current interest, such as the civil rights movement, is frequently so fervent that history is used to confirm our prejudices rather than to increase our understanding; and historians, legal or otherwise, who use the past as the whipping boy to

---

[46] POUND, *op. cit. supra* note 36, at 11.

[47] See MANNHEIM, IDEOLOGY AND UTOPIA: AN INTRODUCTION TO THE SOCIOLOGY OF KNOWLEDGE (1936). For an interesting and important recent study of this subject, see STARK, THE SOCIOLOGY OF KNOWLEDGE (1960).

[48] Mason, *On Teaching Legal History Backwards,* 18 J. LEGAL ED. 155 (1966).

[49] Inaugural Address of Michael Oakeshott, Professor of Politics, University College, London, 1956.

demonstrate the efficacy of their own views accomplish very little of merit. Certainly they do not promote the "sense of history" that I believe to be so sadly lacking.

Still, bearing the danger in mind, I think Legal History courses can profitably concentrate on issues arising in more recent, rather than more remote times. By interpreting Legal History broadly, and by emphasizing semi-modern as well as medieval topics and issues, I think law students can come to understand better the legal system of which they are to be a part. I think they will thereby also acquire a healthy respect for the past—which is the beginning of wisdom.

Of course Legal History cannot, any more than any other subject, include everything. Limits of time, as well as limits of knowledge are too real to ignore. Yet they are not, I trust, limitations that are so imposing as to defeat the purpose of the subject itself. Legal History is all too often Legalistic History. That it need not, and that it should not be.

VII.

In offering the foregoing suggestions I have hinted at, without having overtly revealed, an assumed ideal role of the legal historian. Recognizing the unattainable nature of most worthwhile ideals, it might not be amiss, and indeed it may be my duty, to disclose the ideal underlying this Article.

At the turn of the century Maitland somewhat disconsolately found himself wondering why the history of English law had never been written, and if it would ever be written. He could only find hope, if hope it could be called, in failure: in some barrister who, tired of waiting for clients who never came, turned to the dust of the past.[50] The ideal historian in whom I put my hope is rather of a different order, one perhaps more akin to Martin Luther's ideal than to Maitland's. "Whoever wishes to write history," said Luther, "must have the heart of a lion." [51] And so it is today with those historians who aspire to write nonscientific history.

In the first place I envision an historian who regards "history" as being something more than a science. As we have seen, the science of history, like all sciences, is essentially an intellectual process by

---

[50] 1 MAITLAND, *op. cit. supra* note 3, at 495–96.

[51] LUTHER, *Preface to Galeatius Capella's History*, in 4 CAREER OF THE REFORMER (34 LUTHER'S WORKS) 275, 277 (Spitz ed. 1960).

624

which complex compounds ("human problems" or "burning issues" in the case of history) are broken down into constituent parts, each of which is then subjected to minute analysis. And the analysts of each constituent part, such as the "Legal Historians" who analyze the law, go their own scholarly ways. The assumption is, presumably, that at some happy time in the future, master-minds will pick up the pieces and put them together again.

It may be so. In the meantime, however, the fare is rather thin. And it is for that reason that I have urged a broader conception of Legal History. Classes of law students come and go—wielders, if you will, of the a-historical tool of law—while our Herodotuses, Gibbons and Spenglers refuse to come forward to help us. We can ill afford to wait longer. To paraphrase Justice Holmes, three generations of analysts are enough.

625

What then is the function, the prime 20th century function, of the legal historian? It is, I say (and I am, alas, still talking ideally)—to synthesize. By synthesis I do not mean works of epic proportions (though the historian who could describe Anglo-American law in a single chapter as accurately as Gibbon did the Roman Law in Chapter XLIV of his *magnum opus,* is surely to be applauded and encouraged). I mean rather works that attempt, on the one hand, to conjoin changes in law with more general extra-legal movements and, on the other hand, to correlate contemporaneous developments in diverse fields of law with each other. An example of the former is a book in which Morton White convincingly showed how several independent intellectual movements afoot at the end of the 19th century—the philosophies of Peirce, James and Dewey, the history of Beard and Robinson, the economics of Veblen and the legal pragmatism of Holmes—all shared a common base in what he called "The Revolt Against Formalism." [52] An example of the latter would be a study that sought to relate, and to explain the concomitant demise of (or attacks on) fault as a basis of tort liability, guilt as the key to criminal responsibility and debt as a term of moral obliquoy in bankruptcy.

The historian who regards synthesis as his function, and law as his province, is hard to find, largely because historians teach their students to be analysts. It is well that they do so. Hopefully, however, we can inspire some to be more. Certainly they can help us to understand our current conception of "law" better, as well as to enliven our single legal link with the past—Legal History.

---

[52] White, Social Thought in America: The Revolt Against Formalism (1957).